D1372269

The
RIVERSIDE READER

For Dean Johnson

Our Editor, Mentor, and Friend

As part of Houghton Mifflin's ongoing commitment to the environment, this text has been printed on recycled paper.

The RIVERSIDE READER

SEVENTH EDITION

Joseph F. Trimmer
Ball State University

Maxine Hairston
University of Texas at Austin

Houghton Mifflin Company   Boston New York

Editor in Chief: Patricia A. Coryell
Senior Sponsoring Editor: Suzanne Phelps Weir
Editorial Assistant: Becky Wong
Project Editor: Jane Lee
Editorial Assistant: Talia Kingsbury
Associate Production/Design Coordinator: Christine Gervais
Senior Manufacturing Coordinator: Jane Spelman
Marketing Manager: Cindy Graff Cohen
Marketing Assistant: Sarah Donelson

Acknowledgments appear on pages 703–707.

Copyright © 2002 by Houghton Mifflin Company. All rights reserved.

No part of this work may be reproduced or transmitted in any form or by any means, electronic or mechanical, including photocopying and recording, or by any information storage or retrieval system without the prior written permission of the copyright owner unless such copying is expressly permitted by federal copyright law. With the exception of nonprofit transcription in Braille, Houghton Mifflin is not authorized to grant permission for further uses of copyrighted selections reprinted in this text without the permission of their owners. Permission must be obtained from the individual copyright owners as identified herein. Address requests for permission to make copies of Houghton Mifflin material to College Permissions, Houghton Mifflin Company, 222 Berkeley Street, Boston, MA 02116-3764.

Printed in the U.S.A.

Library of Congress Catalog Card Number: 2002102452

ISBN: 0-618-26233-4

123456789-FFG-05 04 03 02

CONTENTS

In her acceptance speech for the 1993 Nobel Prize for Literature, this African-American author uses imagery and metaphor to both deplore and celebrate the power of language.

An author, himself a member of two groups who often experience prejudice and verbal abuse, argues that attempts to prohibit and penalize so-called hate speech can lead to practices worse than the offenses they seek to prevent.

In a fantasy about the future, Vonnegut creates a disturbing picture of a world in which the government uses extraordinary measures to ensure that everyone is equal.

RESOURCES FOR WRITING   549
(Thematic Unit—The Internet)

In her account of how she moved from hating e-mail to loving it, this writer and editor describes the ways in which this new kind of communication has altered her life.

In describing his early experiences with a word processor, this teacher, writer, and editor explains how and why he learned to master the new technology of writing with a computer.

A writer whose specialty is the history of business draws a provocative comparison between the ways in which the intercontinental railroad of the nineteenth century and today's Internet have affected their eras.

THEMATIC TABLE OF CONTENTS

The Other

Women

Teaching and Learning

Arts and Leisure

Science and Technology

Business and Ethics

PREFACE

The seventh edition of *The Riverside Reader,* like its predecessors, presents essays by acknowledged masters of prose style, including George Orwell, Flannery O'Connor, and Maya Angelou, along with many new voices such as Judith Ortiz Cofer, Natalie Angier, John Berendt, and Wendy Lesser. Almost half of the selections are new to this edition. As always, introductions, readings, study questions, and writing assignments are simple, clear, and cogent.

NEW FEATURES IN THE SEVENTH EDITION

Resources for Writing, a thematically organized final section, focuses on the subject of the **Internet** and includes seven essays (each exemplifying one rhetorical mode) and one short story. The writing assignments following each reading encourage students to use what they already know to *respond, analze,* and *argue* about the texts.

Documenting Sources provides instructions for documenting sources in the format of the latest Modern Language Association (MLA) style. Special attention is given to documenting electronic sources. The chapter concludes with a student paper, Gwen Vickery's "Is Anybody Out There?: The Value of Chat Groups on the Internet," that explores a provocative subject by drawing on several electronic sources as well as several of the essays that appear in **Resources for Writing.**

The **Glossary** provides extended definitions of key rhetorical terms. Each definition refers students to a particularly effective example in the text.

ENDURING FEATURES IN THE SEVENTH EDITION

At the center of *The Riverside Reader* is our desire to assist students in their reading and writing by helping them to understand the interaction between the two processes:

- The **connection between the reading and writing process** is highlighted in the general introduction. The familiar terminology of *purpose, audience,* and strategy provides a framework for the introduction and for subsequent study questions and writing assignments.

- **Guidelines for Writing an Essay** is paired with **Guidelines for Reading an Essay** to enhance and advance the students' understanding of the reading/writing connection.

- A **new annotated essay** appears in the general introduction—"The Problems with Hypertext" by David Shenk. The annotations illustrate how a reader responds to reading by writing.

- In each section introduction, an **annotated paragraph by a professional writer,** such as an excerpt from Maxine Hong Kingston's "A Song for a Barbarian Reed Pipe," concisely demonstrates reading and writing at work.

- In each section introduction, a **paragraph by a student writer,** such as Lauren Briner's "Deloris," is followed by questions about writing strategy.

- A **Points to Remember** list concludes each section introduction and provides a convenient summary of the essential tasks and techniques of each strategy.

- This edition of *The Riverside Reader* contains **thirty-three new selections,** among them Andre Dubus's "Digging," Julia Alverez's "Grounds for Fiction," and Toni Morrison's "The Bird in Our Hand." The complete collection, which includes popular essays from previous editions, provides a variety of readings to engage the interest of all students.

- A **Thematic Table of Contents** is provided for teachers who wish to organize their course by themes or issues.

- Selections in the **Persuasion and Argument** section are paired to present different perspectives on the issues of race, family, politics, and language. This feature reflects our continuing emphasis on analytical and interpretive reading and writing.

- A **short story** concludes each section to provide an interesting perspective on a particular writing strategy and to give students opportunities to broaden their reading skills. New to this edition are Witi Ihimaera's "His First Ball" and William Gibson's "Burning Chrome."

- **Study questions and writing assignments** throughout the book have been extensively revised.

THE RIVERSIDE TRADITION

The first seven sections in this reader are arranged in a sequence that is familiar to most writing teachers. Beginning with narration and description, moving through the five expository patterns, and ending with persuasion and argument, these sections group readings according to traditional writing strategies.

The readings within each section have been chosen to illustrate what the section introductions say they illustrate: there are no strange hybrids or confusing models. Within each section, the selections are arranged in ascending order of length and complexity. The readings at the beginning are generally shorter and simpler than those near the end. The ultimate purpose of *The Riverside Reader* is to produce writing. For that reason, the writing assignments in this book are presented as the culminating activity of each section. Six assignments at the end of each section ask students to write essays that cover a range of writing tasks from personal response to analysis and argument.

Instructor's Resource Manual

The new *Instructor's Resource Manual* by Rai Peterson of Ball State University is available to any instructor using *The Riverside Reader*. The manual includes extensive rhetorical analysis of each essay and story, reading quizzes and vocabulary lists, and additional student essays and writing assignments. The manual also includes advice on teaching the reading and writing strategies.

ACKNOWLEDGMENTS

We are grateful to the following writing instructors who have provided extensive commentary on *The Riverside Reader* for this revision:

Cullen Bailey Burns, Century College, MN
Thomas P. Coakley, Mount Aloysisus College, PA
Julie Comine, Kirkwood Community College, IA
James P. Friel, SUNY Farmingdale
Stephen Hathaway, Wichita State University
Lana L. Hurt, Lord Fairfax Community College, VA
Alice E. Sink, High Point University, NC
Patrice R. Troutman, Wayne State College, NE
Samuel S. Turner, Cuyamaca Community College, CA
Lisa N. Woodside, Holy Family College, PA

We are also grateful to our students for allowing us to reprint their work in this edition: Lauren Briner, Sara Temple, Nathan Harms, Gareth Tucker, Jason Utesch, Emily Linderman, Jim Saloman, and Gwen Vickery. A special thanks goes to Linda Rabadi and Donna Ferguson for helping us prepare the manuscript. And, of course, our debt to all our students is ongoing.

J. F. T.
M. H.

INTRODUCTION

As a college student, you are necessarily a reader and a writer. Not that either role is new to you, but when you're doing college work, the stakes are high and how well you do depends, at least in part, on how well you read and write. It also depends on your learning to connect the two processes.

Why? Because the reading and writing processes mirror each other. As you become a more skillful reader, you will also become a better writer. And the more you write, the more you will come to enjoy the clear and engaging writing of others. Reading a well-crafted essay carefully is like watching a well-made movie on two levels: on one level you just enjoy the plot and action of the movie, but on another level you can be aware of and appreciate the photography, the acting, or the special effects.

BECOMING A SKILLFUL READER

Step One

The first time you read one of the essays or short stories in this book, read quickly; move straight through and get a general idea what it's about, enjoying it because it's entertaining or interesting. Unless you get lost or confused, don't go back and don't stop to analyze. When you finish, read the questions or comment that follows each selection. They should start you thinking about the topic of the piece and prepare you for the second reading.

Step Two

Now go back and read the selection again, this time more slowly. Get a pencil and straight edge ready to underline key sentences and summarize main points in the margins. Most serious and experienced readers do this kind of active reading almost routinely when they read to absorb content. If they don't own the book, they buy it or photocopy parts of it so they can read with pencil in hand because they know that annotating the material will help them master it and provide cues when they need to respond to what they've read. The sample essay at the end of this introduction shows how one experienced reader underlined and annotated a short essay and responded to the author's ideas.

Also keep a piece of paper ready to jot down ideas and reactions about what the piece of writing means for you. The phrase "for you" is important because a piece of writing never means exactly the same thing to different readers. Nor should it. You are a special reader who brings unique experiences and attitudes to what you're reading, and you create your own meaning when you combine what you know and feel with what the writer is saying. For example, as you read the essay "Uniforms," you may compare an author's account of the benefits of youngsters' wearing school uniforms with the experience you had when you went to a school that required uniforms. Or you might analyze your feelings about your own secure life when you contrast it with the account of a homeless person in "My Daily Dives in the Dumpster."

When you've finished your second reading, jot down some ideas that came to you as you read and what points of the author you might challenge. We believe that if you try this method of interacting with what you read and use the Guidelines for Reading an Essay on pages 8–10, you can become a good reader who enjoys reading serious material and knows how to analyze and react to it.

READING TO BECOME MORE AWARE OF THE WRITING PROCESS

As you read and react to a piece of writing, you can sharpen your own writing skills by thinking consciously about the process that the author of a piece went through as he or she wrote it. Try to get into the writer's mind and watch him or her at work—you may get some ideas that could help you get started with your own writing. For example:

Ask About Purpose

We know that most writers have goals when they write, certain things they want to accomplish through their writing. So ask yourself,

a. Why is the author writing? What does she or he hope to achieve?
b. Does the author tell me that purpose directly? If not, how can I determine it?
c. Do you think the author succeeded?

Ask About Audience

We know that most writers—especially professionals—write for a definite audience and tailor their writing to meet that audience's needs and expectations. So ask yourself,

a. For whom is the author writing? Why did she or he choose that audience?
b. What does the author know—or assume—about that audience? How does that knowledge or assumption shape what he or she writes?

Ask About Strategies

You can learn from other writers by noticing how they work and what kinds of strategies or appeals they use. So ask yourself,

a. What plan did the author seem to follow in organizing the essay?
b. What strategies does the writer use? Is he or she telling stories, citing evidence, making an argument, comparing and contrasting, or what?

Do we guarantee that you will become a better writer by learning to analyze a professional writer's work? No, of course we don't. But we do believe that if you work at reading critically and responsively, you will learn something about the craft of writing. When you do, writing will become a less intimidating and more manageable process.

READING TO LEARN ABOUT WRITING STRATEGIES

In *The Riverside Reader* you will find essays and short stories that comment on events and concerns that affect all our lives—contrasting ethnic values and experiences, environmental concerns, racial issues, and women's roles, to name just a few. The essays connect to other strands in your college education and are as pertinent in sociology, history, or anthropology courses as they are in a college writing course. In the short stories you can see how fiction writers deal with similar issues through using narrative and dialogue. The last section of the book, Resources for Writing, focuses on issues raised by the Internet and its impact on our society.

Common Writing Strategies

The essays in *The Riverside Reader* are arranged according to common patterns of organization that have been serving writers well for centuries: *narration and description, process analysis, comparison and contrast, division and classification, definition, cause and effect,* and *persuasion and argument.* These patterns can serve as *strategies* for the development of ideas in writing. Study how professional writers use these traditional strategies in their writing. If you know from your reading how these strategies are used, you will be able to choose one that fits your writing situation. For example, if you notice how Maya Angelou uses narrative to dramatize racial stereotyping, you may see how you can relate an incident from your life to illustrate a point. If you are convinced by Cathy Young's claim that radical feminists are harming the cause of women's liberation by portraying women as victims, you may want to use the same kind of cause-and-effect argument in a paper for sociology or ethnic studies.

Not that you have to limit yourself to a single strategy for the entire paper—certainly professional writers don't. Often, however, they do structure a piece of writing around one central pattern, and for *The Riverside Reader* we have chosen essays with one dominant strategy so that you can see particularly strong examples of each strategy in action.

Strategies for Your Writing

You can also use the traditional strategies to generate resources and then transform them into writing. Suppose you are trying to get started writing an essay on the early impressionist painters for a humanities course. One way to start thinking would be to *define* the impressionist school of painting. Another would be to explore what *caused* the rise of impressionism in the nineteenth century—what were the artists in the movement reacting to? Another potentially rich approach would be to *compare* these painters to other painters of the time. You could also *describe* an important early impressionist painting or relate a *narrative* about one of the early painters. Each of the strategies provides a kind of special lens for viewing your topic, a different way of looking at it so that you can see its possibilities. When you become aware of how these lenses work—how each one helps you see and shape your subject—you can select one strategy or combine two or three to draft and revise your essay. That is the procedure you can follow in Resources for Writing. Each selection in that section uses one of the common writing strategies to explore a different aspect of the Internet. As you read these selections, recalling what you know about that topic, you can expand and shift your perspective on the subject, uncovering all sorts of resources to develop in your writing.

USING THE *RIVERSIDE READER*

The Riverside Reader will help you become an active, critical reader who can grasp the essential ideas an author presents in an essay and respond to and evaluate those ideas. At the start of every section in the book, an introduction previews the kind of essays you will find there—comparison and contrast, process analysis, or definition, for example. The introduction also gives you clues about what to look for as you read, and concludes with Points to Remember. Next comes a professional paragraph and a student paragraph that illustrates how that kind of writing works.

A headnote appears before each essay and short story to tell you about the author's background and his or her professional credentials. After each essay you'll find questions to help you think about specific elements in it and about what the author is trying to accomplish. After the short story at the end of each section, you'll find a comment that highlights some of its main points. At the end of each section of essays, there are writing assignments that create opportunities for you to connect your own experiences and insights to the reading in that section.

On pages 8–10 we offer a set of questions entitled Guidelines for Reading an Essay. In our everyday leisure reading, most of us wouldn't want or need a set of guidelines to work from—often we read so casually that we'd have a hard time answering many probing questions about what we've read. That's fine. No one wants to be taking tests on his or her recreational reading. But when we read to absorb ideas and understand the writer's purpose and strategies, reading becomes a serious process, something that we need to approach thoughtfully and systematically. We hope these guidelines will help.

After the Guidelines, you will find a sample analysis of David Shenk's essay "The Problem with Hypertext"; the analysis and annotations show one experienced reader's summary comments on and response to Shenk's essay. Also included are two possible writing topics that emerged from a careful reading of the piece. The Introduction to *The Riverside Reader* closes with Guidelines for Writing an Essay, a brief review of the writing process that should help you to get started with your own writing.

Guidelines for Reading an Essay

I. READ THE ESSAY THROUGH COMPLETELY

a. Begin by paying attention to the title. Does it preview the subject of the essay for you? If not, what do you think it means?

b. Read slowly, looking up key words if necessary, but don't stop to reread unless you really get lost.

c. Identify the date when the essay was first written. How important is that date to the theme of the essay?

d. When you finish, stop to think about your reaction to the essay. Did you find it powerful? Moving? Persuasive? Confusing? Why do you think it affected you as it did?

e. If after you finish, you're not sure what the author is saying, go over the essay again, this time with a pencil in your hand. Underline what look like key points and write brief summaries in the margin. (See the annotated essay at the end of this section.) Put question marks next to points you don't understand.

II. ANALYZE YOUR RESPONSE

a. What experience of your own, if any, does the essay bring to your mind? How do you think that experience affects your response?

b. Jot down questions the essay raises. If you strongly disagree with some part, ask yourself, "What would I say to the author if he or she asked me what I think?"

c. Did the essay make you feel good? Angry? Excited? Argumentative? Why?

III. ANALYZE THE AUTHOR'S PURPOSE

a. What do you think the author wanted to accomplish with the essay? What clues does he or she give you?

b. What do you know about the writer's experience, knowledge, or background that helps you understand the purpose of this essay? How does the essay seem to grow out of her or his experience?

c. Consider how well the writer achieved his or her purpose with you. What worked and what didn't?

IV. ANALYZE THE WRITER'S AUDIENCE

a. Try to identify the writer's original audience for this essay. Was it first published as a magazine article? A section of a book? Did it come off the web or from a radio program? What do you think that first audience would be like?

b. What beliefs or values does the author assume the audience shares with him or her? In your case, how justified is that assumption?

c. What knowledge or experience does the author assume readers have?

d. To what extent do you think you're like the readers the author had in mind when writing the essay? How does that similarity—or lack of it—affect your response to the essay?

V. ANALYZE AND EVALUATE WHAT STRATEGIES THE WRITER USES

a. The most effective writers engage their readers' interest at the very beginning of an essay. How effectively does the opening of the essay do that?

b. Can you identify the key pattern of the essay—description, narration, comparison and contrast, or cause and effect? How does that pattern serve the author's purpose?

c. Look for the skillful use of metaphor, analogy, personal experience, appeal to authority, and so on. How do they work for the author?

VI. WHAT SOCIAL, POLITICAL, OR ECONOMIC ISSUES DOES THE ESSAY RAISE?

a. What important issue do you think the essay raises? Does it make a contribution to the ongoing discussion of that issue?

b. What important developments, if any, have occurred in the area the author is writing about since the essay was written? Do those developments have an impact on the essay's effectiveness?

c. What impact do you think the essay may have had on its original readers? Why?

Sample Analysis of an Essay

DAVID SHENK

David Shenk was born in Cincinnati, Ohio, in 1966 and educated at Brown University. He has worked as a radio commentator and producer for National Public Radio (NPR) and as a magazine and Internet columnist. Although Shenk is known for his anti-information, Luddite inclinations, he is not against technology per se. His commentaries are often cautionary tales. His books include *Skeleton Key: A Dictionary for Deadheads* (1994), *Data Smog: Surviving the Information Glut* (1997), and *The End of Patience: Cautionary Notes on the Information Revolution* (1999). In "The Problem with Hypertext," originally broadcast on NPR's *All Thing Considered* and reprinted from *The End of Patience,* Shenk suggests that while hypertext may be a useful tool, it should not "govern the way we think."

The author uses a straightforward title, "The Problem with Hypertext," so the reader clearly knows what to expect. He then opens his essay with an attention-catching image of an alien creature that could have come straight from the *X-Files,* one whose eyes and ears look and work differently from ours because they've evolved from different thought processes over a period of ten thousand years or more.

But, he reminds us in paragraph 2, we don't look or think like that imaginary creature. We still operate in a linear world where we reason from cause to effect and we read stories that have a beginning, a middle, and an end. That's the process our brain expects; it's not ready for us to start a train of thought, then have hypertext links take us in so many directions that we never reach a conclusion. If we succumb to hypertext, we're not reading, we're surfing. As an example of hypertext gone berserk, he points to the opening paragraph of Jane Austen's novel *Pride and Prejudice* as it appears on a website. Four hypertext links have been inserted, and the changes send the reader off in four different directions before she can even get started on the story.

In paragraphs 5 and 6, Shenk cautions his readers not to become so enchanted with hypertext as a research tool that they let it lure them into wandering through information in a disjointed and purposeless way. Just because hypertext is a new technology doesn't mean it should displace the older but still very powerful technology of linear reading. Hypertext can be an excellent tool, but if not used carefully, it can hinder rather than help logical thinking. Traditional narrative, on the other hand, "offers the reader a journey with a built-in purpose." He reinforces his advice by connecting it to references that are familiar to his readers: *The New Yorker, Huckleberry Finn,* George Orwell, and allusions to "surfing."

The Problem with Hypertext

<table>
<tr><td>Someday we may evolve into different form</td><td>Someday, perhaps tens of thousands of year from now, the human form may be very different. Our eyes might point in different directions, our ears may process different channels of sound in distinct parts of the brain, and we might even talk and think in fragmented hyperspeak.</td><td>Images from science fiction — believable?</td></tr>
<tr><td>But now we process ideas linearly</td><td>Until then, we are all stuck in a linear world. We can dabble in hyperfiction and so-called dense TV as forms of entertainment, and as thought experiments. But let us not forget that</td><td></td></tr>
</table>

our brains and our society are better served by
The Adventures of Huckleberry Finn and *The New* — Is this necessar-
Yorker. Our sentences work best when they have — ily true?

We expect a subject, an object, and a verb. Our stories work
narratives best when they have an ending.

As we surf the Internet, we're in danger of
forgetting this basic truth. With hypertext, end- — Notice he's us-
Internet ings are irrelevant—because no one ever gets to — ing biased lan-
can lead one. Reading gives way to surfing, a meandering, — guage to make
us astray peripatetic journey through a maze of threads. — his point
The surfer creates his or her own narrative, opt-
ing for the most seductive link immediately available. As a research technique, this is superb. As
a mode of thought, however, it has serious
deficiencies.

Faster is not always better, and segmentation
Horrible is not always smarter. If Jane Austen could see
example what her book *Pride and Prejudice* has become
on the World Wide Web, she would faint dead
away. In the first five sentences, there are four — Pretty ridiculous—
invitations to go elsewhere. — I agree

In our restless technological optimism, we
Shouldn't tend to look down on old technologies as infe-
assume rior. But we need to resist this. Some of the
the latest boring old linear technologies, including the one
is always we're using right now, still ride on the cutting
better edge of human intelligence. The works of — He appeals to
George Orwell, E. B. White, and Joan Didion — readers who are
read from the beginning to end not just because — also traditional
of the primitive tools these writers used. Traditional narrative offers the reader a journey with
a built-in purpose; the progression of thought is
specifically designed so that the reader may learn
something not just from the parts of the story,
but also from the story as a whole.

Limitations For all of its advantages, hypertext has no
of hypertext whole. As the web becomes integrated into the

It's only fabric of our lives—mostly to our great benefit—
a tool we should <u>employ hyperlinking as a useful tool,</u>
<u>but be careful not to let it govern the way we</u>
<u>think.</u>

Good
reminder

Possible Writing Topics

1. Using your favorite search engine, pull up on the Internet an article about a topic you're interested in—perhaps antique cars or sign language or a biography of one of your favorite sports or music stars—and notice to what extent the account you're reading is frequently interrupted by links to other sites. Study the article and then write a response of 300 to 500 words to Shenk's essay. If the article has several hyperlinks, to what extent do you agree with him that the hyperlinks interfere with the continuity of the article? In what ways did you find them helpful? Do you think you benefitted by being directed to other sites or were hampered by the additional information the hyperlinks offered you?

2. For an audience of your parents and their contemporaries, write a short essay—three hundred to five hundred words—comparing the process of getting information about a topic by the older traditional methods of looking in books and magazines and getting information by doing a search on the Internet. What are the advantages and disadvantages of each process? (See the suggestions on pages 161–168 for writing comparison and contrast papers.) What cautions does a person looking for information on the Internet need to keep in mind? Illustrate your ideas by using a sample topic—for example, research on backpacking in a wilderness area or learning more about Weimaraner dogs.

Guidelines for Writing an Essay

Writing is a complicated, often messy process that varies from one writing task to another and from one writer to another, so we can't offer you a simple or foolproof formula. Nevertheless, most professional writers do plan ahead about what and how they're going to write, particularly when they are writing informative essays or nonfiction articles. Here we offer you some general guidelines that will help you make plans and get started on your writing assignment.

I. ANALYZE YOUR WRITING SITUATION

Every time you undertake a writing assignment, you're going to be writing in a specific situation that has three components you can identify: (1) a topic, (2) a purpose, (3) an audience. Successful writers keep all these elements in mind as they work. So begin your process by analyzing these elements of your writing situation:

a. Who is your audience and why?
b. What do you want to say?
c. What's your purpose?
d. How can you persuade that audience?

To anchor your first draft, write out a capsule analysis of your writing situation and put it in a prominent place to refer to as you work. For instance, in a political science course you've taken, you may have been surprised by the major social changes brought about in the United States after World War II by groups that had very little money behind them. If you want to write about that phenomenon, you might set up this writing situation:

> *I want to persuade college students who are disillusioned by the impact of money on our political system that small determined groups can bring about important change even if they are poorly financed. I*

will cite the examples of the women's movement, the civil rights movement, and the environmental movement.

Now you have your writing situation in a nutshell, and the beginnings of a thesis sentence.

II. SELECT AND NARROW YOUR TOPIC

a. Decide if you're genuinely interested in your topic, enough so that you want to learn more about it. If you're not, choose something else if you can do so; you'll write better if you enjoy what you're doing.
b. Brainstorm, free-write, and talk to people to generate information about your topic. For instance, your parents or some older friends might remember specific examples from the civil rights or women's movement that you could use.
c. Research your topic to find out what material is available. For instance, if you focus particularly on the civil rights movement of the sixties, you could write about the bus boycott in Montgomery, Alabama, and the role of Rosa Parks in that boycott.
d. Write a tentative thesis sentence to focus your writing; it can always be modified later. For example, "The three grassroots movements that brought about major social change in the United States in the sixties—the environmental movement, the civil rights movement, and the women's movement—were poorly financed and not widely supported, but they had a lasting and dramatic impact on our society."

III. DECIDE ON YOUR PURPOSE IN WRITING

a. Decide what you want to achieve by your writing. Do you want to entertain, inform, persuade, bring about change? You may have more than one goal.
b. Decide what readers you want to reach. For the sample

paper, they might be young people who think you have no political clout unless you have money.

c. What change do you want to bring about? For the sample topic, you might just want your readers to realize that political change is possible.

IV. ANALYZE YOUR AUDIENCE

a. Consider what you know about your audience and how you might appeal to them. For instance, your readers might need to know more about events in the sixties in order to understand your points.

b. What examples might highlight your thesis? For instance, you could use brief accounts of the Montgomery, Alabama, bus boycott or the civil rights march in Selma, Alabama, to illustrate the civil rights movement.

c. Jot down what questions your readers might have and be sure to answer them.

d. Think about a publication in which an essay like yours might be published: for example, *Scholastic* or *Seventeen*. Think about who reads those magazines.

V. DECIDE ON SOME WORKING PLAN AND SELECT SOME STRATEGIES

a. Rough out an outline that puts your main points in order.

b. Jot down ideas as they come to you.

c. Choose some examples to illustrate your points.

d. Decide what form might work well for you; for instance, you might use *narration* by telling stories about some civil rights marches or *definition* by explaining what civil rights are.

e. Find evidence to support your argument.

VI. WRITE A DRAFT, REVISE, AND EDIT

a. Write your first draft, let it sit for several hours, and then reread it. Ask yourself: Have I made my ideas clear? Have I given examples? Will my readers be able to follow my argument? Mark up your draft, indicating where you want to make changes.

b. Write a second draft.

c. Check over the second draft for clarity, completeness, and repetition. Edit for spelling and grammar. If you can, print out a draft and get someone to read it over for errors. Print or type out a final clean copy.

NARRATION
AND
DESCRIPTION

The writer who *narrates* tells a story to make a point. The writer who *describes* evokes the senses to create a picture. Although you can use either strategy by itself, you will probably discover that they work best in combination if you want to write a detailed account of some memorable experience— your first trip alone, a last-minute political victory, a picnic in some special place. When you want to explain what happened, you will need to tell the story in some kind of chronological order, putting the most important events—I took the wrong turn, she made the right speech, we picked the perfect spot—in the most prominent position. When you want to give the texture of the experience, you will need to select words and images that help your readers see, hear, and feel what happened—the road snaked to a dead end, the crowd thundered into applause, the sunshine softened our scowls. When you show and tell in this way, you can help your readers see the meaning of the experience you want to convey.

PURPOSE

You can use narration and description for three purposes. Most simply, you can use them to introduce or illustrate a complicated subject. You might begin an analysis of the energy crisis, for example, by telling a personal anecdote that dramatizes wastefulness. Or you might conclude an argument for gun control by giving a graphic description of a shooting incident. In each case, you are using a few sentences or a detailed description to support some other strategy such as causal analysis or argument.

Writers use narration and description most often not as isolated examples but as their primary method when they are analyzing an issue or theme. For example, you might spend a whole essay telling how you came to a new awareness of patriotism because of your experience in a foreign country. Even though your personal experience would be the center of the essay, your narrative purpose (what happened) and your descriptive purpose (what it felt like) might be linked to other purposes. You might want to *explain* what caused your new awareness (why it happened) or to *argue* that everyone needs such awareness (why everyone should reach the same conclusion you did).

The writers who use narration and description most often are those who write autobiography, history, and fiction. If you choose to write in any of these forms, your purpose will be not so much to introduce an example or tell about an experience as to throw light on your subject. You may explain why events happened as they did or argue that such events should never happen again, but you may choose to suggest your ideas subtly through telling a story or giving a description rather than stating them as direct assertions. Your primary purpose is to report the actions and describe the feelings of people entangled in the complex web of circumstance.

AUDIENCE

As you think about writing an essay using narration and description, consider how much you will need to tell your readers and how much you will need to show them. If you are writing from personal experience, few readers will know the story before you tell it. They may know similar stories or have had similar experiences, but they do not know your story. Because you can tell your story in so many different ways—adding or deleting material to fit the occasion—you need to decide how much information your readers will need. Do they need to know every detail of your story, only brief summaries of certain parts, or some mixture of detail and summary?

In order to decide what details you should provide, you need to think about how much your readers know and what they are going to expect. If your subject is unusual (a trip to see an erupting volcano), your readers will need a lot of information, much of it technical, to understand the novel experience you are going to describe. They will expect an efficient, matter-of-fact description of volcanoes but also want you to give them some sense of how it feels to see one erupting. If your subject is familiar to most people (your experience with lawn sprinklers), your readers will need few technical details to understand your subject. But they will expect you to give them new images and insights that create a fresh vision of your subject—for example, portraying lawn sprinklers as the languid pulse of summer.

STRATEGIES

The writers in this section demonstrate that you need to use certain strategies to write a successful narrative and descriptive essay. For openers, you must recognize that an experience and an essay about that experience are not the same thing. When you have any experience, no matter how long it lasts, your memory of that experience is going to be disorganized and poorly defined, but the essay you write about that experience must have a purpose and be sharply focused. When you want to transform your experience into an essay, start by locating the central **conflict.** It may be (1) between the writer and himself, or herself, as when George Orwell finds himself in a quandary about whether to shoot the elephant; (2) between the writer and others, as when Maya Angelou responds to Mrs. Cullinan and her friends; or (3) between the writer and the environment, as when Judith Ortiz Cofer tries to explain the difference between *individuals* and *social stereotypes.*

Once you have identified the conflict, arrange the action so that your readers know how the conflict started, how it developed, and how it was resolved. This coherent sequence of events is called a **plot.** Sometimes you may want to create a plot that sticks to a simple chronological pattern. In "Keeping the Scorebook," Doris Kearns Goodwin simply begins at the beginning and describes events as they occur. At other times you may want to start your essay in the middle or even near the end of the events you are describing. In "Digging," Andre Dubus concludes his narrative by speculating about a different "middle." The authors choose a pattern according to their purpose: Goodwin wants to describe the evolution of an exciting game; Dubus wants to describe why coming home for lunch would have changed the whole story.

When you figure out what the beginning, middle, and end of your plot should be, you can establish how each event in those sections should be paced. **Pace** is the speed at which the writer recounts events. Sometimes you can narrate events quickly by omitting details, compressing time, and summarizing experience. For example, Cofer summarizes several episodes that reveal her contact with a stereotype. At other times you may want to pace events more slowly and carefully because they are vital to your purpose. You will need to include every detail, expand on time, and present the situation as a fully realized scene rather than in summary form. Dubus creates such a scene when he describes his first morning of "digging."

You can make your scenes and summaries effective by your careful **selection of details.** Just adding more details doesn't satisfy this requirement. You must select those special details that satisfy the needs of your readers and further your purpose in the essay. For example, sometimes you will need to give *objective* or *technical* details to help your readers understand your subject. Cofer provides this kind of detail when she describes the cultural customs of Puerto Rico. At other times you will want to give *subjective* or *impressionistic* details to appeal to your readers' senses. Orwell provides much of this sort of detail as he tries to re-create his physical and psychological response to shooting the elephant. Finally, you may want to present your details so they form a *figurative image* or create a *dominant impression.* Dubus uses both of these strategies: the first when he describes his father's conversation, and the second when he describes his lunch hour.

In order to identify the conflict, organize the plot, vary the pace, and select details for your essay, you need to determine your **point of view:** the person and position of the narrator (*point*) and the attitude toward the experience being presented (*view*). You choose your *person* by deciding whether you want to tell your story as "I" saw it (as Maya Angelou does in her story about her confrontation with Mrs. Cullinan), or as "he" saw it (as Dubus does when he describes his father's life).

You choose your *position* by deciding how close you want to be to the action in time and space. You may be involved in the action or view it from the position of an observer, or you may tell about the events as they are happening or many years after they have taken place. For example, George Orwell, the young police officer, is the chief actor in his narrative, but George Orwell, the author, still wonders, years after the event, why he shot the elephant. You create your attitude—how you view the events you intend to present and interpret—by the person and position you choose for writing your essay. The attitudes of the narrators in the following essays might be characterized as angry (Angelou), nostalgic (Goodwin), perplexed (Cofer), reticent (Dubus), and ambivalent (Orwell).

USING NARRATION AND DESCRIPTION IN PARAGRAPHS

Here are two narration and description paragraphs. The first is written by a professional writer and is followed by an analysis. The second is written by a student writer and is followed by questions.

MAXINE HONG KINGSTON
"A Song for a Barbarian Reed Pipe"

Not all of the children who were silent at American school found a voice at Chinese school. One new teacher said each of us had to get up and recite in front of the class, who was to listen. My sister and I had memorized the lesson perfectly. We said it to each other at home, one chanting, one listening. The teacher called on my sister to recite first. It was the first time a teacher had called on the second-born to go first. My sister was scared. She glanced at me and looked away; I looked down at my desk. I hoped that she could do it because if she could, then I would have to. She opened her mouth and a voice came out that wasn't a whisper, but it wasn't a proper voice either. I hoped that she would not cry, fear breaking up her voice like twigs underfoot. She sounded as if she were trying to sing though weeping and strangling. She did not pause or stop to end the embarrassment. She kept going until she said the last word, and then she sat down. When it was my turn, the same voice came out, a crippled animal running on broken legs.

Sets up conflict

Conflict slows pace; heightens suspense

Appeals to sense

You could hear splinters in my voice, bones rub- Creates new
Confirms bing jagged against one another. I was loud, image
point of though. I was glad I didn't whisper.
view

Comment This paragraph, taken from the final section of *The Woman Warrior*, recounts an embarrassing scene involving two Chinese sisters. Kingston describes how she and her sister prepare for the expected recitation. The conflict occurs when the teacher calls on the second-born sister first—a breach of Chinese etiquette. By describing how she looks down at her desk, Kingston slows the pace and heightens the anxiety of the situation. She then selects details and images to evoke the sound of her sister's and then her own voice as they complete the lesson.

LAUREN BRINER
Deloris

"All right, how do you say 'dollars' in Spanish?" Mrs. Tyrrel was setting the rules for Spanish II, but we wanted the old rules. Last year Mr. Kreuger, who taught Spanish I, loved to throw parties. I guess he thought fiestas would make us want to learn Spanish. What we really wanted was more fiestas. But now, according to Mrs. Tyrrel, the party was over. She peered at us over the top of her glasses looking for a snitch. We avoided her eyes by thumbing the sides of our new books. "Lauren? How about you?" I looked for help. No luck! My party friends were faking it, staring at the unintelligible sentences in *Spanish II*. I was on my own. I looked up at Mrs. Tyrrel. "Lauren?" I was desperate, caught in her gaze. I panicked. In a really hokey accent, I suggested a possible answer, "Dellores?" "Deloris? Who's Deloris? Is she a friend of yours?" Mrs. Tyrrel was laughing. The whole class began laughing, "Deloris! Deloris! Deloris!" The blood rushed to

my face and tears welled in my eyes. So much for
old rules and old friends.

1. How does Briner's description of the two teachers establish the
   conflict in this episode?
2. How do the responses of the teacher and the class to Lauren's
   answer reveal the writer's point of view?

NARRATION AND DESCRIPTION

Points to Remember

1. Focus your narrative on the "story" in your story—
   that is, focus on the conflict that defines the plot.
2. Vary the pace of your narrative so that you can summarize some events quickly and render others as fully
   realized scenes.
3. Supply evocative details to help your readers experience the dramatic development of your narrative.
4. Establish a consistent point of view so that your readers know how you have positioned yourself in your
   story.
5. Represent the events in your narrative so that your
   story makes its point.

Maya Angelou (given name, Marguerita Johnson)
was born in St. Louis, Missouri, in 1928 and
spent her early years in California and Arkansas. A
woman of varied accomplishments, she is a novelist, poet, playwright, stage and screen performer,
composer, and singer. She is perhaps best known
for her autobiographical novels: *I Know Why the
Caged Bird Sings* (1970), *Gather Together in My
Name* (1974), *Singin' and Swingin' and Gettin'
Merry Like Christmas* (1976), *Heart of a Woman*
(1981), *All God's Children Need Traveling Shoes*
(1986), *Wouldn't Take Nothing for My Journey
Now* (1993), *A Brave and Startling Truth* (1995),
and *Oh Pray My Wings Are Gonna Fit Me Well*
(1997). Angelou's poetry is equally well respected
and is published in her *Complete Collected Poems*
(1994). In the following selection from *I Know
Why the Caged Bird Sings,* Angelou recounts how
she maintained her identity in a world of prejudice.

My Name Is Margaret

R ECENTLY A WHITE woman from Texas, who would   1
quickly describe herself as a liberal, asked me about
my hometown. When I told her that in Stamps my grandmother had owned the only Negro general merchandise
store since the turn of the century, she exclaimed, "Why,
you were a debutante." Ridiculous and even ludicrous. But
Negro girls in small Southern towns, whether poverty-
stricken or just munching along on a few of life's necessities,
were given as extensive and irrelevant preparations for adulthood as rich white girls shown in magazines. Admittedly
the training was not the same. While white girls learned to

waltz and sit gracefully with a tea cup balanced on their knees, we were lagging behind, learning the mid-Victorian values with very little money to indulge them. (Come and see Edna Lomax spending the money she made picking cotton on five balls of ecru tatting thread. Her fingers are bound to snag the work and she'll have to repeat the stitches time and time again. But she knows that when she buys the thread.)

We were required to embroider and I had trunkfuls of colorful dishtowels, pillowcases, runners and handkerchiefs to my credit. I mastered the art of crocheting and tatting, and there was a lifetime's supply of dainty doilies that would never be used in sacheted dresser drawers. It went without saying that all girls could iron and wash, but the finer touches around the home, like setting a table with real silver, baking roasts and cooking vegetables without meat, had to be learned elsewhere. Usually at the source of those habits. During my tenth year, a white woman's kitchen became my finishing school.

Mrs. Viola Cullinan was a plump woman who lived in a three-bedroom house somewhere behind the post office. She was singularly unattractive until she smiled, and then the lines around her eyes and mouth which made her look perpetually

---

During my tenth year, a white woman's kitchen became my finishing school.

---

dirty disappeared, and her face looked like the mask of an impish elf. She usually rested her smile until late afternoon when her women friends dropped in and Miss Glory, the cook, served them cold drinks on the closed-in porch.

The exactness of her house was inhuman. This glass went here and only here. That cup had its place and it was an act of impudent rebellion to place it anywhere else. At twelve o'clock the table was set. At 12:15 Mrs. Cullinan sat down to dinner (whether her husband had arrived or not). At 12:16 Miss Glory brought out the food.

It took me a week to learn the difference between a salad plate, a bread plate and a dessert plate.

Mrs. Cullinan kept up the tradition of her wealthy parents. She was from Virginia. Miss Glory, who was a descendant of slaves that had worked for the Cullinans, told me her history. She had married beneath her (according to Miss Glory). Her husband's family hadn't had their money very long and what they had "didn't 'mount to much."

As ugly as she was, I thought privately, she was lucky to get a husband above or beneath her station. But Miss Glory wouldn't let me say a thing against her mistress. She was very patient with me, however, over the housework. She explained the dishware, silverware and servants' bells. The large round bowl in which soup was served wasn't a soup bowl, it was a tureen. There were goblets, sherbet glasses, ice-cream glasses, wine glasses, green glass coffee cups with matching saucers, and water glasses. I had a glass to drink from, and it sat with Miss Glory's on a separate shelf from the others. Soup spoons, gravy boat, butter knives, salad forks and carving platter were additions to my vocabulary and in fact almost represented a new language. I was fascinated with the novelty, with the fluttering Mrs. Cullinan and her Alice-in-Wonderland house.

Her husband remains, in my memory, undefined. I lumped him with all the other white men that I had ever seen and tried not to see.

On our way home one evening, Miss Glory told me that Mrs. Cullinan couldn't have children. She said that she was too delicate-boned. It was hard to imagine bones at all under those layers of fat. Miss Glory went on to say that the doctor had taken out all her lady organs. I reasoned that a pig's organs included the lungs, heart and liver, so if Mrs. Cullinan was walking around without those essentials, it explained why she drank alcohol out of unmarked bottles. She was keeping herself embalmed.

When I spoke to Bailey about it, he agreed that I was right, but he also informed me that Mr. Cullinan had two daughters by a colored lady and that I knew them very well. He added that the girls were the spitting image of their father. I was unable to remember what he looked like, although I had just left him a few hours before, but I thought of the Coleman girls. They were very light-skinned and certainly didn't look very much like their mother (no one ever mentioned Mr. Coleman).

My pity for Mrs. Cullinan preceded me the next morning 11
like the Cheshire cat's smile. Those girls, who could have been her daughters, were beautiful. They didn't have to straighten their hair. Even when they were caught in the rain, their braids still hung down straight like tamed snakes. Their mouths were pouty little cupid's bows. Mrs. Cullinan didn't know what she missed. Or maybe she did. Poor Mrs. Cullinan.

For weeks after, I arrived early, left late and tried very hard 12
to make up for her barrenness. If she had had her own children, she wouldn't have had to ask me to run a thousand errands from her back door to the back door of her friends. Poor old Mrs. Cullinan.

Then one evening Miss Glory told me to serve the ladies 13
on the porch. After I set the tray down and turned toward the kitchen, one of the women asked, "What's your name, girl?" It was the speckled-faced one. Mrs. Cullinan said, "She doesn't talk much. Her name's Margaret."

"Is she dumb?" 14

"No. As I understand it, she can talk when she wants to 15
but she's usually quiet as a little mouse. Aren't you, Margaret?"

I smiled at her. Poor thing. No organs and couldn't even 16
pronounce my name correctly.

"She's a sweet little thing, though." 17

"Well, that may be, but the name's too long. I'd never 18
bother myself. I'd call her Mary if I was you."

I fumed into the kitchen. That horrible woman would 19
never have the chance to call me Mary because if I was starving I'd never work for her. I decided I wouldn't pee on her if her heart was on fire. Giggles drifted in off the porch

and into Miss Glory's pots. I wondered what they could be laughing about.

Whitefolks were so strange. Could they be talking about [20] me? Everybody knew that they stuck together better than the Negroes did. It was possible that Mrs. Cullinan had friends in St. Louis who heard about a girl from Stamps being in court and wrote to tell her. Maybe she knew about Mr. Freeman.

My lunch was in my mouth a second time and I went [21] outside and relieved myself on the bed of four-o'clocks. Miss Glory thought I might be coming down with something and told me to go on home, that Momma would give me some herb tea, and she'd explain to her mistress.

I realized how foolish I was being before I reached the [22] pond. Of course Mrs. Cullinan didn't know. Otherwise she wouldn't have given me two nice dresses that Momma cut down, and she certainly wouldn't have called me a "sweet little thing." My stomach felt fine, and I didn't mention anything to Momma.

That evening I decided to write a poem on being white, [23] fat, old and without children. It was going to be a tragic ballad. I would have to watch her carefully to capture the essence of her loneliness and pain.

The very next day, she called me by the wrong name. Miss [24] Glory and I were washing up the lunch dishes when Mrs. Cullinan came to the doorway. "Mary?"

Miss Glory asked, "Who?" [25]

Mrs. Cullinan, sagging a little, knew and I knew. "I want [26] Mary to go down to Mrs. Randall's and take her some soup. She's not been feeling well for a few days."

Miss Glory's face was a wonder to see. "You mean Mar- [27] garet, ma'am. Her name's Margaret."

"That's too long. She's Mary from now on. Heat that soup [28] from last night and put it in the china tureen and, Mary, I want you to carry it carefully."

Every person I knew had a hellish horror of being "called [29] out of his name." It was a dangerous practice to call a Negro anything that could be loosely construed as insulting because of the centuries of their having been called niggers, jigs, dinges, blackbirds, crows, boots and spooks.

Miss Glory had a fleeting second of feeling sorry for me. 30 Then as she handed me the hot tureen she said, "Don't mind, don't pay that no mind. Sticks and stones may break your bones, but words . . . You know, I been working for her for twenty years."

She held the back door open for me. "Twenty years. I 31 wasn't much older than you. My name used to be Hallelujah. That's what Ma named me, but my mistress give me 'Glory,' and it stuck. I likes it better too."

I was in the little path that ran behind the houses when 32 Miss Glory shouted, "It's shorter too."

For a few seconds it was a tossup over whether I would 33 laugh (imagine being named Hallelujah) or cry (imagine letting some white woman rename you for her convenience). My anger saved me from either outburst. I had to quit the job, but the problem was going to be how to do it. Momma wouldn't allow me to quit for just any reason.

"She's a peach. That woman is a real peach." Mrs. Ran- 34 dall's maid was talking as she took the soup from me, and I wondered what her name used to be and what she answered to now.

For a week I looked into Mrs. Cullinan's face as she called 35 me Mary. She ignored my coming late and leaving early. Miss Glory was a little annoyed because I had begun to leave egg yolk on the dishes and wasn't putting much heart in polishing the silver. I hoped that she would complain to our boss, but she didn't.

Then Bailey solved my dilemma. He had me describe the 36 contents of the cupboard and the particular plates she liked best. Her favorite piece was a casserole shaped like a fish and the green glass coffee cups. I kept his instructions in mind, so on the next day when Miss Glory was hanging out clothes and I had again been told to serve the old biddies on the porch, I dropped the empty serving tray. When I heard Mrs. Cullinan scream, "Mary!" I picked up the casserole and two of the green glass cups in readiness. As she rounded the kitchen door I let them fall on the tiled floor.

I could never absolutely describe to Bailey what happened   37
next, because each time I got to the part where she fell on the floor and screwed up her ugly face to cry, we burst out laughing. She actually wobbled around on the floor and picked up shards of the cups and cried, "Oh, Momma. Oh, dear Gawd. It's Momma's china from Virginia. Oh, Momma, I sorry."

Miss Glory came running in from the yard and the women   38
from the porch crowded around. Miss Glory was almost as broken up as her mistress. "You mean to say she broke our Virginia dishes? What we gone do?"

Miss Cullinan cried louder, "That clumsy nigger. Clumsy   39
little black nigger."

Old speckled-face leaned down and asked, "Who did it,   40
Viola? Was it Mary? Who did it?"

Everything was happening so fast I can't remember   41
whether her action preceded her words, but I know that Mrs. Cullinan said, "Her name's Margaret, goddamn it, her name's Margaret." And she threw a wedge of the broken plate at me. It could have been the hysteria which put her aim off, but the flying crockery caught Miss Glory right over the ear and she started screaming.

I left the front door wide open so all the neighbors could   42
hear.

Mrs. Cullinan was right about one thing. My name wasn't   43
Mary.

For Study and Discussion

QUESTIONS FOR RESPONSE

1. In what ways do you identify with your name? How do you feel when someone mispronounces, changes, or forgets it?
2. What questions do you have about some of the unresolved issues

in the narration? For example, what do you think will happen when Margaret loses her job?

QUESTIONS ABOUT PURPOSE

1. In what sense does Mrs. Cullinan's kitchen serve as Angelou's "finishing school"? What is she supposed to learn there? What does she learn?
2. How does Angelou's description of Mrs. Cullinan's house as *exact* and *inhuman* support her purpose in recounting the events that take place there?

QUESTIONS ABOUT AUDIENCE

1. How does Angelou's comment about the liberal woman from Texas identify the immediate audience for her essay?
2. What assumptions does Angelou make about her other readers when she comments on the laughter of the white women on the porch?

QUESTIONS ABOUT STRATEGIES

1. How does Angelou use the three discussions of her name to organize her narrative? How does she pace the third discussion to provide an effective resolution for her essay?
2. How does Angelou's intention to write a poem about Mrs. Cullinan establish her initial attitude toward her employer? What changes her attitude toward Mrs. Cullinan's "loneliness and pain"?

QUESTIONS FOR DISCUSSION

1. How did you feel about Glory's and Bailey's reactions to the destruction of the fish-shaped casserole? Explain their strengths and weaknesses as a teacher or adviser.
2. Angelou admits that poor black girls in small southern towns and rich white girls in magazines do not receive the same training. What evidence in the essay suggests that both girls were given "extensive and irrelevant preparations for adulthood"?

Doris Kearns Goodwin was born in 1943 in Rockville Centre, New York, and educated at Colby College and Harvard University. She worked in Washington, D.C., at various government agencies, eventually becoming special consultant to President Lyndon Johnson. That appointment enabled her to write *Lyndon Johnson and the American Dream* (1976). She has worked since at Harvard University where she has written *The Fitzgeralds and the Kennedys: An American Saga* (1987) and *No Ordinary Time—Franklin and Eleanor Roosevelt: The Home Front in World War II* (1994), which won the Pulitzer Prize. She has also appeared frequently on television as a historical commentator on current events. In "Keeping the Scorebook," reprinted from her memoir *Wait till Next Year* (1997), Goodwin explains how she recorded the deeds of her favorite baseball team, the Brooklyn Dodgers.

Keeping the Scorebook

W HEN I WAS six, my father gave me a bright-red scorebook that opened my heart to the game of baseball. After dinner on long summer nights, he would sit beside me in our small enclosed porch to hear my account of that day's Brooklyn Dodger game. Night after night he taught me the odd collection of symbols, numbers, and letters that enable a baseball lover to record every action of the game. Our score sheets had blank boxes in which we could draw our own slanted lines in the form of a diamond as we followed players around the bases. Wherever the baserunner's progress stopped, the line stopped. He instructed me to fill in the unused boxes at the end of each inning with an elaborate checkerboard design which made it absolutely clear who had been the last to bat and who would lead off the next inning. By the time I had mastered the art of scorekeeping, a lasting bond had been forged among my father, baseball, and me.

All through the summer of 1949, my first summer as a fan, I spent my afternoons sitting cross-legged before the squat Philco radio which stood as a permanent fixture on our porch in Rockville Centre, on the South Shore of Long Island, New York. With my scorebook spread before me, I attended Dodger games through the courtly voice of Dodger announcer Red Barber. As he announced the lineup, I carefully printed each player's name in a column on the left side of my

2

---

*The nightly recountings to
my father of the Dodgers' progress
provided my first lessons
in the narrative art.*

---

sheet. Then, using the standard system my father had taught me, which assigned a number to each position in the field, starting with a "1" for the pitcher and ending with a "9" for the right fielder, I recorded every play. I found it difficult at times to sit still. As the Dodgers came to bat, I would walk around the room, talking to the players as if they were standing in front of me. At critical junctures, I tried to make a bargain, whispering and cajoling while Pee Wee Reese or Duke Snider stepped into the batter's box: "Please, please, get a hit. If you get a hit now, I'll make my bed every day for a week." Sometimes, when the score was close and the opposing team at bat with men on base, I was too agitated to listen. Asking my mother to keep notes, I left the house for a walk around the block, hoping that when I returned the enemy threat would be over, and once again we'd be up at bat. Mostly, however, I stayed at my post, diligently recording each inning so that, when my father returned from his job as bank examiner for the State of New York, I could re-create for him the game he had missed.

When my father came home from the city, he would 3 change from his three-piece suit into long pants and a short-sleeved sport shirt, and come downstairs for the ritual Manhattan cocktail with my mother. Then my parents would summon me for dinner from my play on the street outside our house. All through dinner I had to restrain myself from telling him about the day's game, waiting for the special time to come when we would sit together on the couch, my scorebook on my lap.

"Well, did anything interesting happen today?" he would 4 begin. And even before the daily question was completed I had eagerly launched into my narrative of every play, and almost every pitch, of that afternoon's contest. It never crossed my mind to wonder if, at the close of a day's work, he might find my lengthy account the least bit tedious. For there was mastery as well as pleasure in our nightly ritual. Through my knowledge, I commanded my father's undivided attention, the sign of his love. It would instill in me an early awareness of the power of narrative, which would introduce a lifetime of storytelling, fueled by the naive confidence that others would find me as entertaining as my father did.

Michael Francis Aloysius Kearns, my father, was a short 5 man who appeared much larger on account of his erect bearing, broad chest, and thick neck. He had a ruddy Irish complexion, and his green eyes flashed with humor and vitality. When he smiled his entire face was transformed, radiating enthusiasm and friendliness. He called me "Bubbles," a pet name he had chosen, he told me, because I seemed to enjoy so many things. Anxious to confirm his description, I refused to let my enthusiasm wane, even when I grew tired or grumpy. Thus excitement about things became a habit, a part of my personality, and the expectation that I should enjoy new experiences often engendered the enjoyment itself.

These nightly recountings of the Dodgers' progress pro-   6
vided my first lessons in the narrative art. From the scorebook, with its tight squares of neatly arranged symbols, I
could unfold the tale of an entire game and tell a story that
seemed to last almost as long as the game itself. At first, I was
unable to resist the temptation to skip ahead to an important
play in later innings. At times, I grew so excited about a
Dodger victory that I blurted out the final score before I had
hardly begun. But as I became more experienced in my
storytelling, I learned to build a dramatic story with a beginning, middle, and end. Slowly, I learned that if I could recount the game, one batter at a time, inning by inning,
without divulging the outcome, I could keep the suspense
and my father's interest alive until the very last pitch. Sometimes I pretended that I was the great Red Barber himself,
allowing my voice to swell when reporting a home run,
quieting to a whisper when the action grew tense, injecting
tidbits about the players into my reports. At critical moments,
I would jump from the couch to illustrate a ball that turned
foul at the last moment or a dropped fly that was scored as
an error.

"How many hits did Roy Campanella get?" my dad would   7
ask. Tracing my finger across the horizontal line that represented Campanella's at bats that day, I would count. "One,
two, three. Three hits, a single, a double, and another single."
"How many strikeouts for Don Newcombe?" It was easy. I
would count the Ks. "One, two . . . eight. He had eight
strikeouts." Then he'd ask me more subtle questions about
different plays—whether a strikeout was called or swinging,
whether the double play was around the horn, whether the
single that won the game was hit to left or right. If I had
scored carefully, using the elaborate system he had taught me,
I would know the answers. My father pointed to the second
inning, where Jackie Robinson had hit a single and then
stolen second. There was excitement in his voice. "See, it's
all here. While Robinson was dancing off second he rattled
the pitcher so badly that the next two guys walked to load
the bases. That's the impact Robinson makes, game after

game. Isn't he something?" His smile at such moments inspired me to take my responsibility seriously.

Sometimes, a particular play would trigger in my father a 8 memory of a similar situation in a game when he was young, and he would tell me stories about the Dodgers when he was a boy growing up in Brooklyn. His vivid tales featured strange heroes such as Casey Stengel, Zack Wheat, and Jimmy Johnston. Though it was hard at first to imagine that the Casey Stengel I knew, the manager of the Yankees, with his colorful language and hilarious antics, was the same man as the Dodger outfielder who hit an inside-the-park home run at the first game ever played at Ebbets Field, my father so skillfully stitched together the past and the present that I felt as if I were living in different time zones. If I closed my eyes, I imagined I was at Ebbets Field in the 1920s for that celebrated game when Dodger right fielder Babe Herman hit a double with the bases loaded, and through a series of mishaps on the base paths, three Dodgers ended up at third base at the same time. And I was sitting by my father's side, five years before I was born, when the lights were turned on for the first time at Ebbets Field, the crowd gasping and then cheering as the summer night was transformed into startling day.

When I had finished describing the game, it was time to 9 go to bed, unless I could convince my father to tally each player's batting average, reconfiguring his statistics to reflect the developments of that day's game. If Reese went 3 for 5 and had started the day at .303, my father showed me, by adding and multiplying all the numbers in his head, that his average would rise to .305. If Snider went 0 for 4 and started the day at .301 then his average would dip four points below the .300 mark. If Carl Erskine had let in three runs in seven innings, then my father would multiply three times nine, divide that by the number of innings pitched, and magically tell me whether Erskine's earned-run average had improved or worsened. It was this facility with numbers that had made it possible for my father to pass the civil-service test and become a bank examiner despite leaving school after the eighth grade. And this job had carried him from a Brooklyn tenement to a house with a lawn on Southard Avenue in Rockville Centre.

All through that summer, my father kept from me the knowledge that running box scores appeared in the daily newspapers. He never mentioned that these abbreviated histories had been a staple feature of the sports pages since the nineteenth century and were generally the first thing he and his fellow commuters turned to when they opened the *Daily News* and the *Herald Tribune* in the morning. I believed that, if I did not recount the games he had missed, my father would never have been able to follow our Dodgers the proper way, day by day, play by play, inning by inning. In other words, without me, his love of baseball would be forever unfulfilled. 10

I had the luck to fall in love with baseball at the start of an era of pure delight for New York fans. In each of the nine seasons from 1949 to 1957—spanning much of my childhood—we would watch one of the three New York teams—the Dodgers, the Giants, or the Yankees—compete in the World Series. In this golden era, the Yankees won five consecutive World Series, the Giants won two pennants and one championship, and my beloved Dodgers won one championship and five pennants, while losing two additional pennants in the last inning of the last game of the season. 11

In those days before players were free agents, the starting lineups remained basically intact for years. Fans gave their loyalty to a team, knowing the players they loved would hold the same positions and, year after year, exhibit the same endearing quirks and irritating habits. And what a storied lineup my Dodgers had in the postwar seasons: Roy Campanella started behind the plate, Gil Hodges at first, Jackie Robinson at second, Pee Wee Reese at short, Billy Cox at third, Gene Hermanski in left, Duke Snider in center, and Carl Furillo in right. Half of that lineup—Reese, Robinson, Campanella, and Snider—would eventually be elected to the Hall of Fame; Gil Hodges and Carl Furillo would likely have been enshrined in Cooperstown had they played in any other decade or for any other club. Never would there be a better time to be a Dodger fan. 12

For Study and Discussion

QUESTIONS FOR RESPONSE

1. What kind of special skill has one of your parents taught you—cooking, fishing, car repair—that has created a "lasting bond" between you?
2. How has the business of contemporary sports changed your loyalties to *your* team?

QUESTIONS ABOUT PURPOSE

1. What does Goodwin learn about the power of narrative by telling her father the story of the day's game?
2. Why is Goodwin so devoted to keeping the scorebook for her father?

QUESTIONS ABOUT AUDIENCE

1. How does Goodwin anticipate the needs and questions of her primary audience (her father)?
2. How does she make this story about old baseball games "come alive" for her contemporary readers?

QUESTIONS ABOUT STRATEGY

1. How does Goodwin learn "to build a dramatic story with a beginning, middle, and end"?
2. How does Goodwin's father use effective narrative strategies to tell his daughter about the games he saw when he was a boy?

QUESTIONS FOR DISCUSSION

1. Why does Goodwin's father fail to mention the box scores published in the daily newspaper?
2. How does Goodwin's attitude toward baseball demonstrate her realization that expecting to enjoy new experiences "often engendered the enjoyment itself."

Judith Ortiz Cofer was born in Hormigueros, Puerto Rico, in 1952. She emigrated to the United States in 1956 and was educated at Augusta College, Florida Atlantic University, and Oxford University. She has taught in the public schools of Palm Beach County, Florida, as well as at several universities such as Miami University and the University of Georgia. Her poetry is collected in *Reading for the Mainland* (1987) and *Terms of Survival* (1987), and her first novel, *The Line of the Sun* (1989), was nominated for the Pulitzer Prize. Her recent books include *The Latin Deli: Prose and Poetry* (1993) and *An Island Like You: Stories of the Barrio* (1995). In "The Myth of the Latin Woman: I Just Met a Girl Named María," reprinted from *The Latin Deli*, Cofer describes several experiences that taught her about the pervasive stereotypes of Latin women.

The Myth of the Latin Woman: I Just Met a Girl Named María

O N A BUS trip to London from Oxford University where I was earning some graduate credits one summer, a young man, obviously fresh from a pub, spotted me and as if struck by inspiration went down on his knees in the aisle. With both hands over his heart he broke into an Irish tenor's rendition of "María" from *West Side Story*. My politely amused fellow passengers gave his lovely voice the round of gentle applause it deserved. Though I was not quite as amused, I managed my version of an English smile: no show

1

of teeth, no extreme contortions of the facial muscles—I was at this time of my life practicing reserve and cool. Oh, that British control, how I coveted it. But María had followed me to London, reminding me of a prime fact of my life: you can leave the Island, master the English language, and travel as far as you can, but if you are a Latina, especially one like me who so obviously belongs to Rita Moreno's gene pool, the Island travels with you.

This is sometimes a very good thing—it may win you that   2
extra minute of someone's attention. But with some people, the same things can make *you* an island—not so much a tropical paradise as an Alcatraz, a place nobody wants to visit. As a Puerto Rican girl growing up in the United States and wanting like most children to "belong," I resented the stereotype that my Hispanic appearance called forth from many people I met.

Our family lived in a large urban center in New Jersey   3
during the sixties, where life was designed as a microcosm of

---

When a Puerto Rican girl dressed in her idea of what is attractive meets a man from the mainstream culture who has been trained to react to certain types of clothing, a clash is likely to take place.

---

my parents' casas on the island. We spoke in Spanish, we ate Puerto Rican food bought at the bodega, and we practiced strict Catholicism complete with Saturday confession and Sunday mass at a church where our parents were accommodated into a one-hour Spanish mass slot, performed by a Chinese priest trained as a missionary for Latin America.

As a girl I was kept under strict surveillance, since virtue   4
and modesty were, by cultural equation, the same as family

honor. As a teenager I was instructed on how to behave as a proper señorita. But it was a conflicting message girls got, since the Puerto Rican mothers also encouraged their daughters to look and act like women and to dress in clothes our Anglo friends and their mothers found too "mature" for our age. It was, and is, cultural, yet I often felt humiliated when I appeared at an American friend's party wearing a dress more suitable to a semiformal than to a playroom birthday celebration. At Puerto Rican festivities, neither the music nor the colors we wore could be too loud. I still experience a vague sense of letdown when I'm invited to a "party" and it turns out to be a marathon conversation in hushed tones rather than a fiesta with salsa, laughter, and dancing—the kind of celebration I remember from my childhood.

I remember Career Day in our high school, when teachers   5 told us to come dressed as if for a job interview. It quickly became obvious that to the barrio girls, "dressing up" sometimes meant wearing ornate jewelry and clothing that would be more appropriate (by mainstream standards) for the company Christmas party than as daily office attire. That morning I had agonized in front of my closet, trying to figure out what a "career girl" would wear because, essentially, except for Marlo Thomas on TV, I had no models on which to base my decision. I knew how to dress for school: at the Catholic school I attended we all wore uniforms; I knew how to dress for Sunday mass, and I knew what dresses to wear for parties at my relatives' homes. Though I do not recall the precise details of my Career Day outfit, it must have been a composite of the above choices. But I remember a comment my friend (an Italian-American) made in later years that coalesced my impressions of that day. She said that at the business school she was attending the Puerto Rican girls always stood out for wearing "everything at once." She meant, of course, too much jewelry, too many accessories. On that day at school, we were simply made the negative models by the nuns who were themselves not credible fashion experts to any of us. But it was painfully obvious to me that to the others, in their tailored skirts and silk blouses, we must have seemed "hopeless" and "vulgar." Though I now know that most adolescents feel out of step much of the time, I also know that for the Puerto Rican girls of my generation that sense was intensified. The way our teachers and classmates looked at us that day in school was just a taste of the culture clash that awaited us in the real world, where prospective employers and men on the street would often misinterpret our tight skirts and jingling bracelets as a come-on.

Mixed cultural signals have perpetuated certain stereotypes—for example, that of the Hispanic woman as the "Hot Tamale" or sexual firebrand. It is a one-dimensional view that the media have found easy to promote. In their special vocabulary, advertisers have designated "sizzling" and "smoldering" as the adjectives of choice for describing not only the foods but also the women of Latin America. From conversations in my house I recall hearing about the harassment that Puerto Rican women endured in factories where the "boss men" talked to them as if sexual innuendo was all they understood and, worse, often gave them the choice of submitting to advances or being fired.

It is custom, however, not chromosomes, that leads us to choose scarlet over pale pink. As young girls, we were influenced in our decisions about clothes and colors by the women—older sisters and mothers who had grown up on a tropical island where the natural environment was a riot of primary colors, where showing your skin was one way to keep cool as well as to look sexy. Most important of all, on the island, women perhaps felt freer to dress and move more provocatively, since, in most cases, they were protected by the traditions, mores, and laws of a Spanish/Catholic system of morality and machismo whose main rule was: *You may look at my sister, but if you touch her I will kill you.* The extended family and church structure could provide a young woman with a circle of safety in her small pueblo on the island; if a man "wronged" a girl, everyone would close in to save her family honor.

This is what I have gleaned from my discussions as an adult   8
with older Puerto Rican women. They have told me about
dressing in their best party clothes on Saturday nights and
going to the town's plaza to promenade with their girlfriends
in front of the boys they liked. The males were thus given an
opportunity to admire the women and to express their admiration in the form of *piropos:* erotically charged street poems
they composed on the spot. I have been subjected to a few
piropos while visiting the Island, and they can be outrageous,
although custom dictates that they must never cross into
obscenity. This ritual, as I understand it, also entails a show
of studied indifference on the woman's part; if she is "decent," she must not acknowledge the man's impassioned
words. So I do understand how things can be lost in translation. When a Puerto Rican girl dressed in her idea of what
is attractive meets a man from the mainstream culture who
has been trained to react to certain types of clothing as a
sexual signal, a clash is likely to take place. The line I first
heard based on this aspect of the myth happened when the
boy who took me to my first formal dance leaned over to
plant a sloppy overeager kiss painfully on my mouth, and
when I didn't respond with sufficient passion said in a resent-
ful tone: "I thought you Latin girls were supposed to mature
early"—my first instance of being thought of as a fruit or
vegetable—I was supposed to *ripen,* not just grow into womanhood like other girls.

It is surprising to some of my professional friends that   9
some people, including those who should know better, still
put others "in their place." Though rarer, these incidents are
still commonplace in my life. It happened to me most recently
during a stay at a very classy metropolitan hotel favored by
young professional couples for their weddings. Late one evening after the theater, as I walked toward my room with my
new colleague (a woman with whom I was coordinating an
arts program), a middle-aged man in a tuxedo, a young girl
in satin and lace on his arm, stepped directly into our path.
With his champagne glass extended toward me, he exclaimed,
"Evita!"

Our way blocked, my companion and I listened as the man 10
half-recited, half-bellowed "Don't Cry for Me, Argentina."
When he finished, the young girl said: "How about a round
of applause for my daddy?" We complied, hoping this would
bring the silly spectacle to a close. I was becoming aware that
our little group was attracting the attention of the other
guests. "Daddy" must have perceived this too, and he once
more barred the way as we tried to walk past him. He began
to shout-sing a ditty to the tune of "La Bamba"—except the
lyrics were about a girl named María whose exploits all
rhymed with her name and gonorrhea. The girl kept saying
"Oh, Daddy" and looking at me with pleading eyes. She
wanted me to laugh along with the others. My companion
and I stood silently waiting for the man to end his offensive
song. When he finished, I looked not at him but at his
daughter. I advised her calmly never to ask her father what
he had done in the army. Then I walked between them and
to my room. My friend complimented me on my cool handling of the situation. I confessed to her that I really had
wanted to push the jerk into the swimming pool. I knew that
this same man—probably a corporate executive, well educated, even worldly by most standards—would not have been
likely to regale a white woman with a dirty song in public.
He would perhaps have checked his impulse by assuming that
she could be somebody's wife or mother, or at least *somebody*
who might take offense. But to him, I was just an Evita or a
María: merely a character in his cartoon-populated universe.

Because of my education and my proficiency with the 11
English language, I have acquired many mechanisms for dealing with the anger I experience. This was not true for my
parents, nor is it true for the many Latin women working at
menial jobs who must put up with stereotypes about our
ethnic group such as: "They make good domestics." This is
another facet of the myth of the Latin woman in the United
States. Its origin is simple to deduce. Work as domestics,
waitressing, and factory jobs are all that's available to women
with little English and few skills. The myth of the Hispanic
menial has been sustained by the same media phenomenon

that made "Mammy" from *Gone with the Wind* America's idea of the black woman for generations; María, the housemaid or counter girl, is now indelibly etched into the national psyche. The big and the little screens have presented us with the picture of the funny Hispanic maid, mispronouncing words and cooking up a spicy storm in a shiny California kitchen.

This media-engendered image of the Latina in the United States has been documented by feminist Hispanic scholars, who claim that such portrayals are partially responsible for the denial of opportunities for upward mobility among Latinas in the professions. I have a Chicana friend working on a Ph.D. in philosophy at a major university. She says her doctor still shakes his head in puzzled amazement at all the "big words" she uses. Since I do not wear my diplomas around my neck for all to see, I too have on occasion been sent to that "kitchen," where some think I obviously belong.   12

One such incident that has stayed with me, though I recognize it as a minor offense, happened on the day of my first public poetry reading. It took place in Miami in a boat-restaurant where we were having lunch before the event. I was nervous and excited as I walked in with my notebook in my hand. An older woman motioned me to her table. Thinking (foolish me) that she wanted me to autograph a copy of my brand new slender volume of verse, I went over. She ordered a cup of coffee from me, assuming that I was the waitress. Easy enough to mistake my poems for menus, I suppose. I know that it wasn't an intentional act of cruelty, yet of all the good things that happened that day, I remember that scene most clearly, because it reminded me of what I had to overcome before anyone would take me seriously. In retrospect I understand that my anger gave my reading fire, that I have almost always taken doubts in my abilities as a challenge—and that the result is, most times, a feeling of satisfaction at having won a convert when I see the cold, appraising eyes warm to my words, the body language change, the smile that indicates that I have opened some   13 avenue for communication. That day I read to that woman and her lowered eyes told me that she was embarrassed at her little faux pas, and when I willed her to look up at me, it was my victory, and she graciously allowed me to punish her with my full attention. We shook hands at the end of the reading, and I never saw her again. She has probably forgotten the whole thing but maybe not.

Yet I am one of the lucky ones. My parents made it possible 14 for me to acquire a stronger footing in the mainstream culture by giving me the chance at an education. And books and art have saved me from the harsher forms of ethnic and racial prejudice that many of my Hispanic *compañeras* have had to endure. I travel a lot around the United States, reading from my books of poetry and my novel, and the reception I most often receive is one of positive interest by people who want to know more about my culture. There are, however, thousands of Latinas without the privilege of an education or the entrée into society that I have. For them life is a struggle against the misconceptions perpetuated by the myth of the Latina as whore, domestic or criminal. We cannot change this by legislating the way people look at us. The transformation, as I see it, has to occur at a much more individual level. My personal goal in my public life is to try to replace the old pervasive stereotypes and myths about Latinas with a much more interesting set of realities. Every time I give a reading, I hope the stories I tell, the dreams and fears I examine in my work, can achieve some universal truth which will get my audience past the particulars of my skin color, my accent, or my clothes.

I once wrote a poem in which I called us Latinas "God's 15 brown daughters." This poem is really a prayer of sorts, offered upward, but also, through the human-to-human channel of art, outward. It is a prayer for communication, and for respect. In it, Latin women pray "in Spanish to an Anglo God / with a Jewish heritage," and they are "fervently hoping / that if not omnipotent, / at least He be bilingual."

For Study and Discussion

QUESTIONS FOR RESPONSE

1. In what ways have people misread your behavior—by focusing on your clothes, your language, or your looks?
2. What strategies do you use to control your anger and resentment when you are misread?

QUESTIONS ABOUT PURPOSE

1. Why does Cofer introduce the conflict between *custom* and *chromosomes*? How does this conflict help explain the concept of *stereotype*?
2. How does this narrative help accomplish Cofer's "personal goal in her public life?"

QUESTIONS ABOUT AUDIENCE

1. In what ways does Cofer use the references to *María* and *Evita* to identify her audience?
2. How does she use the example of the *piropos* to educate her audience?

QUESTIONS ABOUT STRATEGIES

1. How does Cofer use the details of Career Day to explain how a cultural stereotype is perpetuated?
2. How does she manipulate point of view at her "first public poetry reading" to illustrate how she intends to change that stereotype?

QUESTIONS FOR DISCUSSION

1. How does Cofer use *Gone with the Wind* to illustrate how the media creates stereotypes?
2. Why does she put so much emphasis on education? What can it do *for* you? What might it do *to* you?

Andre Dubus (1936–1999) was born in Lake Charles, Louisiana, and educated at McNeese State College and the University of Iowa. He taught writing at universities such as the University of Alabama and Boston University. His work includes novels such as *The Lieutenant* (1967), *Voices from the Moon* (1984), and *House of Sand and Fog* (1999), and several collections of short stories, including *Finding a Girl in America* (1980) and *Dancing After Hours* (1996). In 1986, he barely survived a devastating traffic accident that cost him his leg. He writes about confronting his disability in a series of essays, *Meditations from a Movable Chair* (1998). In "Digging," reprinted from that collection, Dubus remembers the lessons he learned from physical labor.

Digging

T HAT HOT JUNE in Lafayette, Louisiana, I was sixteen, I would be seventeen in August, I weighed 105 pounds, and my ruddy, broad-chested father wanted me to have a summer job. I only wanted the dollar allowance he gave me each week, and the dollar and a quarter I earned caddying for him on weekend and Wednesday afternoons. With a quarter I could go to a movie, or buy a bottle of beer, or a pack of cigarettes to smoke secretly. I did not have a girlfriend, so I did not have to buy drinks or food or movie tickets for anyone else. I did not want to work. I wanted to drive around with my friends, or walk with them downtown, to stand in front of the department store, comb our ducktails, talk, look at girls.

1

My father was a civil engineer, and the district manager for   2
the Gulf States Utilities Company. He had been working for
them since he left college, beginning as a surveyor, wearing
boots and khakis and, in a holster on his belt, a twenty-two
caliber pistol for cottonmouths. At home he was quiet; in the
evenings he sat in his easy chair, and smoked, and read: *Time*,
The Saturday Evening Post, *Collier's*, *The Reader's Digest*,
detective novels, books about golf, and Book-of-the-Month
Club novels. He loved to talk, and he did this at parties I
listened to from my bedroom, and with his friends on the
golf course, and drinking in the clubhouse after playing eighteen holes. I listened to more of my father's conversations

---

*It is time to thank my father for wanting
me to work and telling me I had to work
and buying me lunch and a pith helmet
instead of taking me home to my mother
and sister.*

---

about politics and golf and his life and the world than I ever
engaged in, during the nearly twenty-two years I lived with
him. I was afraid of angering him, seeing his blue eyes, and
reddening face, hearing the words he would use to rebuke
me; but what I feared most was his voice, suddenly and
harshly rising. He never yelled for long, only a few sentences,
but they emptied me, as if his voice had pulled my soul from
my body. His voice seemed to empty the house, too, and,
when he stopped yelling, the house filled with silence. He did
not yell often. That sound was not part of our family life. The
fear of it was part of my love for him.

I was shy with him. Since my forties I have believed that   3
he was shy with me too, and I hope it was not as painful for
him as it was for me. I think my shyness had very little to do

with my fear. Other boys had fathers who yelled longer and more often, fathers who spanked them or, when they were in their teens, slapped or punched them. My father spanked me only three times, probably because he did not know of most of my transgressions. My friends with harsher fathers were neither afraid nor shy; they quarreled with their fathers, provoked them. My father sired a sensitive boy, easily hurt or frightened, and he worried about me; I knew he did when I was a boy, and he told me this on his deathbed, when I was a Marine captain.

My imagination gave me a dual life: I lived in my body, and at the same time lived a life no one could see. All my life I have told myself stories, and have talked in my mind to friends. Imagine my father sitting at supper with my mother and two older sisters and me: I am ten and small and appear distracted. Every year at school there is a bully, sometimes a new one, sometimes the one from the year before. I draw bullies to me, not because I am small, but because they know I will neither fight nor inform on them. I will take their pushes or pinches or punches, and try not to cry, and I will pretend I am not hurt. My father does not know this. He only sees me at supper, and I am not there. I am riding a horse and shooting bad men. My father eats, glances at me. I know he is trying to see who I am, who I will be. 4

Before my teens, he took me to professional wrestling matches because I wanted to go; he told me they were fake, and I did not believe him. We listened to championship boxing matches on the radio. When I was not old enough to fire a shotgun he took me dove hunting with his friends: we crouched in a ditch facing a field, and I watched the doves fly toward us and my father rising to shoot, then I ran to fetch the warm, dead and delicious birds. In summer he took me fishing with his friends; we walked in woods to creeks and bayous and fished with bamboo poles. When I was ten he learned to play golf and stopped hunting and fishing, and on weekends I was his caddy. I did not want to be, I wanted to play with my friends, but when I became a man and left home, I was grateful that I had spent those afternoons 5 watching him, listening to him. A minor league baseball team made our town its home, and my father took me to games, usually with my mother. When I was twelve or so, he taught me to play golf, and sometimes I played nine holes with him; more often and more comfortably, I played with other boys.

If my father and I were not watching or listening to some-   6
thing and responding to it, or were not doing something, but were simply alone together, I could not talk, and he did not, and I felt that I should, and I was ashamed. That June of my seventeenth year, I could not tell him that I did not want a job. He talked to a friend of his, a building contractor, who hired me as a carpenter's helper; my pay was seventy-five cents an hour.

On a Monday morning my father drove me to work. I   7
would ride the bus home and, next day, would start riding the bus to work. Probably my father drove me that morning because it was my first day; when I was twelve he had taken me to a store to buy my first pair of long pants; we boys wore shorts and, in fall and winter, knickers and long socks till we were twelve; and he had taken me to a barber for my first haircut. In the car I sat frightened, sadly resigned, and feeling absolutely incompetent. I had the lunch my mother had put in a brown paper bag, along with a mason jar with sugar and squeezed lemons in it, so I could make lemonade with water from the cooler. We drove to a street with houses and small stores and parked at a corner where, on a flat piece of land, men were busy. They were building a liquor store, and I assumed I would spend my summer handing things to a carpenter. I hoped he would be patient and kind.

As a boy in Louisiana's benevolent winters and hot sum-   8
mers I had played outdoors with friends: we built a club-house, chased each other on bicycles, shot air rifles at birds, tin cans, bottles, trees; in fall and winter, wearing shoulder pads and helmets, we played football on someone's very large side lawn; and in summer we played baseball in a field that a father mowed for us; he also built us a backstop of wood and chicken wire. None of us played well enough to be on a

varsity team; but I wanted that gift, not knowing that it was a gift, and I felt ashamed that I did not have it. Now we drove cars, smoked, drank in nightclubs. This was French Catholic country; we could always buy drinks. Sometimes we went on dates with girls, but more often looked at them and talked about them; or visited them, when several girls were gathered at the home of a girl whose parents were out for the evening. I had never done physical work except caddying, pushing a lawn mower, and raking leaves, and I was walking from the car with my father toward working men. My father wore his straw hat and seersucker suit. He introduced me to the foreman and said: "Make a man of him."

Then he left. The foreman wore a straw hat and looked   9 old; everyone looked old; the foreman was probably thirty-five. I stood mutely, waiting for him to assign me to some good-hearted Cajun carpenter. He assigned me a pickaxe and a shovel and told me to get into the trench and go to work. In all four sides of the trench were files of black men, swinging picks, and shoveling. The trench was about three feet deep and it would be the building's foundation; I went to where the foreman pointed, and laid my tools on the ground; two black men made a space for me, and I jumped between them. They smiled and we greeted each other. I would learn days later that they earned a dollar an hour. They were men with families and I knew this was unjust, as everything else was for black people. But on that first morning I did not know what they were being paid, I did not know their names, only that one was working behind me and one in front, and they were good to me and stronger than I could ever be. All I really knew in those first hours under the hot sun was raising the pickaxe and swinging it down, raising it and swinging, again and again till the earth was loose; then putting the pick on the ground beside me and taking the shovel and plunging it into dirt that I lifted and tossed beside the trench.

I did not have the strength for this: not in my back, my   10 legs, my arms, my shoulders. Certainly not in my soul. I only wanted it to end. The air was very humid, and sweat dripped on my face and arms, soaked my shirts and jeans. My hands gripping the pick or shovel were sore, my palms burned, the muscles in my arms ached, and my breath was quick. Sometimes I saw tiny black spots before my eyes. Weakly I raised the pick, straightening my back, then swung it down, bending my body with it, and it felt heavier than I was, more durable, this thing of wood and steel that was melting me. I laid it on the ground and picked up the shovel and pushed it into the dirt, lifted it, grunted, and emptied it beside the trench. The sun, always my friend till now, burned me, and my mouth and throat were dry, and often I climbed out of the trench and went to the large tin water cooler with a block of ice in it and water from a hose. At the cooler were paper cups and salt tablets, and I swallowed salt and drank and drank, and poured water onto my head and face; then I went back to the trench, the shovel, the pick.

Nausea came in the third or fourth hour. I kept swinging 11 the pick, pushing and lifting the shovel. I became my sick and hot and tired and hurting flesh. Or it became me; so, for an hour or more, I tasted a very small piece of despair. At noon in Lafayette a loud whistle blew, and in the cathedral the bell rang. I could not hear the bell where we worked, but I heard the whistle, and lowered the shovel and looked around. I was dizzy and sick. All the men had stopped working and were walking toward shade. One of the men with me said it was time to eat, and I climbed out of the trench and walked with black men to the shade of the tool shed. The white men went to another shaded place; I do not remember what work they had been doing that morning, but it was not with picks and shovels in the trench. Everyone looked hot but comfortable. The black men sat talking and began to eat and drink. My bag of lunch and jar with lemons and sugar were on the ground in the shade. Still I stood, gripped by nausea. I looked at the black men and at my lunch bag. Then my stomach tightened and everything in it rose, and I went around the corner of the shed where no one could see me and, bending over, I vomited and moaned and heaved until it ended. I went to the water cooler and rinsed my mouth and spat, and then

I took another paper cup and drank. I walked back to the shade and lay on my back, tasting vomit. One of the black men said: "You got to eat."

"I threw up," I said, and closed my eyes and slept for the rest of the hour that everyone—students and workers—had for the noon meal. At home my nineteen-year-old sister and my mother and father were eating dinner, meat and rice and gravy, vegetables and salad and iced tea with a loaf of mint; and an oscillating fan cooled them. My twenty-two-year-old sister was married. At one o'clock the whistle blew, and I woke up and stood and one of the black men said: "Are you all right?"

I nodded. If I had spoken, I may have wept. When I was a boy I could not tell a man what I felt, if I believed what I felt was unmanly. We went back to the trench, down into it, and I picked up the shovel I had left there at noon, and shoveled out all the loose earth between me and the man in front of me, then put the shovel beside the trench, lifted the pick, raised it over my shoulder, and swung it down into the dirt. I was dizzy and weak and hot; I worked for forty minutes or so; then, above me, I heard my father's voice, speaking my name. I looked up at him; he was here to take me home, to forgive my failure, and in my great relief I could not know that I would not be able to forgive it. I was going home. But he said: "Let's go buy you a hat."

Every man there wore a hat, most of them straw, the others baseball caps. I said nothing. I climbed out of the trench, and went with my father. In the car, in a voice softened with pride, he said: "The foreman called me. He said the Nigras told him you threw up, and didn't eat, and you didn't tell him."

"That's right," I said, and shamefully watched the road, and cars with people who seemed free of all torment, and let my father believe I was brave, because I was afraid to tell him that I was afraid to tell the foreman. Quietly we drove to town and he parked and took me first to a drugstore with air-conditioning and a lunch counter, and bought me a 7-Up for my stomach, and told me to order a sandwich. Sweet-smelling women at the counter were smoking. The men in the trench had smoked while they worked, but my body's only desire had been to stop shoveling and swinging the pick, to be with no transition at all in the shower at home, then to lie on my bed, feeling the soft breath of the fan on my damp skin. I would not have smoked at work anyway, with men. Now I wanted a cigarette. My father smoked, and I ate a bacon and lettuce and tomato sandwich.

Then we walked outside, into humidity and the heat and   16
glare of the sun. We crossed the street to the department store where, in the work clothes section, my father chose a pith helmet. I did not want to wear a pith helmet. I would happily wear one in Africa, hunting lions and rhinoceroses. But I did not want to wear such a thing in Lafayette. I said nothing; there was no hat I wanted to wear. I carried the helmet in its bag out of the store and, in the car, laid it beside me. At that place where sweating men worked, I put it on; a thin leather strap looped around the back of my head. I went to my two comrades in the trench. One of them said: "That's a good hat."

I jumped in.   17

The man behind me said: "You going to be all right now."   18

I was; and I still do not know why. A sandwich and a soft   19
drink had not given me any more strength than the breakfast I had vomited. An hour's respite in the car and the cool drugstore and buying the helmet that now was keeping my wet head cool certainly helped. But I had the same soft arms and legs, the same back and shoulders I had demanded so little of in my nearly seventeen years of stewardship. Yet all I remember of that afternoon is the absence of nausea.

At five o'clock the whistle blew downtown and we climbed   20
out of the trench and washed our tools with the hose, then put them in the shed. Dirt was on my arms and hands, my face and neck and clothes. I could have wrung sweat from my shirt and jeans. I got my lunch from the shade. My two comrades said, See you tomorrow. I said I would see them. I went to the bus stop at the corner and sat on the bench. My wet clothes cooled my skin. I looked down at my dirty tennis shoes; my socks and feet were wet. I watched people in passing cars. In one were teenaged boys, and they laughed

and shouted something about my helmet. I watched the car till it was blocks away, then took off the helmet and held it on my lap. I carried it aboard the bus; yet all summer I wore it at work, maybe because my father bought it for me and I did not want to hurt him, maybe because it was a wonderful helmet for hard work outdoors in Louisiana.

My father got home before I did and told my mother and 21 sister the story, the only one he knew, or the only one I assumed he knew. The women proudly greeted me when I walked into the house. They were also worried. They wanted to know how I felt. They wore dresses, they smelled of perfume or cologne, they were drinking bourbon and water, and my sister and father were smoking cigarettes. Standing in the living room, holding my lunch and helmet, I said I was fine. I could not tell the truth to these women who loved me, even if my father were not there. I could not say that I was not strong enough and that I could not bear going back to work tomorrow, and all summer, anymore than I could tell them I did not believe I was as good at being a boy as other boys were: not at sports, or with girls; and now not with a man's work. I was home, where vases held flowers, and things were clean, and our manners were good.

Next morning, carrying my helmet and lunch, I rode the 22 bus to work and joined the two black men in the trench. I felt that we were friends. Soon I felt this about all the black men at work. We were digging the foundation; we were the men and the boy with picks and shovels in the trench. One day the foundation was done. I use the passive voice, because this was a square or rectangular trench, men were working at each of its sides. I had been working with my comrades on the same side for weeks, moving not forward but down. Then it was done. Someone told us. Maybe the contractor was there, with the foreman. Who dug out that last bit of dirt? I only knew that I had worked as hard as I could, I was part of the trench, it was part of me, and it was finished; it was there in the earth to receive concrete and probably never to be seen again. Someone should have blown a bugle, we should have climbed exultant from the trench, gathered to wipe sweat from our brows, drink water, shake hands, then walk together to each of the four sides and marvel at what we had made.

On that second morning of work I was not sick, and at 23 noon I ate lunch with the blacks in the shade, then we all slept on the grass till one o'clock. We worked till five, said goodbye to each other, and they went to the colored section of town, and I rode the bus home. When I walked into the living room, into cocktail hour, and my family asked me about my day, I said it was fine. I may have learned something if I had told them the truth: the work was too hard, but after the first morning I could bear it. And all summer it would be hard; after we finished the foundation, I would be transferred to another crew. We would build a mess hall at a Boy Scout camp and, with a black man, I would dig a septic tank in clay so hard that the foreman kept hosing water into it as we dug; black men and I would push wheelbarrows of mixed cement; on my shoulder I would carry eighty-pound bags of dry cement, twenty-five pounds less than my own weight; and at the summer's end my body would be twenty pounds heavier. If I had told these three people who loved me that I did not understand my weak body's stamina, they may have taught me why something terrible had so quickly changed to something arduous.

It is time to thank my father for wanting me to work and 24 telling me I had to work and getting the job for me and buying me lunch and a pith helmet instead of taking me home to my mother and sister. He may have wanted to take me home. But he knew he must not, and he came tenderly to me. My mother would have been at home that afternoon; if he had taken me to her she would have given me iced tea and, after my shower, a hot dinner. When my sister came home from work, she would have understood, and told me not to despise myself because I could not work with a pickaxe and a shovel. And I would have spent the summer at home, nestled in the love of the two women, peering at my father's face, and yearning to be someone I respected, a varsity second baseman, a halfback, someone cheerleaders and drum majorettes and pretty scholars loved; yearning to be a man among men, and that is where my father sent me with a helmet on my head.

For Study and Discussion

QUESTIONS FOR RESPONSE

1. Have you ever had a summer job that required hard physical labor? How did your body respond to the demands of this work?
2. In what ways did your parents teach you about work?

QUESTIONS ABOUT PURPOSE

1. How do Dubus's father's instructions to the foreman—"Make a man of him"—reveal the narrator's purpose?
2. How is the narrator's admission that he lived a "dual life" revealed in his story?

QUESTIONS ABOUT AUDIENCE

1. How does Dubus's characterization of himself as sensitive and shy help him establish a connection with his audience?
2. How does his friendship with black workmen help him teach his audience something about justice?

QUESTIONS ABOUT STRATEGIES

1. How does Dubus pace his first day at work to reveal the intensity of his efforts?
2. How do Dubus's speculations about what would have happened if he had gone home to lunch help clarify the purpose of the narrative?

QUESTIONS FOR DISCUSSION

1. Why is it difficult—according to Dubus—to tell the truth to friends and family?
2. What does his father's decision to take him to lunch and buy him a pith helmet reveal about the nature of many father-son relationships?

George Orwell, the pen name of Eric Blair (1903–1950), was born in Motihari, Bengal, where his father was employed with the Bengal civil service. He was brought to England at an early age for schooling (Eton), but rather than completing his education at the university, he served with the Indian imperial police in Burma (1922–1927). He wrote about these experiences in his first novel, *Burmese Days.* Later he returned to Europe and worked at various jobs (described in *Down and Out in Paris and London,* 1933) before fighting on the Republican side in the Spanish civil war (see *Homage to Catalonia,* 1938). Orwell's attitudes toward war and government are reflected in his most famous books: *Animal Farm* (1945), *1984* (1949), and *Shooting an Elephant and Other Essays* (1950). In the title essay from the last volume, Orwell reports a "tiny incident" that gave him deeper insight into his own fears and "the real motives for which despotic governments act."

Shooting an Elephant

I N MOULMEIN, IN lower Burma, I was hated by large num- 1
bers of people—the only time in my life that I have been important enough for this to happen to me. I was sub-divisional police officer of the town, and in an aimless, petty kind of way anti-European feeling was very bitter. No one had the guts to raise a riot, but if a European woman went through the bazaars alone somebody would probably spit betel juice over her dress. As a police officer I was an obvious target and was baited whenever it seemed safe to do so. When a nimble Burman tripped me up on the football field and the

referee (another Burman) looked the other way, the crowd yelled with hideous laughter. This happened more than once. In the end the sneering yellow faces of young men that met me everywhere, the insults hooted after me when I was at a safe distance, got badly on my nerves. The young Buddhist priests were the worst of all. There were several thousands of them in the town and none of them seemed to have anything to do except stand on street corners and jeer at Europeans.

All this was perplexing and upsetting. For at that time I had already made up my mind that imperialism was an evil thing and the sooner I chucked up my job and got out of it   2

As soon as I saw the elephant I knew with perfect certainty that I ought not to shoot him.

---

the better. Theoretically—and secretly, of course—I was all for the Burmese and all against their oppressors, the British. As for the job I was doing, I hated it more bitterly than I can perhaps make clear. In a job like that you see the dirty work of Empire at close quarters. The wretched prisoners huddling in the stinking cages of the lock-ups, the gray, cowed faces of the long-term convicts, the scarred buttocks of the men who had been flogged with bamboos—all these oppressed me with an intolerable sense of guilt. But I could get nothing into perspective. I was young and ill educated and I had had to think out my problems in the utter silence that is imposed on every Englishman in the East. I did not even know that the British Empire is dying, still less did I know that it is a great deal better than the younger empires that are going to supplant it. All I knew was that I was stuck between my hatred of the empire I served and my rage against the evil-spirited little beasts who tried to make my job impossible. With one part of my mind I thought of the British Raj as an unbreakable tyranny, as something clamped down, in *saecula saeculorum,* upon the will of prostrate peoples; with another part I thought that the greatest joy in the world would be to drive a bayonet into a Buddhist priest's guts. Feelings like these are the normal by-products of imperialism; ask any Anglo-Indian official, if you can catch him off duty.

One day something happened which in a roundabout way   3 was enlightening. It was a tiny incident in itself; but it gave me a better glimpse than I had had before of the real nature of imperialism—the real motives for which despotic governments act. Early one morning the sub-inspector at a police station the other end of town rang me up on the 'phone and said that an elephant was ravaging the bazaar. Would I please come and do something about it? I did not know what I could do, but I wanted to see what was happening and I got on to a pony and started out. I took my rifle, an old .44 Winchester and much too small to kill an elephant, but I thought the noise might be useful *in terrorem.* Various Burmans stopped me on the way and told me about the elephant's doings. It was not, of course, a wild elephant, but a tame one which had gone "must." It had been chained up, as tame elephants always are when their attack of "must" is due, but on the previous night it had broken its chain and escaped. Its mahout, the only person who could manage it when it was in that state, had set out in pursuit, but had taken the wrong direction and was now twelve hours' journey away, and in the morning the elephant had suddenly reappeared in the town. The Burmese population had no weapons and were quite helpless against it. It had already destroyed somebody's bamboo hut, killed a cow and raided some fruit-stalls and devoured the stock; also it had met the municipal rubbish van and, when the driver jumped out and took to his heels, had turned the van over and inflicted violences upon it.

The Burmese sub-inspector and some Indian constables   4 were waiting for me in the quarter where the elephant had been seen. It was a very poor quarter, a labyrinth of squalid bamboo huts, thatched with palm-leaf, winding all over a steep hillside. I remember that it was a cloudy, stuffy morning at the beginning of the rains. We began questioning the people as to where the elephant had gone and, as usual, failed to get any definite information. That is invariably the case in the East; a story always sounds clear enough at a distance, but the nearer you get to the scene of events the vaguer it becomes. Some of the people said that the elephant had gone in one direction, some said that he had gone in another, some professed not even to have heard of any elephant. I had almost made up my mind that the whole story was a pack of lies, when we heard yells a little distance away. There was a loud, scandalized cry of "Go away, child! Go away this instant!" and an old woman with a switch in her hand came round the corner of a hut, violently shooing away a crowd of naked children. Some more women followed, clicking their tongues and exclaiming; evidently there was something that the children ought not to have seen. I rounded the hut and saw a man's dead body sprawling in the mud. He was an Indian, a black Dravidian coolie, almost naked, and he could not have been dead many minutes. The people said that the elephant had come suddenly upon him round the corner of the hut, caught him with its trunk, put its foot on his back and ground him into the earth. This was the rainy season and the ground was soft, and his face had scored a trench a foot deep and a couple of yards long. He was lying on his belly with arms crucified and head sharply twisted to one side. His face was coated with mud, the eyes wide open, the teeth bared and grinning with an expression of unendurable agony. (Never tell me, by the way, that the dead look peaceful. Most of the corpses I have seen looked devilish.) The friction of the great beast's foot had stripped the skin from his back as neatly as one skins a rabbit. As soon as I saw the dead man I sent an orderly to a friend's house nearby to borrow an elephant rifle. I had already sent back the pony, not wanting it to go mad with fright and throw me if it smelt the elephant.

The orderly came back in a few minutes with a rifle and five cartridges, and meanwhile some Burmans had arrived and told us that the elephant was in the paddy fields below, only a few hundred yards away. As I started forward practically the

5

whole population of the quarter flocked out of the houses and followed me. They had seen the rifle and were all shouting excitedly that I was going to shoot the elephant. They had not shown much interest in the elephant when he was merely ravaging their homes, but it was different now that he was going to be shot. It was a bit of fun to them, and it would be to an English crowd; besides they wanted the meat. It made me vaguely uneasy. I had no intention of shooting the elephant—I had merely sent for the rifle to defend myself if necessary—and it is always unnerving to have a crowd following you. I marched down the hill, looking and feeling a fool, with the rifle over my shoulder and an ever-growing army of people jostling at my heels. At the bottom, when you got away from the huts, there was a metalled road and beyond that a miry waste of paddy fields a thousand yards across, not yet ploughed but soggy from the first rains and dotted with coarse grass. The elephant was standing eight yards from the road, his left side toward us. He took not the slightest notice of the crowd's approach. He was tearing up bunches of grass, beating them against his knees to clean them, and stuffing them into his mouth.

I had halted on the road. As soon as I saw the elephant I knew with perfect certainty that I ought not to shoot him. It is a serious matter to shoot a working elephant—it is comparable to destroying a huge and costly piece of machinery—and obviously one ought not to do it if it can possibly be avoided. And at that distance, peacefully eating, the elephant looked no more dangerous than a cow. I thought then and I think now that his attack of "must" was already passing off; in which case he would merely wander harmlessly about until the mahout came back and caught him. Moreover, I did not in the least want to shoot him. I decided that I would watch him for a little while to make sure that he did not turn savage again, and then go home.

But at that moment I glanced round at the crowd that had followed me. It was an immense crowd, two thousand at the least and growing every minute. It blocked the road for a long distance on either side. I looked at the sea of yellow faces above the garish clothes—faces all happy and excited over this bit of fun, all certain that the elephant was going to be shot. They were watching me as they would watch a conjurer about to perform a trick. They did not like me, but with the magical rifle in my hands I was momentarily worth watching. And suddenly I realized that I should have to shoot the elephant after all. The people expected it of me and I had got to do it; I could feel their two thousand wills pressing me forward, irresistibly. And it was at this moment, as I stood there with the rifle in my hands, that I first grasped the hollowness, the futility of the white man's dominion in the East. Here was I, the white man with his gun, standing in front of the unarmed native crowd—seemingly the leading actor of the piece; but in reality I was only an absurd puppet pushed to and fro by the will of those yellow faces behind. I perceived in this moment that when the white man turns tyrant it is his own freedom that he destroys. He becomes a sort of hollow, posing dummy, the conventionalized figure of a sahib. For it is the condition of his rule that he shall spend his life in trying to impress the "natives," and so in every crisis he has got to do what the "natives" expect of him. He wears a mask, and his face grows to fit it. I had got to shoot the elephant. I had committed myself to doing it when I sent for the rifle. A sahib has got to act like a sahib; he has got to appear resolute, to know his own mind and do definite things. To come all that way, rifle in hand, with two thousand people marching at my heels, and then to trail feebly away, having done nothing— no, that was impossible. The crowd would laugh at me. And my whole life, every white man's life in the East, was one long struggle not to be laughed at.

But I did not want to shoot the elephant. I watched him 8 beating his bunch of grass against his knees with that preoc- cupied grandmotherly air that elephants have. It seemed to me that it would be murder to shoot him. At that age I was not squeamish about killing animals, but I had never shot an elephant and never wanted to. (Somehow it always seems worse to kill a *large* animal.) Besides, there was the beast's owner to be considered. Alive, the elephant was worth at least a hundred pounds; dead, he would only be worth the value of his tusks, five pounds, possibly. But I had got to act quickly.

I turned to some experienced-looking Burmans who had been there when we arrived, and asked them how the elephant had been behaving. They all said the same thing: he took no notice of you if you left him alone, but he might charge if you went too close to him.

It was perfectly clear to me what I ought to do. I ought 9 to walk up to within, say, twenty-five yards of the elephant and test his behavior. If he charged, I could shoot; if he took no notice of me, it would be safe to leave him until the mahout came back. But also I knew that I was going to do no such thing. I was a poor shot with a rifle and the ground was soft mud into which one would sink at every step. If the elephant charged and I missed him, I should have about as much chance as a toad under a steam-roller. But even then I was not thinking particularly of my own skin, only of the watchful yellow faces behind. For at that moment, with the crowd watching me, I was not afraid in the ordinary sense, as I would have been if I had been alone. A white man mustn't be frightened in front of "natives"; and so, in general, he isn't frightened. The sole thought in my mind was that if anything went wrong those two thousand Burmans would see me pursued, caught, trampled on, and reduced to a grinning corpse like that Indian up the hill. And if that happened it was quite probable that some of them would laugh. That would never do. There was only one alternative. I shoved the cartridges into the magazine and lay down on the road to get a better aim.

The crowd grew very still, and a deep, low, happy sigh, as 10 of people who see the theater curtain go up at last, breathed from innumerable throats. They were going to have their bit of fun after all. The rifle was a beautiful German thing with cross-hair sights. I did not then know that in shooting an elephant one would shoot to cut an imaginary bar running from ear-hole to ear-hole. I ought, therefore, as the elephant was sideways on, to have aimed straight at his ear-hole; actually I aimed several inches in front of this, thinking the brain would be further forward.

When I pulled the trigger I did not hear the bang or feel 11 the kick—one never does when a shot goes home—but I heard the devilish roar of glee that went up from the crowd. In that instant, in too short a time, one would have thought, even for the bullet to get there, a mysterious, terrible change had come over the elephant. He neither stirred, nor fell, but every line of his body had altered. He looked suddenly stricken, shrunken, immensely old, as though the frightful impact of the bullet had paralyzed him without knocking him down. At last, after what seemed a long time—it might have been five seconds, I dare say—he sagged flabbily to his knees. His mouth slobbered. An enormous senility seemed to have settled upon him. One could have imagined him thousands of years old. I fired again into the same spot. At the second shot he did not collapse but climbed with desperate slowness to his feet and stood weakly upright, with legs sagging and head drooping. I fired a third time. That was the shot that did for him. You could see the agony of it jolt his whole body and knock the last remnant of strength from his legs. But in falling he seemed for a moment to rise, for as his hind legs collapsed beneath him he seemed to tower upward like a huge rock toppling, his trunk reaching skyward like a tree. He trumpeted, for the first and only time. And then down he came, his belly toward me, with a crash that seemed to shake the ground even where I lay.

I got up. The Burmans were already racing past me across the mud. It was obvious that the elephant would never rise again, but he was not dead. He was breathing very rhythmically with long rattling gasps, his great mound of a side painfully rising and falling. His mouth was wide open—I could see far down into caverns of pale pink throat. I waited a long time for him to die, but his breathing did not weaken. Finally I fired my two remaining shots into the spot where I thought his heart must be. The thick blood welled out of him like red velvet, but still he did not die. His body did not even jerk when the shots hit him, the tortured breathing continued without a pause. He was dying, very slowly and in great agony, but in some world remote from me where not even a bullet could damage him further. I felt that I had got to put an end to that dreadful noise. It seemed dreadful to see the great beast lying there, powerless to move and yet powerless to die, and not even to be able to finish him. I sent back for my small rifle and poured shot after shot into his heart and down his throat. They seemed to make no impression. The tortured gasps continued as steadily as the ticking of a clock.

In the end I could not stand it any longer and went away.   13
I heard later that it took him half an hour to die. Burmans were bringing dahs and baskets even before I left, and I was told they had stripped his body almost to the bones by the afternoon.

Afterward, of course, there were endless discussions about   14
the shooting of the elephant. The owner was furious, but he was only an Indian and could do nothing. Besides, legally I had done the right thing, for a mad elephant has to be killed, like a mad dog, if its owner fails to control it. Among the Europeans opinion was divided. The older men said I was right, the younger men said it was a damn shame to shoot an elephant for killing a coolie, because an elephant was worth more than any damn Coringhee coolie. And afterward I was very glad that the coolie had been killed; it put me legally in the right and it gave me a sufficient pretext for shooting the elephant. I often wondered whether any of the others grasped that I had done it solely to avoid looking a fool.

For Study and Discussion

QUESTIONS FOR RESPONSE

1. How do you feel when you are laughed at? What do you do in order to avoid looking like a fool?
2. How did you react to Orwell's long introduction (paragraphs 1 and 2) to the incident? Were you attentive, bored, or confused? Now that you have finished the essay, reread these two paragraphs. How does your second reading compare with your first?

QUESTIONS ABOUT PURPOSE

1. What thesis about "the real nature of imperialism" does Orwell prove by narrating this "tiny incident"?
2. List the reasons Orwell considers when he tries to decide what to do. According to his conclusion, what was his main purpose in shooting the elephant?

QUESTIONS ABOUT AUDIENCE

1. How does Orwell wish to present himself to his readers in paragraphs 6 through 9? Do you follow the logic of his argument?
2. Which of the three positions stated in the final paragraph does Orwell expect his readers to agree with? Why is he "glad that the coolie had been killed"?

QUESTIONS ABOUT STRATEGIES

1. Although Orwell begins narrating the incident in paragraph 3, we do not see the elephant until the end of paragraph 5. What details do we see? How do they intensify the dramatic conflict?
2. How does Orwell pace the shooting of the elephant in paragraphs 11 and 12? How does the elephant's slow death affect Orwell's point of view toward what he has done?

QUESTIONS FOR DISCUSSION

1. Orwell was young, frightened, and tormented by strangers in a strange land. What parallels do you see between Orwell's plight and the plight of young American soldiers who served in Vietnam?
2. Much of Orwell's essay assumes a knowledge of the words *imperialism* and *despotism*. What do these words mean? How do they apply to the essay? What current events can you identify in which these words might also apply?

Alice Adams (1926–1999) was born in Fredericksburg, Virginia, and educated at Radcliffe College. After twelve years of marriage, she began working at various office jobs, including secretary, clerk, and bookkeeper, while she mastered the skills of a writer. Adams published her first book of fiction, *Careless Love* (1966), at the age of forty. Since that time she has published five widely acclaimed novels, *Families and Survivors* (1975), *Listening to Billie* (1978)—the title refers to the legendary blues singer Billie Holiday—*Rich Rewards* (1980), *Superior Women* (1984), and *Caroline's Daughter* (1991), as well as three collections of short stories, *Beautiful Girl* (1979), *To See You Again* (1982), and *Return Trips* (1985). She has also contributed numerous short stories to magazines such as *The New Yorker, The Atlantic,* and *Paris Review.* Her most recent novel, entitled *After the War* (2000), was published posthumously. The narrator of "Truth or Consequences," reprinted from *To See You Again,* tries to understand the "consequences" that resulted from her truthful answer in a childhood game.

Truth or Consequences

THIS MORNING, WHEN I read in a gossip column that a man named Carstairs Jones had married a famous former movie star, I was startled, thunderstruck, for I knew that he must certainly be the person whom I knew as a child, one extraordinary spring, as "Car Jones." He was a dangerous and disreputable boy, one of what were then called the "truck children," with whom I had a most curious, brief and frightening connection. Still, I noted that in a way I was pleased at such good fortune; I was "happy for him," so to speak, perhaps as a result of sheer distance, so many years. And before I could imagine Car as he might be now, Carstairs Jones, in Hollywood clothes, I suddenly saw, with the most terrific accuracy and bright sharpness of detail, the schoolyard of all those years ago, hard and bare, neglected. And I relived the fatal day, on the middle level of that schoolyard, when we were playing truth or consequences, and I said that I would rather kiss Car Jones than be eaten alive by ants.

Our school building then was three stories high, a formi- 2 dable brick square. In front a lawn had been attempted, some years back; graveled walks led up to the broad, forbidding entranceway, and behind the school were the playing fields, the playground. This area was on three levels: on the upper level, nearest the school, were the huge polished steel frames for the creaking swings, the big green splintery wooden see-saws, the rickety slides—all for the youngest children. On the middle level older girls played hopscotch, various games, or jumped rope—or just talked and giggled. And out on the lowest level, the field, the boys practiced football, or baseball, in the spring.

To one side of the school was a parking space, usually filled 3 with the bulging yellow trucks that brought children from out in the country in to town: truck children, country chil-dren. Sometimes they would go back to the trucks at lunchtime to eat their sandwiches, whatever; almost always there were several overgrown children, spilling out from the trucks. Or Car Jones, expelled from some class, for some new acts of rebelliousness. That area was always littered with trash, wrappings from sandwiches, orange peel, Coke bottles.

Beyond the parking space was an empty lot, overgrown 4 with weeds, in the midst of which stood an abandoned trellis, perhaps once the support of wisteria; now wild honeysuckle almost covered it over.

The town was called Hilton, the seat of a distinguished 5 university, in the middle South. My widowed mother,

Charlotte Ames, had moved there the previous fall (with me, Emily, her only child). I am still not sure why she chose Hilton; she never much liked it there, nor did she really like the brother-in-law, a professor, into whose proximity the move had placed us.

An interesting thing about Hilton, at that time, was that 6 there were three, and only three, distinct social classes. (Negroes could possibly make four, but they were so separate, even from the poorest whites, as not to seem part of the social system at all; they were in effect invisible.) At the scale's top were professors and their families. Next were the townspeople, storekeepers, bankers, doctors and dentists, none of whom had the prestige nor the money they were later to acquire. Country people were the bottom group, families living out on the farms that surrounded the town, people who sent their children in to school on the yellow trucks.

The professors' children of course had a terrific advantage, 7 academically, coming from houses full of books, from parental respect for learning; many of those kids read precociously and had large vocabularies. It was not so hard on most of the town children; many of their families shared qualities with the faculty people; they too had a lot of books around. But the truck children had a hard and very unfair time of it. Not only were many of their parents near-illiterates, but often the children were kept at home to help with chores, and sometimes, particularly during the coldest, wettest months of winter, weather prevented the trucks' passage over the slithery red clay roads of that countryside, that era. A child could miss out on a whole new skill, like long division, and fail tests, and be kept back. Consequently many of the truck children were overage, oversized for the grades they were in.

In the seventh grade, when I was eleven, a year ahead of 8 myself, having been tested for and skipped the sixth (attesting to the superiority of Northern schools, my mother thought, and probably she was right), dangerous Car Jones, in the same class, was fourteen, and taller than anyone.

There was some overlapping, or crossing, among those 9 three social groups; there were hybrids, as it were. In fact, I

was such a crossbreed myself: literally my mother and I were
town people—my dead father had been a banker, but since
his brother was a professor we too were considered faculty
people. Also my mother had a lot of money, making us
further élite. To me, being known as rich was just embarrassing, more freakish than advantageous, and I made my mother
stop ordering my clothes from Best's; I wanted dresses from
the local stores, like everyone else's.

Car Jones too was a hybrid child, although his case was   10
less visible than mine: his country family were distant cousins
of the prominent and prosperous dean of the medical school,
Dean Willoughby Jones. (They seem to have gone in for
fancy names, in all the branches of that family.) I don't think
his cousins spoke to him.

In any case, being richer and younger than the others in   11
my class made me socially very insecure, and I always approached the playground with a sort of excited dread: would
I be asked to join in a game, and if it were dodge ball (the
game I most hated) would I be the first person hit with the
ball, and thus eliminated? Or, if the girls were just standing
around and talking, would I get all the jokes, and know which
boys they were talking about?

Then, one pale-blue balmy April day, some of the older   12
girls asked me if I wanted to play truth or consequences with
them. I wasn't sure how the game went, but anything was
better than dodge ball, and, as always, I was pleased at being
asked.

"It's easy," said Jean, a popular leader, with curly red hair;   13
her father was a dean of the law school. "You just answer the
questions we ask you, or you take the consequences."

I wasn't at all sure what consequences were, but I didn't   14
like to ask.

They began with simple questions. How old are you?   15
What's your middle name?

This led to more complicated (and crueler) ones.   16

"How much money does your mother have?"   17

"I don't know." I didn't, of course, and I doubt that she   18
did either, that poor vague lady, too young to be a widow,

too old for motherhood. "I think maybe a thousand dollars," I hazarded.

At this they all frowned, that group of older, wiser girls, 19 whether in disbelief or disappointment, I couldn't tell. They moved a little away from me and whispered together.

It was close to the end of recess. Down on the playing field 20 below us one of the boys threw the baseball and someone batted it out in a long arc, out to the farthest grassy edges of the field, and several other boys ran to retrieve it. On the level above us, a rutted terrace up, the little children stood in line for turns on the slide, or pumped with furious small legs on the giant swings.

The girls came back to me. "Okay, Emily," said Jean. "Just 21 tell the truth. Would you rather be covered with honey and eaten alive by ants, in the hot Sahara Desert—or kiss Car Jones?"

Then, as now, I had a somewhat literal mind: I thought of 22 honey, and ants, and hot sand, and quite simply I said I'd rather kiss Car Jones.

Well. Pandemonium: Did you hear what she said? Emily 23 would kiss Car Jones! *Car Jones.* The truth—Emily would like to kiss Car Jones! Oh, Emily if your mother only knew! Emily and Car! Emily is going to kiss Car Jones! Emily said she would! Oh, Emily!

The boys, just then coming up from the baseball field, cast 24 bored and pitying looks at the sources of so much noise; they had always known girls were silly. But Harry McGinnis, a glowing, golden boy, looked over at us and laughed aloud. I had been watching Harry timidly for months; that day I thought his laugh was friendly.

Recess being over, we all went back into the schoolroom, 25 and continued with the civics lesson. I caught a few ambiguous smiles in my direction, which left me both embarrassed and confused.

That afternoon, as I walked home from school, two of the 26 girls who passed me on their bikes called back to me, "Car Jones!" and in an automatic but for me new way I squealed out, "Oh no!" They laughed, and repeated, from their distance, "Car Jones!"

The next day I continued to be teased. Somehow the boys 27 had got wind of what I had said, and they joined in with remarks about Yankee girls being fast, how you couldn't tell about quiet girls, that sort of wit. Some of the teasing sounded mean; I felt that Jean, for example, was really out to discomfit me, but most of it was high-spirited friendliness. I was suddenly discovered, as though hitherto I had been invisible. And I continued to respond with that exaggerated, phony squeal of embarrassment that seemed to go over so well. Harry McGinnis addressed me as Emily Jones, and the others took that up. (I wonder if Harry had ever seen me before.)

Curiously, in all this new excitement, the person I thought 28 of least was the source of it all: Car Jones. Or, rather, when I saw the actual Car, hulking over the water fountain or lounging near the steps of a truck, I did not consciously connect him with what felt like social success, new popularity. (I didn't know about consequences.)

Therefore, when the first note from Car appeared on my 29 desk, it felt like blackmail, although the message was innocent, was even kind. "You mustn't mind that they tease you. You are the prettiest one of the girls. C. Jones." I easily recognized his handwriting, those recklessly forward-slanting strokes, from the day when he had had to write on the blackboard, "I will not disturb the other children during Music." Twenty-five times. The note was real, all right.

Helplessly I turned around to stare at the back of the 30 room, where the tallest boys sprawled in their too small desks. Truck children, all of them, bored and uncomfortable. There was Car, the tallest of all, the most bored, the least contained. Our eyes met, and even at that distance I saw that his were not black, as I had thought, but a dark slate blue; stormy eyes, even when, as he rarely did, Car smiled. I turned away quickly, and I managed to forget him for a while.

Having never witnessed a Southern spring before, I was   31
astounded by its bursting opulence, that soft fullness of petal
and bloom, everywhere the profusion of flowering shrubs
and trees, the riotous flower beds. Walking home from
school, I was enchanted with the yards of the stately houses
(homes of professors) that I passed, the lush lawns, the rows
of brilliant iris, the flowering quince and dogwood trees,
crepe myrtle, wisteria vines. I would squint my eyes to see
the tiniest pale-green leaves against the sky.

My mother didn't like the spring. It gave her hay fever,   32
and she spent most of her time languidly indoors, behind
heavily lined, drawn draperies. "I'm simply too old for such
exuberance," she said.

"Happy" is perhaps not the word to describe my own state   33
of mind, but I was tremendously excited, continuously. The
season seemed to me so extraordinary in itself, the colors, the
enchanting smells, and it coincided with my own altered
awareness of myself: I could command attention, I was pretty
(Car Jones was the first person ever to say that I was, after
my mother's long-ago murmurings to a late-arriving baby).

Now everyone knew my name, and called it out as I walked   34
onto the playground. Last fall, as an envious, unknown new
girl, I had heard other names, other greetings and teasing-
insulting nicknames, "Hey, Red," Harry McGinnis used to
shout, in the direction of popular Jean.

The new note from Car Jones said, "I'll bet you hate it   35
down here. This is a cruddy town, but don't let it bother
you. Your hair is beautiful. I hope you never cut it. C. Jones."

This scared me a little: the night before I had been arguing   36
with my mother on just that point, my hair, which was long
and straight. Why couldn't I cut it and curl it, like the other
girls? How had Car Jones known what I wanted to do? I
forced myself not to look at him; I pretended that there was
no Car Jones; it was just a name that certain people had made
up.

I felt—I was sure—that Car Jones was an "abnormal"   37
person. (I'm afraid "different" would have been the word I

used, back then.) He represented forces that were dark and strange, whereas I myself had just come out into the light. I had joined the world of the normal. (My "normality" later included three marriages to increasingly "rich and prominent" men; my current husband is a surgeon. Three children, and as many abortions. I hate the symmetry, but there you are. I haven't counted lovers. It comes to a normal life, for a woman of my age.) For years, at the time of our coming to Hilton, I had felt a little strange, isolated by my father's death, my older-than-most-parents mother, by money. By being younger than other children, and new in town. I could clearly afford nothing to do with Car, and at the same time my literal mind acknowledged a certain obligation.

Therefore, when a note came from Car telling me to meet   38
him on a Saturday morning in the vacant lot next to the school, it didn't occur to me that I didn't have to go. I made excuses to my mother, and to some of the girls who were getting together for Cokes at someone's house. I'd be a little late, I told the girls. I had to do an errand for my mother.

It was one of the palest, softest, loveliest days of that   39
spring. In the vacant lot weeds bloomed like the rarest of flowers; as I walked toward the abandoned trellis I felt myself to be a sort of princess, on her way to grant an audience to a courtier.

Car, lounging just inside the trellis, immediately brought   40
me up short. "You're several minutes late," he said, and I noticed that his teeth were stained (from tobacco?) and his hands were dirty: couldn't he have washed his hands, to come and meet me? He asked, "Just who do you think you are, the Queen of Sheba?"

I am not sure what I had imagined would happen between   41
us, but this was wrong; I was not prepared for surliness, this scolding. Weakly I said that I was sorry I was late.

Car did not acknowledge my apology; he just stared at me,   42
stormily, with what looked like infinite scorn.

Why had he insisted that I come to meet him? And now   43
that I was here, was I less than pretty, seen close up?

A difficult minute passed, and then I moved a little away. 44
I managed to say that I had to go; I had to meet some girls,
I said.

At that Car reached and grasped my arm. "No, first we 45
have to do it."

Do it? I was scared. 46

"You know what you said, as good as I do. You said kiss 47
Car Jones, now didn't you?"

I began to cry. 48

Car reached for my hair and pulled me toward him; he 49
bent down to my face and for an instant our mouths were
mashed together. (Christ, my first kiss!) Then, so suddenly
that I almost fell backward, Car let go of me. With a last look
of pure rage he was out of the trellis and striding across the
field, toward town, away from the school.

For a few minutes I stayed there in the trellis; I was no 50
longer crying (that had been for Car's benefit, I now think)
but melodramatically I wondered if Car might come back and
do something else to me—beat me up, maybe. Then a
stronger fear took over: someone might find out, might have
seen us, even. At that I got out of the trellis fast, out of the
vacant lot. (I was learning conformity fast, practicing up for
the rest of my life.)

I think, really, that my most serious problem was my utter 51
puzzlement: what did it mean, that kiss? Car was mad, no
doubt about that, but did he really hate me? In that case, why
a kiss? (Much later in life I once was raped, by someone to
whom I was married, but I still think that counts; in any case,
I didn't know what he meant either.)

Not sure what else to do, and still in the grip of a monu- 52
mental confusion, I went over to the school building, which
was open on Saturdays for something called Story Hours, for
little children. I went into the front entrance and up to the
library where, to the surprise of the librarian, who may have
thought me retarded, I listened for several hours of tales of
the Dutch Twins, and Peter and Polly in Scotland. Actually
it was very soothing, that long pasteurized drone, hard even
to think about Car while listening to pap like that.

When I got home I found my mother for some reason in   53
a livelier, more talkative mood than usual. She told me that
a boy had called while I was out, three times. Even before
my heart had time to drop—to think that it might be Car,
she babbled on, "Terribly polite. Really, these *bien élevé*
Southern boys." (No, not Car.) "Harry something. He said
he'd call again. But, darling, where were you, all this time?"

I was beginning to murmur about the library, homework,   54
when the phone rang. I answered, and it was Harry McGinnis, asking me to go to the movies with him the following
Saturday afternoon. I said of course, I'd love to, and I giggled
in a silly new way. But my giggle was one of relief; I was saved,
I was normal, after all. I belonged in the world of light, of
lightheartedness. Car Jones had not really touched me.

I spent the next day, Sunday, in alternating states of agita-   55
tion and anticipation.

On Monday, on my way to school, I felt afraid of seeing   56
Car, at the same time that I was both excited and shy at the
prospect of Harry McGinnis—a combination of emotions
that was almost too much for me, that dazzling, golden first
of May, and that I have not dealt with too successfully in later
life.

Harry paid even less attention to me than he had before;   57
it was a while before I realized that he was conspicuously not
looking in my direction, not teasing me, and that that in itself
was a form of attention, as well as being soothing to my
shyness.

I realized too, after a furtive scanning of the back row, that   58
Car Jones was *not at school* that day. Relief flooded through
my blood like oxygen, like spring air.

Absences among the truck children were so unremarkable,   59
and due to so many possible causes, that any explanation at
all for his was plausible. Of course it occurred to me, among
other imaginings, that he had stayed home out of shame for
what he did to me. Maybe he had run away to sea, had joined
the Navy or the Marines? Coldheartedly, I hoped so. In any
case, there was no way for me to ask.

Later that week the truth about Car Jones did come out—   60 at first as a drifting rumor, then confirmed, and much more remarkable than joining the Navy: Car Jones had gone to the principal's office, a week or so back, and had demanded to be tested for entrance (immediate) into high school, a request so unprecedented (usually only pushy academic parents would ask for such a change) and so dumbfounding that it was acceded to. Car took the test and was put into the sophomore high-school class, on the other side of town, where he by age and size—and intellect, as things turned out; he tested high—most rightfully belonged.

I went to a lot of Saturday movies with Harry McGinnis, 61 where we clammily held hands, and for the rest of that spring, and into summer, I was teased about Harry. No one seemed to remember having teased me about Car Jones.

Considering the size of Hilton at that time, it seems sur- 62 prising that I almost never saw Car again, but I did not, except for a couple of tiny glimpses, during the summer that I was still going to the movies with Harry. On both those occasions, seen from across the street, or on the other side of a dim movie house, Car was with an older girl, a high-school girl, with curled hair, and lipstick, all that. I was sure that his hands and teeth were clean.

By the time I had entered high school, along with all those 63 others who were by now my familiar friends, Car was a freshman in the local university, and his family had moved into town. Then his name again was bruited about among us, but this time was an underground rumor: Car Jones was reputed to have "gone all the way"—to have "done it" with a pretty and most popular senior in our high school. (It must be remembered that this was more unusual among the young then than now.) The general (whispered) theory was that Car's status as a college boy had won the girl; traditionally, in Hilton, the senior high-school girls began to date the freshmen in the university, as many and as often as possible. But this was not necessarily true; maybe the girl was simply drawn to Car, his height and his shoulders, his stormy eyes. Or maybe they didn't do it after all.

The next thing I heard about Car, who was by then an authentic town person, a graduate student in the university, was that he had written a play which was to be produced by the campus dramatic society. (Maybe that is how he finally met his movie star, as a playwright? The column didn't say.) I think I read this item in the local paper, probably in a clipping forwarded to me by my mother; her letters were always thick with clippings, thin with messages of a personal nature.

My next news of Car came from my uncle, the French professor, a violent, enthusiastic partisan in university affairs, especially in their more traditional aspects. In scandalized tones, one family Thanksgiving, he recounted to me and my mother, that a certain young man, a graduate student in English, named Carstairs Jones, had been offered a special sort of membership in D.K.E., his own beloved fraternity, and "Jones had *turned it down*." My mother and I laughed later and privately over this; we were united in thinking my uncle a fool, and I am sure that I added, Well, good for him. But I did not, at that time, reconsider the whole story of Car Jones, that most unregenerate and wicked of the truck children.

But now, with this fresh news of Carstairs Jones, and his wife the movie star, it occurs to me that we two, who at a certain time and place were truly misfits, although quite differently—we both have made it: what could be more American dream-y, more normal, than marriage to a lovely movie star? Or, in my case, marriage to the successful surgeon?

And now maybe I can reconstruct a little of that time; specifically, can try to see how it really was for Car, back then. Maybe I can even understand that kiss.

Let us suppose that he lived in a somewhat better than usual farmhouse; later events make this plausible—his family's move to town, his years at the university. Also, I wish him

well. I will give him a dignified white house with a broad
front porch, set back among pines and oaks, in the red clay
countryside. The stability and size of his house, then, would
have set Car apart from his neighbors, the other farm families,
other truck children. Perhaps his parents too were somewhat
"different," but my imagination fails at them; I can easily
imagine and clearly see the house, but not its population.
Brothers? sisters? Probably, but I don't know.

Car would go to school, coming out of his house at the   69
honk of the stained and bulging, ugly yellow bus, which was
crowded with his supposed peers, toward whom he felt both
contempt and an irritation close to rage. Arrived at school,
as one of the truck children, he would be greeted with a total
lack of interest; he might as well have been invisible, or been
black, *unless* he misbehaved in an outright, conspicuous way.
And so he did: Car yawned noisily during history class, he
hummed during study hall and after recess he dawdled
around the playground and came in late. And for these and
other assaults on the school's decorum he was punished in
one way or another, and then, when all else failed to curb his
ways, he would be *held back,* forced to repeat an already
insufferably boring year of school.

One fall there was a minor novelty in school: a new girl   70
(me), a Yankee, who didn't look much like the other girls,
with long straight hair, instead of curled, and Yankee clothes,
wool skirts and sweaters, instead of flowery cotton dresses
worn all year round. A funny accent, a Yankee name: Emily
Ames. I imagine that Car registered those facts about me,
and possibly the additional information that I was almost as
invisible as he, but without much interest.

Until the day of truth or consequences. I don't think Car   71
was around on the playground while the game was going on;
one of the girls would have seen him, and squealed out,
"Oooh, there's Car, there *he is!*" I rather believe that some
skinny little kid, an unnoticed truck child, overheard it all,
and then ran over to where Car was lounging in one of the
school buses, maybe peeling an orange and throwing the

peel, in spirals, out the window. "Say, Car, that little Yankee girl, she says she'd like to kiss you."

"Aw, go on."   72

He is still not very interested; the little Yankee girl is as   73 dumb as the others are.

And then he hears me being teased, everywhere, and   74 teased with his name. "Emily would kiss Car Jones—Emily Jones!" Did he feel the slightest pleasure at such notoriety? I think he must have; a man who would marry a movie star must have at least a small taste for publicity. Well, at that point he began to write me those notes: "You are the prettiest one of the girls" (which I was not). I think he was casting us both in ill-fitting roles, me as the prettiest, defenseless girl, and himself as my defender.

He must have soon seen that it wasn't working out that   75 way. I didn't need a defender, I didn't need him. I was having a wonderful time, at his expense, if you think about it, and I am pretty sure Car did think about it.

Interestingly, at the same time he had his perception of my   76 triviality, Car must have got his remarkable inspiration in regard to his own life: there was a way out of those miserably boring classes, the insufferable children who surrounded him. He would demand a test, he would leave this place for the high school.

Our trellis meeting must have occurred after Car had taken   77 the test, and had known that he did well. When he kissed me he was doing his last "bad" thing in that school, was kissing it off, so to speak. He was also insuring that I, at least, would remember him; he counted on its being my first kiss. And he may have thought that I was even sillier than I was, and that I would tell, so that what had happened would get around the school, waves of scandal in his wake.

For some reason, I would also imagine that Car is one of   78 those persons who never look back; once kissed, I was readily dismissed from his mind, and probably for good. He could concentrate on high school, new status, new friends. Just as, now married to his movie star, he does not ever think of having been a truck child, one of the deprived, the disappointed. In his mind there are no ugly groaning trucks, no hopeless littered playground, no squat menacing school building.

But of course I could be quite wrong about Car Jones. He [79] could be another sort of person altogether; he could be as haunted as I am by everything that ever happened in his life.

COMMENT ON "TRUTH OR CONSEQUENCES"

"Truth or Consequences" is an excellent illustration of how narration and description are used in short fiction. The catalyst for the story is the narrator's reading in a gossip column about Car Jones's marriage to a famous former movie star. His name sparks a memory, and the narrator (Emily) tries to reconstruct the events that occurred during her school years. The story is paced at two speeds: the opening is slow as Emily describes the various social divisions on the playground; the action speeds up once Emily says she would rather kiss Car Jones than be eaten by ants. The plot reaches its climax when Car Jones calls Emily's bluff and asks her to meet him by the trellis near the school. The story concludes as Emily (older and wiser?) continues to wonder about the "truth" and "consequences" of this brief encounter.

Narration and Description as a Writing Strategy

1. Recount the details of an accident or disaster in which you were a witness or a victim. You may wish to retell the events as a reporter would for a front-page story in the local newspaper, or you may recount the events from a more personal point of view, as Maya Angelou does in her description of the "disaster" in Mrs. Cullinan's kitchen. If you were a witness, consider the points of view of the other people involved so that you can give your readers an objective perspective on the event. If you were a victim, slow the pace of the major conflict, which probably occurred quickly, so you can show your readers its emotional impact.

2. Report an experience in which you had to commit an extremely difficult or distasteful deed. You may wish to begin, as George Orwell does, by telling your readers about the conditions you encountered before you confronted the problem of whether to commit the questionable act. Be sure to list all the options you considered before you acted, and conclude by reflecting on your attitude toward your choice. And, of course, make sure to plot your essay so that the *act* is given the central and most dramatic position.

3. In "Keeping the Scorebook," Doris Kearns Goodwin recounts her experience telling the stories of the daily baseball game. Study the lessons she learned about "storytelling." Then make a list of the difficulties your friends and relatives have telling an effective story. Finally, write a narrative illustrating "how to tell a good story" or "how to ruin a good story."

4. Describe a significant event in your life when you were unfairly stereotyped. You may want to point out certain features of your dress or behavior that sent—unknown to you—mixed signals. Like Cofer, you may want to speculate on how these signals were the result of custom or media cartoons.

5. Describe how people who are different are treated within your community. Like Andre Dubus, you may want to document how the shy and sensitive feel shame and attract bullies. Or you may want to describe how you discovered an injustice in your community's way of acknowledging those who are different.

6. Demonstrate the effects of perception on values (how "seeing is believing"). All the writers in this section deal with this subject. Angelou demonstrates how white people's inability to "see" black people distorts their belief about them. Goodwin describes how a scorekeeper's code or a good story can make you believe you are seeing the real thing. Cofer reveals how people from mainstream culture believe that they should be applauded for their ability to perpetuate stereotypes. Dubus recounts how his summer of physical labor changed his body and his thinking. Orwell shows how seeing the crowd's mocking faces convinces him to shoot the elephant. And Emily Ames, the narrator in Alice Adams's short story, tells how her concern for social acceptance made her misread the actions of someone who was different.

PROCESS
ANALYSIS

A **process** is an operation that moves through a series of steps to bring about a desired result. You can call almost any procedure a process, whether it is getting out of bed in the morning or completing a transaction on the stock exchange. A useful way to identify a particular kind of process is by its principal function. A process can be *natural* (the birth of a baby), *mechanical* (starting a car engine), *physical* (dancing), or *mental* (reading).

Analysis is an operation that divides something into its parts in order to understand the whole more clearly. For example, poetry readers analyze the lines of a poem to find meaning. Doctors analyze a patient's symptoms to prescribe

treatment. Politicians analyze the opinions of individual voters and groups of voters to plan campaigns.

If you want to write a process-analysis essay, you need to
go through three steps: (1) divide the process you are going
to explain into its individual steps; (2) show the movement
of the process, step by step, from beginning to end; and (3)
explain how each step works, how it ties into other steps in
the sequence, and how it brings about the desired result.

PURPOSE

Usually you will write a process analysis to accomplish two
purposes: *to give directions* and *to provide information*. Sometimes you might find it difficult to separate the two purposes.
After all, when you give directions about how to do something (hit a baseball), you also have to provide information
on how the whole process works (rules of the game—strike
zone, walks, hits, base running, outs, scoring). But usually
you can separate the two because you're trying to accomplish
different goals. When you give directions, you want to help
your readers do something (change a tire). When you give
information, you want to satisfy your readers' curiosity about
some process they'd like to know about but are unlikely to
perform (pilot a space shuttle).

You might also write a process analysis to demonstrate that
(1) a task that looks difficult is really easy or (2) a task that
looks easy is really quite complex. For instance, you might
want to show that selecting a specific tool can simplify a
complex process (using a microwave oven to cook a six-
course dinner). You might also want to show why it's important to have a prearranged plan to make a process seem simple
(explaining the preparations for an informal television interview).

AUDIENCE

When you write a process-analysis essay, you must think carefully about who your audience will be. First, you need to

decide whether you're writing *to* an audience (giving directions) or writing *for* an audience (providing information). If you are writing *to* an audience, you can address directly readers who are already interested in your subject: "If you want to plant a successful garden, you must follow these seven steps." If you are writing *for* an audience, you can write from a more detached point of view, but you have to find a way to catch the interest of more casual readers: "Although many Americans say they are concerned about nuclear power, few understand how a nuclear power plant works."

Second, you have to determine how wide the knowledge gap is between you and your readers. Writing about a process suggests you are something of an expert in that area. If you can be sure your readers are also experts, you can make certain assumptions as you write your analysis. For instance, if you're outlining courtroom procedure to a group of fellow law students, you can assume you don't have to define the special meaning of the word *brief.*

On the other hand, if you feel sure your intended audience knows almost nothing about a process (or has only general knowledge), you can take nothing for granted. If you are explaining how to operate a VCR to readers who have never used one, you will have to define special terms and explain all procedures. If you assume your readers are experts when they are not, you will confuse or annoy them. If you assume they need to be told everything when they don't, you will bore or antagonize them. And, finally, remember that to analyze a process effectively, you must either research it carefully or have firsthand knowledge of its operation. It's risky to try to explain something you don't really understand.

STRATEGIES

The best way to write a process analysis is to organize your essay according to five parts:

Overview
Special terms

Sequence of steps
Examples
Results

The first two parts help your readers understand the process, the next two show the process in action, and the last one evaluates the worth of the completed process. Begin your analysis with an *overview* of the whole process. To make such an overview, you take these four steps:

1. Define the objective of the process
2. Identify (and number) the steps in the sequence
3. Group some small steps into larger units
4. Call attention to the most important steps or units

For example, Julia Alvarez begins her analysis of how she writes a story by breaking down this process into short steps. Nikki Giovanni makes her recommendations for black students in sequence and then goes on to illustrate some of the common problems that occur with each recommendation.

Each process has its own *special terms* to describe tools, tasks, and methods, and you will have to define those terms for your readers. You can define them at the beginning so your readers will understand the terms when you use them, but often you do better to define them as you use them. Your readers may have trouble remembering specialized language out of context, so it's often practical to define your terms throughout the course of the essay, pausing to explain their special meaning or use the first time you introduce them. Serena Nanda follows this strategy by defining what Indians mean by the bride's "dowry."

When you write a process-analysis essay, you must present the *sequence of steps* clearly and carefully. As you do so, give the reason for each step and, where appropriate, provide these reminders:

1. *Do not omit any steps.* A sequence is a sequence because all steps depend on one another. Nikki Giovanni explains the

importance of going to class to establish "a consistent presence in the classroom."

2. *Do not reverse steps.* A sequence is a sequence because each step must be performed according to a necessary and logical pattern. Lars Eighner reminds readers that if they start eating something before they have inspected it, they are likely to discover moldy bread or sour milk after they have put it into their mouth.

3. *Suspend certain steps.* Occasionally, a whole series of steps must be suspended and another process completed before the sequence can resume. Natalie Angier analyzes how male dolphins must first reach consensus before they start their courtship rituals.

4. *Do not overlook steps within steps.* Each sequence is likely to have a series of smaller steps buried within each step. Julia Alvarez reminds her readers that collecting curious information is not the same as researching it.

5. *Avoid certain steps.* It is often tempting to insert steps that are not recommended but that appear "logical." Serena Nanda discovers that her American logic does not work in an Indian context.

You may want to use several kinds of examples to explain the steps in a sequence:

1. *Pictures.* You can use graphs, charts, and diagrams to illustrate the operation of the process. Although none of the writers in this section uses pictures, Serena Nanda's purpose is to demonstrate how important looks—height, skin color—can be in selecting a bride.

2. *Anecdotes.* Since you're claiming some level of expertise by writing a process analysis, you can clarify your explanation by using examples from your own experience. Eighner uses this method when he describes his experience selecting discarded pizzas and waiting for the "junk" that will be pitched at the end of a semester.

3. *Variants.* You can mention alternative steps to show that the process may not be as rigid or simplistic as it often

appears. Angier suggests that male dolphins can change alliances and courtship procedures every day.

4. *Comparisons.* You can use comparisons to help your readers see that a complex process is similar to a process they already know. Nanda uses this strategy when she compares the complexities of arranging an Indian marriage to the "love matches" made in America.

Although you focus on the movement of the process when you write a process-analysis essay, finally you should also try to evaluate the *results* of that process. You can move to this last part by asking two questions: How do you know it's done? How do you know it's good? Sometimes the answer is simple: the car starts; the trunk opens. At other times, the answer is not so clear: the student may need further instruction; the jury may have difficulty reaching a decision.

USING PROCESS ANALYSIS IN PARAGRAPHS

Here are two process-analysis paragraphs. The first is written by a professional writer and is followed by an analysis. The second is written by a student writer and is followed by questions.

HENRY PETROSKI
The Book on the Bookshelf

Putting a book back on the shelf in such circumstances can be as difficult as putting a sardine back in a can. A bookshelf appears to abhor a vacuum, and so the void that is created when one book is removed is seldom adequate to receive the book again. Like a used air mattress or roadmap, which can never seem to be folded back into the shape in which it came, the book opened seems to have a new dimension when reclosed. Where it once fit it no longer does, and it has to

Makes comparison to another process

Makes another comparison

be used as a wedge to pry apart its formerly tolerant neighbors in order to get a foothold on the shelf. Invariably, the book I push back into its place scrapes along its neighbors and pushes them back a little. Where there is ample room above them, the disturbed books can be re-aligned with a little effort. However, in my office, where I cannot easily reach in to pull the books back out and align their spines, I find myself pushing the whole shelf back a bit to realign them. I cannot just push the books all the way to the rear of the shelf, of course, because they do not all have the same width, and so the shelf of them would present a rather ragged appear-ance. In time, however, so many of the books end up pushed all the way back that I have to take a whole section of them out and reposition them near the front edge of the shelf.

Describes personal anecdote

Provides warning

Comment This paragraph, excerpted from *The Book on the Bookshelf,* analyzes the difficult process of removing and then replacing a book on a bookshelf so that all the books on the shelf remain aligned. The opening sentence creates a vivid image—putting a sardine back in a can—that establishes the difficulty of the process. Petroski makes sure his readers an-ticipate all the things that can go wrong when trying to realign books. And even after the books are realigned, they are so far back on the shelf that he must move whole sections out toward "the front edge of the shelf."

SARA TEMPLE
Making Stained Glass

Before you begin making stained glass, you will need to purchase the right tools—most of which you can find at your local hardware store. First, select a glass cutter. It looks like a steel fork with a wheel at one end. The wheel is the blade that allows you to cut out the shape of each piece of glass. Second, you will need another tool to "break" the glass along the line you have scored with your cutter. I've always called this object "the tool." Tell the hardware clerk what you want and she'll show you what you need. Third, pick out a glass grinder to polish each piece of glass to the right size. Finally, buy a soldering iron to fuse the various pieces of glass into your design. These last two tools can be "pricey," so you may want to find a partner to share the cost. In the process, you may discover that your stained glass will become more creative when you design it with a friend.

1. How does Temple list and describe the special tools needed in the process?
2. What advice does Temple provide about how to purchase and use the "pricey" tools?

PROCESS ANALYSIS

Points to Remember

1. Arrange the steps in your process in an orderly sequence.
2. Identify and explain the purpose of each of the steps in the process.
3. Describe the special tools, terms, and tasks needed to complete the process.
4. Provide warnings, where appropriate, about the consequences of omitting, reversing, or overlooking certain steps.
5. Supply illustrations and personal anecdotes to help clarify aspects of the process.

LARS EIGHNER

Lars Eighner was born in 1948 in Corpus Christi, Texas, and attended the University of Texas at Austin. He held a series of jobs, including work as an attendant at the state mental hospital in Austin, before he became homeless. For five years he drifted between Austin and Hollywood, living on the streets and in abandoned buildings. Then he began to contribute essays to the *Threepenny Review*; these writings are collected in his memoir, *Travels with Lizabeth* (1993). In one of these essays, "My Daily Dives in the Dumpster," Eighner analyzes the "predictable series of stages that a person goes through in learning to scavenge."

My Daily Dives in the Dumpster

I BEGAN DUMPSTER diving about a year before I became homeless. 1

I prefer the term "scavenging" and use the word "scrounging" when I mean to be obscure. I have heard people, evidently meaning to be polite, use the word "foraging," but I prefer to reserve that word for gathering nuts and berries and such which I do also, according to the season and opportunity. 2

I like the frankness of the word "scavenging." I live from the refuse of others. I am a scavenger. I think it a sound and honorable niche, although if I could I would naturally prefer to live the comfortable consumer life, perhaps—and only perhaps—as a slightly less wasteful consumer owing to what I have learned as a scavenger. 3

Except for jeans, all my clothes come from Dumpsters. 4
Boom boxes, candles, bedding, toilet paper, medicine, books,

a typewriter, a virgin male love doll, change sometimes amounting to many dollars: All came from Dumpsters. And, yes, I eat from Dumpsters too.

There are a predictable series of stages that a person goes 5 through in learning to scavenge. At first the new scavenger is filled with disgust and self-loathing. He is ashamed of being seen and may lurk around trying to duck behind

---

Scavenging, more than most other pursuits, tends to yield returns in some proportion to the effort and the intelligence brought to bear.

---

things, or he may try to dive at night. (In fact, this is unnecessary, since most people instinctively look away from scavengers.)

Every grain of rice seems to be a maggot. Everything 6 seems to stink. The scavenger can wipe the egg yolk off the found can, but he cannot erase the stigma of eating garbage from his mind.

This stage passes with experience. The scavenger finds a 7 pair of running shoes that fit and look and smell brand-new. He finds a pocket calculator in perfect working order. He finds pristine ice cream, still frozen, more than he can eat or keep. He begins to understand: People do throw away perfectly good stuff, a lot of perfectly good stuff.

At this stage he may become lost and never recover. All 8 the Dumpster divers I have known come to the point of trying to acquire everything they touch. Why not take it, they reason, it is all free. This is, of course, hopeless, and most divers come to realize that they must restrict themselves to items of relatively immediate utility.

The finding of objects is becoming something of an urban   9
art. Even respectable, employed people will sometimes find
something tempting sticking out of a Dumpster or standing
beside one. Quite a number of people, not all of them of the
bohemian type, are willing to brag that they found this or
that piece in the trash.

But eating from Dumpsters is the thing that separates the   10
dilettanti from the professionals. Eating safely involves three
principles: using the senses and common sense to evaluate
the condition of the found materials; knowing the Dumpsters
of a given area and checking them regularly; and seeking
always to answer the question, Why was this discarded?

Perhaps everyone who has a kitchen and a regular supply   11
of groceries has, at one time or another, eaten half a sandwich
before discovering mold on the bread, or has gotten a mouthful of milk before realizing the milk had turned. Nothing of
the sort is likely to happen to a Dumpster diver because he
is constantly reminded that most food is discarded for a
reason.

Yet perfectly good food can be found in Dumpsters.   12
Canned goods, for example, turn up fairly often in the
Dumpsters I frequent. All except the most phobic people
would be willing to eat from a can even if it came from a
Dumpster. I have few qualms about dry foods such as crackers, cookies, cereal, chips, and pasta if they are free of visible
contaminants and still dry and crisp. Raw fruits and vegetables with intact skins seem perfectly safe to me, excluding, of
course, the obviously rotten. Many are discarded for minor
imperfections that can be pared away. Chocolate is often
discarded only because it has become discolored as the cocoa
butter de-emulsified.

I began scavenging by pulling pizzas out of the Dumpster   13
behind a pizza delivery shop. In general, prepared food requires caution, but in this case I knew what time the shop
closed and went to the Dumpster as soon as the last of the
help left.

Because the workers at these places are usually inexperienced, pizzas are often made with the wrong topping, baked incorrectly, or refused on delivery for being cold. The products to be discarded are boxed up because inventory is kept by counting boxes: A boxed pizza can be written off; an unboxed pizza does not exist. So I had a steady supply of fresh, sometimes warm pizza.

The area I frequent is inhabited by many affluent college students. I am not here by chance; the Dumpsters are very rich. Students throw out many good things, including food, particularly at the end of the semester and before and after breaks. I find it advantageous to keep an eye on the academic calendar.

A typical discard is a half jar of peanut butter—though non-organic peanut butter does not require refrigeration and is unlikely to spoil in any reasonable time. Occasionally I find a cheese with a spot of mold, which, of course, I just pare off, and because it is obvious why the cheese was discarded, I treat it with less suspicion than an apparently perfect cheese found in similar circumstances. One of my favorite finds is yogurt—often discarded, still sealed, when the expiration date has passed—because it will keep for several days, even in warm weather.

I avoid ethnic foods I am unfamiliar with. If I do not know what it is supposed to look or smell like when it is good, I cannot be certain I will be able to tell if it is bad.

No matter how careful I am I still get dysentery at least once a month, oftener in warm weather. I do not want to paint too romantic a picture. Dumpster diving has serious drawbacks as a way of life.

Though I have a proprietary feeling about my Dumpsters, I don't mind my direct competitors, other scavengers, as much as I hate the soda-can scroungers.

I have tried scrounging aluminum cans with an able-bodied companion, and afoot we could make no more than a few dollars a day. I can extract the necessities of life from the Dumpsters directly with far less effort than would be required to accumulate the equivalent value in aluminum. Can scroungers, then, are people who *must* have small amounts of cash—mostly drug addicts and winos.

I do not begrudge them the cans, but can scroungers tend   21
to tear up the Dumpsters, littering the area and mixing the contents. There are precious few courtesies among scavengers, but it is a common practice to set aside surplus items: pairs of shoes, clothing, canned goods, and such. A true scavenger hates to see good stuff go to waste, and what he cannot use he leaves in good condition in plain sight. Can scroungers lay waste to everything in their path and will stir one of a pair of good shoes to the bottom of a Dumpster to be lost or ruined in the muck. They become so specialized that they can see only cans and earn my contempt by passing up change, canned goods, and readily hockable items.

Can scroungers will even go through individual garbage   22
cans, something I have never seen a scavenger do. Going through individual garbage cans without spreading litter is almost impossible, and litter is likely to reduce the public's tolerance of scavenging. But my strongest reservation about going through individual garbage cans is that this seems to me a very personal kind of invasion, one to which I would object if I were a homeowner.

Though Dumpsters seem somehow less personal than gar-   23
bage cans, they still contain bank statements, bills, correspondence, pill bottles, and other sensitive information. I avoid trying to draw conclusions about the people who dump in the Dumpsters I frequent. I think it would be unethical to do so, although I know many people will find the idea of scavenger ethics too funny for words.

Occasionally a find tells a story. I once found a small paper   24
bag containing some unused condoms, several partial tubes of flavored sexual lubricant, a partially used compact of birth control pills, and the torn pieces of a picture of a young man. Clearly, the woman was through with him and planning to give up sex altogether.

Dumpster things are often sad—abandoned teddy bears,   25
shredded wedding albums, despaired-of sales kits. I find dia-
ries and journals. College students also discard their papers;
I am horrified to discover the kind of paper that now merits
an A in an undergraduate course.

Dumpster diving is outdoor work, often surprisingly pleas-   26
ant. It is not entirely predictable; things of interest turn up
every day, and some days there are finds of great value. I am
always very pleased when I can turn up exactly the thing I
most wanted to find. Yet in spite of the element of chance,
scavenging, more than most other pursuits, tends to yield
returns in some proportion to the effort and intelligence
brought to bear.

I think of scavenging as a modern form of self-reliance.   27
After ten years of government service, where everything is
geared to the lowest common denominator, I find work that
rewards initiative and effort refreshing. Certainly I would be
happy to have a sinecure again, but I am not heartbroken to
be without one.

I find from the experience of scavenging two rather deep   28
lessons. The first is to take what I can use and let the rest go.
I have come to think that there is no value in the abstract. A
thing I cannot use or make useful, perhaps by trading, has
no value, however fine or rare it may be. (I mean useful in
the broad sense—some art, for example, I would think valuable.)

The second lesson is the transience of material being. I do   29
not suppose that ideas are immortal, but certainly they are
longer-lived than material objects.

The things I find in Dumpsters, the love letters and rag   30
dolls of so many lives, remind me of this lesson. Many times
in my travels I have lost everything but the clothes on my
back. Now I hardly pick up a thing without envisioning
the time I will cast it away. This, I think, is a healthy state of
mind. Almost everything I have now has already been cast
out at least once, proving that what I own is valueless to
someone.

I find that my desire to grab for the gaudy bauble has been 31
largely sated. I think this is an attitude I share with the very
wealthy—we both know there is plenty more where whatever
we have came from. Between us are the rat-race millions who
have confounded their selves with the objects they grasp and
who nightly scavenge the cable channels looking for they
know not what.

I am sorry for them. 32

For Study and Discussion

QUESTIONS FOR RESPONSE

1. What assumptions do you make about someone sorting through
   a Dumpster?
2. What things that you throw away in the weekly garbage might
   others find valuable?

QUESTIONS ABOUT PURPOSE

1. Why does Eighner prefer the term *scavenging* to *scrounging* or
   foraging to characterize the process he analyzes?
2. In what ways does Eighner's analysis demonstrate that Dumpster
   diving is "a sound and honorable niche"?

QUESTIONS ABOUT AUDIENCE

1. How does Eighner anticipate his audience's reaction to his subject by presenting the "predictable series of stages that a person
   goes through in learning to scavenge"?
2. How do Eighner's "scavenger ethics" enhance his standing with
   his readers?

QUESTIONS ABOUT STRATEGIES

1. How does Eighner use the example of pizza to illustrate the three
   principles of eating from a Dumpster?
2. How does Eighner's analysis of the process of "soda-can
   scrounging" help distinguish that process from "scavenging"?

QUESTIONS FOR DISCUSSION

1. How do the two lessons Eighner has learned demonstrate that his "work" rewards initiative and effort?
2. What attitudes toward consumption and waste does Eighner claim he shares with the very wealthy? Why does he feel sorry for "the rat-race millions"?

Nikki Giovanni was born in 1943 in Knoxville, Tennessee, and was educated at Fisk University, the University of Pennsylvania, and Columbia University. She has taught creative writing at Rutgers University and Virginia Tech and worked for the Ohio Humanities Council and the Appalachian Community Fund. Her poems have appeared in the collections *My House* (1972), *The Women and the Men* (1975), and *Those Who Ride the Night Winds* (1983). Her nonfiction work appears in books such as *Gemini: An Extended Autobiographical Statement on My First Twenty-five Years Being a Black Poet* (1971), *Sacred Cows . . . and Other Edibles* (1988), and *Racism 101* (1994). In "Campus Racism 101," Giovanni tells black students how to succeed at predominantly white colleges.

Campus Racism 101

T HERE IS A bumper sticker that reads: TOO BAD IGNO-   1
RANCE ISN'T PAINFUL. I like that. But ignorance is. We just seldom attribute the pain to it or even recognize it when we see it. Like the postcard on my corkboard. It shows a young man in a very hip jacket smoking a cigarette. In the background is a high school with the American flag waving. The caption says: "Too cool for school. Yet too stupid for the real world." Out of the mouth of the young man is a bubble enclosing the words "Maybe I'll start a band." There could be a postcard showing a jock in a uniform saying, "I don't need school. I'm going to the NFL or NBA." Or one showing a young man or woman studying and a group of young

people saying, "So you want to be white." Or something equally demeaning. We need to quit it.

I am a professor of English at Virginia Tech. I've been here   2
for four years, though for only two years with academic rank. I am tenured, which means I have a teaching position for life, a rarity on a predominantly white campus. Whether from malice or ignorance, people who think I should be at a predominantly Black institution will ask, "Why are you at Tech?" Because it's here. And so are Black students. But even if Black students weren't here, it's painfully obvious that this nation and this world cannot allow white students to go

---

Your job is not to educate white people; it is to obtain an education.

---

through higher education without interacting with Blacks in authoritative positions. It is equally clear that predominantly Black colleges cannot accommodate the numbers of Black students who want and need an education.

Is it difficult to attend a predominantly white college?   3
Compared with what? Being passed over for promotion because you lack credentials? Being turned down for jobs because you are not college-educated? Joining the armed forces or going to jail because you cannot find an alternative to the streets? Let's have a little perspective here. Where can you go and what can you do that frees you from interacting with the white American mentality? You're going to interact; the only question is, will you be in some control of yourself and your actions, or will you be controlled by others? I'm going to recommend self-control.

What's the difference between prison and college? They   4
both prescribe your behavior for a given period of time. They both allow you to read books and develop your writing. They both give you time alone to think and time with your

peers to talk about issues. But four years of prison doesn't give you a passport to greater opportunities. Most likely that time only gives you greater knowledge of how to get back in. Four years of college gives you an opportunity not only to lift yourself but to serve your people effectively. What's the difference when you are called nigger in college from when you are called nigger in prison? In college you can, though I admit with effort, follow procedures to have those students who called you nigger kicked out or suspended. You can bring issues to public attention without risking your life. But mostly, college is and always has been the future. We, neither less nor more than other people, need knowledge. There are discomforts attached to attending predominantly white colleges, though no more so than living in a racist world. Here are some rules to follow that may help:

Go to class. No matter how you feel. No matter how you 5 think the professor feels about you. It's important to have a consistent presence in the classroom. If nothing else, the professor will know you care enough and are serious enough to be there.

Meet your professors. Extend your hand (give a firm hand- 6 shake) and tell them your name. Ask them what you need to do to make an A. You may never make an A, but you have put them on notice that you are serious about getting good grades.

Do assignments on time. Typed or computer-generated. 7 You have the syllabus. Follow it, and turn those papers in. If for some reason you can't complete an assignment on time, let your professor know before it is due and work out a new due date—then meet it.

Go back to see your professor. Tell him or her your name 8 again. If an assignment received less than an A, ask why, and find out what you need to do to improve the next assignment.

Yes, your professor is busy. So are you. So are your parents 9 who are working to pay or help with your tuition. Ask early what you need to do if you feel you are starting to get into academic trouble. Do not wait until you are failing.

Understand that there will be professors who do not like you; 10

there may even be professors who are racist or sexist or both. You must discriminate among your professors to see who will give you the help you need. You may not simply say, "They are all against me." They aren't. They mostly don't care. Since you are the one who wants to be educated, find the people who want to help.

Don't defeat yourself. Cultivate your friends. Know your 11 enemies. You cannot undo hundreds of years of prejudicial thinking. Think for yourself and speak up. Raise your hand in class. Say what you believe no matter how awkward you may think it sounds. You will improve in your articulation and confidence.

Participate in some campus activity. Join the newspaper 12 staff. Run for office. Join a dorm council. Do something that involves you on campus. You are going to be there for four years, so let your presence be known, if not felt.

You will inevitably run into some white classmates who are 13 troubling because they often say stupid things, ask stupid questions—and expect an answer. Here are some comebacks to some of the most common inquiries and comments:

Q: What's it like to grow up in a ghetto?   14
A: I don't know.   15

Q (from the teacher): Can you give us the Black perspective 16 on Toni Morrison, Huck Finn, slavery, Martin Luther King, Jr., and others?
A: I can give you *my* perspective. (Do not take the burden 17 of 22 million people on your shoulders. Remind everyone that you are an individual, and don't speak for the race or any other individual within it.)

Q: Why do all the Black people sit together in the dining 18 hall?
A: Why do all the white students sit together?   19

Q: Why should there be an African-American studies course? 20
A: Because white Americans have not adequately studied the 21

contributions of Africans and African-Americans. Both Black and white students need to know our total common history.

Q: Why are there so many scholarships for "minority" students?   22

A: Because they wouldn't give my great-grandparents their forty acres and the mule.   23

Q: How can whites understand Black history, culture, literature, and so forth?   24

A: The same way we understand white history, culture, literature, and so forth. That is why we're in school: to learn.   25

Q: Should whites take African-American studies courses?   26

A: Of course. We take white-studies courses, though the universities don't call them that.   27

Comment: When I see groups of Black people on campus, it's really intimidating.   28

Comeback: I understand what you mean. I'm frightened when I see white students congregating.   29

Comment: It's not fair. It's easier for you guys to get into college than for other people.   30

Comeback: If it's so easy, why aren't there more of us?   31

Comment: It's not our fault that America is the way it is.   32

Comeback: It's not our fault, either, but both of us have a responsibility to make changes.   33

It's really very simple. Educational progress is a national concern; education is a private one. Your job is not to educate white people; it is to obtain an education. If you take the racial world on your shoulders, you will not get the job done. Deal with yourself as an individual worthy of respect, and make everyone else deal with you the same way. College is a little like playing grown-up. Practice what you want to be. You have been telling your parents you are grown. Now is your chance to act like it.   34

For Study and Discussion

QUESTIONS FOR RESPONSE

1. How have you responded to situations in which you were convinced that your teacher did not like you?
2. How have you felt when a teacher or fellow student placed you in a group (characterized by stereotypes) and then asked you to speak *for* that group?

QUESTIONS ABOUT PURPOSE

1. How does Giovanni explain her reasons for teaching at a predominantly white school?
2. In what ways does the issue of control, particularly self-control, explain the purpose of her advice?

QUESTIONS ABOUT AUDIENCE

1. How do the examples in the first paragraph and the advice in the last paragraph identify Giovanni's primary audience?
2. How does Giovanni's status as professor at a predominantly white college establish her authority to address her audience on "Racism 101"?

QUESTIONS ABOUT STRATEGIES

1. How does Giovanni arrange her advice? Why is her first suggestion—"Go to class"—her *first* suggestion? Why is her last suggestion—"Participate in some campus activity"—her *last* suggestion?
2. How does she use sample questions and answers to illustrate the experience of learning on a white campus?

QUESTIONS FOR DISCUSSION

1. What does Giovanni's attitude toward *individual* as opposed to *group* perspective suggest about the nature of "racism"?
2. How might white students learn as much as black students from following her advice?

Natalie Angier was born in New York City in 1958, and educated at the University of Michigan and Barnard College. She worked as a staff writer for *Discover* and *Time* and as an editor for *Savvy* before becoming the science correspondent for the *New York Times* where she won the Pulitzer Prize for best reporting. Her books include *Natural Obsessions* (1988), *The Beauty of the Beastly* (1995), and *Woman: An Intimate Geography* (1999). In "Dolphin Courtship: Brutal, Cunning, and Complex," reprinted from *The Beauty of the Beastly,* Angier analyzes the complex process by which dolphins mate.

Dolphin Courtship: Brutal, Cunning, and Complex

AS MUCH AS puppies or pandas or even children, dolphins are universally beloved. They seem to cavort and frolic at the least provocation, their mouths are fixed in what looks like a state of perpetual merriment, and their behavior and enormous brains suggest an intelligence approaching that of humans—even, some might argue, surpassing it.

Dolphins are turning out to be exceedingly clever, but not in the loving, utopian-socialist manner that sentimental Flipperophiles may have hoped. Researchers who spent thousands of hours observing the behavior of bottle-nose dolphins off the coast of Australia have discovered that the males form social alliances that are far more sophisticated and devious than any seen in animals other than human beings. In these sleek submarine partnerships, one team of dolphins will

113

recruit the help of another band of males to gang up against a third group, a sort of multitiered battle plan that requires considerable mental calculus.

The purpose of these complex alliances is not exactly sportive. Males collude with their peers in order to steal fertile females from competing bands. And after they succeed in spiriting a female away, the males remain in their tight-knit group and perform a series of feats, at once spectacular and threatening, to guarantee that the female stays in line. Two or three males will surround her, leaping and bellyflopping, swiveling and somersaulting, all in perfect synchrony. Should the female be so unimpressed by the choreography as to attempt to flee, the males will chase after her, bite her, slap

Dolphins become conspicuously charmless when they want to mate or avoid mating.

her with their fins, or slam into her with their bodies. The scientists call this effort to control females "herding," but they acknowledge that the word does not convey the aggressiveness of the act. As the herding proceeds, the sounds of fin swatting and body bashing rumble the waters, and sometimes the female emerges with deep tooth rakes on her sides.

Although biologists have long been impressed with the intelligence and social complexity of bottle-nose dolphins—the type of porpoise often enlisted for marine mammal shows because they are so responsive to trainers—they were nonetheless surprised by the Machiavellian flavor of the males' stratagems. Many primates, including chimpanzees and baboons, are known to form gangs to attack rival camps, but never before had one group of animals been seen to solicit a second to go after a third. Equally impressive, the multipart alliances among dolphins seemed flexible, shifting from day to day depending on the dolphins' needs, whether one group owed a favor to another, and the dolphins' perceptions of what they could get away with. The creatures seemed to be highly opportunistic, which meant that each animal was always computing who was friend and who was foe.

In an effort to thwart male encroachment, female dolphins likewise formed sophisticated alliances, the sisterhood sometimes chasing after an alliance of males that had stolen one of their friends from the fold. What is more, females seemed to exert choice over the males that sought to herd them, sometimes swimming alongside them in apparent contentment, at other times working furiously to escape, and often succeeding. Considered together, the demands of fluid and expedient social allegiances and counterallegiances could have been a force driving the evolution of intelligence among dolphins.

Lest it seem that a dolphin is little more than a thug with fins and a blowhole, biologists emphasize that it is in general a remarkably good-natured and friendly animal, orders of magnitude more peaceful than a leopard or even a chimpanzee. Most of the thirty species of dolphins and small whales are extremely social, forming into schools of several to hundreds of mammals, which periodically break off into smaller clans and come back together again in what is called a fission-fusion society. Among other things, their sociality appears to help them evade sharks and forage more effectively for fish.

Species like the bottle-nose and the spinner dolphins make most of their decisions by consensus, spending hours dawdling in a protected bay, nuzzling one another, and generating an eerie nautical symphony of squeaks, whistles, barks, twangs, and clicks. The noises rise ever louder until they reach a pitch that apparently indicates the vote is unanimous and it is time to take action—say, to go out and fish. "When they're coordinating their decisions, it's like an orchestra tuning up, and it gets more impassioned and more rhythmic," said Dr.

Kenneth Norris, a leader in dolphin research. "Democracy takes time, and they spend hours every day making decisions."

As extraordinary as the music is, dolphins do not possess   8
what can rightly be called a complex language, where one animal can say unequivocally to another "Let's go fishing." But the vocalizations are not completely random. Each bottle-nose dolphin has, for example, its own call sign—a signature whistle unique to that creature. A whistle is generated internally and sounds more like a radio signal than a human whistle. The mother teaches her calf what its whistle will be by repeating the sound over and over. The calf retains that whistle, squealing it out at times as though declaring its presence. On occasion, one dolphin will imitate the whistle of a companion, in essence calling the friend's name.

But dolphin researchers warn against glorifying dolphins   9
beyond the realms of mammaldom. "Everybody who's done research in the field is tired of dolphin lovers who believe these creatures are floating Hobbits," said one dolphin trainer and scientist. "A dolphin is a healthy social mammal, and it behaves like one, sometimes doing things that we don't find very charming."

Dolphins become conspicuously charmless when they   10
want to mate or to avoid being mated. Female bottle-nose dolphins bear a single calf only once every four or five years, so a fertile female is a prized commodity. Because there is almost no size difference between the sexes, a single female cannot be forced to mate by a lone male. That may be part of the reason that males team into gangs.

One ten-year study covered a network of about three   11
hundred male dolphins off western Australia. The researchers discovered that early in adolescence, a male bottle-nose will form an unshakable alliance with one or two other males. They stick together for years, perhaps a lifetime, swimming, fishing, and playing together, and flaunt their fast friendship by always traveling abreast and surfacing in exact synchrony.

Sometimes that pair or triplet is able to woo a fertile female   12
on its own, although what happens once the males have
herded in a female, and whether she goes for one or all of
them, is not known: dolphin copulations occur deep under
water and are almost impossible to witness. Nor do researchers understand how the males determine that a female
is fertile, or at least nearly so, and is thus worth herding.
Males do sometimes sniff around a female's genitals, as
though trying to smell her receptivity; but because bottle-
nose dolphins give birth so rarely, males may attempt to keep
a female around even when she is not ovulating, in the hope
that she will require their services when the prized moment
of estrus arrives.

At other times potential mates are scarce, and male alli-   13
ances grow testy. That is when pairs or triplets seek to steal
females from other groups. They scout out another alliance
of lonely bachelors and, through a few deft strokes of their
pectoral fins or gentle pecks with their mouths, persuade that
pair or triplet to join in the venture.

The pact sealed, the two dolphin gangs then descend on   14
a third group that is herding along a female. They chase and
assault the defending team, and, because there are more of
them, they usually win and take away the female. Significantly,
the victorious joint alliance then splits up, with only one pair
or triplet getting the female; the other team apparently helped
them strictly as a favor.

That buddy-buddy spirit, however, may be fleeting. Two   15
groups of dolphins that cooperated one week may be adver-
saries the next, and a pair of males will switch sides to help a
second group pilfer the same female they had helped the
defending males capture in the first place.

The instability and complications of the mating games may   16
explain why males are so aggressive and demanding toward
the females they do manage to capture. Male pairs or triplets
guard the female ferociously, jerking their heads at her, charging her, biting her, and leaping and swimming about her in
perfect unison, as though turning their bodies into fences.

They may swim up under her, their penises extruded and erect but without attempting penetration. Sometimes a male will make a distinctive popping noise at the female, a vocalization that sounds like a fist rapping on hollow wood. The noise probably indicates "Get over here!" for if the female ignores the pop, the male will threaten or attack her.

At some point, the female mates with one or more of the males, and once she gives birth, the alliance loses interest in her. Female dolphins raise their calves as single mothers for four to five years.

The pressure to cooperate and to compete with their fellows may have accelerated the evolution of the dolphin brain. The dolphin has one of the highest ratios of brain size to body mass in the animal kingdom, and such a ratio is often a measure of intelligence. A similar hypothesis has been proposed for the flowering of intelligence in humans, another big-brained species. Like dolphins, humans evolved in highly social conditions, where kin, friends, and foes are all mingled together, and the resources an individual can afford to share today may become dangerously scarce tomorrow, igniting conflict. In such a setting, few relationships are black or white; it is the capacity to distinguish subtle shades of gray that demands intelligence.

But keep in mind that the dolphin's big brain does not, on its own, rank it as a big thinker. After all, the creature endowed with what may be the largest brain-to-body ratio in nature is none other than the sheep.

For Study and Discussion

QUESTIONS FOR RESPONSE

1. How have you responded to movies about "Flipper" or marine mammal shows featuring dolphins?
2. In what ways has figuring out the friends and foes in your shifting peer groups made you more savvy about social relationships?

QUESTIONS ABOUT PURPOSE

1. Why does Angier begin her essay by characterizing dolphins as "universally beloved"?
2. Why does she end her essay by speculating about the evolution of the dolphin's brain?

QUESTIONS ABOUT AUDIENCE

1. What assumptions does Angier make about her audience when she uses the term "Flipperophiles"?
2. How does she use the testimony of dolphin trainers and researchers to convince her readers that dolphins are not always "charming"?

QUESTIONS ABOUT STRATEGY

1. According to Angier, what are the primary steps in dolphin courtship?
2. How does she account for the steps researchers cannot explain (determining fertility) or have not seen (copulation)?

QUESTIONS FOR DISCUSSION

1. How does Angier's comparison of dolphins to other animals explain the uniqueness of their courtship rituals?
2. In what ways does the male-female behavior of dolphins remind you of the male-female behavior of human beings?

Julia Alvarez was born in New York City in 1950, but was raised in the Dominican Republic until her family was forced to flee the country because her father's involvement in the plot to overthrow dictator Rafael Trujillo was uncovered. She was educated at Middlebury College, Syracuse University, and Bread Loaf School of English and worked as a Poet-in-the-Schools in several states. She then began teaching writing at George Washington University, the University of Illinois, and Middlebury College. Her major works of fiction include *How the Garcia Girls Lost Their Accents* (1991), *In the Time of Butterflies* (1994), *¡YO!* (1996), and *In the Name of Salomé: A Novel* (2000). Her poems appear in *Homecoming* (1984) and *The Other Side/El Otro Lado* (1995). In "Grounds for Fiction," reprinted from *Something to Declare* (1998), Alvarez analyzes the sources and strategies of her writing process.

Grounds for Fiction

E VERY ONCE IN a while after a reading, someone in the audience will come up to me. *Have I got a story for you!* They will go on to tell me the story of an aunt or sister or next-door neighbor, some moment of mystery, some serendipitous occurrence, some truly incredible story. "You should write it down," I always tell them. They look at me as if they've just offered me their family crown jewels and I've refused them. "I'm no writer," they tell me. "You're the writer."

"Oh, you never know," I reply, so as to encourage them. What I should tell them is that writing ideas can't really be traded in an open market. If they could be, writers would be multimillionaires. Who knows what mystery (or madness) it is that drives us to our computers for two, three, four years, in pursuit of some sparkling possibility that looks like dull fact to everyone else's eyes. One way to define a writer is she who is able to make what obsesses her into everyone's obsession. I am thinking of Goethe, whose *Sorrows of Young Werther*, published in 1774, caused a spate of suicides in imitation of its young hero. Young Werther's blue frock coat and yellow waistcoat became the fad. We have all been the victims of someone's too-long slide show of their white-water rafting

> *I told the young man that if he didn't want to spend hours and hours finding out if the kernel of an idea, the glimmer of an inspiration, the flash of a possibility would make a good story, he should give up the* idea *of being a writer.*

trip or their recounting of a convoluted, boring dream. But a Mark Twain can turn that slide show into the lively backdrop of a novel, or a Jorge Luis Borges can take the twist and turn of a dream and wring the meaning of the universe from it.

But aside from talent—and granted, that is a big aside, one that comes and goes and shifts and grows and diminishes, so it is also somewhat unpredictable—how can we tell when we've got it: that seed of experience, of memory, that voice of a character or fleeting image that might just be grounds for fiction? The answer is that we can never tell. And so another way to define a writer is someone who is willing to find out. As James Dickey once explained to an audience, "I work on the process of refining low-grade ore. I get maybe a couple of nuggets of gold out of fifty tons of dirt. It is tough for me. No, I am not inspired."

"Are you all here because you want to muck around in fifty tons of dirt?" I ask my workshop of young writers the first day. Not one hand goes up unless I've told them the Dickey story first.

In fact, my students want to know ahead of time if some idea they have will make a good story. "I mean, before I spend hours and hours on it," one young man explained. I told my students what Mallarmé told his friend the painter Degas, when Degas complained that he couldn't seem to write well although he was "full of ideas." Mallarmés's famous answer was, "My dear Degas, poems are not made out of ideas. Poems are made out of words." I told my student that if a young writer had come up to me and told me that he was going to write a story about a man who wakes up one morning and finds out that he has been turned into a cockroach, I would have told him to forget it. That story would never work. "And I would have stopped Kafka from writing his 'Metamorphosis,'" I concluded, smiling at my student, as if he might be a future Kafka.

"Well, it's just two pages," he grumbled. "And I have this other idea that might be better. About a street person who is getting Alzheimer's."

"Write both stories, and I'll read them and tell you what I think of them," I said. He looked alarmed. So I leveled with him. I told him that if he didn't want to spend hours and hours finding out if the kernel of an idea, the glimmer of an inspiration, the flash of a possibility would make a good story, he should give up the *idea* of wanting to be a writer.

As much as I can break down the process of writing stories, I would say that this is how it begins. I find a detail or image or character or incident or cluster of events. A certain luminosity surrounds them. I find myself attracted. I come forward. I pick it up, turn it around, begin to ask questions, and

spend hours and weeks and months and years trying to answer them.

I keep a folder, a yellow folder with pockets. For a long time ⁹
it had no label because I didn't know what to label it:
WHATCHAMACALLITS, filed under *W*, or also under *W*,
STORY-POEM-WANNABES. Finally, I called the folder
CURIOSIDADES, in Spanish so I wouldn't have to commit
myself to what I was going to do in English with these
random little things. I tell my students this, too, that writing
begins before you ever put pen to paper or your fingers down
on the keyboard. It is a way of being alive in the world. Henry
James's advice to the young writer was to be someone on
whom nothing is lost. And so this is my folder of the little
things that have not been lost on me; news clippings, headlines, inventory lists, bits of gossip that I've already sensed
have an aura about them, the beginnings of a poem or a short
story, the seed of a plot that might turn into a novel or a
query that might needle an essay out of me.

Periodically, when I'm between writing projects and some- ¹⁰
times when I'm in the middle of one and needing a break, I
go through my yellow folder. Sometimes I discard a clipping
or note that no longer holds my attention. But most of my
curiosidades have been in my folder for years, though some
have migrated to new folders, the folders of stories and poems
they have inspired or found a home in.

Here's one of these curiosidades that is now in a folder ¹¹
that holds drafts of a story that turned into a chapter of my
novel *¡YO!* This chapter is in the point of view of Marie
Beaudry, a landlady who, along with other narrators, gets to
tell a story on Yolanda García, the writer. The little curiosity
that inspired Marie's voice was a note I found in the trash of
an apartment I moved into. It has nothing at all to do with
what happens in my story.

> *Re and Mal: Here's the two keys to your father's apt.*
> *Need I say more excepting that's such a rotten thing*

you pulled on him. My doing favors is over as of this
morning. Good luck to you two hard-hearted han-
nahs. I got more feeling in my little finger than the
two of you got in your whole body.

Jinny

I admit that when I read this note, I wanted to move out   12
of that apartment. I felt the place was haunted by the ghost
of the last tenant against whom some violation had been
perpetrated by these two hard-hearted hannahs, Re and Mal.
Over the years that handwritten note stayed in my yellow
folder and eventually gave me the voice of my character Marie
Beaudry.

Here's another scrap from deep inside one of the pockets.   13
It's the title of an article in one of my husband's ophthal-
mological journals: "Treatment of Chronic Postfiltration Hypotony by Intrableb Injection of Autologous Blood." I think
I saved that choice bit of medical babble because of the
delight I took in the jabberwocky phenomenon of that title.

> *'Twas brillig and the slithy toves*
> *Did gyre and postfiltrate the wabe;*
> *All hypotonious was the blood,*
> *And autologous the intrableb.*

I have not yet used it in a story or poem, but who knows,
maybe someday you will look over the shoulder of one of my
characters and see that he is reading this article or writing it.
I can tell you that this delight in words and how we use and
misuse them is a preoccupation of mine.

Maybe because I began my writing life as a poet, the   14
naming of things has always interested me:

> *Mother, unroll the bolts and name*
> *the fabrics from which our clothing came,*
> *dress the world in vocabulary:*
> *broadcloth, corduroy, denim, terry.*

Actually, that poem, "Naming the Fabrics," besides being inspired, of course, by the names of fabrics, was also triggered by something I picked up while reading *The 1961 Better Homes and Garden Sewing Book,* page 45: "During a question and answer period at a sewing clinic, a woman in the audience asked this question: 'I can sew beautifully; my fitting is excellent; the finished dress looks as good as that of any professional—but how do I get up enough courage to cut the fabric?'" I typed out this passage and put it away. A few months later, this fear found its way from my yellow folder to my poem, "Naming the Fabrics":

> *I pay a tailor to cut his suits*
> *from seersucker, duck, tweed, cheviot,*
> *those names make my cutting hand skittish—*
> *either they sound like sex or British.*

Since I myself have no sewing skills to speak of, I didn't know about this fear that seamstresses experience before cutting fabric. Certainly, the year 1961, when this sewing book was published, brings other fears to mind: the Berlin Wall going up; invaders going down to the Bay of Pigs; Trujillo, our dictator of thirty-one years, being assassinated in the Dominican Republic. But this housewife in Indiana had her own metaphysical fears to work out on cloth. "How do I get up enough courage to cut the fabric?" Her preoccupation astonished me and touched me for all kinds of reasons I had to work out on paper.

You might wonder what a "serious writer" was doing 15
reading *The 1961 Better Homes and Garden Sewing Book.* Wouldn't my time have been better spent perusing Milton or Emily Dickinson or even the *New York Review of Books* or *The Nation?* All I can say in my defense is that I believe in Henry James's advice: be someone on whom nothing is lost. Or what Deborah Kerr said in *Night of the Iguana,* "Nothing human disgusts me." I once heard a writer on *Fresh Air* tell Terry Gross that one of the most important things he had ever learned in his life was that you could learn a lot from

people who were dumber than you. You can also learn a lot from publications that are below your literary standards: housekeeping books, cookbooks, manuals, cereal boxes, and the local newspapers of your small town.

These last are the best. Even if some of this "news" is really 16 glorified gossip—so what? Most of our classics are glorified gossip. Think of the Wife of Bath's inventory of husbands or the debutante's hair-rape in "The Rape of the Lock." How about Madame Bovary's seamy affair? Is what happened to Abelard over his Héloïse or to Jason for pissing off Medea any less infamous than the John and Lorena Bobbit story of several years ago? The wonderful Canadian writer Alice Munro admits that she likes reading *People* magazine, and "not just at the checkout stand. I sometimes buy it." She goes on to say that gossip is "a central part of my life. I'm interested in small-town gossip. Gossip has that feeling in it, that one wants to know about life."

I've gotten wonderful stories from the *Addison Inde-* 17 *pendent,* the *Valley Voice,* even the *Burlington Free Press* that would never be reported in the *Wall Street Journal* or the *New York Times:*

11-YEAR-OLD GIRLS TAKE CAR
ON TWO-STATE JOYRIDE

Two 11-year-old girls determined to see a newborn niece secretly borrowed their grandfather's car, piled clothes on the front seat so they could see over the steering wheel and drove more than 10 hours.

Neither one of them had ever driven a car before, said Michael Ray, Mercer County's juvenile case worker. The youngsters packed the Dodge Aries with soda, snacks, and an atlas for their trek from West Virginia to the central Kentucky town of Har-rodsburg. "They were determined to see that baby," said caseworker Ray.

You could write a whole novel about that. In fact, in Mona 18 Simpson's latest novel, *A Regular Guy,* eleven-year-old Jane di Natali is taught by her mother to drive their pickup with wood blocks strapped to the pedals so her short legs can reach them. Little Jane takes off on her own to see her estranged father hundreds of miles away. I wonder if Mona Simpson got her idea for Jane's odyssey from reading about these two eleven-year-olds.

Here's another article I've saved in my yellow folder: 19

MISDIAGNOSED PATIENT FREED AFTER 2 YEARS

A Mexican migrant worker misdiagnosed and kept sedated in an Oregon mental hospital for two years because doctors couldn't understand his Indian dialect is going home.

Adolfo Gonzales, a frail 5-foot-4-inch grape picker who doesn't speak English or Spanish, had been trying to communicate in his native Indian dialect of Trique.

Gonzales, believed to be in his 20s, was born in a village in Oaxaca, Mexico. He was committed in June 1990 after being arrested for indecent exposure at a laundromat. Charges later were dropped.

I couldn't get this story out of my head. First, I was—and am—intensely interested in the whole Scheherazade issue of how important it is to be able to tell our stories to those who have power over us. Second, and more mundanely, I was intensely curious about those charges that were later dropped: indecent exposure at a laundromat. What was Adolfo Gonzales doing taking his clothes off in a laundromat? Why was he in town after a hard day of grape picking? I had to find answers to these questions, and so I started writing a poem. "It's a myth that writers write what they know," the writer Marcie Hershman has written. "We write what it is that we need to know."

> *The next payday you went to town*
> *to buy your girl and to wash your one*
> *set of working clothes.*

In the laundromat, you took them off
to wring out the earth you wanted
to leave behind you.
                    from "Two Years Too Late"

Of course, you don't even have to go to your local paper.   20
Just take a walk downtown, especially if you live in a small
town, as I do. All I have to do is have a cup of coffee at Steve's
Diner or at Jimmy's Weybridge Garage and listen to my
neighbors talking. Flannery O'Connor claimed that most
beginners' stories don't work because "they don't go very far
inside a character, don't reveal very much of the character.
And this problem is in large part due to the fact that these
characters have no distinctive speech to reveal themselves
with." Here are some examples of my fellow Vermonters
talking their very distinctive and revealing speech.

> He's so lazy he married a pregnant woman.
> I'm so hungry I could eat the north end out of a
> southbound skunk.
> The snow's butt-high to a tall cow.
> More nervous than a long-tailed cat in a room full of
> rocking chairs.
> I'm so sick that I'd have to get well to die.

Of course if, like Whitman, you do nothing but listen, you
will also hear all kinds of bogus voices these days, speaking
the new doublespeak. In our litigious, politically overcor-
rected, dizzily spin-doctored age, politicians and public
figures have to use language so that it doesn't say anything
that might upset anyone. Here's a list of nonterms and what
they really stand for:

Sufferer of fictitious disorder syndrome:	Liar
Suboptimal:	Failed
Temporarily displaced inventory:	Stolen
Negative gain in test scores:	Lower test scores
Substantive negative outcome:	Death

We're back to "Treatment of Chronic Postfiltration Hypotony by Intrableb Injection of Autologous Blood," what Ken Macrorie in his wonderful book about expository writing, *Telling Writing,* calls "Engfish"—homogenized, doctored-up, approximate language that can't be traced to a human being.

I tend to agree with what Dickinson once said about   21 poetry, "There are no approximate words in a poem." Auden even went so far as to say that he could pick out a potential poet by a student's answer to the question, "Why do you want to write poetry?" If the student answered, "I have important things to say," then he was not a poet. If he answered, "I like hanging around words listening to what they say," then maybe he was going to be a poet.

I got enmeshed in one such string of words when I visited   22 the United Nations to hear my mother give a speech on violation of human rights. At the door an aide handed me the list of voting member countries and the names caught my eye: Dem Kampuchea, Dem Yemen, Denmark, Djibouti, Dominica, Dominican Republic, Ecuador, Egypt. . . . When I got home, I started writing a poem, ostensibly about hearing my mother give that speech, but really because I wanted to use the names of those countries:

> *I scan the room for reactions,*
> *picking out those countries*
> *guilty of her sad facts.*
> *Kampuchea is absent,*
> *absent, too, the South African delegate.*
> *I cannot find the United States.*
> *Nervous countries predominate,*
> *Nicaragua and Haiti,*
> *Iraq, Israel, Egypt.*
>   *from "Between Dominica and Ecuador"*

But of course, it's not just words that intrigue writers, but the stories, the possibilities of human character that cluster around a bit of history, trivia, gossip.

For instance, Anne Macdonald's book, *Feminine Ingenu-*   23 *ity,* inspired a character trait of the mother in *How the García Girls Lost Their Accents.* According to Macdonald, at the beginning of the twentieth century, 5,535 American women were granted patents for inventions, including a straw-weaving device, an open-eye needle for sewing hot-air balloons, and special planking designed to discourage barnacles from attaching themselves to warships. These intriguing facts gave me a side of the mother's character I would never have thought up on my own. Inspired by the gadgetry of her new country, Laura García sets out to make her mark: soap sprayed from the nozzle head of a shower when you turn the knob a certain way; instant coffee with creamer already mixed in; time-released water capsules for your potted plants when you were away; a key chain with a timer that would go off when your parking meter was about to expire. (And the ticking would help you find your keys easily if you mislaid them.)

Sometimes the inspiration is history. History . . . that sub-   24
ject I hated in school because it was so dry and all about dead people. I wish now my teachers had made me read novels to make the past spring alive in my imagination. For years, I wanted to write about the Mirabal sisters, but I admit I was put off by these grand historical abstractions. It wasn't until I began to accumulate several yellow folders' worth of vivid little details about them that these godlike women became accessible to me. One of my first entries came from my father, who had just returned from a trip to the Dominican Republic: "I met the man who sold the girls pocketbooks at El Gallo before they set off over the mountain. He told me he warned them not to go. He said he took them out back to the stockroom supposedly to show them inventory and explained they were going to be killed. But they did not believe him." I still get goosebumps reading my father's letter dated June 5, 1985. It went in my yellow folder. That pocketbook-buying scene is at the end of the novel I published nine years later.

So what are you to conclude from this tour of my yellow   25
folder? That this essay is just an excuse to take you through

my folder and share my little treasures with you? Well, one thing I don't want you to conclude is that this preliminary woolgathering is a substitute for the real research that starts once you have a poem or story going. In "Naming the Fabrics," for instance, though I was inspired by the plaintive question asked at a sewing clinic, I still had to go down to the fabric store and spend an afternoon with a very kind and patient saleslady who taught me all about gingham and calico, crepe and gauze. I spent days reading fabric books, and weeks working on the poem, and years going back to it, revising it, tinkering with it. For my story, "The Tent," I had to call up the National Guard base near Champaign, Illinois, and get permission from the base commander to go observe his men setting up a tent. ("What exactly do you need this for?" he asked at least half a dozen times.) Sometimes I think the best reason for a writer to have a reputable job like being a professor at a university or a vice president of Hartford Insurance Company is so you can call up those base commanders or bother those salesladies in fabric stores as if you do have a real job. Otherwise, they might think you are crazy and lock you up like poor Adolfo Gonzales.

On the whole, I have found people to be kind and gener-   26
ous with their time, especially when you ask them to talk about something they know and care about. Many people have actually gone beyond kindness in helping me out. I remember calling up the local Catholic priest, bless his heart, who really deserves, I don't know, a plenary indulgence for tolerance in the face of surprise. Imagine getting an early-morning call (my writing day starts at 6:30, but I really don't do this kind of phone calling till about 7:30 since I do want my sources to be lucid). Anyhow, imagine an early-morning call at your rectory from a woman you don't know who asks you what is the name of that long rod priests have with a hole on one end to sprinkle people with holy water? I'd be lying if I tried to make drama out of the phone call and say there was a long pause. Nope. Father John spoke right up, "Ah yes, my aspergill."

One thing I should add—the bad news part of all this fun, 27
but something writers do have to think about in this litigious
age—what is grounds for fiction can also be, alas, grounds
for suing. All three of my novels have been read by my
publisher's lawyer for what might be libelous. Thank goodness Algonquin's lawyer is also a reader who refuses to vacuum all the value out of a book in order to play it safe. Still,
I have had to take drinks out of characters' hands and make
abused ladies disabused and make so many changes in hair
coloring and hairstyle that I could start a literary beauty
parlor.

But even if your fictional ground is cleared of litigious 28
material, there might still be grounds for heartache. Your
family and friends might feel wounded when they can de-
tect—even if no one else can—the shape of the real behind
the form of your fiction. And who would want to hurt those
very people you write for, those very people who share with
you the world you are struggling to understand in your
fiction for their sake as well as your own?

I don't know how to get around this and I certainly 29
haven't figured out what the parameters of my responsibility
are to the real people in my life. One of my theories, which
might sound defensive and self-serving, is that there is no
such thing as straight-up fiction. There are just levels of
distance from our own life experience, the thing that drives
us to write in the first place. In spite of our caution and
precaution, bits of our lives will get into what we write. I have
a friend whose mother finds herself in all his novels, even
historical novels set in nineteenth-century Russia or islands
in the Caribbean where his mother has never been. A novelist
writing about Napoleon might convey his greedy character
by describing him spooning gruel into his mouth, only to
realize that her image of how a greedy man eats comes from
watching her fat Tío Jorge stuff his face with sweet ha-
bichuelas.

I think that if you start censoring yourself as a novelist— 30
this is out of bounds, that is sacrosanct—you will never write

anything. My advice is to write it out, and then decide, by whatever process seems fair to you—three-o'clock-in-the-morning insomniac angst sessions with your soul, or a phone call with your best friend, or a long talk with your sister—what you are going to do about it. More often than not, an upset reaction has more to do with people's wounded vanity or their own unresolved issues with *you* rather than what you've written. I'm not speaking now of meanness or revenge thinly masquerading as fiction, but of a writer's serious attempts to render justice to the world she lives in, which includes, whether she wants it to or not, the people she loves or has tried to love, the people who have been a part of the memories, details, life experiences that form the whole cloth of her reality—out of which, with fear and a trembling hand, she must perforce cut her fiction.

But truly, this is a worry to put out of your head while you are writing. You'll need your energy for the hard work ahead: tons and tons of good *ideas* to process in order to get those nuggets of pure prose. What Yeats once said in his poem, "Dialogue of Self and Soul," could well be the writer's pledge of allegiance:

> *I am content to follow to its source,*
> *every event in action or in thought.*

And remember, no one is probably going to pay you a whole lot of money to do this. You also probably won't save anyone's life with anything you write. But so much does depend on seeing a world in a grain of sand and a heaven in a wildflower. Maybe we are here only to say: house, bridge, aspergill, gingham, calico, gauze. "But to say them," as Rilke said, "remember oh, to say them in a way that the things themselves never dreamed of existing so intensely."

But this is too much of an orchestral close for the lowly little ditty that starts with a newspaper clipping or the feel of a bolt of gingham or a cup of coffee at the Weybridge Garage. The best advice I can give writers is something so dull and simple you'd never save it in your yellow folder. But go ahead and engrave it in your writer's heart. If you want to be a writer, anything in this world is grounds for fiction.

For Study and Discussion

QUESTIONS FOR RESPONSE

1. Have you ever read a news story or overheard some gossip that you think would make a good story? Explain the features that made it "good."
2. Have you ever tried to write about a personal experience that meant a great deal to you? Why were you satisfied or disappointed with the results?

QUESTIONS ABOUT PURPOSE

1. How does Alvarez use Henry James's advice—to be someone on whom nothing is lost—to explain the purpose of the process she is trying to analyze?
2. How does she use "the Scheherazade issue" to explain the purpose of writing?

QUESTIONS ABOUT AUDIENCE

1. In what ways do the people who attend Alvarez's poetry readings serve as the imaginary audience for her essay?
2. How does she use Auden's question to student writers (page 129) to expand her audience?

QUESTIONS ABOUT STRATEGIES

1. Identify the steps in the little paragraph Alvarez uses to "break down the process of writing fiction." What steps are hidden within this sequence?
2. How does Alvarez's "tour" of her CURIOSIDADES help her illustrate the way she *finds* stories?

QUESTIONS FOR DISCUSSION

1. How does Alvarez suggest you solve the problem of the conflict between grounds for fiction and grounds for suing?
2. How does Alvarez support her argument that there is no such thing as "straight-up fiction?"

Serena Nanda was educated at New York University and taught cultural anthropology at John Jay College of Criminal Justice at City University of New York. Her books include *Cultural Anthropology* (1998); *American Cultural Pluralism and Law* (1996); *Neither Man nor Woman: The Hijras of India* (1999), and *Gender Diversity: Cross-Cultured Variations* (2000). Nanda's current research focuses on non-European representations of Europeans in art and performance. In "Arranging a Marriage in India," reprinted from *The Naked Anthropologist: Tales from Around the World* (1992), Nanda contrasts the Indian and American processes of getting married.

Arranging a Marriage in India

Sister and doctor brother-in-law invite correspondence from North Indian professionals only, for a beautiful, talented, sophisticated, intelligent sister, 5′ 3″, slim, M.A. in textile design, father a senior civil officer. Would prefer immigrant doctors, between 26–29 years. Reply with full details and returnable photo.

A well-settled uncle invites matrimonial correspondence from slim, fair, educated South Indian girl, for his nephew, 25 years, smart, M.B.A., green card holder, 5′ 6″. Full particulars with returnable photo appreciated.
—*Matrimonial Advertisements*, India Abroad

I N INDIA, ALMOST all marriages are arranged. Even among 1
the educated middle classes in modern, urban India, marriage is as much a concern of the families as it is of the individuals. So customary is the practice of arranged marriage that there is a special name for a marriage which is not arranged: It is called a "love match."

On my first field trip to India, I met many young men and 2
women whose parents were in the process of "getting them
married." In many cases, the bride and groom would not
meet each other before the marriage. At most they might
meet for a brief conversation, and this meeting would take

*I found it difficult to accept the docile
manner in which this well-educated young
woman awaited the outcome of a process
that would result in her spending the rest of
her life with a man she hardly knew, a
virtual stranger, picked out by her parents.*

place only after their parents had decided that the match was
suitable. Parents do not compel their children to marry a
person who either marriage partner finds objectionable. But
only after one match is refused will another be sought.

As a young American woman in India for the first time, I 3
found this custom of arranged marriage oppressive. How
could any intelligent young person agree to such a marriage
without great reluctance? It was contrary to everything I
believed about the importance of romantic love as the only
basis of a happy marriage. It also clashed with my strongly
held notions that the choice of such an intimate and permanent relationship could be made only by the individuals involved. Had anyone tried to arrange my marriage, I would
have been defiant and rebellious!

At the first opportunity, I began, with more curiosity than 4
tact, to question the young people I met on how they felt
about this practice. Sita, one of my young informants, was a
college graduate with a degree in political science. She had
been waiting for over a year while her parents were arranging
a match for her. I found it difficult to accept the docile

manner in which this well-educated young woman awaited the outcome of a process that would result in her spending the rest of her life with a man she hardly knew, a virtual stranger, picked out by her parents.

"How can you go along with this?" I asked her, in frus- 5 tration and distress. "Don't you care who you marry?"

"Of course I care," she answered. "This is why I must let 6 my parents choose a boy for me. My marriage is too important to be arranged by such an inexperienced person as myself. In such matters, it is better to have my parents' guidance."

I had learned that young men and women in India do not 7 date and have very little social life involving members of the opposite sex. Although I could not disagree with Sita's reasoning, I continued to pursue the subject.

"But how can you marry the first man you have ever met? 8 Not only have you missed the fun of meeting a lot of different people, but you have not given yourself the chance to know who is the right man for you."

"Meeting with a lot of different people doesn't sound like 9 any fun at all," Sita answered. "One hears that in America the girls are spending all their time worrying about whether they will meet a man and get married. Here we have the chance to enjoy our life and let our parents do this work and worrying for us."

She had me there. The high anxiety of the competition to 10 "be popular" with the opposite sex certainly was the most prominent feature of life as an American teenager in the late fifties. The endless worrying about the rules that governed our behavior and about our popularity ratings sapped both our self-esteem and our enjoyment of adolescence. I reflected that absence of this competition in India most certainly may have contributed to the self-confidence and natural charm of so many of the young women I met.

And yet, the idea of marrying a perfect stranger, whom 11 one did not know and did not "love," so offended my American ideas of individualism and romanticism, that I persisted with my objections.

"I still can't imagine it," I said. "How can you agree to marry a man you hardly know?" 12

"But of course he will be known. My parents would never arrange a marriage for me without knowing all about the boy's family background. Naturally we will not rely only on what the family tells us. We will check the particulars out ourselves. No one will want their daughter to marry into a family that is not good. All these things we will know beforehand." 13

Impatiently, I responded, "Sita, I don't mean know the family, I mean, know the man. How can you marry someone you don't know personally and don't love? How can you think of spending your life with someone you may not even like?" 14

"If he is a good man, why should I not like him?" she said. "With you people, you know the boy so well before you marry, where will be the fun to get married? There will be no mystery and no romance. Here we have the whole of our married life to get to know and love our husband. This way is better, is it not?" 15

Her response made further sense, and I began to have second thoughts on the matter. Indeed, during months of meeting many intelligent young Indian people, both male and female, who had the same ideas as Sita. I saw arranged marriages in a different light. I also saw the importance of the family in Indian life and realized that a couple who took their marriage into their own hands was taking a big risk, particularly if their families were irreconcilably opposed to the match. In a country where every important resource in life—a job, a house, a social circle—is gained through family connections, it seemed foolhardy to cut oneself off from a supportive social network and depend solely on one person for happiness and success. 16

Six years later I returned to India to again do fieldwork, this time among the middle class in Bombay, a modern, sophisticated city. From the experience of my earlier visit, I decided to include a study of arranged marriages in my proj- 17 ect. By this time I had met many Indian couples whose marriages had been arranged and who seemed very happy. Particularly in contrast to the fate of many of my married friends in the United States who were already in the process of divorce, the positive aspects of arranged marriages appeared to me to outweigh the negatives. In fact, I thought I might even participate in arranging a marriage myself. I had been fairly successful in the United States in "fixing up" many of my friends, and I was confident that my matchmaking skills could be easily applied to this new situation, once I learned the basic rules. "After all," I thought, "how complicated can it be? People want pretty much the same things in a marriage whether it is in India or America."

An opportunity presented itself almost immediately. A 18 friend from my previous Indian trip was in the process of arranging for the marriage of her eldest son. In India there is a perceived shortage of "good boys," and since my friend's family was eminently respectable and the boy himself personable, well educated, and nice looking, I was sure that by the end of my year's fieldwork, we would have found a match.

The basic rule seems to be that a family's reputation is 19 most important. It is understood that matches would be arranged only within the same caste and general social class, although some crossing of subcastes is permissible if the class positions of the bride's and groom's families are similar. Although dowry is now prohibited by law in India, extensive gift exchanges took place with every marriage. Even when the boy's family do not "make demands," every girl's family nevertheless feels the obligation to give the traditional gifts, to the girl, to the boy, and to the boy's family. Particularly when the couple would be living in the joint family—that is, with the boy's parents and his married brothers and their families, as well as with unmarried siblings—which is still very common even among the urban, upper-middle class in India, the girl's parents are anxious to establish smooth relations between their family and that of the boy. Offering the proper gifts, even when not called "dowry," is often an important factor in influencing the relationship between the bride's and groom's families and perhaps, also, the treatment of the bride in her new home.

In a society where divorce is still a scandal and where, in 20 fact, the divorce rate is exceedingly low, an arranged marriage is the beginning of a lifetime relationship not just between the bride and groom but between their families as well. Thus, while a girl's looks are important, her character is even more so, for she is being judged as a prospective daughter-in-law as much as a prospective bride. Where she would be living in a joint family, as was the case with my friend, the girl's ability to get along harmoniously in a family is perhaps the single most important quality in assessing her suitability.

My friend is a highly esteemed wife, mother, and daugh- 21 ter-in-law. She is religious, soft-spoken, modest, and deferential. She rarely gossips and never quarrels, two qualities highly desirable in a woman. A family that has the reputation for gossip and conflict among its womenfolk will not find it easy to get good wives for their sons. Parents will not want to send their daughter to a house in which there is conflict.

My friend's family were originally from North India. They 22 had lived in Bombay, where her husband owned a business, for forty years. The family had delayed in seeking a match for their eldest son because he had been an Air Force pilot for several years, stationed in such remote places that it had seemed fruitless to try to find a girl who would be willing to accompany him. In their social class, a military career, despite its economic security, has little prestige and is considered a drawback in finding a suitable bride. Many families would not allow their daughters to marry a man in an occupation so potentially dangerous and which requires so much moving around.

The son had recently left the military and joined his fa- 23 ther's business. Since he was a college graduate, modern, and well traveled, from such a good family, and, I thought, quite handsome, it seemed to me that he, or rather his family, was in a position to pick and choose. I said as much to my friend.

While she agreed that there were many advantages on their   24
side, she also said, "We must keep in mind that my son is
both short and dark; these are drawbacks in finding the right
match." While the boy's height had not escaped my notice,
"dark" seemed to me inaccurate; I would have called him
"wheat" colored perhaps, and in any case, I did not realize
that color would be a consideration. I discovered, however,
that while a boy's skin color is a less important consideration
than a girl's, it is still a factor.

An important source of contacts in trying to arrange her   25
son's marriage was my friend's social club in Bombay. Many
of the women had daughters of the right age, and some had
already expressed an interest in my friend's son. I was most
enthusiastic about the possibilities of one particular family
who had five daughters, all of whom were pretty, demure,
and well educated. Their mother had told my friend, "You
can have your pick for your son, whichever one of my daughters appeals to you most."

I saw a match in sight. "Surely," I said to my friend, "we   26
will find one there. Let's go visit and make our choice." But
my friend held back; she did not seem to share my enthusiasm, for reasons I could not then fathom.

When I kept pressing for an explanation of her reluctance,   27
she admitted, "See, Serena, here is the problem. The family
has so many daughters, how will they be able to provide
nicely for any of them? We are not making any demands, but
still, with so many daughters to marry off, one wonders
whether she will even be able to make a proper wedding.
Since this is our eldest son, it's best if we marry him to a girl
who is the only daughter, then the wedding will truly be a
gala affair." I argued that surely the quality of the girls themselves made up for any deficiency in the elaborateness of the
wedding. My friend admitted this point but still seemed
reluctant to proceed.

"Is there something else," I asked her, "some factor I have   28
missed?" "Well," she finally said, "there is one other thing.
They have one daughter already married and living in Bombay. The mother is always complaining to me that the girl's

in-laws don't let her visit her own family often enough. So it makes me wonder, will she be that kind of mother who always wants her daughter at her own home? This will prevent the girl from adjusting to our house. It is not a good thing." And so, this family of five daughters was dropped as a possibility.

Somewhat disappointed, I nevertheless respected my 29 friend's reasoning and geared up for the next prospect. This was also the daughter of a woman in my friend's social club. There was clear interest in this family and I could see why. The family's reputation was excellent; in fact, they came from a subcaste slightly higher than my friend's own. The girl, who was an only daughter, was pretty and well educated and had a brother studying in the United States. Yet, after expressing an interest to me in this family, all talk of them suddenly died down and the search began elsewhere.

"What happened to that girl as a prospect?" I asked one 30 day. "You never mention her any more. She is so pretty and so educated, what did you find wrong?"

"She is too educated. We've decided against it. My hus- 31 band's father saw the girl on the bus the other day and thought her forward. A girl who 'roams about' the city by herself is not the girl for our family." My disappointment this time was even greater, as I thought the son would have liked the girl very much. But then I thought, my friend is right, a girl who is going to live in a joint family cannot be too independent or she will make life miserable for everyone. I also learned that if the family of the girl has even a slightly higher social status than the family of the boy, the bride may think herself too good for them, and this too will cause problems. Later my friend admitted to me that this had been an important factor in her decision not to pursue the match.

The next candidate was the daughter of a client of my 32 friend's husband. When the client learned that the family was looking for a match for their son, he said, "Look no further, we have a daughter." This man then invited my friends to dinner to see the girl. He had already seen their son at the office and decided that "he liked the boy." We all went together for tea, rather than dinner—it was less of a commitment—and while we were there, the girl's mother showed us around the house. The girl was studying for her exams and was briefly introduced to us.

After we left, I was anxious to hear my friend's opinion. 33 While her husband liked the family very much and was impressed with his client's business accomplishments and reputation, the wife didn't like the girl's looks. "She is short, no doubt, which is an important plus point, but she is also fat and wears glasses." My friend obviously thought she could do better for her son and asked her husband to make his excuses to his client by saying that they had decided to postpone the boy's marriage indefinitely.

By this time almost six months had passed and I was 34 becoming impatient. What I had thought would be an easy matter to arrange was turning out to be quite complicated. I began to believe that between my friend's desire for a girl who was modest enough to fit into her joint family, yet attractive and educated enough to be an acceptable partner for her son, she would not find anyone suitable. My friend laughed at my impatience: "Don't be so much in a hurry," she said. "You Americans want everything done so quickly. You get married quickly and then just as quickly get divorced. Here we take marriage more seriously. We must take all the factors into account. It is not enough for us to learn by our mistakes. This is too serious a business. If a mistake is made we have not only ruined the life of our son or daughter, but we have spoiled the reputation of our family as well. And that will make it much harder for their brothers and sisters to get married. So we must be very careful."

What she said was true and I promised myself to be more 35 patient, though it was not easy. I had really hoped and expected that the match would be made before my year in India was up. But it was not to be. When I left India my friend seemed no further along in finding a suitable match for her son than when I had arrived.

Two years later, I returned to India and still my friend had 36 not found a girl for her son. By this time, he was close to thirty, and I think she was a little worried. Since she knew I had friends all over India, and I was going to be there for a year, she asked me to "help her in this work" and keep an eye out for someone suitable. I was flattered that my judgment was respected, but knowing now how complicated the process was, I had lost my earlier confidence as a matchmaker. Nevertheless, I promised that I would try.

It was almost at the end of my year's stay in India that I met a family with a marriageable daughter whom I felt might be a good possibility for my friend's son. The girl's father was related to a good friend of mine and by coincidence came from the same village as my friend's husband. This new family had a successful business in a medium-sized city in central India and were from the same subcaste as my friend. The daughter was pretty and chic; in fact, she had studied fashion design in college. Her parents would not allow her to go off by herself to any of the major cities in India where she could make a career, but they had compromised with her wish to work by allowing her to run a small dressmaking boutique from their home. In spite of her desire to have a career, the daughter was both modest and home-loving and had had a traditional, sheltered upbringing. She had only one other sister, already married, and a brother who was in his father's business. 37

I mentioned the possibility of a match with my friend's son. The girl's parents were most interested. Although their daughter was not eager to marry just yet, the idea of living in Bombay—a sophisticated, extremely fashion-conscious city where she could continue her education in clothing design—was a great inducement. I gave the girl's father my friend's address and suggested that when they went to Bombay on some business or whatever, they look up the boy's family. 38

Returning to Bombay on my way to New York, I told my friend of this newly discovered possibility. She seemed to feel there was potential but, in spite of my urging, would not make any moves herself. She rather preferred to wait for the girl's family to call upon them. I hoped something would come of this introduction, though by now I had learned to rein in my optimism. 39

A year later I received a letter from my friend. The family had indeed come to visit Bombay, and their daughter and my 40 friend's daughter, who were near in age, had become very good friends. During that year, the two girls had frequently visited each other. I thought things looked promising.

Last week I received an invitation to a wedding: My friend's son and the girl were getting married. Since I had found the match, my presence was particularly requested at the wedding. I was thrilled. Success at last! As I prepared to leave for India, I began thinking, "Now, my friend's younger son, who do I know who has a nice girl for him . . . ?" 41

FURTHER REFLECTIONS ON ARRANGED MARRIAGE

The previous essay was written from the point of view of a family seeking a daughter-in-law. Arranged marriage looks somewhat different from the point of view of the bride and her family. Arranged marriage continues to be preferred, even among the more educated, Westernized sections of the Indian population. Many young women from these families still go along, more or less willingly, with the practice, and also with the specific choices of their families. Young women do get excited about the prospects of their marriage, but there is also ambivalence and increasing uncertainty, as the bride contemplates leaving the comfort and familiarity of her own home, where as a "temporary guest" she has often been indulged, to live among strangers. Even in the best situation, she will now come under the close scrutiny of her husband's family. How she dresses, how she behaves, how she gets along with others, where she goes, how she spends her time, her domestic abilities—all of this and much more—will be observed and commented on by a whole new set of relations. Her interaction with her family of birth will be monitored and curtailed considerably. Not only will she leave their home, but with increasing geographic mobility, she may also live very far from them, perhaps even on another continent. Too much expression of her fondness for her own family, or her desire to visit them, may be interpreted as an inability to adjust to her new family, and may become a source of conflict. In an arranged marriage, the burden of adjustment is clearly heavier for a woman than for a man. And that is in the best of situations.

In less happy circumstances, the bride may be a target of resentment and hostility from her husband's family, particularly her mother-in-law or her husband's unmarried sisters, for whom she is now a source of competition for the affection, loyalty, and economic resources of a son or brother. If she is psychologically or even physically abused, her options are limited, as returning to her parents' home or getting a divorce is still very stigmatized. For most Indians, marriage and motherhood are still considered the only suitable roles for a woman, even for those who have careers, and few women can comfortably contemplate remaining unmarried. Most families still consider "marrying off" their daughters as a compelling religious duty and social necessity. This increases a bride's sense of obligation to make the marriage a success, at whatever cost to her own personal happiness.

The vulnerability of a new bride may also be intensified by the issue of dowry that, although illegal, has become a more pressing issue in the consumer conscious society of contemporary urban India. In many cases, where a groom's family is not satisfied with the amount of dowry a bride brings to her marriage, the young bride will be harassed constantly to get her parents to give more. In extreme cases, the bride may even be murdered, and the murder disguised as an accident or a suicide. This also offers the husband's family an opportunity to arrange another match for him, thus bringing in another dowry. This phenomenon, called dowry death, calls attention not just to the "evils of dowry" but also to larger issues of the powerlessness of women as well.

For Study and Discussion

QUESTIONS FOR RESPONSE

1. Have you ever been fixed up on a blind date? How did you feel about spending an evening with someone you didn't know? How did it work out?

2. Have you ever tried to fix people up? Why were you so sure that they would make a good match? How did it work out?

QUESTIONS ABOUT PURPOSE

1. How does Nanda's conversation with Sita help illustrate her thesis that in India marriage is a family, not an individual, decision?
2. How does Sita's criticism of American marriages help Nanda clarify her purpose?

QUESTIONS ABOUT AUDIENCE

1. In what ways does Nanda address her essay to American rather than Indian readers?
2. How does Nanda serve as a substitute for her readers? For example, how does she, and thus her readers, learn about the criteria for a good marriage?

QUESTIONS ABOUT STRATEGIES

1. How does Nanda use the example of the family with five daughters to illustrate the importance of social caste and financial status in Indian marriages?
2. How does Nanda use the example of the well-educated girl to illustrate the importance of finding a good daughter-in-law—as opposed to finding a good wife?

QUESTIONS FOR DISCUSSION

1. What arguments would you use to defend "love matches" as opposed to "arranged marriages"? Compare Anne Roiphe's observation on these issues (pages 190–191).
2. How do issues such as "dowry-death" enable Nanda to present the arranged marriage from the point of view of the bride and her family?

Elizabeth Winthrop was born in 1948 in Washington, D.C., and educated at Sarah Lawrence College. She worked for Harper and Row editing Harper Junior Books before she began her own career as author of books for children. She has written more than thirty such books, including *Bunk Beds* (1972), *Potbellied Possums* (1977), *In My Mother's House* (1988), *The Battle for the Castle* (1993), and *As the Crow Flies* (1998). Winthrop has twice won the PEN Syndicated Fiction Contest, once in 1985 with her story "Bad News" and again in 1990 with "The Golden Darters." In the latter story, reprinted from *American Short Fiction,* a young girl betrays her father by using their creation for the wrong purpose.

The Golden Darters

I WAS TWELVE years old when my father started tying flies. 1
It was an odd habit for a man who had just undergone a serious operation on his upper back, but, as he remarked to my mother one night, at least it gave him a world over which he had some control.

The family grew used to seeing him hunched down close 2
to his tying vise, hackle pliers in one hand, thread bobbin in the other. We began to bandy about strange phrases—foxy quills, bodkins, peacock hurl. Father's corner of the living room was off limits to the maid with the voracious and destructive vacuum cleaner. Who knew what precious bit of calf's tail or rabbit fur would be sucked away never to be seen again?

Because of my father's illness, we had gone up to our 3
summer cottage on the lake in New Hampshire a month

early. None of my gang of friends ever came till the end of
July, so in the beginning of that summer I hung around home
watching my father as he fussed with the flies. I was the only
child he allowed to stand near him while he worked. "Your
brothers bounce," he muttered one day as he clamped the
vise onto the curve of a model-perfect hook. "You can stay
and watch if you don't bounce."

So I took great care not to bounce or lean or even breathe   4
too noisily on him while he performed his delicate maneuvers, holding back hackle with one hand as he pulled off the
final flourish of a whip finish with the other. I had never been
so close to my father for so long before, and while he studied
his tiny creations, I studied him. I stared at the large pores
of his skin, the sleek black hair brushed straight back from
the soft dip of his temples, the jaw muscles tightening and
slackening. Something in my father seemed always to be
ticking. He did not take well to sickness and enforced
confinement.

When he leaned over his work, his shirt collar slipped down   5
to reveal the recent scar, a jagged trail of disrupted tissue.
The tender pink skin gradually paled and then toughened
during those weeks when he took his prescribed afternoon
nap, lying on his stomach on our little patch of front lawn.
Our house was one of the closest to the lake and it seemed
to embarrass my mother to have him stretch himself out on
the grass for all the swimmers and boaters to see.

"At least sleep on the porch," she would say. "That's why   6
we set the hammock up there."

"Why shouldn't a man sleep on his own front lawn if he   7
so chooses?" he would reply. "I have to mow the bloody
thing. I might as well put it to some use."

And my mother would shrug and give up.   8

At the table when he was absorbed, he lost all sense of   9
anything but the magnified insect under the light. Often
when he pushed his chair back and announced the comple-
tion of his latest project to the family, there would be a bit

of down or a tuft of dubbing stuck to the edge of his lip. I
did not tell him about it but stared, fascinated, wondering
how long it would take to blow away. Sometimes it never did,
and I imagine he discovered the fluff in the bathroom mirror
when he went upstairs to bed. Or maybe my mother plucked
it off with one of those proprietary gestures of hers that
irritated my brothers so much.

In the beginning, Father wasn't very good at the fly-tying. 10
He was a large, thick-boned man with sweeping gestures, a
robust laugh, and a sudden terrifying temper. If he had not
loved fishing so much, I doubt he would have persevered
with the fussy business of the flies. After all, the job required
tools normally associated with woman's work. Thread and
bobbins, soft slippery feathers, a magnifying glass, and an
instruction manual that read like a cookbook. It said things
like, "Cut off a bunch of yellowtail. Hold the tip end with
the left hand and stroke out the short hairs."

But Father must have had a goal in mind. You tie flies 11
because one day, in the not-too-distant future, you will attach
them to a tippet, wade into a stream, and lure a rainbow trout
out of his quiet pool.

There was something endearing, almost childish, about his 12
stubborn nightly ritual at the corner table. His head bent
under the standing lamp, his fingers trembling slightly, he
would whisper encouragement to himself, talk his way
through some particularly delicate operation. Once or twice
I caught my mother gazing silently across my brothers' heads
at him. When our eyes met, she would turn away and busy
herself in the kitchen.

Finally, one night, after weeks of allowing me to watch, he 13
told me to take his seat. "Why, Father?"

"Because it's time for you to try one." 14

"That's all right. I like to watch." 15

"Nonsense, Emily. You'll do just fine." 16

He had stood up. The chair was waiting. Across the room, 17
my mother put down her knitting. Even the boys, embroiled
in a noisy game of double solitaire, stopped their wrangling

for a moment. They were all waiting to see what I would do. It was my fear of failing him that made me hesitate. I knew that my father put his trust in results, not in the learning process.

"Sit down, Emily."   18

I obeyed, my heart pounding. I was a cautious, secretive   19
child, and I could not bear to have people watch me doing things. My piano lesson was the hardest hour in the week. The teacher would sit with a resigned look on her face while my fingers groped across the keys, muddling through a sonata that I had played perfectly just an hour before. The difference was that then nobody had been watching.

"—so we'll start you off with a big hook." He had been   20
talking for some time. How much had I missed already?

"Ready?" he asked.   21

I nodded.   22

"All right then, clamp this hook into the vise. You'll be   23
making the golden darter, a streamer. A big flashy fly, the kind that imitates a small fish as it moves underwater."

Across the room, my brothers had returned to their game,   24
but their voices were subdued. I imagined they wanted to hear what was happening to me. My mother had left the room.

"Tilt the magnifying glass so you have a good view of the   25
hook. Right. Now tie on with the bobbin thread."

It took me three tries to line the thread up properly on the   26
hook, each silken line nesting next to its neighbor. "We're going to do it right, Emily, no matter how long it takes."

"It's hard," I said quietly.   27

Slowly I grew used to the tiny tools, to the oddly enlarged   28
view of my fingers through the magnifying glass. They looked as if they didn't belong to me anymore. The feeling in their tips was too small for their large, clumsy movements. Despite my father's repeated warnings, I nicked the floss once against the barbed hook. Luckily it did not give way.

"It's Emily's bedtime," my mother called from the   29
kitchen.

"Hush, she's tying in the throat. Don't bother us now."   30

I could feel his breath on my neck. The mallard barbules   31
were stubborn, curling into the hook in the wrong direction.
Behind me, I sensed my father's fingers twisting in imitation
of my own.

"You've almost got it," he whispered, his lips barely mov-   32
ing. "That's right. Keep the thread slack until you're all the
way around."

I must have tightened it too quickly. I lost control of the   33
feathers in my left hand, the clumsier one. First the gold
mylar came unwound and then the yellow floss.

"Damn it all, now look what you've done," he roared, and   34
for a second I wondered whether he was talking to me. He
sounded as if he were talking to a grown-up. He sounded the
way he had just the night before when an antique teacup had
slipped through my mother's soapy fingers and shattered
against the hard surface of the sink. I sat back slowly, resting
my aching spine against the chair for the first time since we'd
begun.

"Leave it for now, Gerald," my mother said tentatively   35
from the kitchen. Out of the corner of my eye, I could see
her sponging the kitchen counter with small, defiant sweeps
of her hand. "She can try again tomorrow."

"What happened?" called a brother. They both started   36
across the room toward us but stopped at a look from my
father.

"We'll start again," he said, his voice once more under   37
control. "Best way to learn. Get back on the horse."

With a flick of his hand, he loosened the vise, removed my   38
hook, and threw it into the wastepaper basket.

"From the beginning?" I whispered.   39

"Of course," he replied. "There's no way to rescue a mess   40
like that."

My mess had taken almost an hour to create.   41

"Gerald," my mother said again. "Don't you think—"   42

"How can we possibly work with all these interruptions?"   43
he thundered. I flinched as if he had hit me. "Go on upstairs,

all of you. Emily and I will be up when we're done. Go on, for God's sake. Stop staring at us."

At a signal from my mother, the boys backed slowly away   44 and crept up to their room. She followed them. I felt all alone, as trapped under my father's piercing gaze as the hook in the grip of its vise.

We started again. This time my fingers were trembling so   45 much that I ruined three badger hackle feathers, stripping off the useless webbing at the tip. My father did not lose his temper again. His voice dropped to an even, controlled monotone that scared me more than his shouting. After an hour of painstaking labor, we reached the same point with the stubborn mallard feathers curling into the hook. Once, twice, I repinched them under the throat, but each time they slipped away from me. Without a word, my father stood up and leaned over me. With his cheek pressed against my hair, he reached both hands around and took my fingers in his. I longed to surrender the tools to him and slide away off the chair, but we were so close to the end. He captured the curling stem with the thread and trapped it in place with three quick wraps.

"Take your hands away carefully," he said. "I'll do the   46 whip finish. We don't want to risk losing it now."

I did as I was told, sat motionless with his arms around   47 me, my head tilted slightly to the side so he could have the clear view through the magnifying glass. He cemented the head, wiped the excess glue from the eye with a waste feather, and hung my golden darter on the tackle box handle to dry. When at last he pulled away, I breathlessly slid my body back against the chair. I was still conscious of the havoc my clumsy hands or an unexpected sneeze could wreak on the table, which was cluttered with feathers and bits of fur.

"Now, that's the fly you tied, Emily. Isn't it beautiful?"   48 I nodded. "Yes, Father."   49

"Tomorrow, we'll do another one. An olive grouse.   50 Smaller hook but much less complicated body. Look. I'll show you in the book."

As I waited to be released from the chair, I didn't think   51 he meant it. He was just trying to apologize for having lost his temper, I told myself, just trying to pretend that our time together had been wonderful. But the next morning when I came down, late for breakfast, he was waiting for me with the materials for the olive grouse already assembled. He was ready to start in again, to take charge of my clumsy fingers with his voice and talk them through the steps.

That first time was the worst, but I never felt comfortable   52
at the fly-tying table with Father's breath tickling the hair on my neck. I completed the olive grouse, another golden darter to match the first, two muddler minnows, and some others. I don't remember all the names anymore.

Once I hid upstairs, pretending to be immersed in my   53
summer reading books, but he came looking for me.

"Emily," he called. "Come on down. Today we'll start the   54
lead-winged coachman. I've got everything set up for you."

I lay very still and did not answer.   55

"Gerald," I heard my mother say. "Leave the child alone.   56
You're driving her crazy with those flies."

"Nonsense," he said, and started up the dark, wooden   57
stairs, one heavy step at a time.

I put my book down and rolled slowly off the bed so that   58
by the time he reached the door of my room, I was on my feet, ready to be led back downstairs to the table.

Although we never spoke about it, my mother became   59
oddly insistent that I join her on trips to the library or the general store.

"Are you going out again, Emily?" my father would call   60
after me. "I was hoping we'd get some work done on this minnow."

"I'll be back soon, Father," I'd say. "I promise."   61

"Be sure you do," he said.   62

And for a while I did.   63

Then at the end of July, my old crowd of friends from   64
across the lake began to gather and I slipped away to join them early in the morning before my father got up.

The girls were a gang. When we were all younger, we'd   65

held bicycle relay races on the ring road and played down at
the lakeside together under the watchful eyes of our mothers.
Every July, we threw ourselves joyfully back into each other's
lives. That summer we talked about boys and smoked illicit
cigarettes in Randy Kidd's basement and held leg-shaving
parties in her bedroom behind a safely locked door. Randy
was the ringleader. She was the one who suggested we pierce
our ears.

"My parents would die," I said. "They told me I'm not   66
allowed to pierce my ears until I'm seventeen."

"Your hair's so long, they won't even notice," Randy said.   67
"My sister will do it for us. She pierces all her friends' ears at
college."

In the end, only one girl pulled out. The rest of us sat in   68
a row with the obligatory ice cubes held to our ears, waiting
for the painful stab of the sterilized needle.

Randy was right. At first my parents didn't notice. Even   69
when my ears became infected, I didn't tell them. All alone
in my room, I went through the painful procedure of twisting
the gold studs and swabbing the recent wounds with alcohol.
Then on the night of the club dance, when I had changed
my clothes three times and played with my hair in front of
the mirror for hours, I came across the small plastic box with
dividers in my top bureau drawer. My father had given it to
me so that I could keep my flies in separate compartments,
untangled from one another. I poked my finger in and slid
one of the golden darters up along its plastic wall. When I
held it up, the mylar thread sparkled in the light like a jewel.
I took out the other darter, hammered down the barbs of the
two hooks, and slipped them into the raw holes in my earlobes.

Someone's mother drove us all to the dance, and Randy   70
and I pushed through the side door into the ladies' room. I
put my hair up in a ponytail so the feathered flies could twist
and dangle above my shoulders. I liked the way they made
me look—free and different and dangerous, even. And they
made Randy notice.

"I've never seen earrings like that," Randy said. "Where 71
did you get them?"

"I made them with my father. They're flies. You know, for 72
fishing."

"They're great. Can you make me some?" 73

I hesitated. "I have some others at home I can give you," 74
I said at last. "They're in a box in my bureau."

"Can you give them to me tomorrow?" she asked. 75

"Sure," I said with a smile. Randy had never noticed 76
anything I'd worn before. I went out to the dance floor,
swinging my ponytail in time to the music.

My mother noticed the earrings as soon as I got home. 77

"What has gotten into you, Emily? You know you were 78
forbidden to pierce your ears until you were in college. This
is appalling."

I didn't answer. My father was sitting in his chair behind 79
the fly-tying table. His back was better by that time, but he
still spent most of his waking hours in that chair. It was as if
he didn't like to be too far away from his flies, as if something
might blow away if he weren't keeping watch.

I saw him look up when my mother started in with me. 80
His hands drifted ever so slowly down to the surface of the
table as I came across the room toward him. I leaned over so
that he could see my earrings better in the light.

"Everybody loved them, Father. Randy says she wants a 81
pair, too. I'm going to give her the muddler minnows."

"I can't believe you did this, Emily," my mother said in a 82
loud, nervous voice. "It makes you look so cheap."

"They don't make me look cheap, do they, Father?" I 83
swung my head so he could see how they bounced, and my
hip accidentally brushed the table. A bit of rabbit fur floated
up from its pile and hung in the air for a moment before it
settled down on top of the foxy quills.

"For God's sake, Gerald, speak to her," my mother said 84
from her corner.

He stared at me for a long moment as if he didn't know 85

who I was anymore, as if I were a trusted associate who had committed some treacherous and unspeakable act. "That is not the purpose for which the flies were intended," he said.

"Oh, I know that," I said quickly. "But they look good   86
this way, don't they?"

He stood up and considered me in silence for a long time   87
across the top of the table lamp.

"No, they don't," he finally said. "They're hanging upside   88
down."

Then he turned off the light and I couldn't see his face   89
anymore.

COMMENT ON "THE GOLDEN DARTERS"

"The Golden Darters" questions the purpose of learning a particular process. Emily's father decides to tie fishing flies to help him recuperate from back surgery. Although he is clumsy at first, he masters the tools, the procedure, and the artistry of tying. He has a goal in mind—to "attach [the flies] to a tippet, wade into a stream, and lure a rainbow trout out of his quiet pool." Emily's father decides to teach her what he has learned, even though his presence makes her nervous and her mistakes complicate the work process. Emily eventually escapes his obsession and joins her girlfriends to learn other procedures—smoking, leg-shaving, ear-piercing. The last procedure enables Emily to experiment—to wear two yellow darters as earrings to the club dance. Although she dazzles her friends, she disappoints her father, who sees her experiment as a betrayal.

Process Analysis as a Writing Strategy

1. Write an essay for readers of a popular magazine in which you give directions on how to complete a mechanical or artistic project. Like Julia Alvarez, anticipate the resistance of those readers who are certain before they start that they can't do it.
2. Provide information for the members of your writing class on the steps you followed to complete an educational project such as writing a research paper. Like Nikki Giovanni, you may want to explain these steps to a particular group of students.
3. Lars Eighner's "My Daily Dives in the Dumpster" raises significant questions about how our culture views the processes of consuming, disposing, and conserving. Construct a portrait of a conscientious consumer, and then analyze the processes he or she would use to maintain an ethically responsible relationship to the environment.
4. Analyze the various steps in a political process (casting a vote), an economic process (purchasing stock), or a social process (getting married). Assume that your audience watches a lot of television. Explain how the process you are analyzing (finding a spouse) differs from the process they see represented on the tube.
5. Analyze a process that tests the ability to reach consensus and capture others. Like Natalie Angier, you may want to describe the behavioral process of certain animals. Or you may want to analyze the process illustrated in children's play, athletic contests, or human mating games.
6. Analyze a process that confuses or intimidates people, particularly when other people are watching. Elizabeth Winthrop's short story "The Golden Darters" is obviously a good source for this assignment. Your job is to describe the intricate steps of the physical tasks and to speculate on why the presence of the observer (a teacher, a relative, a friend) makes the task so difficult.

COMPARISON AND CONTRAST

Technically speaking, when you **compare** two or more things, you're looking for similarities; and when you **contrast** them, you're looking for differences. In practice, of course, the operations are opposite sides of the same coin, and one implies the other. When you look for what's similar, you will also notice what is different. You can compare things at all levels, from the trivial (plaid shoelaces and plain ones) to the really serious (the differences between a career in medicine and one in advertising). Often when you compare things at a serious level, you do so to make a choice. That's why it's helpful to know how to organize your thinking so that you can analyze similarities and differences in a systematic, useful way that brings out significant differences. It's particularly helpful to have such a system when you are going to write a comparison-and-contrast essay.

PURPOSE

You can take two approaches to writing comparison-and-contrast essays; each has a different purpose. You can make a *strict* comparison, exploring the relationship between things in the same class, or you can do a *fanciful* comparison, looking at the relationship among things from different classes.

When you write a *strict* comparison, you compare only things that are truly alike—actors with actors, musicians with musicians, but *not* actors with musicians. You're trying to find similar information about both your subjects. For instance, what are the characteristics of actors, whether they are movie or stage actors? How are jazz musicians and classical musicians alike, even if their music is quite different? In a strict comparison, you probably also want to show how two things in the same class are different in important ways. Often when you focus your comparison on differences, you do so in order to make a judgment and, finally, a choice. That's one of the main reasons people make comparisons, whether they're shopping or writing.

When you write a *fanciful* comparison, you try to set up an imaginative, illuminating comparison between two things that don't seem at all alike, and you do it for a definite reason: to help explain and clarify a complex idea. For instance, the human heart is often compared to a pump—a fanciful and useful comparison that enables one to envision the heart at work. You can use similar fanciful comparisons to help your readers see new dimensions to events. For instance, you can compare the astronauts landing on the moon to Columbus discovering the New World, or you can compare the increased drug use among young people to an epidemic spreading through part of our culture.

You may find it difficult to construct an entire essay around a fanciful comparison—such attempts tax the most creative energy and can quickly break down. Probably you can use this method of comparison most effectively as a device for enlivening your writing and highlighting dramatic similarities. When you're drawing fanciful comparisons, you're not very likely to be comparing to make judgments or recommend choices. Instead, your purpose in writing a fanciful comparison is to catch your readers' attention and show new connections between unlike things.

AUDIENCE

As you plan a comparison-and-contrast essay, think ahead about what your readers already know and what they're going to expect. First, ask yourself what they know about the items or ideas you're going to compare. Do they know a good deal about both—for instance, two popular television programs? Do they know very little about either item—for instance, Buddhism and Shintoism? Or do they know quite a bit about one but little about the other—for instance, football and rugby?

If you're confident that your readers know a lot about both items (the television programs), you can spend a little time pointing out similarities and concentrate on your reasons for making the comparison. When readers know little about either (Eastern religions), you'll have to define each, using concepts they are familiar with before you can point out important contrasts. If readers know only one item in a pair (football and rugby), then use the known to explain the unknown. Emphasize what is familiar to them about football, and explain how rugby is like it but also how it is different.

As you think about what your readers need, remember they want your essay to be fairly balanced, not 90 percent about Buddhism and 10 percent about Shintoism, or two paragraphs about football and nine or ten about rugby. When your focus seems so unevenly divided, you appear to be using one element in the comparison only as a springboard to talk about the other. Such an imbalance can disappoint your readers, who expect to learn about both.

STRATEGIES

You can use two basic strategies for organizing a comparison-and-contrast essay. The first is the *divided* or *subject-by-subject* pattern. The second is the *alternating* or *point-by-point* pattern.

When you use the *divided* pattern, you present all your information on one topic before you bring in information on the other topic. Mark Twain uses this method in "Two Views of the River." First he gives an apprentice's poetic view, emphasizing the beauty of the river; then he gives the pilot's practical view, emphasizing the technical problems the river poses.

When you use the *alternating* pattern, you work your way through the comparison point by point, giving information first on one aspect of the topic, then on the other. If Mark Twain had used an alternating pattern, he would have given the apprentice's poetic view of a particular feature of the river, then the pilot's pragmatic view of that same feature. He would have followed that pattern throughout, commenting on each feature—the wind, the surface of the river, the sunset, the color of the water—by alternating between the apprentice's and the pilot's points of view.

Although both methods are useful, you'll find that each has benefits and drawbacks. The divided pattern lets you present each part of your essay as a satisfying whole. It works especially well in short essays, such as Twain's, where you're presenting only two facets of a topic and your reader can easily keep track of the points you want to make. Its drawback is that sometimes you slip into writing what seems like two separate essays. When you're writing a long comparison essay about a complex topic, you may have trouble organizing your material clearly enough to keep your readers on track.

The alternating pattern works well when you want to show

the two subjects you're comparing side by side, emphasizing the points you're comparing. You'll find it particularly good for longer essays, such as Laura Bohannan's "Shakespeare in the Bush," when you want to show many complex points of comparison and need to help your readers see how those points match up. The drawback of the alternating pattern is that you may reduce your analysis to an exercise. If you use it for making only a few points of comparison in a short essay on a simple topic, your essay sounds choppy and disconnected, like a simple list.

Often you can make the best of both worlds by *combining strategies.* For example, you can start out using a divided pattern to give an overall, unified view of the topics you're going to compare. Then you can shift to an alternating pattern to show how many points of comparison you've found between your subjects. Deborah Tannen uses a version of this strategy in "Rapport-Talk and Report-Talk." She begins by establishing the difference between private conversations and public speaking; then she uses an alternating pattern within each category to demonstrate the contrasts between the speaking styles of men and women.

When you want to write a good comparison-and-contrast analysis, keep three guidelines in mind: (1) *balance parts,* (2) *include reminders,* and (3) *supply reasons.* Look, for example, at how Scott Russell Sanders balances his own aspirations for the camping trip with his son's criticism of his motives.

Laura Bohannan uses similar strategies when she contrasts her version of *Hamlet* with the African elders' reinterpretation of the play.

USING COMPARISON AND CONTRAST IN PARAGRAPHS

Here are two comparison-and-contrast paragraphs. The first is written by a professional writer and is followed by an analysis. The second is written by a student writer and is followed by questions.

DAVID McCULLOUGH
FDR and Truman

Uses alternating pattern

Both [FDR and Truman] were men of exceptional determination, with great reserves of personal courage and cheerfulness. They were alike
too in their enjoyment of people. (The human
race, Truman once told a reporter, was an "excellent outfit.") Each had an active sense of humor and was inclined to be dubious of those who
did not. But Roosevelt, who loved stories, loved
also to laugh at his own, while Truman was more
of a listener and laughed best when somebody
else told "a good one." Roosevelt enjoyed flattery, Truman was made uneasy by it. Roosevelt
loved the subtleties of human relations. He was
a master of the circuitous solution to problems,
of the pleasing if ambiguous answer to difficult
questions. He was sensitive to nuances in a way
Harry Truman never was and never would be.
Truman, with his rural Missouri background,
and partly, too, because of the limits of his education, was inclined to see things in far simpler
terms, as right or wrong, wise or foolish. He
dealt little in abstractions. His answers to questions, even complicated questions, were nearly
always direct and assured, plainly said, and followed often by a conclusive "And that's all there
is to it," an old Missouri expression, when in
truth there may have been a great deal more "to
it."

Establishes points of comparison

Sets up points of contrast

Expands on significant difference between two men (circuitous versus direct)

Comment This paragraph illustrates how the alternating pattern can be used to point out many levels of comparison
between two subjects. McCullough acknowledges that President Roosevelt and President Truman shared many common
virtues—determination, courage, and cheerfulness. But he
also contrasts (point by point) how the two men's personal

styles—love of complex subtleties (FDR) versus preference for direct simplicity (Truman)—contributed to their uniqueness.

NATHAN M. HARMS
Howard and Rush

Howard [Stern] and Rush [Limbaugh] seem like the ying and yang of talk radio. Howard is thin and shaggy and loves to bash entrenched, stodgy Republicans. Rush is fat and dapper and loves to bash traditional liberal Democrats. Howard, the defender of individual freedom, wants to sleep with every woman in America. Rush, the defender of family values, wants every American woman to stay home and take care of the kids. Although they may think the world works in different ways, Howard and Rush work in the world in the same way. They focus their shows on controversy, belittle those who disagree with them, package their "philosophies" in best-selling books, and thrive on their ability to create publicity and fame for themselves.

1. What specific points of difference does Harms see between Howard Stern and Rush Limbaugh?
2. What major personality trait does Harms suspect they share?

COMPARISON AND CONTRAST
Points to Remember

1. Decide whether you want the pattern of your comparison to focus on complete units (*divided*) or specific features (*alternating*).
2. Consider the possibility of combining the two patterns.
3. Determine which subject should be placed in the first position and why.
4. Arrange the points of your comparison in a logical, balanced, and dramatic sequence.
5. Make sure you introduce and clarify the reasons for making your comparison.

MARK TWAIN

Mark Twain (the pen name of Samuel Clemens, 1835–1910) was born in Florida, Missouri, and grew up in the river town of Hannibal, Missouri, where he watched the comings and goings of the steamboats he would eventually pilot. Twain spent his young adult life working as a printer, a pilot on the Mississippi, and a frontier journalist. After the Civil War, he began a career as a humorist and storyteller, writing such classics as *The Adventures of Tom Sawyer* (1876), *Life on the Mississippi* (1883), *The Adventures of Huckleberry Finn* (1885), and *A Connecticut Yankee in King Arthur's Court* (1889). His place in American writing was best characterized by editor William Dean Howells, who called Twain the "Lincoln of our literature." In "Two Views of the River," taken from *Life on the Mississippi*, Twain compares the way he saw the river as an innocent apprentice to the way he saw it as an experienced pilot.

Two Views of the River

NOW WHEN I had mastered the language of this water, and had come to know every trifling feature that bordered the great river as familiarly as I knew the letters of the alphabet, I had made a valuable acquisition. But I had lost something, too. I had lost something which could never be restored to me while I lived. All the grace, the beauty, the poetry, had gone out of the majestic river! I still keep in mind a certain wonderful sunset which I witnessed when steamboating was new to me. A broad expanse of the river was turned to blood; in the middle distance the red hue brightened into gold, through which a solitary log came floating black and conspicuous; in one place a long, slanting mark lay sparkling upon the water; in another the surface was broken by boiling, tumbling rings that were as many-tinted as an opal; where the ruddy flush was faintest, was a smooth spot that was covered with graceful circles and radiating lines, ever so delicately traced; the shore on our left was densely wooded, and the somber shadow that fell from this forest was broken in one place by a long, ruffled trail that shone like silver; and high above the forest wall a clean-stemmed dead tree waved a single leafy bough that glowed like a flame in the unobstructed splendor that was flowing from the sun.

> *When I mastered the language of the river,*
> *I made a valuable acquisition, but I lost*
> *something too.*

There were graceful curves, reflected images, woody heights, soft distances; and over the whole scene, far and near, the dissolving lights drifted steadily, enriching it every passing moment with new marvels of coloring.

I stood like one bewitched. I drank it in, in a speechless   2
rapture. The world was new to me, and I had never seen anything like this at home. But as I have said, a day came when I began to cease from noting the glories and the charms which the moon and the sun and the twilight wrought upon the river's face; another day came when I ceased altogether to note them. Then, if that sunset scene had been repeated, I should have looked upon it without rapture, and should have commented upon it, inwardly, after this fashion: "This sun means that we are going to have wind to-morrow; that floating log means that the river is rising, small thanks to it; that slanting mark on the water refers to a bluff reef which is going to kill somebody's steamboat one of these nights, if it keeps on stretching out like that; those tumbling 'boils' show

a dissolving bar and a changing channel there; the lines and circles in the slick water over yonder are a warning that that troublesome place is shoaling up dangerously; that silver streak in the shadow of the forest is the 'break' from a new snag, and he has located himself in the very best place he could have found to fish for steamboats; that tall dead tree, with a single living branch, is not going to last long, and then how is a body ever going to get through this blind place at night without the friendly old landmark?"

No, the romance and beauty were all gone from the river. 3 All the value any feature of it had for me now was the amount of usefulness it could furnish toward compassing the safe piloting of a steamboat. Since those days, I have pitied doctors from my heart. What does the lovely flush in a beauty's cheek mean to a doctor but a "break" that ripples above some deadly disease? Are not all her visible charms sown thick with what are to him the signs and symbols of hidden decay? Does he ever see her beauty at all, or doesn't he simply view her professionally, and comment upon her unwholesome condition all to himself? And doesn't he sometimes wonder whether he has gained most or lost most by learning his trade?

For Study and Discussion

QUESTIONS FOR RESPONSE

1. Mark Twain is one of America's most famous historical personalities. Which of his books or stories have you read? What ideas and images from this selection do you associate with his other works?
2. Do you agree with Twain when he argues that an appreciation of beauty depends on ignorance of danger? Explain your answer.

QUESTIONS ABOUT PURPOSE

1. What does Twain think he has gained and lost by learning the river?

2. What does Twain accomplish by *dividing* the two views of the river rather than *alternating* them beneath several headings?

QUESTIONS ABOUT AUDIENCE

1. Which attitude—poetic or pragmatic—does Twain anticipate his readers have toward the river? Explain your answer.
2. How does he expect his readers to answer the questions he raises in paragraph 3?

QUESTIONS ABOUT STRATEGIES

1. What sequence does Twain use to arrange the points of his comparison?
2. Where does Twain use transitional phrases and sentences to match up the parts of his comparison?

QUESTIONS FOR DISCUSSION

1. Besides the pilot and the doctor, can you identify other professionals who lose as much as they gain by learning their trade?
2. How would people whose job is to create beauty—writers, painters, musicians, architects, gardeners—respond to Twain's assertion that knowledge of their craft destroys their ability to appreciate beauty?

SCOTT RUSSELL SANDERS

Scott Russell Sanders was born in Memphis, Tennessee, in 1945 and educated at Brown University and Cambridge University. He teaches creative writing at Indiana University and explores various aspects of life in the Midwest. He is the author of a newspaper column, "One Man's Fiction," which appeared in the *Chicago Sun Times* (1977–1983), and articles published in *North American Review, Omni,* and *New Dimensions.* His books include *Wilderness Plots: Tales About the Settlement of the American Land* (1983), *Fetching the Dead* (1984), *Stone Country* (1985), *The Paradise of Bombs* (1987), and *The Force of Spirit* (2000). In "Mountain Music," reprinted from *Hunting for Hope: A Father's Journey* (1998), Sanders compares his and his son's views of the environment.

Mountain Music

ON A JUNE morning high in the Rocky Mountains of Colorado, snowy peaks rose before me like the promise of a world without grief. A creek brim full of meltwater roiled along to my left, and to my right an aspen grove shimmered with new leaves. Bluebirds darted in and out of holes in the aspen trunks, and butterflies flickered beside every puddle, tasting the succulent mud. Sun glazed the new grass and licked a silver sheen along the boughs of pines.

With all of that to look at, I gazed instead at my son's broad back as he stalked away from me up the trail. Sweat had darkened his gray T-shirt in patches the color of bruises. His shoulders were stiff with anger that would weight his tongue and keep his face turned from me for hours. Anger also made him quicken his stride, gear after gear, until I could no longer keep up. I had forty-nine years on my legs and heart and lungs, while Jesse had only seventeen on his. My left foot ached from old bone breaks and my right knee creaked from recent surgery. Used to breathing among the low, muggy hills of Indiana, I was gasping up here in the alpine air, a mile and a half above sea level. Jesse would not

---

For the previous year or so, no matter how long our spells of serenity, my son Jesse and I had kept falling into quarrels, like victims of malaria breaking out in fever.

---

stop, would not even slow down unless I asked; and I was in no mood to ask. So I slumped against a boulder beside the trail and let him rush on ahead.

This day, our first full one in Rocky Mountain National 3 Park, had started out well. I woke at first light, soothed by the roar of a river foaming along one edge of the camp-ground, and looked out from our tent to find half a dozen elk, all cows and calves, grazing so close by that I could see the gleam of their teeth. Just beyond the elk, a pair of ground squirrels loafed at the lip of their burrow, noses twitching. Beyond the squirrels, a ponderosa pine, backlit by sunrise, caught the wind in its ragged limbs. The sky was a blue slate marked only by the curving flight of swallows.

Up to that point, and for several hours more, the day was 4 equally unblemished. Jesse slept on while I sipped coffee and studied maps and soaked in the early light. We made our plans over breakfast without squabbling: walk to Bridal Veil Falls in the morning, raft on the Cache la Poudre River in the afternoon, return to camp in the evening to get ready for backpacking up into Wild Basin the next day. Tomorrow we would be heavily laden, but today we carried only water and snacks, and I felt buoyant as we hiked along Cow Creek toward the waterfall. We talked easily the whole way, joking and teasing, more like good friends than like father and son. Yet even as we sat at the base of the falls, our shoulders touching, the mist of Bridal Veil cooling our skin, we remained father and son, locked in a struggle that I could only partly understand.

For the previous year or so, no matter how long our spells   5 of serenity, Jesse and I had kept falling into quarrels, like victims of malaria breaking out in fever. We might be talking about soccer or supper, about the car keys or the news, and suddenly our voices would begin to clash like swords. I had proposed this trip to the mountains in hopes of discovering the source of that strife. Of course I knew that teenage sons and their fathers are expected to fight, yet I sensed there was a grievance between us that ran deeper than the usual vexations. Jesse was troubled by more than a desire to run his own life, and I was troubled by more than the pain of letting him go. I wished to track our anger to its lair, to find where it hid and fed and grew, and then, if I could not slay the demon, at least I could drag it into the light and call it by name.

The peace between us held until we turned back from the   6 waterfall and began discussing where to camp the following night. Jesse wanted to push on up to Thunder Lake, near eleven thousand feet, and pitch our tent on snow. I wanted to stop a thousand feet lower and sleep on dry dirt.

"We're not equipped for snow," I told him.   7

"Sure we are. Why do you think I bought a new sleeping   8 bag? Why did I call ahead to reserve snowshoes?"

I suggested that we could hike up from a lower campsite   9 and snowshoe to his heart's content.

He loosed a snort of disgust. "I can't believe you're wimp-   10 ing out on me, Dad."

"I'm just being sensible."   11

"You're wimping out. I came here to see the backcountry,   12
and all you want to do is poke around the foothills."

"This isn't wild enough for you?" I waved my arms at the   13
view. "What do you need—avalanches and grizzlies?"

Just then, as we rounded a bend, an elderly couple came   14
shuffling toward us, hunched over walking sticks, white hair
jutting from beneath their straw hats. They were followed by
three toddling children, each rigged out with tiny backpack
and canteen. Jesse and I stood aside to let them pass, returning nods to their cheery hellos.

After they had trooped by, Jesse muttered, "We're in the   15
wilds, huh, Dad? That's why the trail's full of grandparents
and kids." Then he quickened his pace until the damp blond
curls that dangled below his bill cap were slapping against his
neck.

"Is this how it's going to be?" I called after him. "You're   16
going to spoil the trip because I won't agree to camp on
snow?"

He turned and glared at me. "You're the one who's spoil-   17
ing it, you and your hang-ups. You always ruin everything."

With that, he swung his face away and lengthened his   18
stride and rushed on ahead. I watched his rigid shoulders and
the bruise-colored patches on the back of his T-shirt until he
disappeared beyond a rise. That was when I gave up on
chasing him, slumped against a boulder, and sucked at the
thin air. Butterflies dallied around my boots and hawks kited
on the breeze, but they might have been blips on a screen,
and the whole panorama of snowy peaks and shimmering
aspens and shining pines might have been cut from cardboard, for all the feeling they stirred in me.

The rocks that give these mountains their name are an-   19
cient, nearly a third as old as the earth, but the Rockies
themselves are new, having been lifted up only six or seven
million years ago, and they were utterly new to me, for I had
never seen them before except from airplanes. I had been
yearning toward them since I was Jesse's age, had been learn-

ing about their natural and human history, the surge of stone and gouge of glaciers, the wandering of hunters and wolves. Drawn to these mountains from the rumpled quilt of fields and forests in the hill country of the Ohio Valley, I was primed for splendor. And yet now that I was here I felt blinkered and numb.

What we call landscape is a stretch of earth overlaid with memory, expectation, and thought. Land is everything that is actually *there,* independent of us; landscape is what we allow in through the doors of perception. My own doors had slammed shut. My quarrel with Jesse changed nothing about the Rockies, but changed everything in my experience of the place. What had seemed glorious and vibrant when we set out that morning now seemed bleak and bare. It was as though anger had drilled a hole in the world and leached the color away.

I was still simmering when I caught up with Jesse at the trail head, where he was leaning against our rented car, arms crossed over his chest, head sunk forward in a sullen pose I knew all too well, eyes hidden beneath the frayed bill of his cap. Having to wait for me to unlock the car had no doubt reminded him of another gripe: I carried the only set of keys. Because he was too young to be covered by the rental company's insurance, I would not let him drive. He had fumed about my decision, interpreting it as proof that I mistrusted him, still thought of him as a child. That earlier scuffle had petered out with him grumbling, "Stupid, stupid. I knew this would happen. Why did I come out here? Why?"

The arguments all ran together, playing over and over in my head as we jounced, too fast, along a rutted gravel road toward the highway. The tires whumped and the small engine whined up hills and down, but the silence inside the car was louder. We had two hours of driving to our rendezvous spot for the rafting trip, and I knew that Jesse could easily clamp his jaw shut for that long, and longer. I glanced over at him from time to time, looking for any sign of detente. His eyes were glass.

We drove. In the depths of Big Thompson Canyon, where

the road swerved along a frothy river between sheer rockface and spindly guardrail, I could bear the silence no longer. "So what are my hang-ups?" I demanded. "How do I ruin everything?"

"You don't want to know," he said.   24

"I want to know. What is it about me that grates on you?"   25

I do not pretend to recall the exact words we hurled at   26
one another after my challenge, but I remember the tone and thrust of them, and here is how they have stayed with me:

"You wouldn't understand," he said.   27

"Try me."   28

He cut a look at me, shrugged, then stared back through   29
the windshield. "You're just so out of touch."

"With what?"   30

"With my whole world. You hate everything that's fun.   31
You hate television and movies and video games. You hate my music."

"I like some of your music. I just don't like it loud."   32

"You hate advertising," he said quickly, rolling now. "You   33
hate billboards and lotteries and developers and logging companies and big corporations. You hate snowmobiles and jet skies. You hate malls and fashions and cars."

"You're still on my case because I won't buy a Jeep?" I   34
said, harking back to another old argument.

"Forget Jeeps. You look at any car and all you think is   35
pollution, traffic, roadside crap. You say fast-food's poisoning our bodies and TV's poisoning our minds. You think the Internet is just another scam for selling stuff. You think business is a conspiracy to rape the earth."

"None of that bothers you?"   36

"Of course it does. But that's the *world*. That's where   37
we've got to live. It's not going to go away just because you don't approve. What's the good of spitting on it?"

"I don't spit on it. I grieve over it."   38

He was still for a moment, then resumed quietly. "What's   39
the good of grieving if you can't change anything?"

"Who says you can't change anything?"   40

"*You* do. Maybe not with your mouth, but with your   41
eyes." Jesse rubbed his own eyes, and the words came out

muffled through his cupped palms. "Your view of things is totally dark. It bums me out. You make me feel the planet's dying and people are to blame and nothing can be done about it. There's no room for hope. Maybe you can get by without hope, but I can't. I've got a lot of living still to do. I have to believe there's a way we can get out of this mess. Otherwise what's the point? Why study, why work—why do anything if it's all going to hell?"

That sounded unfair to me, a caricature of my views, and 42 I thought of many sharp replies; yet there was too much truth and too much hurt in what he said for me to fire back an answer. Had I really deprived my son of hope? Was this the deeper grievance—that I had passed on to him, so young, my anguish over the world? Was this what lurked between us, driving us apart, the demon called despair?

"You're right," I finally told him. "Life's meaningless with- 43 out hope. But I think you're wrong to say I've given up."

"It seems that way to me. As if you think we're doomed." 44

"No, buddy, I don't think we're doomed. It's just that 45 nearly everything I care about is under assault."

"See, that's what I mean. You're so worried about the fate 46 of the earth, you can't enjoy anything. We come to these mountains and you bring the shadows with you. You've got me seeing nothing but darkness."

Stunned by the force of his words, I could not speak. If 47 my gloom cast a shadow over Creation for my son, then I had failed him. What remedy could there be for such a be-trayal?

Through all the shouting and then talking and then the 48 painful hush, our car hugged the swerving road, yet I cannot remember steering. I cannot remember seeing the stony canyon, the white mane of the Big Thompson whipping along beside us, the oncoming traffic. Somehow we survived our sashay with the river and cruised into a zone of burger joints and car-care emporiums and trinket shops. I realized how often, how relentlessly, I had groused about just this sort of "commercial dreck," and how futile my complaints must have seemed to Jesse.

He was caught between a chorus of voices telling him that 49 the universe was made for us—that the earth is an inexhaustible warehouse, that consumption is the goal of life, that money is the road to delight—and the stubborn voice of his father saying none of this is so. If his father was right, then much of what humans babble every day—in ads and editorials, in sitcoms and song lyrics, in thrillers and market reports and teenage gab—is a monstrous lie. Far more likely that his father was wrong, deluded, perhaps even mad. . . .

Before leaving for Colorado, I had imagined that he would   50
be able to meet the Rockies with clear eyes, with the freshness of his green age. So long as he was in my company, however, he would see the land through the weather of my moods. And if despair had so darkened my vision that I was casting a shadow over Jesse's world, even here among these magnificent mountains and tumultuous rivers, then I would have to change. I would have to learn to see differently. Since I could not forget the wounds to people and planet, could not unlearn the dismal numbers—the tallies of pollution and population and poverty that foretold catastrophe—I would have to look harder for antidotes, for medicines, for sources of hope.

For Study and Discussion

QUESTIONS FOR RESPONSE

1. Have you ever spent a considerable amount of time traveling alone with one of your parents or children? What did you expect from the trip? How did it turn out?
2. How do you respond to the features—music, clothes, hang-ups—of your parents' or children's world?

QUESTIONS ABOUT PURPOSE

1. How does Sanders explain the purpose of his camping trip with his son?
2. What does he conclude about himself that changes his original purpose?

QUESTIONS ABOUT AUDIENCE

1. How does Sanders remark—"I know teenage sons and their fathers are expected to fight"—help him to identify with his readers?
2. In what ways does Sanders allow his readers to agree with Jesse's side of the argument?

QUESTIONS ABOUT STRATEGIES

1. How does Sanders balance his description of the glorious environment with his bleak mood about Jesse?
2. How does Sanders use the issue of who can drive to prompt the discussion about hang-ups?

QUESTIONS FOR DISCUSSION

1. In what ways is Jesse right—i.e., in what ways does Sanders's grief deprive Jesse of hope?
2. At the end of the essay, Sanders says he will have to change. Given his "hang-ups," where might he find "sources of hope"?

ANNE ROIPHE

Anne Roiphe was born in New York City in 1935 and educated at Sarah Lawrence College. Perhaps best known for the novel *Up the Sandbox!* (1970), her works explore a woman's search for identity in the wake of marriage and divorce. In some of her fiction, *The Pursuit of Happiness* (1991), and nonfiction, *Generation Without Memory: A Jewish Journey in Christian America* (1981), *A Season of Healing: Reflections on the Holocaust* (1988), and *1185 Park Avenue: A Memoir* (1999), Roiphe explores the special issues confronted by Jewish women. In "A Tale of Two Divorces," reprinted from *Women on Divorce* (1995), Roiphe compares two marriages, one that should have ended in divorce and one that did.

A Tale of Two Divorces

E VERY DIVORCE IS a story, and while they can begin to sound the same—sad and cautionary—each one is as unique as a human face. My divorce is the tale of two divorces, one that never was and one that was. The first is the story of my parents' marriage.

My mother was the late fifth child, raised in a large house on Riverside Drive in New York City. Her father, who came to America as a boy from a town outside of Suvalki, Poland, had piled shirts on a pushcart and wandered the streets of the Lower East Side in the 1880s. His pushcart turned into a loft with twenty women sewing shirts for him and before he was twenty-five he owned a small company called Van Heusen Shirts. He was one of the founding members of Beth Israel Hospital and I have a photo of him, shovel in hand, black hat on his head, as the foundation stone is placed in the ground.

My mother grew up, small, plump, nervous, fearful of 3
horses, dogs, cats, cars, water, balls that were hit over nets,
tunnels, and bridges. She was expected to marry brilliantly
into the world of manufacturers of coats, shoes, gowns, store

---

*In twentieth-century America, we place so
much emphasis on romance that we barely
notice the other essentials of marriage that
include economics and child rearing.*

---

owners, prosperous bankers whose sons attended the dozens
of teas and charity events where she—always afraid her hair
was wrong, her conversation dull, her dress wrinkled—tried
to obey the instructions of her older sister and sparkle. A girl
after all had to sparkle. She was under five feet. She was
nearsighted. Without her thick glasses she stumbled, recognized no one, groped the wall for comfort. Her lipstick
tended to smear. She chain-smoked. She lost things. She
daydreamed. Her father died of a sudden heart attack when
she was just thirteen. Her older sisters married millionaires,
her brothers inherited the business. She was herself considered an heiress, a dangerous state for a tremulous girl, whose
soul was perpetually fogged in uncertainty.

At a Z.B.T. Columbia University fraternity party she met 4
my father. He was the Hungarian-born son of a drug salesman who bet the horses and believed that he had missed his
grander destiny. My paternal grandfather was never able to
move his family out from the railroad flat under the Third
Avenue El. His wife, my grandmother, was a statuesque
woman, taller than her husband but overwhelmed by noise,
the turmoil of her American days. She never learned English.
She stayed home in her nightgown and slippers, sleeping long
hours. My father was in law school. He was tall and handsome

with black hair slicked down like Valentino and cold eyes set perfectly in an even face. He was an athlete who had earned his college expenses by working summers as a lifeguard in the Catskills. His shoes were perfectly polished. His white shirt gleamed. He loathed poverty. He claimed to speak no other language than English though he had arrived in America at age nine. He told my mother he loved her. Despite the warnings of her siblings, she believed him. If she was not his dream girl, she was his American dream. They went on their honeymoon to Europe and purchased fine china and linen at every stop.

My father became a lawyer for the family shirt company.   5
He was edgy, prone to yell at others; he ground his teeth. He suffered from migraines. He could tolerate nothing out of place, nothing that wasn't spotless. He joined a club where men played squash, steamed in the sauna, and drank at the bar. He stayed long hours at his club. He told his wife she was unbeautiful. She believed him although the pictures of her at the time tell a different story. They show a young woman with soft amused eyes and a long neck, with a shy smile and a brave tilt of the head. My father explained to my mother that he could never admire a short woman, that long legs were the essence of glamour.

My father began to have other ladies. He would meet them   6
under the clock at the Biltmore, at motels in Westchester. He had ice in his heart, but he looked good in his undershirt. He looked good in his monogrammed shirts. He lost his nonfamily clients. They didn't like his temper, his impatience. It didn't matter. He took up golf and was gone all day Saturday and Sunday in the good weather. He made investments in the stock market. He had a genius for bad bets. My mother made up the heavy losses. She had two children and she lived just as she was expected to do, with servants to take care of the details, to wake with the babies, to prepare the food, to mop the floors. She spent her days playing cards and shopping. She went to the hairdresser two, sometimes three times a week. A lady came to the house to wax her legs and

do her long red nails. She had ulcers, anxiety attacks, panic attacks. In the evening at about five o'clock she would begin to wait for my father to come home. She could do the crossword puzzle in five minutes. She was a genius at canasta, Oklahoma, bridge, backgammon. She joined a book club. She loved the theater and invested cleverly in Broadway shows. She took lessons in French and flower arranging.

At the dinner table, as the food was being served, my father 7 would comment that he didn't like the way my mother wore the barrette in her hair. She would say bitterly that he never liked anything she wore. He would say that she was stupid. She would say that she was not. Their voices would carry. In the kitchen the maid would clutch the side of the sink until her fingernails were white. My mother would weep. My father would storm out of the house, slamming doors, knocking over lamps. She would shout after him, "You don't love me." He would scream at her, "Who could love you?" She would lie in bed with ice cubes on her swollen eyes, chain-smoking Camel cigarettes. She would call her sister for comfort. Her sister would say, "Don't give him an argument." She would say, "I'll try to do better, I really will."

When I was seven years old, she lay in the bathtub soaking 8 and I was sitting on the rim keeping her company. "I could divorce him," she said. "I could do it." Her eyes were puffed. I felt a surge of electricity run through me, adrenaline flowed. "Leave him?" I asked. "Yes," she said. "Should I?" she asked me. "Should I leave him? Would you mind?" I was her friend, her confidante. I did not yet know enough of the world to answer the question. I thought of my home split apart. I thought my father would never see me again. I wondered what I would tell my friends. No one I knew had parents who were divorced. I was afraid. "Who will take care of us?" I asked. My mother let the ashes of her cigarette fall into the tub. "God!" she said. "Help me," she said. But she'd asked the wrong person.

Then she did a brave thing. She went to a psychiatrist. I 9 would wait for her downstairs in the lobby. She would emerge from the elevator after her appointment with her mascara smeared over her cheeks. "When I'm stronger," she said, "I'll leave him." But the years went on. He said she was demanding. He said, "I spend enough time with you. Go to Florida with your sister. Go to Maine with your brother. Stop asking me to talk to you. I've already said everything I want to say." She said, "I need you to admire me. I need you to say you love me." "I do," he said, but then they had a party and I found him in the coat closet with a lady and lipstick all over his face.

He talked about politics. He read history books. He hit   10
on the chin a man who disagreed with him. He yelled at my mother that she had no right to an opinion on anything. He said, "Women with opinions smell like skunks." She said, "He's so smart. He knows so much." She said, "If I leave him no other man will marry me." She said, "I can't leave him."

Week after week, she would say something that irritated   11
him. He would make her cry and then he would scream at her for crying. His screams were howls. If you listened to the sound you would think an animal was trapped and in pain. Dinner after dinner my brother and I would silently try to eat our food as the same old fight began again, built and reached its crescendo.

Finally I was old enough. "Leave him," I said. "I don't   12
know," she said, "maybe." But she couldn't and she wouldn't and the dance between them had turned into a marathon. She quit first. She died at age fifty-two, still married, still thinking, if only I had been taller, different, better. He inherited her money and immediately wed a tall woman, with whom he had been having an affair for many years, whose hands shook when she spoke to him. He called her: "That stupid dame." "That dumb broad," he would say. He went off to his club. He went for long walks. He had migraines.

This was a story of a divorce that should have been.   13

When I was twenty-seven I found myself checking into a   14
fleabag hotel in Juárez. My three-year-old daughter was try-

ing to pull the corncob out of the parrot cage and the parrot was trying to bite her fingers. I was there, my room squeezed between those of the local drunks and prostitutes, to get a divorce. This was a divorce that should have been and was. I had married a man whom I thought was just the opposite of my father. He was a playwright, a philosopher. He was from an old southern family. He talked to me all the time and let me read and type his manuscripts. I worked as a receptionist to support him. Our friends were poets and painters, beatniks and their groupies. I had escaped my mother's home or so I thought. What I didn't notice was that my husband was handsome and thought me plain, that my husband was poor and thought me a meal ticket, that my husband—like my father—was dwarfed of spirit and couldn't imagine another soul beside himself. What I didn't know was that I—like my mother—had no faith, no confidence, no sense that I could fly too. I could even write.

My husband had other women and I thought it was an [15] artist's privilege. My husband said, "If Elizabeth Taylor is a woman, then you must be a hamster." I laughed. My husband went on binges and used up all our money. I thought it was poetic although I was always frightened; bill collectors called. I was always apologizing. We didn't fight so I thought I had achieved matrimonial heaven, a place where of course certain compromises were necessary.

Then after I had a child I thought of love as oxygen and [16] I felt faint. In the middle of the night when I was nursing the baby and my husband was out at the local bar I discovered that loneliness was the name of my condition. I noticed that my husband could not hold his child because he was either too drunk, out of the house, closed into his head, or consumed with nervousness about the applause the outside world was giving or withholding from him. I discovered that I had married a man more like my father than not and that, more like my mother than not, I had become a creature to be pitied. Like moth to flame I was drawn to repeat. My divorce was related to her undivorce, so the generations unfold back to back handing on their burdens—by contami-

nation, memory, experience, identification, one's failure becomes the other's. The courage it takes to really make things
better, to change, is rare and won only at great cost. Yes, we
are responsible for ourselves, but nevertheless our family stories course and curse through our veins: our memories are
not free.

If my mother had been brave enough to go it alone I might   17
have seen myself differently. I might have been brave enough
to let myself be loved the first time around. At least I didn't
wait for my entire life to pass before leaping up and away. So
this is why I listen with tongue in cheek to all the terrible
tales of what divorce has done to the American family. I know
that if my mother had left my father not only her life but
mine too might have been set on more solid ground. I know
that if I had stayed in my marriage my child would have lived
forever in the shadow of my perpetual grief and thought of
herself as I had, unworthy of the ordinary moments of affection and connection.

In twentieth-century America we place so much emphasis   18
on romance that we barely notice the other essentials of
marriage that include economics and child rearing. My
mother was undone by the economic equation in her marriage. Money, which we know to be a part of the bitterness
of divorce, is in there from the beginning, a thread in the
cloak of love, whether we like it or not.

History clunking through our private lives certainly af-   19
fected my mother's marriage and my bad marriage. Woman's
proper role, woman's masochistic stance, immigration, push
to rise in social status, the confusion of money damned my
mother to a lifetime of tears and almost caught me there too.
But history is always present without our always being able
to name its nasty work.

The women's movement, which came too late for my   20
mother, sent some women off adventure bound, free of suburb, unwilling to be sole caretakers to find, at the end of their
rainbow isolation, disappointment, bitterness. The sexual

revolution, which soon after burned like a laser through our towns and sent wives running in circles in search of multiple pleasures, freedom from convention, and distance from the burdens of domesticity, was a balloon that popped long before the arrival of AIDS. We found we were not, after all, in need of the perfect orgasm. We were in need of a body to spoon with in bed, a story we could tell together as well as sexual equality.

But there is more. Divorce is also the terrible knife that 21 rends family asunder, and for the children it can be the tilting, defining moment that marks them ever after, walking wounded, angry, sad souls akimbo, always prone to being lost in a forest of despair. They can be tough, too tough. They can be helpless, too helpless. They can never trust. They can be too trusting. They can accept a stepparent for a while and then revoke their acceptance. They can protest the stepparent for a while and then change their mind, but either way their own parents' divorce hangs over them, threat, reminder, betrayal always possible. My stepdaughter, now a married woman and a mother herself, speaks of her own parents' breakup, which came when she was only seven, as the most terrible moment in her life. As she says this I have only to listen to the tightness in her voice, watch the sight tremble in her hand to know that the divorce seemed to her like an earthquake. The divorce caused a before and after and everything after is tarnished, diminished by what went before.

I wish this were not so. I wish that we could marry a new 22 mate, repair, go on to undo the worst of our mistakes without leaving ugly deep scars across our children's psyches, but we can't. And furthermore the children will never completely forgive us, never understand how our backs were against the wall: They may try to understand our broken vows but they don't. Of course there are other things our children don't forgive us for. If we die, if we withdraw, if we let ourselves drown in misery, addictions, if we fail at work or lose our courage in the face of economic or other adversity, that too will eat at their hearts and spoil their chances for the gold

ring on life's carousel. There are, in other words, many ways
to damage children, and divorce is only the most effective
and perhaps most common of them.

For a while, in the seventies, divorce was everywhere, a   23
panacea for the heart burdened. We were too excited by the
prospects of freedom to see the damage that was done. The
wounds are very severe for both partners and children. It may
be worth it as it would have been for my mother. It may be
necessary, but divorce is never nice. I felt as if the skin had
been stripped from my body the first months after my divorce, and I was only twenty-seven years old. I felt as if I had
to learn anew how to walk in the streets, how to set my face,
how to plot a direction, how to love. I had to admit to failure,
take back my proud words, let others help me. It was a relief,
but it was a disaster. I had lost confidence in my decisions. It
took a long while to gain back what I had lost. I understand
why my mother did not have the strength to do it, although
she should have.

I cannot imagine a world in which divorce would not   24
sometimes occur. Men and women will always fail each other,
miss each others' gestures, change in fatally different ways.
There are men who cannot love, who abuse their wives or
themselves or some substance. There are women who do the
same. There are some disasters that wreck a marriage, a sick
or damaged child, an economic calamity, a professional failure. There are marriages that are simply asphyxiated by daily
life.

But I can imagine a world in which divorce would be rare,   25
in which the madness, meanness, mess of everyday life were
absorbed and managed without social cataclysm. It is perhaps
our American obsession with the romantic that leads to so
much trouble. If we were able to see marriage as largely an
economic, child-rearing institution, as a social encounter involving ambition, class, money, we might be better off. Never
mind our very up-to-date goals of personal fitness and fulfillment; we are still characters, all of us, in a nineteenth-century
novel.

At the moment, now that my children are of marriageable   26 age I have become a believer in the arranged betrothal. Such marriages could not possibly cause more mischief than those that were created by our free will rushing about in heavy traffic with its eyes closed. Perhaps we should consider love as a product of marriage instead of the other way around. Of course those societies that arrange marriages have other tragic stories of bride burning, lifelong miserable submission experienced by women, sexual nightmares, poor young girls and dirty old men. We are the only animal species that cannot seem to figure out how to pair off and raise children without maiming ourselves in the process.

We can bemoan the social disorder caused by divorce until the moon turns to cream cheese, but we are such fragile souls, so easily cast adrift, wounded, set upon by devils of our own making, that no matter how we twist or turn, no system will protect us from the worst. There is cruelty in divorce. There is cruelty in forced or unfortunate marriage. We will continue to cry at weddings because we know how bittersweet, how fragile is the troth. We will always need legal divorce just as an emergency escape hatch is crucial in every submarine. No sense, however, in denying that after every divorce someone will be running like a cat, tin cans tied to its tail: spooked and slowed down.

27

For Study and Discussion

QUESTIONS FOR RESPONSE

1. How have your friends or members of your family reacted to a divorce?
2. How do you characterize divorce—as a failure or liberation? Can you tell a story about a couple that might fit into each category?

QUESTIONS ABOUT PURPOSE

1. In what ways does Roiphe's sentence—"my divorce is the tale of two divorces, one that never was and one that was"—state the purpose of her essay?

2. How do her stories demonstrate her thesis that marriage requires more than romance?

QUESTIONS ABOUT AUDIENCE

1. How does Roiphe's assertion that all divorce stories sound the same, and yet each is as "unique as a human face," help her identify her audience?
2. These two contemporary tales focus on women. How does Roiphe anticipate the responses of her male readers?

QUESTIONS ABOUT STRATEGIES

1. How does Roiphe balance her two stories to demonstrate that although they seem different, her husband was like her father and she was like her mother?
2. How does Roiphe use her stepdaughter's experience to make a transition to the final part of her essay?

QUESTIONS FOR DISCUSSION

1. What effects does Roiphe think the women's movement has had on divorce?
2. How does she justify her assertion that we will always need divorce as "an emergency escape hatch"?

DEBORAH TANNEN

Deborah Tannen was born in 1945 in Brooklyn, New York, and was educated at the State University of New York at Binghamton, Wayne State University, and the University of California at Berkeley. She has taught English at the Hellenic American Union in Athens, Greece; Herbert H. Lehman College of the City University of New York; and Georgetown University. She has contributed articles on language to numerous scholarly books, including *Language and Social Identity* (1982) and *Languages and Linguistics in Context* (1986), and she has written several books on language and gender, including *Gender and Discourse* (1994) and *Talking from 9 to 5* (1994). Tannen's *That's Not What I Meant! How Conversational Style Makes or Breaks Your Relations with Others* (1986) attracted national attention because of its engaging study of the breakdown of communication between the sexes. One of her most recent books is *The Argument Culture: Moving from Debate to Dialogue* (1998). In "Rapport-Talk and Report-Talk," excerpted from *You Just Don't Understand* (1989), Tannen compares the public and private conversational styles of men and women.

Rapport-Talk and Report-Talk

W HO TALKS MORE, then, women or men? The seemingly   1
contradictory evidence is reconciled by the difference between what I call *public* and *private speaking*. More men feel comfortable doing "public speaking," while more women feel comfortable doing "private" speaking. Another

193

way of capturing these differences is by using the terms *report-talk* and *rapport-talk*.

For most women, the language of conversation is primarily   2
a language of rapport: a way of establishing connections and
negotiating relationships. Emphasis is placed on displaying
similarities and matching experiences. From childhood, girls
criticize peers who try to stand out or appear better than
others. People feel their closest connections at home, or in
settings where they *feel* at home—with one or a few people
they feel close to and comfortable with—in other words,

---

*To men, talk is for information. To women,
talk is for interaction.*

---

during private speaking. But even the most public situations
can be approached like private speaking.

For most men, talk is primarily a means to preserve inde-   3
pendence and negotiate and maintain status in a hierarchical
social order. This is done by exhibiting knowledge and skill,
and by holding center stage through verbal performance such
as story-telling, joking, or imparting information. From
childhood, men learn to use talking as a way to get and keep
attention. So they are more comfortable speaking in larger
groups made up of people they know less well—in the broadest sense, "public speaking." But even the most private situations can be approached like public speaking, more like
giving a report than establishing rapport.

PRIVATE SPEAKING: THE WORDY
WOMAN AND THE MUTE MAN

What is the source of the stereotype that women talk a lot?   4
Dale Spender suggests that most people feel instinctively (if
not consciously) that women, like children, should be seen
and not heard, so any amount of talk from them seems like

too much. Studies have shown that if women and men talk equally in a group, people think the women talked more. So there is truth to Spender's view. But another explanation is that men think women talk a lot because they hear women talking in situations where men would not: on the telephone; or in social situations with friends, when they are not discussing topics that men find inherently interesting; or, like the couple at the women's group, at home alone—in other words, in private speaking.

Home is the setting for an American icon that features the silent man and the talkative woman. And this icon, which grows out of the different goals and habits I have been describing, explains why the complaint most often voiced by women about the men with whom they are intimate is "He doesn't talk to me"—and the second most frequent is "He doesn't listen to me."

A woman who wrote to Ann Landers is typical:

> *My husband never speaks to me when he comes home from work. When I ask, "How did everything go today?" he says, "Rough . . ." or "It's a jungle out there." (We live in Jersey and he works in New York City.)*
>
> *It's a different story when we have guests or go visiting. Paul is the gabbiest guy in the crowd—a real spellbinder. He comes up with the most interesting stories. People hang on every word. I think to myself, "Why doesn't he ever tell me these things?"*
>
> *This has been going on for 38 years. Paul started to go quiet on me after 10 years of marriage. I could never figure out why. Can you solve the mystery?*
> —THE INVISIBLE WOMAN

Ann Landers suggests that the husband may not want to talk because he is tired when he comes home from work. Yet women who work come home tired too, and they are nonetheless eager to tell their partners or friends everything that happened to them during the day and what these fleeting, daily dramas made them think and feel.

Sources as lofty as studies conducted by psychologists, as down to earth as letters written to advice columnists, and as sophisticated as movies and plays come up with the same insight: Men's silence at home is a disappointment to women. Again and again, women complain, "He seems to have everything to say to everyone else, and nothing to say to me." 7

The film *Divorce American Style* opens with a conversation in which Debbie Reynolds is claiming that she and Dick Van Dyke don't communicate, and he is protesting that he tells her everything that's on his mind. The doorbell interrupts their quarrel, and husband and wife compose themselves before opening the door to greet their guests with cheerful smiles. 8

Behind closed doors, many couples are having conversations like this. Like the character played by Debbie Reynolds, women feel men don't communicate. Like the husband played by Dick Van Dyke, men feel wrongly accused. How can she be convinced that he doesn't tell her anything, while he is equally convinced he tells her everything that's on his mind? How can women and men have such different ideas about the same conversations? 9

When something goes wrong, people look around for a source to blame: either the person they are trying to communicate with ("You're demanding, stubborn, self-centered") or the group that the other person belongs to ("All women are demanding"; "All men are self-centered"). Some generous-minded people blame the relationship ("We just can't communicate"). But underneath, or overlaid on these types of blame cast outward, most people believe that something is wrong with them. 10

If individual people or particular relationships were to blame, there wouldn't be so many different people having the same problems. The real problem is conversational style. Women and men have different ways of talking. Even with the best intentions, trying to settle the problem through talk 11 can only make things worse if it is ways of talking that are causing trouble in the first place.

BEST FRIENDS

Once again, the seeds of women's and men's styles are sown 12 in the ways they learn to use language while growing up. In our culture, most people, but especially women, look to their closest relationships as havens in a hostile world. The center of a little girl's social life is her best friend. Girls' friendships are made and maintained by telling secrets. For grown women too, the essence of friendship is talk, telling each other what they're thinking and feeling, and what happened that day: who was at the bus stop, who called, what they said, how that made them feel. When asked who their best friends are, most women name other women they talk to regularly. When asked the same question, most men will say it's their wives. After that, many men name other men with whom they do things such as play tennis or baseball (but never just sit and talk) or a chum from high school whom they haven't spoken to in a year.

When Debbie Reynolds complained that Dick Van Dyke 13 didn't tell her anything, and he protested that he did, both were right. She felt he didn't tell her anything because he didn't tell her the fleeting thoughts and feelings he experienced throughout the day—the kind of talk she would have with her best friend. He didn't tell her these things because to him they didn't seem like anything to tell. He told her anything that seemed important—anything he would tell his friends.

Men and women often have very different ideas of what's 14 important—and at what point "important" topics should be raised. A woman told me, with lingering incredulity, of a conversation with her boyfriend. Knowing he had seen his friend Oliver, she asked, "What's new with Oliver?" He replied, "Nothing." But later in the conversation it came out that Oliver and his girlfriend had decided to get married.

"That's nothing?" the woman gasped in frustration and disbelief.

For men, "Nothing" may be a ritual response at the start   15
of a conversation. A college woman missed her brother but
rarely called him because she found it difficult to get talk
going. A typical conversation began with her asking, "What's
up with you?" and his replying, "Nothing." Hearing his
"Nothing" as meaning "There is nothing personal I want to
talk about," she supplied talk by filling him in on her news
and eventually hung up in frustration. But when she thought
back, she remembered that later in the conversation he had
mumbled, "Christie and I got into another fight." This came
so late and so low that she didn't pick up on it. And he was
probably equally frustrated that she didn't.

Many men honestly do not know what women want, and   16
women honestly do not know why men find what they want
so hard to comprehend and deliver.

"TALK TO ME!"

Women's dissatisfaction with men's silence at home is cap-   17
tured in the stock cartoon setting of a breakfast table at which
a husband and wife are sitting: He's reading a newspaper;
she's glaring at the back of the newspaper. In a Dagwood
strip, Blondie complains, "Every morning all he sees is the
newspaper! I'll bet you don't even know I'm here!" Dagwood reassures her, "Of course I know you're here. You're
my wonderful wife and I love you very much." With this, he
unseeingly pats the paw of the family dog, which the wife has
put in her place before leaving the room. The cartoon strip
shows that Blondie is justified in feeling like the woman who
wrote to Ann Landers: invisible.

Another cartoon shows a husband opening a newspaper   18
and asking his wife, "Is there anything you would like to say
to me before I begin reading the newspaper?" The reader
knows that there isn't—but that as soon as he begins reading
the paper, she will think of something. The cartoon highlights the difference in what women and men think talk is

for: To him, talk is for information. So when his wife interrupts his reading, it must be to inform him of something that he needs to know. This being the case, she might as well tell him what she thinks he needs to know before he starts reading. But to her, talk is for interaction. Telling things is a way to show involvement, and listening is a way to show interest and caring. It is not an odd coincidence that she always thinks of things to tell him when he is reading. She feels the need for verbal interaction most keenly when he is (unaccountably, from her point of view) buried in the newspaper instead of talking to her.

Yet another cartoon shows a wedding cake that has, on top, in place of the plastic statues of bride and groom in tuxedo and gown, a breakfast scene in which an unshaven husband reads a newspaper across the table from his disgruntled wife. The cartoon reflects the enormous gulf between the romantic expectations of marriage represented by the plastic couple in traditional wedding costume, and the often disappointing reality represented by the two sides of the newspaper at the breakfast table—the front, which he is reading, and the back, at which she is glaring. 19

These cartoons, and many others on the same theme, are funny because people recognize their own experience in them. What's not funny is that many women are deeply hurt when men don't talk to them at home, and many men are deeply frustrated by feeling they have disappointed their partners, without understanding how they failed or how else they could have behaved. 20

Some men are further frustrated because, as one put it, "When in the world am I supposed to read the morning paper?" If many women are incredulous that many men do not exchange personal information with their friends, this man is incredulous that many women do not bother to read the morning paper. To him, reading the paper is an essential part of his morning ritual, and his whole day is awry if he doesn't get to read it. In his words, reading the newspaper in the morning is as important to him as putting on makeup in the morning is to many women he knows. Yet many 21

women, he observed, either don't subscribe to a paper or
don't read it until they get home in the evening. "I find this
very puzzling," he said. "I can't tell you how often I have
picked up a woman's morning newspaper from her front door
in the evening and handed it to her when she opened the
door for me."

To this man (and I am sure many others), a woman who   22
objects to his reading the morning paper is trying to keep
him from doing something essential and harmless. It's a
violation of his independence—his freedom of action. But
when a woman who expects her partner to talk to her is
disappointed that he doesn't, she perceives his behavior as a
failure of intimacy: He's keeping things from her; he's lost
interest in her; he's pulling away. A woman I will call Rebecca,
who is generally quite happily married, told me that this is
the one source of serious dissatisfaction with her husband,
Stuart. Her term for his taciturnity is *stinginess of spirit*. She
tells him what she is thinking, and he listens silently. She asks
him what he is thinking, and he takes a long time to answer,
"I don't know." In frustration she challenges, "Is there nothing on your mind?"

For Rebecca, who is accustomed to expressing her fleeting   23
thoughts and opinions as they come to her, *saying* nothing
means *thinking* nothing. But Stuart does not assume that his
passing thoughts are worthy of utterance. He is not in the
habit of uttering his fleeting ruminations, so just as Rebecca
"naturally" speaks her thoughts, he "naturally" dismisses his
as soon as they occur to him. Speaking them would give them
more weight and significance than he feels they merit. All her
life she has had practice in verbalizing her thoughts and
feelings in private conversations with people she is close to;
all his life he has had practice in dismissing his and keeping
them to himself. . . .

PUBLIC SPEAKING: THE TALKATIVE MAN AND THE SILENT WOMAN

So far I have been discussing the private scenes in which many   24
men are silent and many women are talkative. But there are

other scenes in which the roles are reversed. Returning to Rebecca and Stuart, we saw that when they are home alone, Rebecca's thoughts find their way into words effortlessly, whereas Stuart finds he can't come up with anything to say. The reverse happens when they are in other situations. For example, at a meeting of the neighborhood council or the parents' association at their children's school, it is Stuart who stands up and speaks. In that situation, it is Rebecca who is silent, her tongue tied by an acute awareness of all the negative reactions people could have to what she might say, all the mistakes she might make in trying to express her ideas. If she musters her courage and prepares to say something, she needs time to formulate it and then waits to be recognized by the chair. She cannot just jump up and start talking the way Stuart and some other men can.

Eleanor Smeal, president of the Fund for the Feminist   25
Majority, was a guest on a call-in radio talk show, discussing abortion. No subject could be of more direct concern to women, yet during the hour-long show, all the callers except two were men. Diane Rehm, host of a radio talk show, expresses puzzlement that although the audience for her show is evenly split between women and men, 90 percent of the callers to the show are men. I am convinced that the reason is not that women are uninterested in the subjects discussed on the show. I would wager that women listeners are bringing up the subjects they heard on *The Diane Rehm Show* to their friends and family over lunch, tea, and dinner. But fewer of them call in because to do so would be putting themselves on display, claiming public attention for what they have to say, catapulting themselves onto center stage.

I myself have been the guest on innumerable radio and   26
television talk shows. Perhaps I am unusual in being completely at ease in this mode of display. But perhaps I am not unusual at all, because, although I am comfortable in the role of invited expert, I have never called in to a talk show I was listening to, although I have often had ideas to contribute. When I am the guest, my position of authority is granted before I begin to speak. Were I to call in, I would be claiming that right on my own. I would have to establish my credibility

by explaining who I am, which might seem self-aggrandizing, or not explain who I am and risk having my comments ignored or not valued. For similar reasons, though I am comfortable lecturing to groups numbering in the thousands, I rarely ask questions following another lecturer's talk, unless I know both the subject and the group very well.

My own experience and that of talk show hosts seems to   27 hold a clue to the difference in women's and men's attitudes toward talk: Many men are more comfortable than most women in using talk to claim attention. And this difference lies at the heart of the distinction between report-talk and rapport-talk.

REPORT-TALK IN PRIVATE

Report-talk, or what I am calling public speaking, does not   28 arise only in the literally public situation of formal speeches delivered to a listening audience. The more people there are in a conversation, the less well you know them, and the more status differences among them, the more a conversation is *like* public speaking or report-talk. The fewer the people, the more intimately you know them, and the more equal their status, the more it is like private speaking or rapport-talk. Furthermore, women feel a situation is more "public"—in the sense that they have to be on good behavior—if there are men present, except perhaps for family members. Yet even in families, the mother and children may feel their home to be "backstage" when Father is not home, "on-stage" when he is: Many children are instructed to be on good behavior when Daddy is home. This may be because he is not home often, or because Mother—or Father—doesn't want the children to disturb him when he is.

The difference between public and private speaking also   29 explains the stereotype that women don't tell jokes. Although some women are great raconteurs who can keep a group spellbound by recounting jokes and funny stories, there are fewer such personalities among women than among men. Many women who do tell jokes to large groups of people come from ethnic backgrounds in which verbal performance is highly valued. For example, many of the great women stand-up comics, such as Fanny Brice and Joan Rivers, came from Jewish backgrounds.

Although it's not true that women don't tell jokes, it is   30
true that many women are less likely than men to tell jokes in large groups, especially groups including men. So it's not surprising that men get the impression that women never tell jokes at all. Folklorist Carol Mitchell studied joke telling on a college campus. She found that men told most of their jokes to other men, but they also told many jokes to mixed groups and to women. Women, however, told most of their jokes to other women, fewer to men, and very few to groups that included men as well as women. Men preferred and were more likely to tell jokes when they had an audience: at least two, often four or more. Women preferred a small audience of one or two, rarely more than three. Unlike men, they were reluctant to tell jokes in front of people they didn't know well. Many women flatly refused to tell jokes they knew if there were four or more in the group, promising to tell them later in private. Men never refused the invitation to tell jokes.

All of Mitchell's results fit in with the picture I have been   31
drawing of public and private speaking. In a situation in which there are more people in the audience, more men, or more strangers, joke telling, like any other form of verbal performance, requires speakers to claim center stage and prove their abilities. These are the situations in which many women are reluctant to talk. In a situation that is more private, because the audience is small, familiar, and perceived to be members of a community (for example, other women), they are more likely to talk.

The idea that telling jokes is a kind of self-display does not   32
imply that it is selfish or self-centered. The situation of joke telling illustrates that status and connection entail each other. Entertaining others is a way of establishing connections with them, and telling jokes can be a kind of gift giving, where the joke is a gift that brings pleasure to receivers. The key issue is asymmetry: One person is the teller and the others are the audience. If these roles are later exchanged— for example, if the joke telling becomes a round in which one person after

another takes the role of teller—then there is symmetry on the broad scale, if not in the individual act. However, if women habitually take the role of appreciative audience and never take the role of joke teller, the asymmetry of the individual joke telling is diffused through the larger interaction as well. This is a hazard for women. A hazard for men is that continually telling jokes can be distancing. This is the effect felt by a man who complained that when he talks to his father on the phone, all his father does is tell him jokes. An extreme instance of a similar phenomenon is the class clown, who, according to teachers, is nearly always a boy.

RAPPORT-TALK IN PUBLIC

Just as conversations that take place at home among friends   33
can be like public speaking, even a public address can be like private speaking: for example, by giving a lecture full of personal examples and stories.

At the executive committee of a fledgling professional   34
organization, the outgoing president, Fran, suggested that the organization adopt the policy of having presidents deliver a presidential address. To explain and support her proposal, she told a personal anecdote: Her cousin was the president of a more established professional organization at the time that Fran held the same position in this one. Fran's mother had been talking to her cousin's mother on the telephone. Her cousin's mother told Fran's mother that her daughter was preparing her presidential address, and she asked when Fran's presidential address was scheduled to be. Fran was embarrassed to admit to her mother that she was not giving one. This made her wonder whether the organization's professional identity might not be enhanced if it emulated the more established organizations.

Several men on the committee were embarrassed by Fran's   35
reference to her personal situation and were not convinced by her argument. It seemed to them not only irrelevant but unseemly to talk about her mother's telephone conversations at an executive committee meeting. Fran had approached the

meeting—a relatively public context—as an extension of the private kind. Many women's tendency to use personal experience and examples, rather than abstract argumentation, can be understood from the perspective of their orientation to language as it is used in private speaking.

A study by Celia Roberts and Tom Jupp of a faculty meeting at a secondary school in England found that the women's arguments did not carry weight with their male colleagues because they tended to use their own experience as evidence, or argue about the effect of policy on individual students. The men at the meeting argued from a completely different perspective, making categorical statements about right and wrong.   36

The same discussion is found in discussions at home. A man told me that he felt critical of what he perceived as his wife's lack of logic. For example, he recalled a conversation in which he had mentioned an article he had read in *The New York Times* claiming that today's college students are not as idealistic as students were in the 1960s. He was inclined to accept this claim. His wife questioned it, supporting her argument with the observation that her niece and her niece's friends were very idealistic indeed. He was incredulous and scornful of her faulty reasoning; it was obvious to him that a single personal example is neither evidence nor argumentation—it's just anecdote. It did not occur to him that he was dealing with a different logical system, rather than a lack of logic.   37

The logic this woman was employing was making sense of the world as a more private endeavor—observing and integrating her personal experience and drawing connections to the experiences of others. The logic the husband took for granted was a more public endeavor—more like gathering information, conducting a survey, or devising arguments by rules of formal logic as one might in doing research.   38

Another man complained about what he and his friends call women's "shifting sands" approach to discussion. These men feel that whereas they try to pursue an argument logically, step by step, until it is settled, women continually   39 change course in mid-stream. He pointed to the short excerpt from *Divorce American Style* quoted above as a case in point. It seemed to him that when Debbie Reynolds said, "I can't argue now. I have to take the French bread out of the oven," she was evading the argument because she had made an accusation—"All you do is criticize"—that she could not support.

This man also offered an example from his own experience.   40 His girlfriend had told him of a problem she had because her boss wanted her to do one thing and she wanted to do another. Taking the boss's view for the sake of argumentation, he pointed out a negative consequence that would result if she did what she wanted. She countered that the same negative consequence would result if she did what the boss wanted. He complained that she was shifting over to the other field of battle—what would happen if she followed her boss's will—before they had made headway with the first— what would happen if she followed her own.

For Study and Discussion

QUESTIONS FOR RESPONSE

1. How would you characterize your own conversational style?
2. How does context affect the way you talk? What situations make you shift styles?

QUESTIONS ABOUT PURPOSE

1. What does Tannen want to demonstrate about the relationship between communication failure and conversational style?
2. How do size (the number of people) and status (those people claiming authority) contribute to Tannen's comparison of rapport-talk and report-talk?

QUESTIONS ABOUT AUDIENCE

1. What assumptions does Tannen make about the probable gender of most of her readers?

2. How does Tannen assume her audience can benefit from her analysis?

QUESTIONS ABOUT STRATEGIES

1. How does Tannen use advice columns, movies, and cartoons to illustrate the problems of domestic communication?
2. How does Tannen use her own experience as a lecturer to compare the way men and women talk in public?

QUESTIONS FOR DISCUSSION

1. Do the men and women you know construct arguments according to Tannen's format? How many men use personal experience as evidence? How many women make categorical assertions?
2. To what extent do conversational styles depend on innate skill (personality type) or learned behavior (acquired habits)? To what extent is it possible (or desirable) to change styles?

LAURA BOHANNAN

Laura Bohannan was born in New York City in 1922 and educated at Smith College, the University of Arizona, and Oxford University. She has taught anthropology at Northwestern University, the University of Chicago, and the University of Illinois, Chicago Circle. She has held several fellowships to conduct research in East Africa which have resulted in books such as *The Tiv of Central Nigeria* (1953) and *A Sourcebook on Tiv Religion* (1972). In "Shakespeare in the Bush," reprinted from *Natural History* magazine, Bohannan compares her version of *Hamlet* with the interpretation of the elders of an African tribe.

Shakespeare in the Bush
An American Anthropologist Set Out to Study the Tiv of West Africa and Was Taught the True Meaning of Hamlet

JUST BEFORE I left Oxford for the Tiv in West Africa, conversation turned to the season at Stratford. "You Americans," said a friend, "often have difficulty with Shakespeare. He was, after all, a very English poet, and one can easily misinterpret the universal by misunderstanding the particular."

I protested that human nature is pretty much the same the whole world over; at least the general plot and motivation of the greater tragedies would always be clear—everywhere—although some details of custom might have to be explained and difficulties of translation might produce other slight changes. To end an argument we could not conclude, my friend gave me a copy of *Hamlet* to study in the African bush: it would, he hoped, lift my mind above its primitive surroundings, and possibly I might, by prolonged meditation, achieve the grace of correct interpretation.

It was my second field trip to that African tribe, and I thought myself ready to live in one of its remote sections—an area difficult to cross even on foot. I eventually settled on the hillock of a very knowledgeable old man, the head of a 3

Before the end of the second month in the bush, grace descended on me. I was quite sure that Hamlet had only one possible interpretation, and that one was universally obvious.

---

homestead of some hundred and forty people, all of whom were either his close relatives or their wives and children. Like the other elders of the vicinity, the old man spent most of his time performing ceremonies seldom seen these days in the more accessible parts of the tribe. I was delighted. Soon there would be three months of enforced isolation and leisure, between the harvest that takes place just before the rising of the swamps and the clearing of new farms when the water goes down. Then, I thought, they would have even more time to perform ceremonies and explain them to me.

I was quite mistaken. Most of the ceremonies demanded 4 the presence of elders from several homesteads. As the swamps rose, the old men found it too difficult to walk from one homestead to the next, and the ceremonies gradually ceased. As the swamps rose even higher, all activities from one came to an end. The women brewed beer from maize and millet. Men, women, and children sat on their hillocks and drank it.

People began to drink at dawn. By midmorning the whole 5 homestead was singing, dancing, and drumming. When it rained, people had to sit inside their huts: there they drank and sang or they drank and told stories. In any case, by noon or before, I either had to join the party or retire to my own hut and my books. "One does not discuss serious matters when there is beer. Come, drink with us." Since I lacked their capacity for the thick native beer, I spent more and more time with *Hamlet*. Before the end of the second month, grace descended on me. I was quite sure that *Hamlet* had only one possible interpretation, and that one universally obvious.

Early every morning, in the hope of having some serious 6 talk before the beer party, I used to call on the old man at his reception hut—a circle of posts supporting a thatched roof above a low mud wall to keep out wind and rain. One day I crawled through the low doorway and found most of the men of the homestead sitting huddled in their ragged cloths on stools, low plank beds, and reclining chairs, warming themselves against the chill of the rain around a smoky fire. In the center were three pots of beer. The party had started.

The old man greeted me cordially. "Sit down and drink." 7 I accepted a large calabash full of beer, poured some into a small drinking gourd, and tossed it down. Then I poured some more into the same gourd for the man second in seniority to my host before I handed my calabash over to a young man for further distribution. Important people shouldn't ladle beer themselves.

"It is better like this," the old man said, looking at me 8 approvingly and plucking at the thatch that had caught in my hair. "You should sit and drink with us more often. Your servants tell me that when you are not with us, you sit inside your hut looking at a paper."

The old man was acquainted with four kinds of "papers": 9 tax receipts, bride price receipts, court fee receipts, and letters. The messenger who brought him letters from the chief used them mainly as a badge of office, for he always knew what was in them and told the old man. Personal letters for the few who had relatives in the government or mission stations were kept until someone went to a large market where there was a letter writer and reader. Since my arrival,

letters were brought to me to be read. A few men also
brought me bride price receipts, privately, with requests to
change the figures to a higher sum. I found moral arguments
were of no avail, since in-laws are fair game, and the technical
hazards of forgery difficult to explain to an illiterate people.
I did not wish them to think me silly enough to look at any
such papers for days on end, and I hastily explained that my
"paper" was one of the "things of long ago" of my country.

"Ah," said the old man. "Tell us."   10

I protested that I was not a storyteller. Storytelling is a   11
skilled art among them; their standards are high, and the
audiences critical—and vocal in their criticism. I protested in
vain. This morning they wanted to hear a story while they
drank. They threatened to tell me no more stories until I told
them one of mine. Finally, the old man promised that no one
would criticize my style "for we know you are struggling with
our language." "But," put in one of the elders, "you must
explain what we do not understand, as we do when we tell
you our stories." Realizing that here was my chance to prove
Hamlet universally intelligible, I agreed.

The old man handed me some more beer to help me on   12
with my storytelling. Men filled their long wooden pipes and
knocked coals from the fire to place in the pipe bowls; then,
puffing contentedly, they sat back to listen. I began in the
proper style, "Not yesterday, not yesterday, but long ago, a
thing occurred. One night three men were keeping watch
outside the homestead of the great chief, when suddenly they
saw the former chief approach them."

"Why was he no longer their chief?"   13

"He was dead," I explained. "That is why they were trou-   14
bled and afraid when they saw him."

"Impossible," began one of the elders, handing his pipe   15
on to his neighbor, who interrupted, "Of course it wasn't the
dead chief. It was an omen sent by a witch. Go on."

Slightly shaken, I continued. "One of these three was a   16
man who knew things"—the closest translation for scholar,
but unfortunately it also meant witch. The second elder
looked triumphantly at the first. "So we spoke to the dead

chief saying, 'Tell us what we must do so you may rest in your grave,' but the dead chief did not answer. He vanished, and they could see him no more. Then the man who knew things—his name was Horatio—said this event was the affair of the dead chief's son, Hamlet."

There was a general shaking of heads round the circle. 17 "Had the dead chief no living brothers? Or was this son the chief?"

"No," I replied. "That is, he had one living brother who 18 became the chief when the elder brother died."

The old men muttered: such omens were matters for chiefs 19 and elders, not for youngsters; no good could come of going behind a chief's back; clearly Horatio was not a man who knew things.

"Yes, he was," I insisted, shooing a chicken away from my 20 beer. "In our country the son is next to the father. The dead chief's younger brother had become the great chief. He had also married his elder brother's widow only about a month after the funeral."

"He did well," the old man beamed and announced to the 21 others, "I told you that if we knew more about Europeans, we would find they really were very like us. In our country also," he added to me, "the younger brother marries the elder brother's widow and becomes the father of his children. Now, if your uncle, who married your widowed mother, is your father's full brother, then he will be a real father to you. Did Hamlet's father and uncle have one mother?"

His question barely penetrated my mind; I was too upset 22 and thrown too far off balance by having one of the most important elements of *Hamlet* knocked straight out of the picture. Rather uncertainly I said that I thought they had the same mother, but I wasn't sure—the story didn't say. The old man told me severely that these genealogical details made all the difference and that when I got home I must ask the elders about it. He shouted out the door to one of his younger wives to bring his goatskin bag.

Determined to save what I could of the mother motif, I 23
took a deep breath and began again. "The son Hamlet was
very sad because his mother had married again so quickly.
There was no need for her to do so, and it is our custom for
a widow not to go to her next husband until she has mourned
for two years."

"Two years is too long," objected the wife, who had ap- 24
peared with the old man's battered goatskin bag. "Who will
hoe your farms for you while you have no husband?"

"Hamlet," I retorted without thinking, "was old enough 25
to hoe his mother's farms himself. There was no need for her
to remarry." No one looked convinced. I gave up. "His
mother and the great chief told Hamlet not to be sad, for the
great chief himself would be a father to Hamlet. Furthermore, Hamlet would be the next chief: therefore he must stay
to learn the things of a chief. Hamlet agreed to remain, and
all the rest went off to drink beer."

While I paused, perplexed at how to render Hamlet's 26
disgusted soliloquy to an audience convinced that Claudius
and Gertrude had behaved in the best possible manner, one
of the younger men asked me who had married the other
wives of the dead chief.

"He had no other wives," I told him. 27

"But a chief must have many wives! How else can he brew 28
beer and prepare food for all his guests?"

I said firmly that in our country even chiefs had only one 29
wife, that they had servants to do their work, and that they
paid them from tax money.

It was better, they returned, for a chief to have many wives 30
and sons who would help him hoe his farms and feed his
people; then everyone loved the chief who gave much and
took nothing—taxes were a bad thing.

I agreed with the last comment, but for the rest fell back 31
on their favorite way of fobbing off my questions: "That is
the way it is done, so that is how we do it."

I decided to skip the soliloquy. Even if Claudius was here 32
thought quite right to marry his brother's widow, there remained the poison motif, and I knew they would disapprove

of fratricide. More hopefully I resumed, "That night Hamlet kept watch with the three who had seen his dead father. The dead chief again appeared, and although the others were afraid, Hamlet followed his dead father off to one side. When they were alone, Hamlet's dead father spoke."

"Omens can't talk!" The old man was emphatic.   33

"Hamlet's dead father wasn't an omen. Seeing him might   34 have been an omen, but he was not." My audience looked as confused as I sounded. "It *was* Hamlet's dead father. It was a thing we call a 'ghost.'" I had to use the English word, for unlike many of the neighboring tribes, these people didn't believe in the survival after death of any individuating part of the personality.

"What is a 'ghost?' An omen?"   35

"No, a 'ghost' is someone who is dead but who walks   36 around and can talk, and people can hear him and see him but not touch him."

They objected. "One can touch zombis."   37

"No, no! It was not a dead body the witches had animated   38 to sacrifice and eat. No one else made Hamlet's dead father walk. He did it himself."

"Dead men can't walk," protested my audience as one   39 man.

I was quite willing to compromise. "A 'ghost' is the dead   40 man's shadow."

But again they objected. "Dead men cast no shadows."   41

"They do in my country," I snapped.   42

The old man quelled the babble of disbelief that arose   43 immediately and told me with that insincere, but courteous, agreement one extends to the fancies of the young, ignorant, and superstitious, "No doubt in your country the dead can also walk without being zombis." From the depths of his bag he produced a withered fragment of kola nut, bit off one end to show it wasn't poisoned, and handed me the rest as a peace offering.

"Anyhow," I resumed, "Hamlet's dead father said that his   44 own brother, the one who became chief, had poisoned him. He wanted Hamlet to avenge him. Hamlet believed this in his heart, for he did not like his father's brother." I took another swallow of beer. "In the country of the great chief, living in the same homestead, for it was a very large one, was an important elder who was often with the chief to advise and help him. His name was Polonius. Hamlet was courting his daughter, but her father and her brother . . . [I cast hastily about for some tribal analogy] warned her not to let Hamlet visit her when she was alone on her farm, for he would be a great chief and so could not marry her."

"Why not?" asked the wife, who had settled down on the edge of the old man's chair. He frowned at her for asking stupid questions and growled, "They lived in the same homestead."

"That was not the reason," I informed them. "Polonius was a stranger who lived in the homestead because he helped the chief, not because he was a relative."

"Then why couldn't Hamlet marry her?"

"He could have," I explained, "but Polonius didn't think he would. After all, Hamlet was a man of great importance who ought to marry a chief's daughter, for in his country a man could have only one wife. Polonius was afraid that if Hamlet made love to his daughter, then no one else would give a high price for her."

"That might be true," remarked one of the shrewder elders, "but a chief's son would give his mistress's father enough presents and patronage to more than make up the difference. Polonius sounds like a fool to me."

"Many people think he was," I agreed. "Meanwhile Polonius sent his son Laertes off to Paris to learn the things of that country, for it was the homestead of a very great chief indeed. Because he was afraid that Laertes might waste a lot of money on beer and women and gambling, or get into trouble by fighting, he sent one of his servants to Paris secretly, to spy out what Laertes was doing. One day Hamlet came upon Polonius's daughter Ophelia. He behaved so oddly he frightened her. Indeed"—I was fumbling for words to express the dubious quality of Hamlet's madness—"the chief and many others had also noticed that when Hamlet talked one could understand the words but not what they meant. Many people thought that he had become mad." My audience suddenly became much more attentive. "The great chief wanted to know what was wrong with Hamlet, so he sent for two of Hamlet's age mates [school friends would have taken long explanation] to talk to Hamlet and find out what troubled his heart. Hamlet, seeing that they had been bribed by the chief to betray him, told them nothing. Polonius, however, insisted that Hamlet was mad because he had been forbidden to see Ophelia, whom he loved."

"Why," inquired a bewildered voice, "should anyone bewitch Hamlet on that account?"   51

"Bewitch him?"   52

"Yes, only witchcraft can make anyone mad, unless, of course, one sees the beings that lurk in the forest."   53

I stopped being a storyteller, took out my notebook and demanded to be told more about these two causes of madness. Even while they spoke and I jotted notes, I tried to calculate the effect of this new factor on the plot. Hamlet had not been exposed to the beings that lurk in the forests. Only his relatives in the male line could bewitch him. Barring relatives not mentioned by Shakespeare, it had to be Claudius who was attempting to harm him. And, of course, it was.   54

For the moment I staved off questions by saying that the great chief also refused to believe that Hamlet was mad for the love of Ophelia and nothing else. "He was sure that something much more important was troubling Hamlet's heart."   55

"Now Hamlet's age mates," I continued, "had brought with them a famous storyteller. Hamlet decided to have this man tell the chief and all his homestead a story about a man who had poisoned his brother because he desired his brother's wife and wished to be chief himself. Hamlet was sure the great chief could not hear the story without making a sign if he was indeed guilty, and then he would discover whether his dead father had told him the truth."   56

The old man interrupted, with deep cunning, "Why should a father lie to his son?" he asked.   57

I hedged: "Hamlet wasn't sure that it really was his dead 58
father." It was impossible to say anything, in that language,
about devil-inspired visions.

"You mean," he said, "it actually was an omen, and he 59
knew witches sometimes send false ones. Hamlet was a fool
not to go to one skilled in reading omens and divining the
truth in the first place. A man-who-sees-the-truth could have
told him how his father died, if he really had been poisoned,
and if there was witchcraft in it; then Hamlet could have
called the elders to settle the matter."

The shrewd elder ventured to disagree. "Because his fa- 60
ther's brother was a great chief, one-who-sees-the-truth
might therefore have been afraid to tell it. I think it was for
that reason that a friend of Hamlet's father—a witch and an
elder—sent an omen so his friend's son would know. Was the
omen true?"

"Yes," I said, abandoning ghosts and the devil; a witch- 61
sent omen it would have to be. "It was true, for when the
storyteller was telling his tale before all the homestead, the
great chief rose in fear. Afraid that Hamlet knew his secret he
planned to have him killed."

The stage set of the next bit presented some difficulties of 62
translation. I began cautiously. "The great chief told Hamlet's mother to find out from her son what he knew. But
because a woman's children are always first in her heart, he
had the important elder Polonius hide behind a cloth that
hung against the wall of Hamlet's mother's sleeping hut.
Hamlet started to scold his mother for what she had done."

There was a shocked murmur from everyone. A man 63
should never scold his mother.

"She called out in fear, and Polonius moved behind the 64
cloth. Shouting, 'A rat!' Hamlet took his machete and slashed
through the cloth." I paused for dramatic effect. "He had
killed Polonius!"

The old men looked at each other in supreme disgust. 65
"That Polonius truly was a fool and a man who knew nothing! What child would not know enough to shout, 'It's me!'"
With a pang, I remembered that these people are ardent
hunters, always armed with bow, arrow, and machete; at the

first rustle in the grass an arrow is aimed and ready, and the hunter shouts "Game!" If no human voice answers immediately, the arrow speeds on its way. Like a good hunter Hamlet had shouted, "A rat!"

I rushed in to save Polonius's reputation. "Polonius did 66 speak. Hamlet heard him. But he thought it was the chief and wished to kill him to avenge his father. He had meant to kill him earlier that evening. . . ." I broke down, unable to describe to these pagans, who had no belief in individual afterlife, the difference between dying at one's prayers and dying "unhousell'd, disappointed, unaneled."

This time I had shocked my audience seriously. "For a man 67 to raise his hand against his father's brother and the one who has become his father—that is a terrible thing. The elders ought to let such a man be bewitched."

I nibbled at my kola nut in some perplexity, then pointed 68 out that after all the man had killed Hamlet's father.

"No," pronounced the old man, speaking less to me than 69 to the young men sitting behind the elders. "If your father's brother has killed your father, you must appeal to your father's age mates; *they* may avenge him. No man may use violence against his senior relatives." Another thought struck him. "But if his father's brother had indeed been wicked enough to bewitch Hamlet and make him mad that would be a good story indeed, for it would be his fault that Hamlet, being mad, no longer had any sense and thus was ready to kill his father's brother."

There was a murmur of applause. *Hamlet* was again a good 70 story to them, but it no longer seemed quite the same story to me. As I thought over the coming complications of plot and motive, I lost courage and decided to skim over dangerous ground quickly.

"The great chief," I went on, "was not sorry that Hamlet 71 had killed Polonius. It gave him a reason to send Hamlet away, with his two treacherous age mates, with letters to a chief of a far country, saying that Hamlet should be killed. But Hamlet changed the writing on their papers, so that the chief killed his age mates instead." I encountered a reproachful glare from one of the men whom I had told undetectable forgery was not merely immoral but beyond human skill. I looked the other way.

"Before Hamlet could return, Laertes came back for his 72 father's funeral. The great chief told him Hamlet had killed Polonius. Laertes swore to kill Hamlet because of this, and because his sister Ophelia, hearing her father had been killed by the man she loved, went mad and drowned in the river."

"Have you already forgotten what we told you?" The old 73 man was reproachful. "One cannot take vengeance on a madman; Hamlet killed Polonius in his madness. As for the girl, she not only went mad, she was drowned. Only witches can make people drown. Water itself can't hurt anything. It is merely something one drinks and bathes in."

I began to get cross. "If you don't like the story, I'll stop." 74

The old man made soothing noises and himself poured me 75 some more beer. "You tell the story well, and we are listening. But it is clear that the elders of your country have never told you what the story really means. No, don't interrupt! We believe you when you say your marriage customs are different, or your clothes and weapons. But people are the same everywhere; therefore, there are always witches and it is we, the elders, who know how witches work. We told you it was the great chief who wished to kill Hamlet, and now your own words have proved us right. Who were Ophelia's male relatives?"

"There were only her father and her brother." Hamlet was 76 clearly out of my hands.

"There must have been many more; this also you must ask 77 of your elders when you get back to your country. From what you tell us, since Polonius was dead, it must have been Laertes who killed Ophelia, although I do not see the reason for it."

We had emptied one pot of beer, and the old men argued 78 the point with slightly tipsy interest. Finally one of them demanded of me, "What did the servant of Polonius say on his return?"

With difficulty I recollected Reynaldo and his mission. "I 79
don't think he did return before Polonius was killed."

"Listen," said the elder, "and I will tell you how it was and 80
how your story will go, then you may tell me if I am right.
Polonius knew his son would get into trouble, and so he did.
He had many fines to pay for fighting, and debts from gambling. But he had only two ways of getting money quickly.
One was to marry off his sister at once, but it is difficult to
find a man who will marry a woman desired by the son of a
chief. For if the chief's heir commits adultery with your wife,
what can you do? Only a fool calls a case against a man who
will someday be his judge. Therefore Laertes had to take the
second way: he killed his sister by witchcraft, drowning her
so he could secretly sell her body to the witches."

I raised an objection. "They found her body and buried 81
it. Indeed Laertes jumped into the grave to see his sister once
more—so, you see, the body was truly there. Hamlet, who
had just come back, jumped in after him."

"What did I tell you?" The elder appealed to the others. 82
"Laertes was up to no good with his sister's body. Hamlet
prevented him, because the chief's heir, like a chief, does not
wish any other man to grow rich and powerful. Laertes would
be angry, because he would have killed his sister without
benefit to himself. In our country he would try to kill Hamlet
for that reason. Is this not what happened?"

"More or less," I admitted. "When the great chief found 83
Hamlet was still alive, he encouraged Laertes to try to kill
Hamlet and arranged a fight with machetes between them.
In the fight both the young men were wounded to death.
Hamlet's mother drank the poisoned beer that the chief
meant for Hamlet in case he won the fight. When he saw his
mother die of poison, Hamlet, dying, managed to kill his
father's brother with his machete."

"You see, I was right!" exclaimed the elder. 84

"That was a very good story," added the old man, "and 85
you told it with very few mistakes. There was just one more
error, at the very end. The poison Hamlet's mother drank

was obviously meant for the survivor of the fight, whichever it was. If Laertes had won, the great chief would have poisoned him, for no one would know that he arranged Hamlet's death. Then, too, he need not fear Laertes' witchcraft; it takes a strong heart to kill one's only sister by witchcraft.

"Sometime," concluded the old man, gathering his ragged 86 toga about him, "you must tell us some more stories of your country. We, who are elders, will instruct you in their true meaning, so that when you return to your own land your elders will see that you have not been sitting in the bush, but among those who know things and who have taught you wisdom."

For Study and Discussion

QUESTIONS FOR RESPONSE

1. What has been your experience reading *Hamlet*? What aspects of the play confuse you?
2. Have you ever tried to tell a story to a group of people who interrupted and misunderstood you? How did you react to the situation?

QUESTIONS ABOUT PURPOSE

1. What belief convinces Bohannan that *Hamlet* is universally intelligible?
2. How does her attempt to tell Hamlet's story prove that her friend was right: "one can easily misinterpret the universal by misunderstanding the particular"?

QUESTIONS ABOUT AUDIENCE

1. How does Bohannan translate concepts—*chief* for *king, farm* for *castle*—to help her African audience understand her story?
2. How does she reveal her frustration and anger in trying to tell her audience what she thought was a simple story?

QUESTIONS ABOUT STRATEGIES

1. How does Bohannan's discussion of Hamlet's *madness* reveal differences in the English and African culture?
2. Ironically, what feature of her version of Hamlet's story convinces her African audience that "people are the same everywhere"?

QUESTIONS FOR DISCUSSION

1. How does Bohannan's audience interpret Hamlet's story? What convinces them that Bohannan's elders have not told her the true story?
2. How do the elders suggest that Hamlet should have resolved his conflict with Claudius? What does this solution suggest about the presumed superiority of the English culture?

Witi Ihimaera was born in 1944 in Gisborne, New Zealand, and educated at the University of Auckland. After working as a newspaper reporter, he accepted a position as a diplomatic officer in New Zealand's Ministry of Foreign Affairs. He began writing to document the two landscapes of New Zealand, the Maori (the indigenous people) and the Pakeha (the Europeans). In particular, he wanted to ensure that "my Maori people were taken into account." His short stories have been collected in *Pounamu, Pounamu* (1972) and *The New Net Goes Fishing* (1976). His novels include *Tangi* (1973) and *Whanau* (1974). He has also edited a collection of Maori writing, *Into the World of Light* (1978). "His First Ball," reprinted from *Dear Miss Mansfield* (1989), recalls a similar story by a Pakeha New Zealander who spent most of her life in England, Katherine Mansfield.

His First Ball

J UST WHY IT was that he, Tuta Wharepapa, should receive 1
the invitation was a mystery to him. Indeed, when it
came, in an envelope bearing a very imposing crest, his
mother mistook it for something entirely different—notice of
a traffic misdemeanour, a summons perhaps, or even worse,
an overdue account. She fingered it gingerly, holding it as far
away from her body as possible—just in case a pair of hands
came out to grab her fortnightly cheque—and said, "Here,
Tuta. It must be a bill." She thrust it quickly at her son before
he could get away and, wriggling her fingers to get rid of the
taint, waited for him to open it.

"Hey—" Tuta said as he stared down at the card. His face 2
dropped such a long way that his mother—her name was

Coral—became alarmed. Visions of pleading in court on his behalf flashed through her mind. "Oh, Tuta, how bad is it?" she said as she prepared to defend her son against all-comers. But Tuta remained speechless and Coral had to grab the card from his hands. "What's this?" she asked. The card was edged with gold:

The Aide-de-Camp in Waiting
Is Desired By Their Excellencies

"Oh, Tuta, what have you done?" Coral said. But Tuta was still in a state of shock. Then, "Read on, Mum," he said.

To Invite Mr Tuta Wharepapa
To A Dance At Government House

Coral's voice drifted away into speechlessness like her son's. Then she compressed her lips and jabbed Tuta with an elbow. "I'm tired of your jokes," she said. "It's not my joke, Mum," Tuta responded. "I know you, Tuta," Coral continued. "True, Mum, honest. One of the boys must be having me on." Coral looked at Tuta, unconvinced. "Who'd want to have *you* at their flash party?" she asked. "Just wait till I get the joker who sent this," Tuta swore to himself. Then Coral began to laugh. "You? Go to Government House? You don't even know how to bow!" And she laughed and laughed so much at the idea that Tuta couldn't take it. "Where are you going, Your Highness?" Coral asked. "To find out who sent this," Tuta replied, waving the offending invitation in her face. "By the time I finish with him—or her—" because he suddenly realised Coral herself might have sent it—"they'll be laughing on the other side of their face." With that, he strode out of the kitchen. "Oh, Tuta?" he heard Coral call, all la-di-da, "If you ore gooing pahst Government Howse please convay may regahrds to—" and she burst out laughing again.

Tuta leapt on to his motorbike and, over the rest of the 3
day, roared around the city calling on his mates from the factory. "It wasn't me, Tuta," Crazy-Joe said as he sank a red ball in the billiard saloon, "but I tell you, man, you'll look

great in a suit." Nor was it Blackjack over at the garage, who said, "But listen, mate, when you go grab some of those Diplo number plates for me, ay?" And neither was it Des, who moonlighted as Desirée Dawn at the strip club, or Sheree, who worked part time at the pinball parlour. "You couldn't take a partner, could you?" Desirée Dawn breathed hopefully. "Nah, you wouldn't be able to fit on my bike," Tuta said—apart from which he didn't think a six-foot transvestite with a passion for pink boas and slit satin dresses would enjoy it all that much. By the end of the day Tuta was no wiser, and when he arrived at Bigfoot's house and found his mate waiting for him in a tiara, he knew that word was getting around. Then it came to him that perhaps the invitation was real after all. Gloria Simmons would know—she was the boss's secretary and knew some lords.

"Oh," Mrs. Simmons whispered reverently as Tuta handed her the crested envelope. She led Tuta into the sitting-room. "It looks real," she said as she held it to the light. Then she opened the envelope and, incredulous, asked, "*You* received this?" Tuta nodded. "You didn't just pick it up on the street," Mrs. Simmons continued, "and put your name on it?" Offended, Tuta shook his head, saying "You don't think I want to go, do you?" Mrs. Simmons pursed her lips and said, "Perhaps there's another Tuta Wharepapa, and you got his invitation in error." And Mrs. Simmons's teeth smiled and said, "In that case, let me ring Government House and let them know." With that, Mrs. Simmons went into another room, where Tuta heard her dialling. Then *her* voice went all la-di-da too as she trilled, "Ooo, Gahverment Howse? May ay speak to the Aide-de-Camp? Ooo, har do yoo do. So sorry to trouble you but ay am ringing to advayse you—" Tuta rolled his eyes—how come everybody he told about the invitation got infected by some kind of disease! Then he became acutely aware that Mrs. Simmons had stopped talking. He heard her gasp. He heard her say in her own lingo, "You mean to tell me that this is for real? That you people actually sent an invite to a—a—boy who packs batteries in a factory?" She put down the telephone and returned to the sitting-room. She was pale but calm as she said, "Tuta dear, difficult though this may be, can you remember the woman who came to look at the factory about two months ago?" Tuta knitted his eyebrows. "Yeah, I think so. That must have been when we opened the new extension." Mrs. Simmons closed her eyes. "The woman, Tuta. The woman." Tuta thought again. "Oh yeah, there *was* a lady, come to think of it, a horsey-looking lady who—" Mrs. Simmons interrupted him. "Tuta, dear, that lady was the wife of the Governor-General."

Dazed, Tuta said, "But she didn't say who she was." And   5
he listened as Mrs. Simmons explained that Mrs. Governor-General had been very impressed by the workers at the factory and that Tuta was being invited to represent them. "Of course you will have to go," Mrs. Simmons said. "One does not say 'No' to the Crown." Then Mrs. Simmons got up and telephoned Tuta's mother. "Coral? Gloria here. Listen, about Tuta, you and I should talk about what is required. What for? Why, when he goes to the ball of course! Now—" *Me? Go to a ball?* Tuta thought. *With all those flash people, all those flash ladies with their crowns and diamonds and emeralds? Not bloody likely—Bigfoot can go, he's already got a tiara, yeah. Not me. They'll have to drag me there. I'm not going. Not me. No fear. No WAY.* But he knew, when he saw the neighbours waiting for him at home that, of course, his mother had already flapped her mouth to everybody. "Oh yes," she was telling the neighbours when Tuta walked in, "it was delivered by special messenger. This dirty big black car came and a man, must have been a flunkey, knocked on the door and—" Then Coral saw Tuta and, "Oh Tuta," she cried, opening her arms to him as if she hadn't seen him for days.

After that, of course, there was no turning back. The boss   6
from the factory called to put the hard word on Tuta. Mrs. Simmons RSVPeed by telephone and—"Just in case, Tuta dear"—by letter and, once that was done, he had to go. The rest of his mates at the factory got into the act, also, cancelling the airline booking he made to get out of town and, from thereon in, followed him everywhere. "Giz a break, fellas,"

Tuta pleaded as he tried to get out, cajole or bribe himself out of the predicament. But Crazy-Joe only said, "Lissen, if you don't get there then I'm—" and he drew a finger across his throat, and Blackjack said, "Hey, man, I know a man who knows a man who can get us a Rolls for the night—" and Bigfoot just handed him the tiara. And boy, did Coral ever turn out to be the walking compendium of What To Do And How To Do It At A Ball. "Gloria says that we have to take you to a tailor so you can hire a suit. Not just any suit and none of your purple numbers either. A black *conservative* suit. And then we have to get you a bowtie and you have to wear black shoes—so I reckon a paint job on your brown ones will do. You've got a white shirt, thank goodness, but we'll have to get some new socks—calf length so that when you sit down people won't see your hairy legs. Now, what else? Oh yes, I've already made an appointment for you to go to have your hair cut, no buts, Tuta, and the boys are taking you there, so don't think you're going to wriggle out of it. By the time that dance comes around we'll have you decked out like the Prince of Wales—" which was just what Tuta was afraid of.

But that was only the beginning. Not only did his appearance have to be radically altered, but his manners had to be brushed up also—and Mrs. Simmons was the first to have a go. "Tuta dear," she said when he knocked on her door. "Do come in. Yes, take your boots off but on THE NIGHT, the shoes stay *on*. Please, come this way. No, Tuta, *after* me, just a few steps behind. Never barge, Tuta and don't shamble along. Be PROUD, Tuta, be HAUGHTY"—and she showed him how to put his nose in the air. Tuta followed her, his nose so high that he almost tripped, into the dining-room. "Voila!" she said. "Ay?" Tuta answered. Mrs. Simmons then realised that this was going to be very difficult. "I said, 'Ta ra!'" She had set the table with a beautiful cloth—and it appeared to be laid with thousands of knives, forks and spoons. "This is what it will be like at the ball," she explained. "Oh boy," Tuta said. "Now, because I'm a lady you must escort me to my seat," Mrs. Simmons said. "Huh? Can't you walk there yourself?" Tuta asked. "Just *do* it," Mrs. Simmons

responded dangerously, and *don't* push me all the way under
the table, Tuta, just to the edge will do—" and then, under
her breath "—Patience, Gloria dear, *patienza*." Once seated,
she motioned Tuta to a chair opposite her. "Gee, thanks," he
said. Mrs. Simmons paused, thoughtfully, and said, "Tuta
dear, when in doubt don't say *anything*. Just shut your
mouth." She shivered, but really, the boy would only understand common language, "—and keep it shut." Then she
smiled. "Now follow every action that I make." Exaggerating
the movements for Tuta's benefit, Mrs. Simmons said, "First,
take up the spoon. No, not that one, *that* one. That's for
your soup, that's for the second course, that's for the third
course, that's for the fourth—" Tuta looked helplessly at her.
"Can't I use the same knives and things all the time?" he
asked. "*Never*," Mrs. Simmons shivered. "Well, what's all
these courses for?" Tuta objected. "Why don't they just stick
all the kai on the table at once?" Mrs. Simmons deigned not
to answer. Instead she motioned to the glasses, saying, "Now
this is for white wine, this for red wine, this for champagne
and this for cognac." Tuta sighed, saying "No beer? Thought
as much." Refusing to hear him. Mrs. Simmons proceeded,
"You sip your wine just like you sip the soup. Like *so*," and
she showed him. "No, Tuta, not too fast. And leave the bowl
on the table, *don't* put it to your lips. No, *don't* slurp. Oh my
goodness. Very GOOD, Tuta! Now wipe your lips with the
napkin." Tuta looked puzzled. "Ay?" he asked. "The paper
napkin on your lap." Mrs. Simmons said. "This hanky thing?"
Tuta responded. "Why, Tuta!" Mrs. Simmons's teeth said,
"How clever of you to work that out. Shall we proceed to
the second course? Good!" Mrs. Simmons felt quite sure that
Professor Higgins didn't have it *this* bad.

　　Then, of course, there was the matter of learning how to
dance—not hot rock but slow *slow* dancing, holding a girl,
"You know," Mrs. Simmons said, "*together*," adding, "and
young ladies at the ball are never allowed to decline." So Tuta
made a date with Desirée Dawn after hours at the club.
Desirée was just overwhelmed to be asked for advice and told
her friends Alexis Dynamite and Chantelle Derrier to help

her. "Lissun, honey," Desirée said as she cracked her gum. "No matter what the dance is, there's always a basic rhythm." Chantelle giggled and said, "Yeah, very basic." Ignoring her, Desirée hauled Tuta on to the floor, did a few jeté's and, once she had limbered up, said, "Now *you* lead," and "Oo, honey, I didn't know you were so masterful." Alexis fluttered her false eyelashes and, "You two don't need music at *all*," she whispered. Nevertheless, Alexis ran the tape and the music boomed across the club floor. "This isn't ball music," Tuta said as he heard the raunch scream out of the saxes. "How do *you* know?" Chantelle responded. And Tuta had the feeling that he wasn't going to learn how to dance in any way except improperly. "Lissun," Desirée said, "Alexis and I will show you. Move your butt over here, Lexie. Now, Tuta honey, just watch. Can ya hear the rhythum? Well you go *boom* and a *boom* and a *boom boom boom*." And Alexis screamed and yelled, "Desirée, he wants to dance with the girl, not *make* her in the middle of the floor." And Chantelle only made matters worse by laughing, "Yeah, you stupid slut, you want him to end up in prison like you?" At which Desirée gasped, walked over to Chantelle, peeled off both Chantelle's false eyelashes, said, "Can you see better? Good," and lammed her one in the mouth. As he exited, Tuta knew he would have better luck with Sheree at the pinball parlour— she used to be good at roller skating and could even do the splits in mid-air.

So it went on. The fitting at the tailor's was duly accomplished ("Hmmmmnnnn," the tailor said as he measured Tuta up. "Your shoulders are too wide, your hips too large, you have shorter legs than you should have but— Hmmmmnnnn"), his hair was trimmed to within an inch of propriety, and he painted his brown shoes black. His lessons continued with Mrs. Simmons, Tuta's mother, the workers from the factory—even the boss—all pitching in to assist Tuta in the etiquette required. For instance: "If you're talking you ask about the weather. This is called polite conversation. You say "Isn't it lovely?" to everything, even if it isn't. You always say "Yes" if you're offered something, even if you don't want it. The man with the medals is *not* the waiter. He is His Excellency. The lady who looks like a horse is not in drag and you should *not* ask if her tiara fell off the same truck as Bigfoot's."

Then, suddenly it was time for Tuta to go to the ball. "Yes, 10 Mum," he said to Coral as she fussed around him with a clothes brush, "I've got a hanky, I've brushed my teeth three times already, the invite is in my pocket—" And when Tuta stepped out the door the whole world was there—the boss, Mrs. Simmons, Crazy-Joe, Blackjack, Bigfoot and others from the factory, Desirée Dawn and the neighbours. "Don't let us down," the boss said. "Not too much food on the fork," Mrs. Simmons instructed. "The third boom is the one that does it," Desirée Dawn called. "Don't forget the Diplo plates," Blackjack whispered. "And don't drink too much of the beer," Coral said. Then, there was the car, a Jaguar festooned with white ribbons and two small dolls on the bonnet. "It's a ball I'm off to," Tuta said sarcastically, "not a wedding." Blackjack shrugged his shoulders. "Best I could do, mate, and this beauty was just sitting there outside the church and—" He got in and started the motor. Tuta sat in the back and, suddenly, Bigfoot and Crazy-Joe were in either side. "The boss's orders," they said. "We deliver you to the door or else—" Outside, Tuta saw the boss draw a line across their necks. The car drew away and as it did so, Mrs. Simmons gave a small scream. "Oh my goodness, I forgot to tell Tuta that if Nature calls he should not use the bushes," she said.

Looking back, Tuta never quite understood how he ever 11 survived that journey. At one point a police car drew level on the motorway, but when they looked over at the Jaguar and saw Tuta he could just imagine their disbelief, Nah. Couldn't possibly . . . Nah. His head was whirling with all the etiquette he had learnt and all the instructions he had to remember. He trembled, squirmed, palpitated and sweated all over the seat. Then he was there, and Blackjack was showing the invitation, and the officer at the gate was looking doubtfully at the wedding decorations, and then "Proceed ahead, sir," the officer said. *What a long drive*, Tuta thought. *What a big*

*palace. And look at all those flash people. And they're all going
in.* "Well, mate," Blackjack said, "Good luck. Look for us in
the car park." And Crazy-Joe said, "Hey, give the missus a
whirl for me, ay?" and with that, and a squeal of tires (Blackjack was always such a show-off), they were gone.
He was alone. Him. Tuta Wharepapa. Standing there. At   12
the entrance way. Inside he heard music and the laughter of
the guests. Then someone grabbed his arm and said, "Come
along!" and before he knew it he was inside and being pro-
pelled along a long hallway. And the young woman who had
grabbed him was suddenly pulled away by her companion,
and Tuta was alone again. *Oh boy,* he thought. *Look at this
red carpet.* He felt quite sure that the paint was running off
his shoes and that there were great big black footmarks all
the way to where he was now standing. Then a voice
BOOMED ahead, and Tuta saw that there was a line of
people in front and they were handing their invitations in to
the bouncer. Tuta joined them. The bouncer was very old
and very dignified—he looked, though, as if he should have
been retired from the job years ago. *Nah,* Tuta thought. *He
couldn't be a bouncer. Must be a toff.* The toff looked Tuta up
and down and thrust out his white-gloved hand. "I got an
invitation," Tuta said. "True. I got one." The toff read the
card and his eyebrows arched. "Your name?" he BOOMED.
"Tuta." Couldn't he read? Then the toff turned away in the
direction of a huge ballroom that stretched right to the end
of the world. The room seemed to be hung with hundreds
of chandeliers and *thousands* of people were either dancing
or standing around the perimeter. There were steps leading
down to the ballroom and, at the bottom, was a man wearing
medals and a woman whose tiara wasn't as sparkly as Bigfoot's—*them.* And Tuta felt *sure,* when the Major-Domo—
for that was who the toff was—stepped forward and opened
his mouth to announce him, that *everybody* must have heard
him BOOM—
"Your Excellencies, Mr. Tutae Tockypocka."   13
Tuta looked for a hole to disappear into. He tried to   14
backpedal down the hallway but there were people behind

him. "No, you got it wrong," he said between clenched teeth to the Major-Domo. "Tutae's a rude word." But the Major-Domo simply sniffed, handed back the invitation, and motioned Tuta down the stairs. Had *they* heard? In trembling anticipation Tuta approached the Governor-General. "Mr. Horrynotta?" the Governor-General smiled. "Splendid that you were able to come along. Dear? Here's Mr. Tutae." And in front of him was Mrs. Governor-General. "Mr. Forrimoppa, how kind of you to come. May I call you Tutae? Please let me introduce you to Lord Wells." And Lord Wells, too. "Mr. Mopperuppa, quite a mouthful, what. Not so with Tutae, what?" *You don't know the half of it,* Tuta thought gloomily. And then Mrs. Governor-General just *had* to, didn't she, giggle and pronounce to all and sundry, "Everybody, you must meet Mr. Tutae." And that's who Tuta became all that evening. "Have you met Mr. Tutae yet? No? Mr. Tutae, this is Mr.—" And Tuta would either shake hands or do a stiff little bow and look around for that hole in the floor. He once made an attempt to explain what "tutae" was but heard Mrs. Simmons's voice: "If in doubt, Tuta, *don't.*" So instead he would draw attention away from that word by asking about the weather. "Do you think it will rain?" he would ask. "Oh, not inside, Mr. Tutae!"—and the word got around that Mr. Tutae was such a wit, so funny, so quaint, that he soon found himself exactly where he didn't want to be—at the centre of attention. In desperation, he asked every woman to dance. "Why, certainly, Mr. Tutae!" they said, because ladies never said no. So he danced with them all—a fat lady, a slim lady, a lady whose bones cracked all the time—and, because he was nervous, he went *boom* at every third step, and *that* word got around too. And as the Governor-General waltzed past he shouted, "Well done, Tutae, jolly good show."

No matter what he tried to do Tuta could never get away   15 from being at the centre of the crowd or at the centre of attention. Instead of being gratified, however, Tuta became more embarrassed. Everybody seemed to laugh at his every word, even when it wasn't funny, or to accept his way of dancing because it was so *daring*. It seemed as if he could get away with anything. At the same time, Tuta suddenly realised that he was the only Maori there and that perhaps people were mocking him. He wasn't a real person to them, but rather an Entertainment. Even when buffet dinner was served, the crowd still seemed to mock him, pressing in upon him with "Have some hors d'oeuvres, Mr. Tutae. Some *escalope* of veal, perhaps? You must try the pâté de foie gras! A slice of *jambon?* What about some langouste? Oh, the raspberry gâteau is just divine!" It was as if the crowd knew very well his ignorance of such delicacies and, by referring to them, was putting him down. In desperation Tuta tried some caviar. "Oh, Mr. Tutae, we can see that you just love caviar!" Tuta gave a quiet, almost dangerous, smile. "Yes," he said. "I think it's just divine."

So it went on. But then, just after the buffet, a Very Important Person arrived and, relieved, Tuta found himself deserted. Interested, he watched as the one who had just arrived became the centre of attention. "It always happens this way," a voice said behind Tuta. "I wouldn't worry about it." Startled, Tuta turned around and saw a huge fern. "Before you," the fern continued, "it was me." Then Tuta saw that a young woman was sitting behind the fern. "I'm not worried," he said to her, "I'm glad." The woman sniffed and said, "You certainly looked as if you were enjoying it." Tuta parted the fronds to get a good look at the woman's face—it was a pleasant face, one which could be pretty if it didn't frown so much. "Shift over," Tuta said. "I'm coming to join you." He sidled around the plant and sat beside her. "My name is—" he began. "Yes, I know," the woman said quickly, "Mr. Tutae." Tuta shook his head vigorously, " *No*, not Tutae. Tuta." The woman looked at him curiously and, "Is there a difference?" she asked. "You better believe it," Tuta said. "Oh—" the woman sniffed. "I'm Joyce."

The music started to play again. Joyce squinted her eyes and Tuta sighed, "Why don't you put on your glasses?" Joyce squealed, "How did you know?" before popping them on and parting the fronds. "I'm a sociology student," Joyce muttered. "Don't you think people's behaviour is just amazing? I mean ay-*may*zing?" Tuta shrugged his shoulders and wondered if Joyce was looking at something he couldn't see. "I mean," Joyce continued, "look at them out there, just *look* at them. This could be India under the Raj. All this British Imperial graciousness and yet the carpet is being pulled from right beneath their feet." Puzzled, Tuta tried to see the ball through Joyce's eyes, but failed. "Ah well," Joyce sighed. Then she put her hand out to Tuta so that he could shake it, saying "Goodbye, Mr. Tuta." Tuta looked at her and, "Are you going?" he asked. "Oh no," Joyce said, "I'm staying here until everybody leaves. But *you* must go out and reclaim attention." Tuta laughed. "That new guy's welcome," he said. "But don't you want to fulfil their expectations?" Joyce asked. Tuta paused, and "If that means what I think it means, no," he said. "Good," Joyce responded, "You are perfectly capable of beating them at their own game. Good luck."

Then, curious, Tuta asked, "What did you mean when you said that before me it had been *you*?" Joyce shifted uneasily, took off her glasses and said, "Well, I'm not a Maori, but I thought it would have been obvious—" *Oh,* Tuta thought, *she's a plain Jane and people have been making fun of her.* "But that doesn't matter to me," Tuta said gallantly. "Really?" Joyce asked. "I'll prove it," Tuta said. "How about having the next dance." Joyce gasped, "Are you *sure*?" Taken aback, Tuta said, "Of course, I'm sure." And Joyce said, "But are you *sure* you're sure!" To show her, Tuta stood up and took her hand. Joyce sighed and shook her head. "Well, don't say I didn't warn you." Then she stood up . . . and up . . . and UP. [18]

"Oh," Tuta said as he parted the fronds to look up at Joyce's face. She must have been six feet six at least. He and Joyce regarded each other miserably. Joyce bit her lip. *Well you asked for it,* Tuta thought. "Come on," he said, "let's have a good time." He reached up, grabbed her waist, put his face against her chest, and they waltzed into the middle of the floor. There, Tuta stood as high on his toes as possible. *Oh, why did I come?* he thought. Then the music ended and [19] he took Joyce back to the fern. "I'm sorry I'm such a bad dancer," she apologised. "I always took the man's part at school." Tuta smiled at her. "That's no sweat. Well—" And he was just about to leave her when he suddenly realised that after all he and Joyce were both outsiders really. And it came to him that, bloody hell, if you could not join them—as if he would really want to do *that*—then, yes, he could beat them if he wanted to. Not by giving in to them, but by being strong enough to stand up to them. Dance, perhaps, but using his own steps. Listen, also, not to the music of the band but to the music in his head. He owed it, after all, to generous but silly wonderful mixed-up Mum, Mrs. Simmons, Desirée Dawn, and the boys—Crazy-Joe, Blackjack and Bigfoot— who were out *there* but wanting to know enough to get *in*. But they needed to come in on their own terms—that's what they would have to learn—as the real people they were and not as carbon copies of the people already on the inside. Once they learnt that, *oh, world, watch out, for your walls will come down in a flash, like Jericho.*

"Look," Tuta said, "how about another dance!" Joyce   20 looked at him in disbelief. "You're a sucker for punishment, aren't you!" she muttered. "Why?" Tuta bowed, mockingly. "Well, for one thing, it would be just divine." At that, Joyce let out a peal of laughter. She stood up again. "Thank you," Joyce whispered. Then, "You know, this is my first ball." And Tuta smiled and "It's *my* first ball too," he said. "From now on, balls like these will never be the same again." He took her hand and the band began to wail a sweet but *oh-so-mean* saxophone solo as he led her on to the floor.

COMMENT ON
"HIS FIRST BALL"

"His First Ball" is a vivid and humorous comparison of cross-cultural misunderstanding. Tuta Wharepapa, a Maori factory worker, is invited to a formal ball thrown by the British government of New Zealand. With coaching from his friends, Tuta polishes his manners and dancing, trying to transform himself into something he is not—a British gentleman. When he arrives at the ball, the British treat him as entertainment rather than as a guest. At the end of this colonial *Pygmalion,* Tuta realizes that he must be his own person—not the creation of the dominant culture.

Comparison and Contrast as a Writing Strategy

1. Select a place in your childhood neighborhood—perhaps a garden, a playground, or a movie theater. Then, in an essay addressed to your writing class, write a short comparison of the way the place used to be and the way it is now. Consider the example of Mark Twain's "Two Views of the River" as you compare your childhood and adult visions. Consider also what you have learned about the place or about yourself by making the comparison. That lesson should help control your decisions about purpose and audience.

2. Select two people who embody similar characteristics—athletes, musicians, movie stars, family members. Then, like Scott Russell Sanders, compare their strengths and weaknesses. Include information on how they might see each other. Cite biographical information that accounts for their similarities and differences.

3. Conduct some research on the conversational patterns in your home (or dormitory) and in your classroom. Keep track of who talks, what they talk about, and how they use conversation—for example, to make friends, to report information, to win approval. Keep track of who doesn't talk and in what situations they are likely to stay silent. Then write an essay in which you compare the patterns of home and school conversation.

4. In "A Tale of Two Divorces," Anne Roiphe contrasts two women's reaction to the same situation. Select a subject you know well—a family celebration—and then compare your version with the way it is represented on television.

5. Write an essay comparing the way two magazines or newspapers cover the same story. Or like Laura Bohannan, compare the way a story might be told in one culture with the way it might be told in another. For example, how would you compare the way the American media and the African media might tell the story of America's last presidential election?

6. Compare and contrast arguments on both sides of a controversial issue such as welfare reform or gun control. Such issues produce controversy because there are legitimate arguments on each side. They also produce controversy because people can simplify them in slogans (Reading is good; television is bad). Select two slogans that present the opposing sides of the controversy you are writing about. Compare and contrast the assumptions, evidence, and logic of both slogans. Like Deborah Tannen, avoid choosing sides. Maintain a neutral tone as you assess the motives, methods, and reasons for each argument.

DIVISION
AND
CLASSIFICATION

Division and **classification** are mental processes that often work together. When you *divide,* you separate something (a college, a city) into sections (departments, neighborhoods). When you *classify,* you place examples of something (restaurants, jobs) into categories or classes (restaurants: moderately expensive, very expensive; jobs: unskilled, semiskilled, and skilled).

When you divide, you move downward from a concept to the subunits of that concept. When you classify, you move upward from specific examples to classes or categories that share a common characteristic. For example, you could *divide* a television news program into subunits such as news, features, editorials, sports, and weather. And you could *classify* some element of that program—such as the editorial commentator on the six o'clock news—according to his or her style, knowledge, and trustworthiness. You can use either division or classification singly, depending on your purpose, but most of the time you will probably use them together when you are writing a classification essay. First you might identify the subunits in a college sports program—football, basketball, hockey, volleyball, tennis; then you could classify them according to their budgets—most money budgeted for football, the least budgeted for volleyball.

PURPOSE

When you write a classification essay, your chief purpose is to *explain*. You might want to explain an established method for organizing information, such as the Library of Congress system, or a new plan for arranging data such as the Internal Revenue Service's latest schedule for itemizing tax deductions. On one level, your purpose in such an essay is simply to show how the system works. At a deeper level, your purpose is to define, analyze, and justify the organizing principle that underlies the system.

You can also write a classification essay to *entertain* or to *persuade*. If you classify to entertain, you have an opportunity to be clever and witty. If you classify to persuade, you have a chance to be cogent and forceful. If you want to entertain, you might concoct an elaborate scheme for classifying fools, pointing out the distinguishing features of each category and giving particularly striking examples of each type. But if you want to persuade, you could explain how some new or controversial plan, such as the metric system or congressional redistricting, is organized, pointing out how the schemes use new principles to identify and organize information. Again, although you may give your readers a great deal of information in such an essay, your main purpose is to persuade them that the new plan is better than the old one.

AUDIENCE

As with any writing assignment, when you write a classification essay, you need to think carefully about what your readers already know and what they need to get from your writing. If you're writing on a new topic (social patterns in a primitive society) or if you're explaining a specialized system of classification (the botanist's procedure for identifying plants), your readers need precise definitions and plenty of illustrations for each subcategory. If your readers already know about your subject and the system it uses for classification (the movies' G, PG, PG–13, R, and NC–17 rating codes), then you don't need to give them an extensive demonstration. In that kind of writing situation, you might want to sketch the system briefly to refresh your readers' memories but then move on, using examples of specific movies to analyze whether the system really works.

You also need to think about how your readers might use the classification system that you explain in your essay. If you're classifying rock musicians, your readers are probably going to regard the system you create as something self-enclosed—interesting and amusing, perhaps something to quibble about, but not something they're likely to use in their everyday lives. On the other hand, if you write an essay classifying stereo equipment, your readers may want to use your system when they shop. For the first audience, you can use an informal approach to classification, dividing your subject into interesting subcategories and illustrating them with vivid examples. For the other audience, you need to be careful and strict in your approach, making sure you divide your topic into all its possible classes and illustrating each class with concrete examples.

STRATEGIES

When you write a classification essay, your basic strategy for organization should be to *divide your subject* into major categories that exhibit a common trait, then subdivide those categories into smaller units. Next, *arrange your categories* into a sequence that shows a logical or a dramatic progression. Finally, *define each of your categories*. First, show how each category is different from the others; then discuss its most vivid examples.

To make this strategy succeed, you must be sure that your classification system is *consistent, complete, emphatic,* and *significant*. Here is a method for achieving this goal. First, when you divide your subject into categories, *apply the same principle of selection to each class*. You may find this hard to do if you're trying to explain a system that someone else has already established but that is actually inconsistent. You have undoubtedly discovered that record stores use overlapping and inconsistent categories. Linda Ronstadt albums, for example, may be found in sections labeled *country, rock, pop, standards,* and *female vocal*. You can avoid such tangles if you create and control your own classification system.

For instance, in "The Extendable Fork" Calvin Trillin classifies eaters by how they eat off other people's plates. James H. Austin follows a similar strategy when he classifies "four kinds of chance." By contrast, the other three writers in this section explain existing systems of classification. In "Shades of Black" Mary Mebane classifies the arbitrary and unfair assessment of students by color and class. In "Modern Friendships," Phillip Lopate classifies friendships according to age. And in "Five and a Half Utopias," Steven Weinberg classifies according to nonsocialist styles.

After you have divided your subject into separate and consistent categories, *make sure your division is complete*. The simplest kind of division separates a subject into two categories: A and Not-A (for example, conformists and nonconformists). This kind of division, however, is rarely encouraged. It allows you to tell your readers about category A (conformists), but you won't tell them much about Not-A (nonconformists). For this reason, you should try to "exhaust" your subject by finding at least three separate categories and by acknowledging any examples that don't fit into the system. When an author writes a formal classification essay, like Phillip Lopate in this section, he or she tries to be definitive—to include everything significant. Even when an author is writing less formal classification essays, such as Trillin's, he or she tries to set up a reasonably complete system. Once you have completed your process of division, *arrange your categories and examples in an emphatic order.* Lopate arranges his categories of friendship from childhood to adulthood. Weinberg arranges his utopias according to various models, with the most controversial—*Green* and *Technological*—coming last. Austin arranges his classification of chance from blind luck to personal sensibility. Mebane arranges her categories into increasingly subtle codes of class and color. The authors of these essays reveal the principal purpose underlying their classification schemes: to show variety in similarity, to point out how concepts change, and to challenge the arbitrariness of an established system.

Finally, *you need to show the significance of your system of classification.* The strength of the classification process is that you can use it to analyze a subject in any number of ways. Its weakness is that you can use it to subdivide a subject into all kinds of trivial or pointless categories. You can classify people by their educational backgrounds, their work experience, or their significant achievements. You can also classify them by their shoe size, the kind of socks they wear, or their tastes in ice cream. Notice that when Mary Mebane explains her classification system, she questions the social and psychological impact it has on self-esteem. Even a writer who chooses a subject that doesn't seem particularly significant—such as Calvin Trillin's eaters—must convince readers that his or her *system* counts in some way, if only because it lays out and demonstrates, consistently and completely, the significant subdivisions of the subject.

USING DIVISION AND CLASSIFICATION IN PARAGRAPHS

Here are two division-and-classification paragraphs. The first is written by a professional writer and is followed by an analysis. The second is written by a student writer and is followed by questions.

WENDELL BERRY
Conservation Is Good Work

Divides conservation into three categories:
1. preservation of wild or "scenic"
2. conservation of natural resources
3. limit, stop, or remedy abuses

There are, as nearly as I can make out, three kinds of conservation currently operating. The first is the preservation of places that are grandly wild or "scenic" or in some other way spectacular. The second is what is called "conservation of natural resources"—That is, of the things of nature that we intend to use: soil, water, timber, and minerals. The third is what you might call industrial troubleshooting: the attempt to limit or stop or remedy the most flagrant abuses of the industrial system. All three kinds of conservation are inadequate, both separately and together.

Concludes that all three are inadequate.

Comment In this paragraph, Wendell Berry points out the "three kinds of conservation currently operating" in our culture. As his last sentence suggests, Berry's purpose for establishing these categories is to demonstrate—in subsequent paragraphs—why they are "inadequate, both separately and together."

GARETH TUCKER
Gentlemen! Start Your Engines

On a typical weekend, most couch potatoes can channel-surf past about a dozen car races. As they watch brightly colored machines circling the track again and again, like images on some manic video game, they may conclude that a race is a race is a race. Actually automobile racing is divided into many subtle subcategories. For example, the three most popular forms can be identified by the image of the car and driver. Stock cars are perceived as souped-up versions of "stock" cars driven by "good ole boys" who talk as if they have just outrun the local police. Indy cars are perceived as masterpieces of engineering driven by "test pilots" who speak the techno-babble of rocket scientists. Formula One cars are almost as technologically advanced as Indy cars, but they still retain the image of the European "Grand Prix" car—the sports car driven by some count who talks as if he's just finished a jolly little tour through the countryside.

1. What principle does Tucker use to establish his three categories?
2. How does his characterization of the race car driver help clarify each category?

DIVISION AND CLASSIFICATION

Points to Remember

1. Determine whether you want to (a) explain an existing system of classification or (b) create your own system.
2. Divide your subject into smaller categories by applying the same principle of selection to each category.
3. Make sure that your division is complete by establishing separate and consistent types of categories.
4. Arrange your categories (and the examples you use to illustrate each category) in a logical and emphatic sequence.
5. Demonstrate the significance of your system by calling your readers' attention to its significance.

Calvin Trillin was born in Kansas City, Missouri, in 1935 and was educated at Yale University. He began his career by working as a reporter for *Time* magazine, then as a columnist for *The New Yorker.* In recent years, he has written a national newspaper column and staged a one-man show off-Broadway. His writing includes two novels, *Runestruck* (1977) and *Floater* (1980); several collections of reporting, *U.S. Journal* (1971), *Killings* (1982), and *American Stories* (1991); a best-selling memoir, *Remembering Denny* (1993); and numerous books of humor, such as *Family Man* (1998). In "The Extendable Fork," reprinted from his syndicated column, Trillin classifies eaters by how they eat off other people's plates.

The Extendable Fork

I N OUR HOUSE, news that the extendable fork had been invented was greeted with varying degrees of enthusiasm. I think it's fair to say that I was the most enthusiastic of all. I eat off of other people's plates. My wife was mildly enthusiastic. She figures that if I use an extendable fork I'm less likely to come away from the table with gravy on my cuff.

People who eat off of other people's plates can be categorized in four types—The Finisher, The Waif, The Researcher and The Simple Thief. I might as well admit right here at the beginning that I am all four.

The Finisher demonstrates concern that food may be left uneaten even though the starving children your mother told you about are still hungry. Once the pace of eating begins to slacken off a bit, he reaches across to spear a roast potato off of someone's plate a nanosecond after saying, "If you're not planning to finish these . . ."

The long-reach eater I think of as The Waif often doesn't   4 order much himself at a restaurant, claiming that he's not terribly hungry or that he's trying to lose weight. Then, he gazes at his dinner companions' plates, like a hungry urchin who has his nose pressed up against the window of a restaurant where enormously fat rich people are slurping oysters and shoveling down mounds of boeuf bourguignon. Occasionally, he murmurs something like, "That looks delicious." Answering "Actually, it's not all that good" does not affect

---

People who eat off other people's plates come in four categories: The Finisher, The Waif, The Researcher, and The Simple Thief.

---

him—although it may slow down The Researcher, who, as he extends his fork usually says something like, "I'm curious how they do these fried onions."

The Simple Thief simply waits for his dining companions   5 to glance away, then confidently grabs what he wants. If he's desperate, he may actually take measures to distract them, saying something like, "Is it my imagination, or could that be Michael Jackson and Lisa Marie Presley at the table over by the door?"

That sort of subterfuge is not necessary, by the way, if the   6 plate I have singled out as a target is my wife's. She does not object to my sampling—a reflection, I've always thought, of her generous heart. In fact, I have said in the past that if a young groom on his honeymoon reaches over for the first time to sample his bride's fettuccine only to be told "Don't you like what you're having?" or "There really isn't that much of this," he knows he's in for a long haul.

Actually, my wife might be called a Finisher herself. If   7 we're having fried chicken, she will stare at what's on my plate after I have indeed finished. "Look at all the chicken you left," she'll say. Or "There's a ton of meat still on that chicken."

Oddly enough, this is precisely the sort of thing that I   8
heard from my mother, who was also fond of saying that I didn't "do a good job" on the chicken. The way my wife eats chicken is to eat every speck of meat off the bones, so that the chicken looks as if it had been staked out on an anthill by a tribe of crazed chicken torturers. She treats a lobster the same way.

I eat more the way a shark eats—tearing off whatever   9
seems exposed and easy to get at. I have suggested, in fact, that in fried-chicken or lobster restaurants we could economize by getting only one order, which I could start and my wife could finish.

My wife's approach to finishing does not, of course, re-   10
quire an extendable fork, but I intend to be an early customer myself. According to an item in the *New York Times,* the fork is nearly two feet long when fully opened. It's being marketed under the name of Alan's X-Tenda Fork.

I might have chosen another name, but this one is,   11
I'll admit, evocative. For me, it conjures up visions of a Limbaugh-sized man named Alan sitting in a restaurant with friends and family. He seems to be engaging in normal conversation, but his tiny eyes dart from plate to plate; occasionally, with a fork as quick as the strike of an adder, he helps with the finishing.

In fact, I can imagine Alan inventing other needed imple-   12
ments—a sort of vacuum tube, for instance, that can suck up french fries from three feet away. I can see him improving on Alan's X-Tenda Fork. He might install a tiny tape recorder in it, so when you pulled it out to its full length and moved it quickly across the table a voice said, "If you're not planning to finish these . . ."

For Study and Discussion

QUESTIONS FOR RESPONSE

1. How do you respond when someone eats off your plate?
2. What explanations do you offer when you want to sample something from someone else's plate?

QUESTIONS ABOUT PURPOSE

1. How does Trillin use the news of the invention of the "extendable fork" to justify his classification of eaters?
2. What purpose does Trillin accomplish by admitting that he fits into all four categories?

QUESTIONS ABOUT AUDIENCE

1. What assumptions does Trillin make about the eating habits of his readers?
2. How do his comments about his wife's and mother's behavior clarify his attitude toward his readers?

QUESTIONS ABOUT STRATEGIES

1. What principle does Trillin use to divide and identify his four types of eaters?
2. How does he use dialogue to illustrate the strategies of each eater?

QUESTIONS FOR DISCUSSION

1. What do books of etiquette say about the practice of eating from another's plate?
2. How does the concept of *finishing* fit into our cultural attitudes toward efficiency and economy?

JAMES H. AUSTIN

James H. Austin was born in 1925 in Cleveland, Ohio, and educated at Brown University and Harvard University Medical School. After an internship at Boston City Hospital and a residency at the Neurological Institute of New York, Austin established a private practice in neurology, first in Protland, Oregon, and then in Denver, Colorado. He currently serves as professor and head of the department of neurology at the University of Colorado Medical School. His major publication, *Chase, Chance, and Creativity: The Lucky Art of Novelty* (1978), addresses the issue of how "chance and creativity interact in biomedical research." His most recent book is *Zen and the Brain: Toward an Understanding of Meditation and Consciousness* (1999). In this essay, published originally in *Saturday Review*, Austin distinguishes four kinds of chance by the way humans react to their environment.

Four Kinds of Chance

WHAT IS CHANCE? Dictionaries define it as something fortuitous that happens unpredictably without discernible human intention. Chance is unintentional and capricious, but we needn't conclude that chance is immune from human intervention. Indeed, chance plays several distinct roles when humans react creatively with one another and with their environment.

We can readily distinguish four varieties of chance if we consider that they each involve a different kind of motor activity and a special kind of sensory receptivity. The varieties of chance also involve distinctive personality traits and differ in the way one particular individual influences them.

Chance I is the pure blind luck that comes with no effort 3
on your part. If, for example, you are sitting at a bridge table
of four, it's "in the cards" for you to receive a hand of all 13
spades, but it will come up only once in every 6.3 trillion
deals. You will ultimately draw this lucky hand—with no
intervention on your part—but it does involve a longer wait
than most of us have time for.

Chance II evokes the kind of luck Charles Kettering had 4
in mind when he said: "Keep on going and the chances are
you will stumble on something, perhaps when you are least

The term serendipity *describes the facility
for encountering unexpected good luck as
the result of accident, general exploratory
behavior, or sagacity.*

---

expecting it. I have never heard of anyone stumbling on
something sitting down."

In the sense referred to here, Chance II is not passive, but 5
springs from an energetic, generalized motor activity. A certain basal level of action "stirs up the pot," brings in random
ideas that will collide and stick together in fresh combinations, lets chance operate. When someone, *anyone*, does
swing into motion and keeps on going, he will increase the
number of collisions between events. When a few events are
linked together, they can then be exploited to have a fortuitous outcome, but many others, of course, cannot. Kettering
was right. Press on. Something will turn up. We may term
this the Kettering Principle.

In the two previous examples, a unique role of the indi- 6
vidual person was either lacking or minimal. Accordingly, as
we move on to Chance III, we see blind luck, but in
camouflage. Chance presents the clue, the opportunity exists,
but it would be missed except by that one person uniquely
equipped to observe it, visualize it conceptually, and fully

grasp its significance. Chance III involves a special receptivity and discernment unique to the recipient. Louis Pasteur characterized it for all time when he said: "Chance favors only the prepared mind."

Pasteur himself had it in full measure. But the classic example of his principle occurred in 1928, when Alexander Fleming's mind instantly fused at least five elements into a conceptually unified nexus. His mental sequences went something like this: (1) I see that a mold has fallen by accident into my culture dish; (2) the staphylococcal colonies residing near it failed to grow; (3) the mold must have secreted something that killed the bacteria; (4) I recall a similar experience once before; (5) if I could separate this new "something" from the mold, it could be used to kill staphylococci that cause human infections.   7

Actually, Fleming's mind was exceptionally well prepared for the penicillin mold. Six years earlier, while he was suffering from a cold, his own nasal drippings had found their way into a culture dish, for reasons not made entirely clear. He noted that nearby bacteria were killed, and astutely followed up the lead. His observations led him to discover a bactericidal enzyme present in nasal mucus and tears, called lysozyme. Lysozyme proved too weak to be of medical use, but imagine how receptive Fleming's mind was to the penicillin mold when it later happened on the scene!   8

One word evokes the quality of the operations involved in the first three kinds of chance. It is *serendipity*. The term describes the facility for encountering unexpected good luck, as the result of: accident (Chance I), general exploratory behavior (Chance II), or sagacity (Chance III). The word itself was coined by the Englishman-of-letters Horace Walpole, in 1754. He used it with reference to the legendary tales of the Three Princes of Serendip (Ceylon), who quite unexpectedly encountered many instances of good fortune on their travels. In today's parlance, we have usually watered down *serendipity* to mean the good luck that comes solely by accident. We think of it as a result, not an ability. We have tended to lose sight of the element of sagacity, by which term   9

Walpole wished to emphasize that some distinctive personal receptivity is involved.

There remains a fourth element in good luck, an unintentional but subtle personal prompting of it. The English Prime Minister Benjamin Disraeli summed up the principle underlying Chance IV when he noted that "we make our fortunes and we call them fate." Disraeli, a politician of considerable practical experience, appreciated that we each shape our own destiny, at least to some degree. One might restate the principle as follows: *Chance favors the individualized action.*

In Chance IV the kind of luck is peculiar to one person, and like a personal hobby, it takes on a distinctive individual flavor. This form of chance is one-man-made, and it is as personal as a signature. . . . Chance IV has an elusive, almost miragelike, quality. Like a mirage, it is difficult to get a firm grip on, for it tends to recede as we pursue it and advance as we step back. But we still accept a mirage when we see it, because we vaguely understand the basis for the phenomenon. A strongly heated layer of air, less dense than usual, lies next to the earth, and it bends the light rays as they pass through. The resulting image may be magnified as if by a telescopic lens in the atmosphere, and real objects, ordinarily hidden far out of sight over the horizon, are brought forward and revealed to the eye. What happens in a mirage then, and in this form of chance, not only appears farfetched but indeed is farfetched.

About a century ago, a striking example of Chance IV took place in the Spanish cave of Altamira.* There, one day in 1879, Don Marcelino de Sautuola was engaged in his hobby of archaeology, searching Altamira for bones and stones. With him was his daughter, Maria, who had asked him if she could come along to the cave that day. The indulgent father had said she could. Naturally enough, he first looked where he had always found heavy objects before, on the *floor* of the cave. But Maria, unhampered by any such preconceptions,

*The cave had first been discovered some years before by an enterprising hunting dog in search of game. Curiously, in 1932 the French cave of Lascaux was discovered by still another dog.

looked not only at the floor but also all around the cave with the open-eyed wonder of a child! She looked up, exclaimed, and then he looked up, to see incredible works of art on the cave ceiling! The magnificent colored bison and other animals they saw at Altamira, painted more than 15,000 years ago, might lead one to call it "the Sistine Chapel of Prehistory." Passionately pursuing his interest in archaeology, de Sautuola, to his surprise, discovered man's first paintings. In quest of science, he happened upon Art.

Yes, a dog did "discover" the cave, and the initial receptivity was his daughter's, but the pivotal reason for the cave paintings' discovery hinged on a long sequence of prior events originating in de Sautuola himself. For when we dig into the background of this amateur excavator, we find he was an exceptional person. Few Spaniards were out probing into caves 100 years ago. The fact that he—not someone else—decided to dig that day in the cave of Altamira was the culmination of his passionate interest in his hobby. Here was a rare man whose avocation had been to educate himself from scratch, as it were, in the science of archaeology and cave exploration. This was no simple passive recognizer of blind luck when it came his way, but a man whose unique interests served as an active creative thrust—someone whose own actions and personality would focus the events that led circuitously but inexorably to the discovery of man's first paintings. 13

Then, too, there is a more subtle matter. How do you give full weight to the personal interests that imbue your child with your own curiosity, that inspire her to ask to join you in your own musty hobby, and that then lead you to agree to her request at the critical moment? For many reasons, at Altamira, more than the special receptivity of Chance III was required—this was a different domain, that of the personality and its actions. 14

A century ago no one had the remotest idea our caveman ancestors were highly creative artists. Weren't their talents rather minor and limited to crude flint chippings? But the paintings at Altamira, like a mirage, would quickly magnify 15 this diminutive view, bring up into full focus a distant, hidden era of man's prehistory, reveal sentient minds and well-developed aesthetic sensibilities to which men of any age might aspire. And like a mirage, the events at Altamira grew out of de Sautuola's heated personal quest and out of the invisible forces of chance we know exist yet cannot touch. Accordingly, one may introduce the term *altamirage* to identify the quality underlying Chance IV. Let us define it as the facility for encountering unexpected good luck as the result of highly individualized action. *Altamirage* goes well beyond the boundaries of serendipity in its emphasis on the role of personal action in chance.

Chance IV is favored by distinctive, if not eccentric, hobbies, personal life-styles, and modes of behavior peculiar to one individual, usually invested with some passion. The farther apart these personal activities are from the area under investigation, the more novel and unexpected will be the creative product of the encounter. 16

For Study and Discussion

QUESTIONS FOR RESPONSE

1. Would you consider yourself a lucky or an unlucky person? What evidence would you use to support your case?
2. Do you agree with Austin's assessment of the dictionary's definitions of the word *chance*? How would you define the word?

QUESTIONS ABOUT PURPOSE

1. What elements of human behavior and attitude does Austin demonstrate by dividing chance into four varieties?
2. What relationship does Austin discover between the words "luck," "serendipity," "sagacity," and "altamirage"?

QUESTIONS ABOUT AUDIENCE

1. What assumptions does Austin make about his readers when he offers them *the best example* rather than several examples to illustrate each category?
2. How does Austin's attitude toward his audience change during the essay? For example, why does he speak directly to his readers when he explains Chance I but address them more formally in his discussion of other categories?

QUESTIONS ABOUT STRATEGIES

1. How does Austin arrange his four categories? Why doesn't he give equal treatment to each category?
2. How does Austin use transitions and summaries to clarify the differences between the major categories? In particular, see paragraphs 6 and 9.

QUESTIONS FOR DISCUSSION

1. What incidents in your personal experience would support Austin's classification system? How many examples can you cite in each category?
2. What do you think is the relationship between *ability* and *result*? For example, what is your opinion of Disraeli's assertion that "we make our fortunes and we call them fate"?

MARY MEBANE

Mary Mebane was born in 1933 in Durham, North Carolina, and educated at North Carolina Central University and the University of North Carolina. She taught in the public schools of North Carolina before moving on to teaching writing at the University of South Carolina and the University of Wisconsin. She has written essays for the *New York Times;* a two-act play, *Take a Sad Song* (1975); and two volumes of her autobiography, *Mary: An Autobiography* (1981) and *Mary, Wayfarer* (1983). In "Shades of Black," excerpted from the first autobiographical volume, Mebane reveals how class and color have been used to classify members of the African-American community.

Shades of Black

D URING MY FIRST week of classes as a freshman, I was   1
stopped one day in the hall by the chairman's wife, who was indistinguishable in color from a white woman. She wanted to see me, she said.

This woman had no official position on the faculty, except   2
that she was an instructor in English; nevertheless, her summons had to be obeyed. In the segregated world there were (and remain) gross abuses of authority because those at the pinnacle, and even their spouses, felt that the people "under" them had no recourse except to submit—and they were right except that sometimes a black who got sick and tired of it would go to the whites and complain. This course of action was severely condemned by the blacks, but an interesting thing happened—such action always got positive results.

Power was thought of in negative terms: I can deny someone something, I can strike at someone who can't strike back, I can ride someone down; that proves I am powerful. The concept of power as a force for good, for affirmative response to people or situations, was not in evidence.

When I went to her office, she greeted me with a big smile. 3 "You know," she said, "you made the highest mark on the verbal part of the examination." She was referring to the examination that the entire freshman class took upon entering the college. I looked at her but I didn't feel warmth, for in spite of her smile her eyes and tone of voice were saying, "How could this black-skinned girl score higher on the verbal than some of the students who've had more advantages than she? It must be some sort of fluke. Let me talk to her." I felt it, but I managed to smile my thanks and back off. For here at North Carolina College at Durham, as it had been since the beginning, social class and color were the primary criteria used in determining status on the campus.

First came the children of doctors, lawyers, and college 4 teachers. Next came the children of public-school teachers, businessmen, and anybody else who had access to more money than the poor black working class. After that came the

---

At my college, social class and color were the primary criteria in determining status on campus.

---

bulk of the student population, the children of the working class, most of whom were the first in their families to go beyond high school. The attitude toward them was: You're here because we need the numbers, but in all other things defer to your betters.

The faculty assumed that light-skinned students were more 5 intelligent, and they were always a bit nonplussed when a dark-skinned student did well, especially if she was a girl. They had reason to be appalled when they discovered that I planned to do not only well but better than my light-skinned peers.

I don't know whether African men recently transported to   6
the New World considered themselves handsome or, more important, whether they considered African women beautiful in comparison with Native American Indian women or immigrant European women. It is a question that I have never heard raised or seen research on. If African men considered African women beautiful, just when their shift in interest away from black black women occurred might prove to be an interesting topic for researchers. But one thing I know for sure: by the twentieth century, really black skin on a woman was considered ugly in this country. This was particularly true among those who were exposed to college.

Hazel, who was light brown, used to say to me, "You are   7
dark, but not *too* dark." The saved commiserating with the damned. I had the feeling that if nature had painted one more brushstroke on me, I'd have had to kill myself.

Black skin was to be disguised at all costs. Since a black   8
face is rather hard to disguise, many women took refuge in ludicrous makeup. Mrs. Burry, one of my teachers in elementary school, used white face powder. But she neglected to powder her neck and arms, and even the black on her face gleamed through the white, giving her an eerie appearance. But she did the best she could.

I observed all through elementary and high school that for   9
various entertainments the girls were placed on the stage in order of color. And very black ones didn't get into the front row. If they were past caramel-brown, to the back row they would go. And nobody questioned the justice of these decisions—neither the students nor the teachers.

One of the teachers at Wildwood School, who was from   10
the Deep South and was just as black as she could be, had been a strict enforcer of these standards. That was another irony—that someone who had been judged outside the realm

of beauty herself because of her skin tones should have adopted them so wholeheartedly and applied them herself without question.

One girl stymied that teacher, though. Ruby, a black cherry of a girl, not only got off the back row but off the front row as well, to stand alone at stage center. She could outsing, outdance, and outdeclaim everyone else, and talent proved triumphant over pigmentation. But the May Queen and her Court (and in high school, Miss Wildwood) were always chosen from among the lighter ones.

When I was a freshman in high school, it became clear that a light-skinned sophomore girl named Rose was going to get the "best girl scholar" prize for the next three years, and there was nothing I could do about it, even though I knew I was the better. Rose was caramel-colored and had shoulder-length hair. She was highly favored by the science and math teacher, who figured the averages. I wasn't. There was only one prize. Therefore, Rose would get it until she graduated. I was one year behind her, and I would not get it until after she graduated.

To be held in such low esteem was painful. It was difficult not to feel that I had been cheated out of the medal, which I felt that, in a fair competition, I perhaps would have won. Being unable to protest or do anything about it was a traumatic experience for me. From then on I instinctively tended to avoid the college-exposed, dark-skinned male, knowing that when he looked at me he saw himself and, most of the time, his mother and sister as well, and since he had rejected his blackness, he had rejected theirs and mine.

Oddly enough, the lighter-skinned black male did not seem to feel so much prejudice toward the black black woman. It was no accident, I felt, that Mr. Harrison, the eighth-grade teacher, who was reddish-yellow himself, once protested to the science and math teacher about the fact that he always assigned sweeping duties to Doris and Ruby Lee, two black black girls. Mr. Harrison said to them one day, right in the other teacher's presence, "You must be some bad girls. Every day I come down here ya'll are sweeping." The science and math teacher got the point and didn't ask them to sweep anymore.

Uneducated black males, too, sometimes related very well 15 to the black black woman. They had been less firmly indoctrinated by the white society around them and were more securely rooted in their own culture.

Because of the stigma attached to having dark skin, a black 16 black woman had to do many things to find a place for herself. One possibility was to attach herself to a light-skinned woman, hoping that some of the magic would rub off on her. A second was to make herself sexually available, hoping to attract a mate. Third, she could resign herself to a more chaste life-style—either (for the professional woman) teaching and work in established churches or (for the uneducated woman) domestic work and zealous service in the Holy and Sanctified churches.

Even as a young girl, Lucy had chosen the first route. Lucy 17 was short, skinny, short-haired, and black black, and thus unacceptable. So she made her choice. She selected Patricia, the lightest-skinned girl in the school, as her friend, and followed her around. Patricia and her friends barely tolerated Lucy, but Lucy smiled and doggedly hung on, hoping that some who noticed Patricia might notice her, too. Though I felt shame for her behavior, even then I understood.

As is often the case of the victim agreeing with and adopt- 18 ing the attitudes of oppressor, so I have seen it with black black women. I have seen them adopt the oppressor's attitude that they are nothing but "sex machines," and their supposedly superior sexual performance becomes their sole reason for being and for esteeming themselves. Such women learn early that in order to make themselves attractive to men they have somehow to shift the emphasis from physical beauty to some other area—usually sexual performance. Their constant talk is of their desirability and their ability to gratify a man sexually.

I knew two such women well—both of them black black. 19 To hear their endless talk of sexual conquests was very sad. I have never seen the category that these women fall into described anywhere. It is not that of promiscuity or nympho-mania. It is the category of total self-rejection: "Since I am black, I am ugly, I am nobody. I will perform on the level that they have assigned to me." Such women are the pitiful results of what not only white America but also, and more important, black America has done to them.

Some, not taking the sexuality route but still accepting   20 black society's view of their worthlessness, swing all the way across to intense religiosity. Some are staunch, fervent work-ers in the more traditional Southern churches—Baptist and Methodist—and others are leaders and ministers in the lower status, more evangelical Holiness sects.

Another avenue open to the black black woman is excel-   21 lence in a career. Since in the South the field most accessible to such women is education, a great many of them prepared to become teachers. But here, too, the black black woman had problems. Grades weren't given to her lightly in school, nor were promotions on the job. Consequently, she had to prepare especially well. She had to pass examinations with flying colors or be left behind; she knew that she would receive no special consideration. She had to be overqualified for a job because otherwise she didn't stand a chance of getting it—and she was competing only with other blacks. She had to have something to back her up: not charm, not personality—but training.

The black black woman's training would pay off in the   22 1970's. With the arrival of integration the black black woman would find, paradoxically enough, that her skin color in an integrated situation was not the handicap it had been in an all-black situation. But it wasn't until the middle and late 1960s, when the post-1945 generation of black males arrived on college campuses, that I noticed any change in the situ-ation at all. *He* wore an afro and *she* wore an afro, and sometimes the only way you could tell them apart was when his afro was taller than hers. Black had become beautiful, and the really black girl was often selected as queen of various campus activities. It was then that the dread I felt at dealing with the college-educated black male began to ease. Even now, though, when I have occasion to engage in any type of transaction with a college-educated black man, I gauge his age. If I guess he was born after 1945, I feel confident that the transaction will turn out all right. If he probably was born before 1945, my stomach tightens, I find myself taking shallow breaths, and I try to state my business and escape as soon as possible.

For Study and Discussion

QUESTIONS FOR RESPONSE

1. How do you respond when you or your friends are judged by some physical feature—weight, height, hair?
2. How do you and your friends identify various social classes? What assumptions do you make about people in each class?

QUESTIONS ABOUT PURPOSE

1. Why does Mebane use the concept of power to introduce her classification?
2. How does Mebane use her essay to explain the impulse of the victim to adopt the attitudes of the oppressor?

QUESTIONS ABOUT AUDIENCE

1. Does Mebane envision her readers as primarily black or primarily white, primarily men or primarily women? Explain your answer.
2. In what way do you think Mebane's system may apply to the attitudes of today's African-American students? Explain your answer.

QUESTIONS ABOUT STRATEGIES

1. How does Mebane classify her college classmates by color and class? What assumptions do her teachers make about black black working-class women?
2. What options does Mebane suggest are available to black black women? How are these options enforced?

QUESTIONS FOR DISCUSSION

1. How did the civil rights movement of the 1950s and black consciousness movement of the 1960s change the African-American community's definition of beauty?
2. Do subtle judgments about class and color still control the power structure of the African-American community? In what way?

Phillip Lopate was born in Jamaica Heights, New York, in 1943 and educated at Columbia University. He taught creative writing with the Teachers and Writers Collaborative in the New York Public Schools before devoting his full attention to his own writing. He has contributed fiction to *Paris Review*, poetry to *Yale Literary Review*, and film criticism to the *Cinemabook*. His essays have appeared in collections such as *Against Joie de Vivre* (1989); he has also edited numerous writing collections such as *The Anchor Essay Annual* (1997) and *Writing New York: A Literary Anthology* (2000). In "Modern Friendships," reprinted from *Against Joie de Vivre*, Lopate classifies his changing attitude toward various kinds of "friends."

Modern Friendships

I S THERE ANYTHING left to say about friendship after so 1
many great essayists have picked over the bones of the
subject? Probably not. Aristotle and Cicero, Seneca and Montaigne, Bacon and Samuel Johnson, Hazlitt, Emerson, and Lamb have all taken their cracks at it; since the ancients, friendship has been a sort of examination subject for the personal essayist. It is partly the very existence of such wonderful prior models that lures the newcomer to follow in the others' footsteps, and partly a self-referential aspect of the genre, since the personal essay is itself an attempt to establish a friendship on the page between writer and reader.

Friendship has been called "love without wings," implying 2
a want of lyrical afflatus. On the other hand, the Stoic definition of love ("Love is the attempt to form a friendship inspired by beauty") seems to suggest that friendship came first.

Certainly a case can be made that the buildup of affection and the yearning for more intimacy, without the release of sexual activity, keeps friends in a state of sweet-sorrowful itchiness that has as much romantic quality as a love affair. We know that a falling-out between two old friends can leave a deeper and more perplexing hurt than the ending of a love affair, perhaps because we are more pessimistic about the latter's endurance from the start.

Our first attempted friendships are within the family. It is   3
here we practice the techniques of listening sympathetically

Friendship is a school for character,
allowing us to study in great detail and
over time temperaments very different from
our own.

and proving that we can be trusted, and learn the sort of kindness we can expect in return. I have a sister, one year younger than I, who often took care of me when I was growing up. Once, when I was about fifteen, unable to sleep and shivering uncontrollably with the start of a fever, I decided in the middle of the night to go into her room and wake her. She held me, performing the basic service of a friend—presence—and the chills went away.

There is something tainted about these family friendships,   4
however. This same sister, in her insecure adolescent phase, told me: "You love me because I'm related to you, but if you were to meet me for the first time at a party, you'd think I was a jerk and not worth being your friend." She had me in a bind: I had no way of testing her hypothesis. I should have argued that even if our bond was not freely chosen, our decision to work on it had been. Still, we are quick to dismiss the partiality of our family members when they tell us we are

talented, cute, or lovable; we must go out into the world and seduce others.

It is just a few short years from the promiscuity of the sandbox to the tormented, possessive feelings of a fifth grader who has just learned that his best and only friend is playing at another classmate's house after school. There may be worse betrayals in store, but probably none is more influential than the sudden fickleness of an elementary school friend who has dropped us for someone more popular after all our careful, patient wooing. Often we lose no time inflicting the same betrayal on someone else, just to ensure that we have got the victimization dynamic right.

What makes friendships in childhood and adolescence so poignant is that we need the chosen comrade to be everything in order to rescue us from the gothic inwardness of family life. Even if we are lucky enough to have several companions, there must be a Best Friend, knightly dubbed as though victor of an Arthurian tournament.

I clung to the romance of the Best Friend all through high school, college, and beyond, until my university circle began to disperse. At that point, in my mid-twenties, I also "acted out" the dark competitive side of friendship that can exist between two young men fighting for a place in life and love, by doing the one unforgivable thing: sleeping with my best friend's girl. I was baffled at first that there was no way to repair the damage. I lost this friendship forever, and came away from that debacle much more aware of the amount of injury that friendship can and cannot sustain. Perhaps I needed to prove to myself that friendship was not an all-permissive, resilient bond, like a mother's love, but something quite fragile. Precisely because Best Friendship promotes such a merging of identities, such seeming boundarylessness, the first major transgression of trust can cause the injured party to feel he is fighting for his violated soul against his darkest enemy. There is not much room to maneuver in a best friendship between unlimited intimacy and unlimited mistrust.

Still, it was not until the age of thirty that I reluctantly abandoned the Best Friend expectation and took up a more pluralistic model. At present, I cherish a dozen friends for their unique personalities, without asking that any one be my soul-twin. Whether this alteration constitutes a movement toward maturity or toward cowardly pragmatism is not for me to say. It may be that, in refusing to depend so much on any one friend, I am opting for self-protection over intimacy. Or it may be that, as we advance into middle age, the life problem becomes less that of establishing a tight dyadic bond and more one of making our way in a broader world, "society." Indeed, since Americans have so indistinct a notion of society, we often try to put friendship networks in its place. If a certain intensity is lost in the pluralistic model of friendship, there is also the gain of being able to experience all of one's potential, half-buried selves, through witnessing the spectacle of the multiple fates of our friends. Since we cannot be polygamists in our conjugal life, at least we can do so with friendship. As it happens, the harem of friends, so tantalizing a notion, often translates into feeling pulled in a dozen different directions, with the guilty sense of having disappointed everyone a little. It is also a risky, contrived enterprise to try to make one's friends behave in a friendly manner toward each other: if the effort fails one feels obliged to mediate; if it succeeds too well, one is jealous.

Whether friendship is intrinsically singular and exclusive, 9
or plural and democratic, is a question that has vexed many commentators. Aristotle distinguished three types of friendship in *The Nicomachean Ethics:* "friendship based on utility," such as businessmen cultivating each other for benefit; "friendship based on pleasure," like young people interested in partying; and "perfect friendship." The first two categories Aristotle calls "qualified and superficial friendships," because they are founded on circumstances that could easily change; the last, which is based on admiration for another's good character, is more permanent, but also rarer, because good men "are few." Cicero, who wrote perhaps the best treatise on friendship, also insisted that what brings true friends together is "a mutual belief in each other's goodness." This insistence on virtue as a precondition for true friendship may

strike us as impossibly demanding: who, after all, feels himself good nowadays? And yet, if I am honest, I must admit that the friendships of mine which have lasted longest have been with those whose integrity, or humanity, or strength to bear their troubles I continue to admire. Conversely, when I lost respect for someone, however winning he otherwise remained, the friendship petered away almost immediately. "Remove respect from friendship," said Cicero, "and you have taken away the most splendid ornament it possesses."

Montaigne distinguished between friendship, which he saw as a once-in-a-lifetime experience, and the calculating worldly alliances around him, which he thought unworthy of the name. In paying tribute to his late friend Etienne de la Boetie, Montaigne wrote: "Having so little time to last, and having begun so late, for we were both grown men, and he a few years older than I, it could not lose time and conform to the pattern of mild and regular friendships, which need so many precautions in the form of long preliminary association. Our friendship has no other model than itself, and can be compared only with itself. It is not one special consideration, nor two, nor three, nor four, nor a thousand: it is I know not what quintessence of all this mixture, which, having seized my whole will, led it to plunge and lose itself in his; which, having seized his whole will, led it to plunge and lose itself in mine, with equal hunger, equal rivalry. . . . So many coincidences are needed to build up such a friendship that it is a lot if fortune can do it once in three centuries." This seems a bit high hat: since the sixteenth century, our expectations of friendship may have grown more plebeian. Even Emerson, in his grand romantic essay on the subject, allowed as how he was not up to the Castor-and-Pollux standard: "I am not quite so strict in my terms, perhaps because I have never known so high a fellowship as others." Emerson contents himself with a circle of intelligent men and women, but warns us not to throw them together: "You shall have very useful and cheering discourse at several times with two several men, but let all three of you come together, and you shall not have one new and hearty word. Two may talk and one may hear, but three cannot take part in a conversation of the most sincere and searching sort."

Friendship is a long conversation. I suppose I could imagine a nonverbal friendship revolving around shared physical work or sport, but for me, good talk is the point of the thing. Indeed, the ability to generate conversation by the hour is the most promising indication, during its uncertain early stages, that a possible friendship will take hold. In the first few conversations there may be an exaggeration of agreement, as both parties angle for adhesive surfaces. But later on, trust builds through the courage to assert disagreement, through the tactful acceptance that differences of opinion will have to remain.   11

Some view like-mindedness as both the precondition and product of friendship. Myself, I distrust it. I have one friend who keeps assuming that we see the world eye-to-eye. She is intent on enrolling us in a flattering aristocracy of taste, on the short "we" list against the ignorant "they"; sometimes I do not have the strength to fight her need for consensus with my own stubborn disbelief in the existence of any such inner circle of privileged, cultivated sensibility. Perhaps I have too much invested in a view of myself as idiosyncratic to be eager to join any coterie, even a coterie of two. What attracts me to friends' conversation is the give-and-take, not necessarily that we come out at the same point.   12

"Our tastes and aims and views were identical—and that is where the essence of a friendship must always lie," wrote Cicero. To some extent, perhaps, but then the convergence must be natural, not, as Emerson put it, "a mush of concession. Better be a nettle in the side of your friend than his echo." And Francis Bacon observed that "the best preservative to keep the mind in health is the faithful admonition of a friend."   13

Friendship is a school for character, allowing us the chance to study in great detail and over time temperaments very different from our own. These charming quirks, these contradictions, these nobilities, these blind spots of our friends we track not out of disinterested curiosity: we must have this   14 information before knowing how far we may relax our guard, how much we may rely on them in crises. The learning curve of friendship involves, to no small extent, filling out this picture of the other's limitations and making peace with the results. (With one's own limitations there may never be peace.) Each time I hit up against a friend's inflexibility I am relieved as well as disappointed: I can begin to predict, and arm myself in advance against repeated bruises. I have one friend who is always late, so I bring a book along when I am to meet her. If I give her a manuscript to read and she promises to look at it over the weekend, I start preparing myself for a month-long wait.

Not that one ever gives up trying to educate the friend to 15 one's needs. I approach such matters experimentally: sometimes I will pride myself in tactfully circumventing the friend's predicted limitation, even if it means relinquishing all hope of getting the response I want; at other times I will confront a problem with intentional tactlessness, just to see if any change is still possible.

I have a dear old friend, Richard, who shies away from 16 personal confidences. Years go by without my learning anything about his love life, and he does not encourage the baring of my soul either, much as I like that sort of thing. But we share so many other interests and values that that limitation seems easily borne, most of the time. Once, however, I found myself in a state of emotional despair; I told him I had exhausted my hopes of finding love or success, that I felt suicidal, and he changed the topic, patently embarrassed. I was annoyed both at his emotional rigidity and at my own stupidity—after all, I'd enough friends who ate up this kind of confessional talk, why foist on Richard what I might have predicted he couldn't, or wouldn't, handle? For a while I sulked, annoyed at him for having failed me, but I also began to see my despair through his eyes as melodramatic, childish petulance, and I began to let it go. As it happened, he found other ways during our visit to be so considerate that I ended up feeling better, even without our having had a heart-to-heart talk. I suppose the moral is that a friend can serve as a corrective to our insular miseries simply by offering up his essential otherness.

Though it is often said that with a true friend there is no   17
need to hold anything back ("A friend is a person with whom I may be sincere. Before him I may think aloud," wrote Emerson), I have never found this to be entirely the case. Certain words may be too cruel if spoken at the wrong moment—or may fall on deaf ears, for any number of reasons. I also find with each friend, as they must with me, that some initial resistance, restlessness, psychic weather must be overcome before that tender ideal attentiveness may be called forth.

I have a good friend, Charlie, who is often very distracted   18
whenever we first get together. If we are sitting in a cafe he will look around constantly for the waiter, or be distracted by a pretty woman or the restaurant's cat. It would be foolish for me to broach an important subject at such moments, so I resign myself to waiting the half hour or however long it takes until his jumpiness subsides. Or else I draw this pattern grumpily to his attention. Once he has settled down, however, I can tell Charlie virtually anything, and he me. But the candor cannot be rushed. It must be built up to with the verbal equivalent of limbering exercises.

The Friendship Scene—a flow of shared confidences, rec-   19
ognition's, humor, advice, speculation, even wisdom—is one of the key elements of modern friendships. Compared to the rest of life, this ability to lavish one's best energies on an activity utterly divorced from the profit motive and free from the routines of domination and inequality that affect most relations (including, perhaps, the selfsame friendship at other times) seems idyllic. The Friendship Scene is by its nature not an everyday occurrence. It represents the pinnacle, the fruit of the friendship, potentially ever-present but not always arrived at. Both friends' dim yet self-conscious awareness that they are wandering conversationally toward a goal that they have previously accomplished but which may elude them this time around creates a tension, an obligation to communicate as sincerely as possible, like actors in an improvisation exercise

struggling to shape their baggy material into some climactic form. This very pressure to achieve "quality" communication may induce a sort of inauthentic epiphany, not unlike what happens sometimes in the last ten minutes of a psychotherapy session. But a truly achieved Friendship Scene can be among the best experiences life has to offer.

I remember one such afternoon when Michael, a close 20 writer-friend, and I met at a cafeteria on a balmy Saturday in early spring and talked for three and a half hours. There were no outside time pressures that particular afternoon, a rare occurrence for either of us. At first we caught up with our latest business, the sort of items that might have gone into a biweekly bulletin sent to any number of acquaintances. Then gradually we settled into an area of perplexing unresolved impressions. I would tell Michael about A's chance, seemingly hostile remark toward me at a gathering, and he would report that the normally ebullient B looked secretly depressed. These were the memory equivalents of food grains stuck in our teeth, which we were now trying to free with our tongues: anecdotal fragments I was not even sure had any point, until I started fashioning them aloud for Michael's interest. Together we diagnosed our mutual acquaintances, each other's character, and, from there, the way of the world. In the course of our free associations we eventually descended into what was really bothering us. I learned he was preoccupied with the fate of an old college friend who was dying of AIDS; he, that my father was in poor health and needed two operations. We had touched bottom—mortality—and it was reassuring to settle there awhile. Gradually we rose again, drawn back to the questions of ego and career, craft and romance. It was, as I've said, a pretty day, and we ended up walking through a new mall in Houston, gawking at the window displays of that bland emporium with a reawakened curiosity about the consumer treats of America, our attentions turned happily outward now that we had dwelt long enough in the shared privacies of our psyches.

Contemporary urban life, with its tight schedules and 21 crowded appointment books, has helped to shape modern friendship into something requiring a good deal of intentionality and pursuit. You phone a friend and make a date a week or more in advance; then you set aside an evening, like a tryst, during which to squeeze in all your news and advice, confession and opinion. Such intimate compression may add a romantic note to modern friendships, but it also places a strain on the meeting to yield a high quality of meaning and satisfaction, closer to art than life, thereby increasing the chance for disappointment. If I see certain busy or out-of-town friends only once every six months, we must not only catch up on our lives but convince ourselves within the allotted two hours together that we still share a special affinity, an inner track to each other's psyches, or the next meeting may be put off for years. Surely there must be another, saner rhythm to friendship in rural areas—or maybe not? I think about "the gold old days" when friends would go on walking tours through England together, when Edith Wharton would bundle poor Henry James into her motorcar and they'd drive to the South of France for a month. I'm not sure my friendships could sustain the strain of travel for weeks at a time, and the truth of the matter is that I've gotten used to this urban arrangement of serial friendship "dates," where the pleasure of the rendezvous is enhanced by the knowledge that it will only last, at most, six hours. If the two of us don't happen to mesh that day (always a possibility)—well, it's only a few hours; and if it should go beautifully, one needs an escape hatch from exaltation as well as disenchantment. I am capable of only so much intense, exciting communication before I start to fade; I come to these encounters equipped with a six-hour oxygen tank. Is this an evolutionary pattern of modern friendship, or only a personal limitation?

Perhaps because I conceive of the modern Friendship 22 Scene as a somewhat theatrical enterprise, a one-act play, I tend to be very affected by the "set," so to speak. A restaurant, a museum, a walk in the park through the zoo, even accompanying a friend on shopping errands—I prefer public turf where the stimulation of the city can play a backdrop to our dialogue, feeding it with details when inspiration flags. True, some of the most cherished friendship scenes have occurred around a friend's kitchen table. The problem with restricting the date to one another's houses is that the entertaining friend may be unable to stop playing the host, or may sink too passively into his or her surroundings. Subtle struggles may also develop over which domicile should serve as the venue.

I have a number of *chez moi* friends, friends who always   23 invite me to come to their homes while evading offers to visit mine. What they view as hospitality I see as a need to control the *mise-en-scène* of friendship. I am expected to fit in where they are most comfortable, while they play lord of the manor, distracted by the props of decor, the pool, the unexpected phone call, the swirl of children, animals, and neighbors. Indeed, *chez moi* friends often tend to keep a sort of open house, so that in going over to see them—for a *tête-à-tête*, I had assumed—I will suddenly find their other friends and neighbors, whom they have also invited, dropping in all afternoon. There are only so many Sundays I care to spend hanging out with a friend's entourage before becoming impatient for a private audience.

Married friends who own their own homes are much more   24 apt to try to draw me into their domestic fold, whereas single people are often more sensitive about establishing a discreet space for the friendship to occur. Perhaps the married assume that a bachelor like myself is desperate for home cooking and a little family life. I have noticed that it is not an easy matter to pry a married friend away from mate and milieu. For married people, especially those with children, the home often becomes the wellspring of all their nurturing feelings, and the single friend is invited to partake in the general flow. Maybe there is also a certain tendency on their parts to kill two birds with one stone: they don't see enough of their spouse and kids, and figure they can visit with you all at the same time. And maybe they need one-on-one friendship less, hampered as they are by responsibilities that no amount of camaraderie or discussion can change. Often friendship in these circumstances is not even a pairing, but a mixing together of two sets of parents and children willy-nilly. What would the ancients say about this? In Rome, according to Bacon, "the whole senate dedicated an altar to Friendship, as to a goddess. . . ." From my standpoint, friendship is a jealous goddess. Whenever a friend of mine marries, I have to fight to overcome the feeling that I am being "replaced" by the spouse. I don't mind sharing a friend with his family milieu—in fact I like it, up to a point—but eventually I must get the friend alone, or else, as a bachelor at a distinct power disadvantage, I risk becoming a mere spectator of familial rituals instead of a key player in the drama of friendship.

A person living alone usually has more control over his or 25
her schedule, hence more energy to give to friendship. If anything, the danger is of investing too much emotional energy in one's friends. When a single person is going through a romantic dry spell he or she often tries to extract the missing passion from a circle of friends. This works only up to a point: the frayed nerves of protracted celibacy can lead to hypersensitive imaginings of slights and rejections, during which times one's platonic friends seem to come particularly into the line of fire.

Today, with the partial decline of the nuclear family 26
and the search for alternatives to it, we also see attempts to substitute the friendship web for intergenerational family life. Since psychoanalysis has alerted us to regard the family as a minefield of unrequited love, manipulation, and ambivalence, it is only natural that people may look to friendship as a more supportive ground for relation. But in our longing for an unequivocally positive bond, we should beware of sentimentalizing friendship, as saccharine "buddy" movies or certain feminist novels do, of neutering its problematic, destructive aspects. Besides, friendship can never substitute for the true meaning of family: if nothing else, it will never be able to duplicate the family's wild capacity for concentrating neurosis.

In short, friends can't be your family, they can't be your 27
lovers, they can't be your psychiatrists. But they can be your

friends, which is plenty. For, as Cicero tells us, "friendship is the noblest and most delightful of all the gifts the gods have given to mankind." And Bacon adds: "It is a mere and miserable solitude to want true friends, without which the world is but a wilderness. . . ."

When I think about the qualities that characterize the best 28 friendships I've known, I can identify five: rapport, affection, need, habit, and forgiveness. Rapport and affection can only take you so far; they may leave you at the formal, outer gate of goodwill, which is still not friendship. A persistent need for the other's company, for their interest, approval, opinion, will get you inside the gates, especially when it is reciprocated. In the end, however, there are no substitutes for habit and forgiveness. A friendship may travel for years on cozy habit. But it is a melancholy fact that unless you are a saint you are bound to offend every friend deeply at least once in the course of time. The friends I have kept the longest are those who forgave me for wronging them, unintentionally, intentionally, or by the plain catastrophe of my personality, time and again. There can be no friendship without forgiveness.

For Study and Discussion

QUESTIONS FOR RESPONSE

1. In your life as a student, how many times have you had to write or read an essay on *friendship*? Which ones made the biggest impression on you?
2. How often do you enact the Friendship Scene (page 272)? What is your favorite setting for this scene?

QUESTIONS ABOUT PURPOSE

1. In what way does Lopate distinguish between the classical definition of friendship and friendships shaped by "contemporary urban life"?
2. What evidence does he supply for his argument that "friends can't be your family"?

QUESTIONS ABOUT AUDIENCE

1. Lopate acknowledges that many classical essayists have written about friendship. How does he help his readers understand what these essayists said? Does he agree or disagree with them?
2. He suggests, "The personal essay is an attempt to establish a friendship on the page between writer and reader." In what passages in the essay do you sense that Lopate is trying to establish such a friendship with his readers?

QUESTIONS ABOUT STRATEGIES

1. How does Lopate use maturity as a principle for classifying friendships? What kind of problems occurs among "pluralistic" friends?
2. How does he use the scenes with Richard, Charlie, and Michael to demonstrate the difficulties of sustaining a friendship?

QUESTIONS FOR DISCUSSION

1. Only one of the friends Lopate mentions in this essay is a woman. How do you respond to the famous line in the movie *When Harry Met Sally* that "men and women can't be friends"?
2. What do you think about the five qualities Lopate identifies as characterizing the best friendships? Has he left out an important quality? Explain your answer.

Steven Weinberg was born in New York City in 1933 and educated at Cornell University and Princeton University. His speculations about theoretical physics earned him the Nobel Prize in Physics 1979. His books include *The Discovery of Subatomic Particles* (1983), *The First Three Minutes: A Modern View of the Origin of the Universe* (1988), and *The Quantum Theory of Fields* (1995). In "Five and a Half Utopias," reprinted from the January 2000 issue of the *Atlantic Monthly,* Weinberg classifies five different kinds of societies and then concludes that we are probably better off with half measures than a perfect state.

Five and a Half Utopias

Despite its dismal record, the utopian impulse is by no means extinct. An eminent physicist looks at several of the guises in which utopian thinking is likely to appear during the century ahead—and at the perils that lurk behind each one

I USED TO read a good deal of science fiction when I was a boy. Even though I knew pretty early that I was going to be a scientist, it wasn't the science that interested me in science fiction; it was the vision of future societies that, for better or worse, would be radically different from our own. This led me on from science fiction to utopian literature, to Plato's *Republic,* Thomas More's *Utopia,* and Edward Bellamy's *Looking Backward,* and also to the literature of anti-utopias, to Aldous Huxley's *Brave New World* and George Orwell's *1984.* I have been more interested in other things

1

in recent years, but now that we are starting a new millennium, it is natural to start thinking again about what sort of utopia or anti-utopia might be waiting for us in the future.

There was a great deal of this sort of speculation at the end 2 of the previous century. The characters in Anton Chekhov's

---

We had better watch out for people selling various utopias; each of these visions abandons one or more of the grand causes—equality, liberty, and the quality of life and work—that motivated the best utopian ideas of the past.

Three Sisters (written exactly a hundred years ago) seem captivated by utopian dreams. Here, for instance, is Colonel Vershinin, in Act II:

> *In a century or two, or in a millennium, people will live in a new way, a happier way. We won't be there to see it—but it's why we live, why we work. It's why we suffer. We're creating it. That's the purpose of our existence. The only happiness we can know is to work toward that goal.*

Vershinin's hopes have not worked out so well in this 3 century. The most influential utopian idea of the nineteenth and twentieth centuries was socialism, which has failed everywhere. Under the banner of socialism Stalin's USSR and Mao's China gave us not utopias but ghastly anti-utopias. It is ironic that in the heyday of utopian thinking, in the nineteenth century, Karl Marx himself sneered at utopian thought, and claimed to be guided instead by a science of history. Of course, there is no science of history, but that's almost beside the point. Even if we could decide that some type of government or economy was historically inevitable, as Marx believed communism to be, it would not follow that this would be something we would like. If Marx had been an honest utopian, and recognized his responsibility to describe the society he wanted to bring into being, it might have been clearer from the beginning that the effort would end in tyranny. Hitler's Germany, too, started with utopian rhetoric: socialism combined with a maniac vision of a master race.

Even so, I can't believe that we have seen the last of utopia-mongering. Indeed, five nonsocialist styles of utopia seem (in various combinations) to be emerging in public debate. We had better watch out for people selling these utopias; each of these visions abandons one or more of the grand causes—equality, liberty, and the quality of life and work—that motivated the best utopian ideas of the past. 4

THE FREE-MARKET UTOPIA

Government barriers to free enterprise disappear.
Governments lose most of their functions, serving only to
punish crimes, enforce contracts, and provide
national defense. Freed of artificial restraints, the
world becomes industrialized and prosperous.

This style of utopia has the advantage of not depending on any assumed improvements in human nature, but that doesn't mean we have to like it. If only for the sake of argument, let's say that *something* (productivity? gross national product? Pareto efficiency?) is maximized by free markets. Whatever it is, we still have to decide for ourselves whether this is what we want to be maximized. 5

One thing that is clearly not maximized by free markets is equality. I am talking not about that pale substitute for equality known as equality of opportunity but about equality itself. Whatever purposes may be served by rewarding the talented, I have never understood why untalented people *deserve* less of the world's good things than other people. It is hard to 6 see how equality can be promoted, and a safety net provided for those who would otherwise fall out of the bottom of the economy, unless there is government interference in free markets.

Not everyone has put a high value on equality. Plato did   7 not have much use for it, especially after the Athenian democracy condemned his hero, Socrates. He explained the rigid stratification of his Republic by comparing society to the human soul: the guardians are the rational part; the soldiers are the spirited part; and the peasants and artisans are the baser parts. I don't know whether he was more interested in the self as a metaphor for the state or the state as a metaphor for the self, but at any rate such silly analogies continued for two millennia to comfort the comfortable.

In the course of time the dream of equality grew to be-   8 come an emotional driving force behind utopian thinking. When English peasants and artisans rebelled against feudalism in 1381, their slogan was the couplet preached by John Ball at Blackheath: "When Adam delved, and Eve span, who was then the gentleman?" The French Revolution adopted the goal of equality along with liberty and fraternity; Louis-Philippe-Joseph, duc d'Orléans, wishing to gain favor with the Jacobins, changed his name to Philippe-Egalité. (Neither his new name nor his vote for the execution of Louis XVI saved the duke from the Terror, and he joined the King and thousands of other Frenchmen in the equality of the guillotine.) The central aim of the socialists and anarchists of the nineteenth and twentieth centuries was to end the unequal distribution of wealth. Bellamy followed *Looking Backward* with a sequel titled simply *Equality*. It is a cruel joke of history that in the twentieth century the passion for equality has been used to justify communist states in which everyone was reduced to an equality of poverty. Everyone, that is, except for a small number of politicians and celebrities and their families, who alone had access to good housing, good food, and good medicine. Egalitarianism is perhaps the aspect of utopian thinking that has been most discredited by the failure of communism. These days anyone who urges a more equal distribution of wealth is likely to be charged with trying to revive the class struggle.

Of course, some inequality is inevitable. Everyone knows 9 that only a few people can be concert violinists, factory managers, or major-league pitchers. In revolutionary France the ideal of equality soon gave way to the *carrière ouverte aux talents*. It was said that each soldier in Napoleon's army carried a marshal's baton in his knapsack, but no one expected that many soldiers would get to use it. For my part, I would fight against any proposal to be less selective in choosing graduate students and research associates for the physics department in which I work. But the inequalities of title and fame and authority that follow inexorably from inequalities of talent provide powerful spurs to ambition. Is it really necessary to add gross inequalities of wealth to these other incentives?

This issue cannot be judged on purely economic grounds. 10 Economists tell us that inequality of compensation fulfills important economic functions: just as unequal prices for different foods help in allocating agricultural resources to produce what people want to eat, so unequal rewards for labor and for capital can help in directing people into jobs, and their money into investments, of the greatest economic value. The difference between these various inequalities is that *in themselves*, the relative prices of wheat and rye are of no importance; they only serve the economic function of helping to adjust production and resources. But whatever its economic effects, gross inequality in wealth is itself a social evil, which poisons life for millions.

Those who grew up in comfortable circumstances often 11 have trouble understanding this. They call any effort to reduce inequality "the politics of envy." The best place for the well-to-do to get some feeling for the damage done by inequality may be American literature, perhaps because America led the world in making wealth the chief determinant of class. This damage is poignantly described in the novels of Theodore Dreiser, who grew up poor during the Gilded Age, when inequality of wealth in America was at its height. Or think of Willa Cather's story "Paul's Case." The hopeless longing of the boy Paul for the life of the rich drives him to give up his whole dreary life for a few days of luxury.

Another thing that is manifestly not maximized by free 12 markets is civilization. By "civilization" I mean not just art museums and grand opera but the whole range of public and private goods that are there not merely to help keep us alive but to add quality to our lives. Everyone can make his or her own list; for me, civilization includes classical-music radio stations and the look of lovely old cities. It does not include telemarketing or Las Vegas. Civilization is elitist; only occasionally does it match the public taste, and for this reason it cannot prosper if not supported by individual sacrifices or government action, whether in the form of subsidy, regulation, or tax policy.

The aspect of civilization that concerns me professionally 13 is basic scientific research, like the search for the fundamental laws of nature or for the origins of the universe or of life— research that cannot be justified by foreseeable economic benefits. Along with all the good things that have come from the opening of free-market economies in Eastern Europe, we have seen the devastation in those countries of scientific establishments that cannot turn a profit. In the United States the opening of the telephone industry to free-market forces has led to the almost complete dismantling of pure science at the Bell Laboratories, formerly among the world's leading private scientific-research facilities.

It might be worthwhile to let equality and civilization take 14 their chances in the free market if in return we could expect that the withering of government would serve as a guarantee against oppression. But that is an illusion. For many Americans the danger of tyranny lies not in government but in employers or insurance companies or health-maintenance organizations, from which we need government to protect us. To say that any worker is free to escape an oppressive employer by getting a different job is about as realistic as to say that any citizen is free to escape an oppressive government by emigrating.

THE BEST-AND-BRIGHTEST UTOPIA

Public affairs are put in the hands of an
intelligent and well-educated class of leaders.

This was Plato's vision. In the *Republic* and other dia- 15
logues Plato described a hierarchical society of peasants and soldiers ruled over by a eugenically bred class of "guardians," and in *Critias* he imagined that this was the constitution of ancient Athens, before the war with Atlantis, 9,000 years earlier. In our own times Lee Kuan Yew, the Senior Minister of Singapore, has said that only an elite, consisting of the top three to five percent of a society, can deal effectively with public issues. The rulers of the "People's Republic" of China would probably agree, except that I suppose they would think that three percent is a gross overestimate. Even democratic countries such as France and Japan recruit their powerful bureaucracies from special educational institutions—the Grandes Ecoles and the University of Tokyo.

The claims of Lee Kuan Yew and others for the effective- 16
ness of "Asian model" technocracies look pretty unconvincing after the East Asian economic downturn of the past few years. Even before that, Amartya Sen and other economists had argued that authoritarian governments do not generally perform better economically than democratic ones, and may in fact be more at risk of economic catastrophe. But rule by an elite has much worse drawbacks.

As Alexis de Tocqueville pointed out, even if government 17
by an elite could be trusted to be efficient and public-spirited, it would have the effect of making its citizens into children. And surely we should have learned by now that no such government can be trusted. Behind every Marcus Aurelius is a crazy relative like Commodus, waiting to take over.

There never has been a governing elite in any age that did   18
not eventually come to give priority to its own interests. It
doesn't help to choose the elite from some special segment
of society. Attacking Marxism, the anarchist Mikhail Bakunin
pointed out that it would be impossible to put workers at
the head of government, because then they would cease to
be workers and instead become governors. In *Looking Backward*, Bellamy, like many other socialists, argued that labor
unions would become unnecessary once the means of
production were handed over to a national industrial army,
because then the workers would own their own factories.
This argument was not borne out by the experience of labor in the Soviet Union, to say the least. There is no reason
to imagine that a ruling elite drawn from business leaders
would do any better. H. G. Wells and other utopians have
imagined putting public affairs in the hands of scientists, but
I know my fellow scientists too well to be enthusiastic
about this proposal. Most scientists would rather do their
own research than govern anyone. I have known a number
of academic physics departments in which faculty members
actively compete for the privilege of *not* being department chairman. Anyway, I haven't seen any signs that
scientists would be better than anyone else at running a
country.

Power is not safe in the hands of any elite, but it is not safe   19
in the hands of the people, either. To abandon all constraints
on direct democracy is to submit minorities to the tyranny of
the majority. If it were not for the interposition of an elite
judiciary, the majority in many states might still be enforcing
racial segregation, and at the very least would have introduced prayer sessions in the public schools. It is the majority
that has favored state-imposed religious conformity in Algeria
and Afghanistan and other Islamic countries.

So what is the solution? Whom can we trust to exercise   20
government power? W. S. Gilbert proposed an admirably
simple solution to this problem. In the Savoy opera *Utopia,
Limited,* the King exercises all power but is in constant danger

of being turned over to the Public Exploder by two Wise Men, who explain,

> *Our duty is to spy*
> *Upon our King's illicities,*
> *And keep a watchful eye*
> *On all his eccentricities.*
> *If ever a trick he tries*
> *That savours of rascality,*
> *At our decree he dies*
> *Without the least formality.*

We just have to get used to the fact that in the real world there is no solution, and we can't trust anyone. The best we can hope for is that power be widely diffused among many conflicting government and private institutions, any of which may be allies in opposing the encroachments of others— much as in the United States today.

THE RELIGIOUS UTOPIA

A religious revival sweeps the earth, reversing
the secularization of society that began
with the Enlightenment. Many countries follow
the example of Iran, and accept religious leaders as
their rulers. America returns to its historical
roots as a Christian country. Scientific research
and teaching are permitted only where
they do not corrode religious belief.

It is hard to see why anyone would think that religion is a   21 cure for the world's problems. People have been at each other's throats over differences in religion throughout history, a sad story that continues today in Northern Ireland, the Balkans, the Middle East, Sudan, and India. But even fighting over religion is not as bad as an imposed religious uniformity. Of all the elites that can oppress us, the most dangerous are those bearing the banner of religion. Their

power is greater, because they can threaten punishment in
the next world as well as in this, and their influence is more
intrusive, because it reaches into matters that ought to be left
to private choice, such as sexual practice and family life. In
our own times we have had a taste of what utopias based on
religious uniformity are like, in countries like Iran, Saudi
Arabia, and Afghanistan, where the freedom of women is
sharply limited, and holy war is preached to children.

Religious readers may object that the harm in all these   22
cases is done by perversions of religion, not by religion itself.
But religious wars and persecutions have been at the center
of religious life throughout history. What has changed, that
these now seem to some people in some parts of the world
to be only perversions of true religious belief? Has there been
a new supernatural revelation, or a discovery of lost sacred
writings that put religious teachings in a new light? No—
since the Enlightenment there has been instead a spread of
rationality and humanitarianism that has in turn affected religious belief, leading to a wider spread of religious toleration.
It is not that religion has improved our moral sense but that
a purely secular improvement in our moral values has improved the way religion is practiced here and there. People
ought to be religious or not religious according to whether
they believe in the teachings of religion, not because of any
illusion that religion raises the moral level of society.

THE GREEN UTOPIA

*The world turns away from industrialism and
returns to a simpler style of life. Small communities
grow their own food, build houses and furniture
with their own hands, and use electricity
only to the extent that they can generate it
from sun, wind, or water.*

This is the sort of utopia that appears most often in mod-   23
ern literature—for instance, in the science fiction of Ursula
Le Guin. But modern writers tend to locate their utopias on
other planets. No one has described a rural utopia here on

earth better than William Morris did in 1890, in *News From Nowhere*. (His title, by the way, is an echo of More's *Utopia*, which might come from either the Greek *eu-* + *topos*, meaning "good place," or *ou-* + *topos*, meaning "no place." The second meaning was also picked up by Samuel Butler, in *Erewhon* (1872), which of course is "nowhere" spelled backwards—except that it isn't, which shows how hard it is to be perfect.) In Morris's future England, Hammersmith and Kensington are again small villages; the national government has become unnecessary; and the Houses of Parliament are used to store manure. Morris gives a lovely description of the unpolluted countryside seen by his hero in a long rowing voyage from London to the upper reaches of the Thames. It is all very pretty, but some of us would miss urban London.

It is common for those who don't have to work hard to romanticize hard labor, especially agricultural labor. Shakespeare's Henry V imagines that no king can sleep as soundly as a peasant, [24]

> *Who with a body fill'd and vacant mind*
> *Gets him to rest, cramm'd with distressful bread;*
> *Never sees horrid night, the child of hell,*
> *But, like a lackey, from the rise to set*
> *Sweats in the eye of Phoebus and all night*
> *Sleeps in Elysium; next day after dawn,*
> *Doth rise and help Hyperion to his horse,*
> *And follows so the ever-running year,*
> *With profitable labour, to his grave.*

I doubt that any real peasant would see farm work this way. In the words of Mel Brooks, "It's good to be the king."

Some utopians—like Wells, in *The World Set Free*—would [25] like to restore the natural environment of the past while keeping the benefits of technology, by radically reducing the earth's population. This seems hard on all those who would be unable to enjoy utopia because they had not been born. Others, like Morris, imagine that a nontechnological utopia could support the same population as at present. I don't believe it, but even if I did, I would object to abandoning the technology that gives us heart defibrillators and elementary-particle accelerators. In fact, Morris cheats. He refers to some sort of "force" that helps with necessary work that can't be done by hand; but how could something like this exist without an industrial establishment?

Hostility to technology also promotes hostility to science, [26] which gets additional fuel from the discomfort produced by what science reveals about the world. In a speech at Independence Hall, in Philadelphia, on the Fourth of July in 1994, the Czech poet and statesman Václav Havel protested that "we are not at all just an accidental anomaly . . . we are mysteriously connected to the entire universe." He called for "a science that is new . . . postmodern." One of the items that Havel would like to include in this new science is the Gaia hypothesis, according to which the earth and the living things it supports form a single organism. If the Gaia hypothesis is any more than a poetic way of expressing the obvious fact that life and its environment act on each other, then it is mystical mumbo jumbo, but it has a nice Green tinge that Havel obviously likes. This business of picking out the comforting parts of science and condemning the rest is an old story. The people of future England in *News From Nowhere* engage in some sort of science, about which Morris says only that it is different from the "commercial" science of the nineteenth century. This is an amazing comment on the science of Charles Darwin and James Clerk Maxwell. One gets the impression that the work of science in Morris's utopia consists of collecting pretty rocks and butterflies.

THE TECHNOLOGICAL UTOPIA

The development of information processing, robotics, synthetic materials, and biotechnology increases productive capacity so much that questions about the distribution of wealth become irrelevant. National borders also become irrelevant, as the whole world is connected by a web of fiber-optic cables.

There is a tendency to exaggerate the rate at which our 27
lives will be changed by technology. We still have a whole
year to go before 2001, but I doubt that Arthur C.
Clarke's vision of commercial flights to the moon is going to come
true by then. Individual technologies reach plateaus beyond
which further improvement is not worthwhile. For instance,
the experience of riding in commercial aircraft has not mate-
rially changed since the introduction of the Boeing 707, more
than forty years ago. (The Concorde is an exception that
proves the rule; it has never paid for the cost of its development.) Computer technology clearly has not yet reached its
plateau, but it will—probably when the miniaturization of
solid-state devices runs into the limits imposed by the finite
size of individual atoms. Successful technologies also tend to
be self-limiting once they become available to the general
population. I doubt that it is possible to cross Manhattan
from the East River to the Hudson River faster by automobile
today than it was by horse-drawn streetcar a century ago. The
Internet is already beginning to show the effects of over-
crowding. I tremble at the thought of two billion air-condi-
tioners in a future China and India, each adding its own
exhaust heat to the earth's atmosphere.

Still, however long it may take, new technologies will 28
inevitably bring great changes to our lives. Far from leading
us to utopia, some of these changes may well be frightening.
Technology certainly gives us the power to wreck the environment in which we live. Also, I can't imagine anything
more destructive of common feeling among the world's people than a new medical technology that would extend youth
for decades but would only be affordable by the very rich.

Then there is the problem of what people would do with 29
themselves if technology freed most of them from the necessity of work. As Freud taught, our greatest needs are love and
work. Work gives us a sense of identity and the dignity of
earning our living, and it gives many of us our chief reason
to get out of the house. In "The Machine Stops," E. M.
Forster imagined a world of perfect comfort whose people
are isolated from one another within an all-caring machine.

Their lives are so appalling that the reader is glad when the story's title comes true.

Some utopians imagine that the problem of work will solve 30 itself. Wells vaguely suggested that after technology had brought universal plenty, everyone would become an artist, and Bellamy thought that when workers retired at age forty-five, many of them would take up the arts or the sciences. I can't think of any better way to spread general misery. Even a lover of the arts can read only so much new literature, hear only so much new music, or look at only so many new paintings or sculptures, and in trying to choose the best of these everyone will tend to be drawn to the same works. Consequently, whatever joy they took in the work itself, the great majority of writers, composers, painters, and sculptors would spend their lives without having anyone else notice their work. The same would apply to scientists. By now it is impossible for a theoretical physicist to read all the papers even in some narrow subspecialty, so most articles on theoretical physics have little impact and are soon forgotten.

Morris excluded modern technology from his utopia not 31 only because he was in love with the Middle Ages but also because he wanted to preserve work for people to do. Although modern technology has made work more unsatisfying for many, I think that Morris was wrong in supposing that this is inevitable. The mindless, repetitive quality that makes routine jobs on assembly lines so hateful is also just the thing that would allow them in the future to be done entirely by machines. Technology creates better jobs, from auto mechanic to astronaut. But there is no guarantee that the advance of technology will provide all people with work that they like to do, and in the short run it converts the badly employed into the unemployed.

One of the things that attract some people to technological 32 utopias is the prospect of a world unified by technology. In the utopia of Wells's *The World Set Free* all national boundaries are dissolved; there is a powerful world government, a single world language (English, of course), worldwide adoption of the metric system, and interconvertible currencies with fixed exchange rates. There is still a United States in Bellamy's *Looking Backward,* but its citizens look forward to eventual world unification.

Physicists (who invented the World Wide Web) already 33 participate in an early version of world unification. For instance, throughout the world we share a typesetting code for mathematical symbols known as LaTeX, based on English. I recently did some work on the quantum theory of fields in collaboration with a Catalan physicist who was visiting Kyoto; we sent our equations back and forth between Texas and Japan by e-mail, in LaTeX.

I am not so sure that world unification is an unmixed 34 blessing. It has the side effect of shrinking the psychological space in which we live. A few hundred years ago large areas of the map were blank, leaving the imagination free to fill them with strange peoples and animals. Even Queen Victoria, who, it is said, tried to taste every fruit grown in the British Empire, never had a chance to try a mango or a durian. Now we can fly anywhere, and we buy mangoes in our local supermarkets. This is not my idea of utopia. Wouldn't it be more exciting to eat a mango if it could be done nowhere but in India? What is the good of getting somewhere quickly if it is no different from the place one has left?

More is at stake here than just making travel fun again 35 sometime in the future when everyone can afford it. Isolated by language differences and national boundaries, each of the world's cultures represents a precious link to the past and an opportunity for distinctive new artistic and intellectual creation. All these are put at risk by steps toward world unification.

Now I have said hard things about five different styles of 36 utopia—so what do I have to offer? No easy solutions. There is no simple formula that will tell us how to strike a balance between the dangers from governing elites and those from majority rule or free markets, or between the opportunities and the hazards of new technology. I can't resist offering a utopian vision of my own, but it is a very modest one.

THE CIVILIZED EGALITARIAN
CAPITALIST UTOPIA

*Production remains mostly in the hands of competing
private corporations, overseen by a democratic government that is itself overseen by independent courts; these
corporations continue to use high salaries along with
status and authority to attract workers and managers with
special talents, and dividends to attract capital. Those
who receive a high income are able to keep only part of it;
to prevent the rest of their income from being simply taken
in taxes they give much of it to museums, universities, and
other institutions of their choice, reaping benefits that
range from moral satisfaction to better seats at the opera.
These nonprofit institutions use the donations to invest in
business enterprises, eventually replacing wealthy individuals as the owners of industrial corporations.*

Not very original? No, it is in fact a natural development 37
from some present trends. Nonprofit institutions have been
the fastest-growing sector of the American economy over
the past fifteen years. But the tide of American politics now
seems to be flowing in the opposite direction. We are in the
process of giving up our best weapon against inequality: the
graduated income tax, levied on all forms of income and
supplemented by taxes on legacies. A steeply graduated income tax, if accompanied by generous allowances for the
deduction of charitable contributions, has another virtue: it
amounts to a public subsidy for museums, symphony orchestras, hospitals, universities, research laboratories, and charities
of all sorts, without putting them under the control of government. Oddly, the deductibility of charitable contributions
has been attacked in whole or in part by conservatives like
Steve Forbes and Herbert Stein, even though it has been a
peculiarly American way of achieving government support for
the values of civilization without increasing government
power.

I don't offer this modest utopia with any great fervor, 38
because I have doubts whether men and women will be

content with an individualistic life of love and work and liberty and equality. People have seemed also to need some exciting collective enterprise that, even if destructive, would lift them out of the everyday round of civilized life.

The individualistic lives of propertied European men at 39 the beginning of the twentieth century were about as pleasant as one can imagine: these men moved in a world of elegant cafés, theaters, country houses, and relatively unspoiled countryside; their comforts were seen to by deferential women and servants; and for those who cared about such things, there were exciting innovations in science and the arts. Yet there is plenty of evidence that many of these men were afflicted with such boredom and directionlessness that they felt as they went off to the Great War, in 1914, like "swimmers into cleanness leaping." Now war has become intolerable. Perhaps someday we may find a better common cause in the colonization of the solar system, but that is far off—and even then most people will be left here on earth.

Can we change ourselves enough to be satisfied with a 40 civilized society? The dream that behaviorists and Marxists had of changing human nature seems to me the worst sort of exaggeration of the capabilities of science. In *Three Sisters,* Chekhov has Baron Tuzenbach reply to Vershinin's utopian dreams.

> *Well, maybe we'll fly in balloons, the cut of jackets will be different, we'll have discovered a sixth sense, maybe even developed it—I don't know. But life will be the same—difficult, full of unknowns, and happy. In a thousand years, just like today, people will sigh and say, oh, how hard it is to be alive. They'll still be scared of death, and won't want to die.*

Facing a new millennium we can share some of Vershinin's hopes for utopia, but when it comes to judging the chances of really changing the way we live, no doubt most of us would side with Tuzenbach.

For Study and Discussion

QUESTIONS FOR RESPONSE

1. What utopias have you read about in science fiction or seen on television series or in films? What did you like or dislike about these visions of the future?
2. If you could create a utopia, what would be its distinctive features? Who would you put in charge? How would you define work? How would you distribute wealth?

QUESTIONS ABOUT PURPOSE

1. How does Weinberg's assessment of each utopia support his assertion that each vision "abandons one or more of the grand causes?"
2. How does he use the quotes from Anton Chekhov's *Three Sisters*, at the beginning and end of his essay, to clarify his purpose?

QUESTION ABOUT AUDIENCE

1. How does Weinberg anticipate his readers' limited knowledge about other utopian writers?
2. How does Weinberg assess the behavior and motives of scientists like himself?

QUESTIONS ABOUT STRATEGIES

1. How consistent is Weinberg's principle of classification? Has he overlooked any particular model?
2. How effective is his description of each utopia (in italics)? How does he introduce the problems apparent in each utopia? For example, how do they abandon equality, quality of life, and work?

QUESTIONS FOR DISCUSSION

1. What do you think of Weinberg's "solution"? Do you share his confidence in the tax code and the nonprofit sector? Explain your answer.
2. The word *utopia* means *nowhere*. In what ways are utopian schemes intended as political blueprints? If they are created as entertainment, why should we discuss them as serious options?

Flannery O'Connor (1925–1964) was born in Savannah, Georgia, and was educated at the Women's College of Georgia and the University of Iowa. She returned to her mother's farm near Milledgeville, Georgia, when she discovered that she had contracted lupus erythematosus, the systemic disease that had killed her father and of which she herself was to die. For the last fourteen years of her life, she lived a quiet, productive life on the farm—raising peacocks, painting, and writing the extraordinary stories and novels that won her worldwide acclaim. Her novels, *Wise Blood* (1952), which was adapted for film in 1979, and *The Violent Bear It Away* (1960), deal with fanatical preachers. Her thirty-one carefully crafted stories, combining grotesque comedy and violent tragedy, appear in *A Good Man Is Hard to Find* (1955), *Everything That Rises Must Converge* (1965), and *The Complete Stories* (1971), which won the National Book Award. "Revelation" dramatizes the ironic discoveries a woman makes about how different classes of people fit into the order of things.

Revelation

T HE DOCTOR'S WAITING room, which was very small, was almost full when the Turpins entered and Mrs. Turpin, who was very large, made it look even smaller by her presence. She stood looming at the head of the magazine table set in the center of it, a living demonstration that the room was inadequate and ridiculous. Her little bright black eyes took in all the patients as she sized up the seating situ- 1 ation. There was one vacant chair and a place on the sofa occupied by a blond child in a dirty blue romper who should have been told to move over and make room for the lady. He was five or six, but Mrs. Turpin saw at once that no one was going to tell him to move over. He was slumped down in the seat, his arms idle at his sides and his eyes idle in his head; his nose ran unchecked.

Mrs. Turpin put a firm hand on Claud's shoulder and said   2
in a voice that included anyone who wanted to listen, "Claud, you sit in that chair there," and gave him a push down into the vacant one. Claud was florid and bald and sturdy, somewhat shorter than Mrs. Turpin, but he sat down as if he were accustomed to doing what she told him to.

Mrs. Turpin remained standing. The only man in the room   3
besides Claud was a lean stringy old fellow with a rusty hand spread out on each knee, whose eyes were closed as if he were asleep or dead or pretending to be so as not to get up and offer her his seat. Her gaze settled agreeably on a well-dressed gray-haired lady whose eyes met hers and whose expression said: if that child belonged to me, he would have some manners and move over—there's plenty of room there for you and him too.

Claud looked up with a sigh and made as if to rise.   4
"Sit down," Mrs. Turpin said. "You know you're not   5
supposed to stand on that leg. He has an ulcer on his leg," she explained.

Claud lifted his foot onto the magazine table and rolled   6
his trouser leg up to reveal a purple swelling on a plump marble-white calf.

"My!" the pleasant lady said. "How did you do that?"   7
"A cow kicked him," Mrs. Turpin said.   8
"Goodness!" said the lady.   9
Claud rolled his trouser leg down.   10
"Maybe the little boy would move over," the lady sug-   11
gested, but the child did not stir.

"Somebody will be leaving in a minute," Mrs. Turpin said.   12
She could not understand why a doctor—with as much money as they made charging five dollars a day to just stick

their head in the hospital door and look at you—couldn't afford a decent-sized waiting room. This one was hardly bigger than a garage. The table was cluttered with limp-looking magazines and at one end of it there was a big green glass ash tray full of cigarette butts and cotton wads with little blood spots on them. If she had had anything to do with the running of the place, that would have been emptied every so often. There were no chairs against the wall at the head of the room. It had a rectangular-shaped panel in it that permitted a view of the office where the nurse came and went and the secretary listened to the radio. A plastic fern in a gold pot sat in the opening and trailed its fronds down almost to the floor. The radio was softly playing gospel music.

Just then the inner door opened and a nurse with the highest stack of yellow hair Mrs. Turpin had ever seen put her face in the crack and called for the next patient. The woman sitting beside Claud grasped the two arms of her chair and hoisted herself up; she pulled her dress free from her legs and lumbered through the door where the nurse had disappeared. 13

Mrs. Turpin eased into the vacant chair, which held her tight as a corset. "I wish I could reduce," she said, and rolled her eyes and gave a comic sigh. 14

"Oh, *you* aren't fat," the stylish lady said. 15

"Ooooo I am too," Mrs. Turpin said. "Claud he eats all he wants to and never weighs over one hundred and seventy-five pounds, but me I just look at something good to eat and I gain some weight," and her stomach and shoulders shook with laughter. "You can eat all you want to, can't you, Claud?" she asked, turning to him. 16

Claud only grinned. 17

"Well, as long as you have such a good disposition," the stylish lady said, "I don't think it makes a bit of difference what size you are. You just can't beat a good disposition." 18

Next to her was a fat girl of eighteen or nineteen, scowling into a thick blue book which Mrs. Turpin saw was entitled *Human Development.* The girl raised her head and directed her scowl at Mrs. Turpin as if she did not like her looks. She 19 appeared annoyed that anyone should speak while she tried to read. The poor girl's face was blue with acne and Mrs. Turpin thought how pitiful it was to have a face like that at that age. She gave the girl a friendly smile but the girl only scowled the harder. Mrs. Turpin herself was fat but she had always had good skin, and, though she was forty-seven years old, there was not a wrinkle in her face except around her eyes from laughing too much.

Next to the ugly girl was the child, still in exactly the same position, and next to him was a thin leathery old woman in a cotton print dress. She and Claud had three sacks of chicken feed in their pump house that was in the same print. She had seen from the first that the child belonged with the old woman. She could tell by the way they sat—kind of vacant and white-trashy, as if they would sit there until Doomsday if nobody called and told them to get up. And at right angles but next to the well-dressed pleasant lady was a lank-faced woman who was certainly the child's mother. She had on a yellow sweat shirt and wine-colored slacks, both gritty-looking, and the rims of her lips were stained with snuff. Her dirty yellow hair was tied behind with a little piece of red paper ribbon. Worse than niggers any day, Mrs. Turpin thought. 20

The gospel hymn playing was, "When I looked up and He looked down," and Mrs. Turpin, who knew it, supplied the last line mentally, "And wona these days I know I'll weear a crown." 21

Without appearing to, Mrs. Turpin always noticed people's feet. The well-dressed lady had on red and gray suede shoes to match her dress. Mrs. Turpin had on her good black patent leather pumps. The ugly girl had on Girl Scout shoes and heavy socks. The old woman had on tennis shoes and the white-trashy mother had on what appeared to be bedroom slippers, black straw with gold braid threaded through them—exactly what you would have expected her to have on. 22

Sometimes at night when she couldn't go to sleep, Mrs. Turpin would occupy herself with the question of who she would have chosen to be if she couldn't have been herself. If 23

Jesus had said to her before he made her, "There's only two places available for you. You can either be a nigger or white-trash," what would she have said? "Please, Jesus, please," she would have said, "just let me wait until there's another place available," and he would have said, "No, you have to go right now and I have only those two places so make up your mind." She would have wiggled and squirmed and begged and pleaded but it would have been no use and finally she would have said, "All right, make me a nigger then—but that don't mean a trashy one." And he would have made her a neat clean respectable Negro woman, herself but black.

Next to the child's mother was a red-headed youngish 24
woman, reading one of the magazines and working a piece of chewing gum, hell for leather, as Claud would say. Mrs. Turpin could not see the woman's feet. She was not white-trash, just common. Sometimes Mrs. Turpin occupied herself at night naming the classes of people. On the bottom of the heap were most colored people, not the kind she would have been if she had been one, but most of them; then next to them—not above, just away from—were the white-trash; then above them were the home-owners, and above them the home-and-land-owners, to which she and Claud belonged. Above she and Claud were people with a lot of money and much bigger houses and much more land. But here the complexity of it would begin to bear in on her, for some of the people with a lot of money were common and ought to be below she and Claud and some of the people who had good blood had lost their money and had to rent and then there were colored people who owned their homes and land as well. There was a colored dentist in town who had two red Lincolns and a swimming pool and a farm with registered white-face cattle on it. Usually by the time she had fallen asleep all the classes of people were moiling and roiling around in her head, and she would dream they were all crammed in together in a box car, being ridden off to be put in a gas oven.

"That's a beautiful clock," she said and nodded to her 25
right. It was a big wall clock, the face encased in a brass sunburst.

"Yes, it's very pretty," the stylish lady said agreeably. "And   26
right on the dot too," she added, glancing at her watch.

The ugly girl beside her cast an eye upward at the clock,   27
smirked, then looked directly at Mrs. Turpin and smirked
again. Then she returned her eyes to her book. She was
obviously the lady's daughter because, although they didn't
look anything alike as to disposition, they both had the same
shape of face and the same blue eyes. On the lady they
sparkled pleasantly but in the girl's seared face they appeared
alternately to smolder and to blaze.

What if Jesus had said, "All right, you can be white-trash   28
or a nigger or ugly"!

Mrs. Turpin felt an awful pity for the girl, though she   29
thought it was one thing to be ugly and another to act ugly.

The woman with the snuff-stained lips turned around in   30
her chair and looked up at the clock. Then she turned back
and appeared to look a little to the side of Mrs. Turpin. There
was a cast in one of her eyes. "You want to know wher you
can get you one of themther clocks?" she asked in a loud
voice.

"No, I already have a nice clock," Mrs. Turpin said. Once   31
somebody like her got a leg in the conversation, she would
be all over it.

"You can get you one with green stamps," the woman said.   32
"That's most likely wher he got hisn. Save you up enough,
you can get you most anythang. I got me some joo'ry."

Ought to have got you a wash rag and some soap, Mrs.   33
Turpin thought.

"I get contour sheets with mine," the pleasant lady said.   34

The daughter slammed her book shut. She looked straight   35
in front of her, directly through Mrs. Turpin and on through
the yellow curtain and the plate glass window which made
the wall behind her. The girl's eyes seemed lit all of a sudden
with a peculiar light, an unnatural light like night road signs
give. Mrs. Turpin turned her head to see if there was anything
going on outside that she should see, but she could not see
anything. Figures passing cast only a pale shadow through
the curtain. There was no reason the girl should single her
out for her ugly looks.

"Miss Finley," the nurse said, cracking the door. The 36
gum-chewing woman got up and passed in front of her and
Claud and went into the office. She had on red high-heeled
shoes.

Directly across the table, the ugly girl's eyes were fixed on 37
Mrs. Turpin as if she had some very special reason for dislik-
ing her.

"This is wonderful weather, isn't it?" the girl's mother said. 38

"It's good weather for cotton if you can get the niggers 39
to pick it," Mrs. Turpin said, "but niggers don't want to pick
cotton any more. You can't get the white folks to pick it and
now you can't get the niggers—because they got to be right
up there with the white folks."

"They gonna *try* anyways," the white-trash woman said, 40
leaning forward.

"Do you have one of the cotton-picking machines?" the 41
pleasant lady asked.

"No," Mrs. Turpin said, "they leave half the cotton in the 42
field. We don't have much cotton anyway. If you want to
make it farming now, you have to have a little of everything.
We got a couple of acres of cotton and a few hogs and
chickens and just enough white-face that Claud can look after
them himself."

"One thang I don't want," the white-trash woman said, 43
wiping her mouth with the back of her hand. "Hogs. Nasty
stinking things, a-gruntin and a-rootin all over the place."

Mrs. Turpin gave her the merest edge of her attention. 44
"Our hogs are not dirty and they don't stink," she said.
"They're cleaner than some children I've seen. Their feet
never touch the ground. We have a pig-parlor—that's where
you raise them on concrete," she explained to the pleasant
lady, "and Claud scoots them down with the hose every
afternoon and washes off the floor." Cleaner by far than that
child right there, she thought. Poor nasty little thing. He had
not moved except to put the thumb of his dirty hand into
his mouth.

The woman turned her face away from Mrs. Turpin. "I 45
know I wouldn't scoot down no hog with no hose," she said
to the wall.

You wouldn't have no hog to scoot down, Mrs. Turpin   46
said to herself.

"A-gruntin and a-rootin and a-groanin," the woman mut-   47
tered.

"We got a little of everything," Mrs. Turpin said to the   48
pleasant lady. "It's no use in having more than you can handle
yourself with help like it is. We found enough niggers to pick
our cotton this year but Claud he has to go after them and
take them home again in the evening. They can't walk that
half a mile. No they can't. I tell you," she said and laughed
merrily, "I sure am tired of buttering up niggers, but you got
to love em if you want em to work for you. When they come
in the morning, I run out and I say, 'Hi yawl this morning?'
and when Claud drives them off to the field I just wave to
beat the band and they just wave back." And she waved her
hand rapidly to illustrate.

"Like you read out of the same book," the lady said,   49
showing she understood perfectly.

"Child, yes," Mrs. Turpin said. "And when they come in   50
from the field, I run out with a bucket of icewater. That's the
way it's going to be from now on," she said. "You may as
well face it."

"One thang I know," the white-trash woman said. "Two   51
thangs I ain't going to do: love no niggers or scoot down no
hog with no hose." And she let out a bark of contempt.

The look that Mrs. Turpin and the pleasant lady exchanged   52
indicated they both understood that you had to *have* certain
things before you could *know* certain things. But every time
Mrs. Turpin exchanged a look with the lady, she was aware
that the ugly girl's peculiar eyes were still on her, and she had
trouble bringing her attention back to the conversation.

"When you got something," she said, "you got to look   53
after it." And when you ain't got a thing but breath and
britches, she added to herself, you can afford to come to town
every morning and just sit on the Court House coping and
spit.

A grotesque revolving shadow passed across the curtain   54
behind her and was thrown palely on the opposite wall. Then

a bicycle clattered down against the outside of the building. The door opened and a colored boy glided in with a tray from the drugstore. It had two large red and white paper cups on it with tops on them. He was a tall, very black boy in discolored white pants and a green nylon shirt. He was chewing gum slowly, as if to music. He set the tray down in the office opening next to the fern and stuck his head through to look for the secretary. She was not in there. He rested his arms on the ledge and waited, his narrow bottom stuck out, swaying to the left and right. He raised a hand over his head and scratched the base of his skull.

"You see that button there, boy?" Mrs. Turpin said. "You   55 can punch that and she'll come. She's probably in the back somewhere."

"Is thas right?" the boy said agreeably, as if he had never   56 seen the button before. He leaned to the right and put his finger on it. "She sometime out," he said and twisted around to face his audience, his elbows behind him on the counter. The nurse appeared and he twisted back again. She handed him a dollar and he rooted in his pocket and made the change and counted it out to her. She gave him fifteen cents for a tip and he went out with the empty tray. The heavy door swung too slowly and closed at length with the sound of suction. For a moment no one spoke.

"They ought to send all them niggers back to Africa," the   57 white-trash woman said. "That's wher they come from in the first place."

"Oh, I couldn't do without my good colored friends," the   58 pleasant lady said.

"There's a heap of things worse than a nigger," Mrs.   59 Turpin agreed. "It's all kinds of them just like it's all kinds of us."

"Yes, and it takes all kinds to make the world go round,"   60 the lady said in her musical voice.

As she said it, the raw-complexioned girl snapped her teeth   61 together. Her lower lip turned downwards and inside out, revealing the pale pink inside of her mouth. After a second it rolled back up. It was the ugliest face Mrs. Turpin had ever seen anyone make and for a moment she was certain that the girl had made it at her. She was looking at her as if she had known and disliked her all her life—all of Mrs. Turpin's life, it seemed too, not just all the girl's life. Why, girl, I don't even know you, Mrs. Turpin said silently.

She forced her attention back to the discussion. "It 62 wouldn't be practical to send them back to Africa," she said. "They wouldn't want to go. They got it too good here."

"Wouldn't be what they wanted—if I had anythang to do 63 with it," the woman said.

"It wouldn't be a way in the world you could get all the 64 niggers back over there," Mrs. Turpin said. "They'd be hiding out and lying down and turning sick on you and wailing and hollering and raring and pitching. It wouldn't be a way in the world to get them over there."

"They got over here," the trashy woman said. "Get back 65 like they got over."

"It wasn't so many of them then," Mrs. Turpin explained. 66

The woman looked at Mrs. Turpin as if here was an idiot 67 indeed but Mrs. Turpin was not bothered by the look, considering where it came from.

"Nooo," she said, "they're going to stay here where they 68 can go to New York and marry white folks and improve their color. That's what they all want to do, every one of them, improve their color."

"You know what comes of that, don't you?" Claud asked. 69

"No, Claud, what?" Mrs. Turpin said. 70

Claud's eyes twinkled. "White-faced niggers," he said with 71 never a smile.

Everybody in the office laughed except the white-trash and 72 the ugly girl. The girl gripped the book in her lap with white fingers. The trashy woman looked around her from face to face as if she thought they were all idiots. The old woman in the feed sack dress continued to gaze expressionless across the floor at the high-top shoes of the man opposite her, the one who had been pretending to be asleep when the Turpins came in. He was laughing heartily, his hands still spread out on his knees. The child had fallen to the side and was lying now almost face down in the old woman's lap.

While they recovered from their laughter, the nasal chorus   73
on the radio kept the room from silence.

> *You go to blank blank*
> *And I'll go to mine*
> *But we'll all blank along*
> *To-geth-ther,*
> *And all along the blank*
> *We'll hep eachother out*
> *Smile-ling in any kind of*
> *Weath-ther!*

Mrs. Turpin didn't catch every word but she caught   74
enough to agree with the spirit of the song and it turned her
thoughts sober. To help anybody out that needed it was her
philosophy of life. She never spared herself when she found
somebody in need, whether they were white or black, trash
or decent. And of all she had to be thankful for, she was most
thankful that this was so. If Jesus had said, "You can be high
society and have all the money you want and be thin and
svelte-like, but you can't be a good woman with it," she
would have had to say, "Well don't make me that then. Make
me a good woman and it don't matter what else, how fat or
how ugly or how poor!" Her heart rose. He had not made
her a nigger or white-trash or ugly! He had made her herself
and given her a little of everything. Jesus, thank you! she said.
Thank you thank you thank you! Whenever she counted her
blessings she felt as buoyant as if she weighed one hundred
and twenty-five pounds instead of one hundred and eighty.

"What's wrong with your little boy?" the pleasant lady   75
asked the white-trashy woman.

"He has a ulcer," the woman said proudly. "He ain't give   76
me a minute's peace since he was born. Him and her are just
alike," she said, nodding at the old woman, who was running
her leathery fingers through the child's pale hair. "Look like
I can't get nothing down them two but Co' Cola and candy."

That's all you try to get down em, Mrs. Turpin said to   77
herself. Too lazy to light the fire. There was nothing you
could tell her about people like them that she didn't know

already. And it was not just that they didn't have anything. Because if you gave them everything, in two weeks it would all be broken or filthy or they would have chopped it up for lightwood. She knew all this from her own experience. Help them you must, but help them you couldn't.

All at once the ugly girl turned her lips inside out again.   78
Her eyes fixed like two drills on Mrs. Turpin. This time there was no mistaking that there was something urgent behind them.

Girl, Mrs. Turpin exclaimed silently, I haven't done a thing   79
to you! The girl might be confusing her with somebody else. There was no need to sit by and let herself be intimidated. "You must be in college," she said boldly, looking directly at the girl. "I see you reading a book there."

The girl continued to stare and pointedly did not answer.   80

Her mother blushed at this rudeness. "The lady asked you   81
a question, Mary Grace," she said under her breath.

"I have ears," Mary Grace said.   82

The poor mother blushed again. "Mary Grace goes to   83
Wellesley College," she explained. She twisted one of the buttons on her dress. "In Massachusetts," she added with a grimace. "And in the summer she just keeps right on studying. Just reads all the time, a real book worm. She's done real well at Wellesley; she's taking English and Math and History and Psychology and Social Studies," she rattled on, "and I think it's too much. I think she ought to get out and have fun."

The girl looked as if she would like to hurl them all   84
through the plate glass window.

"Way up north," Mrs. Turpin murmured and thought,   85
well, it hasn't done much for her manners.

"I'd almost rather to have him sick," the white-trash   86
woman said, wrenching the attention back to herself. "He's so mean when he ain't. Look like some children just take natural to meanness. It's some gets bad when they get sick but he was the opposite. Took sick and turned good. He don't give me no trouble now. It's me waitin to see the doctor," she said.

If I was going to send anybody back to Africa, Mrs. Turpin   87
thought, it would be your kind, woman. "Yes, indeed," she
said aloud, but looking up at the ceiling, "it's a heap of things
worse than a nigger." And dirtier than a hog, she added to
herself.

"I think people with bad dispositions are more to be pitied   88
than anyone on earth," the pleasant lady said in a voice that
was decidedly thin.

"I thank the Lord he has blessed me with a good one,"   89
Mrs. Turpin said. "The day has never dawned that I couldn't
find something to laugh at."

"Not since she married me anyways," Claud said with a   90
comical straight face.

Everybody laughed except the girl and the white-trash.   91

Mrs. Turpin's stomach shook. "He's such a caution," she   92
said, "that I can't help but laugh at him."

The girl made a loud ugly noise through her teeth.   93

Her mother's mouth grew thin and tight. "I think the   94
worst thing in the world," she said, "is an ungrateful person.
To have everything and not appreciate it. I know a girl," she
said, "who has parents who would give her anything, a little
brother who loves her dearly, who is getting a good education, who wears the best clothes, but who can never say a
kind word to anyone, who never smiles, who just criticizes
and complains all day long."

"Is she too old to paddle?" Claud asked.   95

The girl's face was almost purple.   96

"Yes," the lady said, "I'm afraid there's nothing to do but   97
leave her to her folly. Some day she'll wake up and it'll be too
late."

"It never hurt anyone to smile," Mrs. Turpin said. "It just   98
makes you feel better all over."

"Of course," the lady said sadly, "but there are just some   99
people you can't tell anything to. They can't take criticism."

"If it's one thing I am," Mrs. Turpin said with feeling, "it's   100
grateful. When I think who all I could have been besides
myself and what all I got, a little of everything, and a good
disposition besides, I just feel like shouting, 'Thank you,

Jesus, for making everything the way it is!' It could have been different!" For one thing, somebody else could have got Claud. At the thought of this, she was flooded with gratitude and a terrible pang of joy ran through her. "Oh thank you, Jesus, Jesus, thank you!" she cried aloud.

The book struck her directly over her left eye. It struck   101
almost at the same instant that she realized the girl was about to hurl it. Before she could utter a sound, the raw face came crashing across the table toward her, howling. The girl's fingers sank like clamps into the soft flesh of her neck. She heard the mother cry out and Claud shout, "Whoa!" There was an instant when she was certain that she was about to be in an earthquake.

All at once her vision narrowed and she saw everything as   102
if it were happening in a small room far away, or as if she were looking at it through the wrong end of a telescope. Claud's face crumpled and fell out of sight. The nurse ran in, then out, then in again. Then the gangling figure of the doctor rushed out of the inner door. Magazines flew this way and that as the table turned over. The girl fell with a thud and Mrs. Turpin's vision suddenly reversed itself and she saw everything large instead of small. The eyes of the white-trashy woman were staring hugely at the floor. There the girl, held down on one side by the nurse and on the other by her mother, was wrenching and turning in their grasp. The doctor was kneeling astride her, trying to hold her arm down. He managed after a second to sink a long needle into it.

Mrs. Turpin felt entirely hollow except for her heart which   103
swung from side to side as if it were agitated in a great empty drum of flesh.

"Somebody that's not busy call for the ambulance," the   104
doctor said in the off-hand voice young doctors adopt for terrible occasions.

Mrs. Turpin could not have moved a finger. The old man   105
who had been sitting next to her skipped nimbly into the office and made the call, for the secretary still seemed to be gone.

"Claud!" Mrs. Turpin called. 106

He was not in his chair. She knew she must jump up and 107 find him but she felt like some one trying to catch a train in a dream, when everything moves in slow motion and the faster you try to run the slower you go.

"Here I am," a suffocated voice, very unlike Claud's, said. 108

He was doubled up in the corner on the floor, pale as 109 paper, holding his leg. She wanted to get up and go to him but she could not move. Instead, her gaze was drawn slowly downward to the churning face on the floor, which she could see over the doctor's shoulder.

The girl's eyes stopped rolling and focused on her. They 110 seemed a much lighter blue than before, as if a door that had been tightly closed behind them was now open to admit light and air.

Mrs. Turpin's head cleared and her power of motion re- 111 turned. She leaned forward until she was looking directly into the fierce brilliant eyes. There was no doubt in her mind that the girl did know her, knew her in some intense and personal way, beyond time and place and condition. "What you got to say to me?" she asked hoarsely and held her breath, wait- ing, as for a revelation.

The girl raised her head. Her gaze locked with Mrs. Tur- 112 pin's. "Go back to hell where you came from, you old wart hog," she whispered. Her voice was low but clear. Her eyes burned for a moment as if she saw with pleasure that her message had struck its target.

Mrs. Turpin sank back in her chair. 113

After a moment the girl's eyes closed and she turned her 114 head wearily to the side.

The doctor rose and handed the nurse the empty syringe. 115 He leaned over and put both hands for a moment on the mother's shoulders, which were shaking. She was sitting on the floor, her lips pressed together, holding Mary Grace's hand in her lap. The girl's fingers were gripped like a baby's around her thumb. "Go on to the hospital," he said. "I'll call and make the arrangements."

"Now let's see that neck," he said in a jovial voice to Mrs.   116
Turpin. He began to inspect her neck with his first two
fingers. Two little moon-shaped lines like pink fish bones
were indented over her windpipe. There was the beginning
of an angry red swelling above her eye. His fingers passed
over this also.

"Lea' me be," she said thickly and shook him off. "See   117
about Claud. She kicked him."

"I'll see about him in a minute," he said and felt her pulse.   118
He was a thin gray-haired man, given to pleasantries. "Go
home and have yourself a vacation the rest of the day," he
said and patted her on the shoulder.

Quit your pattin me, Mrs. Turpin growled to herself.   119

"And put an ice pack over that eye," he said. Then he went   120
and squatted down beside Claud and looked at his leg. After
a moment he pulled him up and Claud limped after him into
the office.

Until the ambulance came, the only sounds in the room   121
were the tremulous moans of the girl's mother, who continued to sit on the floor. The white-trash woman did not take
her eyes off the girl. Mrs. Turpin looked straight ahead at
nothing. Presently the ambulance drew up, a long dark
shadow, behind the curtain. The attendants came in and set
the stretcher down beside the girl and lifted her expertly onto
it and carried her out. The nurse helped the mother gather
up her things. The shadow of the ambulance moved silently
away and the nurse came back in the office.

"That ther girl is going to be a lunatic, ain't she?" the   122
white-trash woman asked the nurse, but the nurse kept on to
the back and never answered her.

"Yes, she's going to be a lunatic," the white-trash woman   123
said to the rest of them.

"Po' critter," the old woman murmured. The child's face   124
was still in her lap. His eyes looked idly out over her knees.
He had not moved during the disturbance except to draw
one leg up under him.

"I thank Gawd," the white-trash woman said fervently, "I   125
ain't a lunatic."

Claud came limping out and the Turpins went home.   126

As their pick-up truck turned into their own dirt road and   127
made the crest of the hill, Mrs. Turpin gripped the window
ledge and looked out suspiciously. The land sloped gracefully
down through a field dotted with lavender weeds and at the
start of the rise their small yellow frame house, with its little
flower beds spread out around it like a fancy apron, sat primly
in its accustomed place between two giant hickory trees. She
would not have been startled to see a burnt wound between
two blackened chimneys.

Neither of them felt like eating so they put on their house   128
clothes and lowered the shade in the bedroom and lay down,
Claud with his leg on a pillow and herself with a damp
washcloth over her eye. The instant she was flat on her back,
the image of a razor-backed hog with warts on its face and
horns coming out behind its ears snorted into her head. She
moaned, a low quiet moan.

"I am not," she said tearfully, "a wart hog. From hell."   129
But the denial had no force. The girl's eyes and her words,
even the tone of her voice, low but clear, directed only to
her, brooked no repudiation. She had been singled out for
the message, though there was trash in the room to whom it
might justly have been applied. The full force of this fact
struck her only now. There was a woman there who was
neglecting her own child but she had been overlooked. The
message had been given to Ruby Turpin, a respectable, hard-
working, church-going woman. The tears dried. Her eyes
began to burn instead with wrath.

She rose on her elbow and the washcloth fell into her hand.   130
Claud was lying on his back, snoring. She wanted to tell him
what the girl had said. At the same time, she did not wish to
put the image of herself as a wart hog from hell into his mind.

"Hey, Claud," she muttered and pushed his shoulder.   131

Claud opened one pale baby blue eye.   132

She looked into it warily. He did not think about any   133
thing. He just went his way.

"Wha, whasit?" he said and closed the eye again.   134

"Nothing," she said. "Does your leg pain you?"   135

"Hurts like hell," Claud said.   136

"It'll quit terreckly," she said and lay back down. In a   137
moment Claud was snoring again. For the rest of the afternoon they lay there. Claud slept. She scowled at the ceiling.
Occasionally she raised her fist and made a small stabbing
motion over her chest as if she was defending her innocence
to invisible guests who were like the comforters of Job,
reasonable-seeming but wrong.

About five-thirty Claud stirred. "Got to go after those   138
niggers," he sighed, not moving.

She was looking straight up as if there were unintelligible   139
handwriting on the ceiling. The protuberance over her eye
had turned a greenish-blue. "Listen here," she said.

"What?"   140

"Kiss me."   141

Claud leaned over and kissed her loudly on the mouth. He   142
pinched her side and their hands interlocked. Her expression
of ferocious concentration did not change. Claud got up,
groaning and growling, and limped off. She continued to
study the ceiling.

She did not get up until she heard the pick-up truck   143
coming back with the Negroes. Then she rose and thrust her
feet in her brown oxfords, which she did not bother to lace,
and stumped out onto the back porch and got her red plastic
bucket. She emptied a tray of ice cubes into it and filled it
half full of water and went out into the back yard. Every
afternoon after Claud brought the hands in, one of the boys
helped him put out hay and the rest waited in the back of the
truck until he was ready to take them home. The truck was
parked in the shade under one of the hickory trees.

"Hi yawl this evening?" Mrs. Turpin asked grimly, appear-   144
ing with the bucket and the dipper. There were three women
and a boy in the truck.

"Us doin nicely," the oldest woman said. "Hi you doin?"   145
and her gaze stuck immediately on the dark lump on Mrs.
Turpin's forehead. "You done fell down, ain't you?" she
asked in a solicitous voice. The old woman was dark and

almost toothless. She had on an old felt hat of Claud's set back on her head. The other two women were younger and lighter and they both had new bright green sunhats. One of them had hers on her head; the other had taken hers off and the boy was grinning beneath it.

Mrs. Turpin set the bucket down on the floor of the truck. "Yawl hep yourselves," she said. She looked around to make sure Claud had gone. "No, I didn't fall down," she said, folding her arms. "It was something worse than that." 146

"Ain't nothing bad happen to you!" the old woman said. She said it as if they all knew that Mrs. Turpin was protected in some special way by Divine Providence. "You just had you a little fall." 147

"We were in town at the doctor's office for where the cow kicked Mr. Turpin," Mrs. Turpin said in a flat tone that indicated they could leave off their foolishness. "And there was this girl there. A big fat girl with her face all broke out. I could look at that girl and tell she was peculiar but I couldn't tell how. And me and her mama was just talking and going along and all of a sudden WHAM! She throws this big book she was reading at me and . . ." 148

"Naw!" the old woman cried out. 149

"And then she jumps over the table and commences to choke me." 150

"Naw!" they all exclaimed, "naw!" 151

"Hi come she do that?" the old woman asked. "What ail her?" 152

Mrs. Turpin only glared in front of her. 153

"Somethin ail her," the old woman said. 154

"They carried her off in an ambulance," Mrs. Turpin continued, "but before she went she was rolling on the floor and they were trying to hold her down to give her a shot and she said something to me." She paused. "You know what she said to me?" 155

"What she say?" they asked. 156

"She said," Mrs. Turpin began, and stopped, her face very dark and heavy. The sun was getting whiter and whiter, 157 blanching the sky overhead so that the leaves of the hickory tree were black in the face of it. She could not bring forth the words. "Something real ugly," she muttered.

"She sho shouldn't said nothin ugly to you," the old woman said. "You so sweet. You the sweetest lady I know." 158

"She pretty too," the one with the hat on said. 159

"And stout," the other one said. "I never knowed no sweeter white lady." 160

"That's the truth befo' Jesus," the old woman said. "Amen! You des as sweet and pretty as you can be." 161

Mrs. Turpin knew exactly how much Negro flattery was worth and it added to her rage. "She said," she began again and finished this time with a fierce rush of breath, "that I was an old wart hog from hell." 162

There was an astounded silence. 163

"Where she at?" the youngest woman cried in a piercing voice. 164

"Lemme see her. I'll kill her!" 165

"I'll kill her with you!" the other one cried. 166

"She b'long in the sylum," the old woman said emphatically. "You the sweetest white lady I know." 167

"She pretty too," the other two said. "Stout as she can be and sweet. Jesus satisfied with her!" 168

"Deed he is," the old woman declared. 169

Idiots! Mrs. Turpin growled to herself. You could never say anything intelligent to a nigger. You could talk at them but not with them. "Yawl ain't drunk your water," she said shortly. "Leave the bucket in the truck when you're finished with it. I got more to do than just stand around and pass the time of day," and she moved off and into the house. 170

She stood for a moment in the middle of the kitchen. The dark protuberance over her eye looked like a miniature tornado cloud which might any moment sweep across the horizon of her brow. Her lower lip protruded dangerously. She squared her massive shoulders. Then she marched into the front of the house and out the side door and started down the road to the pig parlor. She had the look of a woman going single-handed, weaponless, into battle. 171

The sun was a deep yellow now like a harvest moon and 172
was riding westward very fast over the far tree line as if it
meant to reach the hogs before she did. The road was rutted
and she kicked several good-sized stones out of her path as
she strode along. The pig parlor was on a little knoll at the
end of a lane that ran off from the side of the barn. It was a
square of concrete as large as a small room, with a board fence
about four feet high around it. The concrete floor sloped
slightly so that the hog wash could drain off into a trench
where it was carried to the field for fertilizer. Claud was
standing on the outside, on the edge of the concrete, hanging
onto the top board, hosing down the floor inside. The hose
was connected to the faucet of a water trough nearby.

Mrs. Turpin climbed up beside him and glowered down 173
at the hogs inside. There were seven long-snouted bristly
shoats in it—tan with liver-colored spots—and an old sow a
few weeks off from farrowing. She was lying on her side
grunting. The shoats were running about shaking themselves
like idiot children, their little slit pig eyes searching the floor
for anything left. She had read that pigs were the most intelligent animal. She doubted it. They were supposed to be
smarter than dogs. There had even been a pig astronaut. He
had performed his assignment perfectly but died of a heart
attack afterwards because they left him in his electric suit,
sitting upright throughout his examination when naturally a
hog should be on all fours.

A-gruntin and a-rootin and a-groanin. 174

"Gimme that hose," she said, yanking it away from Claud. 175
"Go on and carry them niggers home and then get off that
leg."

"You look like you might have swallowed a mad dog," 176
Claud observed, but he got down and limped off. He paid
no attention to her humors.

Until he was out of earshot, Mrs. Turpin stood on the side 177
of the pen, holding the hose and pointing the stream of water
at the hind quarters of any shoat that looked as if it might
try to lie down. When he had had time to get over the hill,
she turned her head slightly and her wrathful eyes scanned

the path. He was nowhere in sight. She turned back again and seemed to gather herself up. Her shoulders rose and she drew in her breath.

"What do you send me a message like that for?" she said 178 in a low fierce voice, barely above a whisper but with the force of a shout in its concentrated fury. "How am I a hog and me both? How am I saved and from hell too?" Her free fist was knotted and with the other she gripped the hose, blindly pointing the stream of water in and out of the eye of the old sow whose outraged squeal she did not hear.

The pig parlor commanded a view of the back pasture 179 where their twenty beef cows were gathered around the hay-bales Claud and the boy had put out. The freshly cut pasture sloped down to the highway. Across it was their cotton field and beyond that a dark green dusty wood which they owned as well. The sun was behind the wood, very red, looking over the paling of trees like a farmer inspecting his own hogs.

"Why me?" she rumbled. "It's no trash around here, black 180 or white, that I haven't given to. And break my back to the bone every day working. And do for the church."

She appeared to be the right size woman to command the 181 arena before her. "How am I a hog?" she demanded. "Exactly how am I like them?" and she jabbed the stream of water at the shoats. "There was plenty of trash there. It didn't have to be me.

"If you like trash better, go get yourself some trash then," 182 she railed. "You could have made me trash. Or a nigger. If trash is what you wanted why didn't you make me trash?" She shook her fist with the hose in it and a watery snake appeared momentarily in the air. "I could quit working and take it easy and be filthy," she growled. "Lounge about the sidewalks all day drinking root beer. Dip snuff and spit in every puddle and have it all over my face. I could be nasty.

"Or you could have made me a nigger. It's too late for me 183 to be a nigger," she said with deep sarcasm, "but I could act like one. Lay down in the middle of the road and stop traffic. Roll on the ground."

In the deepening light everything was taking on a myste-   184
rious hue. The pasture was growing a peculiar glassy green
and the streak of highway had turned lavender. She braced
herself for a final assault and this time her voice rolled out
over the pasture. "Go on," she yelled, "call me a hog! Call
me a hog again. From hell. Call me a wart hog from hell. Put
that bottom rail on top. There'll still be a top and bottom!"

A garbled echo returned to her.   185

A final surge of fury shook her and she roared, "Who do   186
you think you are?"

The color of everything, field and crimson sky, burned for 187
a moment with a transparent intensity. The question carried
over the pasture and across the highway and the cotton field
and returned to her clearly like an answer from beyond the
wood.

She opened her mouth but no sound came out of it.   188

A tiny truck, Claud's, appeared on the highway, heading   189
rapidly out of sight. Its gears scraped thinly. It looked like a
child's toy. At any moment a bigger truck might smash into
it and scatter Claud's and the niggers' brains all over the road.

Mrs. Turpin stood there, her gaze fixed on the highway,   190
all her muscles rigid, until in five or six minutes the truck
reappeared, returning. She waited until it had had time to
turn into their own road. Then like a monumental statue
coming to life, she bent her head slowly and gazed, as if
through the very heart of mystery, down into the pig parlor
at the hogs. They had settled all in one corner around the
old sow who was grunting softly. A red glow suffused them.
They appeared to pant with a secret life.

Until the sun slipped finally behind the tree line, Mrs.   191
Turpin remained there with her gaze bent to them as if she
were absorbing some abysmal life-giving knowledge. At last
she lifted her head. There was only a purple streak in the sky,
cutting through a field of crimson and leading, like an extension of the highway, into the descending dusk. She raised her
hands from the side of the pen in a gesture hieratic and
profound. A visionary light settled in her eyes. She saw the

streak as a vast swinging bridge extending upward from the earth through a field of living fire. Upon it a vast horde of souls were rumbling toward heaven. There were whole companies of white-trash, clean for the first time in their lives, and bands of black niggers in white robes, and battalions of freaks and lunatics shouting and clapping and leaping like frogs. And bringing up the end of the procession was a tribe of people whom she recognized at once as those who, like herself and Claud, had always had a little of everything and the God-given wit to use it right. She leaned forward to observe them closer. They were marching behind the others with great dignity, accountable as they had always been for good order and common sense and respectable behavior. They alone were on key. Yet she could see by their shocked and altered faces that even their virtues were being burned away. She lowered her hands and gripped the rail of the hog pen, her eyes small but fixed unblinkingly on what lay ahead. In a moment the vision faded but she remained where she was, immobile.

At length she got down and turned off the faucet and   192
made her slow way on the darkening path to the house. In the woods around her the invisible cricket choruses had struck up, but what she heard were the voices of the souls climbing upward into the starry field and shouting hallelujah.

COMMENT ON "REVELATION"

Ruby Turpin, the central character in Flannery O'Connor's "Revelation," is obsessed with the classification process. At night she occupies herself "naming the classes of people": most "colored people" are on the bottom; "next to them— not above, just away from—are the white trash"; and so on. Mrs. Turpin puzzles about the exceptions to her system—the black dentist who owns property and the decent white folks who have lost their money—but for the most part she is certain about her system and her place in it. In the doctor's waiting room, she sizes up the other patients, placing them in their appropriate classes. But her internal and external dialogue reveals the ironies and inconsistencies in her rigid system. Self-satisfied, pleased that Jesus is on her side, she is not prepared for the book on *Human Development* that is thrown at her or the events that follow—the transparent flattery of the black workers, her cleaning of the pig parlor, and finally her vision of the highway to heaven that reveals her real place in God's hierarchy.

Division and Classification as a Writing Strategy

1. Write a column for your local newspaper in which you develop a system for classifying a concept such as trash. You may decide to interpret this word literally, developing a scheme to categorize the type of objects people throw away. Or you may decide to interpret the word figuratively, focusing on things that some people consider worthless— gossip columns, romance magazines, game shows. Here are a few possibilities: although people throw trash away, it won't go away; people's distaste for trash is the cause of its creation; people are so saturated by trash that they accept it as part of their culture with its own subtle subcategories.

2. In an essay addressed to a psychology class, classify various kinds of eaters. Instead of writing a humorous essay like Calvin Trillin's, you may want to write a serious essay that classifies people by what they eat, how fast they eat, or when they eat.

3. Mary Mebane argues that the system of class and color is used to impose power in a negative way. Consider some other system that uses power in a positive way. For example, you may want to classify people by the various ways they empower others.

4. Write an essay that classifies various kinds of bad luck. You may want to follow Austin's pattern by arranging the types of bad luck in an ascending order of complexity.

5. Focus on Phillip Lopate's pluralistic category in "Modern Friendships" and classify it into smaller subcategories. For example, you may wish to draft a feature in which you identify various kinds of "work friends" or you may wish to take on the *When Harry Met Sally* line—explaining why men and women can or cannot be friends.

6. Read Kurt Vonnegut's short story, "Harrison Bergeron," page 537. Then write an essay on the issue of equality. You

may wish to classify the various kinds of inequality evident in Vonnegut's story, or you may wish to support or contest Weinberg's assertion that "inequality of wealth is a social evil."

DEFINITION

As a writer, both in and out of college, you're likely to spend a good deal of time writing definitions. In an astronomy class, you may be asked to explain what the Doppler effect is or what a white dwarf star is. In a literature class, you may be asked to define a sonnet and identify its different forms. If you become an engineer, you may write to define problems your company proposes to solve or to define a new product your company has developed. If you become a business executive, you may have to write a brochure to describe a new service your company offers or draft a letter that defines the company's policy on credit applications.

Writers use definitions to establish boundaries, to show the essential nature of something, and to explain the special qualities that identify a purpose, place, object, or concept and distinguish it from others similar to it. Writers often write extended definitions—definitions that go beyond the one-sentence or one-paragraph explanations that you find in a dictionary or encyclopedia to expand on and examine the essential qualities of a policy, an event, a group, or a trend. Sometimes an extended definition becomes an entire book. Some books are written to define the good life; others are written to define the ideal university or the best kind of government. In fact, many of the books on any current nonfiction best-seller list are primarily definitions. The essays in this section of *The Riverside Reader* are all extended definitions.

PURPOSE

When you write, you can use definitions in several ways. For instance, you can define to *point out the special nature* of something. You may want to show the special flavor of San Francisco that makes it different from other major cities in the world, or you may want to describe the unique features that make the Macintosh computer different from other personal computers.

You can also define to *explain*. In an essay about cross-country skiing, you might want to show your readers what the sport is like and point out why it's less hazardous and less expensive than downhill skiing but better exercise. You might also define to *entertain*—to describe the essence of what it means to be a "good old boy," for instance. Often you define to *inform;* that is what you are doing in college papers when you write about West Virginia folk art or postmodern architecture. Often you write to *establish a standard,* perhaps for a good exercise program, a workable environmental policy, or even the ideal pair of running shoes. Notice that when you define to set a standard, you may also be defining to *persuade,* to convince your reader to accept the ideal you describe. Many definitions are essentially arguments.

Sometimes you may even write to *define yourself.* That is what you are doing when you write an autobiographical statement for a college admissions officer or a scholarship committee, or when you write a job application letter. You hope to give your readers the special information that will distinguish you from all other candidates. When that is your task, you'll profit by knowing the common strategies for defining and by recognizing how other writers have used them.

AUDIENCE

When you're going to use definition in your writing, you can benefit by thinking ahead of time about what your readers expect from you. Why are they reading, and what questions will they want you to answer? You can't anticipate all their questions, but you should plan on responding to at least two kinds of queries.

First, your readers are likely to ask, "What distinguishes what you're writing about? What's typical or different about it? How do I know when I see one?" For example, if you were writing about the Olympic games, your readers would perhaps want to know the difference between today's Olympic games and the original games in ancient Greece. With a little research, you could tell them about several major differences.

Second, for more complex topics you should expect that your readers will also ask, "What is the basic character or the essential nature of what you're writing about? What do you mean when you say 'alternative medicine,' 'Marxist theory,' or 'white-collar crime?'" Answering questions such as these is more difficult, but if you're going to use terms like these in an essay, you have an obligation to define them, using as many strategies as you need to clarify your terms. To define white-collar crime, for instance, you could specify that it is nonviolent, likely to happen within businesses, and involves illegal manipulation of funds or privileged information. You should also strengthen your definition by giving examples that your readers might be familiar with.

STRATEGIES

You can choose from several strategies for defining, using them singly or in combination. A favorite strategy we all use is *giving examples,* something we do naturally when we point to a special automobile we like or show a child a picture of a raccoon in a picture book. Writers use the same method when they describe a scene, create a visual image, or cite a specific instance of something.

Every author in this section uses an abundance of examples. Witold Rybczynski's short piece "One Good Turn" makes an interesting story out of the invention of the wood screw by giving dozens of examples of how important screws are to our world, ending up with dramatic examples of two events that couldn't have happened without screws. John Berendt also uses several entertaining examples of ingenious hoaxes.

You can define by *analyzing qualities* to show what features or traits distinguish the thing you're defining. When you use this strategy, you pick out certain qualities you want your reader to identify with the person, concept, or object you're defining. Richard Rodriguez uses this strategy to show what is special about the adolescents in Los Angeles in his "Growing Up in Los Angeles," pointing out that although rebellion has always been common among American youth, it has a special twist in L.A. Analyzing qualities is David Brooks's primary strategy in "Bobos: The New Upper Class" as he shows members of the new class trying to "reconcile their success with their spirituality, their elite status with their egalitarian ideas."

A similar strategy is *attributing characteristics.* This is Stephen Harrigan's chief tactic in "The Tiger Is God." He begins by describing tigers' characteristic method of attack, points out that zookeepers know that tigers are dangerous, and then identifies tigers as predators whose mission is to kill. Rybczynski describes the essential characteristics of screws that make them different from and superior to nails: they squeeze surfaces together, they don't pop out if the wood dries, and they're stronger and more durable than nails.

One of Berendt's chief strategies is *defining negatively*, showing what something is not. Simple deception or trickery may be a prank, but it is not a hoax. In order to qualify as a hoax, a trick must have something witty and original about it. Alice Walker also defines negatively in "Everyday Use" when the character of the mother suggests that honoring one's heritage doesn't mean hanging on to relics from the past.

Another way to define is by *using analogies*. Rodriguez uses this strategy in "Growing Up in Los Angeles" when he claims that the grafitti done by street gangs is a kind of advertising, comparable to a billboard on Sunset Boulevard. Harrigan uses analogy when he compares the window in the tiger's cage to a portal through which mankind's most primeval terrors flow.

You can also define by *showing functions*. Often the most important feature about an object or belief is what it does. Rybczynski emphasizes function in "One Good Turn"; his chief point about screws is what they can do. Harrigan also focuses on function in "The Tiger Is God," stressing that the primary function of a tiger is to kill; it's a predator.

COMBINING STRATEGIES

Even when you're writing an essay that is primarily a definition, you're not limited to the strategies we've mentioned here. You may want to combine definition with other patterns, as most professional writers do. For example, in "Rapport-Talk and Report-Talk" (see page 193) Deborah Tannen defines men's and women's different styles of communication, then argues from cause and effect to show that many problems between men and woman grow out of these differences. In "A Chinaman's Chance" (page 465) Eric Liu gives his own definition of the American Dream, then argues that young people who feel they have no chance to achieve that dream are mistaken.

Some writers also use narration and description as a way of defining. Maya Angelou defines a certain kind of racist attitude in her story "My Name Is Margaret" (see page 29), and in "Stone Soup" Barbara Kingsolver uses stories about children as a way of defining a strong family (page 478). As you read essays in this section, and especially as you reread them, try to be conscious of the author's strategy. You may find strategies you can incorporate into your own writing.

USING DEFINITION IN PARAGRAPHS

Here are two definition paragraphs. The first is written by a professional writer and is followed by an analysis. The second is written by a student writer and is followed by questions.

JOYCE CAROL OATES
"When Tristram Met Isolde"

Romantic love isn't so much a love that defies conventions, for romantic love is of all love types the most conventional, as a love that arises with seeming spontaneity: unwilled, undirected by others' suggestions or admonitions, raw and unpremeditated and of the heart; not cerebral and not genital. Romantic love is forever in opposition to formal, cultural, and tribal prescriptions of behavior: arranged marriages, for instance, in which brides and their dowries are possessions to be handed over to a bridegroom and his family, or in which titled names are wed in business-like arrangements that have little to do with the feelings of the individuals. Diana, Princess of Wales, would seem to have been a martyr to such an arrangement; her political marriage to Prince Charles ending in dissolution and divorce, and her "quest for personal happiness" (i.e., romantic love) ending in a grotesquely public death on a Parisian boulevard.

Romantic l
is spontane

Opposed to
and restric

Princes
perfect exa

Comment In this paragraph taken from a short essay whose title, "When Tristram met Isolde," invokes the tragic legend of two fatally smitten lovers, the novelist Joyce Carol Oates defines romantic love as an irrational, compulsive emotion that overwhelms all caution and good sense. Those who embrace it are rebelling against the practical economic and social concerns that families in non-Western cultures often value more than spontaneous feelings and individual desires. In both real life and in fiction, the surrender to romantic love often has disastrous consequence. To illustrate her point, Oates calls up what must be the most publicized example of a romantic disaster in the last decade: the death of Princess Diana and her lover in a high-speed automobile crash in that most romantic of cities, Paris.

JASON UTESCH
Personality

"She has a great personality." Translation: she goes to bed early to watch the shopping channel. "He has a great personality." Translation: he tells dirty jokes at funerals. The "p" word is troublesome not only because all the great personalities we've been told about have proved disappointing, but also because all the great personalities we know don't seem to measure up to other people's expectations. Even the old song suggests that personality is a complicated quality to define because to have it a person has to have a special walk, talk, smile, charm, love, and PLUS she (or he) has to have a great big heart.

1. What do you see as Utesch's purpose in listing so many contradictions in the way people define *personality*?
2. What does the writer imply by using the phrase "The 'p' word"?

DEFINITION

Points to Remember

1. Remember that you are obligated to define key terms that you use in your writing—such as Marxism, alternative medicine, nontraditional student.
2. Understand your purpose in defining: to explain, to entertain, to persuade, to set boundaries, or to establish a standard.
3. Understand how writers construct an argument from a definition. For example, by defining the good life or good government, they argue for that kind of life or government.
4. Know the several ways of defining: giving examples, analyzing qualities, attributing characteristics, defining negatively, using analogies, and showing function.
5. Learn to use definition in combination with other strategies, as a basis on which to build an argument, or as supporting evidence.

Witold Rybczynski was born in Edinburgh, Scotland, and educated at the School of Architecture,
McGill University, in Montreal, Canada. He
worked as an architect and planner for Moshe
Safdie on Habitat 67 and as planner of housing
and new towns in northern Canada. He joined the
faculty of McGill University in 1975 and also began working as a consultant to the World Bank,
the United Nations, and the International Research Center. His books include *Taming the Tiger: The Struggle to Control Technology* (1983),
Home: A Short History of an Idea (1986), and *City
Life: Urban Expectations in a New World* (1995).
In "One Good Turn," excerpted from *One Good
Turn: A Natural History of the Screwdriver and the
Screw* (2000), Rybczynski defines the functions of
the tapered and threaded screw.

One Good Turn
How Machine-Made Screws Brought the World Together

S OME YEARS AGO my wife and I built a house. I mean really   1
built it—ourselves, from the ground up. Electricity being unavailable, we used hand tools. I did not have a large
toolbox. It contained different-size saws, a mallet and chisels,
a plane, several hammers (for friends conscripted into our
work force) and, for correcting major mistakes, a heavy
sledge. In addition I had a number of tools for measuring: a
tape, a square, a spirit level and a plumb line. That was all we
needed.

One of the rewards of building something yourself is the   2
pleasure of using tools. Hand tools are really extensions of

the human body, for they have evolved over centuries—millenniums—of trial and error. Power tools are more convenient, of course, but they lack precisely this sense of refinement. Using a clumsy nailing gun is work, but swinging a claw hammer is satisfying work.

Had a medieval carpenter come along—untutored neophytes, we could have used his help—he would have found most of my tools familiar. Indeed, even an ancient Roman carpenter would have found few surprises in my toolbox. He would recognize my plane, a version of his *plana;* he might

3

Without screws, entire fields of science would have languished, navigation would have remained primitive, and naval warfare as well as routine maritime commerce in the 18th and 19th centuries would not have been possible.

---

admire my retractable tape measure, an improvement on his bronze folding *regula.* He would be puzzled by my brace and bit, a medieval invention, but being familiar with the Egyptian bow drill, he would readily infer its purpose. No doubt he would be impressed by my hard steel nails, so much superior to his hand-forged spikes.

Saws, hammers (and nails), chisels, drills and squares all date from the Bronze and early Iron Ages. Many types of modern tools originated even earlier, in the Neolithic period, about 8,000 years ago. In fact, there is only one tool in my toolbox that would puzzle a Roman and a medieval carpenter: my screwdriver. They would understand the principle of screws; after all, Archimedes invented the screw in the third century B.C. Ancient screws were large wood contraptions,

4

used for raising water. One of the earliest devices that used a screw to apply pressure was a Roman clothes press; presses were also used to make olive oil and wine. The Middle Ages applied the same principle to the printing press and to that fiendish torturing device, the thumbscrew. Yet the ordinary screw as a small fixing device was unknown.

Wood screws originated sometime in the 16th century. 5 The first screwdrivers were called turnscrews, flat-bladed bits that could be attached to a carpenter's brace. The inventor of the handheld screwdriver remains unknown, but the familiar tool does not appear in carpenters' toolboxes until after 1800. There was not a great call for screwdrivers, because screws were expensive. They had to be painstakingly made by hand and were used in luxury articles like clocks. It was only after 1850 that wood screws were available in large quantities.

Inexpensive screws are quintessentially modern. Their 6 mass production requires a high degree of precision and standardization. The wood screw also represents an entirely new method of attachment, more durable than nails—which can pop out if the wood dries out or expands. (This makes screws particularly useful in shipbuilding.) The tapered, gimlet-pointed wood screw—like its cousin the bolt—squeezes the two joined pieces together. The more you tighten the screw—or the nut—the greater the squeeze. In modern steel buildings, for example, high-tension bolts are tightened so hard that it is the friction between the two pieces of steel— not the bolt itself—that gives strength to the joint. On a more mundane level, screws enable a vast array of convenient attachments in the home: door hinges, drawer pulls, shelf hangers, towel bars. Perhaps that is why if you rummage around most people's kitchen drawers you will most likely find at least one screwdriver.

Wood screws are stronger and more durable than nails, 7 pegs or staples. But the aristocrat of screws is the precision screw. This was first made roughly—by hand—and later on screw-cutting lathes, which is a chicken-and-egg story, since it was the screw that made machine lathes possible. The machined screw represented a technological breakthrough of epic proportions. Screws enabled the minute adjustment of a variety of precision instruments like clocks, microscopes, telescopes, sextants, theodolites and marine chronometers.

It is not an exaggeration to say that accurately threaded screws changed the world. Without screws, entire fields of science would have languished, navigation would have remained primitive and naval warfare as well as routine maritime commerce in the 18th and 19th centuries would not have been possible. Without screws there would have been no machine tools, hence no industrial products and no Industrial Revolution. Think of that the next time you pick up a screwdriver to pry open a can of paint.

For Study and Discussion

QUESTIONS FOR RESPONSE

1. What do you think you learn about the author himself from this short treatise on hand tools in general and screws in particular? How does that knowledge affect your response to his essay?
2. In one way, Rybczynski has given us a little history lesson about screws. What do you like—or dislike—about that approach?

QUESTIONS ABOUT PURPOSE

1. Why do you think Rybczynski wanted to write this essay? Did he want to instruct, entertain, persuade, provoke action—or is he just a craftsman and writer who is fascinated with tools and simple technology and wants to tell people about his interests?
2. What impact does he want to make when he says "the machined screw represented a technological breakthrough of epic proportions"?

QUESTIONS ABOUT AUDIENCE

1. Who do you think is interested in this sort of short essay? How much would readers need to know about tools in order to enjoy it?

2. Are there indications here that Rybczynski is writing for an older generation? If so, what are those indications, and does their presence necessarily shut out younger people?

QUESTIONS ABOUT STRATEGIES

1. How would you characterize the writing style in this essay? How well do you think it suits the topic?
2. Rybczynski gives the reader an abundance of specific details and historical information; how does this information help him engage his readers' interest?

QUESTIONS FOR DISCUSSION

1. People who have not written much often think they have nothing to say, but Rybczynski shows how a writer can take an apparently ordinary topic and make it interesting. What specialized knowledge about a topic do you have that you could explain to readers in a similar way, giving them informative detail in an interesting manner? For example, such a topic could be shotguns or kaleidoscopes or basketballs or scissors or almost any ordinary implement.
2. In our current Age of Information, with its emphasis on computers and the Internet, who do you know who still works with tools to create things and takes pride in his or her skills? What special satisfaction does that work—perhaps gardening or carpentry or sewing—seem to bring them?

John Berendt was born in Syracuse, New York, in 1939 and was educated at Harvard University. He began his writing career as an associate editor at *Esquire,* before editing *Holiday Magazine* and writing and producing television programs such as *The David Frost Show* and *The Dick Cavett Show.* In 1979, he returned to *Esquire* as a columnist after serving as editor of *New York Magazine* from 1977 to 1979. In 1994, he published his final book, *Midnight in the Garden of Good and Evil,* a "non-fiction novel" about a controversial murder in Savannah, Georgia. The book has since been transformed into a major film by director Clint Eastwood. In "The Hoax," reprinted from *Esquire,* Berendt defines the magical ingredients of a hoax.

The Hoax

W HEN THE HUMORIST Robert Benchley was an under- 1
graduate at Harvard eighty years ago, he and a couple of friends showed up one morning at the door of an elegant Beacon Hill mansion, dressed as furniture repairmen. They told the housekeeper they had come to pick up the sofa. Five minutes later they carried the sofa out the door, put it on a truck, and drove it three blocks away to another house, where, posing as deliverymen, they plunked it down in the parlor. That evening, as Benchley well knew, the couple living in house A were due to attend a party in house B. Whatever the outcome—and I'll get to that shortly—it was guaranteed to be a defining example of how proper Bostonians handle social crises. The wit inherent in Benchley's practical joke elevated it from the level of prank to the more respectable realm of hoax.

To qualify as a hoax, a prank must have magic in it—the 2
word is derived from *hocus-pocus,* after all. Daring and irony
are useful ingredients, too. A good example of a hoax is the
ruse perpetrated by David Hampton, the young black man
whose pretense of being Sidney Poitier's son inspired John
Guare's *Six Degrees of Separation.* Hampton managed to in-
sinuate himself into two of New York's most sophisticated
households—one headed by the president of the public-
television station WNET, the other by the dean of the
Columbia School of Journalism. Hampton's hoax touched a
number of sensitive themes: snobbery, class, race, and sex, all
of which playwright Guare deftly exploited.

Hampton is a member of an elite band of famous impos- 3
tors that includes a half-mad woman who for fifty years

---

*To qualify as a hoax, a prank must have
magic in it. . . .*

---

claimed to be Anastasia, the lost daughter of the assassinated
czar Nicholas II; and a man named Harry Gerguson, who
became a Hollywood restaurateur and darling of society in
the 1930s and 1940s as the ersatz Russian prince Mike Ro-
manoff.

Forgeries have been among the better hoaxes. Fake Ver- 4
meers painted by an obscure Dutch artist, Hans van
Meegeren, were so convincing that they fooled art dealers,
collectors, and museums. The hoax came to light when Van
Meegeren was arrested as a Nazi collaborator after the war.
To prove he was not a Nazi, he admitted he had sold a fake
Vermeer to Hermann Göring for $256,000. Then he owned
up to having created other "Vermeers," and to prove he
could do it, he painted *Jesus in the Temple* in the style of
Vermeer while under guard in jail.

In a bizarre twist, a story much like Van Meegeren's be- 5

came the subject of the book *Fake!*, by Clifford Irving, who in 1972 attempted to pull off a spectacular hoax of his own: a wholly fraudulent "authorized" biography of Howard Hughes. Irving claimed to have conducted secret interviews with the reclusive Hughes, and McGraw-Hill gave him a big advance. Shortly before publication, Hughes surfaced by telephone and denied that he had ever spoken with Irving. Irving had already spent $100,000 of the advance; he was convicted of fraud and sent to jail.

As it happens, we are used to hoaxes where I come from. 6 I grew up just a few miles down the road from Cardiff, New York—a town made famous by the Cardiff Giant. As we learned in school, a farmer named Newell complained, back in 1889, that his well was running dry, and while he and his neighbors were digging a new one, they came upon what appeared to be the fossilized remains of a man twelve feet tall. Before the day was out, Newell had erected a tent and posted a sign charging a dollar for a glimpse of the "giant"—three dollars for a longer look. Throngs descended on Cardiff. It wasn't long before scientists determined that the giant had been carved from a block of gypsum. The hoax came undone fairly quickly after that, but even so—as often happens with hoaxes—the giant became an even bigger attraction *because* it was a hoax. P. T. Barnum offered Newell a fortune for the giant, but Newell refused, and it was then that he got his comeuppance. Barnum simply made a replica and put it on display as the genuine Cardiff Giant. Newell's gig was ruined.

The consequences of hoaxes are what give them spice. 7 Orson Welles's lifelike 1938 radio broadcast of H. G. Wells's *War of the Worlds* panicked millions of Americans, who were convinced that martians had landed in New Jersey. The forged diary of Adolf Hitler embarrassed historian Hugh Trevor-Roper, who had vouched for its authenticity, and *Newsweek* and *The Sunday Times* of London, both of which published excerpts in 1983 shortly before forensic tests proved that there were nylon fibers in the paper it was written on, which wouldn't have been possible had it originated before 1950. The five-hundred-thousand-year-old remains of

Piltdown man, found in 1912, had anthropologists confused about human evolution until 1953, when fluoride tests exposed the bones as an elaborate modern hoax. And as for Robert Benchley's game on Beacon Hill, no one said a word about the sofa all evening, although there it sat in plain sight. One week later, however, couple A sent an anonymous package to couple B. It contained the sofa's slipcovers.

For Study and Discussion

QUESTIONS FOR RESPONSE

1. What hoaxes do you know about or have you been involved in? Which of them had elements that might be described as daring or witty?
2. What's your reaction to those incidents in Berendt's account that involve criminal fraud? How do you explain that reaction?

QUESTIONS ABOUT PURPOSE

1. How do you think Berendt wants you to respond to the tricksters he describes in his essay? To what extent did you respond that way?
2. Berendt's examples of people duped by hoaxes include scientists, a historian, a college president, an eminent publisher, and curators of several museums. What does he accomplish by telling stories about such a wide range of dupes?

QUESTIONS ABOUT AUDIENCE

1. This essay originally appeared in *Esquire* magazine. What traits and attitudes do you think a writer for *Esquire* assumes characterize its readers? (If necessary, browse through an issue of *Esquire* in the library to get a feel for its audience.)
2. Berendt seems to assume that everyone enjoys stories about tricksters getting the best of their victims. In your case, is the assumption justified? Why or why not?

QUESTIONS ABOUT STRATEGIES

1. What does the writer achieve by opening and closing the essay with the anecdote about the sofa?
2. How would you characterize the tone of this essay? What attitude of the writer toward his subject do you think the tone reflects? Do you find that attitude engaging or off-putting?

QUESTIONS FOR DISCUSSION

1. Which of Berendt's anecdotes do you find the most entertaining? Why?
2. When would you say a deception ceases to be a hoax and turns into something else? What examples can you think of?

RICHARD RODRIGUEZ

Richard Rodriguez was born in San Francisco in 1944 and was educated at Stanford, Columbia, and the University of California at Berkeley. The son of Mexican immigrants and unable to speak English when he started school, he eventually went on to earn a master's degree and was awarded a Fulbright fellowship to study English Renaissance literature at the Warburg Institute in London. His compelling and controversial autobiography, *Hunger of Memory: The Education of Richard Rodriguez* (1982), provides details of Rodriguez's experiences in the American educational system and his alienation from his own culture. His recent books include *Days of Obligation: An Argument with My Mexican Father* (1994). In "Growing Up in Los Angeles," Rodriguez tries to define the idea of adolescence as it is acted out in southern California.

Growing Up in Los Angeles

A MERICA'S GREATEST CONTRIBUTION to the world of ideas is adolescence. European novels often begin with a first indelible memory—a golden poplar, or Mama standing in the kitchen. American novels begin at the moment of rebellion, the moment of appetite for distance, the moonless night Tom Sawyer pries open the back-bedroom window, shinnies down the drainpipe, drops to the ground, and runs.

America invented a space—a deferment, a patch of asphalt between childhood and adulthood, between the child's ties to family and the adult's re-creation of family. Within this space, within this boredom, American teenagers are supposed to innovate, to improvise, to rebel, to turn around three times before they harden into adults.

If you want to see the broadcasting center, the trademark capital of adolescence, come to Los Angeles. The great postwar, postmodern, suburban city in Dolby sound was built by restless people who intended to give their kids an unending spring. 3

There are times in Los Angeles—our most American of American cities—when teenagers seem the oldest people around. Many seem barely children at all—they are tough and 4

The baby boom generation transformed youth into a lifestyle, a political manifesto, an aesthetic, a religion.

---

cynical as ancients, beyond laughter in a city that idolizes them. Their glance, when it meets ours, is unblinking.

At a wedding in Brentwood, I watch the 17-year-old daughter of my thrice-divorced friend give her mother away. The mother is dewey with liquid blush. The dry-eyed daughter has seen it all before. 5

I know children in Los Angeles who carry knives and guns because the walk to and from school is more dangerous than their teachers or parents realize. One teenager stays home to watch her younger sister, who is being pursued by a teenage stalker. The girls have not told their parents because they say they do not know how their parents would react. 6

Have adults become the innocents? 7

Adults live in fear of the young. It's a movie script, a boffo science-fiction thriller that has never been filmed but that might well star Jean-Claude Van Damme or Sylvester Stallone. 8

A friend of mine, a heavyweight amateur wrestler, wonders if it's safe for us to have dinner at a Venice Beach restaurant. 9

(There are, he says, 12-year-old gangsters who prowl the neighborhood with guns.)

Some of the richest people in town have figured out how   10
to sell the idea of American adolescence to the world. The children with the most interesting dilemma are the children of 90210. What does adolescence mean when your father is a record producer who drives to work in a Jeep to audition rap groups? What do you do when your father—who has a drug habit and is nowhere around in the years when you are growing up—is an internationally recognizable 50-foot face on the movie screen?

On the other hand: What can it feel like to grow up a   11
teenager in South Central when your mama is on crack and you are responsible for her five kids? Teenagers who never had reliable parents or knew intimacy are having babies. There are teenagers in East L.A. who (literally) spend their young lives searching for family—"blood"—in some gang that promises what they never had.

It is every teenager's dream to "get big." In L.A. you can   12
be very big, indeed. Fame is a billboard along Sunset Boulevard. Mexican-American gangstas pass the Southern California night by writing crypto-nonsense on sides of buildings, because the biggest lesson they have taken from the city is that advertisement is existence. Los Angeles is a horizontal city of separate freeway exits, separate malls, suburb fleeing suburb. Parents keep moving their children away from what they suppose is the diseased inner city. But there is no possibility of a healthy suburb radiant from a corrupt center. *No man is an island entire of itself.* Didn't we learn that in high school?

The children of East L.A. live in the same city as Madonna   13
and Harvard-educated screenwriters who use cocaine for inspiration, selling a believably tarnished vision of the world to children of the crack mothers in Compton.

And look: There's always a TV in the houses of Watts. And   14
it is always on. In the suburbs, white kids watch black rappers on MTV. Suburbanites use TV to watch the mayhem of the inner city. But on the TV in the inner city, they watch the

rest of us. The bejeweled pimp in his gold BMW parodies the Beverly Hills matron on Rodeo Drive.

Elsewhere in America, we like to tell ourselves that Los Angeles is the exception. The truth is that, for all its eccentricity, Los Angeles tells us a great deal about adolescence in rural Kansas. And postmodern L.A. is linked to colonial Boston. Today's gangsta with a tattooed tear on his face is kin to young men fighting Old Man Europe's wars in the trenches of 1914 or 1941, to the young rebels who overthrew Old Man Englande rather than submit to another curfew, and to Judy Garland, who will always be a stagestruck teenager.

The earliest Americans imagined that they had fled the past—motherland, fatherland—and had come upon land that was without history or meaning. By implication, the earliest Americans imagined themselves adolescent, orphans. Their task was self-creation, without benefit or burden of family. The myth that we must each create our own meaning has passed down through American generations.

Young Meriwether Lewis heads out for the territory. He writes to his widowed mother, "I . . . hope therefore you will not suffer yourself to indulge any anxiety for my safety. . . ." The ellipsis is adolescence: estrangement, embarrassment, self-absorption, determination. The adolescent body plumps and furs, bleeds and craves to be known for itself. In some parts of the world, puberty is a secret, a shameful biological event, proof that you have inevitably joined the community of your gender. In America, puberty is the signal to rebel.

American teenagers invent their own tongue, meant to be indecipherable to adult hearing. Every generation of adolescents does it. Adults are left wondering what they mean: *Scrilla. Juking. Woop, woop, woop.*

"Children grow up too quickly," American parents sigh. And yet nothing troubles an American parent so much as the teenager who won't leave home.

Several times in this century, American teenagers have been obliged to leave home to fight overseas. Nineteen-year-old fathers vowed to their unborn children that never again would the youth of the world be wasted by the Potentates of Winter.

My generation, the baby boom generation, was the refoliation of the world. We were the children of mothers who learned how to drive, dyed their hair, used Maybelline, and decorated their houses for Christmas against the knowledge that winter holds sway in the world. Fathers, having returned from blackened theaters of war, used FHA loans to move into tract houses that had no genealogy. In such suburbs, our disillusioned parents intended to ensure their children's optimism. 21

Prolonged adolescence became the point of us—so much the point of me that I couldn't give it up. One night, in the 1950s, I watched Mary Martin, a middle-aged actress, play an enchanted boy so persuasively that her rendition of "I Won't Grow Up" nurtured my adolescent suspicions of anyone over the age of 30. 22

My generation became the first in human history (only hyperbole can suggest our prophetic sense of ourselves) that imagined we might never grow old. 23

Jill, a friend of mine whose fame was an orange bikini, whose face has fallen, whose breasts have fallen, whose hair is gray, is telling me about her son who has just gone to New York and has found there the most wonderful possibilities. My friend's eyes fill with tears. She fumbles in her handbag for the pack of cigarettes she had just sworn off. 24

What's wrong? 25

"Dammit," she says, "I'm a geezer." 26

From my generation arose a culture for which America has become notorious. We transformed youth into a lifestyle, a political manifesto, an aesthetic, a religion. My generation turned adolescence into a commodity that could be sold worldwide by 45-year-old executives at Nike or Warner Bros. To that extent, we control youth. 27

But is it unreasonable for a child to expect that Mick Jagger or Michael Jackson will grow up, thicken, settle, and slow—relinquish adolescence to a new generation? 28

At the Senior Ball, teenagers in the ballroom of the Beverly 29

Hills Hotel, beautiful teenagers in black tie and gowns, try very hard not to look like teenagers. But on the other hand, it is very important not to look like one's parents.

The balancing trick of American adolescence is to stand in-between—neither to be a child nor an adult.   30

Where are you going to college?   31

The question intrudes on the ball like a gong from some great clock. It is midnight, Cinderella. Adolescence must come to an end. Life is governed by inevitabilities and consequences—a thought never communicated in America's rock-and-roll lyrics.   32

American storytellers do better with the beginning of the story than the conclusion. We do not know how to mark the end of adolescence. Mark Twain brings Huck Finn back to Missouri, to Hannibal, and forces his young hero to bend toward inevitability. But Huck yearns, forever, "to light out for the territory . . . because Aunt Sally she's going to adopt me and sivilize me, and I can't stand it."   33

And then comes the least convincing conclusion ever written in all of American literature: THE END, YOURS TRULY, HUCK FINN.   34

For Study and Discussion

QUESTIONS FOR RESPONSE

1. In what ways do Rodriguez's descriptions of teenagers in Los Angeles correspond to the behavior of adolescents that you know? How do they differ?
2. How do you respond to the advertising strategies that the media, especially television, use to appeal to young people? What, if anything, would you like to see changed in those strategies?

QUESTIONS ABOUT PURPOSE

1. Rodriguez projects an angry tone in this article. Toward whom do you think the anger is directed and what does he hope to accomplish by stirring up anger with his readers?

2. What new information or insights about American adolescents did you get from this essay? What do you think Rodriguez wants you to do with that information?

QUESTIONS ABOUT AUDIENCE

1. This article was originally published in *U.S. News and World Report,* a magazine whose readers are generally well educated, fairly prosperous, and in their late thirties or forties. How do you think they view most adolescents, and what might they learn from Rodriguez that could help them with their own children?
2. What different experiences and attitudes about adolescents do readers under thirty bring to this essay? How do you think their experiences affect their response to the essay?

QUESTIONS ABOUT STRATEGIES

1. Probably most of Rodriguez's readers haven't been to Los Angeles. What details does he use to convey the flavor of that city to a stranger? How well do they work to help you envision Los Angeles?
2. Rodriguez uses exaggeration as a strategy. For example, he says that Los Angeles is the most American of cities, he compares a pimp in his gold BMW to a Beverly Hills matron, and he mentions Madonna and the mothers of crack babies in the same sentence. What effects does he achieve with this strategy? How effective do you find it?

QUESTIONS FOR DISCUSSION

1. Rodriguez says that his generation (the baby boomers) turned adolescence into a commodity to be sold worldwide by sports manufacturers and movie producers. How true does that statement ring with you? What examples come to mind?
2. How would you characterize the persona or role that Rodriguez adopts for himself in this essay? Moralist, social critic, cynic, reformer, disenchanted observer? Might you adopt such a persona in an essay you might write? Why?

STEPHEN HARRIGAN

Stephen Harrigan was born in Oklahoma City in 1948 and educated at the University of Texas. After working as a journalist, including a term as senior editor at *Texas Monthly*, Harrigan turned his attention to fiction and screenplays. His novels include *Aransas* (1980) and *Jacob's Well* (1984), and his screenplays include *The Last of His Tribe* (1992) and *The O.J. Simpson Story* (1995). Harrigan has also published two collections of essays, *A Natural State* (1988) and *Comanche Midnight* (1995). In "The Tiger Is God," reprinted from the former collection, Harrigan provides dramatic examples that help define a tiger "just being a tiger."

The Tiger Is God

W HEN TIGERS ATTACK men, they do so in a characteristic way. They come from behind, from the right side, and when they lunge it is with the intent of snapping the neck of the prey in their jaws. Most tiger victims die swiftly, their necks broken, their spinal cords compressed or severed high up on the vertebral column.

Ricardo Tovar, a fifty-nine-year-old keeper at the Houston Zoo, was killed by a tiger on May 12, 1988. The primary cause of death was a broken neck, although most of the ribs on the left side of his chest were fractured as well, and there were multiple lacerations on his face and right arm. No one witnessed the attack, and no one would ever know exactly how and why it took place, but the central nightmarish event was clear. Tovar had been standing at a steel door separating the zookeepers' area from the naturalistic tiger display outside. Set into the door was a small viewing window—only slightly larger than an average television screen—made of wire-reinforced glass. Somehow the tiger had broken the glass, grabbed the keeper, and pulled him through the window to his death.

Fatal zoo accidents occur more frequently than most people realize. The year before Tovar died, a keeper in the Fort Worth Zoo was crushed by an elephant, and in 1985, an employee of the Bronx Zoo was killed by two Siberian tigers—the same subspecies as the one that attacked Tovar—when she mistakenly entered the tiger display while the

> *One point is beyond dispute: A tiger is a predator, its mission on earth is to kill, and in doing so it often displays awesome strength and dexterity.*

animals were still there. But there was something especially haunting about the Houston incident, something that people could not get out of their minds. It had to do with the realization of a fear built deep into our genetic code: the fear that a beast could appear out of nowhere—through a window!—and snatch us away.

The tiger's name was Miguel. He was eleven years old— middle-aged for a tiger—and had been born at the Houston Zoo to a mother who was a wild-caught Siberian. Siberians are larger in size than any of the other subspecies, and their coats are heavier. Fewer than three hundred of them are now left in the frozen river valleys and hardwood forests of the Soviet Far East, though they were once so plentiful in that region that Cossack troops were sent in during the construction of the Trans-Baikal railway specifically to protect the workers from tiger attacks. Miguel was of mixed blood—his father was a zoo-reared Bengal—but his Siberian lineage was dominant. He was a massive 450-pound creature whose disposition had been snarly ever since he was a cub. Some of the other tigers at the zoo were as placid and affectionate as house cats, but Miguel filled his keepers with caution. Oscar Mendietta, a keeper who retired a few weeks before Tovar's death, remembers the way Miguel would sometimes lunge at zoo personnel as they walked by his holding cage, his claws unsheathed and protruding through the steel mesh. "He had," Mendietta says, "an intent to kill."

Tovar was well aware of Miguel's temperament. He had 5 been working with big cats in the Houston Zoo since 1982, and his fellow keepers regarded him as a cautious and responsible man. Like many old-time zookeepers, he was a civil servant with no formal training in zoology, but he had worked around captive animals most of his life (before coming to Houston, he had been a keeper at the San Antonio Zoo) and had gained a good deal of practical knowledge about their behavior. No one regarded Miguel's aggressiveness as aberrant. Tovar and the other keepers well understood the fact that tigers were supposed to be dangerous.

In 1987 the tigers and other cats had been moved from 6 their outdated display cages to brand-new facilities with outdoor exhibit areas built to mimic the animals' natural environments. The Siberian tiger exhibit—in a structure known as the Phase II building—comprised about a quarter of an acre. It was a wide rectangular space decorated with shrubs and trees, a few fake boulders, and a water-filled moat. The exhibit's backdrop was a depiction, in plaster and cement, of a high rock wall seamed with stress fractures.

Built into the wall, out of public view, was a long corridor 7 lined with the cats' holding cages, where the tigers were fed and confined while the keepers went out into the display to shovel excrement and hose down the area. Miguel and the other male Siberian, Rambo, each had a holding cage, and they alternated in the use of the outdoor habitat, since two male tigers occupying the same space guaranteed monumental discord. Next to Rambo's cage was a narrow alcove through which the keepers went back and forth from the corridor into the display. The alcove was guarded by two doors. The one with the viewing window led outside. Another door, made of steel mesh, closed off the interior corridor.

May 12 was a Thursday. Tovar came to work at about 8 six-thirty in the morning, and at that hour he was alone. Rambo was secure in his holding cage and Miguel was outside—it had been his turn that night to have the run of the display.

Thursdays and Sundays were "fast" days. Normally the 9 tigers were fed a daily ration of ten to fifteen pounds of ground fetal calf, but twice a week their food was withheld in order to keep them from growing obese in confinement. The animals knew which days were fast days, and on those mornings they were sometimes balky about coming inside, since no food was being offered. Nevertheless, the tigers had to be secured in their holding cages while the keepers went outside to clean the display. On this morning, Tovar had apparently gone to the viewing window to check the whereabouts of Miguel when the tiger did not come inside, even though the keepers usually made a point of not entering the alcove until they were certain that both animals were locked up in their holding cages. The viewing window was so small and the habitat itself so panoramic that the chances of spotting the tiger from the window were slim. Several of the keepers had wondered why there was a window there at all, since it was almost useless as an observation post and since one would never go through the door in the first place without being certain that the tigers were in their cages.

But that was where Tovar had been, standing at a steel 10 door with a panel of reinforced glass, when the tiger attacked. John Gilbert, the senior zookeeper who supervised the cat section, stopped in at the Phase II building a little after seven-thirty, planning to discuss with Tovar the scheduled sedation of a lion. He had just entered the corridor when he saw broken glass on the floor outside the steel mesh door that led to the alcove. The door was unlocked—it had been opened by Tovar when he entered the alcove to look out the window. Looking through the mesh, Gilbert saw the shards of glass hanging from the window frame and Tovar's cap, watch, and a single rubber boot lying on the floor. Knowing something dreadful had happened, he called Tovar's name, then pushed on the door and cautiously started to enter the alcove. He was only a few paces away from the broken window when the tiger's head suddenly appeared there, filling its jagged frame. His heart pounding, Gilbert backed off, slammed and locked the mesh door behind him and radioed for help.

Tom Dieckow, a wiry, white-bearded Marine veteran of the Korean War, was the zoo's exhibits curator. He was also in charge of its shooting team, a seldom-convened body whose task was to kill, if necessary, any escaped zoo animal that posed an immediate threat to the public. Dieckow was in his office in the service complex building when he heard Gilbert's emergency call. He grabbed a twelve-gauge shotgun, commandeered an electrician's pickup truck, and arrived at the tiger exhibit two minutes later. He went around to the front of the habitat and saw Miguel standing there, calm and unconcerned, with Tovar's motionless body lying face down fifteen feet away. Dieckow did not shoot. It was his clear impression that the keeper was dead, that the harm was already done. By that time the zoo's response team had gathered outside the exhibit. Miguel stared at the onlookers and then picked up Tovar's head in his jaws and started to drag him off.

"I think probably what crossed that cat's mind at that point," Dieckow speculated later, "is 'look at all those scavengers across there that are after my prey. I'm gonna move it.' He was just being a tiger."

Dieckow raised his shotgun again, this time with the intention of shooting Miguel, but because of all the brush and ersatz boulders in the habitat, he could not get a clear shot. He fired into the water instead, causing the startled tiger to drop the keeper, and then fired twice more as another zoo worker discharged a fire extinguisher from the top of the rock wall. The commotion worked, and Miguel retreated into his holding cage.

The Houston Zoo opened a half-hour late that day.

Miguel and all the other big cats were kept inside until zoo officials could determine if it was safe—both for the cats and for the public—to exhibit them again. For a few days the zoo switchboard was jammed with calls from people wanting to express their opinion on whether the tiger should live or die. But for the people at the zoo that issue had never been in doubt.

"It's automatic with us," John Werler, the zoo director, 15 told me when I visited his office a week after the incident. "To what end would we destroy the tiger? If we followed this argument to its logical conclusion, we'd have to destroy every dangerous animal in the zoo collection."

Werler was a reflective, kindly looking man who was obvi- 16 ously weighed down by a load of unpleasant concerns. There was the overall question of zoo safety, the specter of lawsuits, and most recently the public anger of a number of zoo staffers who blamed Tovar's death on the budget cuts, staffing short- ages, and bureaucratic indifference that forced keepers to work alone in potentially dangerous environments. But the dominant mood of the zoo, the day I was there, appeared to be one of simple sadness and shock.

"What a terrible loss," read a sympathy card from the staff 17 of the Fort Worth Zoo that was displayed on a coffee table. "May you gain strength and support to get you through this awful time."

The details of the attack were still hazy, and still eerie to 18 think about. Unquestionably, the glass door panel had not been strong enough, but exactly how Miguel had broken it, how he had killed Tovar—and why—remained the subjects of numb speculation. One point was beyond dispute: A tiger is a predator, its mission on the earth is to kill, and in doing so it often displays awesome strength and dexterity.

An Indian researcher, using live deer and buffalo calves as 19 bait, found that the elapsed time between a tiger's secure grip on the animal's neck and the prey's subsequent death was anywhere from thirty-five to ninety seconds. In other circum- stances the cat will not choose to be so swift. Sometimes a tiger will kill an elephant calf by snapping its trunk and

waiting for it to bleed to death, and it is capable of dragging
the carcass in its jaws for miles. (A full-grown tiger possesses
the traction power of thirty men.) When a mother tiger is
teaching her cubs to hunt, she might move in on a calf,
cripple it with a powerful bite to its rear leg, and stand back
and let the cubs practice on the helpless animal.

Tigers have four long canine teeth—fangs. The two in the   20
upper jaw are tapered along the sides to a shearing edge.
Fourteen of the teeth are molars, for chewing meat and
grinding bone. Like other members of the cat family, tigers
have keen, night-seeing eyes, and their hearing is so acute
that Indonesian hunters—convinced that a tiger could hear
the wind whistling through a man's nose hairs—always kept
their nostrils carefully barbered. The pads on the bottom of
a tiger's paws are surprisingly sensitive, easily blistered or cut
on hot, prickly terrain. But the claws within, five on each
front paw and four in the hind paws, are protected like knives
in an upholstered box.

They are not idle predators; when they kill, they kill to eat.   21
Even a well-fed tiger in a zoo keeps his vestigial repertoire of
hunting behaviors intact. (Captive breeding programs, in
fact, make a point of selecting in favor of aggressive predatory
behavior, since the ultimate hope of these programs is to
bolster the dangerously low stock of free-living tigers.) In the
zoo, tigers will stalk birds that land in their habitats, and they
grow more alert than most people would care to realize when
children pass before their gaze. Though stories of man-eating
tigers have been extravagantly embellished over the centuries,
the existence of such creatures is not legendary. In the Sunderbans, the vast delta region that spans the border of India
and Bangladesh, more than four hundred people have been
killed by tigers in the last decade. So many fishermen and
honey collectors have been carried off that a few years ago
officials at the Sunderbans tiger preserve began stationing
electrified dummies around the park to encourage the tigers
to seek other prey. One percent of all tigers, according to a
German biologist who studied them in the Sunderbans, are
"dedicated" man-eaters: when they go out hunting, they're

after people. Up to a third of all tigers will kill and eat a human if they come across one, though they don't make a special effort to do so.

It is not likely that Miguel attacked Ricardo Tovar out of 22 hunger. Except for the killing wounds inflicted by the tiger, the keeper's body was undisturbed. Perhaps something about Tovar's movements on the other side of the window intrigued the cat enough to make him spring, a powerful lunge that sent him crashing through the glass. Most likely the tiger was surprised, and frightened, and reacted instinctively. There is no evidence that he came all the way through the window. Probably he just grabbed Tovar by the chest with one paw, crushed him against the steel door, and with unthinkable strength pulled him through the window and killed him outside.

John Gilbert, the senior keeper who had been the first on 23 the scene that morning, took me inside the Phase II building to show me where the attack had taken place. Gilbert was a sandy-haired man in his thirties, still shaken and subdued by what he had seen. His recitation of the events was as formal and precise as that of a witness at an inquest.

"When I got to this point," Gilbert said as we passed 24 through the security doors that led to the keepers' corridor, "I saw the broken glass on the floor. I immediately yelled Mr. Tovar's name . . ."

The alcove in which Tovar had been standing was much 25 smaller than I had pictured it, and seeing it firsthand made one thing readily apparent: it was a trap. Its yellow cinder-block walls were no more than four feet apart. The ceiling was made of steel mesh and a door of the same material guarded the exit to the corridor. The space was so confined it was not difficult to imagine—it was impossible *not* to imagine—how the tiger had been able to catch Tovar by surprise with a deadly swipe from his paw.

And there was the window. Covered with a steel plate now, 26 its meager dimensions were still visible. The idea of being hauled through that tiny space by a tiger had an almost supernatural resonance—as if the window were a portal

through which mankind's most primeval terrors were allowed
to pass unobstructed.

Gilbert led me down the corridor. We passed the holding 27
cage of Rambo, who hung his head low and let out a grumbling basso roar so deep it sounded like a tremor in the earth.
Then we were standing in front of Miguel.

"Here he is," Gilbert said, looking at the animal with an 28
expression on his face that betrayed a sad welter of emotions.
"He's quite passive right now."

The tiger was reclining on the floor, looking at us without 29
concern. I noticed his head, which seemed to me wider than
the window he had broken out. His eyes were yellow, and
when the great head pivoted in my direction and Miguel's
eyes met mine I looked away reflexively, afraid of their hypnotic gravity. The tiger stood up and began to pace, his
gigantic pads treading noiselessly on the concrete. The bram-
ble of black stripes that decorated his head was as neatly
symmetrical as a Rorschach inkblot, and his orange fur—conceived by evolution as camouflage—was a florid, provocative
presence in the featureless confines of the cage.

Miguel idly pawed the steel guillotine door that covered 30
the entrance to his cage, and then all of a sudden he reared
on his hind legs. I jumped back a little, startled and dwarfed.
The top of Miguel's head nestled against the ceiling mesh of
his cage, his paws were spread to either side. In one silent
moment, his size and scale seemed to have increased expo-
nentially. He looked down at Gilbert and me. In Miguel's
mind, I suspected, his keeper's death was merely a vignette,
a mostly forgotten moment of fright and commotion that
had intruded one day upon the tiger's torpid existence in the
zoo. But it was hard not to look up at that immense animal
and read his posture as a deliberate demonstration of the
power he possessed.

I thought of Tipu Sultan, the eighteenth-century Indian 31
mogul who was obsessed with the tiger and used its likeness
as his constant emblem. Tipu Sultan's imperial banner had
borne the words "The Tiger Is God." Looking up into
Miguel's yellow eyes I felt the strange appropriateness of

those words. The tiger was majestic and unknowable, a beast of such seeming invulnerability that it was possible to believe that he alone had called the world into being, and that a given life could end at his whim. The truth, of course, was far more literal. Miguel was a remnant member of a species never far from the brink of extinction, and his motivation for killing Ricardo Tovar probably did not extend beyond a behavioral quirk. He had a predator's indifference to tragedy; he had killed without culpability. It was a gruesome and unhappy incident, but as far as Miguel was concerned most of the people at the zoo had reached the same conclusion: he was just being a tiger.

For Study and Discussion

QUESTIONS FOR RESPONSE

1. In your visits to zoos, how have you responded to tigers you've seen? With admiration? With awe? With fear? How do you think reading Harrigan's essay might affect your feelings on any future visit?
2. How do you respond to the zoo professionals' feeling that Miguel was "just being a tiger?" Does that reflect a callous or careless attitude?

QUESTIONS ABOUT PURPOSE

1. What attitude about the tiger do you think Harrigan wants to bring about in his readers?
2. Why does Harrigan go into minute detail about the physical arrangements of the zoo and about the schedules? Why would readers want to know these details?

QUESTIONS ABOUT AUDIENCE

1. On what basis do you think that Harrigan can assume that a general audience would want to read about tigers and about the fatal incident at the Houston Zoo?

2. What questions does Harrigan anticipate that his readers will have? How does he attempt to answer those questions?

QUESTIONS ABOUT STRATEGIES

1. What is the impact on the reader of Harrigan's first paragraph? What tone does it set for the essay?
2. What details does the author give that are most important in defining the nature of the tiger? Pick out three or four specific paragraphs that are most important.

QUESTIONS FOR DISCUSSION

1. In what ways are zoos important institutions in this country? Does their value to the public warrant their cost in money, in risk, and in the treatment of animals?
2. What do you think is the appeal of an article such as this? What special significance does it have that the animal was a tiger rather than another animal that can be just as dangerous, for instance, an elephant or rhinoceros?

DAVID BROOKS

David Brooks was born in Toronto, Canada, in 1961 and educated at the University of Chicago. He has worked as a public reporter for the *Chicago Sun Times* and has published articles in the *New York Times,* the *Washington Post* and *The New Yorker.* He is currently senior editor of *The Weekly Standard,* a contributing editor at *Newsweek,* and a commentator on National Public Radio. His books include *Bobos in Paradise: The New Upper Class and How They Got There* (2000). In "Bobos: The New Upper Class," excerpted from *Bobos in Paradise,* Brooks defines the features of bohemians, radicals, and bourgeois achievers that create "bobos."

Bobos: The New Upper Class

T HE HARDEST OF the hard-core sixties radicals believed   1
the only honest way out was to reject the notion of success altogether: drop out of the rat race, retreat to small communities where real human relationships would flourish. But that sort of utopianism was never going to be very popular, especially among college grads. Members of the educated class prize human relationships and social equality, but as for so many generations of Americans before them, achievement was really at the core of the sixties grads' value system. They were meritocrats, after all, and so tended to define themselves by their accomplishments. Most of them were never going to drop out or sit around in communes smelling flowers, raising pigs, and contemplating poetry. Moreover, as time went by, they discovered that the riches of the universe were lying at their feet.

At first, when the great hump of baby boom college gradu-   2 ates entered the workforce, having a college degree brought few financial rewards or dramatic life changes. As late as 1976, the labor economist Richard Freeman could write a book called *The Overeducated American,* arguing that higher education didn't seem to be paying off in the marketplace. But the information age kicked in, and the rewards for education grew and grew. In 1980, according to labor market specialist Kevin Murphy of the University of Chicago, college gradu-

---

The great achievement of the educated elites in the 1990s was to create a way of living that lets you be an affluent success and at the same time a free-spirit rebel.

---

ates earned roughly 35 percent more than high school graduates. But by the mid-1990s, college graduates were earning 70 percent more than high school graduates, and those with graduate degrees were earning 90 percent more. The wage value of a college degree had doubled in 15 years.

The rewards for intellectual capital have increased while the rewards for physical capital have not. That means that even liberal arts majors can wake up one day and find themselves suddenly members of the top-income brackets. A full professor at Yale who renounced the capitalist rat race finds himself making, as of 1999, $113,100, while a professor at Rutgers pulls in $103,700 and superstar professors, who become the object of academic bidding wars, now can rake in more than $300,000 a year. Congressional and presidential staffers top out at $125,000 (before quintupling that when they enter the private sector), and the journalists at national publications can now count on six-figure salaries when they hit middle age, not including lecture fees. Philosophy and math majors head for Wall Street and can make tens of millions of dollars from their quantitative models. America has always had a lot of lawyers, and now the median income for that burgeoning group is $72,500, while income for the big-city legal grinds can reach seven figures. And super-students still flood into medicine—three-quarters of private practitioners net more than $100,000. Meanwhile, in Silicon Valley there are more millionaires than people. In Hollywood television scriptwriters make $11,000 to $13,000 a week. And in New York top magazine editors, like Anna Wintour of *Vogue*, make $1 million a year, which is slightly more than the head of the Ford Foundation. And these dazzling incomes flow not only to the baby boomers, who might still find them surprising, but to all the subsequent generations of college graduates as well, most of whom have never known a world without $4 million artists' lofts, $350-a-night edgy hotels, avant-garde summer homes, and the rest of the accoutrements of the countercultural plutocracy.

The information age has produced entirely new job categories, some of which seem like practical jokes, though you wouldn't know it from the salaries: creativity officer, chief knowledge officer, team spirit coordinator. Then there are the jobs that nobody dreamed of in high school: Web page designer, patent agent, continuity writer, foundation program officer, talk show booker, and on and on. The economy in this era is such that oddballs like Oliver Stone become multimillionaire moguls and slouchy dropouts like Bill Gates get to run the world. Needless to say, there are still gypsy scholars scraping by while looking for a tenure-track position, and there are still poor saps in the publishing industry parlaying their intelligence into obscenely small paychecks. But the whole thrust of the information age has been to reward education and widen the income gap between the educated and the uneducated. Moreover, the upper middle class has grown from a small appendage of the middle class into a distinct demographic hump populated largely by people with fancy degrees. Within a few years, barring a severe economic downturn, there will be 10 million American households with incomes over $100,00 a year, up from only 2 million in 1982.

Consider the cultural and financial capital of that large group, and you begin to appreciate the social power of the upper middle class. Many of the members of the educated elite didn't go out hungry for money. But money found them. And subtly, against their will, it began to work its way into their mentality.

The members of the educated elite find they must change   5
their entire attitude first toward money itself. When they were poor students, money was a solid. It came in a chunk with every paycheck, and they would gradually chip little bits off to pay the bills. They could sort of feel how much money they had in their bank account, the way you can feel a pile of change in your pocket. But as they became more affluent, money turned into a liquid. It flows into the bank account in a prodigious stream. And it flows out just as quickly. The earner is reduced to spectator status and is vaguely horrified by how quickly the money is flowing through. He or she may try to stem the outward flow in order to do more saving. But it's hard to know where to erect the dam. The money just flows on its own. And after a while one's ability to stay afloat through all the ebbs and flows becomes a sign of accomplishment in itself. The big money stream is another aptitude test. Far from being a source of corruption, money turns into a sign of mastery. It begins to seem deserved, natural. So even former student radicals begin to twist the old left-wing slogan so that it becomes: From each according to his abilities, to each according to his abilities.

The educated elites not only earn far more money than   6
they ever thought they would but now occupy positions of enormous responsibility. We're by now all familiar with modern-day executives who have moved from SDS to CEO, from LSD to IPO. Indeed, sometimes you get the impression the Free Speech movement produced more corporate executives than Harvard Business School.

What's more amazing is the growth of lucrative industries   7
in which everybody involved is a member of the educated class. Only about 20 percent of the adult population of America possesses a college degree, but in many large cities and

suburban office parks, you can walk from office to office, for mile upon mile, and almost everybody in the place will have a sheepskin in the drawer. Educated elites have taken over much of the power that used to accrue to sedate old WASPs with dominating chins. Economists at the International Monetary Fund jet around the world reshaping macroeconomic policies. Brainiacs at McKinsey & Company swoop down on corporate offices run by former college quarterbacks and issue reports on how to merge or restructure.

The educated elites have even taken over professions that used to be working class. The days of the hard-drinking blue-collar journalist, for example, are gone forever. Now if you cast your eye down a row at a Washington press conference, it's: Yale, Yale, Stanford, Emory, Yale, and Harvard. Political parties, which were once run by immigrant hacks, are now dominated by communications analysts with Ph.D.s. If you drive around the old suburbs and follow the collarless-shirt bohemians home from their organic fruit stands, you notice they have literally moved into the houses of the old stockbroker elite. They are sleeping in the old elite's beds. They are swamping the old elite's institutions. As the novelist Louis Auchincloss summarized it, "The old society has given way to the society of accomplishment." Dumb good-looking people with great parents have been displaced by smart, ambitious, educated, and antiestablishment people with scuffed shoes.

Over the past 30 years, in short, the educated class has gone from triumph to triumph. They have crushed the old WASP elite culture, thrived in an economy that lavishly rewards their particular skills, and now sit atop many of the same institutions they once railed against. But all this has created a gnawing problem. How do they make sure they haven't themselves become self-satisfied replicas of the WASP elite they still so forcefully denounce?

Those who want to win educated-class approval must confront the anxieties of abundance: how to show—not least to themselves—that even while climbing toward the top of the ladder they have not become all the things they still profess to hold in contempt. How to navigate the shoals between their affluence and their self-respect. How to reconcile their success with their spirituality, their elite status with their egalitarian ideals. Socially enlightened members of the educated elite tend to be disturbed by the widening gap between rich and poor and are therefore made somewhat uncomfortable by the fact that their own family income now tops $80,000. Some of them dream of social justice yet went to a college where the tuition costs could feed an entire village in Rwanda for a year. Some once had "Question Authority" bumper stickers on their cars but now find themselves heading start-up software companies with 200 people reporting to them. The sociologists they read in college taught that consumerism is a disease, and yet now they find themselves shopping for $3,000 refrigerators. They took to heart the lessons of *Death of a Salesman,* yet now find themselves directing a sales force. They laughed at the plastics scene in *The Graduate* but now they work for a company that manufactures . . . plastic. Suddenly they find themselves moving into a suburban house with a pool and uncomfortable about admitting it to their bohemian friends still living downtown.

Though they admire art and intellect, they find themselves 11 living amidst commerce, or at least in that weird hybrid zone where creativity and commerce intersect. This class is responsible for more yards of built-in bookshelf space than any group in history. And yet sometimes you look at their shelves and notice deluxe leather-bound editions of all those books arguing that success and affluence is a sham: *Babbitt, The Great Gatsby, The Power Elite, The Theory of the Leisure Class.* This is an elite that has been raised to oppose elites. They are affluent yet opposed to materialism. They may spend their lives selling yet worry about selling out. They are by instinct antiestablishmentarian yet somehow sense they have become a new establishment.

The members of this class are divided against themselves, 12 and one is struck by how much of their time is spent earnestly wrestling with the conflict between their reality and their ideals. They grapple with the trade-offs between equality and privilege ("I believe in public schooling, but the private school just seems better for my kids"), between convenience and social responsibility ("These disposable diapers are an incredible waste of resources, but they are so easy"), between rebellion and convention ("I know I did plenty of drugs in high school, but I tell my kids to Just Say No").

But the biggest tension, to put it in the grandest terms, is 13 between worldly success and inner virtue. How do you move ahead in life without letting ambition wither your soul? How do you accumulate the resources you need to do the things you want without becoming a slave to material things? How do you build a comfortable and stable life for your family without getting bogged down in stultifying routine? How do you live at the top of society without becoming an insufferable snob?

These educated elites don't despair in the face of such 14 challenges. They are the Résumé Gods. They're the ones who aced their SATs and succeeded in giving up Merlot during pregnancy. If they are not well equipped to handle the big challenges, no one is. When faced with a tension between competing values, they do what any smart privileged person bursting with cultural capital would do. They find a way to have both. They reconcile opposites.

The grand achievement of the educated elites in the 1990s 15 was to create a way of living that lets you be an affluent success and at the same time a free-spirit rebel. Founding design firms, they find a way to be an artist and still qualify for stock options. Building gourmet companies like Ben & Jerry's or Nantucket Nectars, they've found a way to be dippy hippies and multinational corporate fat cats. Using William S. Burroughs in ads for Nike sneakers and incorporating Rolling Stones anthems into their marketing campaigns, they've reconciled the antiestablishment style with the corporate imperative. Listening to management gurus who tell them to thrive on chaos and unleash their creative potential, they've reconciled the spirit of the imagination with service to the bottom line. Turning university towns like Princeton and Palo Alto into entrepreneurial centers, they have recon-

ciled the highbrow with the high tax bracket. Dressing like
Bill Gates in worn chinos on his way to a stockholders'
meeting, they've reconciled undergraduate fashion with up-
per-crust occupations. Going on eco-adventure vacations,
they've reconciled aristocratic thrill-seeking with social concern. Shopping at Benetton or the Body Shop, they've
brought together consciousness-raising and cost control.

When you are amidst the educated upscalers, you can   16
never be sure if you're living in a world of hippies or the
stockbrokers. In reality you have entered the hybrid world in
which everybody is a little of both.

Marx told us that classes inevitably conflict, but sometimes   17
they just blur. The values of the bourgeois mainstream culture
and the values of the 1960s counterculture have merged.
That culture war has ended, at least within the educated class.
In its place that class has created a third culture, which is a
reconciliation between the previous two. The educated elites
didn't set out to create this reconciliation. It is the product
of millions of individual efforts to have things both ways. But
it is now the dominant tone of our age. In the resolution
between the culture and the counterculture, it is impossible
to tell who co-opted whom, because in reality the bohemians
and the bourgeois co-opted each other. They emerge from
this process as bourgeois bohemians, or Bobos.

For Study and Discussion

QUESTIONS FOR RESPONSE

1. What elements in your life do you see that reflect the kind of
   contradictions Brooks writes about? For example, you may be
   concerned about conserving natural resources but at the same
   time drive a sports utility vehicle, or you may deplore the use of
   child labor in underdeveloped countries but at the same time buy
   athletic shoes made in those countries. How much do such
   contradictions bother you?
2. Who do you know from the 1960s era who was involved in the
   kind of antiestablishment activities that Brooks describes? To

what extent do those people seem to fit into Brooks's Bobo category? Give some examples.

QUESTIONS ABOUT PURPOSE

1. What do you see as Brooks's main purpose or purposes? To inform? To entertain? To stimulate action? To educate for change? On what do you base your answer?
2. What image or persona of himself do you think Brooks wants to project in this essay? What details in the essay give you that impression?

QUESTIONS ABOUT AUDIENCE

1. This essay was excerpted from a popular book called *Bobos in Paradise*. Brooks says in the introduction to his book that he is describing the ideology, manners, and morals of today's educated elite. Who do you think Brooks assumes will be interested in reading about that elite, and why?
2. To what extent do you feel that you are or are likely to become the kind of person Brooks is describing? How does that judgment affect your response to the essay?

QUESTIONS ABOUT STRATEGIES

1. One of Brooks's principal strategies is antithesis, combining opposites in the same sentence or paragraph. How does he strengthen that strategy with specifics?
2. Brooks is a senior editor of a national weekly magazine, writes frequently for other major publications, and is a commentator for National Public Radio. What examples of his journalistic skills do you find in this essay?

QUESTIONS FOR DISCUSSION

1. What do you see as the connection between our contemporary culture of information and the rise of this new class of bourgeois bohemians that Brooks describes?
2. How can one work out a manner of living that enables one to live prosperously and yet be socially responsible?

ALICE WALKER

Alice Walker was born in 1944 in Eatonton, Georgia, attended Spelman College in Atlanta, and graduated from Sarah Lawrence College. She then became active in the civil rights movement, helping to register voters in Georgia, teaching in the Head Start program in Mississippi, and working on the staff of the New York City welfare department. In subsequent years, she began her own writing career while teaching at Wellesley College, the University of California at Berkeley, and Brandeis University. Her writing reveals her interest in the themes of sexism and racism, themes she embodies in her widely acclaimed novels: *The Third Life of Grange Copeland* (1970), *Meridian* (1976), *The Color Purple* (1982), and *Possessing the Secret of Joy* (1992). Her stories, collected in *In Love and Trouble: Stories of Black Women* (1973) and *You Can't Keep a Good Woman Down* (1981); and essays, found in *Living by the Word* (1988) and *The Same River Twice* (1996), examine the complex experiences of black women. "Everyday Use," reprinted from *In Love and Trouble*, focuses on a reunion that reveals two contrasting attitudes toward the meaning of family heritage.

Everyday Use
For Your Grandmama

I WILL WAIT for her in the yard that Maggie and I made so clean and wavy yesterday afternoon. A yard like this is more comfortable than most people know. It is not just a yard. It is like an extended living room. When the hard clay is swept clean as a floor and the fine sand around the edges lined with tiny, irregular grooves anyone can come and sit and look up into the elm tree and wait for the breezes that never come inside the house.

Maggie will be nervous until after her sister goes: she will   2
stand hopelessly in corners homely and ashamed of the burn scars down her arms and legs, eyeing her sister with a mixture of envy and awe. She thinks her sister has held life always in the palm of one hand, that "no" is a word the world never learned to say to her.

You've no doubt seen those TV shows where the child who   3
has "made it" is confronted, as a surprise, by her own mother and father, tottering in weakly from backstage. (A pleasant surprise, of course: What would they do if parent and child came on the show only to curse out and insult each other?) On TV mother and child embrace and smile into each other's faces. Sometimes the mother and father weep, the child wraps them in her arms and leans across the table to tell how she would not have made it without their help. I have seen these programs.

Sometimes I dream a dream in which Dee and I are sud-   4
denly brought together on a TV program of this sort. Out of a dark and soft-seated limousine I am ushered into a bright room filled with many people. There I meet a smiling, gray, sporty man like Johnny Carson who shakes my hand and tells me what a fine girl I have. Then we are on the stage and Dee is embracing me with tears in her eyes. She pins on my dress a large orchid, even though she has told me once that she thinks orchids are tacky flowers.

In real life I am a large, big-boned woman with rough,   5
man-working hands. In the winter I wear flannel nightgowns to bed and overalls during the day. I can kill and clean a hog as mercilessly as a man. My fat keeps me hot in zero weather. I can work all day, breaking ice to get water for washing. I can eat pork liver cooked over the open fire minutes after it comes steaming from the hog. One winter I knocked a bull calf straight in the brain between the eyes with a sledge

hammer and had the meat hung up to chill before nightfall. But of course all this does not show on television. I am the way my daughter would want me to be: a hundred pounds lighter, my skin like an uncooked barley pancake. My hair glistens in the hot bright lights. Johnny Carson has much to do to keep up with my quick and witty tongue.

But that is a mistake. I know even before I wake up. Who   6 ever knew a Johnson with a quick tongue? Who can even imagine me looking a strange white man in the eye? It seems to me I have talked to them always with one foot raised in flight, with my head turned in whichever way is farthest from them. Dee, though. She would always look anyone in the eye. Hesitation was no part of her nature.

"How do I look, Mama?" Maggie says, showing just   7 enough of her thin body enveloped in pink skirt and red blouse for me to know she's there, almost hidden by the door.

"Come out into the yard," I say.   8

Have you ever seen a lame animal, perhaps a dog run over   9 by some careless person rich enough to own a car, sidle up to someone who is ignorant enough to be kind to him? That is the way my Maggie walks. She has been like this, chin on chest, eyes on ground, feet in shuffle, ever since the fire that burned the other house to the ground.

Dee is lighter than Maggie, with nicer hair and a fuller   10 figure. She's a woman now, though sometimes I forget. How long ago was it that the other house burned? Ten, twelve years? Sometimes I can still hear the flames and feel Maggie's arm sticking to me, her hair smoking and her dress falling off her in little black papery flakes. Her eyes seemed stretched open, blazed open by the flames reflected in them. And Dee. I see her standing off under the sweet gum tree she used to dig gum out of; a look of concentration on her face as she watched the last dingy gray board of the house fall in toward the red-hot brick chimney. Why don't you do a dance around the ashes? I'd wanted to ask her. She had hated the house that much.

I used to think she hated Maggie, too. But that was before 11
we raised the money, the church and me, to send her to
Augusta to school. She used to read to us without pity;
forcing words, lies, other folks' habits, whole lives upon us
two, sitting trapped and ignorant underneath her voice. She
washed us in a river of make-believe, burned us with a lot of
knowledge we didn't necessarily need to know. Pressed us to
her with the serious way she read, to shove us away at just
the moment, like dimwits, we seemed about to understand.

Dee wanted nice things. A yellow organdy dress to wear 12
to her graduation from high school; black pumps to match a
green suit she'd made from an old suit somebody gave me.
She was determined to stare down any disaster in her efforts.
Her eyelids would not flicker for minutes at a time. Often I
fought off the temptation to shake her. At sixteen she had a
style of her own: and knew what style was.

I never had an education myself. After second grade the 13
school was closed down. Don't ask me why: in 1927 colored
asked fewer questions than they do now. Sometimes Maggie
reads to me. She stumbles along good-naturedly but can't
see well. She knows she is not bright. Like good looks and
money, quickness passed her by. She will marry John Thomas
(who has mossy teeth in an earnest face) and then I'll be free
to sit here and I guess just sing church songs to myself.
Although I never was a good singer. Never could carry a tune.
I was always better at a man's job. I used to love to milk till
I was hoofed in the side in '49. Cows are soothing and slow
and don't bother you, unless you try to milk them the wrong
way.

I have deliberately turned my back on the house. It is three 14
rooms, just like the one that burned, except the roof is tin;
they don't make shingle roofs any more. There are no real
windows, just some holes cut in the sides, like the portholes
in a ship, but not round and not square, with rawhide holding
the shutters up on the outside. This house is in a pasture,
too, like the other one. No doubt when Dee sees it she will

want to tear it down. She wrote me once that no matter where we "choose" to live, she will manage to come see us. But she will never bring her friends. Maggie and I thought about this and Maggie asked me, "Mama, when did Dee ever *have* any friends?"

She had a few. Furtive boys in pink shirts hanging about on washday after school. Nervous girls who never laughed. Impressed with her they worshiped the well-turned phrase, the cute shape, the scalding humor that erupted like bubbles in lye. She read to them.   15

When she was courting Jimmy T she didn't have much time to pay to us, but turned all her faultfinding power on him. He *flew* to marry a cheap gal from a family of ignorant flashy people. She hardly had time to recompose herself.   16

When she comes I will meet—but there they are!   17

Maggie attempts to make a dash for the house, in her shuffling way, but I stay her with my hand. "Come back here," I say. And she stops and tries to dig a well in the sand with her toe.   18

It is hard to see them clearly through the strong sun. But even the first glimpse of leg out of the car tells me it is Dee. Her feet were always neat-looking, as if God himself had shaped them with a certain style. From the other side of the car comes a short, stocky man. Hair is all over his head a foot long and hanging from his chin like a kinky mule tail. I hear Maggie suck in her breath. "Uhnnnh," is what it sounds like. Like when you see the wriggling end of a snake just in front of your foot on the road. "Uhnnnh."   19

Dee next. A dress down to the ground, in this hot weather. A dress so loud it hurts my eyes. There are yellows and oranges enough to throw back the light of the sun. I feel my whole face warming from the heat waves it throws out. Earrings, too, gold and hanging down to her shoulders. Bracelets dangling and making noises when she moves her arm up to shake the folds of the dress out of her armpits. The dress is loose and flows, and as she walks closer, I like it. I hear Maggie go "Uhnnnh" again. It is her sister's hair. It stands straight up like the wool on a sheep. It is black as night and   20 around the edges are two long pigtails that rope about like small lizards disappearing behind her ears.

"Wa-su-zo-Tean-o!" she says, coming on in that gliding 21 way the dress makes her move. The short stocky fellow with the hair to his navel is all grinning and he follows up with "Asalamalakim, my mother and sister!" He moves to hug Maggie but she falls back, right up against the back of my chair. I feel her trembling there and when I look up I see the perspiration falling off her chin.

"Don't get up," says Dee. Since I am stout it takes some- 22 thing of a push. You can see me trying to move a second or two before I make it. She turns, showing white heels through her sandals, and goes back to the car. Out she peeks next with a Polaroid. She stoops down quickly and lines up picture after picture of me sitting there in front of the house with Maggie cowering behind me. She never takes a shot without making sure the house is included. When a cow comes nibbling around the edge of the yard she snaps it and me and Maggie *and* the house. Then she puts the Polaroid in the back seat of the car, and comes up and kisses me on the forehead.

Meanwhile Asalamalakim is going through the motions 23 with Maggie's hand. Maggie's hand is limp as a fish, and probably as cold, despite the sweat, and she keeps trying to pull it back. It looks like Asalamalakim wants to shake hands but wants to do it fancy. Or maybe he don't know how people shake hands. Anyhow, he soon gives up on Maggie.

"Well," I say. "Dee." 24

"No, Mama," she says. "Not 'Dee,' Wangero Leewanika 25 Kemanjo!"

"What happened to 'Dee'?" I wanted to know. 26

"She's dead," Wangero said. "I couldn't bear it any longer 27 being named after the people who oppress me."

"You know as well as me you was named after your aunt 28 Dicie," I said. Dicie is my sister. She named Dee. We called her "Big Dee" after Dee was born.

"But who was *she* named after?" asked Wangero. 29

"I guess after Grandma Dee," I said. 30

"And who was she named after?" asked Wangero. 31

"Her mother," I said, and saw Wangero getting tired. 32
"That's about as far back as I can trace it," I said. Though,
in fact, I probably could have carried it back beyond the Civil
War through the branches.

"Well," said Asalamalakim, "there you are." 33

"Uhnnnh," I heard Maggie say. 34

"There I was not," I said, "before 'Dicie' cropped up in 35
our family, so why should I try to trace it that far back?"

He just stood there grinning, looking down on me like 36
somebody inspecting a Model A car. Every once in a while
he and Wangero sent eye signals over my head.

"How do you pronounce this name?" I asked. 37

"You don't have to call me by it if you don't want to," 38
said Wangero.

"Why shouldn't I?" I asked. "If that's what you want us 39
to call you, we'll call you."

"I know it might sound awkward at first," said Wangero. 40

"I'll get used to it," I said. "Ream it out again." 41

Well, soon we got the name out of the way. Asalamalakim 42
had a name twice as long and three times as hard. After I
tripped over it two or three times he told me to just call him
Hakim-a-barber. I wanted to ask him was he a barber, but I
didn't really think he was, so I didn't ask.

"You must belong to those beef-cattle peoples down the 43
road," I said. They said "Asalamalakim" when they met you,
too, but they didn't shake hands. Always too busy: feeding
the cattle, fixing the fences, putting up salt-lick shelters,
throwing down hay. When the white folks poisoned some of
the herd the men stayed up all night with rifles in their hands,
I walked a mile and half just to see the sight.

Hakim-a-barber said, "I accept some of their doctrines, 44
but farming and raising cattle is not my style." (They didn't
tell me, and I didn't ask, whether Wangero [Dee] had really
gone and married him.)

We sat down to eat and right away he said he didn't eat 45
collards and pork was unclean. Wangero, though, went on
through the chitlins and corn bread, the greens and everything else. She talked a blue streak over the sweet potatoes.

Everything delighted her. Even the fact that we still used the benches her daddy made for the table when we couldn't afford to buy chairs.

"Oh, Mama!" she cried. Then turned to Hakim-a-barber. 46 "I never knew how lovely these benches are. You can feel the rump prints," she said, running her hands underneath her and along the bench. Then she gave a sigh and her hand closed over Grandma Dee's butter dish. "That's it!" she said. "I knew there was something I wanted to ask you if I could have." She jumped up from the table and went over in the corner where the churn stood, the milk in its clabber by now. She looked at the churn and looked at it.

"This churn top is what I need," she said. "Didn't Uncle 47 Buddy whittle it out of a tree you all used to have?"

"Yes," I said. 48

"Uh huh," she said happily. "And I want the dasher, too." 49

"Uncle Buddy whittle that, too?" asked the barber. 50

Dee (Wangero) looked up at me. 51

"Aunt Dee's first husband whittled the dash," said Maggie 52 so low you almost couldn't hear her. "His name was Henry, but they called him Stash."

"Maggie's brain is like an elephant's," Wangero said, 53 laughing. "I can use the churn top as a centerpiece for the alcove table," she said, sliding a plate over the churn, "and I'll think of something artistic to do with the dasher."

When she finished wrapping the dasher the handle stuck 54 out. I took it for a moment in my hands. You didn't even have to look close to see where hands pushing the dasher up and down to make butter had left a kind of sink in the wood. In fact, there were a lot of small sinks; you could see where thumbs and fingers had sunk into the wood. It was beautiful light yellow wood, from a tree that grew in the yard where Big Dee and Stash had lived.

After dinner Dee (Wangero) went to the trunk at the foot 55 of my bed and started rifling through it. Maggie hung back in the kitchen over the dishpan. Out came Wangero with two quilts. They had been pieced by Grandma Dee and then Big Dee and me had hung them on the quilt frames on the front porch and quilted them. One was in the Lone Star pattern. The other was Walk Around the Mountain. In both of them were scraps of dresses Grandma Dee had worn fifty and more years ago. Bits and pieces of Grandpa Jarrell's Paisley shirts. And one teeny faded blue piece, about the size of a penny matchbox, that was from Great Grandpa Ezra's uniform that he wore in the Civil War.

"Mama," Wangero said sweet as a bird. "Can I have these old quilts?"   56

I heard something fall in the kitchen, and a minute later the kitchen door slammed.   57

"Why don't you take one or two of the others?" I asked. "These old things was just done by me and Big Dee from some tops your grandma pieced before she died."   58

"No," said Wangero. "I don't want those. They are stitched around the borders by machine."   59

"That'll make them last better," I said.   60

"That's not the point," said Wangero. "These are all pieces of dresses Grandma used to wear. She did all this stitching by hand. Imagine!" She held the quilts securely in her arms, stroking them.   61

"Some of the pieces, like those lavender ones, come from old clothes her mother handed down to her," I said, moving up to touch the quilts. Dee (Wangero) moved back just enough so that I couldn't reach the quilts. They already belonged to her.   62

"Imagine!" she breathed again, clutching them closely to her bosom.   63

"The truth is," I said, "I promised to give them quilts to Maggie, for when she marries John Thomas."   64

She gasped like a bee had stung her.   65

"Maggie can't appreciate these quilts!" she said. "She'd probably be backward enough to put them to everyday use."   66

"I reckon she would," I said. "God knows I been saving 'em for long enough with nobody using 'em. I hope she will!" I didn't want to bring up how I had offered Dee (Wangero) a quilt when she went away to college. Then she had told me they were old-fashioned, out of style.   67

"But they're *priceless!*" she was saying now, furiously; for 68
she has a temper. "Maggie would put them on the bed and
in five years they'd be in rags. Less than that!"

"She can always make some more," I said. "Maggie knows 69
how to quilt."

Dee (Wangero) looked at me with hatred. "You just will 70
not understand. The point is these quilts, *these* quilts!"

"Well," I said, stumped. "What would *you* do with them?" 71

"Hang them," she said. As if that was the only thing you 72
could do with quilts.

Maggie by now was standing in the door. I could almost 73
hear the sound her feet made as they scraped over each other.

"She can have them, Mama," she said, like somebody used 74
to never winning anything, or having anything reserved for
her. "I can 'member Grandma Dee without the quilts."

I looked at her hard. She had filled her bottom lip with 75
checkerberry snuff and it gave her face a kind of dopey,
hangdog look. It was Grandma Dee and Big Dee who taught
her how to quilt herself. She stood there with her scarred
hands hidden in the folds of her skirt. She looked at her sister
with something like fear but she wasn't mad at her. This was
Maggie's portion. This was the way she knew God to work.

When I looked at her like that something hit me in the 76
top of my head and ran down to the soles of my feet. Just
like when I'm in church and the spirit of God touches me
and I get happy and shout. I did something I never had done
before: hugged Maggie to me, then dragged her on into the
room, snatched the quilts out of Miss Wangero's hands and
dumped them into Maggie's lap. Maggie just sat there on my
bed with her mouth open.

"Take one or two of the others," I said to Dee. 77

But she turned without a word and went out to Hakim- 78
a-barber.

"You just don't understand," she said, as Maggie and I 79
came out to the car.

"What don't I understand?" I wanted to know. 80

"Your heritage," she said. And then she turned to Maggie, 81
kissed her and said, "You ought to try to make something of

yourself, too, Maggie. It's really a new day for us. But from the way you and Mamma still live you'd never know it."

She put on some sunglasses that hid everything above the   82
tip of her nose and her chin.

Maggie smiled; maybe at the sunglasses. But a real smile,   83
not scared. After we watched the car dust settle I asked Maggie to bring me a dip of snuff. And then the two of us sat there just enjoying, until it was time to go in the house and go to bed.

COMMENT ON "EVERYDAY USE"

Alice Walker's "Everyday Use" describes a difference between a mother's and her visiting daughter's understanding of the word "heritage." For Mama and her daughter Maggie, heritage is a matter of everyday living, of "everyday use." For Mama's other daughter, Dee (Wangero), however, heritage is a matter of style, a fashionable obsession with one's roots. These comparisons are revealed first in Walker's description of the physical appearance of the characters. Mama is fat and manly, and Maggie bears the scars from a fire. By contrast, Dee (Wangero) is beautiful and striking in her brightly colored African dress, earrings, sunglasses, and Afro hairstyle. Next, Walker compares the characters' skills. Mama can butcher a hog or break ice to get water, and Maggie is able to make beautiful quilts. Dee (Wangero), on the other hand, thinks of herself as outside this domestic world, educated by books to understand the cultural significance of her heritage. The problem posed by the debate over family possessions is whether heritage is an object to be preserved, like a priceless painting, or a process, to be learned, like the creation of a quilt.

Definition as a Writing Strategy

1. Reread the strategies section on pages 328–330. Then for your classmates and instructor, write a definition essay about your high school that will give your audience a vivid idea of what that high school was like. What was valued most in the school? Describe some of the admired students. What were the most important activities? Define by giving examples, analyzing qualities, attributing characteristics, drawing analogies when possible, and telling stories about particular individuals that illustrate the flavor and character of the school. This kind of assignment provides a great opportunity to tell stories about people.

2. For a challenging assignment focusing on a person, pick someone you find especially interesting—an athlete such as Tiger Woods, a businessperson such as Bill Gates or Michael Dell, an entertainment personality such as Oprah Winfrey or Barbra Streisand, a public figure such as Jesse Jackson or Justice Ruth Ginsberg. Through a computer search, locate several magazine articles on that person, and read them. Be sure to use substantial articles, not just items from gossip columns. Write a definition essay in which you describe the person—his or her professional activities and personal interests—trying to bring out the unique traits that have made the person successful. Remember that anecdotes are useful in this kind of essay. Your hypothetical audience could be readers of a magazine like *Parade* or *Esquire*.

3. If you are a person with special knowledge about a particular kind of animal, reread Harrigan's essay, "The Tiger Is God," paying special attention to his strategies for defining the nature of the tiger. Then write an essay in which you describe and define a breed or type of animal you know well. Some possibilities are the cutting horse, the dressage horse, hunting dogs or sheep dogs, a particular breed of dog such as Golden Retrievers or Weimaraners, or a particular breed of cat such as Burmese or Russian

Blues. Certainly there are many other possibilities. Use concrete details and examples of particular actions that illustrate the animal's distinctive temperament and behavior.

4. Choose a term that interests you—for example, *camaraderie, sportsmanship, sex appeal, gutsiness, good taste*—and for your campus newspaper write a guest column defining that term with examples and anecdotes. What are the necessary characteristics of someone who has the quality? What is the opposite quality? Who epitomizes the term for you?

5. Richard Rodriguez's "Growing Up in Los Angeles" defines one kind of adolescent, a young person who seems to be the product of that city of glitz and excesses. Write a similar essay, though shorter and less complex, that defines one kind of adolescent in the community where you grew up. You could describe what such a person wears, what extracurricular activities he or she excels at, what he or she drives, and so on. Some possibilities are a rodeo cowboy from west Texas, a gymnast, a member of the school band, a debater, a computer genius, or a popular athlete. You could create a character that would be a composite of several young people you knew. Your audience could be your classmates and instructor.

6. Writers and speakers often argue from definition, trying to get their audiences to agree with or approve of something by defining it positively (for example, a good education) or to criticize something by defining it negatively (for example, a bad grading policy). Drawing on material and information you are getting in one of your courses, write a paper suitable for that course defining a concept, policy, theory, or event either negatively or positively. For a course in early childhood development, you could define a good day-care center. For a chemistry course, you could do a process paper on how to set up a good laboratory experiment. For a government course, you could define a well-run local campaign. For a speech course, you could define an effective speaking style.

CAUSE
AND
EFFECT

If you are like most people, you were born curious and will stay that way all your life, always wondering why things happen, wanting to know reasons. You want to know why the wind blows or what makes some young people dye their hair green, but you also want to know how to control your life and your environment. You can't have that control unless you understand **causes.** That is why so much writing is cause-and-effect writing. You need it to help you understand more about your world so you can improve it. Writing about causes plays an important role in almost all the professions, and it certainly figures prominently in writing in college.

You also want to know about **effects.** Will A lead to B? And also to C, D, and E? Such questions also arise partly from pure curiosity—a youngster will pull any string or push any button just to find out what will happen—but they stem too from a need to regulate your life, to understand how your acts affect the lives of others. You want to predict consequences so you can manage your existence in ways that other creatures cannot manage theirs. You see an effect and look for explanations, usually in writing; and when you try to explain an effect to someone else, you often do it in writing.

PURPOSE

When you write cause-and-effect essays, you're likely to have one of three purposes. Sometimes you want to *explain* why something happened or what might be likely to happen under certain circumstances. Daniel Goleman is writing that kind of essay in "Peak Performance: Why Records Fall" when he explains how new knowledge about training practices and about human mental capacities have led to athletic feats that seemed impossible only a few decades ago. At other times, you might write a cause-and-effect paper to *speculate* about an interesting topic—for instance, to speculate why a new computer game has become so popular or what the effects of a new kind of body suit will be for competitive swimmers.

Often writers use cause-and-effect patterns to *argue.* In fact, that may be the purpose for which they are used most frequently, particularly when someone is writing a policy statement or a proposal. Carl Sagan writes this kind of argument in "Science and Hope" when he shows what will happen if the general public is ignorant about science. This kind of cause-and-effect argument works particularly well when you are making an argument to pragmatic readers who pride themselves on their common sense. If you can show them that a certain policy will have bad effects, they're likely to be persuaded.

AUDIENCE

When you begin to analyze your audience for a cause-and-effect argument, it helps to think of them as jurors to whom you are going to present a case. You can make up a list of questions just as a lawyer would to help him or her formulate an argument. For example:

- How should I prepare my readers for my argument? What background information do they need?
- What kind of evidence are they likely to want? Factual, statistical, anecdotal?
- How much do I have to explain? Will they have enough context to understand my points and make connections without my spelling them out?

Like a trial lawyer, you're trying to establish a chain of cause and effect. Perhaps you can't establish absolute proof, but you can show probability. The format for such arguments can be

- State your claim early, usually in the first paragraph.
- Show the connection you want to establish.
- Present your supporting evidence.
- Repeat your claim in your conclusion.

STRATEGIES

One good strategy in cause-and-effect arguments is drawing analogies. Cathy Young does this in "Keeping Women Weak" when she draws an analogy between paranoia and suspicion in the Soviet Union, where she grew up, and radical feminists' tendency to see sexism and oppression in virtually all male-female relationships. You could use the same kind of argument if you wanted to write a cause-and-effect paper claiming that a culture that glorifies male competition, particularly in bruising sports such as football, shouldn't be surprised at gangs and street violence among young men. You could seek support for your argument by doing key word searches with the entries Violence + Sports or Gangs + Competition.

When you are arguing about effects, you want your audience to accept your analysis of a situation and agree that behavior Y is the result of event X. Robert Coles uses this pattern throughout his essay "Uniforms" when he argues that requiring young people to dress in a certain way puts pressure on them to control their behavior and become part of a respected community. Although Coles isn't dogmatic—that's never his style—he firmly asserts that clothes send signals and that uniforms can help young people who are adrift to find a direction.

You could use the same kind of pattern if you wanted to argue, for instance, that physical punishment is almost never a good idea for children or anyone else. To support your claim you would need to research the issue and then cite studies that show the effects of violence on both those who receive it and those who practice it.

You don't have to write every cause-and-effect paper to prove something or as if you were conducting a major court case. You can also write interesting speculative papers in which you theorize about certain trends—for instance, wearing baseball caps backward or athletic shoes with the laces untied—and try to find who initiated the trends and why. Or you could write satirically about some of the annoyances in our culture—for instance, the 800 "help" numbers that keep you on hold or phone menus that go on forever.

POTENTIAL PITFALLS IN CAUSE-AND-EFFECT PAPERS

Although cause and effect is a powerful writing strategy, it can also be a hazardous one. When it comes to dealing with the difficult, ongoing problems of people and societies, you can almost never prove simple cause-and-effect relationships. Many serious human problems really have no good, single solutions because our lives and cultures are so complex. Thus, to keep from looking naive or poorly informed, avoid hasty statements such as "I know what causes X, and we can fix it if we just do Y." To avoid such pitfalls, you should observe the following cautions in writing about cause and effect.

First, as in all expository writing, be careful about how much you claim. Instead of insisting that if A happens, B is inevitable, write, "I believe if A occurs, B is very likely to happen" or "B will probably follow if A happens." For instance, you might feel absolutely sure that if the university opened a child-care center for students' children, attendance at classes would be higher, but you can't prove it. You would gain more credibility with university administrators if you were careful not to overstate your case.

Second, be careful not to oversimplify cause-and-effect connections. Experienced writers and observers know that most major problems and important events have not one cause but several. Daniel Goleman makes this clear in "Peak Performance: Why Records Fall" when he points out that many elements have contributed to better performance among athletes—better coaching, improved equipment, and more knowledge about physiology. Nevertheless, he points out, intensive, longer practicing seems to be the major cause of better performance in most activities.

A less complicated, because more easily analyzed, effect that one might explore is the significant decline in deaths from heart disease in the United States in the last thirty years. There are many reasons for this decline, not just one or two. Increasingly, people smoke less, eat healthier foods, exercise more, and try to control their blood pressure. New treatments for heart problems also make a difference. Thus, prudent writers qualify their claims about causes and effects by using phrases such as "a major cause," "an important result," or "an immediate effect." Also take care to distinguish between immediate and obvious causes for an occurrence and longer range and less apparent causes. For example, you might think that the decline in teen pregnancies in the United States in the last decade has resulted from government mandated Abstinence Only sex education programs in the schools, but it's important to consider that there are probably also more complex causes such as education about AIDS and more available contraceptives.

And avoid confusing coincidence or simple sequence with valid cause and effect. Just because X follows Y doesn't mean that Y caused X—such assumptions are the basis of superstitions. If a decrease in fatalities in auto accidents follows a rise in gasoline prices, you shouldn't assert that people are having fewer accidents because the high cost of gasoline is causing them to drive less. That would be a hard connection to prove; a drop in fatalities could also come from more cars having side airbags and from Congress having lowered the limit of alcohol in blood tests for drivers to .8 percent.

So working with cause and effect in a paper can be tricky and complex. That doesn't mean, however, that you should refrain from using cause-and-effect explanations or arguments until you are absolutely sure of your ground. You can't always wait for certainty to make an analysis or a forecast. The best you can do is observe carefully, speculate intelligently, and add qualifications.

USING CAUSE AND EFFECT IN PARAGRAPHS

Here are two cause-and-effect paragraphs. The first is written by a professional writer and is followed by an analysis. The second is written by a student writer and is followed by questions.

JONATHAN WEINER
Elephant Evolution

For poachers, elephants with big tusks were prime targets. Elephants with small tusks were more likely to be passed over, and those with no tusks at all were not shot. In effect, though no one realized it at the time, African elephants in places where poaching was rife were under enormous selection pressure for tusklessness. And in fact, elephant watchers in the most heavily poached areas began noticing more and more

Sets up evidence

Shows effect

tuskless elephants in the wild. Andrew Dobson, an ecologist at Princeton, has compiled graphs of this trend, tracing the evolution of tusklessness in five African wildlife preserves, Ambroseli, Mikumi, Tsavo East, Tsavo West, and Queen Elizabeth. In Ambroseli, where the elephants are relatively safe, the proportion of tuskless female elephants is small, just under a few percent. But in Mikumi, a park where the elephants are heavily poached, tusklessness is rising. The longer each generation lives the fewer tusks the elephants carry. Among females aged five through ten about 10 percent are tuskless; among females aged thirty to thirty-five, about 50 percent are tuskless.

Statistics that support his point

Comment In this paragraph taken from his book *The Beak of the Finch*, which documents the evolutionary patterns two scientists have traced by measuring the beaks of finches on an isolated island in the Galápagos, the science writer Jonathan Weiner shows how poaching on elephant preserves in Africa has directly affected the physical characteristics of the elephants on those preserves. He sets up a direct "If-Then" cause-and-effect equation. When poachers killed the elephants with the largest tusks because those tusks were in the greatest demand, fewer elephants who carried the genes for that characteristic were left to breed. Therefore fewer elephants with large tusks appeared in subsequent generations. By citing the graphs that an identified academic ecologist compiled from observations in five specific wildlife preserves, Weiner shores up his cause-and-effect argument; he's not relying only on hearsay evidence or casual observation.

EMILY LINDERMAN
Barrier-Free Design

Many merchants view the Americans with Disabilities Act as expensive social engineering. They have established an attractive and affordable space for their businesses. Their customers seem satisfied. Then the federal government requires them to provide accessible ramps and elevators, wider doorways and halls, larger bathrooms, and lower drinking fountains. Seen from another perspective, however, making these changes may pay off in the long run. How many times have you tried to move furniture into a building or up to the third floor? How many times have you tried to find a place for your packages in a cramped bathroom stall? And how many times have you had to lift your little brother up to the fountain to get a drink? All customers, not simply disabled customers, will benefit from and reward merchants who invest in these barrier-free buildings.

1. Whom do you think Linderman is addressing with her argument for the benefits of barrier-free buildings?
2. How does the significance of the extra benefits that Linderman mentions compare with the significance of the benefits that the Disabilities Act was designed to provide?

CAUSE AND EFFECT

Points to Remember

1. Remember that in human events you can almost never prove direct, simple, cause and effect relationships. Qualify your claims.
2. Be careful not to oversimplify your cause-and-effect statements; be cautious about saying that a cause always produces a certain effect or that a remedy never succeeds.
3. Distinguish between the immediate, obvious cause of something and more long-range, less apparent causes for that effect.
4. Avoid confusing coincidence or simple sequence with cause and effect; because B follows A doesn't mean that A caused B.
5. Build your cause-and-effect argument as a trial lawyer would. Present as much evidence as you can and argue for your hypothesis.

Carl Sagan (1934–1996) was born in New York City and educated at the University of Chicago. He taught astronomy at Harvard University and Cornell University and served as director of the Laboratory of Planetary Studies. In his extraordinary career, he worked as an experimenter on many NASA missions to outer space; an adviser (and board member) to many of the world's most influential organizations—National Institute for the Environment, and Global Forum of Spiritual and Parliamentary Leaders on Human Survival— and the president of his own television studio, which produced the award-winning public television series *Cosmos* (1980). His books include *Planetary Education* (1970), *The Dragons of Eden: Speculations on the Evolution of Human Intelligence* (1977), *Pale Blue Dot: A Vision of the Human Future in Space* (1994), and *Billions and Billions: Thoughts on Life and Death at the Birth of the Millennium* (1997). In "Science and Hope," reprinted from *The Demon-Haunted World: Science as the Candle in the Dark* (1995), Sagan explains why science helps citizens make intelligent decisions about our global environment.

Science and Hope

FOR ME, THERE are four main reasons for a concerted effort to convey science—in radio, TV, movies, newspapers, books, computer programs, theme parks, and classrooms—to every citizen. In all uses of science, it is insufficient—indeed it is dangerous—to produce only a small, highly competent, well-rewarded priesthood of professionals. Instead, some fundamental understanding of the findings and methods of science must be available on the broadest scale.

- Despite plentiful opportunities for misuse, science can be   2
the golden road out of poverty and backwardness for
emerging nations. It makes national economies and the
global civilization run. Many nations understand this. It is

---

*Science alerts us to the perils introduced by
our world-altering technologies, especially to
the global environment on which our
lives depend.*

---

why so many graduate students in science and engineering
at American universities—still the best in the world—are
from other countries. The corollary, one that the United
States sometimes fails to grasp, is that abandoning science
is the road back into poverty and backwardness.

- Science alerts us to the perils introduced by our world-   3
altering technologies, especially to the global environment
on which our lives depend. Science provides an essential
early warning system.

- Science teaches us about the deepest issues of origins, na-   4
tures, and fates—of our species, of life, of our planet, of the
Universe. For the first time in human history we are able
to secure a real understanding of some of these matters.
Every culture on Earth has addressed such issues and valued their importance. All of us feel goosebumps when we
approach these grand questions. In the long run, the greatest gift of science may be in teaching us, in ways no other
human endeavor has been able, something about our cos-
mic context, about where, when, and who we are.

- The values of science and the values of democracy are   5
concordant, in many cases indistinguishable. Science and

democracy began—in their civilized incarnations—in the same time and place, Greece in the seventh and sixth centuries B.C. Science confers power on anyone who takes the trouble to learn it (although too many have been systematically prevented from doing so). Science thrives on, indeed requires, the free exchange of ideas; its values are antithetical to secrecy. Science holds to no special vantage points or privileged positions. Both science and democracy encourage unconventional opinions and vigorous debate. Both demand adequate reason, coherent argument, rigorous standards of evidence and honesty. Science is a way to call the bluff of those who only pretend to knowledge. It is a bulwark against mysticism, against superstition, against religion misapplied to where it has no business being. If we're true to its values, it can tell us when we're being lied to. It provides a mid-course correction to our mistakes. The more widespread its language, rules, and methods, the better chance we have of preserving what Thomas Jefferson and his colleagues had in mind. But democracy can also be subverted more thoroughly through the products of science than any pre-industrial demagogue ever dreamed.

Finding the occasional straw of truth awash in a great   6
ocean of confusion and bamboozle requires vigilance, dedication, and courage. But if we don't practice these tough habits of thought, we cannot hope to solve the truly serious problems that face us—and we risk becoming a nation of suckers, a world of suckers, up for grabs by the next charlatan who saunters along.

For Study and Discussion

QUESTIONS FOR RESPONSE

1. How well informed do you think you are about important scientific issues in our society? How competent do you feel

to judge the accuracy of scientific news that you hear or read?

2. What have been your sources of information about science— for example, science museums, television programs such as *Cosmos* or *Nova*, theme parks such as Epcot Center, or computer programs? How well do you think such sources serve young people?

QUESTIONS ABOUT PURPOSE

1. Sagan makes a strong statement of purpose in his first paragraph. How would you summarize that purpose?
2. What does Sagan see as some of the dangers caused by scientific ignorance? Pick out one of those dangers; how real does it seem in our society?

QUESTIONS ABOUT AUDIENCE

1. In this selection, Sagan obviously wants to reach lay people, not his fellow scientists. Why does he seek this particular audience?
2. How can this lay audience achieve the scientific know-how that Sagan thinks is important for our time?

QUESTIONS ABOUT STRATEGIES

1. Sagan has had an eminent scientific career but he also wrote popular books and contributed frequently to mass market magazines such as the Sunday supplement, *Parade*. What is it about his writing style that helps him appeal to large groups of readers who are relatively uninformed about science?
2. What is the special appeal for Americans of the arguments Sagan makes in paragraph 5, beginning "The values of science and the values of democracy are concordant . . . ?"

QUESTIONS FOR DISCUSSION

1. Toward the end of the essay, Sagan asserts that science and democracy nourish each other, but he also warns that science can be used to subvert democracy. Under what circumstances might

such subversion happen? Do you know of instances where it has happened?

2. Sagan mentions theme parks as one source of scientific information. If you have been to a theme park such as Epcot Center at Disney World, what is your opinion of their kind of scientific education?

ANDREW C. REVKIN

Andrew C. Revkin was born in Providence, Rhode Island, in 1956 and educated at Brown University and Columbia University. Revkin has worked as a journalist covering subjects ranging from murder in the Amazon to the crash of TWA Flight 800, from the plight of the working poor in America to the persistent pollution of the Hudson River. Since 1995, he has been a reporter for the *New York Times*, focusing on environmental issues affecting the metropolitan region. His books include *The Burning Season* (1990) and *Global Warming: Understanding the Forecast* (1992). His current book project, *The Last Shaman*, is the life story of a hereditary chief from a British Columbia Indian tribe. In "Some Big Ideas Wash Up One Bulb at a Time," reprinted from the *New York Times*, Revkin explains why the complex causes of environmental pollution make us feel helpless.

Some Big Ideas Wash Up One Bulb at a Time

PEOPLE REALLY GET around. From the poles to the peaks to the ocean floor, humans have probed and cut and burned and drilled and left their mark.

The human assault on the planet usually does not make headlines unless there is a sudden calamity—giant fires in Indonesia or radioactivity escaping from a nuclear plant in Chernobyl. So we are most attuned to environmental problems of that kind—not the subtle, slow types.

But those subtle, slow-moving processes bear watching. Sometimes, they creep up in surprising ways.

I got my first such surprise in 1979, when, shortly after 4
college, I ended up serving as first mate on a circumnavigat-
ing sailboat. We anchored one day in the lee of an uninhab-
ited volcanic heap of Mars-like rock called Zuqar Island,
in the south end of the Red Sea. The island was so remote
that one chart labeled it "terra nullis." No one claimed it. If
ever a place could be called the middle of nowhere, this was
it.

I felt awfully lucky to be in such an unspoiled place, with 5
black, bed-sized manta rays gliding in the shallows and no
sound but the wind and waves.

I rowed ashore and went for a hike, clambering across a 6
sere landscape of crusty rocks, which cracked underfoot like

> *The human assault on the planet usually*
> *does not make headlines unless there is a*
> *sudden calamity.*

pottery shards. I reached the windward side and walked to
the beach, which was littered, heaped and piled with—light
bulbs.

There were yardlong fluorescent tubes and heavy spot- 7
lights, delicate incandescent globes and flashlight bulbs as big
as a pea. They lay in drifts, unbroken, above the highest tide
line. Others that had shattered clinked musically with each
lapping wave.

Who could have done such a thing? 8

After a moment of reflection, it dawned on me that the 9
light-bulb litter was not the fault of any individual. It must
have been a consequence of the incessant parade of container
and cargo ships plying the Red Sea. I envisioned a tanker
crewman on his night watch unscrewing a burned-out bulb
and, without a thought, tossing it over.

Over the years, ship after passing ship would add up to a 10 lot of bulbs bobbing around. Every once in a while, one would be carried by a wave or the wind far enough above the island's surf line that it would remain an unseen icon of the modern age.

I was not a reporter then, but things like piles of light bulbs 11 on a faraway beach made me want to write about the effect of humans on the environment. Once I became a journalist, I began reporting on all kinds of environmental issues. One small story, in a way, summed up a lot.

It was about a construction crew in the San Fernando 12 Valley in Los Angeles that had been digging a hole for a parking-lot foundation. The crew reached a certain depth, and suddenly gasoline began welling up from the earth.

They had not struck a hidden pipeline. The gasoline, as it 13 turned out, had leaked from a buried, rusting storage tank at a service station a few hundred yards away. It had been leaking almost indiscernibly for years, quart by quart, pooling atop the aquifer in the porous soil and drifting down the block, waiting for someone to dig a hole.

I saw the results of a similar slow degradation a few years 14 ago when I spent time with an Indian tribe in Kitamaat Village, on the coast of British Columbia, about 500 miles north of Vancouver. The village is across a bay from a large aluminum refinery built by Alcan Aluminum.

In his office, the elected chief of the Haisla tribe, Gerald 15 Amos, showed me a glass pint jar half-filled with mercury. He said a Haisla contractor had been hired to take down a work shed on the Alcan property. While dismantling a toilet, he undid the U-shaped trap in the plumbing and found it full of the liquid metal. Someone must have been pouring something containing mercury down the toilet for years, which left a constant residue trapped in the pipes.

In an ideal world, we could look ahead a few decades and 16 figure out that dumping a few dribs of mercury down a toilet, or dropping a bulb over the rail, might eventually have an undesirable effect.

But often the offending activity seems so innocuous that 17 it hardly registers on a person's consciousness, let alone his conscience. It's just one bulb, right?

And, of course, we don't live in an ideal world. We actually   18
live in a very muddled, complicated one. As a result, even
when people do think ahead, they can end up taking the
wrong action.

Brazil, for example, passed laws decades ago protecting the   19
valuable Brazil nut trees of the Amazon. When ranchers
cleared rain forests, towering specimens of the tree remained—standing alone on otherwise denuded land. But
without the surrounding forest, the bees that pollinated the
Brazil nut flowers could not thrive, so few of the remaining
trees produce nuts.

Nature's complexity can also hide early signs that we are   20
having an impact.

Even something as big as a sharp shift in climate as a result   21
of human pollution can be hard to see immediately. For one
thing, its first manifestations—the baby steps—can be ob-
scured by all the natural variability in the natural world.

Year by year, decade by decade, the globe has its comple-   22
ment of hot flashes and cold spells, thanks to El Niño and La
Niña, a squiggly jet stream and the rest.

As Starley Thompson, a scientist at the National Center   23
for Atmospheric Research in Boulder, Colo., put it, the challenge of recognizing global warming amid the ups and downs
of weather is like trying to discern cornstalks rising in a weedy
field.

In Dr. Thompson's scenario, at first there are lots of green   24
sprouting things; at some point, the cornstalks finally stand
out, clear for everyone to see. With climate change, it's all
still a bit weedy.

What it boils down to is that you will never read a front-   25
page headline that says "Earth's Temperature Soars Overnight—Coasts Flooded, Crops Ruined." All those things may
happen, but spread over decades and scattered across the
globe.

So we're a little stuck. We have the general idea that bad   26
things may come from doubling the amount of heat-trapping
gases in the air as a result of burning fossil fuels. But because
there is much disagreement—and more uncertainty—about

the precise dimensions of the problem, we find it hard to settle on a set of concrete actions to cut these so-called greenhouse gases.

It may be that we are condemned to mounting belated, intensive responses once the consequences of slow shifts are evident.   27

That might not be so bad. After all, humans have a good track record at crash programs: the United States did O.K. after being jogged by Sputnik, Pearl Harbor and other surprises. And there can be unanticipated benefits from doing nothing. Sometimes, problems take care of themselves.   28

Consider all those stranded light bulbs in the Red Sea. No need to go clean them up. Let global warming raise the sea level slightly, and they may simply float away.   29

For Study and Discussion

QUESTIONS FOR RESPONSE

1. What examples have you seen or do you know about where the environmental carelessness of some group caused serious damage to a place? What was your reaction to that instance?
2. What kind of regulations would be necessary to prevent such damage? What do you think public reaction would be to such regulations?

QUESTIONS ABOUT PURPOSE

1. What realizations do you think the author wants his readers to come to about how we live?
2. What specific actions, if any, do you think the author would like to have his readers take? Why?

QUESTIONS ABOUT AUDIENCE

1. This article was originally published in the *New York Times*. What assumptions do you make about the environmental awareness of regular readers of that newspaper?

2. How effective do you find the author's examples for most college students? Why?

QUESTIONS ABOUT STRATEGIES

1. How does the author set the stage for the striking scene he reveals in the last sentence of paragraph 6?
2. What is the tone of the last paragraph in the essay? Why do you think the author concludes in this way?

QUESTIONS FOR DISCUSSION

1. What practices do you see in your community or on your campus that may lead to unfortunate environmental consequences? Who can be held responsible for these practices?
2. Our American love affair with the automobile has a variety of environmental consequences. What are some of them and how could we deal with them?

ROBERT COLES

Robert Coles was born in Boston, Massachusetts, in 1929 and educated at Harvard University and Columbia Medical School. He worked as a member of the psychiatric staff at several hospitals before assuming the position of professor of psychiatry and medical humanities at the Harvard Medical School. Although he has contributed essays to journals as diverse as *The Atlantic* and the *American Journal of Psychiatry,* he is best known for his multivolume study of children in various stressful situations, *Children of Crisis* (1967–1978). He has also written books such as *Erik H. Erikson: The Growth of His Work* (1970); *Irony in the Mind's Life: Essays on Novels by James Agee, Elizabeth Bowen and George Eliot* (1974); *The Call of Stories* (1989); *The Call of Service* (1993); and, together with his wife, Jane Hallowell Coles, the multivolume *Women of Crisis* (1978–1980). His recent books include *The Secular Mind* (1999) and *Lives of Moral Leadership* (2000). In "Uniforms," reprinted from *Harvard Diary II,* Coles describes the possible effects of wearing a uniform.

Uniforms

WE HAVE BEEN hearing a good deal, of late, about the value of uniforms as a means of encouraging young people to be more disciplined, law-abiding. The rationale goes like this: children and young people need a sense of order; need firm rules with respect to how they ought to look, behave; need to feel themselves very much part of particular institutions whose educational and ethical principles are meant to strengthen our various communities and, by exten- 1 sion, our nation—and uniforms help address that necessary psychological and moral aspect of child-rearing. Not that clothes in and of themselves possess magical transformative powers. A child (or adult) bent on being rowdy, mean, hurtful, criminal can do so wearing a coat and tie, and shoes polished to a sparkle, whereas youngsters who appear to certain fastidious and formal adults as slobs and worse (their pants uncreased and wrinkled, their shirts sloppily worn) can be conscientious, decent, considerate, kindly—respectful of

> *In a sense, all clothes are . . . symbolic—*
> *we send signals, thereby, as to who we are,*
> *what we hold dear, with whom we wish to*
> *connect, and affiliate ourselves.*

others, if not respectful of the notion some of us have as to how they ought to be attired. Moreover, for some young people, such casual, laid-back garb is itself a uniform—to appear relaxed and "cool" is felt to be a mandatory manner of self-presentation.

For years, actually, I have heard the word "uniform" used by certain Harvard college students of mine, who have arrived in Cambridge from small towns in the South or the Midwest, and aren't familiar with a kind of constraint that is imposed by indirection: "I went to a Catholic school in Minnesota, and we were told we didn't all have to wear the same kind of blouse and skirt and socks and shoes, the way it used to be—but, you know, we did have to wear some kind of blouse and skirt: I mean, no jeans and no T-shirts. So, when I came here I wasn't as uptight as some people I met here [during the first days of orientation] who came from schools where there really were uniforms and everyone had to wear them, be dressed the same. But it doesn't take long to discover that there's a 'uniform' here too—and if you don't wear it, you'll pay a price. I mean [I had, obviously, asked] here, if you wear a skirt and blouse to class, you can feel out of it: too formal. Here, the scruffier the better, that's what you learn right off, boy or girl! There's a way to dress when you go to class, just as there was when I was in high school, only the clothes are different—and Lord help you at breakfast if you come into the dining room looking neat and tidy, and your hair is combed and you're wearing a dress (a dress!) and some jewelry, a bracelet or a necklace: people will think you're on your way to a job interview, or something has *happened*—you have to go to a hospital, or a funeral, or church, something unusual! You'll hear, 'Is everything all right?' Now, I hear myself thinking those words—if I get the urge to wear clothes that are just the slightest bit 'formal,' the way I used to all the time! If I told my roommates or others in the [freshman] dorm what I've just said, they'd think I was odd—making a case out of nothing, one guy put it when I got into a discussion with him about all this, and made the mistake of pointing out that all the boys here wear khakis or jeans, and sneakers, the dirtier the better, and open shirts, work shirts, a lot of them, as if we're in a logging camp out West!"

She was exaggerating a little, but her essential point was quite well taken—that in a setting where studied informality rules supreme, and where individualism is highly touted, there are, nevertheless, certain standards with respect to the desirable, the decidedly unattractive, so that a dress code certainly asserts itself, however informally, unofficially: a uniform of sorts, as the young man she mentioned did indeed agree to call it, a range of what is regarded as suitable, and what is unusual, worth observing closely, even paying the notice of a comment, a question. Nor is such a college environment all that unusual, with respect to a relative consistency of attire that is, surely, more apparent to the outsider. We all tend to fall in line, accommodate the world (of work, of study, of travel and relaxation, of prayer) we have chosen, for varying lengths of time, to join. We take notice of others, ascertain a given norm, with respect to what is (and is not) worn, and make the necessary choices for our wardrobe, our use—or we don't do so, thereby, of course, for one reason or another of our own, setting ourselves apart, even as others promptly do the same in the way they regard us.

All of the above is unsurprising: the stuff of our daily 4 unselfconscious living, yet, an aspect of our existence that ought to be remembered when a topic such as "uniforms" is brought up for public consideration—a necessary context. Still, these days, when the subject of "uniforms" comes up, it is meant to help us consider how to work more effectively in our schools with young people who are in trouble, who aren't doing well in school, who may be drop-outs and already up to no good—well on their way to delinquency, criminality. To ask such individuals (to demand of them when they are under the jurisdiction of a court) that they adhere to a certain dress code is to put them on due and proper notice: a certain kind of behavior is expected, and no ifs, ands, buts—the uniform as an exterior instance of what has to take place within: obedience, self-restraint, a loyalty to institutional authority. True, to repeat, clothes don't make us decent, cooperative, respectful human beings, in and of themselves—but they are an aspect of the way we present ourselves to others, and they are also daily reminders to us of the world to which we belong, and by extension, the values and customs and requirements of that world. To tell a child, a young man or woman, that he or she has to "shape up" in a certain way, dress in a certain manner, speak a certain language (and not another kind!) is to indicate a determination that a particular community's jurisdiction, its sovereignty will be asserted, maintained, upheld, from moment to moment.

I hear all the time, of course, that in our fancy private 5 schools and colleges such an institutional insistence with regard to dress has been, by and large, abandoned in the name of a modern individualism, a lack of pretentiousness, a respect for our variousness, a refusal of "authoritarianism," of the "repressiveness" of yore. To be sure, clothes can be a badge, an instrument of fearful, blind submission, of snobbish, cliquish affiliation, of gratuitous and relentless and unthinking indoctrination. On the other hand, as mentioned earlier, even the most vigorously iconoclastic, even those righteously enamored of a social or political or educational privatism that resists compliance with any number of conventions or habits, will not easily escape their own, ironic nod (and more) to social cohesion—one uniform replacing another, ties and skirts abandoned in a compulsory stampede for jeans or sweatpants, or for undershirts become all there is above the waist.

Many of the youngsters I have met, taught in ghetto   6
schools, many of the youngsters I've known who are in trouble at first-rate suburban or private school, have enormous need for "control": they haven't learned to subordinate their impulses to the needs of others; they are self-absorbed to their own detriment, never mind the harm that such a tenaciously reflexic egoism can cause to others in a classroom, on a team, a playground, anywhere in a neighborhood. Such boys and girls, such youths can often be desperately in search of the very commitment to an (educational, religious, civic) community they seem flagrantly to refuse, scorn. Indeed, their only hope may be the moment when a school or judge acts on behalf of a rehabilitative or corrective program that draws the line, insists that a uniform be a step (a mere step, but nonetheless, a significant first move) toward integration into a world outside any given self, a world in which others count, are respected, a world of obedience and self-control, as well as self-regard and self-assertion (the nature of the mix is all-important).

In a sense then all clothes are, as Freud, not to mention   7
Shakespeare, reminded us, symbolic—we send signals, thereby, as to who we are, what we hold dear, with whom we wish to connect, affiliate ourselves. Moreover, it works both ways: we receive messages with respect to our appearance from the nation, the culture, the various institutions or communities to which we belong (or which we are *told* we must join, such as the schools)—as anyone will realize upon visiting a foreign land, a different continent, but also while here at home, where what we wear can tell a lot about our hopes,

inclinations, dispositions, aspirations, loyalties, and, too, our fears and worries, and worse. Small wonder then, that uniforms worn by young people adrift, wayward in various ways, can bring a promise of direction, can offer a community with a shared purpose certain values and ideals, all of which, literally, are worn on the sleeves of its members. Of course, the heart of the matter is a person's interior moral life, but some of us badly need to be reminded, again and again, that there are others out there to whom, so to speak, we belong, and of whom we have to think with consideration and respect. We do, indeed, dress for those others, not only for ourselves—and for all of us that daily gesture has meaning, even as for some of us such a gesture may mark the beginning of a life that itself has, finally, come to possess some meaning.

For Study and Discussion

QUESTIONS FOR RESPONSE

1. If you or someone close to you wore uniforms to school, what effect do you think they had on those who wore them? Give some examples.
2. Would you say there is an unofficial uniform on your campus? If so, what is it and why do you think it has been adopted? How strong do you think the pressure is to conform?

QUESTIONS ABOUT PURPOSE

1. What significant points does Coles make about the role that clothes play in most of our lives? How valid do you find his reasoning?
2. How does Coles suggest that uniforms can play a part in helping young people to establish their place in a community?

QUESTIONS ABOUT AUDIENCE

1. The original audience for this essay probably consisted of Coles's colleagues and other adults who know of and are interested in his work with children. In what ways do you think that the

response of those readers and those of first-year college students are likely to differ?

2. What negative feelings do many people have about uniforms that Coles has to overcome in order to make his argument? What do you think is the source of those feelings?

QUESTIONS ABOUT STRATEGIES

1. In the course of the essay, what details does Coles reveal about his professional dealings with children? What weight do those details give to his argument?

2. What kind of reasoning does Coles use to counteract the reaction against school uniforms that he knows many students are likely to have?

QUESTIONS FOR DISCUSSION

1. What are some of "the constraints imposed by indirection," as Coles puts it (paragraph 2), that you feel in your life? What would the result be if you defied some of those constraints?

2. What are some of the common reasons school administrators and parents give for wanting youngsters to wear school uniforms? What is your response to those reasons?

DANIEL GOLEMAN

Daniel Goleman was born in 1946 in Stockton, California, and was educated at Amherst College and Harvard University. After working for several years as a professor of psychology, he began his career as an editor for *Psychology Today*. He has contributed more than fifty articles to psychology journals and has written a dozen books, including *The Meditative Mind* (1988), *The Creative Spirit* (1992), *Mind, Body Medicine: How to Use Your Mind for Better Health* (1993), *Emotional Intelligence* (1995), and *Working with Emotional Intelligence* (1998). In "Peak Performance: Why Records Fall," reprinted from a 1994 *New York Times* article, Goleman analyzes how dedication to practice contributes to "peak performances."

Peak Performance: Why Records Fall

THE OLD JOKE—How do you get to Carnegie Hall? Practice, practice, practice—is getting a scientific spin. Researchers are finding an unexpected potency from deliberate practice in world-class competitions of all kinds, including chess matches, musical recitals and sporting events.

Studies of chess masters, virtuoso musicians and star athletes show that the relentless training routines of those at the top allow them to break through ordinary limits in memory and physiology, and so perform at levels that had been thought impossible.

World records have been falling inexorably over the last century. For example, the marathon gold medalist's time in the 1896 Olympics Games was, by 1990, only about as good as the qualifying time for the Boston Marathon.

"Over the last century Olympics have become more and more competitive, and so athletes steadily have had to put in more total lifetime hours of practice," said Dr. Michael Mahoney, a psychologist at the University of North Texas in Denton, who helps train the United States Olympic weight-lifting team. "These days you have to live your sport." 4

That total dedication is in contrast to the relatively leisurely attitude taken at the turn of the century, when even world-class athletes would train arduously for only a few months before their competition. 5

"As competition got greater, training extended to a whole season," said Dr. Anders Ericsson, a psychologist at Florida 6

Through their hours of practice, elite performers of all kinds master shortcuts that give them an edge.

State University in Tallahassee who wrote an article on the role of deliberate practice for star performance recently in the journal *American Psychologist.* "Then it extended through the year, and then for several years. Now the elite performers start their training in childhood. There is a historical trend toward younger starting ages, which makes possible a greater and greater total number of hours of practice time."

To be sure, there are other factors at work: coaching methods have become more sophisticated, equipment has improved and the pool of people competing has grown. But new studies are beginning to reveal the sheer power of training itself. 7

Perhaps the most surprising data show that extensive practice can break through barriers in mental capacities, particularly short-term memory. In short-term memory, information is stored for the few seconds that it is used and then fades, as 8 in hearing a phone number which one forgets as soon as it is dialed.

The standard view, repeated in almost every psychology 9 textbook, is that the ordinary limit on short-term memory is for seven or so bits of information—the length of a phone number. More than that typically cannot be retained in short-term memory with reliability unless the separate units are "chunked," as when the numbers in a telephone prefix are remembered as a single unit.

But, in a stunning demonstration of the power of sheer 10 practice to break barriers in the mind's ability to handle information, Dr. Ericsson and associates at Carnegie-Mellon University have taught college students to listen to a list of as many as 102 random digits and then recite it correctly. After 50 hours of practice with differing sets of random digits, four students were able to remember up to 20 digits after a single hearing. One student, a business major not especially talented in mathematics, was able to remember 102 digits. The feat took him more than 400 hours of practice.

The ability to increase memory in a particular domain is 11 at the heart of a wide range high-level performance, said Dr. Herbert Simon, professor of computer science and psychology at Carnegie-Mellon University and a Nobel laureate. Dr. Ericsson was part of a team studying expertise led by Dr. Simon.

"Every expert has acquired something like this memory 12 ability" in his or her area of expertise, said Dr. Simon. "Memory is like an index; experts have approximately 50,000 chunks of familiar units of information they recognize. For a physician, many of those chunks are symptoms."

A similar memory training effect, Dr. Simon said, seems 13 to occur with many chess masters. The key skill chess players rehearse in practicing is, of course, selecting the best move. They do so by studying games between two chess masters and guessing the next move from their own study of the board as the game progresses.

Repeated practice results in a prodigious memory for chess 14 positions. The ability of some chess masters to play blindfolded, while simply told what moves their opponents make, has long been known; in the 1940's Adrian DeGroot, himself a Dutch grandmaster, showed that many chess masters are able to look at a chess board in midgame for as little as five seconds and then repeat the position of every piece on the board.

Later systematic studies by Dr. Simon's group showed that the chess masters' memory feat was limited to boards used in actual games; they had no such memory for randomly placed pieces. "They would see a board and think, that reminds me of Spassky versus Lasker," said Dr. Simon.   15

This feat of memory was duplicated by a college student who knew little about chess, but was given 50 hours of training in remembering chess positions by Dr. Ericsson in a 1990 study.   16

Through their hours of practice, elite performers of all kinds master shortcuts that give them an edge. Dr. Bruce Abernathy, a researcher at the University of Queensland in Australia, has found that the most experienced players in racquet sports like squash and tennis are able to predict where a serve will land by cues in the server's posture before the ball is hit.   17

A 1992 study of baseball greats like Hank Aaron and Rod Carew by Thomas Hanson, then a graduate student at the University of Virginia in Charlottesville, found that the all-time best hitters typically started preparing for games by studying films of the pitchers they would face, to spot cues that would tip off what pitch was about to be thrown. Using such fleeting cues demands rehearsing so well that the response to them is automatic, cognitive scientists have found.   18

The maxim that practice makes perfect has been borne out through research on the training of star athletes and artists. Dr. Anthony Kalinowski, a researcher at the University of Chicago, found that swimmers who achieved the level of national champion started their training at an average age of 10, while those who were good enough to make the United States Olympic teams started on average at 7. This is the same age difference found for national and international chess champions in a 1987 study.   19

Similarly, the best violinists of the 20th century, all with   20 international careers as soloists for more than 30 years, were found to have begun practicing their instrument at an average age of 5, while violinists of only national prominence, those affiliated with the top music academy in Berlin, started at 8, Dr. Ericsson found in research reported last year in *The Psychological Review.*

Because of limits on physical endurance and mental alertness, world-class competitors—whether violinists or weight lifters—typically seem to practice arduously no more than four hours a day, Dr. Ericsson has found from studying a wide variety of training regimens.   21

"When we train Olympic weight lifters, we find we often have to throttle back the total time they work out," said Dr. Mahoney. "Otherwise you find a tremendous drop in mood, and a jump in irritability, fatigue and apathy."   22

Because their intense practice regimen puts them at risk for burnout or strain injuries, most elite competitors also make rest part of their training routine, sleeping a full eight hours and often napping a half-hour a day, Dr. Ericsson found.   23

Effective practice focuses not just on the key skills involved, but also systematically stretches the person's limits. "You have to tweak the system by pushing, allowing for more errors at first as you increase your limits," said Dr. Ericsson. "You don't get benefits from mechanical repetition, but by adjusting your execution over and over to get closer to your goal."   24

Violin virtuosos illustrate the importance of starting early in life. In his 1993 study Dr. Ericsson found that by age 20 top-level violinists in music academies had practiced a lifetime total of about 10,000 hours, while those who were slightly less accomplished had practiced an average of about 7,500 hours.   25

A study of Chinese Olympic divers, done by Dr. John Shea of Florida State University, found that some 11-year-old divers had spent as many hours in training as had 21-year-old American divers. The Chinese divers started training at age 4.   26

"It can take 10 years of extensive practice to excel in   27 anything," said Dr. Simon. "Mozart was 4 when he started composing, but his world-class music started when he was about 17."

Total hours of practice may be more important than time spent in competition, according to findings not yet published by Dr. Neil Charness, a colleague of Dr. Ericsson at Florida State University. Dr. Charness, comparing the rankings of 107 competitors in the 1993 Berlin City Tournament, found that the more time they spent practicing alone, the higher their ranking as chess players. But there was no relationship between the chess players' rankings and the time they spent playing others. 28

As has long been known, the extensive training of an elite athlete molds the body to fit the demands of a given sport. What has been less obvious is the extent of these changes. 29

"The sizes of hearts and lungs, joint flexibility and bone strength all increase directly with hours of training," said Dr. Ericsson. "The number of capillaries that supply blood to trained muscles increases." 30

And the muscles themselves change, Dr. Ericsson said. Until very recently, researchers believed that the percentage of muscle fiber types was more than 90 percent determined by heredity. Fast-twitch muscles, which allow short bursts of intense effort, are crucial in sports like weight lifting and sprinting, while slow-twitch muscles, richer in red blood cells, are essential for endurance sports like marathons. "Muscle fibers in those muscles can change from fast twitch to slow twitch, as the sport demands," said Dr. Ericsson. 31

Longitudinal studies show that years of endurance training at champion levels leads athletes' hearts to increase in size well beyond the normal range for people their age. 32

Such physiological changes are magnified when training occurs during childhood, puberty and adolescence. Dr. Ericsson thinks this may be one reason virtually all top athletes today began serious practice as children or young adolescents, though some events, like weight training, may be exceptions because muscles need to fully form before intense lifting begins. 33

The most contentious claim made by Dr. Ericsson is that 34

practice alone, not natural talent, makes for a record-breaking performance. "Innate capacities have very little to do with becoming a champion," said his colleague, Dr. Charness. "What's key is motivation and temperament, not a skill specific to performance. It's unlikely you can get just any child to apply themselves this rigorously for so long."

But many psychologists argue that the emphasis on prac-   35
tice alone ignores the place of talent in superb performance. "You can't assume that random people who practice a lot will rise to the top," said Dr. Howard Gardner, a psychologist at Harvard University. Dr. Ericsson's theories "leave out the question of who selects themselves—or are selected—for intensive training," adding, "It also leaves out what we most value in star performance, like innovative genius in a chess player or emotional expressiveness in a concert musician."

Dr. Gardner said: "I taught piano for many years, and   36
there's an enormous difference between those who practice dutifully and get a little better every week, and those students who break away from the pack. There's plenty of room for innate talent to make a difference over and above practice time. Mozart was not like you and me."

For Study and Discussion

QUESTIONS FOR RESPONSE

1. Think of some top performers who started very young—for instance, violinist Midori, chess prodigy Bobby Fisher, or tennis player Jennifer Capriati. What do you know about their subsequent lives? To what extent can you generalize about such individuals?
2. If you hope to be a top performer in your chosen field, does this essay encourage you or discourage you? Explain why.

QUESTIONS ABOUT PURPOSE

1. What message do you think the experts quoted in this essay are giving to young people who want to excel in something? What do you see as the impact of that message?

2. What role do you think science plays in sports these days? What is your feeling about that role?

QUESTIONS ABOUT AUDIENCE

1. What groups of readers do you see as people who would particularly benefit from learning about the research reported here? In what way would they benefit?
2. How would the value system of a reader—that is, the complex of things that the reader thinks is important—affect the way he or she responds to this essay?

QUESTIONS ABOUT STRATEGIES

1. What is the impact of Goleman's pointing out that the marathon runner who won an Olympic gold medal a hundred years ago could barely qualify for the Boston Marathon today?
2. How does Goleman's use of diverse authorities strengthen his essay?

QUESTIONS FOR DISCUSSION

1. What impact do you think the new realities about becoming a winner will have on the families of young artists and athletes? How might it differ among families?
2. What factors in a competitor's performance that are not discussed here might affect his or her achievement? How important are those elements?

Cathy Young was born in 1963 in Moscow, in the former Soviet Union, and was educated at Rutgers University. After writing a weekly column for the college newspaper, she began contributing articles to the *New York Times* and *American Spectator.* One year after graduating from Rutgers, she published *Growing Up in Moscow: Memoirs of a Soviet Girlhood* (1989). Her current book is *Cease-fire!: Why Women and Men Must Join Forces to Achieve Truce Equality* (1999). In "Keeping Women Weak," reprinted from *NEXT: Young American Writers on the New Generation* (1994), Young analyzes the effects of feminism on her generation's attitudes toward women's liberation.

Keeping Women Weak

N OT LONG AGO, I attended a conference on women's research and activism in the nineties, attended by dozens of feminist academics, writers, and public figures. At the wrap-up session, a middle-aged history professor from the Midwest introduced a discordant note into the spirit of celebration. "The fact," she said, "is that young women just aren't interested in feminism or feminist ideas, even though they are leading feminist lives—planning to become lawyers, doctors, professionals. What is it about feminism, and about our approach, that puts young women off?"

In response, some blamed "the backlash," others "homophobia." One woman protested that there *were* young feminists out there, citing sexual harassment lawsuits filed by high-school girls—apparently a greater accomplishment than merely preparing for a career. Another declared that what feminist educators needed to give their students was "an understanding of the power dynamic," not "quote-unquote objectivity." (Could it be something about comments like these that turns female students off?) Missing from this picture was any serious discussion of what modern feminism has to offer modern young women.

Feminism meant a great deal to me when I came to the   3
United States thirteen years ago, after a childhood spent in the Soviet Union. Indeed, one of the things that elated me the most about America was women's liberation.

The society in which I had grown up was one that officially   4
proclaimed sexual equality and made it a point of great pride

---

*The new radical feminism seeks to regulate
personal relationships to a degree
unprecedented since the Puritans roamed
the earth.*

---

yet stereotyped men and women in ways reminiscent of the American fifties. At school, we had mandatory home economics for girls and shop for boys, a practice no one thought of challenging. At the music school for the gifted where my mother taught piano, to say that someone played "like a girl"—pleasantly, neatly, and without substance—was a commonly used putdown; in literary reviews, the highest compliment to be paid a woman writer or poet was that she wrote like a man.

As I approached college age, I learned that there was tacit   5
but widely known discrimination against women in the college-entrance exams, on the assumption that a less-capable male would in the end be a more valuable asset than a bright female, who would have boys and makeup and marriage on her mind. And all too many smart, ambitious girls seemed to accept this injustice as inevitable, assuming simply that they had to be twice as good as the boys to prove themselves.

It was just as unquestioningly accepted that housework,   6
including the arduous task of Soviet shopping, was women's
work; when the problem of women's excessive double burden at home and on the job was mentioned at all, the proposed solution was always for men to be paid more and for
women to spend more time at home, not for men to pitch
in with domestic chores. And although my parents' relationship was an uncommonly equal one, my father still quoted
to me the dictum (coming from Karl Marx, a thinker he
generally did not regard as much of an authority) that
"woman's greatest strength is her weakness."

My discovery of America was also a discovery of femi-   7
nism—not only *Ms.* magazine and *The Feminine Mystique* but
also the open and straightforward manner of young American
women I met. This was in stark contrast to the style that so
many Russian women reverently equated with "femininity"—
a more-or-less affected air of capriciousness and frailty, a
flirtatious deference to men. I admired the easy camaraderie
between boys and girls on American college campuses, the
independence and self-confidence of young women who invited guys on dates and picked up the tab, drove when they
were out with male companions, and wouldn't let anyone
treat them like frail, helpless little things.

Those early impressions may have been too optimistic,   8
perhaps somewhat superficial, perhaps incomplete. But I
don't think they were wrong.

Becoming an American as a teenager in 1980, I joined the   9
first generation of American women who had grown up assuming not only that they would work most of their lives but
also that they were the equals of men and that they could be
anything they wanted to be (except maybe a full-time home-
maker). This was also the first generation, really, to have
grown up after the sexual revolution—at a time when, at least
among the educated, the nice-girls-don't sexual standard
vanished almost completely. In a somewhat dizzying reversal
of traditional norms, many girls felt embarrassed telling their
first lovers that they were virgins (at least that's how I felt).

Of course new choices meant new pressures. I never   10
thought a world of sexual equality would be a utopia of peace

and harmony. I did believe that our generation of women, and men, was on its way to achieving a world in which people were judged as individuals and not on the basis of their gender; a world in which men and women worked and loved in equal partnership—even if, inevitably, they continued every so often to make each other miserable and furious.

And then something funny happened on the way to that 11 feminist future. We were told that we were victims, with little control over our lives and our choices; we were told that we needed to be protected.

When the right said that women were victimized by career 12 opportunities and sexual freedom, it didn't matter much—at least to the middle-class, college-educated women who were the main beneficiaries of these new opportunities. Who, in those social circles, was going to listen to people who said that wives should obey their husbands and stick to the kitchen and nursery—to Phyllis Schlafly or Jerry Falwell, notorious reactionaries with little impact on mass culture?

But the message of victimhood also came from the feminist 13 left. Everywhere around us, we were told, was a backlash seeking to snatch from us the freedoms we had gained. We were told that we were the targets of a hidden war and had better start acting like one, searching for subtle signs of enemy forays everywhere. If we believed that we had never experienced gender-based injustice and had never felt particularly restricted by our gender, we were not just naive but dangerous: we were turning our backs on feminism and fostering the myth that its major battles had been won.

Whenever a campus study has shown that young people of 14 both sexes increasingly share the same values and aspirations and that most college women are quite confident of their ability to succeed in the workplace and to combine family and career, older feminists seem far from pleased. Their warnings—oh, just wait until these young women get a taste of the real world and find that they still face prejudice and discrimination—can sound almost gleeful.

Older feminists talk a good line about empowering young 15 women and letting them speak in their own voices; but that goes only as long as these voices say all the approved things. At a university workshop on peer sexual harassment in schools I attended in the spring of 1993, some of the panelists complained that many girls didn't seem to understand what sexual harassment was; when boys made passes or teased them sexually they just shrugged it off, or they thought it was funny and actually liked it. "They need to be educated," one speaker said earnestly, "that the boys aren't just joking around with you, that it's harassment."

Ignored in all this discussion was intriguing evidence of   16
the assertive, even aggressive sexuality of many of today's teenage girls, who apparently do a bit of harassing of their own. If girls seemed to revel in sexual attention, that could only be a sign of "low self-esteem" or inability to say no.

Judging by all those complaints about the unraised con-   17
sciousness of the young, the preoccupation with the sexual and other victimization of high-school and college females is not coming, by and large, from young women themselves. Most of them, I believe, tend to regard all the extreme rhetoric as a sort of background noise; if they think about feminism at all, they often decide that they want no part of it—even if they're all for equal rights. The kind of feminists they usually see in their midst may further contribute to this alienation.

When I was still in college, I began to notice, along-   18
side the spirited, independent, ambitious young women I admired, a different product of the feminist age: the ever-vigilant watchdog on the alert for signs of sexism. Occasionally, she made a good point; when our environmental science professor blamed overpopulation in part on Third World women "choosing" to have lots of babies, a student spoke up to note that for most Third World women, childbearing was hardly a matter of choice.

More typical, alas, was the young woman in my human   19
sexuality class who was constantly pouncing on the professor for saying something like "People who suffer from premature ejaculation . . ." ("Are you implying that only men are people?"). When he had the audacity to cite data indicating that

some rapists were motivated primarily by hatred of women and the desire to dominate them but others were driven primarily by sexual impulses, she went ballistic: "The ONLY thing that causes rape is men wanting to control and terrorize women, and you're trying to make it SEXY!" Later, this person bragged about having caused the poor prof "a lot of trouble" by filing a complaint with the dean.

Paranoid is a red-flag word to many feminists—understandably so, since it has been used all too often to dismiss women's rightful concerns about sexism. But what other word can come to mind when a woman claims that her writing instructor's selection of a sample of bad writing—a conservative Christian screed linking pornography and communism—was a personal insult directed at her, since she had sometimes worn a Women Against Pornography button in school?   20

And what can one expect when Naomi Wolf, a writer hailed as a trailblazer of a new "Third Wave" of feminism for the younger generation, urges women to undertake—and men, to gracefully (and gratefully) second—"the arduous, often boring, nonnegotiable *daily chore of calling attention to sexism*" (emphasis mine)? In the essay "Radical Heterosexuality, or, How to Love a Man and Save Your Feminist Soul" (published in the twentieth-anniversary issue of *Ms.*), Wolf describes how even well-intentioned men tend to be blind to the horrific things women have to put up with: 21

> Recently, I walked down a New York City avenue with a woman friend, X, and a man friend, Y. I pointed out to Y the leers, hisses, and invitations to sit on faces. Each woman saw clearly what the other woman saw, but Y was baffled. . . . A passerby makes kissy-noises with his tongue while Y is scrutinizing the menu of the nearest bistro. "There, there! Look! Listen!" we cried. "What? Where? Who?" wailed poor Y, valiantly, uselessly spinning.

Like poor Y, I am baffled. God knows, I've been taking walks in Manhattan at least once or twice a week for nearly   22 thirteen years now, and not a single invitation to sit on a face, not even a single hiss as far as I recall—nothing more dramatic than the occasional "You look gorgeous today" or "That's a pretty outfit," and certainly nothing like the constant barrage Wolf describes. Even the time I wore a new dress that exposed much more cleavage than I realized, all it cost me was one fairly tame remark (as I was stepping into a subway car, a man who was stepping off stared at my bosom and muttered, "Very nice"). Applied to everyday life and interpersonal relations, "eternal vigilance is the price of liberty" strikes me as a rather disastrous motto to adopt.

Like all would-be revolutionaries, the radical feminists seek 23 to subordinate private life to ideology—an endeavor that I find, quite simply, frightening. You don't have to spend part of your life under a totalitarian system (though maybe it helps) to realize that social and political movements that subordinate life to ideology have a nasty way of turning coercive, whether it's the mass violence of communism or the neo-Puritan controls of "P.C."

This is not to say that there is no room for rethinking 24 traditional attitudes, on things ranging from who picks up the check in the restaurant to who takes care of the baby. Millions of women and men are grappling with these issues at home and in the workplace, some more successfully than others. But that doesn't mean they have to walk around with their eyes glued to a microscope.

Eternal vigilance is a tempting trap for post-baby-boomer 25 feminists. It has been often remarked that women of earlier generations had to struggle against visible and overt barriers, such as being denied admission to law school, or told that only men need apply for certain jobs or that married women shouldn't work. It seemed that once such barriers dropped, equality would come quickly. It didn't quite turn out that way; there were other, more insidious roadblocks, from a working mother's guilt over taking a business trip to a professor's unconscious tendency to call on the boys in the class. The problem, however, is that subtle sexism is an elusive target, with plenty of room for error and misinterpretation. If you complain to your professor that you find the course work too difficult and he says, "Well, I've always thought girls didn't belong in this class anyway," there's not a shadow of a doubt that he's a sexist pig. But suppose he says, "Hey, start working harder or drop the class, but don't come whining to me." Is he being insensitive to you as a woman? (An incident of this sort figured in a recent sex-discrimination suit at the University of Minnesota.) Or is he simply a blunt fellow who believes people should stand on their own two feet and who would have treated a male student exactly the same? And if he had been tough on a man but sensitive and solicitous toward a woman student, wouldn't that have been exactly the kind of paternalism feminists used to oppose?

But then, certain aspects of cutting-edge feminism do 26 smack of a very old-fashioned paternalism, a sort of chivalry without the charm. At some campus meetings, it is considered P.C. for men who are first in line for the microphone to cede their place to a woman in order to ensure that female speakers—apparently too timid to just get up and get in line—get a proper hearing. Ladies first?

Definitions of "hostile environment" sexual harassment 27 often seem like a throwback to prefeminist, if not positively Victorian, standards of how to treat a lady: no off-color jokes, no sexual remarks, no swearing and, God forbid, no improper advances. Surveys purporting to gauge the prevalence of harassment lump together sexual blackmail—demands for sex as a condition of promotion, good grades, or other rewards—with noncoercive advances from coworkers or fellow students, with sexual jokes or innuendo, "improper staring" or "winking."

Well, guess what: women too make off-color jokes and 28 risqué comments, and even sexual advances. Sure, many women at one time or another also have to deal with obnoxious, lecherous, and/or sexist jerks. But in most cases, especially if the man is not a superior, they're perfectly capable of putting a jerk back in his place. Of course, radical feminists such as Catharine MacKinnon tell us that there is *always* an imbalance of power between a man and a woman: even if you're studying for an MBA and have a prestigious job lined up, you're still powerless. Now there's a message guaranteed to build up self-confidence and self-esteem.

A video on sexual harassment, broadcast on public television twice in January 1993 and available free through an 800 number, includes a segment on a university experiment in which unwitting male students are assigned to supervise the computer work of an attractive girl. Before leaving them alone, the male research assistant pretends to take small liberties with the young woman (putting a hand on her shoulder, bending closely over her) while explaining the work process, and in most cases the male student proceeds to imitate this behavior or even push it a little further. 29

Then, the young woman—who, of course, has known what's been going on the whole time—talks on camera about how the experience has helped her understand what it's like to feel powerless. But doesn't this powerlessness have at least something to do with the fact that she was undoubtedly instructed not to show displeasure? Is it such a good idea to teach young women that, short of legal intervention, they have no way of dealing with such annoyances? 30

I don't believe that our views or our allegiances are determined solely or primarily by age. Still, one might have expected our generation to articulate a feminism rooted in the experience of women who have never felt subordinated to men, have never felt that their options were limited by gender in any significant way or that being treated as sexual beings diminished their personhood. This is not, of course, the experience of all young women; but it is the experience of many, and an experience that should be taken as a model. Perhaps those of us who have this positive view of our lives and our relationships with men have not lived up to our responsibility to translate that view into a new feminist vision. 31

In an *Esquire* article about sexual politics and romantic love on campus in the nineties, Janet Viggiani, then assistant dean for coeducation at Harvard, was quoted as saying, "I think young women now are very confused. . . . They don't have many models for how to be strong females and feminine. Many of their models are victim models—passive, weak, 32 endangered." In recent years, feminist activism has focused almost entirely on negatives, from eating disorders to sexual violence and abuse. Sadly, these problems are all too real, and they certainly should be confronted; what they should not be is the central metaphor for the female condition or for relations between women and men, or for feminism. What does it mean when the only time young women and girls think of feminism is not when they think of achievement but when they think of victimization?

The emphasis on victimhood has had an especially dramatic effect on attitudes toward sexuality. We didn't revel in our sexual freedom for too long; as if the shadow of AIDS weren't bad enough, sex was suddenly fraught with danger and violence as much as possibilities of pleasure, or even more so. A cartoon in the *Nation* shows a girl grooming herself before a mirror, with the caption, "Preparing for a date"— and in the next frame, a boy doing the same, with the caption, "Preparing for a date rape." Pamphlets on sexual assault warn that one out of every five dates ends in a rape, and that up to 25 percent of college women become victims: "Since you can't tell who has the potential for rape by simply looking, be on your guard with every man."

If these numbers are true, women would be well advised either to forswear dating altogether or to carry a can of Mace on every date. But what about these numbers? When one looks at how they are obtained, and how rape is defined, it becomes clear that the acquaintance-rape hysteria not only gives young women an exaggerated picture of the dangers they face in the company of men but essentially demeans women, absolving or stripping them of all responsibility for their behavior.

The question is not whether a woman's provocative dress, flirtatious behavior, or drinking justifies sexual assault; that attitude is now on the wane, for which the women's movement certainly deserves credit. It's not even a question of whether a woman should have to fight back and risk injury to prove that she did not consent to sex. The latest crusade makes a woman a victim of rape if she did not rebuff a man's sexual advances because she was too shy or didn't want to hurt his feelings, or if she had sex while drunk (not passed out, just sufficiently intoxicated so that her inhibitions were loosened) and felt bad about it afterwards. In a typical scenario, a couple is making out and then the woman pulls back and says, "I really think we shouldn't," and the man draws her back toward him, *nonforcibly,* and continues to fondle her, or says, "Oh come on, you know you want it," and eventually they end up having sex. If the woman feels that the intercourse was "unwanted," she can—according to the anti-date-rape activists—claim to be a victim, no different from the woman who's attacked at knifepoint in a dark, empty parking lot.

A few years ago, I was at the apartment of an ex-boyfriend 36 with whom I was still on friendly terms; after a couple of beers, we started kissing. When his hand crept under my skirt, I suddenly sobered up and thought of several good reasons why I should not go to bed with the guy. I wriggled out of his arms, got up, and said, "That's enough." Undaunted, he came up from behind and squeezed my breasts. I rammed my elbow into his chest, forcefully enough to make the point, and snapped, "Didn't you hear me? I said, enough."

Some people might say that I overreacted (my ex- 37 boyfriend felt that way), but the logic of modern-day radical feminists suggests the opposite: that I displayed a heroism that cannot be required of any woman in a situation like that because she could expect the guy to beat her up, to maim her, even if he hadn't made any threats or shown any violent tendencies. A "reasonable" woman would have passively submitted and then cried rape.

Even "no means no" is no longer enough; some activists 38 want to say that yes means no, or at least the absence of an explicit yes means no. Feminist legal theorist MacKinnon suggests that much of what our society regards as consensual sex hardly differs from rape and that, given women's oppression, it is doubtful "whether consent is a meaningful concept" at all. Which is to say that, like underage children and the mentally retarded, women are to be presumed incapable of valid consent. MacKinnon's frequent ally, polemicist Andrea Dworkin, states bluntly that all intercourse is rape.

This reasoning is still very far from mainstream acceptance. 39 Even MacKinnon only expresses such views when addressing fairly narrow and converted audiences, not when she's interviewed on TV. Yet a 1992 report by the Harvard Date Rape Task Force recommended that university guidelines define rape as "any act of sexual intercourse that occurs without the expressed consent of the person." What does this mean—that a consent form must be signed before a date? Or that, as a couple moves toward the bed after passionate and mutual heavy petting, the man should ask the woman if she's quite sure she wants to? (A friend who just graduated from college tells me that some men are actually beginning to act that way.) And perhaps he has to keep asking every time: the couple's prior sexual relationship, the advocates say, makes no difference whatsoever.

Clearly, this vision leaves no room for spontaneity, for 40 ambiguity, for passionate, wordless, animal sex. What's more, it is, in the end, deeply belittling to women, who apparently cannot be expected to convey their wishes clearly or to show a minimum of assertiveness. It also perpetuates a view of woman as the passive and reticent partner who may or may not want sex and man as the pursuer who is naturally presumed to want it: *she* is not required to ask for *his* consent (even though, given some current definitions, plenty of women must have committed rape at least a few times in their lives; I'm sure I have). Sex is something men impose on women. We're back full circle to fragile, chaste, nineteenth-century womanhood.

And some people think that's good. Recently, I got into a 41 discussion with a conservative Catholic male who vehemently argued that the campaign against date rape was nothing more than a distorted expression of women's legitimate rejection of sexual freedom, a thing so contrary to their chaste natures. Casual sex, he said, makes women (but not men) feel cheap and used, and what they're doing now is using the extreme language of rape to describe this exploitation; things were really better under the much-maligned double standard, when women were expected to say no to sex, and thus accorded more protection from male lust. To some conservatives, the outcry about sexual harassment confirms what conservatives have known all along: women want to be put on a pedestal and treated like ladies; they find sexual advances insulting because they are chaster than men.

I don't think that's true. Most young women have no wish   42 to return to the days when they were branded as sluts if they said yes. It may be, however, that this generation's confusion over sexual boundaries has to do with the pains of transition from one set of morals to another, of contradictory cultural messages: the traditional ones of chastity as the basis of female self-respect and reputation and the new ones of sexual liberation and female desire. Sometimes, we may not think we're "cheap" if we go to bed with a man we just met—at least, we're no worse than the guy is for going to bed with a woman he just met—yet when we wake up the next morning we may find that *he* thinks less of us but not of himself. And we may find, to our chagrin, that feminine coyness is not quite as extinct as we might like to think. The other day, a very liberated fortysomething friend of mine breezily said, "Oh, of course no modern woman says no when she means yes." Alas, recent studies (done by feminist researchers) show that *by their own admission,* about half of college women sometimes do.

But there may be another reason, too, for this generation's   43 susceptibility to the victim mentality: overconfidence in the perfectibility of life. The sexual-liberation rhetoric itself overlooked the complexity of human emotions and fostered the belief that sexual relationships could be free of all manipulation or unfair pressure. More generally, there is the idealistic arrogance of middle-class boys and girls who have grown up in a sheltered, affluent environment, accustomed to the notion that getting one's way is a basic right. The old cliché "Life isn't fair" is not only unpopular nowadays but profoundly suspect, seen as a smokescreen designed by the oppressors to keep the oppressed—women and minorities, in particular—in their place. Yes, it has been used for such purposes often enough. But often it happens to be true, and to disregard that is to invite disastrous consequences—like the belief that anyone, male or female, is entitled to an annoyance-free life.

The danger in the new radical feminism is not only that it   44
legitimizes what is, deep down, an extremely retrograde view of women; it also seeks to regulate personal relationships to a degree unprecedented since the Puritans roamed the earth. If you feel that a man has enticed or pressured you into having unwanted sex, you don't confront him and call him a manipulative creep; you run to a campus grievance committee and demand redress. If you don't like the way a coworker has been putting his hand on your shoulder, you don't have to tell him to stop it—you can go and file a lawsuit instead. Courts and law-enforcement authorities are being asked to step into situations where, short of installing hidden cameras in every bedroom and every office hallway, they have no way of finding out on whose side the truth is. Of course, many millions of women and men remain relatively unaffected by this relentless politicization of the personal. Still, the damage is being done.

Again, it may be my Soviet background that makes me   45
especially sensitive to the perils of this aggressive, paternalistic interventionism. In the Soviet *ancien régime,* it was not uncommon to report one's unfaithful spouse to the Communist party bureau at his (or, less commonly, her) workplace, and conflicts between husband and wife—particularly if both were party members—were often settled at public meetings that satisfied both the voyeuristic and the viciously moralistic impulses of the other comrades.

What are we going to be, then? Assertive, strong women   46
(and sometimes, surely, also needy and vulnerable, because we *are* human), seeing ourselves as no better or worse than men; aware of but not obsessed with sexism; interested in loving and equal relationships but with enough confidence in ourselves, and enough understanding of human foibles, to know better than to scrutinize every move we or our partners

make for political incorrectness? Or full-time agents of the gender-crimes police?

Women's liberation is not yet a completed task. Sexism still   47
lingers and injustice toward women still exists, particularly in the distribution of domestic tasks. We are still working on new standards and values to guide a new, equal relationship between men and women. But "Third Wave" feminism, which tries to fight gender bias by defining people almost entirely in terms of gender, is not the way to go.

We need a "Third Way" feminism that rejects the excesses   48
of the gender fanatics *and* the sentimental traditionalism of the Phyllis Schlaflys; one that does not seek special protections for women and does not view us as too socially disadvantaged to take care of ourselves. Because on the path that feminism has taken in the past few years, we are allowing ourselves to be treated as frail, helpless little things—by our would-be liberators.

For Study and Discussion

QUESTIONS FOR RESPONSE

1. For women: Describe an incident with a man in which someone might have seen you as a victim. What was your own reaction to the incident?
2. For men: How do you distinguish for yourself between behavior you mean to be friendly and attentive and behavior that might be interpreted as sexist or patronizing?

QUESTIONS ABOUT PURPOSE

1. What changes in behavior and attitude among today's college students do you think Young wants to help bring about with this essay? How could those changes come about?
2. What does Young mean by claiming that "the new radical feminism . . . legitimizes . . . an extremely retrograde view of women"? See paragraph 44.

QUESTIONS ABOUT AUDIENCE

1. Most of us write for readers with whom we believe we share experiences and concerns. To what extent do you feel that you share Young's experiences and concerns, and how does that feeling affect the way you respond to her essay?
2. Assuming that Young realizes she is not likely to persuade the radical feminists she is criticizing, to what other groups do you think she directs her essay? Give some of their characteristics.

QUESTIONS ABOUT STRATEGIES

1. How does Young go about establishing her credentials as a modern young woman who is concerned about women's issues?
2. How does Young use material from her seventeen years in Russia to strengthen her argument? How well does the strategy work?

QUESTIONS FOR DISCUSSION

1. What do you see as the differences between pioneer feminists such as Gloria Steinem and Betty Friedan—often called radicals in their day—and those feminists of today whom Young calls "radical"?
2. What are some of the consequences for members of a group who become persuaded that they are victims?

SANDRA CISNEROS

Sandra Cisneros was born in 1954 in Chicago and spent much of her childhood living in Chicago and Mexico City. A graduate of the University of Iowa Writer's Workshop, she has taught writing at the University of California at Berkeley and the University of Michigan. She has also taught in the San Antonio Public Schools and worked as literary director of the Guadalupe Cultural Arts Center. She has contributed stories and poems to periodicals such as *Imagine, Contact II,* and *Revista Chicano-Riquena.* Her poems appear in *Bad Boys* (1980), *The Rodrigo Poems* (1985), *My Wicked, Wicked Ways* (1987), and *Loose Woman* (1994); her stories are collected in *Woman Hollering Creek* (1991). Cisneros's book for young adults, *The House on Mango Street* (1983), won the American Book Award. In "One Holy Night," reprinted from *Woman Hollering Creek,* Cisneros's narrator analyzes the impact of her "holy night" with a man who claims he is descended from Mayan kings.

One Holy Night

About the truth, if you give it to a person, then he has
power over you. And if someone gives it to you, then they
have made themselves your slave. It is a strong magic.
You can never take it back.
— Chaq Uxmal Paloquín

H E SAID HIS name was Chaq. Chaq Uxmal Paloquín. 1
That's what he told me. He was of an ancient line of
Mayan kings. Here, he said, making a map with the heel of

434

his boot, this is where I come from, the Yucatán, the ancient cities. This is what Boy Baby said.

It's been eighteen weeks since Abuelita chased him away with the broom, and what I'm telling you I never told nobody, except Rachel and Lourdes, who know everything. He said he would love me like a revolution, like a religion. Abuelita burned the pushcart and sent me here, miles from home, in this town of dust, with one wrinkled witch woman who rubs my belly with jade, and sixteen nosy cousins.

I don't know how many girls have gone bad from selling cucumbers. I know I'm not the first. My mother took the crooked walk too, I'm told, and I'm sure my Abuelita has her own story, but it's not my place to ask.

Abuelita says it's Uncle Lalo's fault because he's the man of the family and if he had come home on time like he was supposed to and worked the pushcart on the days he was told to and watched over his goddaughter, who is too foolish to look after herself, nothing would've happened, and I wouldn't have to be sent to Mexico. But Uncle Lalo says if they had never left Mexico in the first place, shame enough would have kept a girl from doing devil things.

I'm not saying I'm not bad. I'm not saying I'm special. But I'm not like the Allport Street girls, who stand in doorways and go with men into alleys.

All I know is I didn't want it like that. Not against the bricks or hunkering in somebody's car. I wanted it to come undone like gold thread, like a tent full of birds. The way it's supposed to be, the way I knew it would be when I met Boy Baby.

But you must know, I was no girl back then. And Boy Baby was no boy. Chaq Uxmal Paloquín. Boy Baby was a man. When I asked him how old he was he said he didn't know. The past and the future are the same thing. So he seemed boy and baby and man all at once, and the way he looked at me, how do I explain?

I'd park the pushcart in front of the Jewel food store Saturdays. He bought a mango on a stick the first time. Paid for it with a new twenty. Next Saturday he was back. Two mangoes, lime juice, and chili powder, keep the change. The

third Saturday he asked for a cucumber spear and ate it slow.
I didn't see him after that till the day he brought me Kool-Aid
in a plastic cup. Then I knew what I felt for him.

Maybe you wouldn't like him. To you he might be a bum.   9
Maybe he looked it. Maybe. He had broken thumbs and
burnt fingers. He had thick greasy fingernails he never cut
and dusty hair. And all his bones were strong ones like a
man's. I waited every Saturday in my same blue dress. I sold
all the mango and cucumber, and then Boy Baby would come
finally.

What I knew of Chaq was only what he told me, because   10
nobody seemed to know where he came from. Only that he
could speak a strange language that no one could understand,
said his name translated into boy, or boy-child, and so it was
the street people nicknamed him Boy Baby.

I never asked about his past. He said it was all the same   11
and didn't matter, past and the future all the same to his
people. But the truth has a strange way of following you, of
coming up to you and making you listen to what it has to
say.

Night time. Boy Baby brushes my hair and talks to me in   12
his strange language because I like to hear it. What I like to
hear him tell is how he is Chaq, Chaq of the people of the
sun, Chaq of the temples, and what he says sounds sometimes
like broken clay, and at other times like hollow sticks, or like
the swish of old feathers crumbling into dust.

He lived behind Esparza & Sons Auto Repair in a little   13
room that used to be a closet—pink plastic curtains on a
narrow window, a dirty cot covered with newspapers, and a
cardboard box filled with socks and rusty tools. It was there,
under one bald bulb, in the back room of the Esparza garage,
in the single room with pink curtains, that he showed me the
guns—twenty-four in all. Rifles and pistols, one rusty musket,
a machine gun, and several tiny weapons with mother-of-
pearl handles that looked like toys. So you'll see who I am,
he said, laying them all out on the bed of newspapers. So
you'll understand. But I didn't want to know.

The stars foretell everything, he said. My birth. My son's.   14
The boy-child who will bring back the grandeur of my people

from those who have broken the arrows, from those who have pushed the ancient stones off their pedestals.

Then he told how he had prayed in the Temple of the 15 Magician years ago as a child when his father had made him promise to bring back the ancient ways. Boy Baby had cried in the temple dark that only the bats made holy. Boy Baby who was man and child among the great and dusty guns lay down on the newspaper bed and wept for a thousand years. When I touched him, he looked at me with the sadness of stone.

You must not tell anyone what I am going to do, he said. 16 And what I remember next is how the moon, the pale moon with its one yellow eye, the moon of Tikal, and Tulum, and Chichén, stared through the pink plastic curtains. Then something inside bit me, and I gave out a cry as if the other, the one I wouldn't be anymore, leapt out.

So I was initiated beneath an ancient sky by a great and 17 mighty heir—Chaq Uxmal Paloquín. I, Ixchel, his queen.

The truth is, it wasn't a big deal. It wasn't any deal at all. 18 I put my bloody panties inside my T-shirt and ran home hugging myself. I thought about a lot of things on the way home. I thought about all the world and how suddenly I became a part of history and wondered if everyone on the street, the sewing machine lady and the *panadería* saleswomen and the woman with two kids sitting on the bus bench didn't all know. *Did I look any different? Could they tell?* We were all the same somehow, laughing behind our hands, waiting the way all women wait, and when we find out, we wonder why the world and a million years made such a big deal over nothing.

I know I was supposed to feel ashamed, but I wasn't 19 ashamed. I wanted to stand on top of the highest building, the top-top floor, and yell, *I know.*

Then I understood why Abuelita didn't let me sleep over 20 at Lourdes's house full of too many brothers, and why the Roman girl in the movies always runs away from the soldier, and what happens when the scenes in love stories begin to fade, and why brides blush, and how it is that sex isn't simply a box you check *M* or *F* on in the test we get at school.

I was wise. The corner girls were still jumping into their 21 stupid little hopscotch squares. I laughed inside and climbed the wooden stairs two by two to the second floor rear where me and Abuelita and Uncle Lalo live. I was still laughing when I opened the door and Abuelita asked, Where's the pushcart?

And then I didn't know what to do. 22

It's a good thing we live in a bad neighborhood. There 23 are always plenty of bums to blame for your sins. If it didn't happen the way I told it, it really could've. We looked and looked all over for the kids who stole my pushcart. The story wasn't the best, but since I had to make it up right then and there with Abuelita staring a hole through my heart, it wasn't too bad.

For two weeks I had to stay home. Abuelita was afraid the 24 street kids who had stolen the cart would be after me again. Then I thought I might go over to the Esparza garage and take the pushcart out and leave it in some alley for the police to find, but I was never allowed to leave the house alone. Bit by bit the truth started to seep out like a dangerous gasoline.

First the nosy woman who lives upstairs from the laundro- 25 mat told my Abuelita she thought something was fishy, the pushcart wheeled into Esparza & Sons every Saturday after dark, how a man, the same dark Indian one, the one who never talks to anybody, walked with me when the sun went down and pushed the cart into the garage, that one there, and yes we went inside, there where the fat lady named Concha, whose hair is dyed a hard black, pointed a fat finger.

I prayed that we would not meet Boy Baby, and since the 26 gods listen and are mostly good, Esparza said yes, a man like that had lived there but was gone, had packed a few things and left the pushcart in a corner to pay for his last week's rent.

We had to pay $20 before he would give us our pushcart 27 back. Then Abuelita made me tell the real story of how the cart had disappeared, all of which I told this time, except for that one night, which I would have to tell anyway, weeks later, when I prayed for the moon of my cycle to come back, but it would not.

When Abuelita found out I was going to *dar a luz,* she cried until her eyes were little, and blamed Uncle Lalo, and Uncle Lalo blamed this country, and Abuelita blamed the infamy of men. That is when she burned the cucumber pushcart and called me a *sinvergüenza* because I *am* without shame.

28

Then I cried too—Boy Baby was lost from me—until my head was hot with headaches and I fell asleep. When I woke up, the cucumber pushcart was dust and Abuelita was sprinkling holy water on my head.

29

Abuelita woke up early every day and went to the Esparza garage to see if news about that *demonio* had been found, had Chaq Uxmal Paloquín sent any letters, any, and when the other mechanics heard that name they laughed, and asked if we had made it up, that we could have some letters that had come for Boy Baby, no forwarding address, since he had gone in such a hurry.

30

There were three. The first, addressed "Occupant," demanded immediate payment for a four-month-old electric bill. The second was one I recognized right away—a brown envelope fat with cake-mix coupons and fabric-softener samples—because we'd gotten one just like it. The third was addressed in a spidery Spanish to a Señor C. Cruz, on paper so thin you could read it unopened by the light of the sky. The return address a convent in Tampico.

31

This was to whom my Abuelita wrote in hopes of finding the man who could correct my ruined life, to ask if the good nuns might know the whereabouts of a certain Boy Baby— and if they were hiding him it would be of no use because God's eyes see through all souls.

32

We heard nothing for a long time. Abuelita took me out of school when my uniform got tight around the belly and said it was a shame I wouldn't be able to graduate with the other eighth graders.

33

Except for Lourdes and Rachel, my grandma and Uncle 34
Lalo, nobody knew about my past. I would sleep in the big
bed I share with Abuelita same as always. I could hear
Abuelita and Uncle Lalo talking in low voices in the kitchen
as if they were praying the rosary, how they were going to
send me to Mexico, to San Dionisio de Tlaltepango, where
I have cousins and where I was conceived and would've been
born had my grandma not thought it wise to send my mother
here to the United States so that neighbors in San Dionisio
de Tlaltepango wouldn't ask why her belly was suddenly big.

I was happy. I liked staying home. Abuelita was teaching 35
me to crochet the way she had learned in Mexico. And just
when I had mastered the tricky rosette stitch, the letter came
from the convent which gave the truth about Boy Baby—
however much we didn't want to hear.

He was born on a street with no name in a town called 36
Miseria. His father, Eusebio, is a knife sharpener. His mother,
Refugia, stacks apricots into pyramids and sells them on a
cloth in the market. There are brothers. Sisters too of which
I know little. The youngest, a Carmelite, writes me all this
and prays for my soul, which is why I know it's all true.

Boy Baby is thirty-seven years old. His name is Chato 37
which means fat-face. There is no Mayan blood.

I don't think they understand how it is to be a girl. I don't 38
think they know how it is to have to wait your whole life. I
count the months for the baby to be born, and it's like a ring
of water inside me reaching out and out until one day it will
tear from me with its own teeth.

Already I can feel the animal inside me stirring in his own 39
uneven sleep. The witch woman says it's the dreams of wea-
sels that make my child sleep the way he sleeps. She makes
me eat white bread blessed by the priest, but I know it's the
ghost of him inside me that circles and circles, and will not
let me rest.

Abuelita said they sent me here just in time, because a little 40
later Boy Baby came back to our house looking for me, and

she had to chase him away with the broom. The next thing we hear, he's in the newspaper clippings his sister sends. A picture of him looking very much like stone, police hooked on either arm . . . *on the road to* Las Grutas de Xtacum-bilxuna, *the Caves of the Hidden Girl* . . . *eleven female bodies . . . the last seven years* . . .

Then I couldn't read but only stare at the little black-and-white dots that make up the face I am in love with.   41

All my girl cousins here either don't talk to me, or those   42 who do, ask questions they're too young to know *not* to ask. What they want to know really is how it is to have a man, because they're too ashamed to ask their married sisters.

They don't know what it is to lay so still until his sleep   43 breathing is heavy, for the eyes in the dim dark to look and look without worry at the man-bones and the neck, the man-wrist and man-jaw thick and strong, all the salty dips and hollows, the stiff hair of the brow and sour swirl of sideburns, to lick the fat earlobes that taste of smoke, and stare at how perfect is a man.

I tell them, "It's a bad joke. When you find out you'll be   44 sorry."

I'm going to have five children. Five. Two girls. Two boys.   45 And one baby.

The girls will be called Lisette and Maritza. The boys I'll   46 name Pablo and Sandro.

And my baby. My baby will be named Alegre, because life   47 will always be hard.

Rachel says that love is like a big black piano being pushed   48 off the top of a three-story building and you're waiting on the bottom to catch it. But Lourdes says it's not that way at all. It's like a top, like all the colors in the world are spinning so fast they're not colors anymore and all that's left is a white hum.

There was a man, a crazy who lived upstairs from us when   49 we lived on South Loomis. He couldn't talk, just walked

around all day with this harmonica in his mouth. Didn't play
it. Just sort of breathed through it, all day long, wheezing,
in and out, in and out.

This is how it is with me. Love I mean.   50

COMMENT ON "ONE HOLY NIGHT"

In her story "One Holy Night" Sandra Cisneros uses a first-
person narrative to take us into the mind of a fourteen-year-
old girl who has romanticized her seduction—really rape—by
a stranger into "one holy night," a night that leaves her
pregnant. Sure that she is better than the girls who slip into
alleys with boys, the girl imagines her first sexual experience
will be as if something will "come undone like gold thread,
like a tent full of birds." And because her seducer convinces
her that he is like a god, the descendant of an ancient line of
Mayan kings, and that his son will be the boy-child who will
bring back the grandeur of his people, she thinks of losing
her virginity as an initiation "beneath an ancient sky" that
makes her his queen. Her romanticism and her longing to be
someone special betray her into giving herself to a man she
really knows nothing about.

Reality takes over when she is sent away to relatives to have
her baby, still mooning over the child's father and convinced
she's still in love with him. The truth about that father is
stark, even dangerous. He was a thirty-seven-year-old man
from nowhere with no trace of Mayan blood, much less royal
blood. It's also probable that he has killed and hidden the
bodies of eleven women. But at the end, we're still not quite
sure if the title "One Holy Night" is ironic or if the girl will
always look back on her sex with a stranger as "one holy
night."

Cause and Effect as a Writing Strategy

1. For a short opinion piece in some magazine you enjoy reading, write an essay in which you describe the fashions adopted by a certain group of people and then theorize about why the fashion is popular and how it affects the behavior of the people who follow it. Give specific examples that illustrate the fashion.

    Some possibilities that you might consider:

- Where did the fashion of untied shoelaces on athletic shoes come from and why? Of baseball caps turned backward? Of tattered jeans?
- In an office you know, what does casual attire on Fridays look like and how does it affect the behavior of people who adopt it?
- How do instructors dress on your campus? What do you see as the message of their attire?
- What was the approved attire in your high school? How did it influence the behavior of those who observed it most faithfully?
- What was approved prom attire in your high school? How did those clothes influence the behavior of the people who wore them?
- What is the accepted clothes style for the place where you work? How do you think the style affects the employees and the people they serve?

2. For an editorial in your campus newspaper, write an essay of between 300 and 500 words about an incident on your campus that involved allegations of racist or sexist behavior. In your editorial, take sides. In your opinion, were the people who claimed they had been discriminated against justified in their accusations? Were they indeed victims, and if so, what should their response have been? If you don't think they were justified in the complaint, explain why.

Conclude with a suggestion about how such incidents might be avoided in the future.

3. You may strongly disagree with one of the cause-and-effect essays in this section and want to refute what the author is saying or at least argue against a part of his or her thesis. If so, develop a paper by supposing that the writer has appeared as a speaker in your college's Ideas and Issues lecture series and has given his or her essay as a talk. Write your counterargument as a guest editorial for your campus newspaper, assuming that your readers will be other students and the college faculty.

Here are some of the strategies you might use for your argument:

a. Challenge the cause-and-effect relationships that the author claims.

b. Citing information you have from different sources or from your experience, argue that the writer's conclusions are faulty.

c. Challenge the accuracy of some of the writer's evidence, or show weak links in his or her reasoning.

d. Show that the writer has failed to take certain things into account about his or her readers or their situation and has thus weakened the thesis of the essay.

e. Demonstrate that the writer has let his or her biases distort the argument.

f. Show that the writer claims too much, more than the evidence warrants.

Keep in mind how skillfully the writers in this section of the book use facts and examples to support their essays, and be sure you do the same.

4. Write an essay for your classmates telling why you have chosen the profession you currently plan to go into. What are your reasons? Why do you think it will be rewarding? What caused you to choose this profession? Whom do you know in the profession, and how have their experiences affected your choice? What kind of training and education will be necessary, and what sacrifices, both financial and personal, might be involved? What kind of conflicts, if any,

do you think you might experience between your personal and professional lives? What effects do you think those conflicts might have on you?

5. Movies, on and off television, play a major role in modern culture, yet no one seems to have a clear idea of how much influence they have on young people. Write a short essay, perhaps for the movie section of your local newspaper, in which you speculate about the influence a very popular movie or kind of movie has on the under twenty-one viewers who are a major market for Hollywood. Mention specific movies and discuss ways in which they could influence young viewers.

   As an alternative topic, consider this. American movies, particularly action movies with stars like Bruce Willis and Tom Cruise, are extremely popular in other countries. What effect do you think such movies—name some you've seen recently—may have on the image of the United States abroad? If you're a student from another country, draw on your own experience in seeing American movies and discuss how they colored your opinions.

6. For an editorial or feature article in your local or campus newspaper, write an account of an environmental problem you have heard about in your community or your state. Such a problem might be a toxic waste dump close to a neighborhood, a leaky natural gas or oil pipeline that caused hazards, or the accumulation in the walls of a school of a substance that made students and teachers ill. Do some research in the files of your local paper or on the Web to find out the causes of the problem and how long it existed before someone noticed. Conclude by speculating what might be done to prevent such problems from developing in the future.

PERSUASION
AND
ARGUMENT

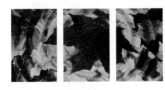

Intuitively, you already know a good deal about **argument.**
For one thing, you use it all the time as you go through the
day talking or writing and making claims and giving reasons.
But you also live surrounded by arguments. They come not
only from people you talk to and deal with in everyday
personal or business situations, but also from television, radio, newspapers, subway posters, billboards, and signs and
brochures of all kinds. Any time someone is trying to persuade you to buy something, contribute money, take action,
make a judgment, or change your mind about anything, that
person is arguing with you.

This introduction offers an overview of some important argument theory, tips about the kinds of argument that you can make, points to keep in mind as you write arguments, and some tips about pitfalls you should avoid. Remember that what we offer here barely scrapes the surface of the complex topic of argument and persuasion. If you want to learn more about argument theory and about writing good arguments, you can find several useful books in your college bookstore or through an online book seller.

KINDS OF ARGUMENTS

Traditionally, arguments fall into three categories: Logical, Emotional, and Ethical. *Logical arguments* appeal to the reason; they depend primarily on evidence and logic. *Emotional arguments* appeal to the feelings; they depend heavily on images and connotative language. *Ethical arguments* appeal on the basis of the writer or speaker's character. In practice, of course, most writers and speakers combine all of these appeals when they try to persuade or convince their audiences. All the writers in this section combine reason and emotion, but some appeal more strongly to the feelings, depending heavily on imagery and figurative language, while others try to make a strong rational appeal, citing historical evidence and giving examples. And all of them use various strategies to give readers the impression that they're ethical; that is, that they have integrity and character.

It's important to remember that rational arguments aren't necessarily better than emotional arguments. Some occasions call for appeals to pride, loyalty, and compassion, for using vivid metaphors and images, and for strong language that touches the passions. When someone is speaking at a political rally or at a graduation or award ceremony, the audience is probably more interested in stories and images than in logical analysis and data. The kind of writing done for such occasions is called *ceremonial discourse,* and often it's successful precisely because it is emotional. The speech by Martin Luther

King, Jr., "I Have a Dream" and Toni Morrison's "The Bird in Our Hand" fit into this category. When you write arguments for your college courses or in your work, however, you should plan on appealing primarily to reason and on providing strong evidence and clear examples. Your writing situation is *not* ceremonial; you're now writing to convince a thoughtful and skeptical audience, one that expects you to make a good case for your position. Again, take your cue from courtroom lawyers: state your case and prove it.

Notice that the eight essays in this section, Argument and Persuasion, are arranged in pairs. Each pair treats a single topic, but the writers take different points of view on that topic. The topic of the first two essays is racism; for the second two essays, it's marriage and child rearing; for the third pair, it's civic responsibility; for the last pair, the topic is how language is used. As you read these essays and compare them, ask yourself which ones are primarily rational and which are primarily emotional. Also ask yourself for each pair, "Which author do I find most convincing?"

PURPOSE

When you hear the term *argument,* you may automatically connect it with controversy and conflict. That's not necessarily the case, however, particularly in academic writing. There—and at other times too—you may have many purposes other than winning a dispute.

Sometimes you may argue *to support a cause.* For instance, you might write an editorial in favor of subsidized child care on your campus. You may also argue *to urge people to action* or *to promote change*—for instance, when you write a campaign brochure or a petition to reduce student fees. Sometimes you may argue *to refute a theory*—perhaps a history paper claiming that antislavery sentiment was not the chief cause of the Civil War. You can also write arguments *to arouse sympathy*—for better laws against child abuse, for example; *to stimulate interest*—for more participation in student government; *to win agreement*—to get condominium residents to agree to abolish regulations against pets; and *to provoke anger*—to arouse outrage against a proposed tax. And, of course, you might incorporate several of these purposes into one piece of writing.

AUDIENCE

When you write arguments, you must think about your readers. Who are they, what do they know, what do they believe, and what do they expect? Unless you can answer these questions at least partially, you cannot expect to write an effective argument. There simply is no such thing as a good argument in the abstract, separated from its purpose and its audience. Any argument you write is a good one only if it does what you want it to do with the particular readers who are going to read it. So by no later than the second draft of any argument you write, you need to know why you are writing and for whom you are writing.

Often it's not easy to analyze your readers. You have to work partly by instinct. Sometimes you adjust the tone of your writing almost automatically to suit a particular group of readers, and often you know intuitively that certain strategies won't work with certain readers. But you don't have to depend only on hunches. Working through a set of questions as part of your preparation to write will yield important information about your readers and will help you gradually form a sense of audience to guide you as you write and revise.

If you are trying to choose an audience for your paper, ask yourself the following questions:

1. Who is likely to be interested in what I am writing about?
2. What groups could make the changes I'm arguing for?

When you know the answers to these questions, you can direct your writing to readers to whom you have something to say—otherwise, there's little point in writing.

Once you have settled on your audience, ask yourself these questions:

1. What do my readers already know about my topic?
   a. What experience and knowledge do they have that I can use?
   b. Can I use specialized language? Should I?
   c. How can I teach them something they want to know?
2. How do my readers feel about my topic?
   a. What shared values can I appeal to?
   b. What prejudices or preconceptions must I pay attention to?
   c. What kind of approach will work best with them—casual or formal, objective or personal, factual or anecdotal?
3. What questions will my readers want me to answer?

You may find it especially useful to write out the answers to that last question.

When you have worked your way through all of these questions, either as a brainstorming exercise or in a prewriting group discussion, you'll have a stronger sense of who your readers are and how you can appeal to them.

STRATEGIES

When you are writing arguments, you can use a wide range of strategies, but most of them will fall into one of these three categories: *emotional appeal, logical appeal,* or *ethical appeal.*

Emotional Appeal

You argue by emotional or nonlogical appeal when you appeal to the emotions, the senses, and to personal biases or prejudices. You incorporate such appeals into your writing when you use *connotative language* that elicits feelings or reactions—words like *melancholy, crimson, slovenly,* or *villainous.* Usually you're also using nonlogical appeal when you use *figurative language*—metaphors, allusions, or colorful phrases that make the reader draw comparisons or make associations. Phrases like "environmental cancer" or "industrial Goliath" evoke images and comparisons and play on the emotions.

Creating a tone is also a nonlogical strategy and an important one. The tone you choose can exert a powerful force on your readers, catching their attention, ingratiating you into their favor, conveying an air of authority and confidence. You can establish a friendly, close-to-your-reader tone by using contractions and the pronouns *I, we,* and *you.* You can create a relaxed tone by bringing in humor or personal anecdote, or you can give your writing an air of authority and detachment by avoiding personal pronouns and writing as objectively as possible.

All the writers in this section use emotional appeal, but those who rely on it most heavily are Martin Luther King, Jr., and Toni Morrison. That's not surprising since both speeches are for major ceremonial occasions, and both authors feel passionately about their topics: King's topic is racial discrimination and denied opportunities and Morrison's is the abuse of language to oppress people. Other authors in the section use emotionally appealing examples— Barbara Kingsolver, for instance, and Jonathan Rauch—but their language is less connotative.

Logical Appeal

You employ logical or rational strategies when you appeal mainly to your readers' intelligence, reason, and common sense. Your chief strategies are

> Making claims and supporting them
> Giving testimony
> Citing authorities
> Arguing from precedent
> Drawing comparisons and analogies
> Arguing from cause and effect

Jonathan Rauch's "In Defense of Prejudice" is primarily a rational argument because he argues from precedent and from cause and effect: what has happened historically when some authority has decided to penalize free speech. So is Paul Rogat Loeb's "Soul of a Citizen" because he gives evidence about change that has come about because some citizen was willing to work for it. Eric Liu argues logically when he cites the past experience of minorities in the United States to argue that minorities can succeed in this country.

Ethical Appeal

Ethical appeal is the most subtle appeal and often the most powerful because it comes from the character and reputation of the author, not directly from words. All the writers in this section use ethical appeal, but it works most effectively for Martin Luther King, Jr., because it rests on his record as a fighter for civil rights and his history of being willing to sacrifice for his beliefs. Toni Morrison's ethical appeal is strong from the very circumstance of her having won the Nobel Prize for Literature.

But the others' ethical appeal is also strong. Liu's comes from his own experience and that of his family; Kingsolver's from her personal experience in raising a child by herself; Barbara Dafoe Whitehead's from her calm tone and obvious concern for children; and Rauch's from his position as one whose religion and sexual orientation have made him vulnerable to oppression. As a novice writer, you're not yet in a position to convince through your reputation, but if you show your readers that you are knowledgeable, thoughtful, have done your homework, and care about your topic, you're likely to succeed with your arguments.

POTENTIAL PITFALLS IN ARGUMENT

This brief introduction to argument cannot point out all the things that can go wrong in arguments—the so-called logical fallacies—but adhering to the following guidelines should keep you from getting into too much trouble.

1. *Don't claim too much.* Avoid suggesting that the proposal you're arguing for will solve all the problems involved—for instance, implying that legalizing drugs would get rid of drug-related crimes or that openly paying college football players would eliminate recruitment scandals. Settle for suggesting that your ideas may be worth considering or that you have thought of a new approach.

2. *Don't oversimplify complex issues.* Usually when an issue is serious enough and interesting enough for you to spend your time writing about it, it's a complicated matter with a tangled history and involves difficult issues. If you try to reduce it to simplistic terms and come up with an easy solution, you'll lose credibility quickly. Instead, acknowledge that the matter defies easy analysis but suggest that some things could be done.

3. *Support your arguments with concrete evidence and specific proposals, not with generalizations and conventional sentiments.* Always assume you are arguing for skeptical readers who expect you to demonstrate your case and won't be impressed by opinion alone. You can hold their interest and gain their respect only if you teach them something as you argue and present an old problem in a new light.

As you read the essays in this section, try to identify how these writers are arguing and what strategies they are using to convince you. As you get in the habit of reading arguments analytically and appreciatively, you will move toward writing arguments more easily and effectively. None of these strategies is new, after all, and seeing what other writers have done can give you an idea of what is possible.

USING PERSUASION AND ARGUMENT IN PARAGRAPHS

Here are two persuasive paragraphs. The first is written by a professional writer and is followed by an analysis. The second is written by a student and is followed by questions.

NICHOLAS LEMANN
The Promised Land

During the first half of the twentieth century, it was at least possible to think of race as a Southern issue. The South, and only the South, had to contend with the contradiction between the national creed of democracy and the local reality of a caste system; consequently the South lacked the optimism and confidence that characterized the country as a whole. The great black migration made race a national issue in the second half of the century—an integral part of the politics, the social thought, and the organization of everyday life in the United States. Not coincidentally, by the time the migration was over, the country had acquired a good measure of the tragic sense that had previously been confined to the South. Race relations stood out nearly everywhere as the one thing most plainly wrong in America, the flawed portion of the great tableau, the chief generator of doubt about how essentially noble the whole national enterprise really was.

Until 1950 one could think only the South had race problems

After 1950 black migration to North

Had to realize racism a national problem

Comment In this paragraph from the first chapter of Nicholas Lemann's book *The Promised Land,* the author lays out one of the central arguments of the book: the migration of blacks from the South to the North after World War II forced Americans to realize that racial discrimination and its consequences constituted a national problem and was not simply a remnant of the South's defeat in the Civil War. They could no longer claim that America was a great democracy with liberty and justice for all. Once hundreds of thousands of blacks were living in the North, the struggle for equal rights and fair treatment began to permeate the political, economic, and social life of the whole nation. Lemann is particularly eloquent in the last sentence when he says "Race relations stood out as . . . the flawed portion of the great tableau, the chief generator of doubt about how essentially noble the whole national enterprise really was."

JIM F. SALOMAN
Genetic Engineering

We need to regulate experiments in genetic engineering. Scientists can reconfigure the genetic makeup of an organism. They can literally change life. But without appropriate controls, such tampering can lead to unpredictable and violent results. What would happen if scientists were able to resurrect an extinct species that would reverse the order of natural selection? And what would happen if they produced a superior organism that destroyed the balance of our present ecosystem? And what would happen if they started "creating" people for particular tasks? They could design aggressive men to fight wars and passive women to breed children. Whole new social classes could be created, some genetically advanced, some genetically restricted. If we are to protect the rights of individuals and prevent evolutionary chaos, we must create a thoughtful public policy that protects us from our own scientific experiments.

1. How might Saloman go on to develop this paragraph into a full-length persuasive essay?
2. Saloman gives several examples of what he calls "unpredictable and violent results." How would you evaluate the persuasive value of the several generalizations that he gives as examples of such results?

ARGUMENT AND PERSUASION

Points to Remember

1. Remember that in order to argue well, you must understand your audience and know your purpose.

2. Understand the three principal kinds of appeal: emotional appeal, the appeal to feelings and senses; logical appeal, the appeal to intelligence and reason; and ethical appeal, the appeal from the character and competence of the author. The most effective arguments combine all three.

3. Construct an argument as a lawyer would construct a case to present to a jury; state your assertions and back them up with evidence and reason, appealing to your readers' intellect and feelings.

4. Always assume your audience is intelligent, although some members of it may be uninformed on a particular issue.

5. Avoid three common pitfalls: (a) don't overstate your claims; (b) be careful not to oversimplify complex issues; and (c) support your arguments with concrete evidence, not generalizations.

Martin Luther King, Jr. (1929–1968) was born in Atlanta, Georgia, and was educated at Morehouse College, Crozer Theological Seminary, and Boston University. Ordained a Baptist minister in his father's church in 1947, King soon became involved in civil rights activities in the South. In 1957 he founded the Southern Christian Leadership Conference and established himself as America's most prominent spokesman for nonviolent racial integration. In 1963 he was named *Time* magazine's Man of the Year; in 1964 he was given the Nobel Peace Prize. In 1968 he was assassinated in Memphis, Tennessee. His writing includes *Letter from Birmingham Jail* (1963), *Why We Can't Wait* (1964), and *Where Do We Go from Here: Chaos or Community?* (1967). "I Have a Dream" is the famous speech King delivered at the Lincoln Memorial at the end of the March on Washington in 1963 to commemorate the one hundredth anniversary of the Emancipation Proclamation. King argues that realization of the dream of freedom for all American citizens is long overdue.

I Have a Dream

FIVE SCORE YEARS ago, a great American, in whose symbolic shadow we stand, signed the Emancipation Proclamation. This momentous decree came as a great beacon light of hope to millions of Negro slaves who had been seared in the flames of withering injustice. It came as a joyous daybreak to end the long night of captivity. 1

But one hundred years later, we must face the tragic fact 2

that the Negro is still not free. One hundred years later, the life of the Negro is still sadly crippled by the manacles of segregation and the chains of discrimination. One hundred years later, the Negro lives on a lonely island of poverty in the midst of a vast ocean of material prosperity. One hundred years later, the Negro is still languishing in the corners of American society and finds himself an exile in his own land. So we have come here today to dramatize an appalling condition.

In a sense we have come to our nation's Capitol to cash a check. When the architects of our republic wrote the magnificent words of the Constitution and the Declaration of

---

There will be neither rest nor tranquility in America until the Negro is granted his citizenship rights.

Independence, they were signing a promissory note to which every American was to fall heir. This note was a promise that all men would be guaranteed the unalienable rights of life, liberty, and the pursuit of happiness.

It is obvious today that America has defaulted on this promissory note insofar as her citizens of color are concerned. Instead of honoring this sacred obligation, America has given the Negro people a bad check; a check which has come back marked "insufficient funds." But we refuse to believe that the bank of justice is bankrupt. We refuse to believe that there are insufficient funds in the great vaults of opportunity of this nation. So we have come to cash this check—a check that will give us upon demand the riches of freedom and the security of justice. We have also come to this hallowed spot to remind America of the fierce urgency of *now.* This is no time to engage in the luxury of cooling off or to take the tranquilizing drug of gradualism. *Now* is the time to make real the promises of Democracy. *Now* is the time to rise from the dark and desolate valley of segregation to the sunlit path of racial justice. *Now* is the time to open the doors of opportunity to all of God's children. *Now* is the time to lift our nation from the quicksands of racial injustice to the solid rock of brotherhood.

It would be fatal for the nation to overlook the urgency   5
of the moment and to underestimate the determination of the Negro. This sweltering summer of the Negro's legitimate discontent will not pass until there is an invigorating autumn of freedom and equality. 1963 is not an end, but a beginning. Those who hope that the Negro needed to blow off steam and will now be content will have a rude awakening if the nation returns to business as usual. There will be neither rest nor tranquility in America until the Negro is granted his citizenship rights. The whirlwinds of revolt will continue to shake the foundations of our nation until the bright day of justice emerges.

But there is something I must say to my people who stand   6
on the warm threshold which leads into the palace of justice. In the process of gaining our rightful place we must not be guilty of wrongful deeds. Let us not seek to satisfy our thirst for freedom by drinking from the cup of bitterness and hatred. We must forever conduct our struggle on the high plane of dignity and discipline. We must not allow our creative protest to degenerate into physical violence. Again and again we must rise to the majestic heights of meeting physical force with soul force. The marvelous new militancy which has engulfed the Negro community must not lead us to a distrust of all white people, for many of our white brothers, as evidenced by their presence here today, have come to realize that their destiny is tied up with our destiny and their freedom is inextricably bound to our freedom. We cannot walk alone.

And as we walk, we must make the pledge that we shall   7
march ahead. We cannot turn back. There are those who are asking the devotees of civil rights, "When will you be satisfied?" We can never be satisfied as long as the Negro is the victim of the unspeakable horrors of police brutality. We

can never be satisfied as long as our bodies, heavy with the fatigue of travel, cannot gain lodging in the motels of the highways and the hotels of the cities. We cannot be satisfied as long as the Negro's basic mobility is from a smaller ghetto to a larger one. We can never be satisfied as long as a Negro in Mississippi cannot vote and a Negro in New York believes he has nothing for which to vote. No, no, we are not satisfied, and we will not be satisfied until justice rolls down like waters and righteousness like a mighty stream.

I am not unmindful that some of you have come here out of great trials and tribulations. Some of you have come fresh from narrow jail cells. Some of you have come from areas where your quest for freedom left you battered by the storms of persecution and staggered by the winds of police brutality. You have been the veterans of creative suffering. Continue to work with the faith that unearned suffering is redemptive. 8

Go back to Mississippi, go back to Alabama, go back to South Carolina, go back to Georgia, go back to Louisiana, go back to the slums and ghettoes of our northern cities, knowing that somehow this situation can and will be changed. Let us not wallow in the valley of despair. 9

I say to you today, my friends, that in spite of the difficulties and frustrations of the moment I still have a dream. It is a dream deeply rooted in the American dream. 10

I have a dream that one day this nation will rise up and live out the true meaning of its creed: "We hold these truths to be self-evident; that all men are created equal." 11

I have a dream that one day on the red hills of Georgia the sons of former slaves and the sons of former slaveowners will be able to sit down together at the table of brotherhood. 12

I have a dream that the state of Mississippi, a desert state sweltering with the heat of injustice and oppression, will be transformed into an oasis of freedom and justice. 13

I have a dream that my four little children will one day live in a nation where they will not be judged by the color of their skin but by the content of their character. 14

I have a dream today. 15

I have a dream that the state of Alabama, whose governor's 16 lips are presently dripping with the words of interposition and nullification, will be transformed into a situation where little black boys and black girls will be able to join hands with little white boys and white girls and walk together as sisters and brothers.

I have a dream today. 17

I have a dream that one day every valley shall be exalted, 18 every hill and mountain shall be made low, the rough places will be made plain, and the crooked places will be made straight, and the glory of the Lord shall be revealed, and all flesh shall see it together.

This is our hope. This is the faith with which I return to 19 the South. With this faith we will be able to hew out of the mountain of despair a stone of hope. With this faith we will be able to transform the jangling discords of our nation into a beautiful symphony of brotherhood. With this faith we will be able to work together, to pray together, to struggle together, to go to jail together, to stand up for freedom together, knowing that we will be free one day.

This will be the day when all of God's children will be able 20 to sing with new meaning.

> *My country, 'tis of thee*
> *Sweet land of liberty,*
> *Of thee I sing:*
> *Land where my fathers died,*
> *Land of the pilgrims' pride,*
> *From every mountainside*
> *Let freedom ring.*

And if America is to be a great nation this must become 21 true. So let freedom ring from the prodigious hilltops of New Hampshire. Let freedom ring from the mighty mountains of New York. Let freedom ring from the heightening Alleghenies of Pennsylvania!

Let freedom ring from the snowcapped Rockies of 22 Colorado!

Let freedom ring from the curvaceous peaks of California!   23
But not only that; let freedom ring from Stone Mountain   24
of Georgia!
Let freedom ring from Lookout Mountain of Tennessee!   25
Let freedom ring from every hill and molehill of Missis-   26
sippi. From every mountainside, let freedom ring.

When we let freedom ring, when we let it ring from every   27
village and every hamlet, from every state and every city, we
will be able to speed up that day when all of God's children,
black men and white men, Jews and Gentiles, Protestants and
Catholics, will be able to join hands and sing in the words of
the old Negro spiritual, "Free at last! free at last! thank God
almighty, we are free at last!"

For Study and Discussion

QUESTIONS FOR RESPONSE

1. What experiences of injustice have you had (or perhaps witnessed, read about, or seen in a movie) that help you to identify with King's dreams and feel the force of his speech?
2. What did you already know about the life of King and of his place in modern U.S. history that prepared you for reading "I Have a Dream"? How well did the speech live up to what you expected of it?

QUESTIONS ABOUT PURPOSE

1. King has at least two strong messages. One message is local and immediate; the other one is national and long range. How would you summarize those two messages?
2. How does King use his speech to reinforce his belief in nonviolence as the appropriate tool in the struggle for civil rights?

QUESTIONS ABOUT AUDIENCE

1. King gave this speech to a huge live audience that had come to Washington for a march for freedom and civil rights. How much

larger is the national audience he is addressing, and why is that audience also important?

2. This speech is one of the most widely anthologized of modern speeches. What audiences does it continue to appeal to and why?

QUESTIONS ABOUT STRATEGIES

1. How does King draw on metaphor to engage his listeners' feelings of injustice and give them hope for a new day? What are some of the most powerful metaphors?

2. In what way do King's talents as a minister serve his purposes in the speech? What African-American leader today do you think most resembles King in style and in mission?

QUESTIONS FOR DISCUSSION

1. If King were alive today, almost forty years after this speech, how much of his dream do you think he would feel has come true? Look particularly at the visions he speaks of in paragraph 7 and paragraphs 11 through 16.

2. What elements in the speech reveal those qualities that contributed to King's power as a major civil rights leader, effective with whites as well as with blacks?

Eric Liu was born in Poughkeepsie, New York, in 1968 and was educated at Yale University. He worked as a legislative aide for Senator David Boren of Oklahoma and then as a speechwriter for Secretary of State Warren Christopher and President Bill Clinton. He is currently the publisher and editor of *The Next Progressive,* a journal of opinion, the editor of *NEXT: Young American Writers on the New Generation* (1994), and the author of *The Accidental Asian: Notes of a Native Speaker* (1998). In "A Chinaman's Chance: Reflections on the American Dream," reprinted from *NEXT,* Liu argues that the American Dream is more about seizing opportunity than about claiming prosperity.

A Chinaman's Chance: Reflections on the American Dream

A LOT OF people my age seem to think that the American Dream is dead. I think they're dead wrong.

Or at least only partly right. It is true that for those of us in our twenties and early thirties, job opportunities are scarce. There looms a real threat that we will be the first American generation to have a lower standard of living than our parents.

But what is it that we mean when we invoke the American Dream?

In the past, the American Dream was something that held people of all races, religions, and identities together. As James Comer has written, it represented a shared aspiration among

all Americans—black, white, or any other color—"to provide
well for themselves and their families as valued members of a
democratic society." Now, all too often, it seems the American Dream means merely some guarantee of affluence, a
birthright of wealth.

At a basic level, of course, the American Dream is about   5
prosperity and the pursuit of material happiness. But to me,
its meaning extends beyond such concerns. To me, the dream
is not just about buying a bigger house than the one I grew
up in or having shinier stuff now than I had as a kid. It also
represents a sense of opportunity that binds generations to-

> *I want to prove that a Chinaman's chance*
> *is as good as anyone else's.*

gether in commitment, so that the young inherit not only
property but also perseverance, not only money but also a
mission to make good on the strivings of their parents and
grandparents.

The poet Robert Browning once wrote that "a man's reach   6
must exceed his grasp—else what's a heaven for?" So it is in
America. Every generation will strive, and often fail. Every
generation will reach for success, and often miss the mark.
But Americans rely as much on the next generation as on the
next life to prove that such struggles and frustrations are not
in vain. There may be temporary setbacks, cutbacks, reces-
sions, depressions. But this is a nation of second chances. So
long as there are young Americans who do not take what they
have—or what they can do—for granted, progress is always
possible.

My conception of the American Dream does not take   7
progress for granted. But it does demand the *opportunity* to
achieve progress—and values the opportunity as much as the
achievement. I come at this question as the son of immi-

grants. I see just as clearly as anyone else the cracks in the idealist vision of fulfillment for all. But because my parents came here with virtually nothing, because they did build something, I see the enormous potential inherent in the ideal.

I happen still to believe in our national creed: freedom and opportunity, and our common responsibility to uphold them. This creed is what makes America unique. More than any demographic statistic or economic indicator, it animates the American Dream. It infuses our mundane struggles—to plan a career, do good work, get ahead—with purpose and possibility. It makes America the only country that could produce heroes like Colin Powell—heroes who rise from nothing, who overcome the odds. 8

I think of the sacrifices made by my own parents. I appreciate the hardship of the long road traveled by my father— one of whose first jobs in America was painting the yellow line down a South Dakota interstate—and by my mother— whose first job here was filing pay stubs for a New York restaurant. From such beginnings, they were able to build a comfortable life and provide me with a breadth of resources—through arts, travel, and an Ivy League education. It was an unspoken obligation for them to do so. 9

I think of my boss in my first job after college, on Capitol Hill. George is a smart, feisty, cigar-chomping, take-no-shit Greek-American. He is about fifteen years older than I, has different interests, a very different personality. But like me, he is the son of immigrants, and he would joke with me that the Greek-Chinese mafia was going to take over one day. He was only half joking. We'd worked harder, our parents doubly harder, than almost anyone else we knew. To people like George, talk of the withering of the American Dream seems foreign. 10

It's undeniable that principles like freedom and opportunity, no matter how dearly held, are not enough. They can inspire a multiracial March on Washington, but they can not bring black salaries in alignment with white salaries. They can draw wave after wave of immigrants here, but they can not provide them the means to get out of our ghettos and barrios 11 and Chinatowns. They are not sufficient for fulfillment of the American Dream.

But they are necessary. They are vital. And not just to the 12 children of immigrants. These ideals form the durable thread that weaves us all in union. Put another way, they are one of the few things that keep America from disintegrating into a loose confederation of zip codes and walled-in communities.

What alarms me is how many people my age look at our 13 nation's ideals with a rising sense of irony. What good is such a creed if you are working for hourly wages in a dead-end job? What value do such platitudes have if you live in an urban war zone? When the only apparent link between homeboys and housepainters and bike messengers and investment bankers is pop culture—MTV, the NBA, movies, dance music— then the social fabric is flimsy indeed.

My generation has come of age at a time when the country 14 is fighting off bouts of defeatism and self-doubt, at a time when racism and social inequities seem not only persistent but intractable. At a time like this, the retreat to one's own kind is seen by more and more of my peers as an advance. And that retreat has given rise again to the notion that there are essential and irreconcilable differences among the races— a notion that was supposed to have disappeared from American discourse by the time my peers and I were born in the sixties.

Not long ago, for instance, my sister called me a "banana." 15

I was needling her about her passion for rap and hip-hop 16 music. Every time I saw her, it seemed, she was jumping and twisting to Arrested Development or Chubb Rock or some other funky group. She joked that despite being the daughter of Chinese immigrants, she was indeed "black at heart." And then she added, lightheartedly, "You, on the other hand— well, you're basically a banana." Yellow on the outside, but white inside.

I protested, denied her charge vehemently. But it was too 17 late. She was back to dancing. And I stood accused.

Ever since then, I have wondered what it means to be 18 black, or white, or Asian "at heart"—particularly for my generation. Growing up, when other kids would ask whether I was Chinese or Korean or Japanese, I would reply, a little petulantly, "American." Assimilation can still be a sensitive subject. I recall reading about a Korean-born Congressman who had gone out of his way to say that Asian-Americans should expect nothing special from him. He added that he was taking speech lessons "to get rid of this accent." I winced at his palpable self-hate. But then it hit me: Is this how my sister sees me?

There is no doubt that minorities like me can draw [19] strength from our communities. But in today's environment, anything other than ostentatious tribal fealty is taken in some communities as a sign of moral weakness, a disappointing dilution of character. In times that demand ever-clearer thinking, it has become too easy for people to shut off their brains: "It's a black/Asian/Latino/white thing," says the variable T-shirt. "You wouldn't understand." Increasingly, we don't.

The civil-rights triumphs of the sixties and the cultural [20] revolutions that followed made it possible for minorities to celebrate our diverse heritages. I can appreciate that. But I know, too, that the sixties—or at least, my generation's grainy, hazy vision of the decade—also bequeathed to young Americans a legacy of near-pathological race consciousness.

Today's culture of entitlement—and of race entitlement in [21] particular—tells us plenty about what we get if we are black or white or female or male or old or young.

It is silent, though, on some other important issues. For [22] instance: What do we "get" for being American? And just as importantly, What do we owe? These are questions around which young people like myself must tread carefully, since talk of common interests, civic culture, responsibility, and integration sounds a little too "white" for some people. To the new segregationists, the "American Dream" is like the old myth of the "Melting Pot": an oppressive fiction, an opiate for the unhappy colored masses.

How have we allowed our thinking about race to become [23] so twisted? The formal obstacles and the hateful opposition to civil rights have long faded into memory. By most external measures, life for minorities is better than it was a quarter century ago. It would seem that the opportunities for tolerance and cooperation are commonplace. Why, then, are so many of my peers so cynical about our ability to get along with one another?

The reasons are frustratingly ambiguous. I got a glimpse of this when I was in college. It was late in my junior year, and as the editor of a campus magazine, I was sitting on a panel to discuss "The White Press at Yale: What Is to Be Done?" The assembly hall was packed, a diverse and noisy crowd. The air was heavy, nervously electric. 24

Why weren't there more stories about "minority issues" in the Yale *Daily News*? Why weren't there more stories on Africa in my magazine, the foreign affairs journal? How many "editors of color" served on the boards of each of the major publications? The questions were volleyed like artillery, one round after another, punctuated only by the applause of an audience spoiling for a fight. The questions were not at all unfair. But it seemed that no one—not even those of us on the panel who *were* people of color—could provide, in this context, satisfactory answers. 25

Toward the end of the discussion, I made a brief appeal for reason and moderation. And afterward, as students milled around restlessly, I was attacked: for my narrowmindedness—How dare you suggest that Yale is not a fundamentally prejudiced place!—for my simplemindedness—Have you, too, been co-opted? 26

And for my betrayal—Are you just white inside? 27

My eyes were opened that uncomfortably warm early summer evening. Not only to the cynical posturing and the combustible opportunism of campus racial politics. But more importantly, to the larger question of identity—my identity—in America. Never mind that the aim of many of the loudest critics was to generate headlines in the very publications they denounced. In spite of themselves—against, it would seem, their true intentions—they got me to think about who I am. 28

In our society today, and especially among people of my generation, we are congealing into clots of narrow commonality. We stick with racial and religious comrades. This tribal 29 consciousness-raising can be empowering for some. But while America was conceived in liberty—the liberty, for instance, to associate with whomever we like—it was never designed to be a mere collection of subcultures. We forget that there is in fact such a thing as a unique American identity that transcends our sundry tribes, sets, gangs, and cliques.

I have grappled, wittingly or not, with these questions of 30 identity and allegiance all my life. When I was in my early teens, I would invite my buddies overnight to watch movies, play video games, and beat one another up. Before too long, my dad would come downstairs and start hamming it up— telling stories, asking gently nosy questions, making corny jokes, all with his distinct Chinese accent. I would stand back, quietly gauging everyone's reaction. Of course, the guys loved it. But I would feel uneasy.

What was then cause for discomfort is now a source of 31 strength. Looking back on such episodes, I take pride in my father's accented English; I feel awe at his courage to laugh loudly in a language not really his own.

It was around the same time that I decided that continued 32 attendance at the community Chinese school on Sundays was uncool. There was no fanfare; I simply stopped going. As a child, I'd been too blissfully unaware to think of Chinese school as anything more than a weekly chore, with an annual festival (dumplings and spring rolls, games and prizes). But by the time I was a peer-pressured adolescent, Chinese school seemed like a badge of the woefully unassimilated. I turned my back on it.

Even as I write these words now, it feels as though I am 33 revealing a long-held secret. I am proud that my ancestors— scholars, soldiers, farmers—came from one of the world's great civilizations. I am proud that my grandfather served in the Chinese Air Force. I am proud to speak even my clumsy brand of Mandarin, and I feel blessed to be able to think idiomatically in Chinese, a language so much richer in nuance and subtle poetry than English.

Belatedly, I appreciate the good fortune I've had to be the 34 son of immigrants. As a kid, I could play Thomas Jefferson in the bicentennial school play one week and the next week play the poet Li Bai at the Chinese school festival. I could come home from an afternoon of teen slang at the mall and sit down to dinner for a rollicking conversation in our family's hybrid of Chinese and English. I understood, when I went over to visit friends, that my life was different. At the time, I just never fully appreciated how rich it was.

Yet I know that this pride in my heritage does not cross   35 into prejudice against others. What it reflects is pride in what my country represents. That became clear to me when I went through Marine Corps Officer Candidates' School. During the summers after my sophomore and junior years of college, I volunteered for OCS, a grueling boot camp for potential officers in the swamps and foothills of Quantico, Virginia.

And once I arrived—standing 5'4", 135 pounds, bespec-   36 tacled, a Chinese Ivy League Democrat—I was a target straight out of central casting. The wiry, raspy-voiced drill sergeant, though he was perhaps only an inch or two taller than I, called me "Little One" with as much venom as can be squeezed into such a moniker. He heaped verbal abuse on me, he laughed when I stumbled, he screamed when I hesi-tated. But he also never failed to remind me that just because I was a little shit didn't mean I shouldn't run farther, climb higher, think faster, hit harder than anyone else.

That was the funny thing about the Marine Corps. It is,   37 ostensibly, one of the most conservative institutions in the United States. And yet, for those twelve weeks, it represented the kind of color-blind equality of opportunity that the rest of society struggles to match. I did not feel uncomfortable at OCS to be of Chinese descent. Indeed, I drew strength from it. My platoon was a veritable cross section of America: forty young men of all backgrounds, all regions, all races, all levels of intelligence and ability, displaced from our lives (if only for a few weeks) with nowhere else to go.

Going down the list of names—Courtemanche, Dough-   38 erty, Grella, Hunt, Liu, Reeves, Schwarzman, and so on— brought to mind a line from a World War II documentary I once saw, which went something like this: The reason why it seemed during the war that America was as good as the rest

of the world put together was that America *was* the rest of
the world put together.

Ultimately, I decided that the Marines was not what I   39
wanted to do for four years and I did not accept the second
lieutenant's commission. But I will never forget the day of
the graduation parade: bright sunshine, brisk winds, the band
playing Sousa as my company passed in review. As my mom
and dad watched and photographed the parade from the
rafters, I thought to myself: this is the American Dream in all
its cheesy earnestness. I felt the thrill of truly being part of
something larger and greater than myself.

I do know that American life is not all Sousa marches and   40
flag-waving. I know that those with reactionary agendas often
find it convenient to cloak their motives in the language of
Americanism. The "American Party" was the name of a major
nativist organization in the nineteenth century. "America
First" is the siren song of the isolationists who would withdraw this country from the world and expel the world from
this country. I know that our national immigration laws were
once designed explicitly to cut off the influx from Asia.

I also know that discrimination is real. I am reminded of   41
a gentle old man who, after Pearl Harbor, was stripped of his
possessions without warning, taken from his home, and
thrown into a Japanese internment camp. He survived, and
by many measures has thrived, serving as a community leader
and political activist. But I am reluctant to share with him my
wide-eyed patriotism.

I know the bittersweet irony that my own father—a strong   42
and optimistic man—would sometimes feel when he was
alive. When he came across a comically lost cause—if the
Yankees were behind 14–0 in the ninth, or if Dukakis was
down ten points in the polls with a week left—he would often
joke that the doomed party had "a Chinaman's chance" of
success. It was one of those insensitive idioms of a generation
ago, and it must have lodged in his impressionable young
mind when he first came to America. It spoke of a perceived
stacked deck.

I know, too, that for many other immigrants, the dream   43

simply does not work out. Fae Myenne Ng, the author of
Bone, writes about how her father ventured here from China
under a false identity and arrived at Angel Island, the deten-
tion center outside the "Gold Mountain" of San Francisco.
He got out, he labored, he struggled, and he suffered "a
bitter no-luck life" in America. There was no glory. For him,
Ng suggests, the journey was not worth it.

But it is precisely because I know these things that I want   44
to prove that in the long run, over generations and across
ethnicities, it *is* worth it. For the second-generation American, opportunity is obligation. I have seen and faced racism.
I understand the dull pain of dreams deferred or unmet. But
I believe still that there is so little stopping me from building
the life that I want. I was given, through my parents' labors,
the chance to bridge that gap between ideals and reality. Who
am I to throw away that chance?

Plainly, I am subject to the criticism that I speak too much   45
from my own experience. Not everyone can relate to the
second-generation American story. When I have spoken like
this with some friends, the issue has been my perspective.
*What you say is fine for you. But unless you grew up where I did,
unless you've had people avoid you because of the color of your
skin, don't talk to me about common dreams.*

But are we then to be paralyzed? Is respect for different   46
experiences supposed to obviate the possibility of shared aspirations? Does the diversity of life in America doom us to a
fractured understanding of one another? The question is
basic: Should the failure of this nation thus far to fulfill its
stated ideals incapacitate its young people, or motivate us?

Our country was built on, and remains glued by, the idea   47
that everybody deserves a fair shot and that we must work
together to guarantee that opportunity—the original American Dream. It was this idea, in some inchoate form, that drew
every immigrant here. It was this idea, however sullied by
slavery and racism, that motivated the civil-rights movement.
To write this idea off—even when its execution is spotty—to
let American life descend into squabbles among separatist
tribes would not just be sad. It would be a total mishandling
of a legacy, the squandering of a great historical inheritance.

Mine must not be the first generation of Americans to lose   48
America. Just as so many of our parents journeyed here to
find their version of the American Dream, so must young
Americans today journey across boundaries of race and class
to rediscover one another. We are the first American generation to be born into an integrated society, and we are accustomed to more race mixing than any generation before us.
We started open-minded, and it's not too late for us to stay
that way.

Time is of the essence. For in our national political culture   49
today, the watchwords seem to be *decline* and *end*. Apocalyptic visions and dark millennial predictions abound. The end
of history. The end of progress. The end of equality. Even
something as ostensibly positive as the end of the Cold War
has a bittersweet tinge, because for the life of us, no one in
America can get a handle on the big question, "What Next?"

For my generation, this fixation on endings is particularly   50
enervating. One's twenties are supposed to be a time of
widening horizons, of bright possibilities. Instead, America
seems to have entered an era of limits. Whether it is the
difficulty of finding jobs from some place other than a temp
agency, or the mountains of debt that darken our future, the
message to my peers is often that this nation's time has come
and gone; let's bow out with grace and dignity.

A friend once observed that while the Chinese seek to   51
adapt to nature and yield to circumstance, Americans seek to
conquer both. She meant that as a criticism of America. But
I interpreted her remark differently. I *do* believe that America
is exceptional. And I believe it is up to my generation to revive
that spirit, that sense that we do in fact have control over our
own destiny—as individuals and as a nation.

If we are to reclaim a common destiny, we must also reach   52
out to other generations for help. It was Franklin Roosevelt
who said that while America can't always build the future for
its youth, it can—and must—build its youth for the future.
That commitment across generations is as central to the
American Dream as any I have enunciated. We are linked,
black and white, old and young, one and inseparable.

I know how my words sound. I am old enough to perceive   53 my own naïveté but young enough still to cherish it. I realize that I am coming of age just as the American Dream is showing its age. Yet I still have faith in this country's unique destiny—to create generation after generation of hyphenates like me, to channel this new blood, this resilience and energy into an ever more vibrant future for *all* Americans.

And I want to prove—for my sake, for my father's sake,   54
and for my country's sake—that a Chinaman's chance is as good as anyone else's.

For Study and Discussion

QUESTIONS FOR RESPONSE

1. Do you endorse or discount Liu's argument? How do you think your family background and history affect your response?
2. How would you define the American Dream? To what extent do you think it has been or will be fulfilled for you?

QUESTIONS ABOUT PURPOSE

1. To what criticisms *about* his generation is Liu responding? To what criticisms *from* his generation is he responding?
2. What specific attitudes among young people does Liu challenge?

QUESTIONS ABOUT AUDIENCE

1. Liu wrote this essay for a 1994 book titled *NEXT: Young American Writers on the New Generation,* a book he conceived of and also edited. What kind of readers do you think he envisioned for the book? How do you think you fit into that group?
2. What do you think Liu's appeal might be to generations older than his? Why?

QUESTIONS ABOUT STRATEGIES

1. What is the impact of Liu's writing about his parents' experience?
2. Liu was once one of President Clinton's speechwriters. What strategies does he use that he might have learned through that experience?

QUESTIONS FOR DISCUSSION

1. What evidence, if any, do you see that students are splitting into separate groups on your campus? What is your view of such splits? Why?

2. What factors in Liu's life and experiences do you think played a significant part in his success in college and beyond? How would those factors affect his outlook on life?

BARBARA KINGSOLVER

Barbara Kingsolver was born in Annapolis, Maryland, in 1955 and educated at DePauw University and the University of Arizona. She began her writing career as a technical writer in the office of arid studies, then began working as a freelance journalist before publishing her first novel, *The Bean Trees* (1988). Her other novels include *Animal Dreams* (1990), *The Poisonwood Bible* (1998), and *Prodigal Summer* (2000). She has published short stories in *Homeland and Other Stories* (1989), poems in *Another America: Otra América* (1992), and essays in *High Tide in Tucson: Essays from Now or Never* (1995). In "Stone Soup," reprinted from *High Tide in Tucson*, Kingsolver argues that there is not necessarily one best model for a successful family.

Stone Soup

IN THE CATALOG of family values, where do we rank an occasion like this? A curly-haired boy who wanted to run before he walked, age seven now, a soccer player scoring a winning goal. He turns to the bleachers with his fists in the air and a smile wide as a gap-toothed galaxy. His own cheering section of grown-ups and kids all leap to their feet and hug each other, delirious with love for this boy. He's Andy, my best friend's son. The cheering section includes his mother and her friends, his brother, his father and step-mother, a stepbrother and stepsister, and a grandparent. Lucky is the child with this many relatives on hand to hail a proud accomplishment. I'm there too, witnessing a family fortune. But in spite of myself, defensive words take shape in my head. I am thinking: I dare *anybody* to call this a broken home.

Families change, and remain the same. Why are our names 2
for home so slow to catch up to the truth of where we live? When I was a child, I had two parents who loved me 3
without cease. One of them attended every excuse for attention I ever contrived, and the other made it to the ones with higher production values, like piano recitals and appendicitis.

Arguing about whether nontraditional families deserve pity or tolerance is a little like the medieval debate about left-handedness as a mark of the devil.

So I was a lucky child too. I played with a set of paper dolls called "The Family of Dolls," four in number, who came with the factory-assigned names of Dad, Mom, Sis, and Junior. I think you know what they looked like, at least before I loved them to death and their heads fell off.

Now I've replaced the dolls with a life. I knit my days 4
around my daughter's survival and happiness, and am proud to say her head is still on. But we aren't the Family of Dolls. Maybe you're not, either. And if not, even though you are statistically no oddity, it's probably been suggested to you in a hundred ways that yours isn't exactly a real family, but an impostor family, a harbinger of cultural ruin, a slapdash substitute—something like counterfeit money. Here at the tail end of our century, most of us are up to our ears in the noisy business of trying to support and love a thing called family. But there's a current in the air with ferocious moral force that finds its way even into political campaigns, claiming there is only one right way to do it, the Way It Has Always Been.

In the face of a thriving, particolored world, this narrow 5 view is so pickled and absurd I'm astonished that it gets airplay. And I'm astonished that it still stings.

Every parent has endured the arrogance of a child-   6
unfriendly grump sitting in judgment, explaining what those kids of ours really need (for example, "a good licking"). If we're polite, we move our crew to another bench in the park. If we're forthright (as I am in my mind, only, for the rest of the day), we fix them with a sweet imperious stare and say, "Come back and let's talk about it after you've changed a thousand diapers."

But it's harder somehow to shrug off the Family-of-Dolls   7
Family Values crew when they judge (from their safe distance) that divorced people, blended families, gay families, and single parents are failures. That our children are at risk, and the whole arrangement is messy and embarrassing. A marriage that ends is not called "finished," it's called *failed*. The children of this family may have been born to a happy union, but now they are called *the children of divorce*.

I had no idea how thoroughly these assumptions overlaid   8
my culture until I went through divorce myself. I wrote to a friend: "This might be worse than being widowed. Overnight I've suffered the same losses—companionship, financial and practical support, my identity as a wife and partner, the future I'd taken for granted. I am lonely, grieving, and hard-pressed to take care of my household alone. But instead of bringing casseroles, people are acting like I had a fit and broke up the family china."

Once upon a time I held these beliefs about divorce: that   9
everyone who does it could have chosen not to do it. That it's a lazy way out of marital problems. That it selfishly puts personal happiness ahead of family integrity. Now I tremble for my ignorance. It's easy, in fortunate times, to forget about the ambush that could leave your head reeling: serious mental or physical illness, death in the family, abandonment, financial calamity, humiliation, violence, despair.

I started out like any child, intent on being the Family of   10
Dolls. I set upon young womanhood believing in most of the doctrines of my generation: I wore my skirts four inches

above the knee. I had the Barbie with her zebra-striped swimsuit and a figure unlike anything found in nature. And I understood the Prince Charming Theory of Marriage, a quest for Mr. Right that ends smack dab where you find him. I did not completely understand that another whole story *begins* there, and no fairy tale prepared me for the combination of bad luck and persistent hope that would interrupt my dream and lead me to other arrangements. Like a cancer diagnosis, a dying marriage is a thing to fight, to deny, and finally, when there's no choice left, to dig in and survive. Casseroles would help. Likewise, I imagine it must be a painful reckoning in adolescence (or later on) to realize one's own true love will never look like the soft-focus fragrance ads because Prince Charming (surprise!) is a princess. Or vice versa. Or has skin the color your parents didn't want you messing with, except in the Crayola box.

It's awfully easy to hold in contempt the straw broken   11 home, and that mythical category of persons who toss away nuclear family for the sheer fun of it. Even the legal terms we use have a suggestion of caprice. I resent the phrase "irreconcilable differences," which suggests a stubborn refusal to accept a spouse's little quirks. This is specious. Every happily married couple I know has loads of irreconcilable differences. Negotiating where to set the thermostat is not the point. A nonfunctioning marriage is a slow asphyxiation. It is waking up despised each morning, listening to the pulse of your own loneliness before the radio begins to blare its raucous gospel that you're nothing if you aren't loved. It is sharing your airless house with the threat of suicide or other kinds of violence, while the ghost that whispers, "Leave here and destroy your children," has passed over every door and nailed it shut. Disassembling a marriage in these circumstances is as much *fun* as amputating your own gangrenous leg. You do it, if you can, to save a life—or two, or more.

I know of no one who really went looking to hoe the   12 harder row, especially the daunting one of single parenthood. Yet it seems to be the most American of customs to blame the burdened for their destiny. We'd like so desperately to believe in freedom and justice for all, we can hardly name that rogue bad luck, even when he's a close enough snake to bite us. In the wake of my divorce, some friends (even a few close ones) chose to vanish, rather than linger within striking distance of misfortune.

But most stuck around, bless their hearts, and if I'm any the wiser for my trials, it's from having learned the worth of steadfast friendship. And also, what not to say. The least helpful question is: "Did you want the divorce, or didn't you?" Did I want to keep that gangrenous leg, or not? How to explain, in a culture that venerates choice: two terrifying options are much worse than none at all. Give me any day the quick hand of cruel fate that will leave me scarred but blameless. As it was, I kept thinking of that wicked third-grade joke in which some boy comes up behind you and grabs your ear, starts in with a prolonged tug, and asks, "Do you want this ear any longer?" 13

Still, the friend who holds your hand and says the wrong thing is made of dearer stuff than the one who stays away. And generally, through all of it, you live. My favorite fictional character, Kate Vaiden (in the novel by Reynolds Price), advises: "Strength just comes in one brand—you stand up at sunrise and meet what they send you and keep your hair combed." 14

Once you've weathered the straits, you get to cross the tricky juncture from casualty to survivor. If you're on your feet at the end of a year or two, and have begun putting together a happy new existence, those friends who were kind enough to feel sorry for you when you needed it must now accept you back to the ranks of the living. If you're truly blessed, they will dance at your second wedding. Everybody else, for heaven's sake, should stop throwing stones. 15

Arguing about whether nontraditional families deserve pity or tolerance is a little like the medieval debate about left-handedness as a mark of the devil. Divorce, remarriage, single parenthood, gay parents, and blended families simply are. They're facts of our time. Some of the reasons listed by 16 sociologists for these family reconstructions are: the idea of marriage as a romantic partnership rather than a pragmatic one; a shift in women's expectations, from servility to self-respect and independence; and longevity (prior to antibiotics no marriage was expected to last many decades—in Colonial days the average couple lived to be married less than twelve years). Add to all this, our growing sense of entitlement to happiness and safety from abuse. Most would agree these are all good things. Yet their result—a culture in which serial monogamy and the consequent reshaping of families are the norm—gets diagnosed as "failing."

For many of us, once we have put ourselves Humpty-Dumpty-wise back together again, the main problem with our reorganized family is that other people think we have a problem. My daughter tells me the only time she's uncomfortable about being the child of divorced parents is when her friends say they feel sorry for her. It's a bizarre sympathy, given that half the kids in her school and nation are in the same boat, pursuing childish happiness with the same energy as their married-parent peers. When anyone asks how *she* feels about it, she spontaneously lists the benefits: our house is in the country and we have a dog, but she can go to her dad's neighborhood for the urban thrills of a pool and sidewalks for roller-skating. What's more, she has three sets of grandparents! 17

Why is it surprising that a child would revel in a widened family and the right to feel at home in more than one house? Isn't it the opposite that should worry us—a child with no home at all, or too few resources to feel safe? The child at risk is the one whose parents are too immature themselves to guide wisely; too diminished by poverty to nurture; too far from opportunity to offer hope. The number of children in the U.S. living in poverty at this moment is almost unfathomably large: twenty percent. There are families among us that need help all right, and by no means are they new on the landscape. The rate at which teenage girls had babies in 1957 (ninety-six per thousand) was twice what it is now. That remarkable statistic is ignored by the religious right—prob- 18 ably because the teen birth rate was cut in half mainly by legalized abortion. In fact, the policy gatekeepers who coined the phrase "family values" have steadfastly ignored the desperation of too-small families, and since 1979 have steadily reduced the amount of financial support available to a single parent. But, this camp's most outspoken attacks seem aimed at the notion of families getting too complex, with add-ons and extras such as a gay parent's partner, or a remarried mother's new husband and his children.

To judge a family's value by its tidy symmetry is to purchase a book for its cover. There's no moral authority there. The famous family comprised of Dad, Mom, Sis, and Junior living as an isolated economic unit is not built on historical bedrock. In *The Way We Never Were,* Stephanie Coontz writes, "Whenever people propose that we go back to the traditional family, I always suggest that they pick a ballpark date for the family they have in mind." Colonial families were tidily disciplined, but their members (meaning everyone but infants) labored incessantly and died young. Then the Victorian family adopted a new division of labor, in which women's role was domestic and children were allowed time for study and play, but this was an upper-class construct supported by myriad slaves. Coontz writes, "For every nineteenth-century middle-class family that protected its wife and child within the family circle, there was an Irish or German girl scrubbing floors . . . a Welsh boy mining coal to keep the home-baked goodies warm, a black girl doing the family laundry, a black mother and child picking cotton to be made into clothes for the family, and a Jewish or an Italian daughter in a sweatshop making 'ladies' dresses or artificial flowers for the family to purchase." 19

The abolition of slavery brought slightly more democratic arrangements, in which extended families were harnessed together in cottage industries; at the turn of the century came a steep rise in child labor in mines and sweatshops. Twenty percent of American children lived in orphanages at the time; their parents were not necessarily dead, but couldn't afford to keep them. 20

During the Depression and up to the end of World War II, 21
many millions of U.S. households were more multigenera-
tional than nuclear. Women my grandmother's age were
likely to live with a fluid assortment of elderly relatives, in-
laws, siblings, and children. In many cases they spent virtually
every waking hour working in the company of other
women—a companionable scenario in which it would be
easier, I imagine, to tolerate an estranged or difficult spouse.
I'm reluctant to idealize a life of so much hard work and so
little spousal intimacy, but its advantage may have been resilience. A family so large and varied would not easily be
brought down by a single blow: it could absorb a death, long
illness, an abandonment here or there, and any number of
irreconcilable differences.

The Family of Dolls came along midcentury as a great 22
American experiment. A booming economy required a mo-
bile labor force and demanded that women surrender jobs to
returning soldiers. Families came to be defined by a single
breadwinner. They struck out for single-family homes at an
earlier age than ever before, and in unprecedented numbers
they raised children in suburban isolation. The nuclear family
was launched to sink or swim.

More than a few sank. Social historians corroborate that 23
the suburban family of the postwar economic boom, which
we have recently selected as our definition of "traditional,"
was no panacea. Twenty-five percent of Americans were poor
in the mid-1950s, and as yet there were no food stamps. Sixty
percent of the elderly lived on less than $1,000 a year, and
most had no medical insurance. In the sequestered suburbs,
alcoholism and sexual abuse of children were far more widespread than anyone imagined.

Expectations soared, and the economy sagged. It's hard 24
to depend on one other adult for everything, come what may.
In the last three decades, that amorphous, adaptable structure
we call "family" has been reshaped once more by economic
tides. Compared with fifties families, mothers are far more
likely now to be employed. We are statistically more likely to
divorce, and to live in blended families or other extranuclear

arrangements. We are also more likely to plan and space our children, and to rate our marriages as "happy." We are less likely to suffer abuse without recourse, or to stare out at our lives through a glaze of prescription tranquilizers. Our aged parents are less likely to be destitute, and we're half as likely to have a teenage daughter turn up a mother herself. All in all, I would say that if "intact" in modern family-values jargon means living quietly desperate in the bell jar, then hip-hip-hooray for "broken." A neat family model constructed to service the Baby Boom economy seems to be returning gradually to a grand, lumpy shape that human families apparently have tended toward since they first took root in the Olduvai Gorge. We're social animals, deeply fond of companionship, and children love best to run in packs. If there is a *normal* for humans, at all, I expect it looks like two or three Families of Dolls, connected variously by kinship and passion, shuffled like cards and strewn over several shoeboxes.

The sooner we can let go of the fairy tale of families   25 functioning perfectly in isolation, the better we might embrace the relief of community. Even the admirable parents who've stayed married through thick and thin are very likely, at present, to incorporate other adults into their families— household help and baby-sitters if they can afford them, or neighbors and grandparents if they can't. For single parents, this support is the rock-bottom definition of family. And most parents who have split apart, however painfully, still manage to maintain family continuity for their children, creating in many cases a boisterous phenomenon that Constance Ahrons in her book *The Good Divorce* calls the "binuclear family." Call it what you will—when ex-spouses beat swords into plowshares and jump up and down at a soccer game together, it makes for happy kids.

Cinderella, look, who needs her? All those evil stepsisters?   26 That story always seemed like too much cotton-picking fuss over clothes. A childhood tale that fascinated me more was the one called "Stone Soup," and the gist of it is this: Once upon a time, a pair of beleaguered soldiers straggled home to a village empty-handed, in a land ruined by war. They were famished, but the villagers had so little they shouted evil words and slammed their doors. So the soldiers dragged out a big kettle, filled it with water, and put it on a fire to boil. They rolled a clean round stone into the pot, while the villagers peered through their curtains in amazement.

"What kind of soup is that?" they hooted. 27

"Stone soup," the soldiers replied. "Everybody can have 28 some when it's done."

"Well, thanks," one matron grumbled, coming out with a 29 shriveled carrot. "But it'd be better if you threw this in."

And so on, of course, a vegetable at a time, until the whole 30 suspicious village managed to feed itself grandly.

Any family is a big empty pot, save for what gets thrown 31 in. Each stew turns out different. Generosity, a resolve to turn bad luck into good, and respect for variety—these things will nourish a nation of children. Name-calling and suspicion will not. My soup contains a rock or two of hard times, and maybe yours does too. I expect it's a heck of a bouillabaise.

For Study and Discussion

QUESTIONS FOR RESPONSE

1. To what extent does the makeup of your family or the families of some of your close friends fit what Kingsolver calls the "traditional family," that is, a father, stay-at-home mother, and two or three children? How do your experiences with different kinds of families affect your response to Kingsolver's essay?

2. The phrase "family values" is an often ambiguous term, used by various factions for their own political purposes. How would you define the term in what seems to you an honest and legitimate way? What do you think Kingsolver's definition of family values might be?

QUESTIONS ABOUT PURPOSE

1. In paragraphs 19 through 23, Kingsolver gives several snapshots of what so-called traditional families have actually looked like for

the past several decades. What do you think she hopes to accomplish with these accounts?

2. What new insights do you think Kingsolver wants her readers to have about the divorce process?

QUESTIONS ABOUT AUDIENCE

1. What experience with divorce, single parenthood, and the step-families created by second marriages do you think today's readers under forty are likely to have? How do those experiences affect the way they are likely to respond to an essay like this?
2. What details in the essay suggest that Kingsolver feels she is writing more for women than for men?

QUESTIONS ABOUT STRATEGIES

1. Kingsolver has published several successful novels, two of which—*The Bean Trees* and *Pigs in Heaven*—tell the story of a single mother who adopts and raises a child. What strategies do you see in this essay that you think might have come from her talent for writing fiction?
2. Kingsolver draws examples from two sources: from her own experience and observations and from historical examples from previous eras. What are the strengths of examples from each of these sources?

QUESTIONS FOR DISCUSSION

1. The variety of households in most communities suggests that there are several models for effective families. Drawing on your own experiences, describe one or two models that you have seen work well.
2. Kingsolver suggests that she's been severely criticized at times for being a divorced woman who is raising a child without a husband. Do you think such criticisms are common and, if so, how justified do you believe them to be?

BARBARA DAFOE WHITEHEAD

Barbara Dafoe Whitehead was born in Rochester, Minnesota, in 1944 and educated at the University of Wisconsin and the University of Chicago. She has contributed articles to *Commonweal,* the *New York Times* and the *Wall Street Journal.* Her most controversial article, "Dan Quayle Was Right," published in the *Atlantic Monthly,* refers to former Vice President Dan Quayle's criticism of the television show "Murphy Brown" because its title character chose to have a baby without being married. She has also written another controversial article for *Atlantic Monthly,* "The Failure of Sex Education." These articles have led to books such as *The Divorce Culture* (1997) and *Goodbye to Girlhood: What's Troubling Girls and What We Can Do About It* (1999). In "Women and the Future of Fatherhood," excerpted from *The Divorce Culture,* Whitehead argues that even the best mothers cannot be good fathers.

Women and the Future of Fatherhood

MUCH OF OUR contemporary debate over fatherhood is   1
governed by the assumption that men can solve the fatherhood problem on their own. The organizers of last year's Million Man March asked women to stay home, and the leaders of Promise Keepers and other grass-roots fatherhood movements whose members gather with considerably less fanfare simply do not admit women.

There is a cultural rationale for the exclusion of women.   2

The fatherhood movement sees the task of reinstating responsible fatherhood as an effort to alter today's norms of masculinity and correctly believes that such an effort cannot succeed unless it is voluntarily undertaken and supported by men. There is also a political rationale in defining fatherlessness as a men's issue. In the debate about marriage and parenthood, which women have dominated for at least 30 years, the fatherhood movement gives men a powerful collective voice and presence.

Yet however effective the grass-roots movement is at stir- 3
ring men's consciences and raising their consciousness, the fatherhood problem will not be solved by men alone. To be sure, by signaling their commitment to accepting responsi-

---

*The notion of marriage as a union between
two sovereign selves may be inadequate to
define a relationship that carries with it the
obligations, duties, and sacrifices
of parenthood.*

---

bility for the rearing of their children, men have taken the essential first step. But what has not yet been acknowledged is that the success of any effort to renew fatherhood as a social fact and a cultural norm also hinges on the attitudes and behavior of women. Men can't be fathers unless the mothers of their children allow it.

Merely to say this is to point to how thoroughly marital 4
disruption has weakened the bond between fathers and children. More than half of all American children are likely to spend at least part of their lives in one-parent homes. Since the vast majority of children in disrupted families live with their mothers, fathers do not share a home or a daily life with their children. It is much more difficult for men to make the

kinds of small, routine, instrumental investments in their children that help forge a good relationship. It is hard to fix a flat bike tire or run a bath when you live in another neighborhood or another town. Many a father's instrumental contribution is reduced to the postal or electronic transmission of money, or, all too commonly, to nothing at all. Without regular contact with their children, men often make reduced emotional contributions as well. Fathers must struggle to sustain close emotional ties across time and space, to "be there" emotionally without being there physically. Some may pick up the phone, send a birthday card, or buy a present, but for many fathers, physical absence also becomes emotional absence.

Without marriage, men also lose access to the social and emotional intelligence of women in building relationships. 5 Wives teach men how to care for young children, and they also encourage children to love their fathers. Mothers who do not live with the father of their children are not as likely as married mothers to represent him in positive ways to the children; nor are the relatives who are most likely to have greatest contact with the children—the mother's parents, brothers, and sisters—likely to have a high opinion of the children's father. Many men are able to overcome such obstacles, but only with difficulty. In general, men need marriage in order to be good fathers.

If the future of fatherhood depends on marriage, however, 6 its future is uncertain. Marriage depends on women as well as men, and women are less committed to marriage than ever before in the nation's history. In the past, women were economically dependent on marriage and assumed a disproportionately heavy responsibility for maintaining the bond, even if the underlying relationship was seriously or irretrievably damaged. In the last third of the 20th century, however, as women have gained more opportunities for paid work and the availability of child care has increased, they have become less dependent on marriage as an economic arrangement. Though it is not easy, it is possible for women to raise children on their own. This has made divorce far more attractive as a remedy for an unsatisfying marriage, and a growing number of women have availed themselves of the option.

Today, marriage and motherhood are coming apart. Re-   7
marriage and marriage rates are declining even as the rates of divorce remain stuck at historic highs and childbearing outside marriage becomes more common. Many women see single motherhood as a choice and a right to be exercised if a suitable husband does not come along in time.

The vision of the "first stage" feminism of the 1960s and   8
'70s, which held out the model of the career woman unfettered by husband or children, has been accepted by women only in part. Women want to be fettered by children, even to the point of going through grueling infertility treatments or artificial insemination to achieve motherhood. But they are increasingly ambivalent about the ties that bind them to a husband and about the necessity of marriage as a condition of parenthood. In 1994, a National Opinion Research survey asked a group of Americans. "Do you agree or disagree: one parent can bring up a child as well as two parents together." Women split 50/50 on the question; men disagreed by more than two to one.

And indeed, women enjoy certain advantages over men in   9
a society marked by high and sustained levels of family breakup. Women do not need marriage to maintain a close bond to their children, and thus to experience the larger sense of social and moral purpose that comes with raising children. As the bearers and nurturers of children and (increasingly) as the sole breadwinners for families, women continue to be engaged in personally rewarding and socially valuable pursuits. They are able to demonstrate their feminine virtues outside marriage.

Men, by contrast, have no positive identity as fathers out-   10
side marriage. Indeed, the emblematic absent father today is the infamous "deadbeat dad." In part, this is the result of efforts to stigmatize irresponsible fathers who fail to pay alimony and child support. But this image also reflects the

fact that men are heavily dependent on the marriage partnership to fulfill their role as fathers. Even those who keep up their child support payments are deprived of the social importance and sense of larger purpose that comes from providing for children and raising a family. And it is the rare father who can develop the qualities needed to meet the new cultural ideal of the involved and "nurturing" father without the help of a spouse.

These differences are reflected in a growing virtue gap. 11 American popular culture today routinely recognizes and praises the achievements of single motherhood, while the widespread failure of men as fathers has resulted in a growing sense of cynicism and despair about men's capacity for virtuous conduct in family life. The enormously popular movie *Waiting to Exhale* captures the essence of this virtue gap with its portrait of steadfast mothers and deadbeat fathers, morally sleazy men and morally unassailable women. And women feel free to vent their anger and frustration with men in ways that would seem outrageous to women if the shoe were on the other foot. In *Operating Instructions* (1993), her memoir of single motherhood, Ann LaMott mordantly observes, "On bad days, I think straight white men are so poorly wired, so emotionally unenlightened and unconscious that you must approach each one as if he were some weird cross between a white supremacist and an incredibly depressing T. S. Eliot poem."

Women's weakening attachment to marriage should not 12 be taken as a lack of interest in marriage or in a husband-wife partnership in child rearing. Rather, it is a sign of women's more exacting emotional standards for husbands and their growing insistence that men play a bigger part in caring for children and the household. Given their double responsibilities as breadwinners and mothers, many working wives find men's need for ego reinforcement and other forms of emotional and physical upkeep irksome and their failure to share housework and child care absolutely infuriating. (Surveys show that husbands perform only one-third of all household tasks even if their wives are working full-time.) Why should men be treated like babies? women complain. If men fail to meet their standards, many women are willing to do without them. Poet and polemicist Katha Pollitt captures the prevailing sentiment: "If single women can have sex, their own homes, the respect of friends and interesting work, they don't need to tell themselves that any marriage is better than none. Why not have a child on one's own? Children are a joy. Many men are not."

For all these reasons, it is important to see the fatherhood   13 problem as part of the larger cultural problem of the decline of marriage as a lasting relationship between men and women. The traditional bargain between men and women has broken down, and a new bargain has not yet been struck. It is impossible to predict what that bargain will look like—or whether there will even be one. However, it is possible to speculate about the talking points that might bring women to the bargaining table. First, a crucial proviso: there must be recognition of the changed social and economic status of women. Rightly or wrongly, many women fear that the fatherhood movement represents an effort to reinstate the status quo ante, to repeal the gains and achievements women have made over the past 30 years and return to the "separate spheres" domestic ideology that put men in the workplace and women in the home. Any effort to rethink marriage must accept the fact that women will continue to work outside the home.

Therefore, a new bargain must be struck over the division   14 of paid work and family work. This does not necessarily mean a 50/50 split in the work load every single day, but it does mean that men must make a more determined and conscientious effort to do more than one-third of the household chores. How each couple arrives at a sense of what is fair will vary, of course, but the goal is to establish some mutual understanding and commitment to an equitable division of tasks.

Another talking point may focus on the differences in the   15 expectations men and women have for marriage and intimacy.

Americans have a "best friends" ideal for marriage that includes some desires that might in fact be more easily met by a best friend—someone who doesn't come with all the complicated entanglements of sharing a bed, a bank account, and a bathroom. Nonetheless, high expectations for emotional intimacy in marriage often are confounded by the very different understandings men and women have of intimacy. Much more than men, women seek intimacy and affection through talking and emotional disclosure. Men often prefer sex to talking, and physical disrobing to emotional disclosing. They tend to be less than fully committed to (their own) sexual fidelity, while women view fidelity as a crucial sign of commitment. These are differences that the sexes need to engage with mutual recognition and tolerance.

In renegotiating the marital bargain, it may also be useful to acknowledge the biosocial differences between mothers and fathers rather than to assume an androgynous model for the parental partnership. There can be a high degree of flexibility in parental roles, but men and women are not interchangeable "parental units," particularly in their children's early years. Rather than struggle to establish identical tracks in career and family lives, it may be more realistic to consider how children's needs and well-being might require patterns of paid work and child rearing that are different for mothers and fathers but are nevertheless equitable over the course of a lifetime. 16

Finally, it may be important to think and talk about marriage in another kind of language than the one that suffuses our current discourse on relationships. The secular language of "intimate relationships" is the language of politics and psychotherapy, and it focuses on individual rights and individual needs. It can be heard most clearly in the personal-ad columns, a kind of masked ball where optimists go in search of partners who respect their rights and meet their emotional needs. These are not unimportant in the achievement of the contemporary ideal of marriage, which emphasizes egalitarianism and emotional fulfillment. But this notion of marriage 17 as a union of two sovereign selves may be inadequate to define a relationship that carries with it the obligations, duties, and sacrifices of parenthood. There has always been a tension between marriage as an intimate relationship between a man and a woman and marriage as an institutional arrangement for raising children, and though the language of individual rights plays a part in defining the former, it cannot fully describe the latter. The parental partnership requires some language that acknowledges differences, mutuality, complementarity, and, more than anything else, altruism.

There is a potentially powerful incentive for women to respond to an effort to renegotiate the marriage bargain, and that has to do with their children. Women can be good mothers without being married. But especially with weakened communities that provide little support, children need levels of parental investment that cannot be supplied solely by a good mother, even if she has the best resources at her disposal. These needs are more likely to be met if the child has a father as well as a mother under the same roof. Simply put, even the best mothers cannot be good fathers. 18

For Study and Discussion

QUESTIONS FOR RESPONSE

1. In paragraph 9, Whitehead says that "women enjoy certain advantages over men in a society marked by high and sustained levels of family breakup." Considering your own experience and that of people you know well, how do you respond to this claim?
2. In her first paragraph, Whitehead talks about "the fatherhood problem." How would you describe that problem in our society? Or do you think it even exists? Why do you say so?

QUESTIONS ABOUT PURPOSE

1. What changes in women's behaviors and attitudes would Whitehead like to bring about?

2. What changes in men's behaviors and attitudes would Whitehead like to bring about?

QUESTIONS ABOUT AUDIENCE

1. Whom do you see as the principal audience that Whitehead hopes to reach with this essay, men or women? On what do you base your answer?
2. What differences in responses to this article would you expect from readers over forty and those under forty?

QUESTIONS ABOUT STRATEGIES

1. Whitehead's argument is built on strong statements like this: "Today, marriage and motherhood are coming apart," and "Men have no positive identity as fathers outside marriage." In light of your own observations about today's families, how credible do you find these statements? Why?
2. Although Whitehead is writing about a topic that often generates a great deal of emotion, she is careful not to sound angry or to blame anyone. How does her argument benefit from her maintaining this moderate tone?

QUESTIONS FOR DISCUSSION

1. In paragraph 15 Whitehead says that men and women have crucial differences in their expectations about marriage and family. Judging by the people you know who have married recently or who plan to marry soon, what do you think women expect? What do men expect?
2. What important contributions (other than money) do you think a father makes to a child's upbringing that can't be adequately taken care of by a mother? Are there other individuals who can make those contributions?

PAUL ROGAT LOEB

Paul Rogat Loeb was born in Berkeley, California, in 1952 and educated at Stanford University and the New School for Social Research. He has worked as a bartender at the Village Gate Jazz Club, a freelance writer for magazines such as the *Village Voice, Mother Earth News,* and *New West,* and a frequent lecturer at universities such as Harvard and Massachusetts Institute of Technology. His books include *Hope in Hard Times: American Peace Movement and the Reagan Era* (1987), *Generation at the Crossroads: Apathy and Action on the American Campus* (1994), and *Soul of a Citizen: Living with Conviction in a Cynical Time* (1999). In "Soul of a Citizen," excerpted from the latter book, Loeb argues that ordinary people can bring about social change.

Soul of a Citizen
Living with Conviction in a Cynical Time

M OST AMERICANS ARE thoughtful, caring, generous. We try to do our best by family and friends. We'll even stop to help a fellow driver stranded by a roadside breakdown, or give spare change to a stranger. But increasingly, a wall separates each of us from the world outside, and from others who have taken refuge in their own private sanctuaries. How can we renew the public participation that's the very soul of democratic citizenship?

To be sure, the issues we face are complex. It's hard to comprehend the moral implications of a world in which Nike pays Michael Jordan millions to appear in its ads while workers at its foreign shoe factories toil away for pennies a day. The 500 richest people on the planet now control more wealth than the poorest 3 billion, half the human population. Is it possible even to grasp this extraordinary imbalance? And, more important, how do we begin to redress it?

Certainly we need to decide for ourselves whether particular causes are wise or foolish. But we also need to believe that our individual involvement is worthwhile, that what we might

---

Our impulses toward involvement are dampened by a culture that demeans idealism, enshrines cynicism, and makes us feel naive for caring about our fellow humans or the planet we inhabit.

---

do in the public sphere will not be in vain. The challenge is as much psychological as political. As the Ethiopian proverb says, "He who conceals his disease cannot be cured."

We need to understand our cultural diseases—callousness, shortsightedness, denial—and learn what it will take to heal our society and our souls. How did so many of us become convinced that we can do nothing to affect the future our children and grandchildren will inherit? And how have others managed to work powerfully for change?

Pete Knutson is one of my oldest friends. During 25 years as a commercial fisherman in Washington and Alaska, he has been forced to respond to the steady degradation of salmon spawning grounds. He could have accepted this as fate and focused on getting a maximum share of the dwindling fish populations. Instead, he gradually built an alliance between Washington fishermen, environmentalists, and Native American tribes, and persuaded them to demand that habitat be preserved and restored.

Cooperation didn't come easily. Washington's fishermen are historically individualistic and politically mistrustful. But with their new allies, they pushed for cleaner spawning streams, preservation of the Endangered Species Act, and increased water flow over regional dams to help boost salmon runs. Fearing that these measures would raise electricity costs or restrict development opportunities, aluminum companies and other large industrial interests bankrolled a statewide referendum, Initiative 640, to regulate fishing nets in a way that would eliminate small family operations.

At first, those who opposed 640 thought they had no 7 chance of success: They were outspent, outstaffed, outgunned. Similar initiatives backed by similar corporate interests had already passed in Florida, Louisiana, and Texas. But the opponents refused to give up. Pete and his coworkers enlisted major environmental groups to campaign against the initiative. They worked with the media to explain the larger issues at stake and focus public attention on the measure's powerful financial backers. On election day in November 1995, Initiative 640 was defeated. White fishermen, Native American activists, and Friends of the Earth staffers threw their arms around each other in victory. "I'm really proud of you, Dad," Pete's 12-year-old son kept repeating. Pete was stunned.

We often think of social involvement as noble but imprac- 8 tical. Yet it can serve enlightened self-interest and the interests of others simultaneously, giving us a sense of connection and purpose nearly impossible to find in private life. "It takes energy to act," says Pete. "But it's more draining to bury your anger, convince yourself you're powerless, and swallow whatever's handed to you."

We often don't know where to start. Most of us would like 9 to see people treated more justly and the earth accorded the respect it deserves. But we mistrust our own ability to make a difference. The magnitude of the issues at hand has led too many of us to conclude that social involvement isn't worth the cost.

Such resignation isn't innate or inevitable. It's what psy- 10 chologists call learned helplessness, a systematic way of ignoring the ills we see and leaving them for others to handle. We find it unsettling even to think about crises as profound as the extinction of species, depletion of the ozone layer, destruction of the rainforests, and desperate urban poverty. We're taught to doubt our voices, to feel that we lack either the time to learn about and articulate the issues or the standing to speak out and be heard. To get socially involved, we believe, requires almost saintlike judgment, confidence, and character—standards we can never meet. Our impulses toward involvement are dampened by a culture that demeans idealism, enshrines cynicism, and makes us feel naive for caring about our fellow human beings or the planet we inhabit.

A few years ago, on Martin Luther King Day, I was inter- 11
viewed on CNN along with Rosa Parks. "Rosa Parks was the woman who wouldn't go to the back of the bus," said the host. "That set in motion the yearlong bus boycott in Montgomery. It earned Rosa Parks the title of 'mother of the civil rights movement.'"

The host's description—the standard rendition of the 12
story—stripped the boycott of its context. Before refusing to give up her bus seat to a white person, Parks had spent 12 years helping to lead the local NAACP chapter. The summer before, she had attended a 10-day training session at the Highlander Center, Tennessee's labor and civil rights organizing school, where she'd met older activists and discussed the Supreme Court decision banning "separate but equal" schools. Parks had become familiar with previous challenges to segregation: another Montgomery bus boycott, 50 years earlier; a bus boycott in Baton Rouge two years before Parks was arrested; and an NAACP dilemma the previous spring, when a young Montgomery woman had also refused to move to the back of the bus. The NAACP had considered a legal challenge but decided the unmarried, pregnant woman would be a poor symbol for a campaign.

In short, Parks didn't make a spur-of-the-moment deci- 13
sion. She was part of a movement for change at a time when

success was far from certain. This in no way diminishes her historical importance, but it reminds us that this powerful act might never have taken place without the humble, frustrating work that preceded it.

We elevate a few people to hero status—especially during 14 times of armed conflict—but most of us know next to nothing of the battles ordinary men and women fought to preserve freedom, expand democracy, and create a more just society. Many have remarked on America's historical amnesia, but its implications are hard to appreciate without recognizing how much identity dissolves in the absence of memory. We lose the mechanisms that grassroots social movements have used successfully to shift public sentiment and challenge entrenched institutional power. Equally lost are the means by which participants eventually managed to prevail.

Think about how differently one can frame Rosa Parks' 15 historic action. In the prevailing myth, Parks—a holy innocent—acts almost on a whim, in isolation. The lesson seems to be that if any of us suddenly got the urge to do something heroic, that would be great. Of course most of us wait our entire lives for the ideal moment.

The real story is more empowering: It suggests that change 16 is the product of deliberate, incremental action. When we join together to shape a better world, sometimes our struggles will fail or bear only modest fruits. Other times they will trigger miraculous outpourings of courage and heart. We can never know beforehand what the consequences of our actions will be.

For Study and Discussion

QUESTIONS FOR RESPONSE

1. What issues do you know about in your community that people have worked for or given money to in order to bring about improvement—for example, abolishing the death penalty, blocking development in an environmentally sensitive area, or keeping

hazardous waste from being dumped close to the city? How do volunteers contribute to these efforts? What evidence can you cite that such volunteers make a difference?

2. What issues, if any, do you feel so strongly about that you would be willing to march in a parade and carry a banner, write a letter to the editor, or contribute a day's salary in order to bring about change? Whom do you know who has become involved in this way?

QUESTIONS ABOUT PURPOSE

1. Loeb states his purpose straightforwardly in his first paragraph by asking "How can we renew the public participation that's the very soul of democratic citizenship?" What response does he hope to get from his readers by using the term "we"?

2. The subtitle of the book from which Loeb drew this argument is "Living with Conviction in a Cynical Time." How does he go about persuading people not to be cynical?

QUESTIONS ABOUT AUDIENCE

1. Why would college students be a group of readers that Loeb would be especially eager to reach? Historically, what part have they played in bringing about social change?

2. Loeb is associated with the Center for Ethical Leadership in Seattle and has written a book titled *Soul of a Citizen*. What groups of people would be likely to be interested in such a center or read such a book? What goals and values would they probably have?

QUESTIONS ABOUT STRATEGIES

1. What effect does Loeb get by telling about Rosa Parks' long involvement with the civil rights struggle before her action set off the Montgomery bus boycott?

2. Loeb asserts that social involvement can give one a sense of connection and purpose. How does he illustrate that claim in the article?

QUESTIONS FOR DISCUSSION

1. What important changes in America have been brought about by ordinary people getting involved in protests and demonstra-

tions even when the forces against such change seemed overwhelming?

2. Loeb says that we live in a culture of cynicism that stifles idealism. To what extent do you think people around you are cynical about doing good works and what contributes to that cynicism?

Sven Birkerts was born in Pontiac, Michigan, in 1951 and educated at the University of Michigan. After working in a bookstore in Ann Arbor, Michigan, Birkerts became a lecturer in the expository writing program at Harvard University. He began writing literary criticism—*The Artificial Wilderness: Essays on 20th Century Literature* (1987) and *The Electric Life: Essays on Modern Poetry* (1989)— before turning his attention to the problems of the Information Age in his widely discussed book, *The Gutenberg Elegies: The Fate of Reading in an Electronic Age* (1994). In "Confessions of a Nonpolitical Man," reprinted from *Readings* (1999), Birkerts argues that political issues are too complex for people to act on their beliefs.

Confessions of a
Nonpolitical Man

I'M FORCED TO face a difficult fact: I will do nothing overt—nothing political—to further causes I believe in. An awful admission. Certainly there is no dearth of causes, all asking for our most committed support. What is wrong with me that I cannot bestir myself to do anything more than sign an occasional petition, write out a small check?

Somewhere not all that deep within, I know—or suspect— that the blockage represents a failing. And I would like to—I think—change myself, to think my way through to an understanding of things out of which action would result naturally.

But how? I am not apathetic. I admire those who feel the compulsion to act out their beliefs and find meaningful ways to do so—but I do not join. The obvious defense is that these activities are useless, that they will not stay the course of the world or stop the powers that be from enacting their schemes. But such an argument is beside the point. Protest and activism have hastened the withdrawal of troops from Vietnam; brought about important legislative victories for blacks; pressured the South African government to end apartheid policies; forced the shutdown of flawed nuclear facilities. The charge of uselessness will not stick.

What stops me is, in part, the sheer complexity of offenses.   4 A total situation—a mesh of social and economic components, a labyrinth congruent with society's deeper structure—

> *I admire those who feel the compulsion to act out their beliefs and find meaningful ways to do so—but I do not join.*

begs a total response. And a total response is impossible. Logic, of course, protests—one cannot do everything; one should not therefore do nothing. I could put my voice and body on the line on behalf of some small part of the web. Others would be doing the same for other parts. Perhaps some collective results could be achieved.

The logic is incontestable, but I remain inert. Maybe the   5 culprit is laziness; or, to raise it to a Deadly Sin, sloth. But sloth is a disease of the will, and when I will something, I can be tirelessly active.

Selfishness? The belief that I will be giving more than I get   6 back? Maybe. It's not as though I haven't made those calculations, balancing the time and caloric output required to swell the ranks of a demonstration by my humble numerical presence. I have to deem what I do—think, read, write—to be part of the struggle: the larger one, which works to ensure the survival of spirit, free inquiry, humanness in a world where these qualities are threatened. I am not greedy of the time because I want to work on my stamp collection. The heavenly powers could grant me bonus days with the stipulation that they not be used for reading or writing, and I still would not hasten to the march.

Why, then, am I paralyzed? Because I do not believe there is a division between the political sphere of life and the others. I see the various levels of perception, action, and consequence as interfused, a continuum. It is therefore fundamentally false to mark out one such area as requiring us especially.   7

This sounds as though I claim for myself some exalted private agenda and urge on others the tasks I cannot bring myself to do. I do not mean it this way. My point is that some people are bent in a certain way; they feel a call to do the obscure labor of perceiving and processing the larger current shifts. It does not seem possible to do both—to pursue a clear picture of these inchoate weather patterns and to engage in specified, directed activity. The continuum, the psyche's economy, will not allow it.   8

My place, then, is at the desk with my books and thoughts. I hope that my words promote the humane values, that they exert some small influence on people who do act. But who can say how these indeterminate forces move through the world?   9

For Study and Discussion

QUESTIONS FOR RESPONSE

1. Birkerts sees himself as a humanist who stands for the traditional values of our culture; he has written a book called *The Gutenberg Elegies* in which he deplores the decline of reading in this so-called Information Age. How would you respond to such a complaint?

2. To what extent do you sympathize with Birkerts' "confession" about why he is not political? Does his attitude seem sensible to you?

QUESTIONS ABOUT PURPOSE

1. Why do you think Birkerts feels he has to explain his reasons for being nonpolitical?
2. Why does Birkerts tell the reader that he does occasionally sign a petition or write a small check for some cause?

QUESTIONS ABOUT AUDIENCE

1. To whom do you think Birkerts is appealing when he says, "My place is at my desk with my books and my thoughts"? Would you make that statement about yourself? Why?
2. Birkerts seems to divide his audience into two groups: doers and thinkers. What do you think he risks by identifying himself with the thinkers?

QUESTIONS ABOUT STRATEGIES

1. This essay was taken from a collection of Birkerts's writings and reprinted in the magazine *Utne Reader* next to Loeb's essay "Soul of a Citizen." What do you think the magazine editor had in mind in juxtaposing the two pieces?
2. What do you think Birkerts accomplishes with the negative statements that he might be lazy or selfish or that he remains inert?

QUESTIONS FOR DISCUSSION

1. What situations can you think of where problems are so complex that it becomes difficult to know what action, if any, you should take? Under those circumstances, how should one act?
2. What do you think Birkerts means when he says in paragraph 4 that "a total situation—a mesh of social and economic components—begs a total response"? What would a total response consist of? When is such a response possible?

TONI MORRISON

Toni Morrison was born in Lorain, Ohio, in 1931 and educated at Harvard University and Cornell University. After teaching for several years, Morrison began working in publishing, advancing to the position of senior editor at Random House. She then began her own literary career with a series of stunning novels about troubled characters who overcome the racist society that warps and impedes their growth: *The Bluest Eye* (1969); *Song of Solomon* (1977), which won the National Book Award; and *Beloved* (1987), which won the Pulitzer Prize. Some of her other novels include *Tar Baby* (1981), *Jazz* (1992), and *Paradise* (1998). In 1992, Morrison was awarded the Nobel Prize for Literature. In "The Bird in Our Hand: Is It Living or Dead?" Morrison's Nobel Prize Acceptance Speech, she uses her narrative powers to deplore and celebrate the power of language.

The Bird in Our Hand: Is It Living or Dead?
Nobel Prize Acceptance Speech, 1993

MEMBERS OF THE
SWEDISH ACADEMY,
LADIES AND GENTLEMEN:

NARRATIVE HAS NEVER been merely entertainment for me. 1 It is, I believe, one of the principal ways in which we absorb knowledge. I hope you will understand, then, why I begin these remarks with the opening phrase of what must be the oldest sentence in the world, and the earliest one we remember from childhood: "Once upon a time . . ."

"Once upon a time there was an old woman. Blind but   2
wise." Or was it an old man? A guru, perhaps. Or a *griot*

---

*Sexist language, racist language, theistic
language—all are typical of the policing
languages of mastery, and cannot, do not,
permit new knowledge or encourage the
mutual exchange of ideas.*

---

soothing restless children. I have heard this story, or one
exactly like it, in the lore of several cultures.

"Once upon a time there was an old woman. Blind. Wise."   3

In the version I know the woman is the daughter of slaves,   4
black, American, and lives alone in a small house outside of
town. Her reputation for wisdom is without peer and without
question. Among her people she is both the law and its
transgression. The honor she is paid and the awe in which
she is held reach beyond her neighborhood to places far away;
to the city where the intelligence of rural prophets is the
source of much amusement.

One day the woman is visited by some young people who   5
seem to be bent on disproving her clairvoyance and showing
her up for the fraud they believe she is. Their plan is simple:
they enter her house and ask the one question the answer to
which rides solely on her difference from them, a difference
they regard as a profound disability: her blindness. They stand
before her, and one of them says,

"Old woman, I hold in my hand a bird. Tell me whether it
is living or dead."

She does not answer, and the question is repeated. "Is the
bird I am holding living or dead?"

Still she does not answer. She is blind and cannot see her   6
visitors, let alone what is in their hands. She does not know

their color, gender or homeland. She only knows their motive.

The old woman's silence is so long, the young people have 7 trouble holding their laughter.

Finally she speaks, and her voice is soft but stern. "I don't 8 know," she says. "I don't know whether the bird you are holding is dead or alive, but what I do know is that it is in your hands. It is in your hands."

Her answer can be taken to mean: if it is dead, you have 9 either found it that way or you have killed it. If it is alive, you can still kill it. Whether it is to stay alive is your decision. Whatever the case, it is your responsibility.

For parading their power and her helplessness, the young 10 visitors are reprimanded, told they are responsible not only for the act of mockery but also for the small bundle of life sacrificed to achieve its aims. The blind woman shifts attention away from assertions of power to the instrument through which that power is exercised.

Speculation on what (other than its own frail body) that 11 bird in the hand might signify has always been attractive to me, but especially so now, thinking as I have been about the work I do that has brought me to this company. So I choose to read the bird as language and the woman as a practiced writer.

She is worried about how the language she dreams in, 12 given to her at birth, is handled, put into service, even withheld from her for certain nefarious purposes. Being a writer, she thinks of language partly as a system, partly as a living thing over which one has control, but mostly as agency—as an act with consequences. So the question the children put to her, "Is it living or dead?," is not unreal, because she thinks of language as susceptible to death, erasure; certainly imperiled and salvageable only by an effort of the will. She believes that if the bird in the hands of her visitors is dead, the custodians are responsible for the corpse. For her a dead language is not only one no longer spoken or written, it is unyielding language content to admire its own paralysis. Like statist language, censored and censoring. Ruthless in its policing duties, it has no desire or purpose other than to maintain the free range of its own narcotic narcissism, its own exclusivity and dominance. However moribund, it is not without effect, for it actively thwarts the intellect, stalls conscience, suppresses human potential. Unreceptive to interrogation, it cannot form or tolerate new ideas, shape other thoughts, tell another story, fill baffling silences. Official language smitheried to sanction ignorance and preserve privilege is a suit of armor, polished to shocking glitter, a husk from which the knight departed long ago. Yet there it is; dumb, predatory, sentimental. Exciting reverence in schoolchildren, providing shelter for despots, summoning false memories of stability, harmony among the public.

She is convinced that when language dies, out of careless-   13
ness, disuse, indifference, and absence of esteem, or killed by fiat, not only she herself but all users and makers are accountable for its demise. In her country children have bitten their tongues off and use bullets instead to iterate the void of speechlessness, of disabled and disabling language, of language adults have abandoned altogether as a device for grappling with meaning, providing guidance, or expressing love. But she knows tongue-suicide is not only the choice of children. It is common among the infantile heads of state and power merchants whose evacuated language leaves them with no access to what is left of their human instincts, for they speak only to those who obey, or in order to force obedience.

The systematic looting of language can be recognized by   14
the tendency of its users to forgo its nuanced, complex, mid-wifery properties, replacing them with menace and subjugation. Oppressive language does more than represent violence; it is violence; does more than represent the limits of knowledge; it limits knowledge. Whether it is obscuring state language or the faux language of mindless media; whether it is the proud but calcified language of the academy or the commodity-driven language of science; whether it is the malign language of law-without-ethics, or language designed for the estrangement of minorities, hiding its racist plunder in its literary cheek—it must be rejected, altered and exposed. It is the language that drinks blood, laps vulnerabilities, tucks its

fascist boots under crinolines of respectability and patriotism as it moves relentlessly toward the bottom line and the bottomed-out mind. Sexist language, racist language, theistic language—all are typical of the policing languages of mastery, and cannot, do not, permit new knowledge or encourage the mutual exchange of ideas.

The old woman is keenly aware that no intellectual mercenary or insatiable dictator, no paid-for politician or demagogue, no counterfeit journalist would be persuaded by her thoughts. There is and will be rousing language to keep citizens armed and arming; slaughtered and slaughtering in the malls, courthouses, post offices, playgrounds, bedrooms and boulevards; stirring, memorializing language to mask the pity and waste of needless death. There will be more diplomatic language to countenance rape, torture, assassination. There is and will be more seductive, mutant language designed to throttle women, to pack their throats like pâté-producing geese with their own unsayable, transgressive words; there will be more of the language of surveillance disguised as research; of politics and history calculated to render the suffering of millions mute; language glamorized to thrill the dissatisfied and bereft into assaulting their neighbors; arrogant pseudo-empirical language crafted to lock creative people into cages of inferiority and hopelessness.

Underneath the eloquence, the glamour, the scholarly associations, however stirring or seductive, the heart of such language is languishing, or perhaps not beating at all—if the bird is already dead.

She has thought about what could have been the intellectual history of any discipline if it had not insisted upon, or been forced into, the waste of time and life that rationalizations for and representations of dominance required—lethal discourses of exclusion blocking access to cognition for both the excluder and the excluded.

The conventional wisdom of the Tower of Babel story is that the collapse was a misfortune. That it was the distraction or the weight of many languages that precipitated the tower's failed architecture. That one monolithic language would have expedited the building, and heaven would have been reached. Whose heaven, she wonders? And what kind? Perhaps the achievement of Paradise was premature, a little hasty if no one could take the time to understand other languages, other views, other narratives. Had they, the heaven they imagined might have been found at their feet. Complicated, demanding, yes, but a view of heaven as life; not heaven as post-life.

She would not want to leave her young visitors with the   19
impression that language should be forced to stay alive merely to be. The vitality of language lies in its ability to limn the actual, imagined and possible lives of its speakers, readers, writers. Although its poise is sometimes in displacing experience, it is not a substitute for it. It arcs toward the place where meaning may lie. When a President of the United States thought about the graveyard his country had become, and said, "The world will little note nor long remember what we say here. But it will never forget what they did here," his simple words were exhilarating in their life-sustaining properties because they refused to encapsulate the reality of 600,000 dead men in a cataclysmic race war. Refusing to monumentalize, disdaining the "final word," the precise "summing up," acknowledging their "poor power to add or detract," his words signal deference to the uncapturability of the life it mourns. It is the deference that moves her, that recognition that language can never live up to life once and for all. Nor should it. Language can never "pin down" slavery, genocide, war. Nor should it yearn for the arrogance to be able to do so. Its force, its felicity, is in its reach toward the ineffable.

Be it grand or slender, burrowing, blasting or refusing to   20
sanctify; whether it laughs out loud or is a cry without an alphabet, the choice word or the chosen silence, unmolested language surges toward knowledge, not its destruction. But who does not know of literature banned because it is interrogative; discredited because it is critical; erased because alternate? And how many are outraged by the thought of a self-ravaged tongue?

Word-work is sublime, she thinks, because it is generative;   21 it makes meaning that secures our difference, our human difference—the way in which we are like no other life.

We die. That may be the meaning of life. But we *do* language. That may be the measure of our lives.

"Once upon a time . . ." Visitors ask an old woman a question. Who are they, these children? What did they make of that encounter? What did they hear in those final words: "The bird is in your hands"? A sentence that gestures toward possibility, or one that drops a latch? Perhaps what the children heard was, "It is not my problem. I am old, female, black, blind. What wisdom I have now is in knowing I cannot help you. The future of language is yours."

They stand there. Suppose nothing was in their hands. Suppose the visit was only a ruse, a trick to get to be spoken to, taken seriously as they have not been before. A chance to interrupt, to violate the adult world, its miasma of discourse about them. Urgent questions are at stake, including the one they have asked: "Is the bird we hold living or dead?" Perhaps the question meant: "Could someone tell us what is life? What is death?" No trick at all; no silliness. A straightforward question worthy of the attention of a wise one. An old one. And if the old and wise who have lived life and faced death cannot describe either, who can?

But she does not; she keeps her secret, her good opinion of herself, her gnomic pronouncements, her art without commitment. She keeps her distance, enforces it and retreats into the singularity of isolation, in sophisticated, privileged space.

Nothing, no word follows her declaration of transfer. That silence is deep, deeper than the meaning available in the words she has spoken. It shivers, this silence, and the children, annoyed, fill it with language invented on the spot.

"Is there no speech," they ask her, "no words you can give us that help us break through your dossier of failures? through the education you have just given us that is no education at all because we are paying close attention to what you have done as well as to what you have said? to the barrier you have erected between generosity and wisdom?

"We have no bird in our hands, living or dead. We have

only you and our important question. Is the nothing in our hands something you could not bear to contemplate, to even guess? Don't you remember being young, when language was magic without meaning? When what you could say, could not mean? When the invisible was what imagination strove to see? When questions and demands for answers burned so brightly you trembled with fury at not knowing?

"Do we have to begin consciousness with a battle heroes 29 and heroines like you have already fought and lost, leaving us with nothing in our hands except what you have imagined is there? Your answer is artful, but its artfulness embarrasses us and ought to embarrass you. Your answer is indecent in its self-congratulation. A made-for-television script that makes no sense if there is nothing in our hands.

"Why didn't you reach out, touch us with your soft 30 fingers, delay the sound bite, the lesson, until you knew who we were? Did you so despise our trick, our modus operandi, that you could not see that we were baffled about how to get your attention? We are young. Unripe. We have heard all our short lives that we have to be responsible. What could that possibly mean in the catastrophe this world has become; where, as a poet said, 'nothing needs to be exposed since it is already barefaced'? Our inheritance is an affront. You want us to have your old, blank eyes and see only cruelty and mediocrity. Do you think we are stupid enough to perjure ourselves again and again with the fiction of nationhood? How dare you talk to us of duty when we stand waist deep in the toxin of your past?

"You trivialize us and trivialize the bird that is not in our 31 hands. Is there no context for our lives? No song, no literature, no poem full of vitamins, no history connected to experience that you can pass along to help us start strong? You are an adult. The old one, the wise one. Stop thinking about saving your face. Think of our lives and tell us your particularized world. Make up a story. Narrative is radical, creating us at the very moment it is being created. We will not blame you if your reach exceeds your grasp; if love so ignites your words that they go down in flames and nothing is left but their scald. Or if, with the reticence of a surgeon's hands, your words suture only the places where blood might flow. We know you can never do it properly—once and for all. Passion is never enough; neither is skill. But try. For our sake and yours forget your name in the street; tell us what the world has been to you in the dark places and in the light. Don't tell us what to believe, what to fear. Show us belief's wide skirt and the stitch that unravels fear's caul. You, old woman, blessed with blindness, can speak the language that tells us what only language can: how to see without pictures. Language alone protects us from the scariness of things with no names. Language alone is meditation.

"Tell us what it is to be a woman so that we may know 32 what it is to be a man. What moves at the margin. What it is to have no home in this place. To be set adrift from the one you knew. What it is to live at the edge of towns that cannot bear your company.

"Tell us about ships turned away from shorelines at Easter, 33 placenta in a field. Tell us about a wagonload of slaves, how they sang so softly their breath was indistinguishable from the falling snow. How they knew from the hunch of the nearest shoulder that the next stop would be their last. How, with hands prayered in their sex, they thought of heat, then sun. Lifting their faces as though it was there for the taking. Turning as though there for the taking. They stop at an inn. The driver and his mate go in with the lamp, leaving them humming in the dark. The horse's void steams into the snow beneath its hooves and the hiss and melt are the envy of the freezing slaves.

"The inn door opens: a girl and a boy stop away from its 34 light. They climb into the wagon bed. The boy will have a gun in three years, but now he carries a lamp and a jug of warm cider. They pass it from mouth to mouth. The girl offers bread, pieces of meat and something more: a glance into the eyes of the one she serves. One helping for each man, two for each woman. And a look. They look back. The next stop will be their last. But not this one. This one is warmed."

It's quiet again when the children finish speaking, until the 35 woman breaks into the silence.

"Finally," she says. "I trust you now. I trust you with the 36 bird that is not in your hands because you have truly caught it. Look. How lovely it is, this thing we have done—together."

For Study and Discussion

QUESTIONS FOR RESPONSE

1. What dominant impression do you get from Morrison's speech? How do you think she creates that impression?
2. Who are some of the groups that Morrison condemns for misusing language? What is your response to those condemnations?

QUESTIONS ABOUT PURPOSE

1. Morrison's essay is about something common and important to all of us: language. What insights does she want her listeners to come to about language and its power in their lives?
2. Morrison makes heavy use of metaphor, connotation, and imagery. What do you see as her purpose in using such language?

QUESTIONS ABOUT AUDIENCE

1. Morrison's immediate audience was the small, select group of intellectuals who choose the Nobel Prize winner, but she knew her address would be published and reach a much broader audience. What particular groups among that broader audience do you think she especially wants to reach?
2. A writer who attacks groups of people usually alienates those groups, and they cease to listen or read. What people might Morrison alienate with this essay?

QUESTIONS ABOUT STRATEGIES

1. Consider the image of holding a bird in your hand; what feelings toward that bird does the image trigger for you? Now consider what Morrison accomplishes by saying "I choose to read the bird as language."
2. Morrison is the African-American author of several successful novels; some of the best known are *The Bluest Eye, Sula,* and *Tar*

Baby. What are some ways in which she uses her talent for writing fiction to achieve her purposes in this essay?

QUESTIONS FOR DISCUSSION

1. Morrison sees language as a very powerful instrument and describes some of the ways in which she believes it is abused. What experiences have you had or have heard about in which you think speakers or writers abused the power of language?
2. What adjectives would you use to describe the way Morrison herself uses language in this essay? Why?

JONATHAN RAUCH

Jonathan Rauch was born in Phoenix, Arizona, in 1960 and educated at Yale University. He worked as a reporter for various newspapers before he began contributing essays to periodicals such as the *Atlantic Monthly, New Republic,* and the *New York Times.* He has also been a regular commentator on Cable News Network (CNN) and Cable Satellite Public Affairs Network (C-SPAN). His books include *The Outnation: A Search for the Soul of Japan* (1992), *Kindly Inquisitors: The New Attacks on Free Thought* (1993), and *Government's End: Why Washington Stopped Working* (1999). In "In Defense of Prejudice," reprinted from *Kindly Inquisitors,* Rauch argues that the attempts to limit hate speech can lead to practices worse than the offenses they seek to prevent.

In Defense of Prejudice
Why Incendiary Speech Must Be Protected

THE WAR ON prejudice is now, in all likelihood, the most 1
uncontroversial social movement in America. Opposition to "hate speech," formerly identified with the liberal left, has become a bipartisan piety. In the past year, groups and factions that agree on nothing else have agreed that the public expression of any and all prejudices must be forbidden. On the left, protesters and editorialists have insisted that Francis L. Lawrence resign as president of Rutgers University for describing blacks as "a disadvantaged population that doesn't have that genetic, hereditary background to have a higher average." On the other side of the ideological divide, Ralph Reed, the executive director of the Christian Coalition, responded to criticism of the religious right by calling a press

conference to denounce a supposed outbreak of "namecalling, scapegoating, and religious bigotry." Craig Rogers, an evangelical Christian student at California State University, recently filed a $2.5 million sexual-harassment suit against a lesbian professor of psychology, claiming that anti-male bias in one of her lectures violated campus rules and left him feeling "raped and trapped."

In universities and on Capitol Hill, in workplaces and   2
newsrooms, authorities are declaring that there is no place for racism, sexism, homophobia, Christian-bashing, and other forms of prejudice in public debate or even in private

---

The campaigns to eradicate prejudice—all of them, the speech codes and workplace restrictions and mandatory therapy for accused bigots and all the rest—should stop, now.

---

thought. "Only when racism and other forms of prejudice are expunged," say the crusaders for sweetness and light, "can minorities be safe and society be fair." So sweet, this dream of a world without prejudice. But the very last thing society should do is seek to utterly eradicate racism and other forms of prejudice.

I suppose I should say, in the customary I-hope-I-don't-   3
sound-too-defensive tone, that I am not a racist and that this is not an article favoring racism or any other particular prejudice. It is an article favoring intellectual pluralism, which permits the expression of various forms of bigotry and always will. Although we like to hope that a time will come when no one will believe that people come in types and that each type belongs with its own kind, I doubt such a day will ever arrive. By all indications, *Homo sapiens* is a tribal species for

whom "us versus them" comes naturally and must be continually pushed back. Where there is genuine freedom of expression, there will be racist expression. There will also be people who believe that homosexuals are sick or threaten children or—especially among teenagers—are rightful targets of manly savagery. Homosexuality will always be incomprehensible to most people, and what is incomprehensible is feared. As for anti-Semitism, it appears to be a hardier virus than influenza. If you want pluralism then you get racism and sexism and homophobia, and communism and fascism and xenophobia and tribalism, and that is just for a start. If you want to believe in intellectual freedom and the progress of knowledge and the advancement of science and all those other good things, then you must swallow hard and accept this: for as thickheaded and wayward an animal as us, the realistic question is how to make the best of prejudice, not how to eradicate it.

Indeed, "eradicating prejudice" is so vague a proposition   4
as to be meaningless. Distinguishing prejudice reliably and nonpolitically from non-prejudice, or even defining it crisply, is quite hopeless. We all feel we know prejudice when we see it. But do we? At the University of Michigan, a student said in a classroom discussion that he considered homosexuality a disease treatable with therapy. We was summoned to a formal disciplinary hearing for violating the school's policy against speech that "victimizes" people based on "sexual orientation." Now, the evidence is abundant that this particular hypothesis is wrong, and any American homosexual can attest to the harm that the student's hypothesis has inflicted on many real people. But was it a statement of prejudice or of misguided belief? Hate speech or hypothesis? Many Americans who do not regard themselves as bigots or haters believe that homosexuality is a treatable disease. They may be wrong, but are they all bigots? I am unwilling to say so, and if you are willing, beware. The line between a prejudiced belief and a merely controversial one is elusive, and the harder you look the more elusive it becomes. "God hates homosexuals" is a

statement of fact, not of bias, to those who believe it; "American criminals are disproportionately black" is a statement of bias, not of fact, to those who disbelieve it.

Who is right? You may decide, and so may others, and   5
there is no need to agree. That is the great innovation of intellectual pluralism (which is to say, of post-Enlightenment science, broadly defined). We cannot know in advance or for sure which belief is prejudice and which is truth, but to advance knowledge we don't need to know. The genius of intellectual pluralism lies not in doing away with prejudices and dogmas but in channeling them—making them socially productive by pitting prejudice against prejudice and dogma against dogma, exposing all to withering public criticism. What survives at the end of the day is our base of knowledge.

What they told us in high school about this process is very   6
largely a lie. The Enlightenment tradition taught us that science is orderly, antiseptic, rational, the province of detached experimenters and high-minded logicians. In the popular view, science stands for reason against prejudice, open-mindedness against dogma, calm consideration against passionate attachment—all personified by pop-science icons like the magisterially deductive Sherlock Holmes, the coolly analytic Mr. Spock, the genially authoritative Mr. Science (from our junior-high science films). Yet one of science's dirty secrets is that although science as a whole is as unbiased as anything human can be, scientists are just as biased as anyone else, sometimes more so. "One of the strengths of science," writes the philosopher of science David L. Hull, "is that it does not require that scientists be unbiased, only that different scientists have different biases." Another dirty secret is that, no less than the rest of us, scientists can be dogmatic and pigheaded. "Although this pigheadedness often damages the careers of individual scientists," says Hull, "it is beneficial for the manifest goal of science," which relies on people to invest years in their ideas and defend them passionately. And the dirtiest secret of all, if you believe in the antiseptic popular

view of science, is that this most ostensibly rational of enterprises depends on the most irrational of motives—ambition,
narcissism, animus, even revenge. "Scientists acknowledge
that among their motivations are natural curiosity, the love
of truth, and the desire to help humanity, but other induce-
ments exist as well, and one of them is to 'get that son of a
bitch,'" says Hull. "Time and again, scientists whom I interviewed described the powerful spur that 'showing that son of
a bitch' supplied to their own research."

Many people, I think, are bewildered by this unvarnished   7
and all too human view of science. They believe that for a
system to be unprejudiced, the people in it must also be
unprejudiced. In fact, the opposite is true. Far from eradicating ugly or stupid ideas and coarse or unpleasant motives,
intellectual pluralism relies upon them to excite intellectual
passion and redouble scientific effort. I know of no modern
idea more ugly and stupid than that the Holocaust never
happened, nor any idea more viciously motivated. Yet the
deniers' claims that the Auschwitz gas chambers could not
have worked led to closer study and, in 1993, research showing, at last, how they actually did work. Thanks to prejudice
and stupidity, another opening for doubt has been shut.

An enlightened and efficient intellectual regime lets a mil-   8
lion prejudices bloom, including many that you or I may
regard as hateful or grotesque. It avoids any attempt to stamp
out prejudice, because stamping out prejudice really means
forcing everyone to share the same prejudice, namely that of
whoever is in authority. The great American philosopher
Charles Sanders Peirce wrote in 1877: "When complete
agreement could not otherwise be reached, a general massa-
cre of all who have not thought in a certain way has proved
a very effective means of settling opinion in a country." In
speaking of "settling opinion," Peirce was writing about one
of the two or three most fundamental problems that any
human society must confront and solve. For most societies
down through the centuries, this problem was dealt with in
the manner he described: errors were identified by the
authorities—priests, politburos, dictators—or by mass opin-

ion, and then the error-makers were eliminated along with their putative mistakes. "Let all men who reject the established belief be terrified into silence," wrote Peirce, describing this system. "This method has, from the earliest times, been one of the chief means of upholding correct theological and political doctrines."

Intellectual pluralism substitutes a radically different doctrine: we kill our mistakes rather than each other. Here I draw on another great philosopher, the late Karl Popper, who pointed out that the critical method of science "consists in letting our hypotheses die in our stead." Those who are in error are not (or are not supposed to be) banished or excommunicated or forced to sign a renunciation or required to submit to "rehabilitation" or sent for psychological counseling. It is the error we punish, not the errant. By letting people make errors—even mischievous, spiteful errors (as, for instance, Galileo's insistence on Copernicanism was taken to be in 1633)—pluralism creates room to challenge orthodoxy, think imaginatively, experiment boldly. Brilliance and bigotry are empowered in the same stroke.

Pluralism is the principle that protects and makes a place in human company for that loneliest and most vulnerable of all minorities, the minority who is hounded and despised among blacks and whites, gays and straights, who is suspect or criminal among every tribe and in every nation of the world, and yet on whom progress depends: the dissident. I am not saying that dissent is always or even usually enlightened. Most of the time it is foolish and self-serving. No dissident has the right to be taken seriously, and the fact that Aryan Nation racists or Nation of Islam anti-Semites are unorthodox does not entitle them to respect. But what goes around comes around. As a supporter of gay marriage, for example, I reject the majority's view of family, and as a Jew I reject its view of God. I try to be civil, but the fact is that most Americans regard my views on marriage as a reckless assault on the most fundamental of all institutions, and many people are more than a little discomfited by the statement "Jesus Christ was no more divine than anybody else" (which is why so few people ever say it). Trap the racists and anti-Semites, and you lay a trap for me too. Hunt for them with eradication in your mind, and you have brought dissent itself within your sights.

The new crusade against prejudice waves aside such warn-   11
ings. Like earlier crusades against antisocial ideas, the mission is fueled by good (if cocksure) intentions and a genuine sense of urgency. Some kinds of error are held to be intolerable, like pollutants that even in small traces poison the water for a whole town. Some errors are so pernicious as to damage real people's lives, so wrongheaded that no person of right mind or goodwill could support them. Like their forebears of other stripe—the Church in its campaigns against heretics, the McCarthyites in their campaigns against Communists—the modern anti-racist and anti-sexist and anti-homophobic campaigners are totalists, demanding not that misguided ideas and ugly expressions be corrected or criticized but that they be eradicated. They make war not on errors but on error, and like other totalists they act in the name of public safety—the safety, especially, of minorities.

The sweeping implications of this challenge to pluralism   12
are not, I think, well enough understood by the public at large. Indeed, the new brand of totalism has yet even to be properly named. "Multiculturalism," for instance, is much too broad. "Political correctness" comes closer but is too trendy and snide. For lack of anything else, I will call the new anti-pluralism "purism," since its major tenet is that society cannot be just until the last traces of invidious prejudice have been scrubbed away. Whatever you call it, the purists' way of seeing things has spread through American intellectual life with remarkable speed, so much so that many people will blink at you uncomprehendingly or even call you a racist (or sexist or homophobe, etc.) if you suggest that expressions of racism should be tolerated or that prejudice has its part to play.

The new purism sets out, to begin with, on a campaign   13
against words, for words are the currency of prejudice, and

if prejudice is hurtful then so must be prejudiced words. "We are not safe when these violent words are among us," wrote Mari Matsuda, then a UCLA law professor. Here one imagines gangs of racist words swinging chains and smashing heads in back alleys. To suppress bigoted language seems, at first blush, reasonable, but it quickly leads to a curious result. A peculiar kind of verbal shamanism takes root, as though certain expressions, like curses or magical incantations, carry in themselves the power to hurt or heal—as though words were bigoted rather than people. "Context is everything," people have always said. The use of the word "nigger" in *Huckleberry Finn* does not make the book an "act" of hate speech—or does it? In the new view, this is no longer so clear. The very utterance of the word "nigger" (at least by a non-black) is a racist act. When a *Sacramento Bee* cartoonist put the word "nigger" mockingly in the mouth of a white supremacist, there were howls of protest and 1,400 canceled subscriptions and an editorial apology, even though the word was plainly being invoked against racists, not against blacks.

Faced with escalating demands of verbal absolutism, news- 14 papers issue lists of forbidden words. The expressions "gyp" (derived from "Gypsy") and "Dutch treat" were among the dozens of terms stricken as "offensive" in a much-ridiculed (and later withdrawn) *Los Angeles Times* speech code. The University of Missouri journalism school issued a *Dictionary of Cautionary Words and Phrases,* which included "*Buxom:* Offensive reference to a woman's chest. Do not use. See 'Woman.' *Codger:* Offensive reference to a senior citizen."

As was bound to happen, purists soon discovered that 15 chasing around after words like "gyp" or "buxom" hardly goes to the roots of the problem. As long as they remain bigoted, bigots will simply find other words. If they can't call you a kike then they will say Jewboy, Judas, or Hebe, and when all those are banned they will press words like "oven" and "lampshade" into their service. The vocabulary of hate is potentially as rich as your dictionary, and all you do by banning language used by cretins is to let them decide what the rest of us may say. The problem, some purists have concluded, must therefore go much deeper than laws: it must go to the deeper level of ideas. Racism, sexism, homophobia, and the rest must be built into the very structure of American society and American patterns of thought, so pervasive yet so insidious that, like water to a fish, they are both omnipresent and unseen. The mere existence of prejudice constructs a society whose very nature is prejudiced.

This line of thinking was pioneered by feminists, who 16 argued that pornography, more than just being expressive, is an act by which men construct an oppressive society. Racial activists quickly picked up the argument. Racist expressions are themselves acts of oppression, they said. "All racist speech constructs the social reality that constrains the liberty of non-whites because of their race," wrote Charles R. Lawrence III, then a law professor at Stanford. From the purist point of view, a society with even one racist is a racist society, because the idea itself threatens and demeans its targets. They cannot feel wholly safe or wholly welcome as long as racism is present. Pluralism says: There will always be some racists. Marginalize them, ignore them, exploit them, ridicule them, take pains to make their policies illegal, but otherwise leave them alone. Purists say: That's not enough. Society cannot be just until these pervasive and oppressive ideas are searched out and eradicated.

And so what is now under way is a growing drive to 17 eliminate prejudice from every corner of society. I doubt that many people have noticed how far-reaching this anti-pluralist movement is becoming.

In universities: Dozens of universities have adopted codes 18 proscribing speech or other expression that (this is from Stanford's policy, which is more or less representative) "is intended to insult or stigmatize an individual or a small number of individuals on the basis of their sex, race, color, handicap, religion, sexual orientation or national and ethnic origin." Some codes punish only persistent harassment of a targeted individual, but many, following the purist doctrine that even one racist is too many, go much further. At Penn, an administrator declared: "We at the University of Pennsylvania have guaranteed students and the community that they can live in a community free of sexism, racism, and homophobia." Here is the purism that gives "political correctness" its distinctive combination of puffy high-mindedness and authoritarian zeal.

In school curricula: "More fundamental than eliminating 19 racial segregation has to be the removal of racist thinking, assumptions, symbols, and materials in the curriculum," writes theorist Molefi Kete Asante. In practice, the effort to "remove racist thinking" goes well beyond striking egregious references from textbooks. In many cases it becomes a kind of mental engineering in which students are encouraged to see prejudice everywhere; it includes teaching identity politics as an antidote to internalized racism; it rejects mainstream science as "white male" thinking; and it tampers with history, installing such dubious notions as that the ancient Greeks stole their culture from Africa or that an ancient carving of a bird is an example of "African experimental aeronautics."

In criminal law: Consider two crimes. In each, I am beaten 20 brutally; in each, my jaw is smashed and my skull is split in just the same way. However, in the first crime my assailant calls me an "asshole"; in the second he calls me a "queer." In most states, in many localities, and, as of September 1994, in federal cases, these two crimes are treated differently: the crime motivated by bias—or deemed to be so motivated by prosecutors and juries—gets a stiffer punishment. "Longer prison terms for bigots," shrilled Brooklyn Democratic Congressman Charles Schumer, who introduced the federal hate-crimes legislation, and those are what the law now provides. Evidence that the assailant holds prejudiced beliefs, even if he doesn't actually express them while committing an offense, can serve to elevate the crime. Defendants in hate-crimes cases may be grilled on how many black friends they have and whether they have told racist jokes. To increase a prison sentence only because of the defendant's "prejudice" (as gauged by prosecutor and jury) is, of course, to try minds and punish beliefs. Purists say, Well, they are dangerous minds and poisonous beliefs.

In the workplace: Though government cannot constitu- 21 tionally suppress bigotry directly, it is now busy doing so indirectly by requiring employers to eliminate prejudice. Since the early 1980s, courts and the Equal Employment Opportunity Commission have moved to bar workplace speech deemed to create a hostile or abusive working environment for minorities. The law, held a federal court in 1988, "does require that an employer take prompt action to prevent . . . bigots from expressing their opinions in a way that abuses or offends their co-workers," so as to achieve "the goal of eliminating prejudices and biases from our society." So it was, as UCLA law professor Eugene Volokh notes, that the EEOC charged that a manufacturer's ads using admittedly accurate depictions of samurai, kabuki, and sumo were "racist" and "offensive to people of Japanese origin"; that a Pennsylvania court found that an employer's printing Bible verses on paychecks was religious harassment of Jewish employees; that an employer had to desist using gender-based job titles like "foreman" and "draftsman" after a female employee sued.

On and on the campaign goes, darting from one outbreak   22
of prejudice to another like a cat chasing flies. In the American Bar Association, activists demand that lawyers who express "bias or prejudice" be penalized. In the Education Department, the civil-rights office presses for a ban on computer bulletin board comments that "show hostility toward a person or group based on sex, race or color, including slurs, negative stereotypes, jokes or pranks." In its security checks for government jobs, the FBI takes to asking whether applicants are "free of biases against any class of citizens," whether, for instance, they have told racist jokes or indicated other "prejudices." Joke police! George Orwell, grasping the close relationship of jokes to dissent, said that every joke is a tiny revolution. The purists will have no such rebellions.

The purist campaign reaches, in the end, into the mind   23
itself. In a lecture at the University of New Hampshire, a professor compared writing to sex ("You and the subject become one"); he was suspended and required to apologize, but what was most insidious was the order to undergo university-approved counseling to have his mind straightened out. At the University of Pennsylvania, a law lecturer said, "We have ex-slaves here who should know about the Thir-

teenth Amendment"; he was banished from campus for a year and required to make a public apology, and he, too, was compelled to attend a "sensitivity and racial awareness" session. Mandatory re-education of alleged bigots is the natural consequence of intellectual purism. Prejudice must be eliminated!

Ah, but the task of scouring minds clean is Augean. "Nobody escapes," said a Rutgers University report on campus prejudice. Bias and prejudice, it found, cross every conceivable line, from sex to race to politics: "No matter who you are, no matter what the color of your skin, no matter what your gender or sexual orientation, no matter what you believe, no matter how you behave, there is somebody out there who doesn't like people of your kind." Charles Lawrence writes: "Racism is ubiquitous. We are all racists." If he means that most of us think racist thoughts of some sort at one time or another, he is right. If we are going to "eliminate prejudices and biases from our society," then the work of the prejudice police is unending. They are doomed to hunt and hunt and hunt, scour and scour and scour.

What is especially dismaying is that the purists pursue prejudice in the name of protecting minorities. In order to protect people like me (homosexual), they must pursue people like me (dissident). In order to bolster minority self-esteem, they suppress minority opinion. There are, of course, all kinds of practical and legal problems with the purists' campaign: the incursions against the First Amendment; the inevitable abuses by prosecutors and activists who define as "hateful" or "violent" whatever speech they dislike or can score points off of; the lack of any evidence that repressing prejudice eliminates rather than inflames it. But minorities, of all people, ought to remember that by definition we cannot prevail by numbers, and we generally cannot prevail by force. Against the power of ignorant mass opinion and group prejudice and superstition, we have only our voices. If you doubt that minorities' voices are powerful weapons, think of the lengths to which Southern officials went to silence the Reverend Martin Luther King Jr. (recall that the city commissioner of Montgomery, Alabama, won a $500,000 libel suit, later overturned in *New York Times* v. *Sullivan* [1964], regarding an advertisement in the *Times* placed by civil-rights leaders who denounced the Montgomery police). Think of how much gay people have improved their lot over twenty-five years simply by refusing to remain silent. Recall the Michigan student who was prosecuted for saying that homosexuality is a treatable disease, and notice that he was black. Under that Michigan speech code, more than twenty blacks were charged with racist speech, while no instance of racist speech by whites was punished. In Florida, the hate-speech law was invoked against a black man who called a policeman a "white cracker"; not so surprisingly, in the first hate-crimes case to reach the Supreme Court, the victim was white and the defendant black.

In the escalating war against "prejudice," the right is already learning to play by the rules that were pioneered by the purist activists of the left. Last year leading Democrats, including the President, criticized the Republican Party for being increasingly in the thrall of the Christian right. Some of the rhetoric was harsh ("fire-breathing Christian radical right"), but it wasn't vicious or even clearly wrong. Never mind: when Democratic Representative Vic Fazio said Republicans were "being forced to the fringes by the aggressive political tactics of the religious right," the chairman of the Republican National Committee, Haley Barbour, said, "Christian-bashing" was "the left's preferred form of religious bigotry." Bigotry! Prejudice! "Christians active in politics are now on the receiving end of an extraordinary campaign of bias and prejudice," said the conservative leader William J. Bennett. One discerns, here, where the new purism leads. Eventually, any criticism of any group will be "prejudice."

Here is the ultimate irony of the new purism: words, which pluralists hope can be substituted for violence, are redefined by purists *as* violence. "The experience of being called 'nigger,' 'spic,' 'Jap,' or 'kike' is like receiving a slap in the face," Charles Lawrence wrote in 1990. "Psychic injury is no less an injury than being struck in the face, and it often is far more severe." This kind of talk is commonplace today. Epithets, insults, often even polite expressions of what's taken to be prejudice are called by purists "assaultive speech," "words that wound," "verbal violence." "To me, racial epithets are not speech," one University of Michigan law professor said. "They are bullets." In her speech accepting the 1993 Nobel Prize for Literature in Stockholm, Sweden, the author Toni Morrison said this: "Oppressive language does more than represent violence; it is violence."

It is not violence. I am thinking back to a moment on the   28
subway in Washington, a little thing. I was riding home late one night and a squad of noisy kids, maybe seventeen or eighteen years old, noisily piled into the car. They yelled across the car and a girl said, "Where do we get off?"

A boy said, "Farragut North."   29

The girl: "*Faggot* North!"   30

The boy: "Yeah! Faggot North!"   31

General hilarity.   32

First, before the intellect resumes control, there is a mo- 33
ment of fear, an animal moment. Who are they? How many of them? How dangerous? Where is the way out? All of these things are noted preverbally and assessed by the gut. Then the brain begins an assessment: they are sober, this is probably too public a place for them to do it, there are more girls than boys, they were just talking, it is probably nothing.

They didn't notice me and there was no incident. The   34
teenage babble flowed on, leaving me to think. I became interested in my own reaction: the jump of fear out of nowhere like an alert animal, the sense for a brief time that one is naked and alone and should hide or run away. For a time, one ceases to be a human being and becomes instead a faggot.

The fear engendered by these words is real. The remedy   35
is as clear and as imperfect as ever: protect citizens against violence. This, I grant, is something that American society has never done very well and now does quite poorly. It is no solution to define words as violence or prejudice as oppression, and then by cracking down on words or thoughts

pretend that we are doing something about violence and oppression. No doubt it is easier to pass a speech code or hate-crimes law and proclaim the streets safer than actually to make the streets safer, but the one must never be confused with the other. Every cop or prosecutor chasing words is one fewer chasing criminals. In a world rife with real violence and oppression, full of Rwandas and Bosnias and eleven-year-olds spraying bullets at children in Chicago and in turn being executed by gang lords, it is odious of Toni Morrison to say that words are violence.

Indeed, equating "verbal violence" with physical violence   36 is a treacherous, mischievous business. Not long ago a writer was charged with viciously and gratuitously wounding the feelings and dignity of millions of people. He was charged, in effect, with exhibiting flagrant prejudice against Muslims and outrageously slandering their beliefs. "What is freedom of expression?" mused Salman Rushdie a year after the ayatollahs sentenced him to death and put a price on his head. "Without the freedom to offend, it ceases to exist." I can think of nothing sadder than that minority activists, in their haste to make the world better, should be the ones to forget the lesson of Rushdie's plight: for minorities, pluralism, not purism, is the answer. The campaigns to eradicate prejudice— all of them, the speech codes and workplace restrictions and mandatory therapy for accused bigots and all the rest— should stop, now. The whole objective of eradicating prejudice, as opposed to correcting and criticizing it, should be repudiated as a fool's errand. Salman Rushdie is right, Toni Morrison wrong, and minorities belong at his side, not hers.

For Study and Discussion

QUESTIONS FOR RESPONSE

1. Rauch cites examples from several universities where students and faculty have been censured for saying or writing things that were considered racist, sexist, homophobic, or anti-Semitic; in some cases individuals have lost their jobs or been required to undergo

counseling designed to change their attitudes. Does such an environment prevail at your college or university, and if so, what is your response to it? Why do you think you feel as you do?

2. Almost everyone has, at some time, been hurt by prejudiced and offensive speech directed toward him or her. What was your response in such a situation? What consequences would you wish for the person who offended you to suffer?

QUESTIONS ABOUT PURPOSE

1. What does Rauch see as the long-range consequences of some authorities deciding what kind of speech should be protected and what kinds should be prohibited and penalized?

2. Some might say that, condensed to its simplest form, Rauch's argument is that "sticks and stones may break my bones, but names can never hurt me." How does the insight he hopes to give his readers go far beyond such a folk saying?

QUESTIONS ABOUT AUDIENCE

1. This article was originally published in *Harper's* magazine, a magazine of opinion and inquiry that has been published in the United States for more than one hundred years for educated and informed readers. What knowledge of history can Rauch assume this audience has? How does he use that knowledge of history as the basis for his argument?

2. Why is an American audience likely to be sympathetic to Rauch's argument? How might someone from a different culture respond differently? Why?

QUESTIONS ABOUT STRATEGIES

1. Rauch argues against the currently popular belief that offensive language should be regulated and penalized, yet he points out that as a Jewish homosexual, he fits into two groups that are often verbally abused. How does his giving you this information affect his argument?

2. What strategy is Rauch using in paragraphs 8 and 9? What effect does he achieve with the points he makes here?

QUESTIONS FOR DISCUSSION

1. If, as Rauch says, people shouldn't be prohibited from or punished for expressing prejudice, even when they are deliberately

offensive, how do you think one can respond constructively to a person or group who makes racist or sexist remarks?

2. In the last two paragraphs of his essay, Rauch says directly in paragraph 25 that Toni Morrison is wrong when she says in her essay "The Bird in Our Hand" (paragraph 14) that "oppressive language does more than represent violence; it is violence. . ." Compare Morrison's argument in paragraphs 14 and 15 with Rauch's argument in his last two paragraphs. How do their arguments differ? Which one do you find more effective and why?

KURT VONNEGUT, JR.

Kurt Vonnegut, Jr., was born in 1922 in Indian-
apolis, Indiana, and attended Cornell University,
where he studied biochemistry before being
drafted into the infantry in World War II. Vonnegut was captured by the Germans at the Battle
of the Bulge and sent to Dresden, where he
worked in the underground meat locker of a
slaughterhouse. He miraculously survived the Al-
lied firebombing of Dresden and, following the
war, returned to the United States to study anthropology at the University of Chicago and to
work for a local news bureau. In 1947 Vonnegut
accepted a position writing publicity for the General Electric Research Laboratory in Schenectady,
New York, but left the company in 1950 to work
on his own writing. His first three novels, *Player
Piano* (1952), a satire on the tyrannies of corporate automation; *The Sirens of Titan* (1959), a
science-fiction comedy on the themes of free will
and determination; and *Cat's Cradle* (1963), a
science fantasy on the amorality of atomic scientists, established Vonnegut's reputation as a writer
who could blend humor with serious insights into
the human experience. His most successful novel,
Slaughterhouse-Five, or the Children's Crusade
(1969), is based on his wartime experiences in
Dresden. His other works include *God Bless You,
Mr. Rosewater* (1966), *Breakfast of Champions*
(1973), *Jailbird* (1979), *Palm Sunday* (1981),
Galápagos (1985), *Hocus Pocus* (1990), and
Timequake (1997). His best-known short stories
are collected in *Canary in the Cat House* (1961)
and *Welcome to the Monkey House* (1968). "Harrison Bergeron," reprinted from the latter collection, is the story of the apparatus that a future
society must create to make everyone equal.

Harrison Bergeron

THE YEAR WAS 2081, and everybody was finally equal.   1
They weren't only equal before God and the law. They
were equal every which way. Nobody was smarter than anybody else. Nobody was better looking than anybody else.
Nobody was stronger or quicker than anybody else. All this
equality was due to the 211th, 212th, and 213th Amendments to the Constitution, and to the unceasing vigilance of
agents of the United States Handicapper General.

Some things about living still weren't quite right, though.   2
April, for instance, still drove people crazy by not being
springtime. And it was in that clammy month that the H-G
men took George and Hazel Bergeron's fourteen-year-old
son, Harrison, away.

It was tragic, all right, but George and Hazel couldn't   3
think about it very hard. Hazel had a perfectly average intelligence, which meant she couldn't think about anything except in short bursts. And George, while his intelligence was
way above normal, had a little mental handicap radio in his
ear. He was required by law to wear it at all times. It was
tuned to a government transmitter. Every twenty seconds or
so, the transmitter would send out some sharp noise to keep
people like George from taking unfair advantage of their
brains.

George and Hazel were watching television. There were   4
tears on Hazel's cheeks, but she'd forgotten for the moment
what they were about.

On the television screen were ballerinas.   5

A buzzer sounded in George's head. His thoughts fled in   6
panic, like bandits from a burglar alarm.

"That was a real pretty dance, that dance they just did,"   7
said Hazel.

"Huh?" said George.   8

"That dance—it was nice," said Hazel.   9

"Yup," said George. He tried to think a little about the   10
ballerinas. They weren't really very good—no better than
anybody else would have been, anyway. They were burdened

with sashweights and bags of birdshot, and their faces were masked, so that no one, seeing a free and graceful gesture or a pretty face, would feel like something the cat drug in. George was toying with the vague notion that maybe dancers shouldn't be handicapped. But he didn't get very far with it before another noise in his ear radio scattered his thoughts.

George winced. So did two of the eight ballerinas. 11

Hazel saw him wince. Having no mental handicap herself, 12 she had to ask George what the latest sound had been.

"Sounded like somebody hitting a milk bottle with a ball 13 peen hammer," said George.

"I'd think it would be real interesting, hearing all the 14 different sounds," said Hazel, a little envious. "All the things they think up."

"Um," said George. 15

"Only, if I was Handicapper General, you know what I 16 would do?" said Hazel. Hazel, as a matter of fact, bore a strong resemblance to the Handicapper General, a woman named Diana Moon Glampers. "If I was Diana Moon Glampers," said Hazel, "I'd have chimes on Sunday—just chimes. Kind of in honor of religion."

"I could think, if it was just chimes," said George. 17

"Well—maybe make 'em real loud," said Hazel. "I think 18 I'd make a good Handicapper General."

"Good as anybody else," said George. 19

"Who knows better'n I do what normal is?" said Hazel. 20

"Right," said George. He began to think glimmeringly 21 about his abnormal son who was now in jail, about Harrison, but a twenty-one-gun salute in his head stopped that.

"Boy!" said Hazel, "that was a doozy, wasn't it?" 22

It was such a doozy that George was white and trembling, 23 and tears stood on the rims of his red eyes. Two of the eight ballerinas had collapsed on the studio floor, were holding their temples.

"All of a sudden you look so tired," said Hazel. "Why 24 don't you stretch out on the sofa, so's you can rest your handicap bag on the pillows, honeybunch." She was referring to the forty-seven pounds of birdshot in a canvas bag, which was padlocked around George's neck. "Go on and rest the

bag for a little while," she said. "I don't care if you're not
equal to me for a while."

George weighed the bag with his hands. "I don't mind   25
it," he said. "I don't notice it any more. It's just a part of
me."

"You been so tired lately—kind of wore out," said Hazel.   26
"If there was just some way we could make a little hole in
the bottom of the bag, and just take out a few of them lead
balls. Just a few."

"Two years in prison and two thousand dollars fine for   27
every ball I took out," said George. "I don't call that a
bargain."

"If you could just take a few out when you came home   28
from work," said Hazel. "I mean—you don't compete with
anybody around here. You just set around."

"If I tried to get away with it," said George, "then other   29
people'd get away with it—and pretty soon we'd be right
back to the dark ages again, with everybody competing
against everybody else. You wouldn't like that, would you?"

"I'd hate it," said Hazel.   30

"There you are," said George. "The minute people start   31
cheating on laws, what do you think happens to society?"

If Hazel hadn't been able to come up with an answer to   32
this question, George couldn't have supplied one. A siren was
going off in his head.

"Reckon it'd fall all apart," said Hazel.   33

"What would?" said George blankly.   34

"Society," said Hazel uncertainly. "Wasn't that what you   35
just said?"

"Who knows?" said George.   36

The television program was suddenly interrupted for a   37
news bulletin. It wasn't clear at first as to what the bulletin
was about, since the announcer, like all announcers, had a
serious speech impediment. For about half a minute, and in
a state of high excitement, the announcer tried to say, "Ladies
and gentlemen—"

He finally gave up, handed the bulletin to a ballerina to   38
read.

"That's all right—" Hazel said to the announcer, "he tried. 39
That's the big thing. He tried to do the best he could with
what God gave him. He should get a nice raise for trying so
hard."

"Ladies and gentlemen—" said the ballerina, reading the 40
bulletin. She must have been extraordinarily beautiful, because the mask she wore was hideous. And it was easy to see
that she was the strongest and most graceful of all the dancers, for her handicap bags were as big as those worn by
two-hundred-pound men.

And she had to apologize at once for her voice, which was 41
a very unfair voice for a woman to use. Her voice was a warm,
luminous, timeless melody. "Excuse me—" she said, and she
began again, making her voice absolutely uncompetitive.

"Harrison Bergeron, age fourteen," she said in a grackle 42
squawk, "has just escaped from jail, where he was held on
suspicion of plotting to overthrow the government. He is a
genius and an athlete, is under-handicapped, and should be
regarded as extremely dangerous."

A police photograph of Harrison Bergeron was flashed on 43
the screen upside down, then sideways, upside down again,
then right side up. The picture showed the full length of
Harrison against a background calibrated in feet and inches.
He was exactly seven feet tall.

The rest of Harrison's appearance was Halloween and 44
hardware. Nobody had ever borne heavier handicaps. He had
outgrown hindrances faster than the H-G men could think
them up. Instead of a little ear radio for a mental handicap,
he wore a tremendous pair of earphones, and spectacles with
thick wavy lenses. The spectacles were intended to make him
not only half blind, but to give him whanging headaches
besides.

Scrap metal was hung all over him. Ordinarily, there was 45
a certain symmetry, a military neatness to the handicaps issued to strong people, but Harrison looked like a walking
junkyard. In the race of life, Harrison carried three hundred
pounds.

And to offset his good looks, the H-G men required that 46

he wear at all times a red rubber ball for a nose, keep his
eyebrows shaved off, and cover his even white teeth with
black caps at snaggle-tooth random.

"If you see this boy," said the ballerina, "do not—I repeat,   47
do not—try to reason with him."

There was the shriek of a door being torn from its hinges.   48

Screams and barking cries of consternation came from the   49
television set. The photograph of Harrison Bergeron on the
screen jumped again and again, as though dancing to the tune
of an earthquake.

George Bergeron correctly identified the earthquake, and   50
well he might have—for many was the time his own home
had danced to the same crashing tune. "My God—" said
George, "that must be Harrison!"

The realization was blasted from his mind instantly by the   51
sound of an automobile collision in his head.

When George could open his eyes again, the photograph   52
of Harrison was gone. A living, breathing Harrison filled the
screen.

Clanking, clownish, and huge, Harrison stood in the cen-   53
ter of the studio. The knob of the uprooted studio door was
still in his hand. Ballerinas, technicians, musicians, and announcers cowered on their knees before him, expecting to
die.

"I am the Emperor!" cried Harrison. "Do you hear? I am   54
the Emperor! Everybody must do what I say at once!" He
stamped his foot and the studio shook.

"Even as I stand here—" he bellowed, "crippled, hobbled,   55
sickened—I am a greater ruler than any man who ever lived!
Now watch me become what I *can* become!"

Harrison tore the straps of his handicap harness like wet   56
tissue paper, tore straps guaranteed to support five thousand
pounds.

Harrison's scrap-iron handicaps crashed to the floor.   57

Harrison thrust his thumbs under the bars of the padlock   58
that secured his head harness. The bar snapped like celery.
Harrison smashed his headphones and spectacles against the
wall.

He flung away his rubber-ball nose, revealed a man that 59
would have awed Thor, the god of thunder.

"I shall now select my Empress!" he said, looking down 60
on the cowering people. "Let the first woman who dares rise
to her feet claim her mate and her throne!"

A moment passed, and then a ballerina arose, swaying like 61
a willow.

Harrison plucked the mental handicap from her ear, 62
snapped off her physical handicaps with marvelous delicacy.
Last of all, he removed her mask.

She was blindingly beautiful. 63

"Now—" said Harrison, taking her hand, "shall we show 64
the people the meaning of the word dance? Music!" he commanded.

The musicians scrambled back into their chairs, and Har- 65
rison stripped them of their handicaps, too. "Play your best,"
he told them, "and I'll make you barons and dukes and earls."

The music began. It was normal at first—cheap, silly, false. 66
But Harrison snatched two musicians from their chairs,
waved them like batons as he sang the music as he wanted it
played. He slammed them back into their chairs.

The music began again and was much improved. 67

Harrison and his Empress merely listened to the music for 68
a while—listened gravely, as though synchronizing their
heartbeats with it.

They shifted their weights to their toes. 69

Harrison placed his big hands on the girl's tiny waist, 70
letting her sense the weightlessness that would soon be hers.

And then, in an explosion of joy and grace, into the air 71
they sprang!

Not only were the laws of the land abandoned, but the law 72
of gravity and the laws of motion as well.

They reeled, whirled, swiveled, flounced, capered, gam- 73
boled, and spun.

They leaped like deer on the moon. 74

The studio ceiling was thirty feet high, but each leap 75
brought the dancers nearer to it.

It became their obvious intention to kiss the ceiling. 76

They kissed it. 77

And then, neutralizing gravity with love and pure will, they 78
remained suspended in air inches below the ceiling, and they
kissed each other for a long, long time.

It was then that Diana Moon Glampers, the Handicapper 79
General, came into the studio with a double-barreled ten-
gauge shotgun. She fired twice, and the Emperor and the
Empress were dead before they hit the floor.

Diana Moon Glampers loaded the gun again. She aimed 80
it at the musicians and told them they had ten seconds to get
their handicaps back on.

It was then that the Bergerons' television tube burned out. 81

Hazel turned to comment about the blackout to George. 82
But George had gone out into the kitchen for a can of beer.

George came back in with the beer, paused while a handi- 83
cap signal shook him up. And then he sat down again. "You
been crying?" he said to Hazel.

"Yup," she said. 84

"What about?" he said. 85

"I forgot," she said. "Something real sad on television." 86

"What was it?" he said. 87

"It's all kind of mixed up in my mind," said Hazel. 88

"Forget sad things," said George. 89

"I always do," said Hazel. 90

"That's my girl," said George. He winced. There was the 91
sound of a rivetting gun in his head.

"Gee—I could tell that one was a doozy," said Hazel. 92

"You can say that again," said George. 93

"Gee—" said Hazel, "I could tell that one was a doozy." 94

COMMENT ON "HARRISON BERGERON"

Known for his offbeat and sometimes bizarre vision of reality, Kurt Vonnegut, Jr., has created in "Harrison Bergeron" a science fiction story full of black humor and grotesque details. The society he creates in the story is reminiscent of the society pictured in Orwell's *1984*, totally controlled by a government that invades and interferes in every facet of its citizens' lives. In a travesty of the famous declaration that "All men are created equal," the government has set out to legislate equality. Vonnegut portrays the results of such legislation in macabre images of people forced to carry weighted bags to reduce their strength, wear grotesque masks to conceal their beauty, and suffer implants in their brain to disrupt their thinking. When a fourteen-year-old boy, Harrison Bergeron, shows signs of excellence, he is first arrested, then ruthlessly destroyed when he throws off his restraints and literally rises to the top.

Underneath the farce, Vonnegut has created a tragic picture of a culture so obsessed with equality that people must be leveled by decree. Mediocrity reigns; any sign of excellence or superiority threatens law and order and must be suppressed immediately. Ultimately, of course, such a society will perish because it will kill its talent and stagnate.

Vonnegut wrote this story in 1961, after the repressive Stalinist regime that wiped out thousands of leaders and intellectuals in Russia; it precedes by a few years the disastrous era of Mao's Red Guards in China, when hundreds of thousands of intellectuals and artists were killed or imprisoned in the name of equality. Is Vonnegut commenting on the leveling tendencies of these totalitarian societies? Or does he see such excesses reflected in our own society? No one knows, but it's the genius of artists to prod us to think about such concerns.

Persuasion and Argument as a Writing Strategy

1. Reread several of the essays in this section, and decide which one or two appeal to you most. Then analyze your response to those essays—to their topic, their tone, their vocabulary, their use of personal anecdotes or narratives, and to the kind of arguments the author presented. Why do you think you liked your one or two choices better than the rest or found them more convincing? What was it about them that appealed to you, a college student, even though you were not the intended reader for that essay? Finally, draw a general conclusion about what you think the author or authors have done that made their work effective for you and what lesson you could take for your own writing.

2. Reread "I Have a Dream" by Martin Luther King, Jr., and "A Chinaman's Chance" by Eric Liu. Write an essay comparing King's dreams and hopes for African Americans with the American Dream that Liu wants to hang on to for his generation. What components of the two dreams are similar? To what extent do you think King and Liu would agree with each other? Conclude on a personal note by sketching out your own version of the American Dream and indicating how you hope to achieve it.

3. For an opinion column for your campus newspaper or perhaps for an on-line magazine like *Salon,* write a persuasive essay pointing out the advantages and rewards of investing substantial chunks of time in learning to navigate the Internet. Such advantages could be financial, recreational, academic, or intellectual—or you might argue that the Internet is just a lot of fun. On the other hand, you could write a comparable essay for the same audience pointing out the disadvantages and frustrations of investing your time on the Internet. For either essay, use specific examples of items you've encountered on the Net and

describe personal experiences to illustrate your claims and enliven your writing.

4. Write a persuasive article for either your hometown newspaper or your campus newspaper in which you try to get a local company or industry to contribute its support to a civic project, either one that exists or one that you design. Such a project might be restoring dilapidated homes for people who need housing, sponsoring a literacy project, or sponsoring a remodeling project for a public playground. Be specific about how the company could help and how it would benefit. You might reread the introduction to this section to help you frame your argument and establish your tone.

5. For an audience of your classmates and your instructor, write an essay in which you give examples of Toni Morrison's use of images and vivid language and her appeals to emotion in "The Bird in Our Hand." Compare her strategies with the cause-and-effect propositions and the appeals to historical precedents that Jonathan Rauch uses in "In Defense of Prejudice." Give several examples from each author. In your conclusion, explain which author's appeal you would find most effective if these writers were addressing an audience of college students.

6. By having a core of basic requirements that everyone must meet in order to get a degree, most colleges and universities affirm that to be considered educated, a person needs to have mastered a certain body of knowledge. Usually the requirements include history, literature, and science courses, and often some courses in philosophy and fine arts. Check out the requirements for a liberal arts degree at your institution. Then, for an audience of your classmates and instructor, discuss what the required courses should cover. For instance, should everyone have to take American history and literature, should everyone have to pass a proficiency test in writing and mathematics, should everyone have to take at least two science courses? Or are requirements superfluous and stifling? Support your argument with reasons and evidence.

RESOURCES
FOR
WRITING

As you worked your way through this book, you discovered that you already possess many resources for reading and writing. You read essays on a wide variety of subjects. You encountered new and complicated information shaped by unusual and unsettling assertions. But you discovered experiences and feelings that you recognize—the challenge of learning, the ordeal of disappointment, the cost of achievement. As you examined these essays, you realized that you had something to say about your reading, something to contribute to the writers' interpretation of some complex subjects. Your reading revealed your resources for writing.

Your work with this book has also enabled you to identify and practice using patterns that at each stage of the writing process will help you transform your resources into writing. In the beginning, these patterns give rise to questions that you might ask about any body of information.

Suppose you want to write an essay on women's contributions to science. You might begin by asking why so few women are ranked among the world's great scientists. You might continue asking questions: What historical forces have discouraged women from becoming scientists (cause and effect)? How do women scientists define problems, analyze evidence, formulate conclusions (process analysis), and do they go about these processes in ways different from the ways used by men scientists (comparison and contrast)? If women scientists look at the world differently from the way men do, does this difference have an effect on the established notions of inquiry (argument)? Such questions work like the different lenses you attach to a camera: each lens gives you a slightly different perspective on your subject.

Your initial questions enable you to envision your subject from different perspectives. Answering one question encourages you to develop your subject according to a purpose associated with one of the common patterns of organization. For instance, if you decide to write about your first scuba dive, your choice of purpose seems obvious: to answer the question, What happened? You would then proceed to write a narrative essay. In drafting this essay, however, you may discover questions you had not anticipated, such as: What factors led to the development of scuba diving? How do you use scuba equipment? How is scuba diving similar to or different from swimming?

Responding to these new questions forces you to decide whether your new information develops or distorts your draft. The history of underwater diving—from diving bells to diving suits to self-contained equipment—may help your readers see a context for your narrative. On the other hand, such information may confuse them, distracting them from your original purpose: to tell what happened.

As you struggle with your new resources, you may decide that your original purpose no longer drives your writing. You may decide to change your purpose and write a cause-and-effect essay. Instead of telling what happened on your first scuba dive, you might decide to use your personal experience, together with some reading, to write a more scientific essay analyzing the effects of underwater swimming on your senses of sight and hearing.

This book has helped you make such decisions by showing you how the common patterns of organization evoke different purposes, audiences, and strategies. In this final section, you will have the opportunity to make such decisions about a new collection of resources—an anthology of writing on the subject of the Internet.

Before you begin reading these selections, take an initial inventory.

- What kind of direct experience have you had with the Internet?
    In an average day, how often do you log on?
    What do you use it for?
    What kind of odd or surprising information have you found while browsing?
- What kind of indirect experience have you had with the Internet?
    How often do the people in your family use it?
    How do your fellow students use it?
    How do your teachers expect you to use it?
- What do you know about the place of the Internet in American culture?
    How old is the Internet?
    What improvements have been made since it was first launched?
    Why is access to the Internet seen as a major social issue in our public debates?
    Why has the Internet become as commonplace as the telephone?

What do you believe about the Internet?
In what ways is it the major technological advance of
our time?
In what way does it simply complicate our lives by
providing more information than anyone can use?

Thinking about such questions will remind you of the
extensive resources you bring to the subject of the Internet.
It is a subject that touches all of our lives in some way. And
it affects our behavior in countless other ways—what we do
with our spare time, with whom we associate, how we spend
our money, and how we think about ourselves (i.e., informed
citizens or information dropouts).

After you have made a preliminary inventory of your
knowledge and attitudes toward the Internet, read the writings in this section. You will notice that each selection asks
you to look at the Internet from a different perspective:

1. *What happened? (Narration and Description).* Wendy
   Lesser recounts her resistance to and then her immersion
   in the world of e-mail.
2. *How do you do it? (Process Analysis).* William Zinsser analyzes the process of using the keyboard on this "new"
   writing tool.
3. *How is it similar to or different from something else? (Comparison and Contrast).* John Steele Gordon compares the
   major technology breakthrough of the nineteenth century—the railroad—with the major technology breakthrough of our time—the Internet.
4. *What kind of subdivision does it contain? (Division and
   Classification).* Dave Barry classifies the strange and useless
   websites he has found on the web.
5. *How would you characterize it? (Definition).* Laura Miller
   defines the traditional frontier as a way of exposing the
   problems with the phrase—*electronic frontier.*
6. *How did it happen? (Cause and Effect).* M. Kadi analyzes
   the flaws in the analysis that suggests the Internet will
   bring about world understanding.

7. *How can you prove it? (Persuasion and Argument).* Evan
   I. Schwartz argues that virtual communities may reinforce
   communities in real space and time.

The collection ends with William Gibson's story, "Burning
Chrome," a science fiction tale about two hackers who try to
circumvent the global systems of computer security. The
story raises all sorts of questions about neuroelectronics,
computer security, and social policy.

As you examine these selections, keep track of how your
reading expands your resources—provoking memories, adding information, and suggesting questions you had not considered when you made your initial inventory about the
Internet. Because this information will give you new ways to
think about your original questions, you will want to explore
your thinking in writing.

The assignments that follow each selection suggest several
ways that you can use these resources for writing:

1. You can *respond* to the essay by shaping a similar experience
   according to its method of organization.
2. You can *analyze* the essay to discover how the writer uses
   specific strategies to communicate a purpose to an audience.
3. You can use the essay as a springboard for an essay that
   argues a similar thesis in a different context.
4. You can *compare* the essay to other selections in the anthology that raise similar questions about the Internet. At
   the end of each writing assignment, one or two selections
   are suggested as Resources for Comparison.

Drawing on your experience, reading, and familiarity with
writing strategies, you are ready to work up a writing assignment on any subject.

WENDY LESSER

Wendy Lesser was born in Santa Monica, California, in 1952 and educated at Howard University, Kings College (Cambridge University), and the University of California, Berkeley. She worked for several years for a public policy consulting firm before becoming the founding editor of *Threepenny Review.* Her books include *The Life Below the Ground: A Study of the Subterranean in Literature and History* (1987), *His Other Half: Men Looking at Women Through Art* (1991), *Pictures at an Execution* (1993), and *The Amateur: An Independent Life of Letters* (1999). In "The Conversion," reprinted from the journal *Creative Nonfiction* (1996), Lesser describes how e-mail altered her life.

The Conversion

I RESISTED E-MAIL for at least two or three years. Many of my Berkeley friends are academics, so they got it automatically as part of their jobs and then annoyingly sang its praises. "It replaces long-distance phone calls!" "You can dig up old recipes from libraries across the Midwest!" "It allows you to communicate instantaneously with colleagues from South Africa!" None of these seemed like things I particularly wanted to do. Moreover, I had strong if somewhat irrational reasons for resisting. I did not want my computer talking on the phone to anyone else's computer, because who knew what could happen once you opened up those lines? I wasn't just worried about viruses, though those were indeed a concern; but how could you be sure that someone wouldn't sneak through the e-mail door and thereby penetrate your hard disk, stealing or at any rate messing up your closely held documents? I preferred to keep my computer chaste and self-contained, aloof from all potential communicants. And then, I didn't see the point of getting those unreadable little messages that seemed to go on forever, with little or no punctuation. To judge by the e-mail I had read in newspapers and magazines (the kind that was always reproduced to show how fun and liberating this new mode of communication was), these emissions were somewhere below the level of the

---

Like all tools, e-mail is more than just a simple replacement of the previous technology—it acts on you as well as you on it, and it acts in ways you can't always predict.

---

worst unsolicited manuscripts I habitually receive in the course of editing a literary magazine. Why should I want to read *more* of the stuff, especially on a barely legible computer screen? What was the good of a technological form that erased the boundary between intimate friends and total strangers, reducing everyone to a digital printout? Where was *handwriting* in all this? Where was *personal style*?

I should interrupt my screed to say that I am not a complete antitechnologist. I watch more television than just about anyone I know, and believe that *Hill Street Blues* and *NYPD Blue* are among the major artistic achievements of late twentieth-century America. I use the latest (well, the second-latest) desktop publishing equipment to put out my magazine, and rely on a rather complex database software to organize its subscriber list. I adore the fax machine and have long considered it the single greatest invention since the telephone—the fax machine, after all, respects and transmits handwriting, just as the telephone conveys the nuances of the individual voice. I am not, that is, a hermit. I constantly employ and enjoy electronic transmissions of all sorts, and I do not feel that they in any way sap my capacity to be an Emersonian individual. On the contrary, they enhance it: without all my little machines, I could not make a living as a self-employed, self-designated arbiter of cultural taste. In Emerson's time, you had to inherit a comfortable income if you wished to subsist as a man of letters; in our day, technology can substitute for and even generate the freeing effects of wealth.

But for some reason this dashing perspective, this reso- 3 lutely cheerful optimism about mechanical progress, did not make a dent in my fear of e-mail. From the perspective of one who has now crossed the great divide, I can see that my phobia stemmed in part from a category error. That is, I thought that "e-mail" and "the Internet" were identical: I believed that in order to communicate with my friends and colleagues, I would have to place myself squarely in front of all the oncoming lanes of traffic in the Information Superhighway. Worse: I was persuaded that those snippets of generic e-mail clipped from the bulletin boards of the Internet represented what my own friends would sound like if I had to talk to them by computer. I wrongly supposed that the machine controlled its own content, that the medium (as we used to say, *pace* McLuhan, in the '60s) would be the message.

Why I should have believed Marshall McLuhan in this 4 respect when I had long since discarded his views on television is a question that perhaps requires a cultural psychotherapist to answer. (I don't know that there *is* such a thing as a cultural psychotherapist, but since I have recently learned of something called "ecopsychology"—which is designed to help us bond with Mother Earth—I assume there are no limits.) For some reason, fear makes us believe in false prophets, the more apocalyptic the better. Clinging to the printed pages of my old-fashioned literary quarterly and my beloved cloth- and paperbound books, I thought that e-mail spelt the end of reading as I knew it. After all, you couldn't do it in the bathtub.

Well, there are lots of things you can't do in the bathtub 5
and even I have to admit that doesn't make them useless or
unacceptable. I wouldn't want to read a novel or even a
ten-page story on e-mail, and faced with that little message
screen, I probably couldn't compose an essay worth printing.
But for daily correspondence, electronic mail has become my
essential instrument. And like all tools, it is more than just a
simple replacement of the previous technology—it acts on
you as well as you on it, and it acts in ways you can't always
predict. In effect, e-mail has restored the personal letter to
my life.

If you are like me, you went through a phase when per- 6
sonal letters occupied a central place in your existence. You
were probably in your late teens or early twenties. Possibly
you were living away from home for the first time, or perhaps
you had just embarked on your first long-term (and long-
distance) love affair, or maybe you were traveling alone
through Europe, or all of the above. The mail became your
lifeline, and you honored it accordingly. You poured everything into your letters—the engaging details of daily existence, the special sights, the serious emotions, the witty
observations—to such an extent that even journal-keeping,
by comparison, seemed onerous and redundant. You tailored
each letter to the personality of the recipient, delightedly
imagining the eventual response to the in-jokes of a shared
history. You received as good as you gave, and each day's mail
delivery marked an emotional high or low point. And then,
at some point, you grew out of all this, and household bills,
business letters, magazines, and fund-raising pleas came to fill
your mailbox instead.

Just as personal letters define a phase in an individual's life, 7
so do they also define a period in Western history. I didn't
realize this until I read P. N. Furbank's review of the *Oxford
Book of Letters*, wherein he remarks

> . . . *how deprived the ancient world was, not having
> discovered the secret of personal letters—long, spon-
> taneous, chatty letters, as funny as they can be made
> but not always just funny, and coming nice and*

> *often—the sort of letters you might have got if you*
> *had known Henry James or Bernard Shaw or Philip*
> *Larkin. You would have been expected to answer*
> *them, and that would have been marvelous too, at*
> *least for oneself. It would be like enjoying a second*
> *life.*

Exactly. And, as Furbank goes on to say, "The ancients knew nothing of this. With what leaden spirits one would have received a letter from Cicero! One may hazard that this best kind of letter-writing began in the eighteenth century and really came into its own in the nineteenth." Not coincidentally, this was just when the postal system was reaching a pinnacle of service, in terms of frequency and reliability.

For one of the keys to the pleasure of letters lies in that 8 half-buried little phrase, "and coming nice and often." In London, where P. N. Furbank lives, mail is still delivered twice a day, and a letter posted first-class will reach its destination anywhere in the United Kingdom by the next day. It is still possible to keep up a satisfying personal correspondence under such circumstances. For the rest of the world, however, mail is generally too slow to gratify the needs of the moment. You might choose to rely on the stamp and envelope on special occasions, or for particularly delicate communications, or if (like a young person in her teens or twenties) you live on a very limited budget; but when you have something important to say, you're much more likely to pick up the telephone.

The crisis in my attitude toward e-mail occurred when I 9 realized that I would no longer be able to afford the telephone. I was about to leave America for four months, and to indulge in long-distance calling from Europe would be ruinously expensive. Nor could I tolerate waiting the two weeks it would take for the round-trip communication by post. It was e-mail or nothing.

One problem with e-mail, though, is that it takes two 10 actively willing participants. Anyone in the modern world can receive a postal letter, but only those with an e-mail hookup can receive e-mail. So I had to get my near and dear to join up at the same time I did. Among those I had to persuade was a writer in New York, a friend of twenty years' standing on whom I normally lavish at least one long-distance phone call a day. As he is even more of a Luddite than I am, this was no easy task.

"I feel very resistant to the idea," he explained.   11

"I know, I know," I said. "I've already been resistant for   12
three years, so can't we take it as done?"

Finally, I just cheated. I ordered *his* CompuServe intro-   13
ductory package when I ordered my own, knowing that when the user-friendly software slipped through his mail slot, he would be unable to resist trying it on. (Or, to put it more truthfully: I planned to make life miserable for him via telephone until he got around to applying his e-mail diskettes.)

It was slow to catch on. At first my friend and I used e-mail   14
mainly as a toy, in between the more substantial communication of our transcontinental phone calls, and most of our electronic conversation was metaconversation, in that it dealt with the ins and outs of using e-mail. But when I left California on a Wednesday night, arrived in London on a Thursday morning, hooked up my computer, received my New York friend's welcoming message, and instantly e-mailed back—well, that was a revelation for both of us. Soon we were up to three or even four exchanges a day. The five-hour time difference meant nothing: he could post a note before he went to sleep, and I would receive it when I woke up the next day. And what I discovered, to my enormous pleasure, was that the electronic mode did not wash out his characteristic tones. On the contrary, he sounded in his virtual incarnation exactly as he did in real life: wry, observant, dryly affectionate, subtle, and sharp. Personal style, it turned out, did not get blotted out by the machine. In some ways it was even enhanced, with new opportunities for humorous self-expression and literary allusion afforded by the title spaces in our messages. "Internettled," his title bar announced when he had been fiddling all day to make the machine do something new. "Later the Same Day," I called one of my frequent

messages, echoing Grace Paley. And it was inevitable, given the technology, that we would soon feel inspired to use E. M. Forster's "Only connect."

Even in our differing responses to the availability of e-mail, 15 my friend and I were faithful to our respective personalities. Something of a self-styled loner, he built up a tiny, highly selective list of e-mail addresses and mailed only to those two or three people. (His willful resistance to technological self-education may have had something to do with this. "How do you communicate with those outside our parish?" he once complained, stumped by the difficulty of crossing over from CompuServe to America Online or Prodigy.)

I, on the other hand, verged on epistolary promiscuity. 16 Within my first week on-line, I had mailed to a number of my Berkeley pals, a long-lost classmate in Tasmania, three Londoners, my husband at his work address, my stepson at college, my father, my sister, a good friend who had temporarily moved to St. Louis, and my exercise teacher. I became an e-mail maniac, checking in every hour or so and collapsing with disappointment if I got the empty-mailbox beep. I found myself waxing expansive onscreen, chatting on about virtually nothing. I was responding, I now think, to the special enticements of the form's mixed nature—at once private and public, solitary and communal, so that it seems to combine the two oldest types of American writing, the diary and the sermon. With e-mail, you begin with the former, alone at your desk, and end (if you use your "multiple send" button) with the latter, broadcasting to the whole congregation.

One of the first responses I got from old e-mail hands, 17 when I contacted them with my newly acquired address, was scorn at the impersonal nature of my mailing moniker. Everybody else, it appeared, had managed to craft idiosyncratic, sometimes poetic, always memorable labels for themselves. Using the loose conventions set up by most e-mail providers, they had come up with word combinations that were nearly as distinctive as their own names (and that often incorporated those names into the address). But CompuServe allowed for no such creativity: we were simply allocated a number. "Your address sounds like something from the Planet Zog," one of my correspondents wrote. Another mocked me for my long resistance to e-mail. "This is just the kind of address I would expect a confirmed Luddite to get," he noted. "Those who resist the machine are doomed to be punished by it."

Whatever form it takes, your e-mail address becomes a part 18 of your permanent identity in a way that no mere phone number can. For one thing, you can't hide it. You can make an obscene phone call from an anonymous number or mail a poison pen letter without giving a return address, but your e-mail message carries its provenance in its heading. This necessary mutuality is both e-mail's virtue and its curse. That is, you have to consider before engaging in any communication whether you want to hear *from* someone as well as speak *to* him, because he will thereafter possess your address. There are no one-way assaults in the world of e-mail: if you launch a missive, you automatically open yourself up to a counter-attack.

And unlike a phone number, which can be as temporary 19 as your present whereabouts, your e-mail address travels with you. I had exactly the same CompuServe number during my European stay as during my normal Berkeley life. People seeking to contact me didn't have to know I was out of the country or even out of the office. Sometimes I would amuse myself by trying to imagine where my virtual mailbox was located. Did it float somewhere in the fourth dimension, rushing into my computer only when it was actually consulted? Or did it hover somewhere over the Atlantic, relaying messages between my temporarily European self and my North American correspondents? I had been told it was in cyberspace—but what kind of space *was* that, exactly? Thinking such thoughts is a bit like trying to imagine how one's voice gets through those little telephone wires into the other person's receiver, only more so. You regress to your childhood self, for whom all such concepts are made concrete and miniature: the little person inside the telephone receiver, the tiny mailbox inside the computer. And the fact that my computer was itself a laptop (a ridiculously compact mechanism which, the dealer told me, was more powerful than the huge computer that had flown the first man to the moon) made the miniaturization imagery even more credible.

I discovered just how portable my e-mail was when a thief 20 crept into my house and walked off with my computer. One day I had been happily communicating with the entire world, the next I was reduced to virtual silence. My anxiety at the loss of my equipment was exacerbated by my sense of all the messages I was missing. I had become dependent on my daily fix, and the burglar, as if guessing at this aspect of my psychology, had even cut the phone wire that led into the computer—a symbolic act, easily remedied by the purchase of a new wire, but one that drove home for me my feeling of violent interruption. "I feel as if I'm hemorrhaging information," I told my husband. But information was only the half of it. All the little pieces of *me* that I had been feeding into cyberspace were loosed into the world, never to return.

Yet when I got a new computer, hooked myself back up 21 to CompuServe, and checked my old mailbox, there it still was, just as if no interruption had ever occurred. My e-mail had been patiently waiting for me out there in Nowhere Land, the messages accumulating until I was once again able to pick them up. The beauty of the system, it turns out, is precisely that it's *not* connected to any physical object. They can steal the transmitting device from you, but the mail service continues unabated in its ideal Platonic form—temporarily inaccessible, maybe, but always ready to be picked up. I had my answer to Bishop Berkeley's question: if the tree had fallen in cyberspace, the sound could simply have waited decades or generations or millennia until someone came along to hear it, and *then* it would have existed. In this respect, as in so much else, e-mail's qualities are strangely mixed. It is both speedy to the point of instantaneousness, and arrested in a state of timelessness.

So have I lost my soul to e-mail? I think not. Of course, 22 proper use of it requires some mastery, and particularly self-mastery. One's initial subservience to the medium's surprising delights is inevitably a bit enslaving. (But this must have been true of all new media, even the cave paint at Lascaux.) Still, once it has been brought under control and made to function in the life you have already constructed for yourself, e-mail can be a great gift. If you keep all those strangers and business connections and mass-directory people off your screen, it can be, as Furbank put it, "like enjoying a second life." You will be rewarded with all the old-fashioned pleasures of the intimate personal letter. You will be offered, in other words, the chance to *gain* a soul rather than lose one. As an agnostic, I'm not even sure I believe in the very idea of a soul; but if I had to say where it resides, I would point to the thing in us that allows us to be and have intimate friends. And e-mail, by bringing back personal correspondence, reintroduces us to the form of writing that best enables us to know and acknowledge friendship.

Topics for Writing
Narration and Description

1. *Respond.* Research the way you use e-mail with family and friends. How often do you check your screen? How long are your messages? How long can you wait for a reply before you become impatient? Use your own experience to write an advice column for your local paper describing the proper use of e-mail. In particular, explain why it "requires some mastery, and particularly self-mastery." (*Resources for Comparison:* Maya Angelou, "My Name Is Margaret," page 29; George Orwell, "Shooting an Elephant," page 64).

2. *Analyze.* Consider Lesser's admiration for the personal letter. Did you ever write such letters, or did someone in your family write such letters? Or are you part of the generation who transmitted personal messages by telephone? In an essay for your communications class, analyze how effective e-mail enables people to carry on a conversation. You may want to consider the e-mail documents of your friends, describing their special addresses, jargon, and secret codes. (*Resources for Comparison:* Doris Kearns Goodwin, "Keeping the Scorebook," page 37; Alice Adams, "Truth or Consequences," page 74).

3. *Argue.* In an e-mail posted to all your friends, provide some evidence to support Lesser's argument that e-mail "reintroduces us to the form of writing that best enables us to know and acknowledge friendships." Consider your mailing list carefully before you send your message. Remember your readers have the ability to reply instantly. Some of your friends may want to read such theorizing; others may wonder if you have broken the rules of the game by revealing too much about yourself and your need for correspondence. (*Resources for Comparison:* Judith Ortiz Cofer, "The Myth of the Latin Woman: I Just Met a Girl Named María," page 44; Andre Dubus, "Digging," page 53).

WILLIAM ZINSSER

William Zinsser was born in New York City in
1922 and educated at Princeton University. He
has worked as a journalist for the *New York Herald
Tribune,* a writing teacher at Yale University, and
an executive editor of the Book-of-the-Month
Club. Zinsser's books include a novel, *The Para-
dise Bit* (1967); a biography, *Willie and Dwike: An
American Profile* (1984); a popular writing textbook, *On Writing Well: An Informal Guide to
Writing Nonfiction* (1976); and several anthologies devoted to particular kinds of writing such as
Inventing the Truth: The Art and Craft of Memoir
(1987), *Worlds of Childhood: The Art and Craft of
Writing for Children* (1990), and *They Went: The
Art and Craft of Travel Writings* (1991). In 1983,
Zinsser wrote *Writing with a Word Processor,* using
his own anxieties about what was then a new
"writing machine" as his main example. In "The
Keyboard," reprinted from that book, Zinsser explains the process of composing with this now all
too familiar technology.

The Keyboard

W E COME NOW to the all-important keyboard. Every- 1
thing else is secondary—the disks, the "memory,"
the printer. Like the strings and hammers of a piano, they
exist only to execute what the person at the keyboard transmits from his mind to his fingers.

I felt comfortable at the keyboard of my word processor 2
almost immediately because I've been typing all my life. On
the whole I'm not manually adept—I can't sew on a button
and I can hardly open a boiled egg. But I can do two things

well that require more motor coordination than sewing on a button: I can type and I can play the piano. I can probably do these things because I want to do these things. I definitely want to play the piano more than I want to open boiled eggs.

What this means is that someone starting on a word processor without being able to type well—or at all—must want to be able to use the machine. Dexterity, I suspect, is ultimately in the head, not the hands. But you shouldn't be scared off. Learning to type isn't one of life's hardest tasks; 3

The cursor and the DELETE *key become the writer's twin companions as he ranges over the screen, rewriting and rearranging, cutting and condensing.*

---

millions of people have done it. I taught myself very early by the inelegant hunt-and-peck method and only later learned the touch system. To use the word processor I just had to master a few new keys—mainly the four cursor keys, the DELETE key, the BACKSPACE key and the ENTER key.

Here, briefly, is how they work. 4

The cursor is a line of light that moves across the screen 5 as you write. It is only as wide as one letter and it is always directly under the space where you want to type next. If it isn't, you can move it to where you *do* want to type next. It is, in short, a pointer. You move the cursor around like a pointer to tell the machine, "I want the next thing I type to go right here."

Much of the time, of course, the cursor will be at rest 6 where you stopped typing a sentence, waiting for your next sentence. When you start that sentence the cursor will start moving again, staying one space to the right of every letter that you type. You can use the space bar to move it another space to the right, just as you use the space bar on a typewriter to move the carriage. If you want to start a new paragraph at the end of a sentence, push the RET (carriage return) key and the cursor will move down to the next line.

Four different keys enable you to move the cursor in four 7 different directions: left, right, up, down. Each key has an arrow to indicate which way it makes the cursor move. When you press a key it moves the cursor one space. But if you hold the key down it moves the cursor rapidly across the screen, or up and down the screen.

If you want to move the cursor even faster—and you often 8 do—you can press a special key called CODE together with the cursor key. This instructs the cursor to move instantly as far as it can go in the direction of the arrow. At the end of a line, for example, you may want to go back to the beginning of the line to correct the first word. Press the CODE key and the *left* arrow key; the cursor will be there faster than you can see it go. Or if you're at the bottom of a page and you want to see what's at the top of the page, press the CODE key and the *up* arrow: the screen will display the top portion of the page, and the cursor will be under the first letter of the first word.

The *up* and *down* cursor keys are what you use to bring 9 more lines of what you have written into view. A page will accommodate sixty-one lines of typing, but the screen can only display twenty lines at a time. This means that if you want to see what you wrote in an earlier paragraph that's no longer on the screen, you have to "scroll" the page into view, using the *up* cursor key to bring the preceding lines down. (You use the *down* cursor to bring lower lines up.) How this affects the act of writing—not being able to look at more than a small chunk of your work—I'll consider in a later chapter. Now I just want to explain how the various keys work.

What makes the system so enjoyable is that anything you 10 type at the location of the cursor will displace what is already there. It won't lose the existing sentences; it will just push them to the right. This means that wherever you place the cursor you can insert a new word, a new phrase, a new sentence, or any number of new paragraphs. Assume, for instance, you want to insert a new sentence in this paragraph—after the sentence that begins: "It won't lose." Just move the cursor back until it's under the *T* in "This means . . ." As you time your new sentence, the existing sentence ("This means . . .") will move to the right, one space at a time, accommodating as much as you want to add. Then the expanded paragraph will regroup itself in tidy lines.

Often, of course, when you put something new into a 11 paragraph you will also want to take something out. Much of the inserting that you do with the cursor, for instance, will consist of replacing one word with a better word. When you type in the better word, the one that you are discarding will move along to the right. Then you have to delete it with the DELETE key. Thus the cursor and the DELETE key become the writer's twin companions as he ranges over the screen, rewriting and rearranging, cutting and condensing. I soon learned to use them with pleasure, for I'm well aware that very few sentences are born perfect. Almost every sentence has, among other failings, more words than it needs. To get rid of the extra words with the mere flick of an electronic wand is enormously satisfying.

Which brings us to the DELETE key. 12

When you want to delete anything from the screen, move 13 the cursor to the letter where you want to start deleting. You may want to delete only one letter. Move the cursor under that letter and press DELETE. The letter will instantly be framed in a box of green light that is brighter than all the other letters. The green box encloses what you have told the machine you want to delete. Simultaneously the screen asks you: DELETE WHAT? If the box correctly expresses your wishes, press ENTER and the doomed letter will vanish.

But you will usually want to delete more than one letter— 14 in fact, whole words, clauses, sentences. What then?

Again, move the cursor to the first letter in the sequence 15 of words that you want to get rid of. Press DELETE. The screen will ask: DELETE WHAT? You will tell it what to delete.

How will you do this? Here's a passage from Thoreau's   16
Walden that we can tinker with:

> *For my part, I could easily do without the post-office.*
> *I think there are very few important communica-*
> *tions that are made through it. To speak critically, I*
> *never received more than one or two letters in my*
> *life—I wrote this some years ago—that were worth*
> *the postage. And I am sure that I never read any*
> *memorable news in a newspaper. If we read of one*
> *man robbed, or murdered, or killed by an accident,*
> *or one house burned, or one vessel wrecked, or one*
> *steamboat blown up, or one cow run over on the*
> *Western Railroad, or one mad dog killed, or one lot*
> *of grasshoppers in the winter, we never need read of*
> *another. One is enough.*

Assume that you want to delete the first three words. You   17
can do it in various ways. First, move the cursor under the *F*
and press the DELETE key. Only the *F* will be boxed in green
light. Move the cursor another space to the right. The *o* will
also be boxed in green. Keep moving the cursor to the right
and each successive letter, plus the comma and the space, will
be boxed in green. Press ENTER; the first three words and the
comma and the space will disappear, and the remaining words
("I could easily . . .") will slide over to the left, replacing what
has gone.

But this is a slow and bothersome method: you have to   18
press the cursor key thirteen times to blanket all the characters you want to delete. Much swifter solutions are available.
They operate on a simple principle: After the system asks
"DELETE WHAT?" it will delete everything through and including whatever character you strike on the keyboard next.

For example (going back to Thoreau), if you start with the   19
cursor under the first *F*, press DELETE and then press a comma,
the machine will highlight in a green box all the characters it
encounters until it finds the first comma—in this case, the
comma after "part." Press ENTER and the first three words and

the comma will go. But you'll still be left with a space that you don't want. The cursor will be poised at that space, having deleted all the preceding characters. Press DELETE, press ENTER, and the space will go. That's a two-step delete, which is better than a thirteen-step delete.

But there's a still easier method—one that quickly became   20 habitual for me. That method is to use the space bar as the instruction for deleting. Remember that the machine thinks of a space as just another character, like a letter of the alphabet. Therefore if the machine asks "DELETE WHAT?" and you press the space bar once, the machine will delete everything through and including the first space. For example (going back to Thoreau again), if you press the space bar three times, you will see highlighted in a green box the first three words ("For my part") plus the comma and the final space. Press ENTER and the deleting is instantly done.

The great advantage of the space-bar method is that much   21 of your deleting will consist of just one word plus the space that follows it. This is true, for instance, when you substitute one word for another. Suppose you don't like the word "easily" in Thoreau's first sentence and want to replace it with "happily." Move the cursor under the e in "easily" and type the new word in. "Easily" will make room for it by moving along to the right, but you still have to get rid of it. Move the cursor under the e in "easily," press DELETE, press the space bar, and press ENTER. "Easily" will go and your spacing will be correct.

You'll also find a lot of brief phrases—three or four words   22 long—that are ripe for deleting. They are clutter phrases, separated from the rest of the sentence by commas, which don't do any real work: "on the whole," "I might add," "in a very real sense." Now you can kill them off with one quick tap of the DELETE key and three or four quick taps of the space bar. Consider, as an exercise, how you might thin out the nine forms of "news" cited by Thoreau in the sentence beginning "If we read." You could prune the list very rapidly if you wanted to. (I wouldn't want to; Thoreau usually knew what he was doing.)

You'll soon get these various patterns in your eye and learn   23 to make the combination of moves that will do your deleting with the greatest speed and economy.

Suppose, for example, you want to delete Thoreau's entire 24 first sentence. Put the cursor under the first *F,* press DELETE, and then press a period. Press ENTER and the machine will delete everything through the period after "post-office." Or suppose you want to delete Thoreau's first two sentences. Press the period twice. The machine will highlight everything through the first period (after "post-office") and will proceed until it meets a second period (after "it"). Everything in the first two sentences will be instantly highlighted. Look at it and make sure it's what you want to delete. If it is, press ENTER and the first two sentences will go.

The trick is to look ahead in your copy to find some 25 distinctive letter or character that the machine will race ahead to reach. It might be a quotation mark closing a quotation. Your eye tells you that you want to delete the entire quotation, which might consist of many sentences. If you press a period you will delete only the first sentence; if you press a quotation mark you'll delete the entire quotation.

The dash is another punctuation mark that serves this 26 function. For example: if you want to delete the parenthetical phrase in the middle of Thoreau's third sentence—"I wrote this some years ago"—just put the cursor under the first dash and instruct the machine to delete everything through the second dash.

Still another key that you can use as a final marker is the 27 RET (carriage return) key. To the machine this key denotes the end of a paragraph. Therefore if you want to delete an entire paragraph, just press the RET key, and all the sentences in the paragraph will be framed in light green. Press ENTER and they will vanish.

This is always a heady moment—the moment when you 28 can make so much writing just disappear. But it's also somewhat scary. Fortunately, you always have a chance to review your decision before you press the fateful ENTER. If you see that you highlighted more words than you want to delete, don't panic. Just press CANCEL and start over.

There's one other method of deleting, which works on a 29

different principle. But it's the method that you'll use more than any other. This is because it's not for making decisions about the writing, but for erasing common typing mistakes. Even the best typists make a lot of mistakes. The machine knows this and has given you the BACKSPACE key to wipe your sins away. This is one area, at least, where it has no Calvinist hang-ups about human fallibility.

The ENTER key simply erases every character that it meets as it moves backward through what you have just written. It erases one letter at a time with each press of the key; if you hold the key down it moves faster. This makes the key ideal for instantly correcting wrong letters and leaving no mess. There's no xxx'ing, no erasing, no white-out.   30

Assume that you hit an extra key in this sentdence. Just backspace over it: the period and the last five letters will vanish, and then you'll type the last four letters and the period again. The whole job takes five seconds—and takes less thought and fewer different moves than the DELETE key.   31

All these decisions soon become instinctive. You begin to know at a glance which keys will do the fastest job of deleting the words and letters you want to get rid of.   32

The keys that I've just described are the ones you'll use constantly: the four cursor keys, DELETE, ENTER and BACKSPACE. I'll mention several others and end this brief tour of the keyboard.   33

GO TO is a key that tells the machine to go to a certain page. You know you stopped typing yesterday in the middle of page 22, and that's where you want to resume today. You could get there by starting on page 1 and pressing the down cursor key; eventually you would reach page 22. Instead, press GO TO. The machine will ask you to type the number of the page where you want to go. Type "22," press GO TO and you'll instantly see the cursor poised at the top of that page.   34

FIND is a key that reaches the same goal by a different route. You don't remember the page where you stopped writing. But you do remember that you were working on a passage where you used a proper name or an unusual word that you   35 hadn't used up to that point. Let's say the name was Xerxes. (This is the passage with your brilliant allusion to the Persian Wars.) Press FIND. The machine will ask: FIND WHAT? Type "Xerxes" and press ENTER. The machine will clunk self-importantly for a few seconds and the page that you're looking for will appear on the screen, with the cursor under the X. If you're looking for that charming reference to ptarmigan . . . but you get the point. The machine will move through a body of writing until it finds a combination of letters that hasn't previously appeared.

MOVE is a key that you will put to many uses. It will move 36
any chunk of writing from one place to another. You can move sentences around within a paragraph, for instance, or to another paragraph. You can move whole paragraphs. You can move material from one page to another, or even from one diskette to another. When you press the MOVE key, the screen will ask MOVE WHAT? You indicate with the cursor the material that you want to move. Then the screen will ask MOVE WHAT? You take the cursor to the place where you want the material to go. Then you press ENTER and pray. Remarkably, the material gets moved.

END is the key that you press when you finish writing—and 37
before you take the diskette out. When you press END everything that you have just written will be transferred to your work diskette and added to what you have already stored there. If you take your diskette out before you press END you will lose what you have just written. This will also happen— you will lose what you have just written—if you turn the power switch off before you press END.

Obviously it's very important to press END whenever you're 38
going to stop writing. Make this not only a discipline; make it a reflex. After you press END, the next thing you'll see on the screen will be a menu with a list of tasks to choose from. Whenever you see a menu, you can safely take your diskettes out. Then you can turn off the power.

Then you're on your own power. 39

Topics for Writing
Process Analysis

1. *Respond.* Zinsser says that he feels comfortable at the computer's keyboard. Do you remember the first time you worked on a computer? What specific functions (keys) intimidated or frustrated you? Write a humorous column for your college newspaper on "Keyboard Phobias"—the keys that people avoid because they produce trouble. (*Resources for Comparison:* Natalie Angier, "Dolphin Courtship: Brutal, Cunning, and Complex," page 113; Julia Alvarez, "Grounds for Fiction," page 120).

2. *Analyze.* Zinsser's essay was written only fifteen years ago, but it now appears badly out of date—as if he were trying to provide instructions for using a pencil or a telephone. In fact, many of the procedures he describes are no longer necessary because of the many functions we can perform by using a mouse to point and click on icons. Analyze his advice, pointing out those features that contemporary writers would find useful and useless. (*Resources for Comparison:* Serena Nanda, "Arranging a Marriage in India," page 136; Elizabeth Winthrop, "The Golden Darters," page 149).

3. *Argue.* Although Zinsser quotes Thoreau, he does so to explain how the word processing system works. But Thoreau's argument that he could do without the post office does raise an important issue for our time. Does e-mail, and the various sites on the web, allow us to make important communications, or does it produce information garbage? Interview a few of your teachers to gather opinions on each side of Thoreau's argument and then draft your side. (*Resources for Comparison:* Lars Eighner, "My Daily Dives in the Dumpster," page 99; Nikki Giovanni, "Campus Racism," page 107).

John Steele Gordon was born in New York City
in 1944 and educated at Vanderbilt University.
After working for several years as a production
editor for Harper and Row Publishers, Gordon
devoted his full attention to his own writing. Gordon's overland expeditions to places such as India,
East Africa, and Mexico resulted in *Overlanding:
How to Explore the World on Four Wheels* (1975).
His other books include *The Scarlet Woman of
Wall Street* (1988), *Hamilton's Blessing: The Extraordinary Life and Times of Our National Debt*
(1997), and *The Great Game: The Emergence of
Wall Street as a World Power, 1653–2000* (1999).
In "The Golden Spike," reprinted from *Forbes*
magazine, Gordon compares the Internet revolution to the railroad revolution more than a century
ago.

The Golden Spike

*The Internet is most analogous to the railroad
revolution more than a century ago.*

THE INTERNET IN the 1990s is just like the railroads in   1
the 1840s. It is still in its infancy, its growth is explod-
ing, and no one yet knows how to make money at it. It also
performs the same economic function: connecting things.
And there is no more potent force than connecting buyers
and sellers. The GDP of an economy, after all, is nothing
more than the sum of all these connections. The more buyers
and sellers there are, the greater the wealth generated. That's
why the railroad was the seminal invention of the 19th century and the Internet will undoubtedly be of the 21st.

It is hard to imagine just how wretched the overland 2 transportation system was before the railroads, even in well-developed Europe. Indeed, *system* is hardly the word for a spotty network of roads, many of which were hardly better than paths. The Great North Road, the major highway through the north of England in the 18th century, had potholes so large that men and horses are known to have drowned in them. This meant that goods, except for luxuries, had to be transported by river or sea or they could not be transported at all.

As an underdeveloped country, and one of continental size 3 at that, the young United States' overland transportation problems dwarfed those of Europe. Worse, most East Coast

---

Just as the railroads—the application of the steam engine—were the prime agent of the creative destruction of the preindustrial world, so the Internet—an application of the computer—is becoming the prime agent in shaping the postindustrial world.

---

rivers were navigable for only short distances inland. As a result, there really was no "American economy." Instead there was a myriad of local ones. Most food was consumed locally, and most goods were locally produced by artisans such as blacksmiths. The railroads changed all that in less than 30 years.

When Andrew Jackson made his way from Nashville to 4 Washington, D.C., for his inauguration in 1829, he traveled by coach and required a month for the journey. Thirty years later it was possible to make the trip in three days. Because of the speed and ease of railroads, the volume of passenger traffic increased enormously as well. Before the new technology, passenger traffic between Charleston, South Carolina, and Augusta, Georgia, was handled by a single stagecoach making three round-trips a week. Five years after rail service opened between the two cities, traffic was averaging more than 2,600 passengers a month.

But it was the railroads' ability to haul freight, not people,   5
that transformed the world. Before its arrival, shipping a ton of goods 400 miles could easily quadruple the price. But by rail, the same ton of goods could be shipped in a fraction of the time and at one-twentieth of the cost. No wonder the multitude of separate economies began to vanish. "Two generations ago," wrote Arthur Hadley, a Yale economics professor, in 1885, "the expense of cartage was such that wheat had to be consumed within 200 miles of where it was grown. Today, the wheat of Dakota, the wheat of Russia, and the wheat of India come into direct competition. The supply at Odessa is an element in determining the price in Chicago."

Sound familiar? With the Internet, it is information and   6
data that can be moved much more quickly and cheaply. According to a Morgan Stanley Dean Witter report, buying airline tickets over the Internet results in an 87% reduction in the distribution cost. Banking online is an 89% reduction. While the railroads produced a national market, the Internet is producing a truly global one. An example: India's software development services now compete with China's, which compete with Silicon Valley's.

A NEW STREET

At first most railroads were locally financed by the people and   7
businessmen who stood to benefit from the new transportation. But the securities issued by these new companies often made their way to Wall Street and played a major part in the growth of the American financial market. In the 1820s and early 1830s, state and federal bonds and bank shares dominated securities trading, and business was often less than brisk. On March 16, 1830, a mere 31 shares changed hands on the New York Stock and Exchange Board (as the NYSE

was then known). By the 1850s, however, average volume had multiplied manyfold, and two-thirds of the issues being sold there were railroad stocks and bonds. With the American economy not yet able to generate enough capital internally, many of these issues were sold to European investors, especially in Britain, despite the 10-day delay in communication across the Atlantic.

Today, the Internet also is remaking Wall Street, and not just with the upstart online companies, 24-hour trading, or the new electronic exchanges. Volumes and prices have reached all-time highs, thanks in large measure to companies trading on the hope of the Internet. Nor is the craziness of the stock prices unique to our time. Because the Erie Railroad had an erratic, often crooked, management, and an odd route (it ran between Dunkirk on Lake Erie and Piermont on the Hudson River—two towns of no commercial importance whatsoever), it became known as "the scarlet woman of Wall Street," the most notorious railroad stock of the 19th century. But many railroad stocks soared and plunged in the early days of the industry as the potential profits and the practical realities intersected with the greed and fear of investors.

BIGGER IS BETTER

It wasn't long before the small, local railway lines began to merge into larger and larger entities, at first regional and then national in scope. In 1853, the New York Central was stitched together out of 10 local lines running between Buffalo and Albany. When Cornelius (nicknamed "Commodore") Vanderbilt took control in 1867, he quickly merged it with his Hudson River Railroad, running from Manhattan to Albany, and then with the Lake Shore and Michigan Southern Railway, running west to Chicago. Carrying millions of tons of freight between the nation's two largest cities built the fabulous row of Vanderbilt mansions on Fifth Avenue.

With the growth of national and international markets, economies of scale became possible in nearly all industries, and they quickly began to grow to take advantage of them.

Instead of each village blacksmith making horseshoes from scratch, one factory could produce horseshoes by the hundreds of thousands at a fraction of the cost per unit. It was precisely to take advantage of such possibilities that many industries began to merge into larger entities and then into the "trusts" that have been a bogeyman of American politics ever since. But despite the supposed threat of "monopoly pricing," the cost of manufactured goods fell relentlessly as the 19th century progressed. In 1911, when Standard Oil was broken up, the price of kerosene was only about one-third of what it had been in 1870, when Standard Oil was formed.

Retailing, as well, could become national in scope, thanks 11
to the railroads. Sears Roebuck, Montgomery Ward, and Woolworth could not have offered such low prices and grown into such vast enterprises if they had not had the railroads to deliver their goods. Catalog companies, of course, threatened local retailers and forced them to lower their prices in order to compete effectively. This played no small part in making possible the fact that the period between the Civil War and World War I was an era completely without inflation, despite an economy that was—even with recurrent and severe depressions—growing explosively.

Internet retailers such as Amazon.com are doing to the 12
American economy exactly what Sears and Montgomery Ward did more than a century ago. Amazon is forcing local retailers to compete on a national scale. It is reducing prices and changing how businesses interact with their suppliers and consumers.

While the railroads themselves greatly increased the de- 13
mand for some goods, they also almost single-handedly gave birth to new industries. The need for rails built the iron and then the steel industries in both Europe and America, the measure of economic power by the dawn of the 20th century. They, in turn, vastly expanded the mining industry. In a classic example of the synergy that is seldom recognized but is so much a part of economic history, the telegraph companies that sprang up after Samuel Morse demonstrated his invention in 1844 soon realized that the rights-of-way of the

railroads were the perfect paths along which to string their lines. (Today, companies laying fiber-optic cable have discovered the same thing.) The railroads also saw that the telegraph could be used as a signaling system, allowing trains to move much more quickly and safely (and thus more cheaply) on the often single-track lines of the early days.

The Internet is proving equally synergistic. It has sparked 14 growth in nearly all sectors of high tech and no doubt will propel the wireless, PDA, and multimedia industries forward. It was not until 1946 that half the households in the country had their own telephones. Half a century later, thanks to the Internet, it is not unusual for middle-class households to have two, three, and even four telephone lines.

CREATIVE DISTINCTION

By the 20th century the railroads' endless ramifications had 15 produced our modern economic world. And much of our domestic politics have centered on devising rules needed to distribute fairly the vast wealth created by that world. (These regulations haven't always worked, of course. The Interstate Commerce Commission, established to protect the public from price gouging by the railroad companies, quickly evolved into a government-sponsored price-fixing cartel that devastated the American railroad industry in the long term.) In the future, we can expect much of our energy will go to figuring out how to distribute the vast wealth created by the Internet.

Just as the railroads—the application of the steam engine— 16 were the prime agent of the creative destruction of the pre-industrial world, so the Internet—an application of the computer—is becoming the prime agent in shaping the postindustrial world. And it is doing so a lot quicker than the railroads, which were expensive to build. The Erie Railroad, hardly a model of efficient management, to be sure, cost $23.5 million at a time when that sum was roughly what the federal government was spending per year. The Internet, on the other hand, has been dirt cheap to create.

Much of the infrastructure, such as telephone lines and 17

personal computers, already existed. Anyone can go into business as an Internet service provider with little more than a server costing a few thousand dollars and some telephone lines. A Web page can be established so easily and at so little cost that millions of teenagers have already done so. Thus it is no surprise that the Progress and Freedom Foundation reports that the Internet has spread to 25% of American households in only seven years, whereas the telephone took 35 years, five times as long, to reach that penetration. Nearly 40% of the American adult population now uses the Internet at home, work, or the local library.

TRAIN WRECK

The railroads overbuilt wildly in the decades after the Civil War, often for competitive rather than economic reasons. In the 1880s and 1890s, as depression hit, two-thirds of the railroad tracks in the United States passed through receivership and were reorganized by the great Wall Street banks such as J. P. Morgan and Kuhn Loeb. This, of course, greatly strengthened the power of these banks. (In the first quarter of the 20th century, J. P. Morgan's was probably the most powerful bank that ever existed.) But it also made it possible for the banks to impose needed reforms. At that time, it was the banks and the stock exchange, not the government, that required publicly traded companies to adopt generally accepted accounting principles and independent accountants to certify their books. 18

The Internet will not escape a shakeout of its own at some point. Most of the thousands of entrepreneurs who rushed in at the first sign of opportunity will fall by the wayside, their fortunes as evanescent as rainbows. 19

The pieces, if the history of the railroads is any guide, will be picked up by people who at first stood on the sidelines. Commodore Vanderbilt never built a railroad in his life. Instead he bought badly run ones, restructured them, merged them into efficient operations, and managed them superbly. (No Vanderbilt railroad went through reorganization at the hands of the banks.) He thus created the largest fortune of 20 the railroad era and died the richest self-made man in the world.

Who the Commodore Vanderbilts of the Internet will be   21 is impossible to say at this point. (If I could, I wouldn't be spending my time writing magazine articles!) But whoever they turn out to be, they're going to make the old Commodore look like a welfare case.

Topics for Writing
Comparison and Contrast

1. *Respond.* In an essay written for the business section of your local newspaper, describe your experiences buying something on the Internet—concert tickets, clothes, CDs. Explain how the process works, and then provide some cautionary notes about how to avoid difficulty. Whenever possible help your readers understand the process by comparing it with more familiar methods of buying goods and services. (*Resources for Comparison:* Mark Twain, "Two Views of the River," page 169; Scott Russell Sanders, "Mountain Music," page 173).

2. *Analyze.* Gordon suggests that like many of the railroad stocks, the Internet stocks will soar and plunge and finally shake out a few winners that might be bought by a single person or corporation. Select a stock that you think might be a winner—even though it has had a recent history of extreme volatility. Analyze the reasons for its possible success, making comparisons to other stocks in its same class that have failed or succeeded. Try to reassure your readers, or would-be investors, that the stock is worth the risk. (*Resources for Comparisons:* Anne Roiphe, "A Tale of Two Divorces," page 182; Deborah Tannen, "Rapport-Talk and Report-Talk," page 193).

3. *Argue.* Gordon argues that despite the economic turmoil they created, the railroads made purchasing goods easier and less expensive. In the process, however, the products of local culture were eliminated in favor of products that could be made, shipped, and sold to national markets. In a column for the style section of your newspaper, make the case for the products of your local culture. Argue that a national and global economy wipes out the market for unique products and personal services. (*Resources for Comparison:* Laura Bohannan, "Shakespeare in the Bush," page 208; Witi Ihimaera, "His First Ball," page 223).

Dave Barry was born in Armonk, New York, in 1947 and educated at Haverford College. He worked as a reporter for several daily newspapers and the Associated Press and was a lecturer on effective writing for businesses before he began his career as a freelance humor columnist—first with the *Miami Herald* and then in national syndication. He has published his columns in over twenty-five books, most of them best-sellers. They include *Babies and Other Hazards of Sex* (1984), *Dave Barry Slept Here* (1989), and *Dave Barry's Complete Guide to Guys: A Fairly Short Book* (1995). In "Selected Web Sites," reprinted from *Dave Barry in Cyberspace* (1996), Barry classifies some of the silly and outrageous material that passes for information on the Internet.

Selected Web Sites[1]

At Last:
Proof That Civilization Is Doomed

A COMMON CRITICISM of the Internet is that it is domi- 1
nated by the crude, the uninformed, the immature, the smug, the untalented, the repetitious, the pathetic, the hostile, the deluded, the self-righteous, and the shrill. This criticism overlooks the fact that the Internet also offers—for the savvy individual who knows where to look—the tasteless and the borderline insane.

I am thinking here mainly of the World Wide Web. 2
Whereas much of the Internet relies strictly on text, the Web is multimedia; this means that if, for example, you're setting

---

[1] I want to thank the good (weird, but good) people on the alt.fan group who suggested many of these sites.—BARRY'S NOTE.

up a Web site devoted to exploring the near-universal human fear that a *Star Wars* character wants to consume your gonads, you can present this issue in both words *and* pictures (I'll have more on this issue later in this chapter[2]). You can also greatly advance the frontiers of scientific knowledge regarding Spam.

In researching this chapter, I spent many, many hours 3 exploring the World Wide Web. My time was divided as follows:

Activity	Time Spent
Typing insanely complex Web addresses	2%
Waiting for what seemed like at least two academic semesters per Web page while the computer appeared to do absolutely nothing	93%
Reading snippy messages stating that there is no such Web address	2%
Retyping insanely complex Web addresses	2%
Actually looking at Web pages	1%

As you can see, it can take quite a while for a Web page to 4 appear on your screen. The reason for the delay is that, when you type in a Web address, your computer passes it along to

---

Do not assume that all *Web sites are a total waste of time; the actual figure is only about 99.999997 percent.*

---

another computer, which in turn passes it along to another computer, and so on through as many as five computers before it finally reaches the workstation of a disgruntled U.S.

[2] This is a good reason to stop reading this chapter right now.—BARRY'S NOTE.

Postal Service employee, who throws it in the trash. So when browsing the Web, you will almost certainly encounter lengthy delays, which means that it's a good idea to have something else to do while you're waiting, such as reroofing your house.

Anyway, by virtue of being diligent and not having a real job, I was eventually able to get through to quite a few Web pages, and in this chapter I'm going to describe some of the more memorable ones. But before I do, I want to stress three points: 5

- All the pages described here are real; I did not make any of them up, not even the virtual toilet.
- What you see here represents just a teensy-tiny fraction of the thousands upon thousands of Web pages, with new ones being created constantly. Do not assume, from what you see in this chapter, that *all* Web pages are a total waste of time; the actual figure is only about 99.999997 percent.
- By the time you read this, you may not be able to visit all of these pages. I visited most of them in mid-1996; some of them may have since gone out of existence for various reasons, such as that their creators were recalled to their home planets.

But this chapter is not intended as an exhaustive list: I just want to give you an idea of some of the stuff that's out there. So fasten your seat belt, and let's visit some of the fascinating rest stops on the Information Superhighway. We'll start, appropriately enough, with: 6

THE TOILETS OF MELBOURNE, AUSTRALIA

http://minyos.xx.rmit.edu.au/~s9507658/toilet/

If you're thinking about taking a trip to Melbourne, Australia, the first question you ask yourself is: "What will the toilets be like?"   7

The answer can be found at this Web site, which offers   8

detailed reviews of selected Melbourne-area toilets. Here are some actual excerpts:

- "What a great day for a drive! Mild weather. A nice lunch. A scenic walk. First-rate toilets."
- "The other notable thing about the toilets was the toilet paper holders. They were Bowscott continuous toilet paper holders that were actually positioned up high enough."
- "On the way we stopped at Eastland shopping centre—home of the best public toilets I have seen so far. They were clean, open, and the toilet roll holders were free moving. As with the Lysterfield Lake toilets, one of the basin-style urinals was positioned lower for kids. The hand dryer was fantastic too. It was a compact, automatic Mirage dryer. Even though it was much smaller than other hand dryers, it blew out plenty of hot air."

And that is not all: From this Web site, you can jump to some of the many, *many* other toilet-related Web sites, including a Virtual Public Restroom ("The Toilet of the Web"[3]), where you can write a virtual message and leave a virtual "poopie."[4]   9

GIANT COLLECTION OF VIOLA JOKES

http://www.mit.edu/people/jcb/viola-jokes.html

If you're like most people, you frequently remark to yourself: 10
"Darn it! I have an important business presentation to make today, and I would love to 'break the ice' by opening with a viola joke, but I don't know any fresh ones!"

Well, you will never have to make that statement again,   11
not after you visit this Web page. This is a *huge* collection of viola jokes. I suppose it's possible that somebody, some-where, has compiled an even *bigger* collection of viola jokes,

---

[3] *http://www.auburn.edu/~carltjm/restroom.html*—BARRY'S NOTE.
[4] Don't ask.—BARRY'S NOTE.

but I seriously doubt that this could be done without the aid of powerful illegal stimulants.

Much of the viola-joke humor appears to be based on the premise that viola players are not the brightest or most talented members of the orchestra:

Q. *How can you tell when a violist is playing out of tune?*
A. The bow is moving.

Q. *What do you call a violist with two brain cells?*
A. Pregnant.

Some of the jokes are probably a lot more hilarious if you know something about classical music. I'm sure, for example, that many orchestra professionals slap their thighs when they hear this one:

Q. *How do you get a violist to play a passage pianissimo tremolando?*
A. Mark it "solo."

Ha ha! "Mark it 'solo'!" Whew!

Anyway, I was genuinely surprised by this Web page. I always thought of classical orchestras as somber operations where most of the musicians are very serious and hunched over to the point of bowel disorder. I had no idea that there was this level of wackiness, especially not in the string section. (The woodwinds, of course, are a different story; those dudes and dudettes are out of *control*.)

GUIDE TO CRACKERS

http://mathlab.sunysb.edu/%7Eelijah/cstuff/index.html

This is one of those ideas that you never in a million years would have had yourself, but as soon as you see it, you smack your forehead and say: "Huh?"

This page features photographs of various types of

crackers—Cheez-Its, Ritz Bits, etc.—actual size. When you click on a cracker, you go to a page that gives you packaging and nutritional information. You are also encouraged to donate crackers, especially "rare and unusual crackers."

I am *sure* there is a good reason. 18

HUMAN TESTICLE CONSUMPTION:

Mr. T Ate My Balls
http://www.cen.uiuc.edu/~nkpatel/mr.t/index.html

Chewbacca Ate My Balls
http://www.cen.uiuc.edu/~nkpatel/chewbacca/
index.html

There are some things in life that it is better to just not even 19
think about, and one of those things is the question of what, exactly, led to the creation of these pages.

In summary, these pages present pictures of Mr. T and 20
Chewbacca expressing—by means of comic book-style speech and thought balloons—the dramatic theme that they would like to eat your testicles.

For example, in the opening scene of the "Chewbacca Ate 21
My Balls" page, Chewbacca is thinking, "I wish I had some BALLS to munch on . . ." In the next scene, he is thinking: "Your balls are MINE!!" And then, in a dramatic plot development reminiscent of the work of playwright Arthur Miller, Chewbacca thinks, "What? Mr. T already got yours?"

These sites also feature a Guest Book, where visitors can 22
leave comments. The comments that I read were all very complimentary. People really respond to a universal theme like this. I myself had to lie down for a while.

THE SPAM CAM

http://www.fright.com/cgi-bin/spamcam

If you have the slightest doubt that the Internet is good for 23
science, you should look at this page, and then you will have much more serious doubts.

This page is billed as "The page that seeks to answer the question: IS SPAM ORGANIC?" It presents close-up photographs of scientific experiments showing what happens when Spam and other types of foods are left sitting out for long periods of time. What happens is—get ready for a major scientific breakthrough—everything gets *really* disgusting. 24

For a while there was also a very popular Web site[5] set up by college students wishing to determine what happens to Twinkies when they are heated with torches, dropped from tall buildings, etc.,[6] but when I tried to check it out, it had been closed down by lawyers. Perhaps by the time you read this book, it will be back in operation again. Or perhaps the entire Internet will have been closed down by lawyers. Or perhaps college students will have started dropping lawyers from tall buildings. You never know with the future. 25

PIERCING MILDRED

http://streams.com/pierce/

Who says there is no culture on the Internet? You will, after you visit this site. This is a game where you get to select a character—either Mildred or Maurice—and then you pierce that person's body parts, or decorate her or him with designer scars. Mildred and Maurice also sometimes get infected, so sometimes you have to purchase antibiotic ointment. 26

You may think this sounds like a fairly perverted game, but ask yourself: Is it *really* that different from Mr. and Mrs. Potato Head? 27

BANANA LABELS OF THE WORLD

http://www.staff.or.jp/whoiswho/ikka/bananadir/ bananalabels.html

If you thought that there were basically only a couple of types of banana labels, then a visit to this site will quickly convince you that you are a stupid idiot. This site presents pictures of hundreds of banana labels, including labels commemorating 28

---

[5] *http://www.owlnet.rice.edu/~gouge/twinkies.html*—BARRY'S NOTE.
[6] It turns out that pretty much nothing happens.—BARRY'S NOTE.

historic events such as the 50th anniversary of Miss Chiquita, not to mention a label from a Big Frieda's Burro Banana. This site will also direct you to *other* banana-label pages.[7] And you are invited to send in banana labels, including "virtual banana labels," which I assume means labels for virtual bananas. (My feeling about this is: fine, but they'd better not come out with virtual beer.)

WAVE TO THE CATS

http://hogwild.hamjudo.com/cgi-bin/wave

This is the perfect Web site[8] to show to the skeptic who thinks you can't do anything useful or practical on the Internet. At this site, you can click on a button that activates a motor at a remote location; the motor is attached to a large fiberboard hand, which waves back and forth at some cats, if the cats happen to be in the room at the time. You can't actually *see* this; you just get the warm feeling of satisfaction that comes from knowing that you are causing a remote, simulated hand to wave at remote, possibly nonexistent cats. You also get a nice "Thank you for your wave" message from the Web page author, as well as his description of the way the cats usually react to the hand ("Master will stare at it when it moves; the other three cats, Callie, Mutant, and Katrina, just ignore it").

I know what you're thinking, but to my knowledge, there currently is no "Spay the Cats" Web site.

TROJAN ROOM COFFEE MACHINE

http://www.cl.cam.ac.uk/coffee/coffee.html

If you go to this page, you can, merely by clicking your mouse, see, from anywhere in the world, an up-to-the-second video image of the coffee machine in the Trojan Room of the University of Cambridge Computer Laboratory in England. It would be virtually impossible to calculate the time that has

---

[7] *Of course* there are other banana-label pages.—BARRY'S NOTE.
[8] This is one of many cool sites I found out about through the highly recommended Center for the Easily Amused, located at *http://www.amused.com/*—BARRY'S NOTE.

been saved by disseminating this information via the Web, as opposed to previous methods.

CAPTAIN AND TENNILLE APPEARANCES

http://www.vcnet.com/moonlight/ CTAPPEARANCES

This page lists upcoming personal appearances by the Captain   32 and Tennille. Using this information, you can find out exactly where this veteran duo will be making their own special brand of musical magic so that you can arrange to be on the diametrically opposite side of the Earth when they perform "Muskrat Love."

CURSING IN SWEDISH

http://www.bart.nl/~sante/enginvek.html

This is the most thorough on-line course in Swedish cursing   33 that I am aware of. It is scholarly, well-organized, and professional-looking; and if your computer has sound, you can click on individual phrases, and your computer will curse at you in Swedish.

Here are some of the practical Swedish curses you can learn   34 on this Web site (I swear I am not making these up):

> *Han var en jävel på att fiska.*
> *He was bloody good at fishing.*
> *Satan! Ungen pissade på sig!*
> *Hell! The kid wet his trousers!*
> *Pubkillarna var ena jävlar på att pissa.*
> *The guys at the pub were masterly at pissing.*
> *Jag tappade den jävla tvålen*
> *I dropped the f**king soap.*
> *Det vore himla roligt om du kom till festen.*
> *It would be heavenly if you could take part in the party.*

Kukjävel!
F**king f**ker!
Festen kommer att gå åt skogen!
The party will be a real flop!

And of course the one curse you *constantly* find yourself   35
needing to express whenever you're in Sweden . . .

När jag blir av med gipset skall du få se på sjutton!
Just wait until I have gotten rid of the plaster!

DUTCH TRAFFIC SIGNS [9]

http://www.eeb.ele.tue.nl:80/traffic/warning-e.html

Without this site, I would never have known that the Dutch   36
have a traffic sign that means "squalls."

FEDERAL CORPSE SLICE PHOTOS

http://www.nlm.nih.gov/research/visible/photos.html

On this site you can see images taken from the government's   37
Visible Human Project, in which two actual deceased humans, one male and one female, were frozen in gelatin and
sliced into very thin slices for the benefit of science. I know
what you're wondering: You're wondering where the government got the corpses. You will be relieved to learn that
the answer is: *not* from the Internal Revenue Service Division
of Taxpayer Compliance.

Or so they claim.   38

PEOPLE WITH TOASTERS

**http://www.berksys.com/www/promotions/
uNurtoaster.html**

This page features photographs of people with their toasters.   39

---

[9] I found this site, along with many other excellent ones, at a *very* useful
site called Useless Pages, *http://www.chaco.com/useless/index.html.* Check it
out.—BARRY'S NOTE.

FABIO

http://redwood.northcoast.com/ ~shojo/Fabio/fabio.html

This page features photographs of the romantic superstar [40] mega-hunk Fabio with his toaster.

No, seriously, the photographs depict the romantic super- [41] star mega-hunk posing in a manner that reveals his deeply passionate sensitive innermost feelings about what a stud-muffin he is. What makes this site great is that you can click on the photographs, and, if your computer has sound, Fabio will say things to you, such as "Your caress is my command." Apparently he doesn't realize that you're caressing him with a mouse pointer.

DEFORMED FROG PICTURES

http://www.mncs.k12.mn.us/frog/picts.html

One summer day in 1995 some students at the Minnesota [42] New Country School were on a Nature Studies hike. They started catching frogs, and after a bit they noticed that many of the frogs did not appear to meet standard frog specifica-tions in terms of total number of legs, eyes, etc. So the students started a Frog Project to study this phenomenon. If you visit this Web page, you can read about their work and see actual photographs of the frogs; this will help you to become more aware of the environment, pollution, and other important topics, unless you're the kind of sicko who just wants to look at deformed frogs.

MUSICAL SAND

http://www.yo.rim.or.jp/~smiwa/index.html

If you are interested in information on musical sand (and who [43] is not?), this is really the only place to go. This Web site offers information in both Japanese and a language that is some-what reminiscent of English. The introduction states:

All information concerning Musical Sand in the world ("singing sand" on beach and "booming sand" in desert) will concentrate in this home pages. Singing properties of the sand is very sensitive to pollution, and that may be play a sensor for it.

To my regret, musical sand is on the brink of a critical position to be exterminated. If cleaning air and sea however, musical sand plays wonderful sound with action of wind and wave for us. I make show you World of Musical Sand that Mother Nature polished by spending eternal time.

Think of it: Endangered sand! [44]

If your computer has sound capability, you can actually [45] listen to some singing sand. It is not easy, on the printed page, to describe the eerie, almost unearthly beauty of the sound that the sand makes; the best words I can come up with are "like a vacuum cleaner trying to suck up a dead cow." I for one would hate to see Earth lose a resource like this, and I hereby urge Sting and Willie Nelson to hold some kind of benefit concert.

EXPLODING WHALE

http://www.xmission.com:80/~grue/whale

On this site you can see pictures of the now-famous incident[10] [46] in which the Oregon State Highway Division, attempting to dispose of a large and aromatic dead whale that had washed up on the beach, decided to—why not?—blow it up with half a ton of dynamite.

The theory was that the whale would be converted from [47] one large unit into many small Whale McNuggets, which would then be eaten by seagulls. Unfortunately, this is not what happened. What happened was, following a massive

[10] About ten years ago, I saw a videotape of this incident, made by a local TV station. I wrote a column about it, and somebody unfamiliar with the copyright laws put that column on the Internet. The result is that for years now, people have been sending me my own column, often with notes saying, "You should write a column, about this!"—BARRY'S NOTE.

blast,[11] large chunks of rotting whale blubber, some of them large enough to dent a car roof, rained down upon spectators several hundred yards away, and there was *still* an extremely large chunk of dead whale lying on the beach. This was not Seagull Chow. A seagull capable of eating this chunk would have to be the size of the Lincoln Memorial.

The moral here is, if another dead whale washes up on the 48 beach in Oregon, the authorities should probably not turn the disposal job over to the State Highway Division. But if they do, I hope they sell tickets.

WORLD RECORD BARBECUE IGNITION

http://ghg.ecn.purdue.edu/oldindex.html

If this Web page doesn't make you proud to be an American, 49 then I frankly don't know what will. This site presents the ultimate result of the effort by members of the Purdue University engineering department to see how fast they could get the barbecue charcoal ignited at their annual picnic. They started by blowing the charcoal with a hair dryer; then, in subsequent years, they escalated to using a propane torch, an acetylene torch, and then compressed pure oxygen.

At this point, they were lighting the charcoal very fast, but 50 for these guys, "very fast" was not good enough. These guys had a dream, and that dream was to ignite their charcoal faster than anybody had ever done before. And thus they hit upon the idea of using liquid oxygen, the kind used in rocket engines. On this Web page you can see photos and video of an engineer named George Goble using long wooden handles to dump a bucket of liquid oxygen onto a grill containing 60 pounds of charcoal; this is followed by a fireball that, according to Goble, reached 10,000 degrees Fahrenheit. The charcoal was ready for cooking in *three seconds.*

Next time Oregon has a whale problem, maybe it should 51 call *these* guys.

[11] Talk about booming sands.—BARRY'S NOTE.

FLAMING POP-TART EXPERIMENT
http://www-personal.umich.edu/ ~gmbrown/tart/

It is a well-known scientific fact[12] that if you put a Kellogg's 52
brand strawberry Pop-Tart into a toaster and hold the toaster
lever down so that it can't pop up, after about five minutes,
the Pop-Tart will turn into the Blowtorch Snack Pastry from
Hell, shooting dramatic blue flames as much as a foot out of
the toaster slots.

If you visit this Web page, you can see actual photos of an 53
experiment demonstrating this spectacular phenomenon. I
urge you, however, *not* to attempt to duplicate this experiment unless you are a trained science professional using
somebody else's toaster, because we are talking about a powerful force with the potential for great destruction. We can
only be grateful that the Nazis never learned how to harness
it, although historians strongly suspect that they were working on it near the end.

Let me repeat that the Web sites described in this chapter 54
represent just a tiny fraction of what's out there. What you
really need to do is get on the Web and start poking around
for yourself. You'll quickly discover that what you've read
about here exemplifies some of the *saner* thinking going on.
So go ahead! Get on the Web! In my opinion, it's WAY more
fun than television, and what harm can it do?

OK, it can kill brain cells by the billions. But you don't 55
need brain cells. You have a computer.

---

[12] This has been verified on the David Letterman show.—BARRY'S NOTE.

Topics for Writing
Division and Classification

1. *Respond.* Since Dave Barry conducted his experiment exploring the World Wide Web in 1996, many aspects of the technology have changed. Most computers are faster. The addition of sound and video has made many websites more appealing. And the use of hyperlinks has enabled browsers to search for many other sites. Record the time spent on various activities during one of your browsing sessions. Then classify those activities in a "How to" essay for your local newspaper. (*Resources for Comparison:* Calvin Trillin, "The Extendable Fork," page 246; James H. Austin, "Four Kinds of Chance," page 250).

2. *Analyze.* Study Barry's footnotes for a website that looks promising—e.g., <http://www.amused.com>. Then use that resource to look for a site that you find appealing. Then in a letter addressed to Barry, analyze the way this site frames its subject, presents its text, and manipulates its sound and graphics. Demonstrate why, by comparison to the sites Barry has selected, this site is informative and useful. (*Resources for Comparison:* Phillip Lopate, "Modern Friendships," page 265; Flannery O'Connor, "Revelation," page 297).

3. *Argue.* Barry argues that 99.999997 percent of the sites on the web are useless. But one could just as easily argue that 99.99% of the books and magazines published each year are useless. Find a particularly informative website—e.g., Library of Congress, Smithsonian Institution, Museum of Modern Art—and demonstrate why its availability and accessible navigation make browsing the web worth the effort. (*Resources for Comparison:* Mary Mebane, "Shades of Black," pages 257; Steven Weinberg, "Five and a Half Utopias," page 279).

Laura Miller was born in San Diego, California, in 1960 and educated at the University of California, Berkeley. She is the co-founder and New York editorial director of Salon.com, one of the most widely read electronic journals. She has also contributed articles to the *New York Times,* the *Washington Post,* the *Village Voice,* and *Wired.* Her most recent book is *The Salon.com Reader's Guide to Contemporary Authors* (2000). In "Women and Children First: Gender and the Settling of the Electronic Frontier," reprinted from *Resisting the Virtual Life: The Culture and Politics of Information* (1995), she challenges the popular notion that women are intimidated by cyberspace.

Women and Children First: Gender and the Settling of the Electronic Frontier

WHEN *NEWSWEEK* (MAY 16, 1994) ran an article entitled "Men, Women and Computers," all hell broke out on the Net, particularly on the on-line service I've participated in for six years, The Well (Whole Earth 'Lectronic Link). "Cyberspace, it turns out," declared *Newsweek*'s Nancy Kantrowitz, "isn't much of an Eden after all. It's marred by just as many sexist ruts and gender conflicts as the Real World. . . . Women often feel about as welcome as a system crash." "It was horrible. Awful, poorly researched, unsubstantiated drivel," one member wrote, a sentiment echoed throughout some 480 postings.

However egregious the errors in the article (some sources

1

2

maintain that they were incorrectly quoted), it's only one of several mainstream media depictions of the Net as an environment hostile to women. Even women who had been complaining about on-line gender relations found themselves increasingly annoyed by what one Well member termed the "cyberbabe harassment" angle that seems to typify media

---

When the mainstream media generalize about women's experiences on line in ways that just happen to uphold the most conventional and pernicious gender stereotypes, they can expect to be greeted with howls of disapproval from women who refuse to acquiesce in these roles and pass them on to other women.

---

coverage of the issue. Reified in the pages of *Newsweek* and other journals, what had once been the topic of discussions by insiders—on-line commentary is informal, conversational, and often spontaneous—became a journalistic "fact" about the Net known by complete strangers and novices. In a matter of months, the airy stuff of bitch sessions became widespread, hardened stereotypes.

At the same time, the Internet has come under increasing   3
scrutiny as it mutates from an obscure, freewheeling web of computer networks used by a small elite of academics, scientists, and hobbyists to . . . well, nobody seems to know exactly what. But the business press prints vague, fevered prophecies of fabulous wealth, and a bonanza mentality has blossomed. With it comes big business and the government, intent on regulating this amorphous medium into a manageable and profitable industry. The Net's history of informal self-regulation and its wide libertarian streak guarantee that

battles like the one over the Clipper chip (a mandatory de-
coding device that would make all encrypted data readable
by federal agents) will be only the first among many.

Yet the threat of regulation is built into the very mythos   4
used to conceptualize the Net by its defenders—and gender
plays a crucial role in that threat. However revolutionary the
technologized interactions of on-line communities may seem,
we understand them by deploying a set of very familiar metaphors from the rich figurative soup of American culture.
Would different metaphors have allowed the Net a different,
better historical trajectory? Perhaps not, but the way we
choose to describe the Net now encourages us to see regulation as its inevitable fate. And, by examining how gender
roles provide a foundation for the intensification of such
social controls, we can illuminate the way those roles pro-
scribe the freedoms of men as well as women.

For months I mistakenly referred to the EFF (an organi-   5
zation founded by John Perry Barlow and Lotus 1-2-3 designer Mitch Kapor to foster access to, and further the
discursive freedom of, on-line communications) as "The
Electronic Frontier Foundation." Once corrected, I was
struck by how intimately related the ideas "frontier" and
"freedom" are in the Western mythos. The *frontier*, as a realm
of limitless possibilities and few social controls, hovers, grail-
like, in the American psyche, the dream our national identity
is based on, but a dream that's always, somehow, just vanish-
ing away.

Once made, the choice to see the Net as a frontier feels   6
unavoidable, but it's actually quite problematic. The word
"frontier" has traditionally described a place, if not land then
the limitless "final frontier" of space. The Net, on the other
hand, occupies precisely no physical space (although the computers and phone lines that make it possible do). It is a
completely bodiless, symbolic thing with no discernible
boundaries or location. The land of the American frontier did
not become a "frontier" until Europeans determined to conquer it, but the continent existed before the intention to
settle it. Unlike land, the Net was created by its pioneers.

Most peculiar, then, is the choice of the word "frontier"   7
to describe an artifact so humanly constructed that it only
exists as ideas or information. For central to the idea of the
frontier is that it contains no (or very few) other people—
fewer than two per square mile according to the nineteenth-
century historian Frederick Turner. The freedom the frontier
promises is a liberation from the demands of society, while
the Net (I'm thinking now of Usenet) has nothing but society
to offer. Without other people, news groups, mailing lists,
and files simply wouldn't exist and e-mail would be purposeless. Unlike real space, cyberspace must be shared.

Nevertheless, the choice of a spatial metaphor (credited to   8
the science-fiction novelist William Gibson, who coined the
term "cyberspace"), however awkward, isn't surprising. Psychologist Julian Jaynes has pointed out that geographical
analogies have long predominated humanity's efforts to conceptualize—map out—consciousness. Unfortunately, these
analogies bring with them a heavy load of baggage comparable to Pandora's box: open it and a complex series of problems have come to stay.

The frontier exists beyond the edge of settled or owned   9
land. As the land that doesn't belong to anybody (or to
people who "don't count," like Native Americans), it is on
the verge of being acquired; currently unowned, but still
ownable. Just as the ideal of chastity makes virginity sexually
provocative, so does the unclaimed territory invite settlers,
irresistibly so. Americans regard the lost geographical frontier
with a melancholy, voluptuous fatalism—we had no choice
but to advance upon it and it had no alternative but to
submit. When an EFF member compares the Clipper chip to
barbed wire encroaching on the prairie, doesn't he realize the
surrender implied in his metaphor?

The psychosexual undercurrents (if anyone still thinks of   10
them as "under") in the idea of civilization's phallic intrusion
into nature's passive, feminine space have been observed,
exhaustively, elsewhere. The classic Western narrative is actually far more concerned with social relationships than
conflicts between man and nature. In these stories, the fron-

tier is a lawless society of men, a milieu in which physical
strength, courage, and personal charisma supplant institutional authority and violent conflict is the accepted means of
settling disputes. The Western narrative connects pleasurably
with the American romance of individualistic masculinity;
small wonder that the predominantly male founders of the
Net's culture found it so appealing.

When civilization arrives on the frontier, it comes dressed 11
in skirts and short pants. In the archetypal 1939 movie *Dodge
City,* Wade Hatton (Errol Flynn) refuses to accept the position of marshal because he prefers the footloose life of a trail
driver. Abbie Irving (Olivia de Haviland), a recent arrival
from the civilized East, scolds him for his unwillingness to
accept and advance the cause of law; she can't function (in
her job as crusading journalist) in a town governed by brute
force. It takes the accidental killing of a child in a street brawl
for Hatton to realize that he must pin on the badge and clean
up Dodge City.

In the Western mythos, civilization is necessary because 12
women and children are victimized in conditions of freedom.
Introduce women and children into a frontier town and the
law must follow because women and children must be protected. Women, in fact, are usually the most vocal proponents
of the conversion from frontier justice to civil society.

The imperiled women and children of the Western narra- 13
tive make their appearance today in newspaper and magazine
articles that focus on the intimidation and sexual harassment
of women on line and reports of pedophiles trolling for
victims in computerized chat rooms. If on-line women successfully contest these attempts to depict them as the beleaguered prey of brutish men, expect the pedophile to assume
a larger profile in arguments that the Net is out of control.

In the meantime, the media prefer to cast women as the 14
victims, probably because many women actively participate in
the call for greater regulation of on-line interactions, just as
Abbie Irving urges Wade Hatton to bring the rule of law to
Dodge City. These requests have a long cultural tradition,
based on the idea that women, like children, constitute a

peculiarly vulnerable class of people who require special protection from the elements of society men are expected to confront alone. In an insufficiently civilized society like the frontier, women, by virtue of this childlike vulnerability, are thought to live under the constant threat of kidnap, abuse, murder, and especially rape.

Women, who have every right to expect that crimes against 15 their person will be rigorously prosecuted, should nevertheless regard the notion of special protections (chivalry, by another name) with suspicion. Based as it is on the idea that women are inherently weak and incapable of self-defense and that men are innately predatory, it actually reinforces the power imbalance between the sexes, with its roots in the concept of women as property, constantly under siege and requiring the vigilant protection of their male owners. If the romance of the frontier arises from the promise of vast stretches of unowned land, an escape from the restrictions of a society based on private property, the introduction of women spoils that dream by reintroducing the imperative of property in their own persons.

How does any of this relate to on-line interactions, which 16 occur not on a desert landscape but in a complex, technological society where women are supposed to command equal status with men? It accompanies us as a set of unexamined assumptions about what it means to be male or female, assumptions that we believe are rooted in the imperatives of our bodies. These assumptions follow us into the bodiless realm of cyberspace, a forum where, as one scholar put it, "participants are washed clean of the stigmata of their real 'selves' and are free to invent new ones to their tastes." Perhaps some observers feel that the replication of gender roles in a context where the absence of bodies supposedly makes them superfluous proves exactly how innate those roles are. Instead, I see in the relentless attempts to interpret on-line interactions as highly gendered, an intimation of just how artificial, how created, our gender system is. If it comes "naturally," why does it need to be perpetually defended and reasserted?

Complaints about the treatment of women on line fall into 17
three categories: that women are subjected to excessive, unwanted sexual attention, that the prevailing style of on-line
discussion turns women off, and that women are singled out
by male participants for exceptionally dismissive or hostile
treatment. In making these assertions, the *Newsweek* article
and other stories on the issue do echo grievances that some
on-line women have made for years. And, without a doubt,
people have encountered sexual come-ons, aggressive debating tactics, and ad hominem attacks on the Net. However,
individual users interpret such events in widely different ways,
and to generalize from those interpretations to describe the
experiences of women and men as a whole is a rash leap
indeed.

I am one of many women who don't recognize their own 18
experience of the Net in the misogynist gauntlet described
above. In researching this essay, I joined America Online and
spent an hour or two "hanging out" in the real-time chat
rooms reputed to be rife with sexual harassment. I received
several "instant messages" from men, initiating private conversations with innocuous questions about my hometown
and tenure on the service. One man politely inquired if I was
interested in "hot phone talk" and just as politely bowed out
when I declined. At no point did I feel harassed or treated
with disrespect. If I ever want to find a phone-sex partner, I
now know where to look but until then I probably won't
frequent certain chat rooms.

Other women may experience a request for phone sex or 19
even those tame instant messages as both intrusive and insulting (while still others maintain that they have received
much more explicit messages and inquiries completely out of
the blue). My point isn't that my reactions are the more
correct, but rather that both are the reactions of women, and
no journalist has any reason to believe that mine are the
exception rather than the rule.

For me, the menace in sexual harassment comes from the 20
underlying threat of rape or physical violence. I see my body
as the site of my heightened vulnerability as a woman. But

on line—where I have no body and neither does anyone else—I consider rape to be impossible. Not everyone agrees. Julian Dibble, in an article for *The Village Voice*, describes the repercussions of a "rape" in a multiuser dimension, or MUD, in which one user employed a subprogram called a "voodoo doll" to cause the personae of other users to perform sexual acts. Citing the "conflation of speech and act that's inevitable in any computer-mediated world," he moved toward the conclusion that "since rape can occur without any physical pain or damage, then it must be classified as a crime against the mind." Therefore, the offending user had committed something on the same "conceptual continuum" as rape. Tellingly, the incident led to the formation of the first governmental entity on the MUD.

No doubt the cyber-rapist (who went by the nom de 21 guerre Mr. Bungle) appreciated the elevation of his mischief-making to the rank of virtual felony: all of the outlaw glamour and none of the prison time (he was exiled from the MUD). Mr. Bungle limited his victims to personae created by women users, a choice that, in its obedience to prevailing gender roles, shaped the debate that followed his crimes. For, in accordance with the real-world understanding that women's smaller, physically weaker bodies and lower social status make them subject to violation by men, there's a troubling notion in the real and virtual worlds that women's minds are also more vulnerable to invasion, degradation, and abuse.

This sense of fragility extends beyond interactions with 22 sexual overtones. The *Newsweek* article reports that women participants can't tolerate the harsh, contentious quality of on-line discussions, that they prefer mutual support to heated debate, and are retreating wholesale to women-only conferences and newsgroups. As someone who values on-line forums precisely because they mandate equal time for each user who chooses to take it and forestall various "alpha male" rhetorical tactics like interrupting, loudness, or exploiting the psychosocial advantages of greater size or a deeper voice, I find this perplexing and disturbing. In these laments I hear the reluctance of women to enter into the kind of robust debate that characterizes healthy public life, a willingness to let men bully us even when they've been relieved of most of their traditional advantages. Withdrawing into an electronic purdah where one will never be challenged or provoked, allowing the ludicrous ritual chest-thumping of some users to intimidate us into silence—surely women can come up with a more spirited response than this.

And of course they can, because besides being riddled with 23 reductive stereotypes, media analyses like *Newsweek*'s simply aren't accurate. While the on-line population is predominantly male, a significant and vocal minority of women contribute regularly and more than manage to hold their own. Some of The Well's most bombastic participants are women, just as there are many tactful and conciliatory men. At least, I think there are, because, ultimately, it's impossible to be sure of anyone's biological gender on line. "Transpostites," people who pose as members of the opposite gender, are an established element of Net society, most famously a man who, pretending to be a disabled lesbian, built warm and intimate friendships with women on several CompuServe forums.

Perhaps what we should be examining is not the triumph 24 of gender differences on the Net, but their potential blurring. In this light, *Newsweek*'s stout assertion that in cyberspace "the gender gap is real" begins to seem less objective than defensive, an insistence that on-line culture is "the same" as real life because the idea that it might be different, when it comes to gender, is too scary. If gender roles can be cast off so easily, they may be less deeply rooted, less "natural" than we believe. There may not actually be a "masculine" or "feminine" mind or outlook, but simply a conventional way of interpreting individuals that recognizes behavior seen as in accordance with their biological gender and ignores behavior that isn't.

For example, John Seabury wrote in the *New Yorker* (June 25 6, 1994) of his stricken reaction to his first "flame," a colorful slice of adolescent invective sent to him by an unnamed technology journalist. Reading it, he begins to "shiver" like a burn victim, an effect that worsens with repeated readings.

He writes that "the technology greased the words . . . with a kind of immediacy that allowed them to slide easily into my brain." He tells his friends, his coworkers, his partner—even his mother—and, predictably, appeals to CompuServe's management for recourse—to no avail. Soon enough, he's talking about civilization and anarchy, how the liberating "lack of social barriers is also what is appalling about the net," and calling for regulation.

As a newcomer, Seabury was chided for brooding over a 26 missive that most Net veterans would have dismissed and forgotten as the crude potshot of an envious jerk. (I can't help wondering if my fellow journalist ever received hate mail in response to his other writings; this bit of e-mail seems comparable, par for the course when one assumes a public profile.) What nobody did was observe that Seabury's reaction—the shock, the feelings of violation, the appeals to his family and support network, the bootless complaints to the authorities—reads exactly like many horror stories about women's trials on the Net. Yet, because Seabury is a man, no one attributes the attack to his gender or suggests that the Net has proven an environment hostile to men. Furthermore, the idea that the Net must be more strictly governed to prevent the abuse of guys who write for the *New Yorker* seems laughable—though who's to say that Seabury's pain is less than any woman's? Who can doubt that, were he a woman, his tribulations would be seen as compelling evidence of Internet sexism?

The idea that women merit special protections in an envi- 27 ronment as incorporeal as the Net is intimately bound up with the idea that women's minds are weak, fragile, and unsuited to the rough and tumble of public discourse. It's an argument that women should recognize with profound mistrust and resist, especially when we are used as rhetorical pawns in a battle to regulate a rare (if elite) space of gender ambiguity. When the mainstream media generalize about women's experiences on line in ways that just happen to uphold the most conventional and pernicious gender stereotypes, they can expect to be greeted with howls of disapproval from women who refuse to acquiesce in these roles and pass them on to other women.

And there are plenty of us, as The Well's response to the 28 *Newsweek* article indicates. Women have always participated in on-line communications, women whose chosen careers in technology and the sciences have already marked them as gender-role resisters. As the schoolmarms arrive on the electronic frontier, their female predecessors find themselves cast in the role of saloon girls, their willingness to engage in "masculine" activities like verbal aggression, debate, or sexual experimentation marking them as insufficiently feminine, or "bad" women. "If that's what women on line are like, I must be a Martian," one Well woman wrote in response to the shrinking female technophobes depicted in the *Newsweek* article. Rather than relegating so many people to the status of gender aliens, we ought to reconsider how adequate those roles are to the task of describing real human beings.

Topics for Writing
Definition

1. *Respond.* Watch several western movies. Then respond to one that features the themes Miller defines as essential to the "western narrative": the conflict between a lawless society of men and the civilizing influences of women. You may find a western in which gender roles are not so predictable. For example, you may find a western film in which women are independent, self-sufficient, and powerful. Whichever film you select, review it for the student paper—pointing out the features of its frontier theme. (*Resources for Comparison:* Richard Rodriguez, "Growing Up in Los Angeles," page 343; Stephen Harrigan, "The Tiger Is God," page 350).

2. *Analyze.* Print the text of a conversation in a chat room. Try to identify—by name, style, or interchange—the gender of the participants. Do the women in this virtual space write/act like women? Do the men write like stereotypical males—using sexual come-ons, aggressive debating tactics, and ad hominen attacks? Based on your analysis write an essay for first-time chat room users explaining why (1) sexual differences are the same in the virtual world as they are in the real world or (2) sexual identity seems more blurred, more artificial in the virtual world than in the real world. (*Resources for Comparison:* John Berendt, "The Hoax," page 338; Alice Walker, "Everyday Use," page 370).

3. *Argue.* Consider the arguments for and against government regulations of the Internet. Do women and children need protection? Does regulating infringe on free speech? What about installing some kind of chip that would block sexual harassment or predators? Do the rules of free speech—often invoked in defense of published pornography—apply to cyberspace? Define your position and then cite cases that support it. You can find examples on web-

sites for both positions on the Family Virtues Network or the American Civil Liberties Union. (*Resources for Comparison:* Witold Rybczynski, "One Good Turn," page 333; David Brooks, "Bobos: The New Upper Class," page 361).

M . K A D I

M. Kadi was born in Oakland, California, in 1962 and educated at the University of California, Berkeley. She worked as a computer consultant for fifteen years and then began writing about the cultural and economic issues in cyberspace. Her articles have appeared in anthologies such as the *Utne Reader*, on-line journals such as *h2so4*, and various textbooks on writing and argument. In "Welcome to Cyberbia," Kadi analyzes how money dictates who moves into a virtual community.

Welcome to Cyberbia
Money Dictates Who Moves into a Virtual Community

Computer networking offers the soundest basis for world peace that has yet been presented. Peace must be created on the bulwark of understanding. International computer net works will knit together the peoples of the world in bonds of mutual respect; its possibilities are vast, indeed.
—*SCIENTIFIC AMERICAN*, JUNE 1994

COMPUTER BULLETIN BOARD services offer up the glories 1 of e-mail, the thought provocation of newsgroups, the sharing of ideas implicit in public posting, and the interaction of real-time chats. The fabulous, wonderful, limitless world of communication is just waiting for you to log on. Sure. Yeah. Right. What this whole delirious, interconnected, global community of a world needs is a little reality check.

Let's face facts. The U.S. government by and large foots   2
the bill for the Internet, through maintaining the structural
(hardware) backbone, including, among other things, fund-
ing to major universities. As surely as the Department of
Defense started this whole thing, AT&T or Ted Turner is
going to end up running it, so I don't think it's too unrealistic
to take a look at the Net as it exists in its commercial form

---

*Between the monetary constraints and the
sheer number of topics and individual posts,
the great Information Highway is not a
place where you will enter an "amazing
web of new people, places, and ideas."*

---

in order to expose some of the realities lurking behind the
regurgitated media rhetoric and the religious fanaticism of
net junkies.

The average person, J. Individual, has an income. How   3
much of J. Individual's income is going to be spent on
computer connectivity? Does $120 a month sound reason-
able? Well, you may find that a bit too steep for your pock-
etbook, but the brutal fact is that $120 is a "reasonable"
monthly amount. The major on-line services have a monthly
service charge of approximately $15. Fifteen dollars to join
the global community, communicate with a diverse group of
people, and access the world's largest repository of knowledge since the Alexandrian library doesn't seem unreasonable, does it? But don't overlook the average per-hour
connection rate of $3 (which can skyrocket upwards of $10,
depending on your modem speed and service). You might
think that you are a crack whiz with your communications
software—that you are rigorous and stringent and never, ever

respond to e-mail or a forum while you're on-line—but let me tell you that no one is capable of logging on efficiently every time. Thirty hours per month is a realistic estimate for on-line time spent by a single user engaging in activities beyond primitive e-mail. Now consider that the average, one-step-above-complete-neophyte user has at least two distinct BBS (bulletin board system) accounts, and do the math. Total monthly cost: $120. Most likely, that's already more than the combined cost of your utility bills. How many people are prepared to double their monthly bills for the sole purpose of connectivity?

In case you think 30 hours a month is an outrageous estimate, think of it in terms of television. Thirty hours a month in front of a television is simply the evening news plus a weekly *Seinfeld/Frasier* hour. Thirty hours a month is less time than the average car-phone owner spends on the phone while commuting. Even a conscientious geek, logging on for e-mail and the up-to-the-minute news that only the net services can provide, is probably going to spend 30 hours a month on-line. And, let's be truthful here, 30 hours a month ignores shareware downloads, computer illiteracy, real-time chatting, interactive game playing, and any serious forum following, which by nature entail a significant amount of scrolling and/or downloading time.

If you are really and truly going to use the net services to connect with the global community, the hourly charges are going to add up pretty quickly. Take out a piece of paper, pretend you're writing a check, and print out "One hundred and twenty dollars—" and tell me again, how diverse is the on-line community?

That scenario aside, let's pretend that you have as much time and as much money to spend on-line as you damn well want. What do you actually do on-line?

Well, you download some cool shareware, you post technical questions in the computer user group forums, you check your stocks, you read the news and maybe some reviews— hey, you've already passed that 30-hour limit! But, of course, since computer networks are supposed to make it easy to reach out and touch strangers who share a particular obsession or concern, you are participating in the on-line forums, discussion groups, and conferences.

Let's review the structure of forums. For the purposes of 8 this essay, we will examine the smallest of the major user-friendly commercial services—America Online (AOL). There is no precise statistic available (at least none that the company will reveal—you have to do the research by HAND!!!) on exactly how many subject-specific discussion areas (folders) exist on America Online. Any on-line service is going to have zillions of posts—contributions from users—pertaining to computer usage (the computer games area of America Online, for example, breaks into 500 separate topics with over 100,000 individual posts), so let's look at a less popular area: the "Lifestyles and Interests" department.

For starters, as I write this, there are 57 initial categories 9 within the Lifestyles and Interests area. One of these categories is Ham Radio. Ham Radio? How can there possibly be 5,909 separate, individual posts about Ham Radio? There are 5,865 postings in the Biking (and that's just bicycles, not motorcycles) category. Genealogy—22,525 posts. The Gay and Lesbian category is slightly more substantial—36,333 posts. There are five separate categories for political and issue discussion. The big catchall topic area, the Exchange, has over 100,000 posts. Servicewide (on the smallest service, remember) there are over a million posts.

You may want to join the on-line revolution, but obviously 10 you can't wade through everything that's being discussed—you need to decide which topics interest you, which folders to browse. Within the Exchange alone (one of 57 subdivisions within one of another 50 higher divisions) there are 1,492 separate topic-specific folders—each containing a rough average of 50 posts, but many containing closer to 400. (Note: America Online automatically empties folders when their post totals reach 400, so total post numbers do not reflect the overall historical totals for a given topic. Sometimes the posting is so frequent that the "shelf life" of a given post is no more than four weeks.)

So, there you are, J. Individual, ready to start interacting 11 with folks, sharing stories and communicating. You have narrowed yourself into a single folder, three tiers down in the America Online hierarchy, and now you must choose between nearly 1,500 folders. Of course, once you choose a few of these folders, you will then have to read all the posts in order to catch up, be current, and not merely repeat a previous post.

A polite post is no more than two paragraphs long (a 12 screenful of text, which obviously has a number of intellectually negative implications). Let's say you choose 10 folders (out of 1,500). Each folder contains an average of 50 posts. Five hundred posts, at, say, one paragraph each, and you're now looking at the equivalent of a 200-page book.

Enough with the stats. Let me back up a minute and 13 present you with some very disturbing, but rational, assumptions. J. Individual wants to join the on-line revolution, to connect and communicate. But J. is not going to read all one million posts on AOL. (After all, J. has a second on-line service.) Exercising choice is J. Individual's God-given right as an American, and, by gosh, J. Individual is going to make some decisions. So J. is going to ignore all the support groups—after all, J. is a normal, well-adjusted person, and all of J.'s friends are normal, well-adjusted people; what does J. need to know about alcoholism or incest victims? J. Individual is white. So J. Individual is going to ignore all the multicultural folders. J. couldn't give a hoot about gender issues and does not want to discuss religion or philosophy. Ultimately, J. Individual does not engage in topics that do not interest J. Individual. So who is J. meeting? Why, people who are *just like* J.

J. Individual has now joined the electronic community. 14 Surfed the Net. Found some friends. *Tuned in, turned on, and geeked out.* Traveled the Information Highway and, just a few miles down that great democratic expressway, J. Individual has settled into an electronic suburb.

Are any of us so very different? It's my time and my money 15
and I am not going to waste any of it reading posts by
disgruntled Robert-Bly drum-beating men's-movement boys
who think that they should have some say over, for instance,
whether or not I choose to carry a child to term simply
because a condom broke. I know where I stand. I'm an adult.
I know what's up and I am not going to waste my money
arguing with a bunch of neanderthals.

Oh yeah; I am so connected, so enlightened, so open to 16
the opposing viewpoint. I'm out there, meeting all kinds of
people from different economic backgrounds (who have
$120 a month to burn), from all religions (yeah, right, like
anyone actually discusses religion anymore from a user standpoint), from all kinds of different ethnic backgrounds and
with all kinds of sexual orientations (as if any of this ever
comes up outside of the appropriate topic folder).

People are drawn to topics and folders that interest them 17
and therefore people will only meet people who are interested
in the same topics in the same folders. Rarely does anyone
venture into a random folder just to see what others (the
Other?) are talking about.

Basically, between the monetary constraints and the sheer 18
number of topics and individual posts, the great Information
Highway is not a place where you will enter an "amazing web
of new people, places, and ideas." One does not encounter
people from "all walks of life" because there are too many
people and too many folders. Diversity might be out there
(and personally I don't think it is), but the simple fact is that
the average person will not encounter it because with one
brain, one job, one partner, one family, and one life, no one
has the time!

Just in case these arguments based on time and money 19
aren't completely convincing, let me bring up a historical
reference. Please take another look at the opening quote of
this essay, from *Scientific American*. It was featured in their
50 Years Ago Today column. Where you read "computer
networking," the quote originally contained the word *television*. Amusing, isn't it?

Topics for Writing
Cause and Effect

1. *Respond.* Review the *Favorites* that you have added to the "bookmark" section of your Internet exchange. How diverse is your list? What kinds of sites are missing? Respond to Kadi's assertion that individuals do not seek out people or ideas that are different. Use your own list—or revised list—to analyze how the Internet has caused you to meet people just like you or people with a different point of view. (*Resources for Comparison:* Robert Coles, "Uniforms," page 402; Sandra Cisneros, "One Holy Night," page 433).

2. *Analyze.* Kadi analyzes the cost of logging on to the Internet. Collect some evidence of your own. How much do the students you know pay in monthly charges for "connecting"? Does this charge inevitably exclude certain people? Who? Using your research as a resource, write a "reality check" on the assertion that "computer networking offers the soundest basis for world peace that has yet been presented." (*Resources for Comparison:* Carl Sagan, "Science and Hope," page 391; Andrew C. Revkin, "Some Big Ideas Wash Up One Bulb at a Time," page 396).

3. *Argue.* Kadi's position rests on the assumption that although technology—television, car phones, and the Internet—change some details of our life, much of our life remains the same. For example, although "diversity might be out there, the simple fact is that the average person will not encounter it because with one brain, one job, one partner, one family, and one life, no one has the time!" Her argument is convincing; however, instead of accepting her position construct a cause-and-effect analysis to demonstrate that this information highway really does inform and enlighten the average person. (*Resources for Comparison:* Daniel Goleman, "Peak Performance: Why Records Fall," page 409; Cathy Young, "Keeping Women Weak," page 417).

EVAN I. SCHWARTZ

Evan I. Schwartz was born in Brooklyn, New York, in 1964 and educated at Union College, Schenectady, New York. As a journalist, he has been covering the high-tech industry for nearly fifteen years, publishing his articles in the *New York Times, Wired,* and *The Industry Standard.* He has also worked as an editor for *Business Week.* His first book, *Webonomics* (1997), has ranked as Amazon.com's number one best-selling business book. His latest book is *Digital Darwinism: 7 Breakthrough Strategies for Surviving in the Cutthroat Web Economy* (1999). In "Looking for Community on the Internet," first published in the *National Civic Review,* Schwartz argues that virtual communities can offer the same kind of warmth and companionship people have traditionally found in neighborhoods.

Looking for Community on the Internet

What are the human needs that electronic social environments—virtual communities set up on the Internet—seek to satisfy? What is their potential for encouraging the reinforcement of community in real space and time?

C AN A TRULY vibrant community exist in cyberspace? Can a bunch of individuals at isolated computer stations achieve warmth, caring and a shared set of values? Is the Internet becoming a pipeline for surrogate communities in an age of technological omnipresence?   1

Community is not the image of the Internet promoted by government and industry. If you ask the telecommunications   2

619

giants and the media conglomerates racing to build the "info-
tainment" pipeline of the future, they point to a world of
interconnected business people, students, e-mailers, and government workers, all operating with breakneck efficiency and
without leaving their desks. But this image might have little
meaning for the numberless millions of actual Internet users,
who might have a starkly different collective vision for tomorrow's advanced communications technologies. In *The Virtual
Community,* author Howard Rheingold dismisses the now-
popular notion that the public demands a great stream of

---

*The Internet is a spirited web of
conversation individuals can weave
themselves by tapping into their personal
computers' keyboards and powering up their
modems.*

---

interactive entertainment and information. What the people
really want, he argues, is a chance to form meaningful relationships with their far-flung neighbors in the global village.
Dale Dougherty, publisher of the *Global Network Navigator,*
an electronic magazine on the Internet, agrees. The Internet,
he says, is filling a deep need: "We want a feeling of connect-
edness, of having things in common."

The "Net" is an amalgam of electronic bulletin boards,   3
on-line information services, and computer conference sessions—all connected by the same global telecommunications
networks to which our phones are attached. Linking about
20 million people in 100 countries, the U.S. government-
subsidized Internet originated in the Department of Defense
in the 1960s and expanded into elite corporate labs in the
1970s, into American universities in the 1980s, and finally
right into many living rooms in the early 1990s. For now,

communications is mainly confined to written text, but that is changing as the 'Net gains the ability to handle voice, video, and other multimedia information. Already, some cable companies are providing Internet link-ups, and there soon will come a day when people with cheap digital video cameras can transmit their footage to the masses.

The virtual community idea approximates much more   4
closely the real Internet than does the popular metaphor of a superhighway running into people's living rooms. The Internet is a spirited web of conversation individuals can weave themselves by tapping into their personal computers' keyboards and powering up their modems. A virtual community, according to Rheingold, is a group of people who have in all likelihood never met face to face, but who enjoy spending time in cyberspace with one another debating politics, discussing their hobbies, conducting business, spilling their guts, or just flirting and playing games with one another.

Rheingold's book provides a tour of the Internet—a tour   5
that begins from inside the specific virtual community to which Rheingold belongs. Based in San Francisco and known as the WELL (for Whole Earth 'Lectronic Link), Rheingold's local virtual community began in 1985 as an experiment. The idea was to give people access to new tools for group communication, letting them decide on their own how it should be used.

Not surprisingly, the WELL has experienced its greatest   6
growth as a forum for discussing the Grateful Dead. But significantly, the Deadheads on the WELL translate their on-line interactions into face-to-face meetings. Occasionally, the Deadheads and other interest groups hold picnics or concerts. For the most part, the Internet acts as a social leveler: Once on-line, no one can tell if you're black or white, old or young, male or female, sick or well. Perhaps most importantly, no one can tell how unattractive you are—looks have never played a smaller role in human affairs than they do on the Internet.

For Rheingold, the WELL is a place to discuss the joys and   7
problems associated with raising kids. One time, when his

daughter got a tick caught in her scalp, he sat down at his PC, typed in his question, and learned from an on-line fellow named Flash Gordon, M.D., how exactly to remove it. The tick was gone by the time the real pediatrician returned a phone call from the author's wife.

Another bulletin board, Baud Town, also emphasizes community by building itself around the analogy of a town, complete with social norms. New joiners receive a lengthy etiquette message explaining that the bulletin-board community allows no X-rated discussion groups or messages in capital letters (the latter are the equivalent of shouting on-line). The bulletin board community even has its own "Neighborhood Watch," in which users police one another against abuse of the system. All of these efforts help reduce anonymous harassment on-line and make for a "safer" electronic community.   8

The "citizens" of Baud Town have created an environment in which they give and receive support. Users receive comforting messages from fellow users during difficult times, such as divorce, illness or death in their families. Much like WELL users, Baud Townies "date" on-line, taking advantage of the low-pressure atmosphere of the Internet that allows users to get to know each other's personalities before meeting in person.   9

The Internet's capacity to function as a vehicle for community lies in the differences between it and all previous communications media. While telephones are primarily a one-to-one medium and television a few-to-many medium, the hypergrowth of the Internet marks the beginning of many-to-many communication. Greater possibilities lie just over the horizon. In two years, one expert predicts, there will be more users on the Internet than there are people living in California. Within five years, the on-line populace will exceed the number of citizens in any country except India or China. With the Internet's ability to transcend time zones and national boundaries, it could contribute to greater understanding between cultures. On the other hand, the   10 free-flowing dialogue could bring on social upheaval, especially in places like Japan, where communication outside cultures is tightly controlled by the powers that be.

Like physical communities, virtual communities can exert 11 strong pressure on members to conform to behavioral norms and conventions. In April a pair of lawyers in Phoenix, Arizona placed an ad for legal services on the Internet. (Noncommercialization of the Internet is one of the cardinal, if unofficial, rules of the medium.) In response to this transgression, users around the world "flamed" the couple with 30,000 hostile messages. The barrage, according to the *Phoenix Gazette,* caused the local Internet node, Internet Direct, to overload and temporarily shut down. Internet Direct posted apologies for the ad and suspended the lawyers' access to the system. Internet Direct systems administrator Geoff Wheelhouse told the *Gazette,* "[The incident] has given us a bad reputation." Most actual communities work no more effectively.

The United States might be poised to benefit most from 12 virtual communities. Since the convivial atmosphere that still exists in Italian piazzas and Parisian bistros has largely died in the U.S., Americans hunger for a new way to connect with each other. One of Rheingold's sources attributes the decline of public meeting spaces in the U.S. to the nation's "suburbanized, urban-decayed, paved, and malled environment." Others attribute the breakdown of intelligent public discourse to the fact that "the public sphere," particularly the airwaves, has been commoditized and sold off to media moguls and advertisers. The Internet, by contrast, still has a chance to be run by and for the grass roots.

Internet enthusiasts sometimes see virtual community as a 13 panacea for all sorts of social ills. They go a bit far, for example, when they hold out the possibility that the Internet could become a forum for electronic democracy. The people conversing on the Internet and other on-line services are, by and large, not a bunch of civic leaders. The untamed, freewheeling nature of cyberspace means that it is often filled with

every skinhead, Trekkie, religious zealot, and Limbaugh-
wannabe with a new theory on how the world should work.
The Internet is not—at least not yet—a town hall meeting.
But cyberspace community is by no means irrelevant to   14
democracy and citizenship. Because it is not centrally controlled, the Internet is a regular proving ground for the First
Amendment. The "alt.sex.pictures" bulletin board, for example, was once based on a Texas computer. When local authorities began a crackdown, however, the operators of the service
moved it to a computer in Finland literally overnight, causing
an instant surge in network traffic to that part of the world.
At the same time, on bulletin boards and Internet conferences, the faithful can quietly discuss theology and the Bible.
There are bulletin boards for every imaginable subject and
interest group: sex and substance abuse, veterans, vegetarians,
gays and lesbians, animal rights activists, and even one for fat
people (called the "Big Board").

The question is how real these communities are and to   15
what extent they really fill the needs of more traditional
communities. The answer is not entirely clear. The Internet
is uncharted territory both for individuals and communities.
"It's like a boomtown in the old West," says Dougherty.
"The rules are not written yet. With TV, people are controlling you. Here, you are on your own."

Even Internet enthusiasts acknowledge that cyberspace   16
may never be a replacement for true communities. Rheingold, who clearly is caught up in channeling virtual communities as a force for good, expresses openly his reservations
about the Internet as a surrogate community: "Perhaps cyberspace is precisely the *wrong* place to look for the rebirth
of community . . . offering a life-denying simulacrum of real
passion and true commitment to one another." And, he asks,
"If a lonely person chooses to spend many hours a day in an
imaginary society, typing witticisms with strangers on other
continents, is that good or bad?"

The key word in the cyberspace community lexicon is   17
"virtual." Like an elaborate, electronic flight simulator, the
technology is breathtaking and the simulation is compelling.

Only when the users find themselves in the cockpits of real airplanes (or in the midst of real communities) do they realize how limiting "virtual" can really be. Still, for many people, the choice seems to be between a very good simulation of community and no community at all; that choice makes the virtual community look very attractive indeed.

Topics for Writing
Persuasion and Argument

1. *Respond.* Schwartz argues that much of cyberspace is filled with skinheads, Trekkies, religious zealots, and Limbaugh-wannabes. What kind of people have you met on the Internet? Have you ever tried to meet them in person? Respond to Schwartz's argument by writing a column about your experience meeting someone you met in cyberspace in real space. Hopefully, he or she was a reasonable citizen, not one of the zany characters Schwartz describes. (*Resources for Comparison:* Martin Luther King, Jr., "I Have a Dream," page 458; Eric Liu, "A Chinaman's Chance: Reflections on the American Dream," page 465).

2. *Analyze.* Check out the two sites Schwartz mentions: WELL and Baud Town. Analyze the way they present themselves on the screen, their membership requirements, their etiquette messages, and some of their actual exchanges. Using this evidence, argue that these virtual communities do provide users with a chance to form meaningful relationships. You may even want to participate in one of these virtual communities to collect more evidence for your analysis. (*Resources for Comparison:* Paul Rogat Loeb, "Soul of a Citizen," page 498; Sven Birkerts, "Confessions of a Nonpolitical Man," page 505).

3. *Argue.* Schwartz, quoting Howard Rheingold, wonders whether it is good or bad "if a lonely person chooses to spend many hours a day in an imaginary society." Consider each side of this argument. It is a good thing because it helps lonely people find a social life. It is a bad thing because it reinforces their loneliness by supplying them with a phony social life. Collect opinions from your real family and friends, and from those people you have met on line. Then take one side of the argument and write a persuasive essay to "all the lonely people." (*Resources for Comparison:* Toni Morrison, "The Bird in Our Hand," page 509; Jonathan Rauch, "In Defense of Prejudice," page 520).

WILLIAM GIBSON

William Gibson was born in Conway, South Carolina, in 1948 and educated at the University of British Columbia. Gibson began his career in college when he signed up for a course in science fiction. Unwilling to submit a traditional research paper, he accepted his teacher's challenge to write a short story. After graduation, he continued to contribute short stories to magazines such as *Omni* until he published his first novel, *Neuromancer* (1984)—the first novel ever to win all the science fiction awards. Gibson's "cyberpunk" style is also evident in novels such as *Count Zero* (1986), *Mona Lisa Overdrive* (1988), *Virtual Light* (1993), and *Idoru* (1996). In "Burning Chrome," one of Gibson's early stories, he introduces the concept of "cyberspace" as two cyber cowboys play a high-stakes game in multiple dimensions.

Burning Chrome

I T WAS HOT, the night we burned Chrome. Out in the malls and plazas, moths were batting themselves to death against the neon, but in Bobby's loft the only light came from a monitor screen and the green and red LEDs on the face of the matrix simulator. I knew every chip in Bobby's simulator by heart; it looked like your workaday Ono-Sendai VII, the 'Cyberspace Seven,' but I'd rebuilt it so many times that you'd have had a hard time finding a square millimetre of factory circuitry in all that silicon.

We waited side by side in front of the simulator console, watching the time display in the screen's lower left corner.

'Go for it,' I said, when it was time, but Bobby was already there, leaning forward to drive the Russian program into its

slot with the heel of his hand. He did it with the tight grace
of a kid slamming change into an arcade game, sure of winning and ready to pull down a string of free games.

A silver tide of phosphenes boiled across my field of vision   4
as the matrix began to unfold in my head, a 3-D chessboard,
infinite and perfectly transparent. The Russian program
seemed to lurch as we entered the grid. If anyone else had
been jacked into that part of the matrix, he might have seen
a surf of flickering shadow roll out of the little yellow pyramid
that represented our computer. The program was a mimetic
weapon, designed to absorb local colour and present itself as
a crash-priority override in whatever context it encountered.

'Congratulations,' I heard Bobby say. 'We just became an   5
Eastern Seaboard Fission Authority inspection probe. . . .'
That meant we were clearing fiberoptic lines with the cybernetic equivalent of a fire siren, but in the simulation matrix
we seemed to rush straight for Chrome's database. I couldn't
see it yet, but I already knew those walls were waiting. Walls
of shadow, walls of ice.

Chrome: her pretty childface smooth as steel, with eyes   6
that would have been at home on the bottom of some deep
Atlantic trench, cold grey eyes that lived under terrible pressure. They said she cooked her own cancers for people who
crossed her, rococo custom variations that took years to kill
you. They said a lot of things about Chrome, none of them
at all reassuring.

So I blotted her out with a picture of Rikki. Rikki kneeling   7
in a shaft of dusty sunlight that slanted into the loft through
a grid of steel and glass: her faded camouflage fatigues, her
translucent rose sandals, the good line of her bare back as she
rummaged through a nylon gear bag. She looks up, and a
half-blond curl falls to tickle her nose. Smiling, buttoning an
old shirt of Bobby's, frayed khaki cotton drawn across her
breasts.

She smiles.   8

'Son of a bitch,' said Bobby, 'we just told Chrome we're   9
an IRS audit and three Supreme Court subpoenas. . . . Hang
on to your ass. Jack. . . .'

So long, Rikki. Maybe now I see you never.   10
And dark, so dark, in the halls of Chrome's ice.   11

Bobby was a cowboy, and ice was the nature of his game,   12
ice from ICE, Intrusion Countermeasures Electronics. The
matrix is an abstract representation of the relationships between data systems. Legitimate programmers jack into their
employers sector of the matrix and find themselves surrounded by bright geometries representing the corporate
data.

Towers and fields of it ranged in the colourless nonspace   13
of the simulation matrix, the electronic consensus-hallucina-
tion that facilitates the handling and exchange of massive
quantities of data. Legitimate programmers never see the
walls of ice they work behind, the walls of shadow that screen
their operations from others, from industrial-espionage artists
and hustlers like Bobby Quine.

Bobby was a cowboy. Bobby was a cracksman, a burglar,   14
casing mankind's extended electronic nervous system,
rustling data and credit in the crowded matrix, monochrome
nonspace where the only stars are dense concentrations of
information, and high above it all burn corporate galaxies and
the cold spiral arms of military systems.

Bobby was another one of those young-old faces you see   15
drinking in the Gentleman Loser, the chic bar for computer
cowboys, rustlers, cybernetic second-story men. We were
partners.

Bobby Quine and Automatic Jack. Bobby's the thin, pale   16
dude with the dark glasses, and Jack's the mean-looking guy
with the myoelectric arm. Bobby's software and Jack's hard;
Bobby punches console and Jack runs down all the little
things that can give you an edge. Or, anyway, that's what the
scene watchers in the Gentleman Loser would've told you,
before Bobby decided to burn Chrome. But they also
might've told you that Bobby was losing his edge, slowing
down. He was twenty-eight, Bobby, and that's old for a
console cowboy.

Both of us were good at what we did, but somehow that   17 one big score just wouldn't come down for us. I knew where to go for the right gear, and Bobby had all his licks down pat. He'd sit back with a white terry sweatband across his forehead and whip moves on those keyboards faster than you could follow, punching his way through some of the fanciest ice in the business, but that was when something happened that managed to get him totally wired, and that didn't happen often. Not highly motivated, Bobby, and I was the kind of guy who's happy to have the rent covered and a clean shirt to wear.

But Bobby had this thing for girls, like they were his   18
private tarot or something, the way he'd get himself moving. We never talked about it, but when it started to look like he was losing his touch that summer, he started to spend more time in the Gentleman Loser. He'd sit at a table by the open doors and watch the crowd slide by, nights when the bugs were at the neon and the air smelled of perfume and fast food. You could see his sunglasses scanning those faces as they passed, and he must have decided that Rikki's was the one he was waiting for, the wild card and the luck changer. The new one.

I went to New York to check out the market, to see what   19
was available in hot software.

The Finn's place was a defective hologram in the window;   20
METRO HOLOGRAFIX, over a display of dead flies wearing fur coats of grey dust. The scrap's waist-high, inside, drifts of it rising to meet walls that are barely visible behind nameless junk, behind sagging pressboard shelves stacked with old skin magazines and yellow-spined years of *National Geographic*.

'You need a gun,' said the Finn. He looks like a recombo   21
DNA project aimed at tailoring people for high-speed burrowing. 'You're in luck. I got the new Smith and Wesson, the four-oh-eight Tactical. Got this xenon projector slung under the barrel, see, batteries in the grip, throw you a twelve-inch high-noon circle in the pitch dark at fifty yards.

The light source is so narrow, it's almost impossible to spot. It's just like voodoo in a nightfight.'

I let my arm clunk down on the table and started the fingers drumming; the servos in the hand began whining like overworked mosquitoes. I knew that the Finn really hated the sound.

'You looking to pawn that?' He prodded the Duralumin wrist joint with the chewed shaft of a felt-tip pen. 'Maybe get yourself something a little quieter?'

I kept it up. 'I don't need any guns, Finn.'

'Okay,' he said, 'okay,' and I quit drumming. 'I only got this one item, and I don't even know what it is.' He looked unhappy. 'I got it off these bridge-and-tunnel kids from Jersey last week.'

'So when'd you ever buy anything you didn't know what it was, Finn?'

'Wise ass.' And he passed me a transparent mailer with something in it that looked like an audio cassette through the bubble padding. 'They had a passport,' he said. 'They had credit cards and a watch. And that.'

'They had the contents of somebody's pockets, you mean.'

He nodded. 'The passport was Belgian. It was also bogus, looked to me, so I put it in the furnace. Put the cards in with it. The watch was okay, a Porsche, nice watch.'

It was obviously some kind of plug-in military program. Out of the mailer, it looked like the magazine of a small assault rifle, coated with nonreflective black plastic. The edges and corners showed bright metal; it had been knocking around for a while.

'I'll give you a bargain on it, Jack. For old times' sake.'

I had to smile at that. Getting a bargain from the Finn was like God repealing the law of gravity when you have to carry a heavy suitcase down ten blocks of airport corridor.

'Looks Russian to me,' I said. 'Probably the emergency sewage controls for some Leningrad suburb. Just what I need.'

'You know,' said the Finn, 'I got a pair of shoes older than you are. Sometimes I think you got about as much class as those yahoos from Jersey. What do you want me to tell you, it's the keys to the Kremlin? You figure out what the goddamn thing is. Me, I just sell the stuff.'

I bought it.   35

Bodiless, we swerve into Chrome's castle of ice. And we're   36
fast, fast. It feels like we're surfing the crest of the invading program, hanging ten above the seething glitch systems as they mutate. We're sentient patches of oil swept along down corridors of shadow.

Somewhere we have bodies, very far away, in a crowded   37
loft roofed with steel and glass. Somewhere we have microseconds, maybe time left to pull out.

We've crashed her gates disguised as an audit and three   38
subpoenas, but her defences are specifically geared to cope with that kind of official intrusion. Her most sophisticated ice is structured to fend off warrants, writs, subpoenas. When we breached the first gate, the bulk of her data vanished behind core-command ice, these walls we see as leagues of corridor, mazes of shadow. Five separate landlines spurted May Day signals to law firms, but the virus had already taken over the parameter ice. The glitch systems gobble the distress calls as our mimetic subprograms scan anything that hasn't been blanked by core command.

The Russian program lifts a Tokyo number from the un-   39
screened data, choosing it for frequency of calls, average length of calls, the speed with which Chrome returned those calls.

'Okay,' says Bobby, 'we're an incoming scrambler call from   40
a pal of hers in Japan. That should help.'

Ride 'em, cowboy.   41

Bobby read his future in women; his girls were omens,   42
changes in the weather, and he'd sit all night in the Gentleman Loser, waiting for the season to lay a new face down in front of him like a card.

I was working late in the loft one night, shaving down a 43
chip, my arm off and the little waldo jacked straight into the
stump.

Bobby came in with a girl I hadn't seen before, and usually 44
I feel a little funny if a stranger sees me working that way,
with those leads clipped to the hard carbon studs that stick
out of my stump. She came right over and looked at the
magnified image on the screen, then saw the waldo moving
under its vacuum-sealed dust cover. She didn't say anything,
just watched. Right away I had a good feeling about her; it's
like that sometimes.

'Automatic Jack, Rikki. My associate.' 45

He laughed, put his arm around her waist, something in 46
his tone letting me know that I'd be spending the night in a
dingy room in a hotel.

'Hi,' she said. Tall, nineteen or maybe twenty, and she 47
definitely had the goods. With just those few freckles across
the bridge of her nose, and eyes somewhere between dark
amber and French coffee. Tight black jeans rolled to midcalf
and a narrow plastic belt that matched the rose-coloured
sandals.

But now when I see her sometimes when I'm trying to 48
sleep, I see her somewhere out on the edge of all this sprawl
of cities and smoke, and it's like she's a hologram stuck
behind my eyes, in a bright dress she must've worn once,
when I knew her, something that doesn't quite reach her
knees. Bare legs long and straight. Brown hair, streaked with
blond, hoods her face, blown in a wind from somewhere, and
I see her wave goodbye.

Bobby was making a show of rooting through a stack of 49
audio cassettes. 'I'm on my way, cowboy,' I said, unclipping
the waldo. She watched attentively as I put my arm back on.

'Can you fix things?' she asked. 50

'Anything, anything you want, Automatic Jack'll fix it.' I 51
snapped my Duralumin fingers for her.

She took a little simstim deck from her belt and showed 52
me the broken hinge on the cassette cover.

'Tomorrow,' I said, 'no problem.'   53

And my oh my, I said to myself, sleep pulling me down the   54
six flights to the street, *what'll Bobby's luck be like with a
fortune cookie like that? If his system worked, we'd be striking
it rich any night now.* In the street I grinned and yawned and
waved for a cab.

Chrome's castle is dissolving, sheets of ice shadow flicker-   55
ing and fading, eaten by the glitch systems that spin out from
the Russian program, tumbling away from our central logic
thrust and infecting the fabric of the ice itself. The glitch
systems are cybernetic virus analogs, self-replicating and voracious. They mutate constantly, in unison, subverting and
absorbing Chrome's defences.

Have we already paralysed her, or is a bell ringing some-   56
where, a red light blinking? Does she know?

Rikki Wildside, Bobby called her, and for these first few   57
weeks it must have seemed to her that she had it all, the whole
teeming show spread out for her, sharp and bright under the
neon. She was new to the scene, and she had all the miles of
malls and plazas to prowl, all the shops and clubs, and Bobby
to explain the wild side, the tricky wiring on the dark under-
side of things, all the players and their names and their games.
He made her feel at home.

'What happened to your arm?' she asked me one night in   58
the Gentleman Loser, the three of us drinking at a small table
in a corner.

'Hang-gliding,' I said, 'accident.'   59

'Hang-gliding over a wheatfield,' said Bobby, 'place called   60
Kiev. Our Jack's just hanging there in the dark, under a
Nightwing parafoil, with fifty kilos of radar jammer between
his legs, and some Russian asshole accidentally burns his arm
off with a laser.'

I don't remember how I changed the subject, but I did.   61

I was still telling myself that it wasn't Rikki who was   62
getting to me, but what Bobby was doing with her. I'd

known him for a long time, since the end of the war, and I knew he used women as counters in a game, Bobby Quine versus fortune, versus time and the night of cities. And Rikki had turned up just when he needed something to get him going, something to aim for. So he'd set her up as a symbol for everything he wanted and couldn't have, everything he'd had and couldn't keep.

I didn't like having to listen to him tell me how much 63 he loved her, and knowing he believed it only made it worse. He was a past master at the hard fall and the rapid recovery, and I'd seen it happen a dozen times before. He might as well have had NEXT printed across his sunglasses in green Day-Glo capitals, reading to flash out at the first interesting face that flowed past the tables in the Gentleman Loser.

I knew what he did to them. He turned them into em- 64 blems, sigils on the map of his hustler's life, navigation beacons he could follow through a sea of bars and neon. What else did he have to steer by? He didn't love money, in and of itself, not enough to follow its lights. He wouldn't work for power over other people; he hated the responsibility it brings. He had some basic pride in his skill, but that was never enough to keep him pushing.

So he made do with women. 65

When Rikki showed up, he needed one in the worst way. 66 He was fading fast, and smart money was already whispering that the edge was off his game. He needed that one big score, and soon, because he didn't know any other kind of life, and all his clocks were set for hustler's time, calibrated in risk and adrenaline and that supernal dawn calm that comes when every move's proved right and a sweet lump of someone else's credit clicks into your own account.

It was time for him to make his bundle and get out; so 67 Rikki got set up higher and further away than any of the others ever had, even though—and I felt like screaming it at him—she was right there, alive, totally real, human, hungry, resilient, bored, beautiful, excited, all the things she was. . . .

Then he went out one afternoon, about a week before I   68
made the trip to New York to see the Finn. Went out and left
us there in the loft, waiting for a thunderstorm. Half the
skylight was shadowed by a dome they'd never finished, and
the other half showed sky, black and blue with clouds. I was
standing by the bench, looking up at that sky, stupid with the
hot afternoon, the humidity, and she touched me, touched
my shoulder, the half-inch border of taut pink scar that the
arm doesn't cover. Anybody else ever touched me there, they
went on to the shoulder, the neck. . . .

But she didn't do that. Her nails were lacquered black, not   69
pointed, but tapered oblongs, the lacquer only a shade darker
than the carbon-fibre laminate that sheathes my arm. And her
hand went down the arm, black nails tracing a weld in the
laminate, down to the black anodized elbow joint, out to the
wrist, her hand soft-knuckled as a child's, fingers spreading
to lock over mine, her palm against the perforated Duralumin.

Her other palm came up to brush across the feedback pads,   70
and it rained all afternoon, raindrops drumming on the steel
and soot-stained glass above Bobby's bed.

Ice walls flick away like supersonic butterflies made of   71
shade. Beyond them, the matrix's illusion of infinite space.
It's like watching a tape of a prefab building going up; only
the tape's reversed and run at high speed, and these walls are
torn wings.

Trying to remind myself that this place and the gulfs be-   72
yond are only representations, that we aren't 'in' Chrome's
computer, but interfaced with it, while the matrix simulator
in Bobby's loft generates this illusion. . . . The core data
begin to emerge, exposed, vulnerable. . . . This is the far side
of ice, the view of the matrix I've never seen before, the view
that fifteen million legitimate console operators see daily and
take for granted.

The core data tower around us like vertical freight trains,   73
colour-coded for access. Bright primaries, impossibly bright

in that transparent void, linked by countless horizontals in nursery blues and pinks.

But ice still shadows something at the centre of it all: the 74 heart of all Chrome's expensive darkness, the very heart. . . .

It was late afternoon when I got back from my shopping 75 expedition to New York. Not much sun through the skylight, but an ice pattern glowed on Bobby's monitor screen, a 2-D graphic representation of someone's computer defences, lines of neon woven like an Art Deco prayer rug. I turned the console off, and the screen went completely dark.

Rikki's things were spread across my workbench, nylon 76 bags spilling clothes and make-up, a pair of bright red cowboy boots, audio cassettes, glossy Japanese magazines about simstim stars. I stacked it all under the bench and then took my arm off, forgetting that the program I'd bought from the Finn was in the right-hand pocket of my jacket, so that I had to fumble it out left-handed and then get it into the padded jaws of the jeweller's vice.

The waldo looks like an old audio turntable, the kind that 77 played disc records, with the vice set up under a transparent dust cover. The arm itself is just over a centimetre long, swinging out on what would've been the tone arm on one of those turntables. But I don't look at that when I've clipped the leads to my stump; I look at the scope, because that's my arm there in black and white, magnification 40×.

I ran a tool check and picked up the laser. It felt a little 78 heavy; so I scaled my weight-sensor input down to a quarter-kilo per gram and got to work. At 40× the side of the program looked like a trailer truck.

It took eight hours to crack: three hours with the waldo 79 and the laser and four dozen taps, two hours on the phone to a contact in Colorado, and three hours to run down a lexicon disc that could translate eight-year-old technical Russian.

Then Cyrillic alphanumerics started reeling down the 80 monitor, twisting themselves into English halfway down.

There were a lot of gaps, where the lexicon ran up against specialized military acronyms in the readout I'd bought from my man in Colorado, but it did give me some idea of what I'd bought from the Finn.

I felt like a punk who'd gone out to buy a switchblade and come home with a small neutron bomb. 81

Screwed again, I thought. *What good's a neutron bomb in* 82 *a streetfight?* The thing under the dust cover was right out of my league. I didn't even know where to unload it, where to look for a buyer. Someone had, but he was dead, someone with a Porsche watch and a fake Belgian passport, but I'd never tried to move in those circles. The Finn's muggers from the 'burbs had knocked over someone who had some highly arcane connections.

The program in the jeweller's vice was a Russian military 83 icebreaker, a killer-virus program.

It was dawn when Bobby came in alone. I'd fallen asleep 84 with a bag of takeout sandwiches in my lap.

'You want to eat?' I asked him, not really awake, holding 85 out my sandwiches. I'd been dreaming of the program, of its waves of hungry glitch systems and mimetic subprograms; in the dream it was an animal of some kind, shapeless and flowing.

He brushed the bag aside on his way to the console, 86 punched a function key. The screen lit with the intricate pattern I'd seen there that afternoon. I rubbed sleep from my eyes with my left hand, one thing I can't do with my right. I'd fallen asleep trying to decide whether to tell him about the program. Maybe I should try to sell it alone, keep the money, go somewhere new, ask Rikki to go with me.

'Whose is it?' I asked. 87

He stood there in a black cotton jump suit, an old leather 88 jacket thrown over his shoulders like a cape. He hadn't shaved for a few days, and his face looked thinner than usual.

'It's Chrome's,' he said. 89

My arm convulsed, started clicking, fear translated to the 90 myoelectrics through the carbon studs. I spilled the sandwiches; limp sprouts, and bright yellow dairy-produce slices on the unswept wooden floor.

'You're stone crazy,' I said.   91

'No,' he said, 'you think she rumbled it? No way. We'd be   92
dead already. I locked on to her through a triple-blind rental system in Mombasa and an Algerian comsat. She knew somebody was having a look-see, but she couldn't trace it.'

If Chrome had traced the pass Bobby had made at her ice,   93
we were good as dead. But he was probably right, or she'd have had me blown away on my way back from New York. 'Why her, Bobby? Just give me one reason. . . .'

Chrome: I'd seen her maybe half a dozen times in the   94
Gentleman Loser. Maybe she was slumming, or checking out the human condition, a condition she didn't exactly aspire to. A sweet little heart-shaped face framing the nastiest pair of eyes you ever saw. She'd looked fourteen for as long as anyone could remember, hyped out of anything like a normal metabolism on some massive program of serums and hormones. She was as ugly a customer as the street ever produced, but she didn't belong to the street anymore. She was one of the Boys, Chrome, a member in good standing of the local Mob subsidiary. Word was, she'd gotten started as a dealer, back when synthetic pituitary hormones were still proscribed. But she hadn't had to move hormones for a long time. Now she owned the House of Blue Lights.

'You're flat-out crazy, Quine. You give me one sane reason   95
for having that stuff on your screen. You ought to dump it, and I mean *now*. . . .'

'Talk in the Loser,' he said, shrugging out of the leather   96
jacket. 'Black Myron and Crow Jane. Jane, she's up on all the sex lines, claims she knows where the money goes. So she's arguing with Myron that Chrome's the controlling interest in the Blue Lights, not just some figurehead for the Boys.'

'"The Boys," Bobby,' I said. 'That's the operative word   97
there. You still capable of seeing that? We don't mess with the Boys, remember? That's why we're still walking around.'

'That's why we're still poor, partner.' He settled back into   98
the swivel chair in front of the console, unzipped his jump
suit, and scratched his skinny white chest. 'But maybe not for
much longer.'

'I think maybe this partnership just got itself permanently   99
dissolved.'

Then he grinned at me. That grin was truly crazy, feral and   100
focused, and I knew that right then he really didn't give a
shit about dying.

'Look,' I said, 'I've got some money left, you know? Why   101
don't you take it and get the tube to Miami, catch a hopper
to Montego Bay. You need a rest, man. You've got to get
your act together.'

'My act, Jack,' he said, punching something on the key-   102
board, 'never has been this together before.' The neon prayer
rug on the screen shivered and woke as an animation program
cut in, ice lines weaving with hypnotic frequency, a living
mandala. Bobby kept punching, and the movement slowed;
the pattern resolved itself, grew slightly less complex, became
an alternation between two distant configurations. A first-
class piece of work, and I hadn't thought he was still that
good. 'Now,' he said, 'there, see it? Wait. There. There again.
And there. Easy to miss. That's it. Cuts in every hour and
twenty minutes with a squirt transmission to their comsat.
We could live for a year on what she pays them weekly in
negative interest.'

'Whose comsat?'   103

'Zürich. Her bankers. That's her bankbook, Jack. That's   104
where the money goes. Crow Jane was right.'

I stood there. My arm forgot to click.   105

'So how'd you do in New York, partner? You get anything   106
that'll help me cut ice? We're going to need whatever we can
get.'

I kept my eyes on his, forced myself not to look in the   107
direction of the waldo, the jeweller's vice. The Russian program was there, under the dust cover.

Wild cards, luck changers.   108

'Where's Rikki?' I asked him, crossing to the console, 109
pretending to study the alternating patterns on the screen.

'Friends of hers,' he shrugged, 'kids, they're all into sim- 110
stim.' He smiled absently. 'I'm going to do it for her, man.'

'I'm going to think about this, Bobby. You want me to 111
come back, you keep your hands off the board.'

'I'm doing it for her,' he said as the door closed behind 112
me. 'You know I am.'

And down now, down, the program a roller coaster 113
through this fraying maze of shadow walls, grey cathedral
spaces between the bright towers. Headlong speed.

Black ice. Don't think about it. Black ice.   114

Too many stories in the Gentleman Loser; black ice is a 115
part of the mythology. Ice that kills. Illegal, but they aren't
we all? Some kind of neural-feedback weapon, and you connect with it only once. Like some hideous Word that eats the
mind from the inside out. Like an epileptic spasm that goes
on and on until there's nothing left at all. . . .

And we're diving for the floor of Chrome's shadow castle. 116

Trying to brace myself for the sudden stopping of breath, 117
a sickness and final slackening of the nerves. Fear of that cold
Word waiting, down there in the dark.

I went out and looked for Rikki, found her in a café with 118
a boy with Sendai eyes, half-healed suture lines radiating from
his bruised sockets. She had a glossy brochure spread open
on the table, Tally Isham smiling up from a dozen photographs, the Girl with the Zeiss Ikon Eyes.

Her little simstim deck was one of the things I'd stacked 119
under my bench the night before, the one I'd fixed for her
the day after I'd first seen her. She spent hours jacked into
that unit, the contact band across her forehead like a grey
plastic tiara. Tally Isham was her favourite, and with the
contact band on, she was gone, off somewhere in the recorded sensorium of simstim's biggest star. Simulated stimuli:
the world—all the interesting parts, anyway—as perceived by

Tally Isham. Tally raced a black Fokker ground-effect plane across Arizona mesa tops. Tally dived the Truk Island preserves. Tally partied with the superrich on private Greek islands, heartbreaking purity of those tiny white seaports at dawn.

Actually she looked a lot like Tally, same colouring and 120 cheekbones. I thought Rikki's mouth was stronger. More sass. She didn't want to *be* Tally Isham, but she coveted the job. That was her ambition, to be in simstim. Bobby just laughed it off. She talked to me about it, though. 'How'd I look with a pair of these?' she'd ask, holding a full-page headshot, Tally Isham's blue Zeiss Ikons lined up with her own amber-brown. She'd had her corneas done twice, but she still wasn't 20-20; so she wanted Ikons. Brand of the stars. Very expensive.

'You still window-shopping for eyes?' I asked as I sat down. 121
'Tiger just got some,' she said. She looked tired, I thought. 122
Tiger was so pleased with his Sendais that he couldn't help 123 smiling, but I doubted whether he'd have smiled otherwise. He had the kind of uniform good looks you get after your seventh trip to the surgical boutique; he'd probably spend the rest of his life looking vaguely like each new season's media front-runner; not too obvious a copy, but nothing too original, either.

'Sendai, right?' I smiled back. 124
He nodded. I watched as he tried to take me in with his 125 idea of a professional simstim glance. He was pretending that he was recording. I thought he spent too long on my arm. 'They'll be great on peripherals when the muscles heal,' he said, and I saw how carefully he reached for his double espresso. Sendai eyes are notorious for depth-perception defects and warranty hassles, among other things.

'Tiger's leaving for Hollywood tomorrow.' 126
'Then maybe Chiba City, right?' I smiled at him. He didn't 127 smile back. 'Got an offer, Tiger? Know an agent?'

'Just checking it out,' he said quietly. Then he got up and 128 left. He said a quick goodbye to Rikki, but not to me.

'That kid's optic nerves may start to deteriorate inside six 129
months. You know that, Rikki? Those Sendais are illegal in
England, Denmark, lots of places. You can't replace nerves.'

'Hey, Jack, no lectures.' She stole one of my croissants and 130
nibbled at the tip of one of its horns.

'I thought I was your adviser, kid.' 131

'Yeah. Well, Tiger's not too swift, but everybody knows 132
about Sendais. They're all he can afford. So he's taking a
chance. If he gets work, he can replace them.'

'With these?' I tapped the Zeiss Ikon brochure. 'Lot of 133
money, Rikki. You know better than to take a gamble like
that.'

She nodded. 'I want Ikons.' 134

'If you're going up to Bobby's, tell him to sit tight until 135
he hears from me.'

'Sure. It's business?' 136

'Business,' I said. But it was craziness. 137

I drank my coffee, and she ate both my croissants. Then I 138
walked her down to Bobby's. I made fifteen calls, each one
from a different pay phone.

Business. Bad craziness. 139

All in all, it took us six weeks to set the burn up, six weeks 140
of Bobby telling me how much he loved her. I worked even
harder, trying to get away from that.

Most of it was phone calls. My fifteen initial and very 141
oblique enquiries each seemed to breed fifteen more. I was
looking for a certain service Bobby and I both imagined as a
requisite part of the world's clandestine economy, but which
probably never had more than five customers at a time. It
would be one that never advertised.

We were looking for the world's heaviest fence, for a non- 142
aligned money laundry capable of dry-cleaning a megabuck
on-line cash transfer and then forgetting about it.

All those calls were a waste, finally, because it was the Finn 143
who put me on to what we needed. I'd gone up to New York
to buy a new blackbox rig, because we were going broke
paying for all those calls.

I put the problem to him as hypothetically as possible.   144
'Macao,' he said.   145
'Macao?'   146
'The Long Hum family. Stockbrokers.'   147
He even had the number. You want a fence, ask another   148
fence.

The Long Hum people were so oblique that they made   149
my idea of a subtle approach look like a tactical nuke-out.
Bobby had to make two shuttle runs to Hong Kong to get
the deal straight. We were running out of capital, and fast. I
still don't know why I decided to go along with it in the first
place; I was scared of Chrome, and I'd never been all that
hot to get rich.

I tried telling myself that it was a good idea to burn the   150
House of Blue Lights because the place was a creep joint, but
I just couldn't buy it. I didn't like the Blue Lights, because
I'd spent a supremely depressing evening there once, but that
was no excuse for going after Chrome. Actually I halfway
assumed we were going to die in the attempt. Even with that
killer program, the odds weren't exactly in our favour.

Bobby was lost in writing the set of commands we were   151
going to plug into the dead centre of Chrome's computer.
That was going to be my job, because Bobby was going to
have his hands full trying to keep the Russian program from
going straight for the kill. It was too complex for us to
rewrite, and so he was going to try to hold it back for the
two seconds I needed.

I made a deal with a streetfighter named Miles. He was   152
going to follow Rikki the night of the burn, keep her in sight,
and phone me at a certain time. If I wasn't there, or didn't
answer in just a certain way, I'd told him to grab her and put
her on the first tube out. I gave him an envelope to give her,
money and a note.

Bobby really hadn't thought about that, much, how things   153
would go for her if we blew it. He just kept telling me he
loved her, where they were going to go together, how they'd
spend the money.

'Buy her a pair of Ikons first, man. That's what she wants. 154
She's serious about that simstim scene.'

'Hey,' he said, looking up from the keyboard, 'she won't 155
need to work. We're going to make it, Jack. She's my luck.
She won't ever have to work again.'

'Your luck,' I said. I wasn't happy. I couldn't remember 156
when I had been happy. 'You seen your luck around lately?'

He hadn't, but neither had I. We'd both been too busy. 157

I missed her. Missing her reminded me of my one night 158
in the House of Blue Lights, because I'd gone there out of
missing someone else. I'd gotten drunk to begin with, then
I'd started hitting Vasopressin inhalers. If your main squeeze
has just decided to walk out on you, booze and Vasopressin
are the ultimate in masochistic pharmacology; the juice makes
you maudlin and the Vasopressin makes you remember, I
mean really remember. Clinically they use the stuff to counter
senile amnesia, but the street finds its own uses for things. So
I'd bought myself an ultra-intense replay of a bad affair;
trouble is, you get the bad with the good. Go gunning for
transports of animal ecstasy and you get what you said, too,
and what she said to that, how she walked away and never
looked back.

I don't remember deciding to go to the Blue Lights, or 159
how I got there, hushed corridors and this really tacky deco-
rative waterfall trickling somewhere, or maybe just a hologram of one. I had a lot of money that night; somebody had
given Bobby a big roll for opening a three-second window
in someone else's ice.

I don't think the crew on the door liked my looks, but I 160
guess my money was okay.

I had more to drink there when I'd done what I went there 161
for. Then I made some crack to the barman about closet
necrophiliacs, and that didn't go down too well. Then this
very large character insisted on calling me War Hero, which
I didn't like. I think I showed him some tricks with the arm,
before the lights went out, and I woke up two days later in
a basic sleeping module somewhere else. A cheap place, not

even room to hang yourself. And I sat there on that narrow foam slab and cried.

Some things are worse than being alone. But the thing 162 they sell in the House of Blue Lights is so popular that it's almost legal.

At the heart of darkness, the still centre, the glitch systems 163 shred the dark with whirlwinds of light, translucent razors spinning away from us; we hang in the centre of a silent slow-motion explosion, ice fragments falling away forever, and Bobby's voice comes in across light-years of electronic void illusion—

'Burn the bitch down. I can't hold the thing back—' 164

The Russian program, rising through towers of data, blot- 165 ting out the playroom colours. And I plug Bobby's home-made command package into the centre of Chrome's cold heart. The squirt transmission cuts in, a pulse of condensed information that shoots straight up, past the thickening tower of darkness, the Russian program, while Bobby struggles to control that crucial second. An unformed arm of shadow twitches from the towering dark, too late.

We've done it. 166

The matrix folds itself round me like an origami trick. 167

And the loft smells of sweat and burning circuitry. 168

I thought I heard Chrome scream, a raw metal sound, but 169 I couldn't have.

Bobby was laughing, tears in his eyes. The elapsed-time 170 figure in the corner of the monitor read 07:24:05. The burn had taken a little under eight minutes.

And I saw that the Russian program had melted in its slot. 171

We'd given the bulk of Chrome's Zürich account to a 172 dozen world charities. There was too much there to move, and we knew we had to break her, burn her straight down, or she might come after us. We took less than ten per cent for ourselves and shot it through the Long Hum set-up in Macao. They took sixty per cent of that for themselves and kicked what was left back to us through the most convoluted

sector of the Hong Kong exchange. It took an hour before
our money started to reach the two accounts we'd opened in
Zürich.

I watched zeros pile up behind a meaningless figure on the   173
monitor. I was rich.

Then the phone rang. It was Miles. I almost blew the code   174
phrase.

'Hey, Jack, man, I dunno—what's it all about, with this   175
girl of yours? Kinda funny thing here. . . .'

'What? Tell me.'   176

'I been on her, like you said, tight but out of sight. She   177
goes to the Lower, hangs out, then she gets a tube. Goes to
the House of Blue Lights—'

'She what?'   178

'Side door. *Employees* only. No way I could get past their   179
security.

'Is she there now?'   180

'No, man, I just lost her. It's insane down here, like the   181
Blue Lights just shut down, looks like for good, seven kinds
of alarms going off, everybody running, the heat out in riot
gear. . . . Now there's all this stuff going on, insurance guys,
real-estate types, vans with municipal plates. . . .'

'Miles, where'd she go?'   182

'Lost her, Jack.'   183

'Look, Miles, you keep the money in the envelope, right?'   184

'You serious? Hey, I'm real sorry. I—'   185

I hung up.   186

'Wait'll we tell her,' Bobby was saying, rubbing a towel   187
across his bare chest.

'You tell her yourself, cowboy. I'm going for a walk.'   188

So I went out into the night and the neon and let the   189
crowd pull me along, walking blind, willing myself to be just
a segment of that mass organism, just one more drifting chip
of consciousness under the geodesics. I didn't think, just put
one foot in front of another, but after a while I did think,
and it all made sense. She'd needed the money.

I thought about Chrome, too. That we'd killed her, mur-   190
dered her, as surely as if we'd slit her throat. The night that

carried me along through the malls and plazas would be hunting her now, and she had nowhere to go. How many enemies would she have in this crowd alone? How many would move, now they weren't held back by fear of her money? We'd taken her for everything she had. She was back on the street again. I doubted she'd live till dawn.

Finally I remembered the café, the one where I'd met 191 Tiger.

Her sunglasses told the whole story, huge black shades 192 with a telltale smudge of fleshtone paintstick in the corner of one lens. 'Hi, Rikki,' I said, and I was ready when she took them off.

Blue. Tally Isham blue. The clear trademark blue they're 193 famous for, ZEISS IKON ringing each iris in tiny capitals, the letters suspended there like flecks of gold.

'They're beautiful,' I said. Paintstick covered the bruising. 194 No scars with work that good. 'You made some money.'

'Yeah, I did.' Then she shivered. 'But I won't make any 195 more, not that way.'

'I think that place is out of business.' 196

'Oh.' Nothing moved in her face then. The new blue eyes 197 were still and very deep.

'It doesn't matter. Bobby's waiting for you. We just pulled 198 down a big score.'

'No. I've got to go. I guess he won't understand, but I've 199 got to go.'

I nodded, watching the arm swing up to take her hand; it 200 didn't seem to be part of me at all, but she held on to it like it was.

'I've got a one-way ticket to Hollywood. Tiger knows 201 some people I can stay with. Maybe I'll even get to Chiba City.'

She was right about Bobby. I went back with her. He 202 didn't understand. But she'd already served her purpose, for Bobby, and I wanted to tell her not to hurt for him, because I could see that she did. He wouldn't even come out into the hallway after she had packed her bags. I put the bags down and kissed her and messed up the paintstick, and something came up inside me the way the killer program had risen above Chrome's data. A sudden stopping of the breath, in a place where no word is. But she had a plane to catch.

Bobby was slumped in the swivel chair in front of his monitor, looking at his string of zeros. He had his shades on, and I knew he'd be in the Gentleman Loser by nightfall, checking out the weather, anxious for a sign, someone to tell him what his new life would be like. I couldn't see it being very different. More comfortable, but he'd always be waiting for that next card to fall.

I tried not to imagine her in the House of Blue Lights, working three-hour shifts in an approximation of REM sleep, while her body and a bundle of conditioned reflexes took care of business. The customers never got to complain that she was faking it, because those were real orgasms. But she felt them, if she felt them at all, as faint silver flares somewhere out on the edge of sleep. Yeah, it's so popular, it's almost legal. The customers are torn between needing someone and wanting to be alone at the same time, which has probably always been the name of that particular game, even before we had the neuroelectronics to enable them to have it both ways.

I picked up the phone and punched the number for her airline. I gave them her real name, her flight number. 'She's changing that,' I said, 'to Chiba City. That's right. Japan.' I thumbed my credit card into the slot and punched my ID code. 'First class.' Distant hum as they scanned my credit records. 'Make that a return ticket.'

But I guess she cashed the return fare, or else she didn't need it, because she hasn't come back. And sometimes late at night I'll pass a window with posters of simstim stars, all those beautiful, identical eyes staring back at me out of faces that are nearly as identical, and sometimes the eyes are hers, but none of the faces are, none of them ever are, and I see her far out on the edge of all this sprawl of night and cities, and then she waves goodbye.

Topics for Writing a Story

1. *Respond.* Although some of the world Gibson describes seems vaguely familiar, much of it seems other-worldly, a world almost but not yet here. Make a list of all the concepts and terms in the story you do not understand and then draft a letter to Gibson asking him for an explanation. (*Resources for Comparison:* Steven Weinberg, "Five and a Half Utopias," page 279; Kurt Vonnegut, Jr., "Harrison Bergeron," page 537.)

2. *Analyze.* Write an essay for the campus newspaper analyzing the concept of ICE as Gibson uses it in his story. You may want to check on the security systems in your university's computer system to help you illustrate the concept. (*Resources for Comparison:* Doris Kearns Goodwin, "Keeping the Scorebook," page 37; John Berendt, "The Hoax," page 338.)

3. *Argue.* Gibson's story describes the motives (intellectual, financial, sexual) that prompt "cowboys" to engage in "hacking." Argue that hackers actually perform a valuable service by finding the weak spots in computer security. Or argue that hackers are criminals who endanger the computer systems that govern our health and safety. (*Resources for Comparison:* Barbara Kingsolver, "Stone Soup," page 478; Barbara Dafoe Whitehead, "Women and the Future of Fatherhood," page 489.)

DOCUMENTING SOURCES

The essays in *The Riverside Reader* are sources. Many of the writing assignments at the end of each chapter ask you to *analyze* these sources or to use them to support your own ideas. Most academic writing asks you to use sources—from books, journals, magazines, newspapers, and the Internet—to augment and advance the ideas in your writing. Every time you cite a source, or use it in some way, you must *document* it. For example, in the student research paper at the end of this chapter, Gwen Vickery uses the Modern Language Association style to cite two essays (one by M. Kadi and another by Evan I. Schwartz) that appear in the chapter Resources for Writing. (See Vickery, pages 4, 5–6, 13).

This chapter explains the style recommended by the Modern Language Association (MLA) for documenting sources in academic papers. It also analyzes some of the implications of MLA style for your research and composing. More detailed information is given in the *MLA Handbook* and the *MLA Style Manual.*

MLA style has three major features. First, all sources cited in a paper are listed in a section entitled **Works Cited,** which is located at the end of the paper. Second, material borrowed from another source is documented within the text by a brief parenthetical reference that directs readers to the full citation in the list of works cited. Third, numbered footnotes or endnotes are used to present two types of supplementary information: (1) commentary or explanation that the text cannot accommodate and (2) bibliographical notes that contain several source citations.

PREPARING THE LIST OF WORKS CITED

In an academic paper that follows MLA style, the list of works cited is the *only* place where readers will find complete information about the sources you have cited. For that reason, your list must be thorough and accurate.

The list of works cited appears at the end of your paper and, as its title suggests, *lists only the works you have cited in your paper.* Occasionally, your instructor may ask you to prepare a list of works consulted. That list would include not only the sources you cite but also the sources you consulted as you conducted your research. In either case, MLA prefers Works Cited or Works Consulted to the more limited heading Bibliography (literally, "description of books") because those headings are more likely to accommodate the variety of sources—articles, films, Internet sources—that writers may cite in a research paper.

To prepare the list of works cited, follow these general guidelines:

1. Paginate the Works Cited section as a continuation of your text. If the conclusion of your paper appears on

page 8, begin your list on page 9 (unless there is an intervening page of endnotes).

2. Double-space between successive lines of an entry and between entries.

3. Begin the first line of an entry flush left, and indent successive lines five spaces or one-half inch.

4. List entries in alphabetical order according to the last name of the author.

5. If you are listing more than one work by the same author, alphabetize the works according to title (excluding the articles *a, an,* and *the*). Instead of repeating the author's name, type *three* hyphens and a period, and then give the title.

6. Underline the titles of works published independently—books, plays, long poems, pamphlets, periodicals, films.

7. Although you do not *need* to underline the spaces between words, a continuous line is easier to type and guarantees that all features of the title are underlined. Type a continuous line under titles unless you are instructed to do otherwise.

8. If you are citing a book whose title includes the title of another book, underline the main title, but do not underline the other title (for example, A Casebook on Ralph Ellison's Invisible Man).

9. Use quotation marks to indicate titles of short works that appear in larger works (for example, "Minutes of Glory." African Short Stories). Also use quotation marks for song titles and for titles of unpublished works, including dissertations, lectures, and speeches.

10. Use arabic numerals except with names of monarchs (Elizabeth II) and except for the preliminary pages of a work (ii–xix), which are traditionally numbered with roman numerals.

11. Use lowercase abbreviations to identify the parts of a work (for example, *vol.* for *volume*), a named translator (*trans.*), and a named editor (*ed.*). However, when these designations follow a period, they should be capitalized (for example, Woolf, Virginia. A Writer's Diary. Ed. Leonard Woolf).

12. Whenever possible, use appropriate shortened forms for the publisher's name (*Random* instead of *Random House*).
13. Separate author, title, and publication information with a period followed by *one space*.
14. Use a colon and one space to separate the volume number and year of a periodical from the page numbers (for example, Trimmer, Joseph. "Memoryscape: Jean Shepherd's Midwest." Old Northwest 2 (1976): 357–69).

In addition to these guidelines, MLA recommends procedures for documenting an extensive variety of sources, including electronic sources and nonprint materials such as films and television programs. The following models illustrate sources most commonly cited.

Sample Entries: Books

When citing books, provide the following general categories of information:

Author's last name, first name. Book title. Additional information. City of publication: Publishing company, publication date.

Entries illustrating variations on this basic format appear below and are numbered to facilitate reference.

A Book by One Author

1. Boorstin, Daniel J. The Creators: A History of the Heroes of the Imagination. New York: Random, 1992.

Two or More Books by the Same Author

2. Garreau, Joel. Edge City: Life on the New Frontier. New York: Doubleday, 1991.

3. ———. The Nine Nations of North America. Boston: Houghton, 1981.

A Book by Two or Three Authors

4. Vare, Ethlie Ann, and Greg Ptacek. Mothers of Invention: From the Bra to the Bomb: Forgotten Women and Their Unforgettable Ideas. New York: Morrow, 1988.

5. Atwan, Robert, Donald McQuade, and John W. Wright. Edsels, Luckies, and Frigidaires: Advertising the American Way. New York: Dell, 1979.

A Book by Four or More Authors

6. Belenky, Mary Field, et al. Women's Ways of Knowing: The Development of Self, Voice, and Mind. New York: Basic, 1986.

A Book by a Corporate Author

7. Boston Women's Health Book Collective. Our Bodies, Ourselves: A Book by and for Women. New York: Simon, 1973.

A Book by an Anonymous Author

8. Literary Market Place: The Dictionary of American Book Publishing. 1998 ed. New York: Bowker, 1997.

A Book with an Editor

9. Hall, Donald, ed. The Oxford Book of American Literary Anecdotes. New York: Oxford UP, 1981.

A Book with an Author and an Editor

10. Toomer, Jean. Cane. Ed. Darwin T. Turner. New York:
Norton, 1988.

A Book with a Publisher's Imprint

11. Kozol, Jonathan. Illiterate America. New York: Anchor-
Doubleday, 1985.

An Anthology or Compilation

12. Valdez, Luis, and Stan Steiner, eds. Aztlan: An Anthology
of Mexican American Literature. New York: Vintage-
Knopf, 1972.

A Work in an Anthology

13. Silko, Leslie Marmon. "The Man to Send Rain Clouds."
Imagining America: Stories from the Promised
Land. Ed. Wesley Brown and Amy Ling. New York:
Persea, 1991. 191–95.

An Introduction, Preface, Foreword, or Afterword

14. Bernstein, Carl. Afterword. Poison Penmanship: The Gentle Art of Muckraking. By Jessica Mitford. New
York: Vintage-Random, 1979. 275–77.

A Multivolume Work

15. Blotner, Joseph. Faulkner: A Biography. 2 vols. New
York: Random, 1974.

An Edition Other Than the First

16. Chaucer, Geoffrey. The Riverside Chaucer. Ed. Larry D.

Benson. 3rd ed. Boston: Houghton, 1987.

A Book in a Series

17. McClave, Heather, ed. Women Writers of the Short Story.

Twentieth Century Views. Englewood Cliffs: Spec-

trum-Prentice, 1980.

A Republished Book

18. Malamud, Bernard. The Natural. 1952. New York: Avon,

1980.

A Signed Article in a Reference Book

19. Tobias, Richard. "Thurber, James." Encyclopedia Ameri-

cana. 1991 ed.

An Unsigned Article in a Reference Book

20. "Tharp, Twyla." Who's Who of American Women. 17th

ed. 1991–92.

A Government Document

21. United States. Cong. House. Committee on the Judiciary.

Immigration and Nationality Act with Amendments

and Notes on Related Laws. 7th ed. Washington:

GPO, 1980.

Published Proceedings of a Conference

22. Griggs, John, ed. AIDS: Public Policy Dimensions. Proc.

of a conference. 16–17 Jan. 1986. New York:

United Hospital Fund of New York, 1987.

A Translation

23. Giroud, Françoise. Marie Curie: A Life. Trans. Lydia

Davis. New York: Holmes, 1986.

A Book with a Title in Its Title

24. Habich, Robert D. Transcendentalism and the Western

Messenger: A History of the Magazine and Its Con-

tributors, 1835–1841. Rutherford: Fairleigh Dickin-

son UP, 1985.

A Book Published Before 1900

25. Field, Kate. The History of Bell's Telephone. London,

1878.

An Unpublished Dissertation

26. Geissinger, Shirley Burry. "Openness versus Secrecy in

Adoptive Parenthood." Diss. U of North Carolina at

Greensboro, 1984.

A Published Dissertation

27. Ames, Barbara Edwards. Dreams and Painting: A Case

Study of the Relationship between an Artist's

Dreams and Painting. Diss. U of Virginia, 1978.

Ann Arbor: UMI, 1979. 7928021.

Sample Entries: Articles in Periodicals

When citing articles in periodicals, provide the following general categories of information:

Author's last name, first name. "Article title." Periodical ti-

tle Date: inclusive pages.

Entries illustrating variations on this basic format appear below and are numbered to facilitate reference.

A Signed Article from a Daily Newspaper

28. Barringer, Felicity. "Where Many Elderly Live, Signs of

the Future." New York Times 7 Mar. 1993, nat. ed.,

sec. 1: 12.

An Unsigned Article from a Daily Newspaper

29. "Infant Mortality Down; Race Disparity Widens." Wash-

ington Post 12 Mar. 1993: A12.

An Article from a Monthly or Bimonthly Magazine

30. Wills, Garry. "The Words That Remade America: Lincoln

at Gettysburg." Atlantic June 1992: 57–79.

An Article from a Weekly or Biweekly Magazine

31. Trillin, Calvin. "Culture Shopping." New Yorker 15 Feb.

1993: 48–51.

An Article in a Journal with Continuous Pagination

32. Elbow, Peter. "Ranking, Evaluating, and Linking: Sorting

Out Three Forms of Judgment." College English 55

(1993): 187–206.

An Article in a Journal That Numbers Pages in Each Issue Separately

33. Seely, Bruce. "The Saga of American Infrastructure: A
    Republic Bound Together." Wilson Quarterly 17.1
    (1993): 19–39.

An Editorial

34. "A Question of Medical Sight." Editorial. Plain Dealer
    [Cleveland, OH] 11 Mar. 1993: 6B.

A Review

35. Morson, Gary Soul. "Coping with Utopia." Rev. of Soviet
    Civilization: A Cultural History, by Andrei Sin-
    yavsky. American Scholar 61 (1992): 132–38.

An Article Whose Title Contains a Quotation or a Title Within Quotation Marks

36. DeCuir, Andre L. "Italy, England and the Female Artist
    in George Eliot's 'Mr. Gilfil's Love-Story.'" Studies
    in Short Fiction 29 (1992): 67–75.

An Abstract from *Dissertation Abstracts* or *Dissertation Abstracts International*

37. Creek, Mardena Bridges. "Myth, Wound, Accommodation:
    American Literary Responses to the War in Viet-
    nam." DAI 43 (1982): 3539A. Ball State U.

Sample Entries: CD-ROMs

When citing information from CD-ROMs, provide the following general categories of information:

Author's last name, first name. "Article title of printed

    source or printed analogue." Periodical title of printed

    source or printed analogue Date: inclusive pages. Title

    of database. CD-ROM. Name of vendor or computer serv-

    ice. Electronic publication date or date of access.

Entries illustrating variations on this basic format appear below and are numbered to facilitate reference.

CD-ROM: Periodical Publication with Printed Source or Printed Analogue

38. West, Cornel. "The Dilemma of the Black Intellectual."

    Critical Quarterly 29 (1987): 39–52. MLA Interna-

    tional Bibliography. CD-ROM. Silver Platter. Feb.

    1995.

CD-ROM: Nonperiodical Publication

39. Cinemania 97. CD-ROM. Redmond: Microsoft, 1996.

CD-ROM: A Work in More Than One Electronic Medium

40. Mozart. CD-ROM. Laser disk. Union City, CA: Ebook,

    1992.

Sample Entries: Internet and Web Sources

When citing information from Internet and World Wide Web sources, provide the following general categories of information:

Author's last name, first name. "Article title" or Book title.

    Publication information for any printed version. Or sub-

ject line of forum or discussion group. Indication of on-
line posting or home page. Title of electronic journal.
Date of electronic publication. Page numbers or the numbers of paragraphs or sections. Name of institution or
organization sponsoring website. Date of access to the
source <electronic address or URL>.

The speed of change in the electronic world means that
particular features for citing Internet and web sources are
constantly evolving. The best way to confirm the accuracy of your citations is to check the MLA website
(<http://www.mla.org>).

Entries illustrating variations on the basic format appear below and are numbered to facilitate reference.

A Professional Site

41. MLA on the Web. 25 November 1997. Modern Language
        Association of America. 25 Mar. 1998
        <http://www.mla.org>.

A Personal Site

42. Hawisher, Gail. Home page. University of Illinois Urbana-
        Champaign/The Women, Information Technology,
        and Scholarship Colloquium. 18 Mar. 1998
        <http://www.art.uiuc.edu/wits/members/
        hawisher.html>.

A Book

43. Conrad, Joseph. Lord Jim. London: Blackwoods, 1900.
        Oxford Text Archive. 12 July 1993. Oxford Univer-

sity Computing Services. 20 Feb. 1998
<ftp://ota.ox.ac.uk/pub/ota/public/english/
conrad/lordjim.1824>.

A Poem

44. Hampl, Patricia. "Who We Will Love." Woman Before an
    Aquarium. Pittsburgh: U of Pittsburgh P, 1978: 27–
    28. A Poem a Week. Rice University. 13 Mar. 1998
    <http://www.ruf.rice.edu/~alisa/Jun24html>.

An Article in a Reference Database

45. "Women in American History." Britannica Online Vers.
    98.1.1. Nov. 1997. Encyclopedia Britannica. 10 Mar.
    1998 <http://www.britannica.com>.

An Article in a Journal

46. Bieder, Robert A. "The Representation of Indian Bodies
    in Nineteenth-Century American Anthropology." The
    American Indian Quarterly 20.2 (1996). 28 Mar.
    1998
    <http://www./uoknor.edu/aiq/aiq202.html#bieder>.

An Article in a Magazine

47. Levine, Judith. "I Surf, Therefore I Am." Salon 29 July
    1997. 9 Dec. 1997 <http://www.salonmagazine.
    com/July97/mothers/surfing.970729.html>.

A Review

48. Roth, Martha. "A Tantalizing Remoteness." Rev. of Jane

Austen: A Biography by Claire Tomalin. Hungry
Mind Review Winter 1997. 10 Mar. 1998
<http://www.bookwire.com/HMR/nonfiction/read.
review$5376>.

A Posting to a Discussion Group

49. Inman, James. "Re: Technologist." Online Posting. 24
Sept. 1997. Alliance for Computers in Writing. 27
Mar. 1998 <acw-1@unicorn.acs.ttu.edu>

A Personal E-mail Message

50. Penning, Sarah. "Mentor Advice." E-mail to Rai Peterson. 6 May 1995.

Sample Entries: Other Sources
Films; Radio and Television Programs

51. The Last Emperor. Dir. Bernardo Bertolucci. With John
Lone and Peter O'Toole. Columbia, 1987.

52. "If God Ever Listened: A Portrait of Alice Walker." Horizons. Prod. Jane Rosenthal. NPR. WBST, Muncie. 3
Mar. 1984.

53. "The Hero's Adventure." Moyers: Joseph Campbell and
the Power of Myth. Prod. Catherine Tatge. PBS.
WNET, New York. 23 May 1988.

Performances

54. A Walk in the Woods. By Lee Blessing. Dir. Des McAnuff.

With Sam Waterston and Robert Prosky. Booth Theatre, New York. 17 May 1988.

55. Ozawa, Seiji, cond. Boston Symphony Orch. Concert. Symphony Hall, Boston. 30 Sept. 1988.

Recordings

56. Mozart, Wolfgang A. Cosi Fan Tutte. Record. With Kiri Te Kanawa, Frederica von Stade, David Rendall, and Philippe Huttenlocher. Cond. Alain Lombard. Strasbourg Philharmonic Orch. RCA, SRL3-2629, 1978.

57. Simon, Paul. "Under African Skies." Graceland. Audiotape. Warner, 4-25447, 1986.

Works of Art

58. Botticelli, Sandro. Giuliano de' Medici. Samuel H. Kress Collection. National Gallery of Art, Washington.

59. Rodin, Auguste. The Gate of Hell. Rodin Museum, Paris.

Maps and Charts

60. Sonoma and Napa Counties. Map. San Francisco: California State Automobile Assn., 1984.

Cartoons and Advertisements

61. Addams, Charles. Cartoon. New Yorker 22 Feb. 1988: 33.

62. Air France. "The Fine Art of Flying." Advertisement. Travel and Leisure May 1988: 9.

Published and Unpublished Letters

63. Fitzgerald, F. Scott. "To Ernest Hemingway." 1 June

1934. The Letters of F. Scott Fitzgerald. Ed. Andrew
Turnbull. New York: Scribner's, 1963. 308–10.

64. Stowe, Harriet Beecher. Letter to George Eliot. 25 May
1869 Berg Collection, New York: New York Public Library.

Interviews

65. Ellison, Ralph. "Indivisible Man." Interview. By James
Alan McPherson. Atlantic Dec. 1970: 45–60.

66. Diamond, Carol. Telephone interview. 27 Dec. 1988.

Lectures, Speeches, and Addresses

67. Russo, Michael. "A Painter Speaks His Mind." Museum
of Fine Arts. Boston, 5 Aug. 1984.

68. Baker, Houston A., Jr. "The Presidential Address." MLA
Convention. New York, 28 Dec. 1992.

SAMPLE OUTLINE AND DOCUMENTED PAPER

The author of the following research paper used many features of MLA style to document her paper. At her instructor's request, she first submitted a final version of her thesis and outline. Adhering to MLA style, she did not include a title page with her outline or her paper. Instead, she typed her name, her instructor's name, the course title, and the date on separate lines (double-spacing between lines) at the upper left margin. Then, after double-spacing again, she typed the title of her paper, double-spaced, and started the first line of her text. On page 1 and successive pages, she typed her last name and the page number in the upper right-hand corner, as recommended by MLA.

Gwen Vickery

Mr. Johnson

English 104

21 November 1996

Is Anybody Out There?: The Value of Chat Groups

on the Internet

Thesis: Meaningful conversations {in chat groups} are

possible, but finding them might take time.

I. Chat groups have created a cultural controversy.

    A. They provide real support for some people.

    B. They also exclude many people.

II. Chat groups have serious limitations.

    A. People talk only to people like them.

    B. Poor people have no access to these conversa-

       tions.

III. The quality of conversation in chat groups is incon-

   sistent.

    A. Too many charlatans and too few civic leaders

       participate in chat groups.

    B. Too many virtual conversations are simply

       junk conversations.

IV. Despite their problems, chat groups have many

   supporters.

    A. Some need the companionship of conversations.

    B. Some like the freedom of textual identity.

    C. Some look for self-affirmation in textual con-
       versations.

V. Chat groups are here to stay.

    A. Some are good; some are bad.

    B. Individuals will have to decide how much time
       and money to invest in searching for meaning-
       ful conversations.

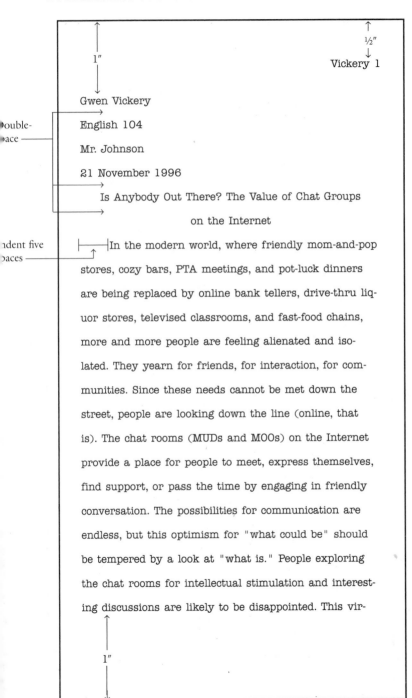

½″

1″

Gwen Vickery

Double-
space

English 104

Mr. Johnson

21 November 1996

Is Anybody Out There? The Value of Chat Groups

on the Internet

Indent five
spaces

In the modern world, where friendly mom-and-pop stores, cozy bars, PTA meetings, and pot-luck dinners are being replaced by online bank tellers, drive-thru liquor stores, televised classrooms, and fast-food chains, more and more people are feeling alienated and isolated. They yearn for friends, for interaction, for communities. Since these needs cannot be met down the street, people are looking down the line (online, that is). The chat rooms (MUDs and MOOs) on the Internet provide a place for people to meet, express themselves, find support, or pass the time by engaging in friendly conversation. The possibilities for communication are endless, but this optimism for "what could be" should be tempered by a look at "what is." People exploring the chat rooms for intellectual stimulation and interesting discussions are likely to be disappointed. This vir-

1″

tual reality has yet to filter out the banality, stupidity,
bigotry, and chauvinism that are all too common in the
real world. If the explorer perseveres, however, he or
she may find a few Masterpiece Theatres amid the thousands of Beavis and Buttheads. Meaningful conversations are possible, but finding them might take time.

When John Perry Barlow's fiancé died of a heart attack, he was overcome with grief and despair. Since he
had been living in New York with his future wife, his
family and friends back home had never met her. Needing to talk, but feeling awkward, he turned to the Internet. He was touched by the responses he received:

Long quotation:
A quotation of
more than four
lines is set off
from text and is
not placed in
quotation marks.

> They told me of their own tragedies and what
> they had done to survive them. As humans
> have done since words were first uttered, we
> shared the second most common human experi-
> ence, death, with an openheartedness that
> would have caused grave uneasiness in physi-
> cal America, where the whole topic is so
> cloaked in denial as to be considered obscene
> (56)

But although Barlow's experience was positive, he
still has reservations about the Internet, especially
about the kinds of people he meets. He feels that

Vickery 3

"women, children, old people, poor people, and the genuinely blind" are conspicuously absent, as are "the illiterate and the continent of Africa" (54). Since he had
been led to believe that cyberspace was teeming with
human diversity, he was disillusioned. He concludes
that cyberspace is inhabited by "white males under 50
with plenty of computer-terminal time, great typing
skills, high math SATs, [and] strongly held opinions on
just about everything" (55). Barlow still uses the Net,
but his enthusiasm has cooled.

M. Kadi would agree with Barlow that the Internet,
hailed as the great social leveler, is really just as dis-
criminatory as real life: "What this whole delirious, interconnected, global community of a world needs is a
little reality check" (57). The cost of subscribing to an
online community such as America Online, Kadi says, is
conservatively estimated at twenty dollars or less per
month. People from the lower economic classes cannot
afford such a luxury. And even if they could afford to
join, would anybody hear their stories or learn from
their experiences? Kadi doesn't think so.

Since the Internet provides an overwhelming selection of topics to choose from, most people are going to

Short quotation:
The quotation is
introduced with
an independent
clause and set
off by a colon.

limit themselves to those discussions that speak to
their immediate concerns:

> So J. is going to ignore all the support groups—
> after all, J. is a normal, well-adjusted person,
> and all of J.'s friends are normal, well-adjusted
> people; what does J. need to know about alco-
> holism or incest victims? J. Individual is white.
> So J. Individual is going to ignore all the multi-
> cultural folders. J. couldn't give a hoot about
> gender issues and does not want to discuss re-
> ligion or philosophy. Ultimately, J. Individual
> does not engage in topics that do not interest
> J. Individual. So who is J. meeting? Why, peo-
> ple who are just like J. (Kadi 59)

When ideas are being discussed that challenge an
individual's belief systems, values, and opinions, does
the average person really stop and listen with an open
mind, provide alternative viewpoints, and work toward
a mutual consensus, or does he/she fight back with insults or simply leave the room?

More and more people are becoming disillusioned
with the promise of Internet diversity, and as they realize that the Internet's demographics mimic real life,
their optimism for a truly democratic online society

fades. Bill Machrone notes, "The Web is not doing a particularly good job of reaching out to the poor and disadvantaged," and he concludes, "The idea of a new
democracy based on electronic pluralism is so far from
reality that it's laughable" (83). Stacy Horn, dismayed
by "the Internet's testosterone-heavy demographics,"
decided to provide private accounts for women (qtd. in
Elmer-Dewitt 56). According to Philip Elmer-Dewitt, this
trend may continue as people "withdraw within their
walled communities and never venture again into the
Internet's public spaces" (56). Some universities have
determined the MUDs are a "frivolous use of computer
systems" and have prohibited their use as a "recreational activity that wastes system resources" (Masinter 1).

Democracy on the Internet is an ideal, a myth, a
pipe dream, and a misrepresentation of reality according to several critics. Not only is Internet access reserved for the economically stable, not only are huge
portions of our population not represented, but the quality of most of the Internet discussions is in a sad state.

Although Evan Schwartz sees the positive potential
of the Internet to serve as a surrogate community, he

> Short quotation:
> Author is being
> identified at the
> beginning of
> the sentence
> and quotation is
> worked into the
> sentence.

does not think that a true "democracy" can exist on
the Net, at least not at this time:

> Internet enthusiasts sometimes see virtual com-
> munity as a panacea for all sorts of social ills.
> They go a bit far, for example, when they hold
> out the possibility that the Internet could be-
> come a forum for electronic democracy. The
> people conversing on the Internet and other on-
> line services are, by and large, not a bunch of
> civic leaders. The untamed, free-wheeling na-
> ture of cyberspace means that it is often filled
> with every skinhead, Trekkie, religious zealot,
> and Limbaugh-wannabe with a new theory on
> how the world should work. The Internet is
> not—at least not now—a town hall meeting.
> (40)

Gary Chapman would agree with this statement.
He is fascinated by the Internet because it has become
a locale where the rude, crude, and socially unacceptable can unabashedly attack those who are trying to
have a genuine conversation. Chapman believes there
are "millions of electronic Walter Mittys" whose only
purpose is to relieve their own aggressions and fanta-

Paraphrase:
Author is iden-
tified at the be-
ginning of the
sentence in
which he is para-
phrased.

sies (14). But even if these pests were eliminated, Chapman's assessment would not improve:

> Even without all the cranks, poseurs, charlatans, fetishists, single-issue monomaniacs, sex-starved lonely hearts, mischievous teenagers, sexists, racists and right-wing haranguers, many participants in unstructured Internet conversations have little of interest to say but a lot of room in which to say it. (14)

If, by some chance, you find a reasonable, interesting person to talk to, you can be assured that your conversation will be "discovered by someone with a hobby horse or an abrasive personality or both, and there are few reliable ways to shunt such people elsewhere" (Chapman 14–15). The prognosis is bad, but despite the mediocrity and the pesky intruders, people are still seduced by the Internet's promise of community.

People are still meeting, still discussing, still flirting (or worse) despite the hazards. Is this good or bad? Rajiv Rao approaches this question with hesitation. Rao states that the Internet does free people from their geography, connecting a multitude of perspectives from around the world, and it does provide a means of securing information twenty-four hours a day, but Rao thinks the psychological price tag for these services

may be higher than we imagined. Cyberfriends can be

made easily, perhaps too easily. "[T]he ease with which

they form these links means that many are likely to be

trivial, shortlived, and disposable—junk friends. We

may be overwhelmed by a continuous static of informa-

tion and casual acquaintance, so that finding true soul

mates will be even harder than it is today" (Rao 98).

In an age where relationships are unstable, divorce is

rampant, and children are abandoned or neglected, the

"if I don't like it I can change rooms or sign off" atti-

tude provided by the Internet may be damaging.

Yet many would disagree. Talk shows parade in

front of the cameras a multitude of happy couples who

met over the Internet. Since their physical identities

were hidden, they judged one another by their conversa-

tions before falling in love. These couples believe that

their love is more "genuine" because it developed from

content (opinions and feelings) as opposed to package

(physical looks). Only time will tell if their predictions

are correct.

Other Internet users do not really care about the

stability of their online relationships. What matters

most to them is the opportunity for conversation, no

Short quotation: Brackets establish quote as a complete sentence.

Vickery 9

matter what the content of those conversations may be. David Boylan, an at-home father raising two young children, often visits "Parent Soup," an ad-supported online community. Boylan states, "In my nine years as a stay-at-home dad, I spent a lot of time saying gah-gah, goo-goo and dying for some intellectual stimulation. The camaraderie is so cool—you can't get that from a magazine" (qtd. in Levine 168–69). Boylan doesn't care if he talks about whooping cough or ticks, as long as he gets to talk. Several homebound mothers have expressed the same sentiment.

Short quotation: quotation *within* source quoted.

So the Internet does provide for one of our most basic needs: companionship. It also gives the people who have access an enormous sense of freedom. Whether a person is trapped within his/her home, disabled, or just plain shy, the Internet allows for movements and encounters at a dizzying speed. Sherry Turkle, author of Life on the Screen, examines the implications of this new form of self-expression and self-determination: "On MUDs, one's body is represented by one's own textual description, so the obese can be slender, the beautiful plain, the 'nerdy' sophisticated" (12). This freedom, Turkle claims, allows "new ways of thinking about evolution, relationships, sexuality, politics, and iden-

Documentation: Both author and title of source are identified in introductory independent clause.

tity" (26). Males are females, old are young, white are
black, and the poor are aristocrats. Since nothing can
be taken for granted in cyberspace, our biases and
prejudices may be exposed, contemplated, and amended.

Summary: Ma-
jor points in sec-
tion of source
are summarized.

Far from being threatening, Turkle believes this experience can be quite liberating. Men who want to experience what women encounter (and vice versa) may do
so thanks to virtual cross-dressing (gender-swapping).
Turkle follows the progress of a thirty-four-year-old
male, an industrial designer, who MUDed as a female
character. As Mairead, a commoner in a medieval
world, he met a nobleman who wanted to marry him
(virtually). Mairead said yes and the services were conducted online. After the marriage, however, this male
engineer was shocked by the way Mairead's virtual husband treated her:

> But everytime [sic] I behave like I'm now going
> to be a countess some day, you know, assert
> myself—as in, "And I never liked this wallpa-
> per anyway"—I get pushed down. The relation-
> ship is pull up, push down. It's an incredibly
> psychologically damaging thing to do to a per-
> son. And the very thing that he liked about
> her—that she was independent, strong, said

Vickery 11

what was on her mind—it is all being bled out

of her. (214)

Although sexism is as prevalent on the Internet as

it is in real life, some men are noticing and experienc-

ing it for the first time. The man in Turkle's case study

is learning that "some of the things that work when

you're a man just backfire when you're a woman"

(214). Although some women pose as males on the In-

ternet in order to experience what it means to be a

man, many pose as a male simply to avoid these kinds

of unpleasant encounters.

For those who do not want to role play, adopt a dif-

ferent identity, or get in touch with a different aspect

of themselves, the Internet can still be a means of vali-

dation. For example, many college graduates are opti-

mistic about their future lives. They imagine a house in

the suburbs, a high-paying job, a spouse and family,

and perhaps a two-car garage. Due to the deplorable

state of the job market, however, these graduates find

themselves trapped in low-paying, intellectually unchal-

lenging jobs, living in unsafe neighborhoods, and iso-

lated from their intellectual peers. Turkle argues that

the Internet helps these people establish a link with

people who will see them as they see themselves:

Documentation: In "block" quotation period goes *before* parenthetical reference. In short quotations the period goes *after* the parenthetical reference.

Vickery 12

Documentation:
Author's name
is cited at begin-
ning of inde-
pendent clause;
quote follows
colon (paren-
thetical refer-
ence follows
quotation).

"MUDs provide them with the sense of a middle-class

peer group. So it is really not that surprising that it is

in virtual social life they feel most like themselves"

(240). This type of self-affirmation is called escapism

by some, therapy by others. Whether it is a way out, a

way back, or a way forward probably depends on the

psychological needs of the individual.

The debate continues. The Internet is said to be a

haven for social misfits, but it is also lauded as a

source of connection and community. Some users find

chat groups organized around topics of interest, such

as parenting skills, literature, or feature films, while

other users find virtual rape and degradation. What is

accepted without question is that such groups are here

to stay. Furthermore, they are "growing faster than

O.J. Simpson's legal bills" (Elmer-Dewitt 50). As in real

life, individuals online will have to decide how much

time and money they want to invest in searching for

meaningful conversations.

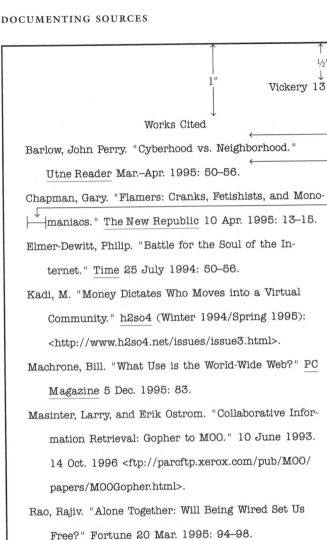

Vickery 13

Works Cited

Barlow, John Perry. "Cyberhood vs. Neighborhood." — Double-space
Utne Reader Mar.–Apr. 1995: 50–56.

Chapman, Gary. "Flamers: Cranks, Fetishists, and Mono- — Indent five
maniacs." The New Republic 10 Apr. 1995: 13–15. spaces

Elmer-Dewitt, Philip. "Battle for the Soul of the Internet." Time 25 July 1994: 50–56.

Kadi, M. "Money Dictates Who Moves into a Virtual — Sample entry:
Community." h2so4 (Winter 1994/Spring 1995): an article in a
<http://www.h2so4.net/issues/issue3.html>. periodical.

Machrone, Bill. "What Use is the World-Wide Web?" PC
Magazine 5 Dec. 1995: 83.

Masinter, Larry, and Erik Ostrom. "Collaborative Infor- — Sample entry:
mation Retrieval: Gopher to MOO." 10 June 1993. date of posting;
14 Oct. 1996 <ftp://parcftp.xerox.com/pub/MOO/ date of access;
papers/MOOGopher.html>. electronic ad-
dress.

Rao, Rajiv. "Alone Together: Will Being Wired Set Us
Free?" Fortune 20 Mar. 1995: 94–98.

Schwartz, Evan. "Looking for Community on the In- — One space
ternet." National Civic Review 84.1 (1995): 37–41.

Turkle, Sherry. Life on Screen: Identity in the Age of — Sample entry: a
the Internet. New York: Simon, 1995. book by one
author.

RHETORICAL GLOSSARY

Abstract

Abstract qualities or characteristics are those we conceive of mentally but cannot see, touch, or hear. For example, *bravery, laziness,* and *perseverance* are abstract terms, and writers often illustrate such terms with examples in order to help readers grasp their significance. For instance, in her essay "Stone Soup" (page 478), Barbara Kingsolver sketches several scenes of children and adults together to show a variety of ways in which the abstract term *family values* can be understood. The opposite of abstract is **concrete,** meaning a term that we

understand because it appeals to the senses, such as *rocky,
sizzling,* or *bright yellow.*

Active Reading

A manner of reading in which one reads intently and consciously, simultaneously reading for meaning and being aware
of one's responses to the content and style. An active reader
often reads with a pencil and ruler in hand, underlining
important phrases or sentences and writing notes in the margin. See the annotated essay "The Problem with Hypertext"
in the Introduction, page 11.

Allusion

A reference to a person, event, or story that is familiar to the
reader, a reference that will help enrich the writer's meaning
because it draws on shared knowledge with the reader. For
instance, on the first page of her essay "Grounds for Fiction"
(page 120), Julia Alvarez makes an allusion to *crown jewels,*
assuming that all her readers will understand this reference to
an object of great value. Allusions work only if the reader
recognizes them; for example, when Alvarez refers to Degas
later in her essay, she is careful to identify him as a painter,
aware that not all her readers would be familiar with the
name.

Analogy

A comparison between two things or concepts that share
certain characteristics although they are not similar in most
ways. Analogies are often used to help clarify an explanation.
Witold Rybczynski is using an analogy in "One Good Turn"
(page 333) when he says, "Hand tools are really extensions
of the human body, for they have evolved over centuries of
trial and error."

Annotate

To make notes or comments about a piece of writing. See the
annotated essay on pages 12–14 of the Introduction.

Argument

A piece of writing or an oral presentation in which an author
or speaker seeks to persuade an audience to accept his or her
beliefs or position by giving reasons and evidence. An argu-

ment doesn't necessarily involve controversy or anger; often it is only a statement intended to present a particular point of view. For example, in "Bobos: The New Upper Class" (page 361), David Brooks makes the argument that the new upper class in America combines many values associated with the 1960s with the respect for money and education associated with the nineties.

Although most arguments combine different kinds of appeal, *emotional arguments* appeal primarily to the passions and the feelings, relying heavily on connotative language and provocative imagery to persuade. In her Nobel Prize–winning address on page 509, Toni Morrison makes a strongly emotional argument. *Rational arguments* rely more on appeals to reason and logic, arguing from precedent and example and trying to establish cause and effect. Steven Weinberg makes a primarily rational argument in "Five and a Half Utopias" on page 279. Writers who want to make an *ethical argument* seek to establish their credentials as persons of authority and trustworthiness. They rely on a good name and a reputation in their field to help convince the audience. In his essay "Science and Hope" (page 391), Carl Sagan argues from cause and effect, but the strong ethical appeal of his essay comes from his international reputation as an eminent scientist and famous writer.

Assumption

Something taken for granted, presumed to be true without need for further explanation or proof. Writers usually make the assumption that their readers have certain knowledge and experiences that they can count on as they present their arguments. In "Shakespeare in the Bush" (page 208), Laura Bohannan shows how her assumptions and those of the tribal elders to whom she was trying to explain *Hamlet* were so wildly different that any understanding was impossible.

Audience

The readers for whom a piece of writing is intended. That audience may be close or distant, a small group or a large number, popular or specialized. Professional writers nearly always tailor their writing toward a particular audience about whom they know a good deal—for example, the readers of the *New York Times* or of *Parade*—and they adapt their vocabulary and style to suit that audience. In the headnote about the author before each essay in *The Riverside Reader* we usually tell you in what other publications the author's work has appeared and where that particular essay originally appeared so you can get a feeling for the kind of reader the author was writing for and how that audience might react. It's important that you, as a college student, are aware that you were not the original audience for these essays and to reflect on how your responses to them might be different from those of the original audience.

Audience Analysis

As you work to develop your writing abilities, few skills are more important to you as a writer than learning how to analyze your audience. Ask yourself: (1) Who am I writing for? (2) What do they expect of me? (3) What knowledge do they already have? (4) What kind of evidence and strategies are they most likely to respond to? And it's important that you learn to project an audience other than your instructor, such as a nonprofessional audience whose interest you must catch and hold. Often it is good practice to imagine your fellow students as the audience for whom you're writing and to gear your language and appeal to them.

Brainstorming

A way of generating ideas and material for writing by thinking about a topic intently and jotting down random thoughts as they occur to you without regard to whether they seem immediately useful and relevant.

Cause and Effect

A mode of writing that explains or persuades by setting up cause-and-effect relationships. In his essay "Some Big Ideas Wash Up One Bulb at a Time" (page 396), Andrew C. Revkin shows how apparently harmless actions—throwing used light bulbs overboard from ships—can cause a serious environmental problem—an accumulation of clinking light bulbs covering an entire tropical beach.

Central Pattern

The dominant mode of exposition in an essay. Most writers use more than one expository pattern when they construct an essay. For example, Serena Nanda combines narration and comparison and contrast in her process essay. "Arranging a Marriage in India" (page 136). In *The Riverside Reader,* however, we have chosen essays that show a central pattern in order to demonstrate how a writer may use a specific pattern as a writing strategy. For example, the central pattern of Andre Dubus's "Digging" (page 53) is narration; the central pattern of Deborah Tannen's "Rapport-Talk and Report-Talk" (page 193) is comparison and contrast.

Classification and Division

A method of organizing an explanation or argument by dividing a topic into distinct parts or classes and discussing the characteristics of those classes. Steven Weinberg does this expertly in "Five and a Half Utopias" (page 279) by identifying five kinds of ideal governments that political theorists have devised, describing those governments, and pointing out the flaws in each of them.

Comparison and Contrast

A popular and convenient way of organizing an essay or article to highlight important ways in which two things or processes can be similar yet different. Mark Twain's classic piece, "Two Views of the River" (page 169), illustrates the method beautifully by contrasting the romantic view of someone who travels down the Mississippi for the first time with the pragmatic view of an experienced river pilot who sees the river as a dangerous waterway that he must analyze in order to navigate safely.

Concept

A broad intellectual notion that captures the essential nature of an idea, system, or process; for example, the concept of affirmative action or the concept of intellectual property. In

"Modern Friendships" (page 265), for example, Phillip Lopate explains the new concept of friendship he has developed as he has matured and made friends with a broad range of people with diverse traits and abilities.

Conclusion

The final paragraph or section of an essay that brings the argument or explanation to appropriate closure and leaves the reader feeling that the author has dealt with all the issues or questions he or she has raised. Good conclusions are challenging to write, and writers sometimes go through several drafts before they are satisfied.

Concrete

Something specific and tangible that can be perceived through the senses; see **Abstract** earlier in *The Riverside Reader* glossary.

Connotation

The added psychological and emotional associations that certain words and phrases carry in addition to their simple meaning. For instance, words like *liberty* and *individualism* carry heavily positive connotations in our culture; they may carry negative connotations in a culture that puts great value on tradition and discipline. All the authors in *The Riverside Reader* use connotation, but two who employ it with particular skill are Martin Luther King, Jr., in "I Have a Dream" (page 458) and Anne Roiphe in "A Tale of Two Divorces" (page 182).

Critical Reading

The critical reader is one who asks questions and analyzes content as he or she reads in order to judge the truth, merit, and general quality of an essay or article. A critical reader might ask, "What is the source of the author's information?," "What evidence does he cite in support of his claim?," and "What organization or special interest might she be affiliated with?" The questions in the margins of "The Problem with Hypertext" (page 11) show evidence of critical reading.

Definition

A type of essay that identifies and gives the qualities of an object, an institution, or a political philosophy in a way that highlights its special characteristics. Authors often use definition when making an argument in order to show that one method or object is superior. Many essays are *extended definitions;* for instance, Witold Rybczynski's "One Good Turn" (page 333) is an essay of definition; in it he describes the essential characteristics of the wood screw and tells its history.

Description

A mode of nonfiction writing that aims to help the reader visualize and grasp the essential nature of an object, an action, a scene, or a person by giving details that reveal the special characteristics and flavor of that person or scene. Most skilled professional writers, like those represented in *The Riverside Reader,* are good at choosing the particular details that give color and interest. Notice how Doris Kearns Goodwin in "Keeping the Scorebook" (page 37) creates details that convey her excitement as she listened to the Dodgers' baseball games when she was a girl.

Division and Classification
See **Classification and Division.**

Documentation

A system used for giving readers information about where the writer found the sources he or she used in an academic paper, a research paper, or a technical report. Writers document their sources by inserting footnotes, endnotes, or in-text citations so that a reader who wants to know more about the topic can easily find the article or book that the author is citing or track down other related articles by the same author. The most common system writers use for documentation in academic papers in writing classes is MLA.

While most authors writing in magazines or books for the general public seldom use formal documentation, many use an informal documentation that lets the reader know where they found the information on which they base their conclusions. Notice that Daniel Goleman does this in "Peak Performance: Why Records Fall" (page 409) by giving the names and the university associations of several researchers whose work he cites. Such informal documentation lends credibility to an article and enhances the writer's authority.

Draft

A preliminary version of a piece of writing that enables an author to get started and develop an idea as he or she writes. Authors often write and revise several drafts before they are satisfied with a piece of writing. In her essay "Grounds for Fiction" (page 120), Julia Alvarez relates how she gathers fragments of miscellaneous information and, through writing drafts, turns them into stories or poems.

Edit

To make small-scale changes in a piece of writing that is close to being complete. Editing may involve changing some word choices, checking for correct spelling and punctuation, eliminating repetition, rearranging sentences or paragraphs, and generally polishing a manuscript into final form before submitting it to an instructor or editor.

Essay

An article or short nonfiction composition that focuses on a specific topic or theme. *The Random House Webster's Unabridged Dictionary* says that an essay is generally "analytical, speculative, or interpretive." Thus a news story would not be an essay, but an opinion piece could be. Nearly all the selections in *The Riverside Reader* qualify as essays. David Brooks's "Bobos: The New Upper Class" (page 361) and Philip Lopate's "Modern Friendships" (page 265) are particularly good examples.

Evidence

Examples that are given to support an assertion or thesis. The term suggests factual data such as scientific observations, historical references, or eyewitness reports rather than personal stories or opinions. Andrew C. Revkin's "Some Big Ideas Wash Up One Bulb at a Time" (page 396) and Natalie

Angier's "Dolphin Courtship" (page 113) are good examples of essays that use evidence effectively.

Example

A specific incident, object, or anecdote used to illustrate and support a claim or expand on an assertion or generalization. Skillful writers know that readers expect and need examples to clarify a statement, develop a thesis sentence, or support an opening assertion. Every writer in *The Riverside Reader* uses examples, but John Berendt's essay "The Hoax" (page 338) consists almost entirely of specific examples that illustrate the distinction he makes between a hoax and a prank.

Figurative Language

Language that uses vivid and sometimes fanciful comparisons to enliven and enrich prose. Such language often takes the form of metaphors that explain an unfamiliar thing or process by comparing it to a familiar thing. Julia Alvarez does this early in her essay "Grounds for Fiction" (page 120) when she quotes the author James Dickey as saying that his writing process was like digging through fifty tons of low-grade ore to come up with two gold nuggets. Natalie Angier, the science writer, is a master at finding the colorful verb or metaphor that conjures up images. Notice those she uses in her essay, "Dolphin Courtship" (page 113), when she talks about female dolphins "chasing after an alliance of males who had stolen one of their friends" and describes the dolphins' maneuvers with verbs like "swiveling and somersaulting," "nuzzling," and "jerking, biting, leaping."

In writing college essays, you should use figurative language carefully because often the assignment is one that calls for rational argument and a serious tone. In such situations, too much figurative language can distract the reader, although an apt metaphor can work well to explain an unfamiliar concept.

Focus

As a verb, to concentrate or emphasize; as a noun, the point of concentration or emphasis. Skillful writers know how to focus their writing on a single central idea or point; they have learned to "write more about less," to narrow their topic down to one that they can explore fully and enrich with details. Witold Rybczynski demonstrates such skill in his essay "One Good Turn" (page 333), by taking a very narrow topic, the wood screw, and writing a rich and informative essay full of fascinating details.

Free-writing

A way to generate ideas for an essay or article by writing down whatever comes into your mind about a topic you have chosen or been assigned, not concerning yourself with organization or style. In free-writing, work quickly to capture ideas. Don't stop to consider whether a phrase or sentence is pertinent or useful—just get it down. After you accumulate a substantial amount of material, you can comb through it to find a starting point for your first draft.

Generalization

A broad statement that makes a general claim or an assertion without giving specific details or supporting evidence. Writers often begin an essay with a generalization, and when readers encounter such a generalization they expect the next sentences and paragraphs to give details and information that expand on and support it. Eric Liu does this in the first sentence of "A Chinaman's Chance" (page 465) when he says, "A lot of people my age seem to think that the American Dream is dead." In "Modern Friendships" (page 265) Phillip Lopate opens with a general question: "Is there anything left to say about friendship after so many great essayists have picked over the bones of the subject?" Both writers quickly shift from the general to the specific and begin to fill out their statements with details.

Headnote

The short introductory passage that comes before each essay in *The Riverside Reader* is a headnote about its author. Its purpose is to give you enough information about the author's age, cultural heritage, and education to help put him or her in some cultural context and to give you a few other pertinent facts, such as what else he has written or where she has published other articles. We provide this information because we believe readers are likely to understand an author's point of view and passions better when they can place his or her work in the larger context of that author's background.

Image

In writing, an impression or visual effect created by an author through the skillful use of language. Toni Morrison creates strong and dramatic images through her impassioned phrases in "A Bird in Our Hand" (page 509). Andrew C. Revkin creates images of a ravaged environment by piling up detailed description in "Some Big Ideas Wash Up One Bulb at a Time" (page 396).

Logic

An intellectual system or process that uses reason and evidence to arrive at conclusions. Often writers construct a logical framework for their arguments, setting up cause-and-effect relationships or establishing a chain of reasoning, but embellish the logic with some figurative and emotional language. Carl Sagan does this in "Science and Hope" (page 391) in the first sentence of his concluding paragraph when he says, "Finding the occasional straw of truth awash in a great ocean of confusion and bamboozle requires vigilance, dedication, and courage."

Metaphor
See **Figurative Language.**

Mode

A style or pattern of writing or discourse that has certain features that characterize it and make it distinctive. The essays in *The Riverside Reader* are classified according to their mode: narration, process, division and classification, definition, argument, and so on. Often a writer combines two or three modes in an essay or article but emphasizes one dominant mode. For example, Andrew C. Revkin uses narration to tell his experiences in "Some Big Ideas Wash Up One Bulb at a Time" (page 396), but his main emphasis is on cause and effect.

Narration

A mode of nonfiction writing that develops an idea or makes a point by telling a story or anecdote. In "Digging" (page 53) Andre Dubus tells the story of how his initiation into hard manual labor at the age of seventeen marked his passage into the world of adults. Writers often combine narration with other patterns of writing to make a point or add human interest to an essay. Judith Ortiz Cofer uses several personal anecdotes to illustrate sexist attitudes toward Latina women in her essay "The Myth of the Latin Woman" (page 44).

Pace

The rate at which an essay or article moves. Writers can create different paces through word choice, sentence length, and the selection of certain kinds of verbs. One can see a dramatic example of changing pace by contrasting the first two paragraphs from Mark Twain's "Two Views of the River" (page 169). In the first paragraph the author creates a dreamy leisurely pace with long sentences filled with rich description and inactive verbs. A few sentences into the second paragraph, the pace changes as he switches from contemplation to analysis. Now the tempo quickens with shorter words and phrases and verbs that depict action.

Paraphrase

A passage that briefly restates the content of a passage in such a way that it retains the original meaning.

Persona

The role or personality a writer assumes in an essay or article. Writers take on a wide range of personas—some possibilities are the disillusioned observer, the committed advocate, the involved narrator, the scolding social critic, or the objective reporter. For instance, in "Soul of a Citizen" (page 498) Paul Rogat Loeb assumes the role of the committed advocate for citizen activism. In "A Tale of Two Divorces" (page 182) Anne Roiphe becomes the involved narrator who wants to teach a lesson by drawing on her own experience. In "Confessions of a Nonpolitical Man" (page 505) Sven Birkerts assumes the persona of the disillusioned observer who has seen so many failed and misguided attempts at solving problems that he no longer is willing to become involved in causes. Writers can and often do assume many different personas as they write for different audiences and different purposes.

Persuasion

The process of using language to get readers to accept one's belief or opinions. Writers use varying strategies to persuade their readers, generally combining reason and emotion. The skillful persuader avoids threats or heavy-handed tactics. In "A Tale of Two Divorces" (page 182) Anne Roiphe engages her readers' interest by telling two stories: one of her mother's marriage, the other of her own. Through them she seeks to persuade her reader that the romantic view of love and marriage can trap women into staying in a bad marriage.

Plagiarism

Plagiarism is using someone else's words or ideas without giving proper credit to the writer of the original. See page 654 for more explanation and useful examples of the appropriate ways to give credit to an author whom you are quoting.

Having another person write a paper or essay that you hand in for credit, whether that person is a friend or someone who writes college papers for money, also constitutes plagiarism and is *never* acceptable. Such an action can have serious consequences, from failing the course to being expelled from an institution. Instructors who have been reading student papers for several years can spot that kind of plagiarism more easily than you might think and have many resources for checking work turned in to them.

Plot

The chain of events that develops a story; through it a writer puts characters into a set of circumstances, describes their behavior, and shows the consequences that ensue.

Point of View

The angle or perspective from which a story or account is told. An account in which the narrator uses "I" and gives an account of an event as it appeared to him or her is called *first-person* point of view. George Orwell's "Shooting an Elephant" (page 64) illustrates this strategy. When the narrator recounts an incident as a detached but fully informed observer, he or she is using the *third-person omniscient* point of view. Flannery O'Connor employs this strategy in "Revelation" (page 297).

Purpose

Authors write with a purpose or a goal. They may wish to inform, to persuade, to explain, to support an assertion, or to entertain. Sometimes they may combine two or more of these purposes, but usually they have a primary goal, one that should be evident to the reader. For instance, in "Arranging a Marriage in India" (page 136) Serena Nanda's primary purpose is to explain why so many young people from India willingly accept the practice of arranged marriages, a custom that seems inexplicable to young Americans. In "Selected Web Sites" (page 584) Dave Barry seeks mainly to entertain his readers.

When you are writing a paper for a college course, you'll do well to think beyond the immediate goal of fulfilling an assignment in order to earn a grade and consider what effect you want to have on your readers. Are you writing to explain, to persuade, to argue for or against a proposal? When you know your purpose, you're better able to choose successful strategies for achieving it.

Quotation

A passage that gives the actual words a writer or speaker has used in an article, book, speech, or conversation. Authors often use quotations to support their arguments: Barbara Dafoe Whitehead employs this strategy several times in "Women and the Future of Fatherhood" (page 489). So does Jonathan Rauch in "In Defense of Prejudice" (page 520). Such passages must always appear in quotation marks in academic papers or, indeed, in any writing done by a responsible author. Writers who fail to give proper credit for a quotation risk losing the respect of their readers or, in college, even getting into considerable trouble. You'll find the proper format for using quotations in Gwen Vickery's "Is Anybody Out There? The Value of Chat Groups on the Internet" (page 669) and in the Documentation section of *The Riverside Reader*.

Refute

To counteract an argument or seek to disprove a claim or proposition. Several of the authors in *The Riverside Reader* are writing to refute what they see as misconceptions. Judith Ortiz Cofer in "The Myth of the Latin Woman" (page 44) wants to disprove the all-too-common assumption that Latin women are sexy and hot-blooded and show that such attitudes are based on false stereotypes. Barbara Kingsolver in "Stone Soup" (page 478) wants to disprove the simplistic view that good family values can flourish only in a traditional two-parent family. Jonathan Rauch wrote "In Defense of Prejudice" (page 520) specifically to refute the attack Toni Morrison makes on prejudicial language in her essay "A Bird in Our Hand" (page 509).

Response

A reader's reaction to what he or she reads is a *response*. Readers can respond in different ways—analytically, critically, emotionally, or approvingly—but in nearly every case that response will come from their own experiences and background: what they know, where they grew up, what kind of culture they lived in, and so on. You might say that they look at an essay through the lens shaped by their own lives, and that lens affects what they see. Such a response is natural and legitimate.

Jonathan Rauch's essay, "In Defense of Prejudice" (page 520), illustrates the point. It is a response to Toni Morrison's essay, "A Bird in Our Hand" (page 509), and his response is conditioned by his being a Jewish man who is gay, but also by a wealth of historical knowledge about the terrible consequences that have ensued over the centuries when a group or government decides to censor speech or thought. Laura Bohannan's essay "Shakespeare in the Bush" (page 208) also delightfully illustrates the ways in which two audiences look through such different lenses that they simply don't see the same thing.

Revise
To make substantial changes in a written draft, changes that may involve narrowing the topic, adding or deleting material, rearranging sections, or rewriting the introduction or conclusion. Don't look at revising as a process of correcting a draft; rather, you develop your essay by the process of revising and often can clarify and strengthen your ideas by the process. Many writers revise an essay through three or four drafts.

Strategy
The means or tactic a writer uses to achieve his or her purpose. In the essays in *The Riverside Reader*, authors use various strategies: narration and description, comparison and contrast, process analysis, cause and effect, and so on.

Summary
A passage that condenses the ideas and content of a long passage in a few sentences or paragraphs; a summary should be objective and accurate.

Testimony
Evidence offered in support of a claim or assertion. The term suggests factual statements given by experts or taken from sources such as historical or government records or from statistical data. Eyewitness accounts are frequently used as testimony. In "Peak Performance: Why Records Fall" (page 409) Daniel Goleman is using testimony when he cites stud-

ies done by several experts and researchers to support his explanation about why records fall.

Thesis Sentence

A comprehensive sentence, usually coming in the first paragraph or so of an essay, that summarizes and previews the main idea the author is going to develop in the essay. Daniel Goleman, in the first sentence of the second paragraph of "Peak Performance: Why Records Fall" (page 409), writes an almost classic thesis sentence that encapsulates the central idea of the essay. Here is the sentence: "Studies of chess masters, virtuoso musicians, and star athletes show that the relentless training routines of those at the top allow them to break through the ordinary limits in memory and physiology, and so perform at levels that had been thought impossible." He goes on to develop each segment of the sentence with examples and testimony.

Tone

The emotional attitude toward their topic that authors convey in their writing. They create tone through the choices they make of words—particularly verbs—of sentence and paragraph length, of styles—formal or informal—and with the kinds of images and figurative language they use. Readers sometimes have trouble finding the exact word for tone; it's an impression you get from writing rather than a quality you discover analytically, and usually we fall back on emotional terms to describe it: angry, engaging, whimsical, passionate, blunt, sarcastic, patronizing, and so on. But tone is an important element in writing, one of which any author should be aware. If your tone antagonizes your readers, they'll quit reading.

In her essay "The Myth of the Latin Woman" (page 44) Judith Ortiz Cofer's tone shifts subtly as her account progresses. At first she seems fairly tolerant of non-Latins who misinterpret cultural dress preferences, but when she begins to tell of the humiliating incidents that she and other Latina women have endured, her tone becomes unmistakably angry. In "The Extendable Fork" (page 246) Calvin Trillin strikes a whimsical tone, one that suits his light topic. He achieves that tone with comical images and dialogue. David Brooks's tone in "Bobos: The New Upper Class" (page 361) is authoritative and a shade sardonic, as if he's amused by the new educated elite who enjoy privilege and power yet want to seem laid back and casual. He creates that tone by displaying a wealth of knowledge about his subject and by drawing ironic comparisons and contrasts.

Works Cited

The list of references and sources that appears at the end of an academic paper or report that uses MLA style and gives the readers enough information about those sources to enable them to evaluate them or use them for further research. On page 652 of the section Documenting Sources you will find a full explanation of this feature.

Writing Process

While there is no single writing process that works for every writer or every writing task, writing specialists have found certain patterns when they analyze how most writers seem to work. They agree that productive writers tend to work through a series of steps in the process of creating an essay or article.

Stage 1. Invention: The process of discovering one's topic and generating material. Typical activities are reading and researching, brainstorming, free-writing, talking with fellow writers, and making rough preliminary outlines.

Stage 2. Drafting: Writing a first version of the paper that puts down ideas in some organized form. Many writers continue to generate ideas as they write and often write two or three drafts before they complete one they think is fairly satisfactory.

Stage 3. Revising and rewriting: reviewing the completed first draft and making substantial changes, perhaps by narrowing the focus, reorganizing, adding and deleting material, or writing a new introduction or conclusion.

Stage 4. Editing, polishing, and proofreading: making minor word changes, polishing style, and checking for spelling and typographical errors.

Writing Situation

Every piece of writing, from a business memo to an inaugural address, is created within some context; that context is the writing situation. Its components are (1) the writer, (2) the topic, (3) the audience, and (4) the purpose. To figure out what your writing situation is for any particular assignment, ask yourself,

- What is my persona or role in this situation?
- What do I want to say?
- To whom am I writing?
- What is my purpose?

By working out an answer to each of these questions before you begin to write, you'll have a good beginning in your effort to turn out a focused and effective product.

ACKNOWLEDGMENTS

ALICE ADAMS From *To See You Again* by Alice Adams. Copyright © 1982 by Alice Adams. Reprinted by permission of Alfred A. Knopf, a Division of Random House, Inc.

JULIA ALVAREZ From *Grounds for Fiction.* Copyright © 1998 by Julia Alvarez. Published by Algonquin Books. Reprinted by permission of Susan Bergholz Literary Services, New York. All rights reserved.

MAYA ANGELOU From *I Know Why the Caged Bird Sings* by Maya Angelou. Copyright © 1969 & renewed 1997 by Maya Angelou. Reprinted by permission of Random House, Inc.

NATALIE ANGIER "Dolphin Courtship: Brutal, Cunning, and Complex" from *The Beauty and the Beastly.* Copyright © 1995 by Natalie Angier. Reprinted by permission of Houghton Mifflin Co. All rights reserved.

JAMES H. AUSTIN Reprinted by author's permission from *Saturday Review/World*, November 2, 1974.

DAVE BARRY From *Dave Barry in Cyberspace* by Dave Barry, copyright © 1996 by Dave Barry. Used by permission of Crown Books, a division of Random House, Inc.

JOHN BERENDT Reprinted by permission from John Berendt.

SVEN BIRKERTS Excerpt from "Reflections of a Nonpolitical Man" copyright 1999 by Sven Birkerts. Reprinted from Readings with the permission of Graywolf Press, Saint Paul, Minnesota, and Utne Reader, July–August 1999.

LAURA BOHANNAN "Shakespeare in the Bush" by Laura Bohannan. Originally appeared in *Natural History*, August–September 1966, pp. 28–33. Reprinted with permission from Laura Bohannan.

DAVID BROOKS Reprinted with the permission of Simon & Schuster, Inc., from *Bobos in Paradise: The New Upper Class and How They Got There* by David Brooks. Copyright © 2000 by David Brooks.

703

SANDRA CISNEROS From *Woman Hollering Creek*. Copyright © 1991 by Sandra Cisneros. Published by Vintage, a division of Random House, Inc., and in hardcover by Random House. Reprinted by permission of Susan Bergholz Literary Services, New York. All rights reserved.

JUDITH ORTIZ COFER "The Myth of the Latin Woman: I Just Met a Girl Named María" by Judith Ortiz Cofer. From *The Latin Deli: Prose and Poetry*. Copyright © 1993. Reprinted by permission of The University of Georgia Press.

ROBERT COLES From *Harvard Diary II* by Robert Coles. Reprinted by permission from The Crossroad Publishing Company.

ANDRE DUBUS From *Meditations from a Movable Chair* by Andre Dubus. Copyright © 1998 by Andre Dubus. Reprinted by permission of Alfred A. Knopf, a Division of Random House, Inc.

LARS EIGHNER Copyright © 1993 by Lars Eighner. From *Travels with Lizbeth* by Lars Eighner. Reprinted by permission of St. Martin's Press, LLC.

WILLIAM GIBSON "Burning Chrome" from *Burning Chrome* by William Gibson. Copyright © 1986 by William Gibson. Reprinted by permission of HarperCollins Publishers, Inc.

NIKKI GIOVANNI "Campus Racism 101" from *Racism 101* by Nikki Giovanni. Copyright © 1994 by Nikki Giovanni. Reprinted by permission of HarperCollins Publishers, Inc.

DANIEL GOLEMAN Daniel Goleman, "Peak Peak Performance: Why Records Fall." *New York Times*. Copyright © 1994 by The New York Company. Reprinted by permission.

DORIS KEARNS GOODWIN Reprinted with the permission of Simon & Schuster from *Wait Till Next Year* by Doris Kearns Goodwin. Copyright © 1997 by Blithedale Productions.

JOHN STEELE GORDON Reprinted by Permission of Forbes Magazine © 2000 Forbes.

STEPHEN HARRIGAN From *The Natural State* by Stephen Harrigan. Copyright © 1988. Reprinted by permission of the author.

WITI IHIMAERA From *Dear Miss Mansfield* by Witi Ihimaera, published by Penguin Books New Zealand. Reprinted by permission.

M. KADI Reprinted by permission from *The Zine h2so4*, San Francisco, CA 94142. M. Kadi is a freelance writer and computer consultant working in New York City. She has degrees in Philosophy and Religious Studies.

MARTIN LUTHER KING, JR. Reprinted by arrangement by The Heirs to the Estate of Martin Luther King, Jr., c/o Writers House, Inc. as agent for the proprietor. Copyright 1963 by Martin Luther King, Jr., copyright renewed 1991 Coretta Scott King.

BARBARA KINGSOLVER "Stone Soup" from *High Tide in Tucson* by Barbara Kingsolver. Copyright © 1995 by Barbara Kingsolver. Reprinted by permission of HarperCollins Publishers, Inc.

MAXINE HONG KINGSTON From *The Woman Warrior* by Maxine Hong Kingston. Copyright © 1975, 1976 by Maxine Hong Kingston. Reprinted by permission of Alfred A. Knopf, a Division of Random House, Inc.

WENDY LESSER Originally printed in *The Graywolf Forum*. Reprinted with permission from the author.

ERIC LIU "A Chinaman's Chance: Reflections on the American Dream" by Eric Liu. Copyright © 1994 by Eric Liu. From *Next: Young American Writers on the New Generation*, edited by Eric Liu. Used by permission of the author and W.W. Norton & Company, Inc.

PAUL ROGAT LOEB Copyright © 1999 by Paul Rogat Loeb. From *Soul of a Citizen* by Paul Rogat Loeb. Reprinted by permission of St. Martin's Press, LLC.

PHILLIP LOPATE Reprinted by permission of The Wendy Weil Agency, Inc. First appeared in *Texas Monthly*. Copyright © 1989.

DAVID McCULLOUGH Reprinted with permission of Simon & Schuster from *Truman* by David McCullough. Copyright © 1992 by David McCullough.

MARY MEBANE "Shades of Black," from *Mary* by Mary Mebane, copyright © 1981 by Mary Elizabeth Mebane. Used by permission of Viking Penguin, a division of Penguin Putnam, Inc.

LAURA MILLER Copyright © 1995 by City Lights Books. Reprinted by permission of City Lights Books.

TONI MORRISON Reprinted by permission of International Creative Management, Inc. Copyright © 1993 by Toni Morrison.

SERENA NANDA Reprinted by permission from Serena Nanda.

JOYCE CAROL OATES Copyright © 1999 by The New York Times Co. Reprinted by permission. All rights reserved.

FLANNERY O'CONNOR "Revelation" from *The Complete Stories* by Flannery O'Connor. Copyright © 1971 by the Estate of Mary Flannery O'Connor. Reprinted by permission of Farrar, Straus and Giroux, LLC.

GEORGE ORWELL "Shooting an Elephant" from *Shooting an Elephant and Other Essays* by George Orwell, copyright 1950 by Sonia Brownell Orwell and renewed 1978 by Sonia Pitt-Rivers, reprinted by permission of Harcourt, Inc.

JONATHAN RAUCH "In Defense of Prejudice: Why incendiary speech must be protected" by Jonathan Rauch. From *Kindly Inquisitors: The New Attacks on Free Thought*. Copyright © 1995 by The University of Chicago Press and the Author.

ANDREW C. REVKIN Reprinted by permission of the author. Andrew C. Revkin writes about the environment for the *New York Times*. He is the author of *The Burning Season: The Murder of Chico Mendes and the Fight for the Amazon Rain Forest* (Houghton Mifflin, 1990) and *Global Warming: Understanding the Forecast* (Abbeville Press, 1992).

RICHARD RODRIGUEZ Copyright, April 7, 1997, *U.S. News & World Report.* Visit us at our web site at www.usnews.com for additional information.

ANNE ROIPHE "A Tale of Two Divorces" from *Women On Divorce: A Bedside Companion* by Peggy Kaganoff and Susan Spano, copyright © 1995 by Anne Roiphe, reprinted by permission of Harcourt, Inc.

WITOLD RYBCZYNSKI "One Good Turn: How Machine-made screws brought the world together" by Witold Rybczynski appeared in *New York Times Magazine,* April 18, 1999. Reprinted with permission from the author.

CARL SAGAN Copyright © 1995 by Carl Sagan, © 2000 by the Estate of Carl Sagan.

SCOTT RUSSELL SANDERS *Hunting for Hope* by Scott Russell Sanders. Copyright © 1998 by Scott Russell Sanders. Reprinted by permission of Beacon Press, Boston.

EVAN I. SCHWARTZ "Looking for Community on the Internet" by Evan Schwartz. From *National Civic Review,* Winter 1995 issue. Reprinted by permission from National Civic League.

DAVID SHENK Reprinted with permission from the author. David Shenk is author of *Data Smog* and *The End of Patience.* An overview of his work can be found online at *www.bigfoot.com/~dshenk.*

DEBORAH TANNEN "Rapport-Talk and Report-Talk" from *You Just Don't Understand* by Deborah Tannen. Copyright © 1990 by Deborah Tannen. Reprinted by permission of HarperCollins Publishers, Inc.

CALVIN TRILLIN "The Extendable Fork"—Copyright © 1995 by Calvin Trillin. Reprinted by permission of Lescher & Lescher, Ltd.

KURT VONNEGUT, JR. "Harrison Bergeron," from *Welcome to the Monkey House* by Kurt Vonnegut, Jr., copyright © 1961 by Kurt Vonnegut, Jr. Used by permission of Dell Publishing, a division of Random House, Inc.

ALICE WALKER "Everyday Use" from *In Love & Trouble: Stories of Black Women,* copyright © 1973 by Alice Walker, reprinted by permission of Harcourt, Inc.

STEVEN WEINBERG © 2000 Steven Weinberg, as first published in *The Atlantic Monthly,* and reprinted in *Facing Up* by Steven Weinberg (Harvard University Press, 2001).

JONATHAN WEINER From *The Beak of the Finch* by Jonathan Weiner. Copyright © 1994 by Jonathan Weiner. Reprinted by permission of Alfred A. Knopf, a Division of Random House, Inc.

BARBARA DAFOE WHITEHEAD From *The Divorce Culture* by Barbara Dafoe Whitehead. Copyright © 1997 by Barbara Dafoe Whitehead. Reprinted by permission from Alfred A. Knopf, a Division of Random House, Inc.

ELIZABETH WINTHROP "The Golden Darters" by Elizabeth Winthrop. First published *in American Short Fiction.* Copyright © 1991 by Elizabeth Winthrop. Reprinted by permission of the author.

CATHY YOUNG "Keeping Women Weak" by Cathy Young. Copyright © 1994 by Cathy Young. From *Next: Young American Writers on the New Generation,* edited by Eric Liu. Used by permission of the author and W.W. Norton & Company, Inc.

WILLIAM K. ZINSSER Copyright © 1983 by William K. Zinsser. Reprinted by permission of the author.

INDEX